SPECIAL INTEREST TOURISM

CONTEXT AND CASES

Edited by **NORMAN DOUGLAS**
NGAIRE DOUGLAS • **ROS DERRETT**

WILEY

John Wiley & Sons Australia, Ltd

First published 2001 by
John Wiley & Sons Australia, Ltd
33 Park Road, Milton, Qld 4064

Offices also in Sydney and Melbourne

Typeset in 10.5/12 pt New Baskerville

National Library of Australia
Cataloguing-in-publication data

Special interest tourism.

  Includes index.
  ISBN 0 471 42171 5.

  1. Tourism. I. Douglas, Norman.
  II. Douglas, Ngaire. III. Derrett, Ros.

338.4791

Printed in Singapore by
Kyodo Printing Co (S'pore) Pte Ltd

10 9 8 7 6 5 4 3 2

CONTENTS ·····································

ACKNOWLEDGEMENTS

It is our pleasure to thank here the numerous people who contributed to this book. The authors of the various chapters responded enthusiastically to requests for submissions and promptly to queries from the editors and the publisher. Of the many institutions and individuals who provided assistance or illustrative material, special thanks are due to the following: Gerry Gerrard and Corinne Fletcher for assistance during the research of the case study in chapter 1; Travel & Tourism Intelligence, London, for permission to use in chapter 11 their special report on health tourism in Europe, *Travel & Tourism Analyst* No. 1, 2000, prepared by consultants Christine Smith and Paul Jenner; the Seniors Card and Office of the Ageing of the Department of Families, Youth and Community Care, Queensland, and in particular Lorna Andrews, Arna Presland and Anna Matthews, for material used in chapter 17; and Jonathan Schofield for assistance during the research of the case study in chapter 18. Chapter 10 was written while the author was employed as an Australian Research Council Postdoctoral Fellow (Indigenous Tourism) in the Department of Leisure and Tourism Studies at the University of Newcastle, New South Wales. Helpful comments were provided by Sue Muloin. Other acknowledgements are made at appropriate places in the book.

At John Wiley & Sons Australia, consistently great support and advice was provided by publishing editor Darren Taylor, publishing assistant Pam Hollander, and project editors Catherine Spedding, Jem Bates and Colleen Foelz. Their persuasive techniques ensured the appearance of the book on schedule. As is evident, Wiley's design team also did its usual excellent work.

Norman Douglas
Ngaire Douglas
Ros Derrett

ABOUT THE EDITORS

Norman Douglas

Norman Douglas is a writer and research consultant. He holds a PhD in Pacific Studies from the Australian National University and has lectured at the University of New South Wales, the University of the South Pacific and the University of Hawaii. He has written extensively for both popular and academic publications on a variety of subjects ranging from missionary history to image analysis. His current research interests include tourism history, cruise tourism and tourism imagery.

Ngaire Douglas

Ngaire Douglas is a senior lecturer at the School of Tourism and Hospitality Management, Southern Cross University. Her PhD from the University of Queensland addresses the history of tourism in Melanesia. She has published widely on a range of issues concerning tourism development in the Pacific Islands, historical dimensions of tourism in Southeast Asia, tourism imagery and cruise tourism and is on the editorial board of the *Asia Pacific Journal of Tourism Research*.

Ros Derrett OAM

Ros Derrett is a lecturer at the School of Tourism and Hospitality Management at Southern Cross University, Lismore. She has worked extensively in education, community development and arts administration in Australia and overseas as a consultant for private enterprise, local government and community event management. She has collaborated with planning authorities on local and national projects. Her research activity reflects her interest in regional community cultural development, cultural tourism and tourism culture with a special focus on festivals.

ABOUT THE CONTRIBUTORS

Robyn Bushell

Robyn Bushell is Associate Professor in the Department of Tourism at the University of Western Sydney, Hawkesbury. Her career spans teaching and researching in environmental health, community health and tourism. Her research interests include tourism planning and the relationship between tourism, sense of place, quality of life and the host community, in addition to the protection and conservation of cultural and biological diversity, the role of interpretation in conservation education and visitor impact management.

Jennifer Craik

Associate Professor Jennifer Craik teaches cultural studies and cultural policy in the School of Film, Media and Cultural Studies at Griffith University, Brisbane. Her publications include *Resorting to Tourism: Cultural Policies for Tourist Development in Australia* (Allen & Unwin, 1991) and *The Face of Fashion: Cultural Studies in Fashion* (Routledge, 1994).

Kay Dimmock

Kay Dimmock is a lecturer at the School of Tourism and Hospitality Management, Southern Cross University, Lismore, New South Wales. She has been studying, researching and teaching tourism and related activities, including festival and event management, since 1995. When not formally studying and teaching tourism issues, she enjoys participating in tourism.

Ross Dowling

Ross Dowling is Associate Professor of Tourism at the School of Marketing, Tourism & Leisure, Edith Cowan University, Joondalup, Western Australia. He is Treasurer of the Ecotourism Association of Australia and is Vice Chairperson of the Forum Advocating Cultural and Ecotourism in Western Australia. He is an international speaker, researcher and consultant on ecotourism and wine tourism. For his contributions to the environment he has been awarded a Mobil Environmental Prize and a New Zealand Conservation Foundation Citation.

Michael Hall

At the time of writing, Professor Michael Hall is Head of the Department of Tourism at the University of Otago in New Zealand and editor of *Current Issues in Tourism*. Michael has written widely on various aspects of tourism, heritage and environmental history. He has a strong interest in special interest tourism and economic development in both rural and urban areas and is currently researching various aspects of cool climate wines, cheeses and regional foods.

Nerilee Hing

Nerilee Hing is a senior lecturer at the School of Tourism and Hospitality Management, Southern Cross University, New South Wales, where she teaches entrepreneurship, gaming management, food and beverage management, and strategic management for tourism and hospitality. She is regional editor for the *International Journal of Contemporary Hospitality Management* and has published widely in a range of tourism, hospitality and management journals.

Les Killion

Les Killion is Head of the School of Marketing and Tourism, Faculty of Business and Law, Central Queensland University, Rockhampton. Les trained as a geographer at the University of New England and completed his doctorate in sociology at the University of Queensland. He has taught at Mitchell College and Canberra CAE in the Graduate Diploma in Outdoor Recreation Management. At Central Queensland University he has been responsible for the Bachelor of Tourism program. Research interests include impacts assessment, rural tourism, and tourism policy and planning.

Richard Mitchell

Richard Mitchell is a senior lecturer in Tourism at La Trobe University in Melbourne and was formerly a lecturer in tourism at the University of Western Sydney. Richard's doctoral studies at the University of Otago focused on New Zealand wine tourism. He continues to reseach wine tourism in Victoria, where he has extended his studies to include the Queen Victoria Markets.

Nigel Morpeth

Nigel Morpeth is a senior lecturer in Tourism Management at Leeds Metropolitan University in the United Kingdom. His research interests include sustainable tourism policy, cycle tourism and community approaches to tourism development. He holds degrees in Government and Politics and Recreation Management and has worked for three British local authority departments within the field of community leisure development. Nigel has published work on cycle tourism, wine tourism, tourism development in Prague and sustainable tourism policy.

Gary Prosser

Gary Prosser is currently Director of Business Development with the Tipperary Institute, Ireland. He was formerly Professor and Head of the School of Tourism and Hospitality Management at Southern Cross University, New South Wales, and Director of the National Centre for Regional Tourism Research, a joint initiative of Tourism Council Australia, the Cooperative Research Centre for Sustainable Tourism and Southern Cross University.

Hein Ruys

Hein Ruys is an associate editor of the *Australian Journal of Hospitality Management*. He recently retired from the University of Queensland but is still involved in educational and industry bodies that deal with tourism issues. His main research interest is the study of the needs and expectations of senior tourists. He has authored or co-authored several journal and conference contributions.

Chris Ryan

Chris Ryan is Professor of Tourism at the University of Waikato, New Zealand. He is editor of *Tourism Management*, and a member of the International Academy for the Study of Tourism and of the 2000 APEC Tourism Ministers' Advisory Committee. His most recent book is *Sex Tourism: Liminalities and Marginal People*, co-authored with Michael Hall and published by Routledge.

Peter Schofield

Peter Schofield is a senior lecturer in Marketing and Tourism Management at the School of Leisure, Hospitality and Food Management, University of Salford, in the United Kingdom. His research interests include the management of heritage-based tourism in urban areas, tourist decision making and behaviour, the strategic marketing of tourism destinations and hospitality service quality management.

Margaret Tiyce

Margaret Tiyce is a part-time lecturer and tutor with the School of Tourism and Hospitality Management at Southern Cross University, Lismore. She has more than 20 years' experience in the organisation, management and marketing of community-based festivals and events. Her research focuses on the impacts of festivals and events on individuals and communities. She also works closely with a range of management agencies and community groups on event planning and management, research and evaluation, visitor management, marketing, and community and regional development.

Robin Trotter

Robin Trotter is a Research Fellow with the Australian Key Centre for Cultural and Media Policy, a joint venture between Griffith University, Queensland University of Technology and the University of Queensland. Her doctoral thesis involved a study of the relationships between museums, heritage and tourism. Currently, she is involved in a range of research projects as well as teaching in the Centre's Master of Arts in Cultural and Media Policy program. Her current research interests include museums and heritage, cultural tourism, and cultural development and planning in both urban and rural communities.

Sherrie Wei

Sherrie Wei received her PhD from the State University of New York at Stony Brook. Currently, she is a lecturer at the School of Natural and Rural Systems Management of the University of Queensland. Her teaching and research interests include marketing research, senior tourism and agribusiness. In the senior tourism area, she has published work on seniors' accommodation needs and the service gap.

Chris Wood

Chris Wood is the Founder/Director of Australians Studying Abroad and has lectured at the University of Melbourne, Monash University, La Trobe University and the Rhode Island School of Design. He has published books on architectural history and travel, and articles on tourism theory, and has scripted and narrated two documentary films on Tuscany. An accomplished photographer with much published work, Chris has acted as group leader and lecturer on educational tours to Europe, the Middle East, the United States, North Africa and Asia.

Heather Zeppel

Heather Zeppel is a lecturer in the Tourism Program, School of Business, James Cook University, Cairns. Her research interests include indigenous tourism, cultural tourism, heritage tourism and festivals. Heather's publications include *Aboriginal Tourism in Australia: A Research Bibliography* (CRC Tourism, 1999) and a co-authored report, *Indigenous Wildlife Tourism in Australia: Wildlife Attractions, Cultural Interpretation and Indigenous Involvement.*

Introduction

The more widespread a human activity becomes, the more likely it is to foster internal diversity. This is as true of politics as it is of education, as true of religion as of recreation. It is strikingly true of the subject of this book — special interest tourism. Hall and Weiler's 1992 *Special Interest Tourism*, now out of print, should be acknowledged as a pioneer study in the field. This book, however, takes a different approach and covers different ground from that important earlier work.

OVERVIEW OF SIT

The expression *special interest tourism* (SIT) probably requires some explanation, although at first glance its meaning may seem self-evident. SIT is defined by Ros Derrett in chapter 1 as 'the provision of customised leisure and recreational experiences driven by the specific expressed interests of individuals and groups'. To some, SIT may simply suggest small-scale, alternative — almost incidental — tourist activities, like bush-walking or bungee jumping. But, as several of our contributors demonstrate, a special interest is not necessarily restricted to a handful of people. Neither do special interest tourists necessarily devote their every recreational minute to the activity: an interest is not an obsession. The tourist may just as easily pursue a special interest within an otherwise conventional holiday. Of course, tourist participation in one category of SIT does not exclude participation in others. Indeed, many tourists engage in a number of SIT categories simultaneously. Though the term may have been coined fairly recently, SIT often incorporates activities with well-defined ante-cedents, as is illustrated below.

The term may also be seen as self-negating — an oxymoron. If it is tourism, then almost by definition it must be a mass pursuit rather than a special interest. Surely, the argument will run, it is the 'traveller' rather than the 'tourist' who pursues special interests. The distinction first drawn by 'lit-erary' traveller Geoffrey Gorer in his dictum 'I am a traveller — thou art a tourist — he, she or they are trippers' (Gorer 1936:232) is still implicit in the advertising of many small tour companies and explicit in the perspec-tive of many travel guides. For example, popular travel guide books such as the Rough Guides and Lonely Planet books, whatever their pretensions in addressing the traveller rather than the tourist, reach out determinedly to a mass market. The distinction, then, if there ever really was one, has long been blurred. Tourists are by definition travellers, and travellers have become increasingly dependent — especially when it comes to accommo-dation and transport — on many of the instruments of mass tourism.

Most modern forms of tourism began as special interests. The famous first tour organised by Thomas Cook in 1841, often seen as the birth of mass tourism, was actually in pursuit of a special interest. Cook's clients (all 570 of them) travelled by train to attend a temperance meeting. Health tourism had its distant origins with the Roman public baths, popular, at least among well-to-do Romans, at a time when few of their contemporaries were taking baths of any kind. In more recent times the spas of Europe (sev-eral of which had Roman origins) and the resort towns of the French and Italian Rivieras were first popularised, though often unintentionally, by the physically dysfunctional, the frail and the consumptive. These unfortunates had gone to thermal springs in Belgium or France, or to the Mediterranean coast to ease or cure their condition and extend their very existence.

Some may have regarded this form of health tourism as a more practical and beneficial alternative to the religious pilgrimage, which was often made for similar reasons. What Lourdes had failed to deliver might be obtained in Menton or San Remo, and in more congenial and salubrious surroundings. As unlikely as it may seem now, the overdeveloped, congested and polluted environments of Nice and Cannes on the French Riviera are the end prod-ucts of a process that began with health tourism — that is, with a form of SIT.

Educational tourism, cultural tourism and heritage tourism (other popular forms of SIT) were born of the Grand Tour, an exercise in pro-ductive leisure focused on Italy and France, and practised particularly by the sons of the British aristocracy as early as the seventeenth century, though it reached the height of its popularity in the late eighteenth cen-tury. At least in its earlier form its participants took the Grand Tour of the cultural heritage of Europe as a way of enhancing their education. They could not have foreseen that education, culture and heritage would be treated by tourism specialists in the early twenty-first century as separate, although not mutually exclusive, categories. 'What would the upper eche-lons of English society have been like', wondered historian John Julius Norwich, 'without the Grand Tour?' (Norwich 1985:6). John Stuart Mill's famous comment on British colonialism — that it represented a 'system of outdoor relief for the British upper classes' — might well have described the Grand Tour's later manifestations, when its educational aspects had begun to give way to routine sightseeing.

As the era of the Grand Tour — with its fixation on classical monuments and the built environment — was declining, another form of special interest travel was being born. Those who regard the appreciation of nature as an inherent human characteristic may be surprised to discover that 'nature tourism' and two of its legacies, environmental tourism and rural tourism (nature tamed and ordered), have their origins in the nineteenth century with the 'rediscovery' of nature. Pioneered in the writings of Jean-Jacques Rousseau and popularised by the Romantic movement, its proponents saw pristine nature as essentially benign and inspirational, rather than the formidable, probably malicious force it was once thought to represent. The notion of a mountain as primarily beautiful rather than menacing is relatively new. In the eighteenth century the great German poet and philosopher Goethe could write that the 'irritating silhouettes and shapeless piles of granite' that constituted mountains could not be 'liked by any kindly man' (Goethe, trans. Auden 1962:52). But by the mid-nineteenth century English author Charles Dickens was entranced by even the most threatening of mountains — volcanoes. 'There is something in the fire and roar, that generates an irresistible desire to get nearer to it', he wrote, after his ascent of Vesuvius (1973:228). Nowadays, climbing active volcanoes in Indonesia, Vanuatu, Hawaii or elsewhere is an increasingly popular tourist activity. Indeed, in modern travel literature mountains so dominate other natural features that the semiologist Roland Barthes, writing about the highly regarded *Blue Guide* travel series, could complain that 'we rarely find plains [and] never plateaux. Only mountains, gorges, defiles and torrents can have access to the pantheon of travel ...' (Barthes, trans. Lavers 1972:74).

For the student of tourism this raises a problem of classification. Are the climbers of Mount Everest simply ambitious 'nature-based' tourists or should they still be considered explorers impelled by the aim of conquest? Serious mountain climbers could probably be classified, in the terms used in this book, as 'hard' adventure tourists, to distinguish them from 'soft' adventurers, whose interests include canoeing and bicycling, for example. Initially, of course, adventure must have played a part in every activity involving a form of transport, since travellers could never be entirely certain of reaching their destination. Indeed, modes of transport have given rise to a number of adventure-based special interest activities. Relatively soon after the invention of the bicycle, and with the benefit of technological advances that enhanced both comfort and safety, cycling enthusiasts formed local and regional associations; since the purpose of the device was to facilitate travel, these associations quickly became known as 'touring clubs'. Thus was born an especially distinctive form of SIT, since many bicyclists would not dream of travelling any other way.

Devotion to a particular form of travel rather than to a specific destination helps to identify another large group of SIT travellers — cruise enthusiasts, who now represent one of international tourism's fastest-growing sectors. The pleasure cruise, as opposed to the mere voyage by sea, shares something with bicycle touring: both are products of an age that produced not only great advances in mechanisation but also greater amounts of leisure time in which to benefit from them. From its inception in 1844 cruising exhibited many of the attributes of a special interest, not all of them desirable. It was not for everyone: a remarkable number of passengers still begin to feel nauseous even before the ship leaves the pier; and it was always an expensive — and therefore elitist — activity. A 'tourist class' was added to some ships only reluctantly and the standards were well below those of the 'true travellers' housed on the upper decks. The democratisation of cruising did not begin in earnest until the 1960s, when one-class vessels became the norm. A reaction to this levelling brought an upsurge in theme cruises catering for very specific tastes. The proliferation of special interest cruises continues today and represents an increasingly large share of the market. Ironically, although the origins of cruising are among the most recent of the many SIT activities and experiences described in this book, its promoters are perhaps the most intent on establishing its historical credentials.

Earlier forms of tourism, including the Grand Tour and many of Thomas Cook's initiatives, were more concerned with cultural objects than with the people who made up the cultures or fashioned the objects. Early guide books, such as Murray's *Guide to India*, paid far more attention to ancient monuments than to people. Where impressive natural spectacle or a significantly venerable built environment was absent, indigenous tourism — that is, travel whose primary motivation is an interest in a destination's native people — might occasionally be a substitute. But generally, if mentioned at all, the indigenes were alluded to only incidentally. The 'peculiar customs of the natives', in a Union Steamship Company's 1909 advertisement for a South Sea Island cruise, are noted *after* the 'coral reef, banana and cocoanut palms, and gorgeous tropical vegetation' (NCSN 1909, unpaged).

The idea of travelling primarily to enjoy local produce does not seem to have occurred to earlier travellers. Many tourists left behind familiar foods and beverages only reluctantly and would complain throughout their journey of the unfamiliar fare they were obliged to consume. English author and physician Tobias Smollett, credited with having 'discovered' the health-giving qualities of the French Riviera for British tourists in the eighteenth century, could not tolerate French food and wine, these days regarded as major reasons for visiting France. 'For my own part, I hate French cookery, and abominate garlic ...', wrote Smollett. 'The wine commonly used in Burgundy is so weak and thin, that you would not drink it in England' (Smollett 1949:72–3). Wine and food tourism is now one of the fastest growing SIT categories, although largely restricted to countries with a European tradition.

To illustrate an earlier suggestion that participation in one category of special interest tourism need not exclude the simultaneous participation in others, one need do little more than refer to an example quoted in the cruise magazine *Porthole*. Ruth Epstein and her friend Sylvie, both in their seventies and passengers on the Carnival cruise ship *Ecstasy*, found themselves male partners within a few hours of embarking. Sylvia 'took up with the ship's photographer, a dashing young man of about 50', according to Ruth's account. Not to be outdone, a short time later Ruth found her eye caught in the ship's casino by the 'enchanting glare' of 'a sprightly young man in his late 20s'. His invitation to take a 'post-gambling stroll' on deck was accepted and was followed by Ruth's discovery that they 'bonded like two souls reunited after centuries apart', despite the age difference. They were married soon after the cruise ended, even though Ruth's friend Sylvia was 'quite peeved that I had snagged a younger man than she did' (www.porthole.com.online). The essential features of three special interest tourism categories — cruising, senior tourism and sex — had thus combined to satisfy consumer expectations. The gambling environment may have been a contributing factor also, but gambling is not examined here.

Many of the chapters in this book focus on one specific special interest activity. Others are concerned with describing the context — geographic or economic, urban or rural, physical or conceptual — in which such activities take place. Although the broad range of tourist interests and activities illustrates the diversity of the subject, by no means are all SIT activities examined here. Subsequent editions of this book or other publications on the subject will introduce other topics as new trends and themes emerge and older ones are subsumed. We must be cautious, however, about introducing a new category to classify every new class of traveller whose interest lies beyond the edges of the conventional. Is soccer hooliganism, which involves purposeful travel — often to a foreign country — by enthusiasts uniformly dedicated to their special interest, a form of SIT? Or, given the large numbers that now participate in it, is it perhaps evolving into a mainstream tourist activity, at least as far as the British are concerned? It was the British, after all, in the person of Thomas Cook, who invented modern mass tourism. Are they now devising variations? This is not as facetious as it may first appear. Already there have been serious discussions about soccer hooliganism as a form of cultural (or sub-cultural) expression, and sports tourism is now seen as a legitimate area of both professional interest and academic study. In mid-2000 the British Tourist Authority announced that its new marketing strategy would centre on sports tourism (PATA June 2000:4).

The common factors that link these apparently unrelated activities so that they may all be termed aspects of SIT will become clearer as you read this book. What will also become evident is that the approach of some contributors to their topics is controversial. If further discussion and debate are generated as a result, then this book will have achieved its main aim — to stimulate as well as instruct. That many of the activities and experiences examined in this book have long pedigrees does not make them any less special. Within the overall framework of tourism they remain distinct pursuits, some with their own distinctive philosophy. A valuable lesson to be learned is that, if SIT is a relatively new term, many of the experiences and activities it encompasses have their roots firmly in the past, some in antiquity. In tourism, as in every other field of human activity, the significance of the past is inescapable.

*I*N THIS BOOK

In this book we demonstrate the complexity of the SIT sector. We explore the ways in which the growing demand for special activities is expressed, how this demand is met and the nature of SIT activity in a wide variety of urban, regional, well-established and newly emerging contexts. Today's special interest tourists want hands-on experience, intellectual challenge, the chance to develop special skills, clear task orientation and encounters that showcase cultural identity. Their search for *authentic* experience can be facilitated through contact with experts and/or participation in 'real' activities rather than events created specifically for visitors. They appreciate opportunities for planning and preparation ahead of their experiences. The global impact of the information age, interest in other languages, concern for the preservation and conservation of heritage and the environment, cultural curiosity and an interest in life-long learning are all represented in the diversity of opportunities offered by SIT providers.

Much of the SIT product is provided by small business. The case studies reveal the important role played by the sole trader, partnership and non-profit association. Motivations for starting up a SIT business are similar to those in any other industry. But with an increasing demand for personalised, specialised service in tourism, successful small business operators must demonstrate confidence, persistence, initiative, resourcefulness, optimism, effective use of feedback, moderate risk taking, long-term commitment and the capacity to tolerate uncertainty. The service provider has to identify with the consumer and prepare a product that satisfies the recognised needs. Highly motivated people interested in developing a tourism enterprise must also familiarise themselves with the appropriate administrative, marketing, financial and operating skills. And they need to know what business they are in: SIT can pose problems for farmers who fail to differentiate their farm-stay accommodation business from their sheep-shearing business; or for the doctor running a health resort alongside a medical clinic; or for the cycle hire company that also has sightseeing interests.

Our study begins by focusing on the individual tourist within the SIT sector. In chapter 1, Ros Derrett outlines the trends in the demand for specific tourism products and services that satisfy the individual consumer's needs. She discusses the delivery of viable specialist services and the management strategies required to satisfy the concerns of all stakeholders in a sustainable manner. Stakeholders can include the host community, tourism partners and government at all levels. A special interest tourist engages with a product or service that satisfies particular interests and needs. Special interest tourists demonstrate a desire for authentic experiences that offer them active, non-exploitative identification with host communities.

Next, Robyn Bushell examines issues relating to host communities and destinations, and the potential for both positive and negative impacts on social and natural environments. In chapter 2 she discusses the role and development of tourism in communities and introduces the concept of *quality of life* and how this impacts on the planning and management of SIT.

She goes on to discuss visitor impact management, introducing approaches and tools designed to monitor and evaluate the impacts of visitors on places and people. This is particularly relevant for many SIT businesses since this sort of tourism experience often relies on close interaction between host and guests and/or guests and the natural environment.

Chapter 3 deals with the economic, psychological, sociological and management perspectives of entrepreneurship. Nerilee Hing identifies small business entrepreneurship as an integral aspect of SIT provision and explores the central role of owner-managers in such ventures. Entrepreneurship has attracted unprecedented attention in the last few decades; it not only creates new employment and avenues for creativity and independence, but also capitalises on market opportunities that are increasingly suitable for small, innovative businesses. These openings include a growing range of niche markets, rapid technological developments and shorter product life-cycles driven by customer demand for better and different products and services. Hing outlines the trends, issues and processes that influence the effective and efficient delivery of business to the SIT market.

In chapter 4 Gary Prosser explains why encouraging tourists to move beyond the major international gateways is important to the tourism industry, regional communities and politicians. Global social and economic change is placing pressure on rural and regional communities in most industrialised countries. Among the driving forces behind the changing nature of regional economies and rural lifestyles are new technologies, free or less restricted trade, the decline of traditional industries, rising unemployment, changing population patterns, faster and more comfortable transport, competing land uses and increased environmental awareness. Regional tourism is represented as tourism in 'concentrated tourist areas', coastal resorts, towns and other urban settlements, and the countryside, hinterland or coastline outside capital cities. It does not rely on particular activities or experiences; rather, its character is determined by the environments in which it takes place.

In chapter 5 Jennifer Craik suggests that cultural tourism concerns forms of tourism that relate to aspects of culture — whether profiling culture, involving cultural experiences, learning about culture or participating in cultural events. For some tourists, cultural experience is the *primary* motivation for their travel. Craik argues that if we are referring solely to this group, then cultural tourism constitutes a *niche* or special interest form of travel. However, other groups of tourists can also be classified as cultural tourists because they take advantage of cultural resources during their travel experience, which has other motivations. For these tourists, culture is a *secondary*, ancillary or contingent motivation. Cultural tourism involves opportunities for tourists to sample cultural precincts, theme parks, heritage sites or centres, museums, galleries, performing arts venues, festivals and even ordinary street life.

The term 'heritage', and changes in its meaning over time, are addressed in chapter 6. Robin Trotter outlines the ways heritage products have been incorporated into a range of institutions, practices and activities, with specific reference to the governmental, institutional, organisational and industry approaches. The notion of heritage as a tourist product raises issues associated with authenticity, preservation versus access, and cultural appropriation. Heritage is an emotive area with connotations of nationhood that link into personal, familial and localised values and histories. When places or objects are first opened up to strangers and to commercial activity, it is not surprising that confrontation surfaces. Trotter discusses the dilemmas facing custodians of heritage and explains how varying agendas are balanced.

Les Killion illustrates the diverse nature of rural tourism in chapter 7. He describes the various geographic and demographic parameters, product-related issues and tourist-experience-related boundaries, while offering a general profile of rural tourists, noting the mix of domestic and international markets for rural tourism products in Australia. Killion discusses the potential of rural tourism to contribute to broader community development and introduces the role of government policy in rural tourism development. Rural tourism is not confined to agriculture and farming. The diversity of its attractions embrace indigenous and European heritage sites; aspects of culture (especially agriculture); industrial tourism; educational tourism; special events; ecological attractions; adventure tourism; wine tourism; and more recently established attractions within the built environment.

Educational tourism tells the stories of places in order to enrich the interactions of travellers with these places. In chapter 8 Christopher Wood defines this type of SIT as a blend of discursive narrative and spatial investigation that sets scholarly analysis of particular sites and events within a global context. Educational travel increases people's capacity to learn about the world by teaching them how to decode places visually, how to see the relationships between places and how to locate places in the evolution of society and culture. Wood suggests that educational tourism may take on an important new role far beyond the activities of educational tour companies. This role is based upon a historical understanding of the relationship between travel, perception and imagination.

Nigel Morpeth poses two questions in chapter 9. Which activity-based tourism forms have the flexibility to satisfy the broad range of motivational requirements of adventure tourists? And is it possible for these tourism activities to operate within the principles of sustainability? This chapter investigates the contemporary applications of cycle tourism, which, Morpeth argues, has the flexibility to satisfy the motivational requirements of adventure tourism. While both 'hard' and 'soft' dimensions of adventure tourism are considered, the soft adventure characteristics of cycle tourism are reviewed within Australian, British and European contexts. This SIT activity exemplifies how sustainable tourism policy ideals can be practically implemented.

Chapter 10 describes how indigenous cultures and peoples are involved in the tourism industry, using a variety of Australian indigenous tourism case studies. Heather Zeppel's review of indigenous tourism in Australia includes recent Aboriginal tourism strategies, tourist promotion of Aboriginal culture and research on Aboriginal tourism. She discusses indigenous tourist attractions including native museums and cultural villages, indigenous festivals or special events, and indigenous arts. Cultural, environmental and spiritual aspects of indigenous heritage and traditions are especially featured. Zeppel describes how Aboriginal groups in Australia are advancing from being exotic tourist attractions to controlling tourism on Aboriginal lands and owning tourism enterprises.

A desire to improve the health has been a motivation in the historical development of tourism ever since wealthy Romans built their seaside villas to escape the pollution of the Imperial city. In more recent times, as Ngaire Douglas describes in chapter 11, amenities aiming to satisfy the health motivations of tourists have been developed both on land, with the growth of spa towns, and at sea, following the British Medical Association's sanctioning of the therapeutic value of sea cruises in the 1870s. In the twenty-first century, with the increasingly frenetic pace of everyday life, it is likely that the pursuit of leisure-time activities that contribute to our health and wellbeing will increase. This will create opportunities for entrepreneurs, large and small, to value-add to existing products or design new products to meet the demand. Here Douglas examines one particular sector of the health tourism industry, the spa and health resort. She outlines the conceptual differences and current state of these facilities in Europe, the United States and Australia.

The last decades of the twentieth century gave rise to two significant international movements. The first was the growing popular concern for conservation and the wellbeing of our environment. The second was the remarkable effect of the jumbo jet on the growth of tourism. In chapter 12 Ross Dowling argues that the inevitable interaction between the two contributed to the growth of environmental tourism. This type of tourism takes many forms, including nature-based tourism, wildlife tourism and eco-tourism. Dowling argues that there are two streams of thought regarding the environment–tourism relationship. The first is that the natural environment is always harmed by tourism and hence the two are necessarily in conflict. The second is that the two have the potential to work together in a symbiotic, mutually beneficial way. The key to the successful growth of environmental tourism is the implementation of sustainable tourism planning and development.

Wine, food and tourism have been closely related for many years. In chapter 13 Michael Hall and Richard Mitchell claim that it is only recently, however, that the important role of wine and food in attracting tourists to a destination has been recognised by governments, researchers and the relevant industries. Wine and food, unique products of the local culture, have significant roles in tourism promotion and potential for local agricultural and economic development. For the tourism industry, wine and food are important aspects of the attractiveness and image of a destination. For the wine and food industries, and especially for small businesses, tourism is a very important way of establishing direct relationships with customers. This chapter identifies these reciprocal roles. Because of the size of the sector and the concentration of research in the area, special attention is given to the characteristics of wine tourism.

Cruising is a complex phenomenon, which, while representing one of tourism's most dynamic growth sectors, remains essentially a special interest. Developments include both bigger ships to accommodate the mass market and smaller, exclusive ships fitted out for the emerging niche market of special interest travellers. In chapter 14 Norman Douglas and Ngaire Douglas introduce some of the essential terminology of cruising, outline its historical growth and discuss the motivations of people who choose to cruise. They describe the development of the cruise business in the Asia–Pacific region, providing examples from Australia, and the methods used to estimate the economic impact of a cruise ship's arrival in port. The recurring imagery used by cruise marketers is also examined. Perceptions of security, comfort and romance play a decisive role among prospective cruise passengers and are dominant features in the marketing programs of cruise companies, large and small.

In chapter 15 Kay Dimmock and Margaret Tiyce propose festivals and events as a popular form of SIT and point to the increasing public demand for celebratory experiences. An enthusiasm for festivals and events is not specific to any particular cultural, religious or community group. Themed public celebrations can often make an important contribution to community pride and wellbeing. While festivals and events differ enormously in size, impact and rationale, they are by definition of limited duration. Dimmock and Tiyce focus on smaller festivals and describe some of the many social, political and economic reasons why a community chooses to host such an event and the potential positive and negative impacts.

Chris Ryan examines the subject of sex tourism primarily from the perspective of consensual encounters. In chapter 16 he seeks to establish what sex tourism is and draws on evidence of the motivations of both sex industry workers and clients. The Sydney Gay and Lesbian Mardi Gras is examined as an example of a product relevant to sex tourism. Ryan argues that the juxtaposition of gay and lesbian celebrations with issues of crime and prostitution arises merely as a consequence of the conceptualisation of sex tourism and that no direct relationship is demonstrated. Ryan admits that the subject of sex tourism is too complex and controversial to be adequately explored in one chapter, but he introduces some of the fundamental issues relating to this niche market.

Hein Ruys and Sherrie Wei focus on seniors as tourists and suggest how tourism service providers can better serve this market segment. It is widely acknowledged that leisure and tourism activities benefit people's health as well as their psychological wellbeing. In chapter 17 Ruys and Wei discuss changes in the travel patterns of older people and the services of tourism providers. Government policies towards tourism for seniors are outlined. For seniors, economic, health and social issues all influence travel motivation and the pattern of travel and activities in which they participate. Lifestyle changes have an impact on the ageing process. The next generation of older tourists will differ from the present one, presenting a continuing challenge for the tourism industry.

Finally, Peter Schofield in chapter 18 draws on both the urban tourism literature and the small business literature to examine urban tourism and, in particular, the role played by small businesses. One of tourism's distinguishing characteristics as a commercial activity, along with its intangible products, is the contribution made by large numbers of small businesses at each tourist destination. Schofield outlines the nature, role and significance of small tourism enterprises (STEs) in the contemporary tourist experience of urban areas. Within this context, he considers the complexity of the urban tourism product, the extent to which small businesses can be described as tourist resources and the role of government policy in the development and management of STEs.

FUTURE DIRECTIONS

All SIT proponents agree that the tourism resource bases — physical, natural and human — are vulnerable to degradation and exploitation through entrenched practices, and that SIT depends on the maintenance of high-quality resources. The case studies that accompany each chapter illustrate such concerns as:

- *socioeconomic impacts:* How can the local economic and social benefits of tourism be maximised?
- *strategic approaches:* How can all environments be integrated into tourism policies and plans?
- *management tools and techniques:* What type of environmental assessment of tourism projects is being undertaken and what types of management, monitoring and accreditation plans are in place?
- *training and education:* What processes can be introduced for both consumers and service providers to ensure environmental awareness and appropriate interpretation?
- *business strategies for sustainable tourism:* What practices ensure delivery of environment-oriented management, best practice industry standards and accreditation, and codes of good practice?
- *financing sustainable tourism:* How can the industry best encourage tourism funding of conservation, appropriate use of tourist taxes, and more collaborative initiatives by private and public bodies?
- *marketing:* How can SIT providers better connect the supply and demand aspects of tourism through marketing strategies for sustainable tourism, defining the responsibilities of tourist boards and tour operators, and extending green symbol schemes?
- *role of government at national, state, regional and local levels:* How can governments and stakeholders be encouraged to settle the debate on legislation versus self-regulation, be urged to adopt practical planning guidelines, and satisfy both community and tourism infrastructure needs?
- *public participation in sustainable SIT:* How can public participation best advance sustainable SIT through community-based initiatives, public feedback and the involvement of non-government organisations?

Development guidelines that safeguard the interests of local people must also ensure the tourist experience genuinely reflects the host community and destination; encourage responsible attitudes to the environment; ensure tourism products are of an appropriate, sustainable scale; encourage local partnerships; and integrate all relevant environments into tourism policies and plans. All stakeholders are demanding such guidelines, which should be fundamental to all policy and planning. The challenge is to maintain a sustainable balance by minimising the physical and social costs of tourism while maximising its economic and social benefits. Strategic approaches should employ appropriate management tools and techniques and incorporate training. Education programs that empower, monitor and evaluate impacts are also essential for sustainable success.

Partnerships for sustainable tourism involve business strategies allowing for the development of industry standards and accreditation, codes of good practice, voluntary actions and environmental audits leading to environment-oriented management. Such strategies encourage initiatives in the public and private sectors. Linking supply and demand through innovative marketing strategies helps promote a greater emphasis on information sharing and collaborative projects, and a greater role for tourism boards and tour operators as well as the media. Public participation in sustainable tourism will encourage greater sensitivity in development and equity and a better response to visitor needs. Community-based initiatives stimulate community empowerment — for example among indigenous people. Government at all levels is being urged to take a greater role in these developments.

All the SIT stakeholders identified in following pages seek to nurture tourism that has positive environmental, economic and sociocultural impacts within a destination. We hope that this book contributes to a greater understanding of how many of these common issues can be productively addressed.

REFERENCES

Barthes, R. (Trans. Lavers, A.). 1972. *Mythologies*. New York: Hill and Wang.

Dickens, C. 1973. *Pictures from Italy*. London: André Deutsch.

Goethe, J. W. von. (Trans. Auden, W. H. & Mayer, E.). 1962. *Italian Journey*. London: William Collins.

Gorer, G. 1936. *Bali and Angkor: A 1930s Pleasure Trip Looking at Life and Death*. London: Michael Joseph.

NCSN. 1909. *Guide to the Northern Coastal Rivers District of New South Wales*. Second Edition. Sydney: North Coast Steam Navigation Co.

Norwich, J. J. 1985. *A Taste for Travel*. London: Macmillan.

PATA (Pacific Asia Travel Association). 2000. *Issues and Trends*. June.

Smollett, T. 1949. *Travels through France and Italy*. London: John Lehman.

Ros Derrett

CHAPTER 1

Special interest tourism:
starting with the individual

LEARNING OBJECTIVES

After reading this chapter, you will have an appreciation of:

■ what special interest tourism (SIT) is and the terms used in the literature to describe it

■ the characteristics and needs of special interest tourists

■ the economic, social and environmental problems associated with SIT

■ the influences on the development of SIT

■ the conditions required for deliberate small-scale tourism development

■ the challenges facing the provision of SIT products and services, including the roles of all stakeholders.

This chapter will explore the demand for specific tourism products and services that satisfy consumer needs. The supply implications will also be discussed, especially the delivery of viable specialist services and the management required to satisfy the concerns of all **stakeholders**, including the **host community**, tourism partners and government at all levels, while maintaining the principles of sustainability.

SIT may be a new term, but it is not a new phenomenon. Many new names have been coined in the literature for the services being offered to participants in 'serious' leisure and tourism. These terms include *alternative, localised, sustainable, endemic, appropriate, cultural, eco, ego, environmental, low impact, new, ethical, responsible, respectful* and *green*. However this sector is labelled, it can be only a partial description of a tourism industry generally designed to cater for large numbers of visitors. SIT, or alternative tourism, has emerged from concerns for the delivery of sustainable tourism. Some characteristics of mass tourism are perceived to be underpinned by unsustainable practices. The literature shows a distinct contrast between the ideal types of 'mass' and 'alternative' tourism.

The tourism industry is a fragmented organisational entity interacting with numerous political, economic, sociocultural and technical environments. The theory and case study approach offered in this chapter will help you to develop a greater understanding of tourism and its subset, SIT, which deals with similar concerns on a different scale.

As you explore SIT experiences and products in this book and elsewhere in your reading, you will encounter an extraordinarily diverse range of special interest opportunities. Examples may include:

- a small-scale tour to an isolated natural environment that actively involves the individual tourist and the operator in **conservation**, **interpretation** and research of a distinctive feature of culture and landscape. This could, for example, be a daunting two-wheeled 15-day tour off the beaten track for 640 kilometres through Ladakh in the Himalayas at heights up to 5000 metres.
- a trip to attend a specific genre music festival simply to listen to the music or to participate in skills-based workshops with experts and meet like-minded enthusiasts
- a five-day bicycle tour of a regional area, sampling the local cuisine and wine and, through 'technical tourism', meeting the people responsible for getting the produce from farm gate to cafe plate
- a lantern-lit tour of Hampton Court Palace, south-west of London. Here Henry VIII (1509–47) learned of the infidelity of his fifth wife, Catherine Howard, while attending chapel. The heritage tourist wishing to learn more of the palace may, during such a tour, imbibe mulled wine and perhaps glimpse (or hear) the beheaded Queen run shrieking through the tapestry-hung gallery she is said to haunt. Guides in period costume share other stories of Tudor intrigues, though organisers say these are not suitable for children!

WHAT IS 'SPECIAL INTEREST TOURISM'?

■ 1.2.1 Definitions *of SIT*

Special interest tourism may be defined as the provision of customised leisure and recreational experiences driven by the specific expressed interests of individuals and groups. A special interest tourist chooses to engage with a product or service that satisfies particular interests and needs, so SIT is tourism undertaken for a distinct and specific reason. Poon (1997:47) suggests that 'new tourism is a phenomenon of large scale packaging of non-standardised leisure services at competitive prices to suit demands of tourists as well as the economic and socioenvironmental needs of destinations'.

■ 1.2.2 Characteristics *of SIT*

SIT is a complex phenomenon characterised by flexible delivery, market segmentation and advances in technology affecting management and distribution. Its often small-scale nature nonetheless requires operators to come to terms with issues similar to those of larger organisations within the tourism system. These include ensuring the delivery of products and services based on ecologically sustainable (ESD) principles; local integration with indigenous ownership and control, where relevant; a response to seasonal and spatial spread of demand; and caring for heritage resources. SIT planners must direct more attention towards the need for balance in the management of impacts, and to the appropriate pace of development and community consultation practices in the planning and development of new enterprises. SIT's labour-intensive nature, its tendency to employ expert personnel, its efforts to maintain the integrity of resources and its creative approach to the mediation between the tourist and the attraction are important considerations for those entering this sector. High-yielding products and services are designed to meet specific needs and are no longer determined by large-scale operations dependent on volume.

Special interest tourists demonstrate a desire for authenticity and real experiences that offer them active identification with host communities in a non-exploitative manner. Individual curiosity, the physical challenges of some environments and ethical considerations all contribute to a rapidly expanding pattern of tourist activity. Such visitors have raised expectations of flexible, personalised service. The active and conscious relationship between hosts and guests, as individuals and communities, in a way that does not degrade the quality of life of either; marketing and management issues; an understanding of the impact of leisure, travel and recreation; the role of government in planning for SIT, and specific ethical and political issues are all part of the emerging SIT landscape.

Read (1980:195) sees SIT as the hub around which the total travel experience is planned and developed. Participants identify strongly with their chosen activity and, through this, the pursuit of serious leisure. Stebbins (1982) suggests this involvement provides a way of finding personal fulfilment. According to Naisbitt (1990):

> The 1990s are characterized by a new respect for the individual as the foundation of society and the basic unit of change. 'Mass' movements are a misnomer. The environmental movement, the women's movement, the anti-nuclear movement were built one consciousness at a time, by an individual persuaded of the possibility of a new reality.

Arguably, mass marketing is no longer the dominant paradigm.

While studying its diverse characteristics, you will need to consider ways in which SIT may be:

- a question of scale or content, depending on the numbers of people involved and their degree of contact with real experiences
- dependent on the attitude and motivation of both provider and participant
- just marketing hype, the latest in faddish packaging, or a real alternative
- dependent on a degree of commercialisation
- a victim to parties whose motives and motivations could be suspect
- devoid of checks and balances, or whether these can be offered by government and the tourism industry.

■ *1.2.3* **Who are** *'special interest tourists'?*

Individuals have special interests. Some individuals are happy to share these interests with others during their travel experiences. Others prefer to limit the number of people with whom they come into contact while on holidays. They concentrate their time, energy and other resources on satisfying a specific leisure aim that allows them to engage with like-minded specialists. Bicycle touring, for example, is increasingly popular. Allenby (2000) suggests that when people are on bicycles they are not voyeurs but are active participants. The options available to cycling enthusiasts range from gentle gastronomic tours through the French countryside to a thigh- and lung-burning ordeal in the Himalayas (Allenby 2000:1). The products or services that meet their needs vary considerably. Some small groups pedal independently or join organised tours; others enter mass events such as the annual NSW Roads and Traffic Authority's RTA Big Ride in which more than 1500 people ride through regional Australia.

Other individuals may have a serious interest in fine art and make extended visits to art galleries to observe, sketch, meet artists or take master classes. Alternatively, busloads of visitors may arrive at the same art gallery as part of a generic tour, which on a given day could include a theme park, local markets and shopping experiences. Some ways to differentiate the mass and special interest tourist are explained in this chapter.

*I*SSUES ASSOCIATED WITH ALTERNATIVE TOURISM

■ *1.3.1* **Critical** *arguments*

There is a demonstrable shift away from mass tourism to niche marketing, which is a response to the increasing sophistication of the travelling public. This shift suggests that traditional attractions are losing appeal. The available products become fragmented and costly to deliver and may require 'reinvention', which involves capital expenditure and changes in policy and marketing by companies and governments. The search for new experiences threatens current investment and provides alternative stresses on infrastructure like roads, transport systems, existing technology and accommodation, and access to sensitive natural locations. The economic, social, cultural and environmental costs are ever under scrutiny. Both public and private sectors see problems with small-scale, personalised tourism traffic. Visitor interest in community-based attractions requires upskilling of inexperienced personnel in tourism management, which demands scarce resources.

Criticism of emerging special interest or alternative tourism identifies limits to its potential for solving the major problems of the global tourism industry (Butler 1990; Wheeler 1991; Stear 1994; Craik 1995; Weaver & Opperman 1999). Arguments advanced include those outlined below.

- Alternative tourism will only spread the negative influences of mass tourism over a wider area.
- It is not realistic to propose that the tourism industry can be controlled by local communities and be self-sustaining.
- The concept of alternative tourism is elitist and middle class.
- The economies of scale of individual operators may be inadequate to implement sustainable practices.
- Alternative tourism places unrealistic faith in education and awareness marketing campaigns.
- Alternative tourism is inequitable because it will increase the cost of travel.
- Proponents of alternative tourism equate it with maintaining the environmental status quo, which is unrealistic in the light of projected increases in world travel.
- SIT is a high-risk strategy that has emerged in the vacuum created by the shift from traditional mass tourism attractions by more sophisticated, better-informed tourists.
- Products are based upon the decline in some industries and are seen as a panacea for regional development (for example, rural crises creating a dependence on farmstay attractions).
- The term 'alternative tourism' can be appropriated by unscrupulous operators.

However, the problems facing both mass and alternative tourism could be addressed with the development of guidelines that:

- secure an appropriate scale of development
- safeguard the interests of the local people
- ensure tourists experience and understand the genuine culture of the destination
- encourage a responsible treatment of the environment
- ensure local economic benefit
- ensure sociocultural, economic and physical harmony.

■ *1.3.2* **Sustainability** *and SIT*

The World Tourism Organisation (WTO 1993, cited in Manning 1999) sponsored an initiative to develop indicators to assist industry managers, regulators and communities in better understanding the future risks of tourism development. The issue was **sustainability**. It can be argued that in recent decades tourism has grown from an exclusive activity called 'travel' to a mass phenomenon, and now there is a movement to advocate a kind of 'back to travel' shift while really moving towards 'megatravel' (Wheeler 1991). At all levels economies, cultures and environments have been transformed. In the 1980s advocates of special interest/soft/low impact/ green/responsible tourism offered an alternative to mass tourism. Some critics (Wheeler 1991; Twining-Ward 1999) argue that alternative tourism diverts attention from the real issues facing the tourism industry and that sustainable tourism development may be a more promising solution.

Sustainability has had an important bearing on the tourism development debate, especially since the release of the Brundtland Report (WCED 1987), the UN Conference on Environment and Development (UNCED) in Rio de Janeiro (1992) and its Agenda 21 manifesto, and the output from the follow-up Kyoto meeting in 1997. Sustainable tourism development is accommodated in the context of wider concerns for community wellbeing.

The sustainability quotient in tourism depends on various factors involving all stakeholders. It implies efforts by stakeholders to renew, nurture, preserve, maintain or increase resources appropriate to their needs. The main components of sustainability, as interpreted by Brundtland (France 1997:12), include revival in growth, change to the quality of growth, meeting basic needs, stabilisation of population, conservation and enhancement of resources, reorientation of technology, risk management and addressing the environment in economic planning. This view demonstrates a strong people-centred ethical stance that places an emphasis on satisfying human needs. This is reflected in the literature of alternative or special interest tourism, with its respect for host communities, sensitivity to social and economic development, ethical environmental resource management and wider participation in decision making.

The numbers of special interest tourists remain low compared with those of mass tourism, which emerged globally in the second half of the twentieth century. The issue of volume is a fundamental problem for tourism development (Wheeler 1997), and special interest or 'responsible' tourism is seen as an alternative approach that addresses some of the concerns for limiting the impacts of mass tourism. Managing the growing impact of these alternative tourists who wish to experience the lifestyle and culture of a host community raises serious issues concerning planning, implementing and monitoring development.

A Pacific Asia Travel Association (PATA) think tank (Oelrichs & Prosser 1992) suggested that 'the tourism industry must be profitable and environmentally sustainable if it is to provide long-term benefits to Australia and the Australian community, but this will not be achieved without a new and different approach to industry planning and development'. The report recognised that an approach that acknowledges the interdependence of tourism, culture and ecology, and that seeks to enhance the benefits of tourism and eliminate or ameliorate its negative consequences, should underpin a values-based approach to tourism planning, management and marketing.

1.4 INFLUENCES ON THE DEVELOPMENT OF SIT

The traditional separation of work and leisure dates back to the late nineteenth century. People now have wider horizons owing to such factors as increased and changing emphasis in their leisure time, advances in technology — from transport to computers — and greater opportunities for dispersal of their discretionary wealth. Leisure activities are pursued not only at home but also on holidays, and this factor has been embraced by the SIT sector.

The leisure time available for people to become tourists is usually in the form of paid leave, public holidays, weekends and retirement. Access to holidays now reflects the existence of a more competitive world economy. Labour markets are more flexible, though employment is less secure. Work hours for some, particularly full-time employees, the more highly skilled and managers, have risen. Many people's working lives start later and finish earlier, providing greater opportunities for travel before and after the working years. Increasing wealth and refinements in air travel have combined with shorter work weeks and more public and paid holidays. These trends have contributed to greater tourism activity; at the same time, many employees are more concerned about job security than taking long holidays.

The tourism market's response to these pressures includes changing patterns to meet the demand for shorter, more frequent and more intensive tourism experiences. This leads to high-yield options for tourism operators: visitors are prepared to spend more but stay for shorter periods, which can provide a better return for tourism investment. There is also an increasing link between holidays and personal interests, and the tourism experience becomes an opportunity to exploit those interests more intensively. Holidays become an essential part of a holistic lifestyle that includes changes of scenery and climate but complements established special interests.

Changes in family life and generational responsibilities, broader economic and lifestyle variations, together with higher expenditures on leisure pursuits, allow for greater segmentation of the tourism market. Consumers do not have as much free time as predicted: indeed, in some industrialised countries there is an imbalance between unemployment for many and overwork for some. Time-poor but money-rich consumers will demand satisfaction and personal development from precisely tailored, flexible products. Retirees, who are free to travel throughout the year and have a wide range of incomes, will make different demands (see chapter 17).

Change is occurring in the way that cultural tourism, for example, is described in the literature and how it is being dealt with in the marketplace. A criterion based upon *what* is visited (such as monuments and artistic events) is being replaced by one that concerns *how* they are visited (Wood 1992). This shift reflects a move from cultural tourism's being represented as a way of protecting monuments *from* tourists, to its use in an 'educative role to teach people to respect them and its economic power to nurture them' (Wood 1992:4). Craik (1995) reflects that cultural tourism consists of customised excursions into other cultures and places to learn about their people, lifestyle, heritage and arts in an informed way that genuinely represents those cultures and their historical contexts (see chapter 5). The changing emphasis in tourism policy, planning and practice in Australia has implications for marketing, programming and management practice in cultural organisations. The significant cultural resources identified include subcultural diversity, festivals, live performances, Aboriginal heritage and regionally specific development.

1.5 MARKETING SIT

SIT, like other tourism sectors, is market driven, responding to the specific needs of enthusiasts for 'travel with a purpose'. Rapid changes have been noted in the ways tourists with particular interests now access the Internet, for example. Providers of SIT products and services are offering more information via the Web and encouraging direct contact prior to meeting their guests. Both parties have greater expectations, with explicit information on sites, destinations and services and with personalised contact already established. This medium addresses the needs of individuals with opportunities for attention to details such as special diets, tour group numbers and customised tourism experiences once the individual's skills, commitment, resources and needs are known.

SIT businesses are using the ten value segments identified by Roy Morgan in conjunction with Ogilvy and Mather (cited in Dickman 1997) (see table 1.1). They offer insights into the psychographic elements of social class, personal values, stage in life cycle and consumer attitudes that could be broadly applied to tourism markets. SIT operators could also select from these behavioural patterns to target specific people.

■ Table 1.1
Value segments

VALUE SEGMENTS	FEATURES
1. Basic Needs (4 per cent of the population)	Refers to the pattern of responses from people who hold traditional views of life, enjoy passive activities and are fairly satisfied with their life. These people are generally retired, pensioners, widowers and people with low incomes.
2. A Fairer Deal (5 per cent)	People who are relatively dissatisfied with their lives, including the highest level of unskilled workers. They are pessimistic, cynical and insecure. They think everyone else has all the fun and they miss out. They feel anger and disillusionment and often hostility to authority.
3. Conventional Family Life (12 per cent)	Life revolves around the home and giving children the life opportunities they deserve. They place a high value on time with family and friends. They strive for financial security and see making money as a way to secure their lifestyle.
4. Traditional Family Life (19 per cent)	These are the over-50 'empty nesters'. They retain a strong commitment to family roles and values and are interested in their extended family. Life centres on home, garden and traditional activities. They are cautious about new things and ideas.
5. Look at Me (13 per cent)	Young, active and unsophisticated, they are self-centred, peer-driven and looking for fun and freedom. They seek a prosperous life and are generally unmarried with no children. They are fashion and trend conscious and socially active. They take their leisure and sport seriously. They are not interested in causes.
6. Something Better (8 per cent)	Probably well-educated, they have responsible jobs, feel confident, ambitious and see themselves as progressive. They want all the good things of life and are prepared to overextend themselves financially to have things now rather than later.
7. Real Conservatives (7 per cent)	They view themselves as conservative in most things. They are asset rich, but income poor; they are interested in security, tradition and stability. They hold conservative social, religious, moral and ethical views.
8. Young Optimists (8 per cent)	They are generally optimistic about the future and most likely to view themselves as middle to upper middle class. They are today's students, computer technologists and professionals. They are career building and travelling.

(continued)

VALUE SEGMENTS	FEATURES
9. Visible Achievers (16 per cent)	Generally over 30 years of age, they enjoy above-average incomes, want personal recognition of their success and are interested in collecting visible signs of achievement. They believe they are in control of their lives and they take an interest in public affairs and politics. They have a strong focus on themselves and their family's needs and desires.
10. Socially Aware (10 per cent)	Socially responsible, community-minded people, they are likely to be involved in community activities and environmental groups, and believe they are progressive and open-minded. They are early adopters of products and ideas and take a global view of the world and political issues.

Source: *Dickman (1997)*

Dickman (1997:32) suggests that providers of specialist tourism, arts, festivals, events and performance products would probably be attempting to reach groups 4, 5, 8, 9 and 10.

Is the alternative/sustainable tourism discussed within the tourism industry and in the wider community just marketing hype? Is there a real alternative to the products provided over recent years, which critics claim have placed unchecked burdens on recipient regions and inflicted a series of catastrophes on local economies, environments and sociocultural development? Segmentation represents a powerful marketing tool because it creates visitor identification. While tourists wishing to participate in special interest products are not homogeneous, specific and differentiated strategies can be pursued by operators, communities and public agencies.

1.6 CONSUMER PROFILE AND DEMAND FOR SIT

The profile of the SIT participant is linked with classic studies that demonstrate the influence of cultural heritage. These analyses include the socio-psychological motivations presented by Crompton (1979), Cohen's (1972) 'drifter' and 'explorer', and Plog's (1974) psychographic continuum. Allocentric behaviour is only one way to categorise the motivations of individual travellers. Classifications such as Smith's (1989) tourist typology and Poon's (1993) 'old' and 'new' tourists — the latter in search of novel experiences as independent travellers, adopting 'new tourism' to meet this need — clearly point to more adventurous, highly individual, self-directed forms of tourism experience. These people journey to find the unfamiliar (Urry 1990).

Krippendorf (1997) points out that little has changed in the responses of individuals to questions posed by psychological tourism research. He suggests the complexity of tourist motivations will offer a truth for all sectors of the tourism market. He maintains travel is still for recuperation and regeneration, for compensation and social integration and for escape. It encourages greater communication, explores other cultures, liberates people from obligations, creates a sense of freedom, self-determination and self-discovery and generates happiness through entertainment.

However, there have been changes in consumer behaviour. The resultant segmentation shows that the values and lifestyles of the 'new consumer' (Poon 1997) are reflected in tourists who are well-educated, better informed, more independent, flexible, spontaneous and unpredictable. Such tourists tend to demonstrate a 'see and enjoy, but do not destroy' attitude. With more travel experience comes a desire for quality experiences and a variety of specific activities to satisfy personal interests.

With changing values has come an interest in *being* rather than *having*, a sensitivity to the biophysical environment, an appreciation of things that are different, an eagerness to participate and a search for the real or natural. Greater flexibility in work hours, higher incomes and frequent short breaks (the average domestic trip lasts four nights and is taken within five hours drive of home) mean that travel has become a way of life. Consumers wish to be in charge during their free time and, in an attempt to be different from the crowd, are more likely to take risks (Poon 1997).

Read (1980, cited in Hall & Weiler 1992) suggests that SIT or **REAL travel** consists of four major elements — *rewarding, enriching, adventuresome* and *learning* experiences. Individuals participating as special interest tourists like to satisfy their curiosity, learn more, appreciate beauty, collect things, improve themselves, express their personalities and receive approval from others. They generally wish to be first in everything and recognised as authorities and influential, so as to have a good story to tell of their experience. They seek to fill their increased leisure time with value-for-money experiences. They expect a high standard of service and to obtain personal prestige or social or cultural advancement from their commitment to specific 'cutting edge' activities. There is an element of fashion or trendsetting in consumer motivations. The self is at the centre of modern consumer society. It ties together issues of choice, identity, status and culture.

Noticeable trends emerging in research into tourism consumer behaviour in recent years have been:
- a shift in interest from traditional tourist attractions to special interest products
- a move from mass tourism to a demand for personalised and sophisticated tourism with a wide range of quality choices
- a growing commitment to the integrity of a region's natural and built environment, and the accompanying landscape and culture
- an interest in nostalgia and acknowledgement of heritage
- increasing numbers of short-stay visits
- a growing awareness of multiculturalism
- increasing interest in the diversity of artform practice
- greater interest in experiencing rather than passive entertainment
- greater desire for accessibility, authenticity, ritual and spectacle.

The film *Jurassic Park* renewed many adults' interest in dinosaurs. Such adults may undertake three-week expeditions with the Dinamation International Society (fabricators of the film's robotic dinos, among other palaeontological projects) to remote corners of Wyoming, in the United States, and exotic Mongolia. Curious, inexperienced participants can take a five-day introductory dig and course called 'Colorado Canyons', held near Grand Junction, Colorado, in the United States.

The Colorado expedition is user-friendly. Participants stay in the Holiday Inn Grand Junction; transportation, several meals (one at Dinosaur Pizza) and a Palaeontology 101 class are included. The dig itself is comparatively posh: white tarps protect participants from the blazing desert sun while fans cool the area and whoosh away inquisitive flies.

'Colorado Canyons' is held six times annually near Dinamation's showplace, Devil's Canyon Science Learning Center, a 7000-square-metre playground for children of all ages. Exhibits include more than 20 amazingly lifelike dinosaur robots (complete with a hatching egg), interactive displays, earthquake simulators and a full-scale laboratory where volunteers prepare fossils for research.

Devil's Canyon lies in the heart of one of the richest fossil deposits in the world in eastern Utah and north-western Colorado. The quarry is noted not only for its numerous and diverse fossils but also for the unusual dimensions of the specimens.

Participants are bombarded with information on the geology of the Morrison Formation where the most important finds are made as well as on the anatomical basics needed to differentiate fossilised bone from rock. The lectures, slide presentations and hikes through the surrounding terrain might appear dryly academic were it not for the enthusiasm of Jim and his team and excited anticipation for the dig itself (days 3 and 4). The site is unexpectedly small yet eerie.

The tools of the trade are humble. Dig kits include knee pads, whisk brooms, camel's hair paintbrushes, dental picks and screwdrivers. A palaeontology dig requires participants to be biologist, surveyor, dental technician, miner, house-cleaner, taxidermist and mechanic all in one. This is meticulous, time-consuming, even tedious work. Each digger has his or her own tiny area to dust and chip.

Souvenirs of the adventure are prepared on day 5, starting with casting take-home specimens — an allosaur's tooth, a mymoorpelta scale — in the laboratory. Panoramic views from Douglas Pass highlight the area's many ecosystems, from subalpine to semi-arid landscapes. Participants collect invertebrate fossils such as 200-million-year-old crickets, fish scales and bird feathers, which the Bureau of Land Management allows civilians to keep.

Rank amateurs are entrusted with digging up valuable fossils. Indeed, as the scientists constantly point out, amateurs have made many of palaeontology's most valuable finds, so there's a tremendous sense of pride and involvement; moreover, the fee for participation helps fund the expedition itself. And participants can actually see the bones unearthed in their natural habitat; no reconstructed skeleton in a museum can reproduce the awe a genuine two-tonne pelvis the size of a VW evokes.

Participants can experience the thrill of an authentic, important palaeontological dig — and perhaps have their name recorded in the scientific annals, or at least in the dig grid.

Source: *Adapted from information supplied by Jordan Simon*

1.7 $\mathcal{S}$UPPLY AND SERVICE

SIT products offer customised packages of experiences developed for niche markets. These products provide unique insights into particular destinations, communities or bodies of knowledge. The emphasis is on experiencing rather than merely seeing landscapes and lifestyles. Each specialist product offers services that include authentic experiences to allow for learning and involvement with local people. Providers of SIT products, therefore, need to ensure that they understand and can deliver on the service characteristics sought by prospective consumers. These include the following:

- The **tourism service provider** recognises the consumer as an individual and understands individual needs.
- The service provider is knowledgeable and is willing to share that knowledge with the consumer.
- The service provider is trustworthy and sincere, just as in a personal relationship.
- The consumer is not intimidated, ignored or neglected by the service provider but, rather, is treated as the focal point of the encounter, not the victim.
- A personal rather than commercial relationship develops that is efficient but relaxed, and warm but competent.

■ 1.7.1 The business *of SIT*

Entrepreneurs wishing to establish SIT businesses generally plan their enterprises like most **small business** operators. After reading chapter 3 you will have a comprehensive understanding of the processes involved. Underpinning the start-up of the SIT business is research. A niche must be identified through observation, personal experience or published industry research. Many businesses are established by people who have already successfully run similar businesses elsewhere. Entrepreneurs with the personal energy to pursue such a commitment need to seek out the capital required to make it a reality. Studies into business failure noted by Hing (in chapter 3) recognise the lack of business experience of many first-time small business operators.

Self-employment in this field is often seen as a means of achieving a life-style choice that can be shared with like-minded tourists. Many bed and breakfast accommodations have been inspired by the owners' personal experience of similar enterprises. The choices made by baby boomers who accept early retirement or superannuation payouts have led to a proliferation of homestay, farmstay and guesthouse accommodation in the Northern Rivers region of New South Wales, whose appealing coastal and rainforest landscapes encourage a relaxed lifestyle for operators and visitors.

Operators wishing to move from one industry to another — for example, from broad acre agriculture to offering rural farmstay hospitality — need self-confidence, optimism, initiative and a willingness to take risks. The operator may bring to the business administrative skills and a degree of financial security through existing ownership of the resources underpinning the proposed business (e.g. land or transportation). However, effective industry networks are also required, as is an understanding of the market-place and a dedication to particular interests that may be shared with visitors, such as kayaking, farming, wine-making, pottery, cooking or other artisanship.

It is also important that the entrepreneur understands the planning, industrial, legal and developmental frameworks in which the business is obliged to operate. An awareness of local conditions, such as zonings peculiar to local government, infrastructure, transport and insurance and licensing regulations, is essential. The scale or geographical location of the operation may place it in conflict with the existing host community and at odds with traditional land use, for example.

The legal form of the organisation chosen will influence the operation, day-to-day management, authority and power within the organisation. Mechanisms to monitor and review the business's operation must be built in. Whether the business takes the form of a sole trader, partnership, company, trust, incorporated association or an enterprise founded on a mix of public and private sector investment, its objectives must be clearly identified. Husband and wife operations often are so busy with the day-to-day running of the business that they neglect 'staff meetings' that would ensure that essential lines of communication are maintained.

Operators need an effective financial plan for the business and an awareness of the true costs. They must understand how to create meaningful data, how to use budgets, monitor cash flow and apply financial discipline, especially where seasonality impinges on the operations. How the business sources finance can be complex. Funding may come from the cash reserves of those who have the business idea, from joint ventures with sympathetic investors or from a number of arrangements made with lending institutions. Advice is available from both private and public sector bodies.

Whether the business is a two-person operation or has a staff of fifty, it is important that all employees have job descriptions, and that appropriate people are allocated tasks that allow for seamless delivery of the product or service. SIT operations also need to keep abreast of industry trends, training, accreditation and best practice, together with changes in legislation.

Image building for the organisation demands a thorough understanding of marketing. Ross and Ross (1990) identify specific areas of concern for small business operators in positioning and pricing the product or service and understanding the use of media for publicity and public relations. Information technology offers small business opportunities to place itself in the global marketplace through the use of websites, e-mail and direct marketing for those special interest tourists who like to be prepared before making a booking.

Operators need to monitor their operations constantly. They can network with the specific interest area in which they conduct their business in order to remain alert to trends, update their skills in any aspect of their operation and regularly review their business objectives to ensure the realistic setting of goals. Associations established by operators in the specific sectors or in particular regions allow for swapping of ideas, bench-marking and reporting of research. Many local councils offer support through their economic development units. Chambers of commerce provide another forum for operators to keep abreast of best practice. Appropriate response to customer feedback is important, as is dialogue with suppliers and residents of the host community, to ensure that markets such as Visiting Friends and Relatives (**VFR travellers**) can be tapped in low seasons. Such dialogue allows for partnerships to be established that will enhance the business's profile. Supporting local events and participation in local promotions can have positive spin-offs for the business. It is important for operators to participate in data collection by various agencies, which may assist their business in the longer term.

■ *1.7.2* **Public** *stakeholders*

Governments at the national, state and regional levels are involved in the provision of tourism services, research and information sharing. Public access land includes forests, national parks, zoos, botanical gardens, heritage sites and river, estuarine or marine reserves. Local governments offer sporting facilities, libraries, museums, galleries, performing arts centres, cultural amenities, civic projects and public parkland, all of which serve as attractions for visitors. Tourists of all kinds identify with many of these facilities and seek to engage actively with them. In Australia state and national transport systems play an integral part in service delivery and are often an end in themselves.

Those managing these services need to address the key principles of quality customer services demanded by the marketplace. They need knowledgeable staff to deliver accurate interpretation of sites, an understanding of the need to limit overuse of property, sensitivity to land ownership issues and appreciation of cultural heritage. Clear, simple and truthful collateral (promotion material) and signage must be present to guide potential customers to the properties and services. Partnerships with other elements of the tourism system to facilitate packages can play an important role. Fundamental to all this is an acknowledgement of the connection between tourism and such specialist areas as indigenous culture, visual arts, conservation of the natural environment and local history.

There may be a tension between what is for the common good and how best to translate the increasing calls for access. Some institutions are introducing user-pays models. Levels of government investment to ensure equity for residents and visitors are constantly under review, and staff are being trained in the ways of marketing through merchandising, media contact and tour guiding. Sometimes it is an uneasy collaboration, and ongoing evaluation of such arrangements has identified opportunities for outsourcing aspects of the operations, such as on-site cafes, souvenir sales and front-of-house management.

Government statistical data on cultural tourism generally focus on visits to formal cultural institutions. Iconic elements of the built environment in Australia's urban centres, such as the Sydney Opera House, the Stockman's Hall of Fame in Longreach or Brisbane's Southbank complex, attract international and domestic tourists alike. And tourists like to shop. Emerging cultural tourism enterprises in the public sector are recognising the opportunities to sell emblematic T-shirts, art or craft works or distribute souvenirs as part of the SIT business.

■ 1.7.3 Community-based *SIT*

'Community, the custodians of the content of Australian tourism, must be enabled to participate in tourism by forming its content. Only if Australians are involved in tourism will it survive' (Wood 1993). This is a substantial premise for the development of tourism sensitive to the concerns of the host community.

Lips (cited in Wood 1992:4) suggests that:

> cultural tourism is the art of participating in another culture, of relating to people and places that have a strong sense of their own identity. It is an approach to tourism that gives tourists credit for intelligence, and promises them some depth of experience and real-life layering that can be explored on many levels.

Participants in this new, alternative and cultural tourism are seeking authentic, informed, quality experiences (Brokensha & Guldberg 1992:30). Authenticity is a personally constructed, contextual and changing concept, but with visitors increasingly wanting 'to do what the locals do' many regional communities are interested in developing distinctive tourism products and services.

Rural communities, for example, are working to establish a dynamic that will make them attractive not only to residents but also to visitors. However, some are concerned about the loss of value-based culture from which the community derived its tradition and identity over generations. Those aspects of community life that visitors may find attractive become commodities and the resultant commercial imperative can bring tension. Local communities express keen interest in being consulted in terms of policy and planning, and in taking responsibility for development and building sustainability into all decisions.

This is particularly evident where communities have developed festivals and events reflecting the lifestyle choices of the residents. There can be resistance to the commercialisation of activity that has become a way of life, but festivals that have amused and entertained locals for generations are now being recognised as opportunities to promote towns, share a specific local pursuit and provide economic gain for communities. The Jacaranda Festival in Grafton in regional New South Wales was established in the 1930s. Beef Week in Casino began in the early 1980s to highlight the importance of a local industry. Both community-based, non-profit volunteer organisations find that the annual programming of their event now has as much to do with tourism marketing as it does with the traditional community entertainment and cultural development.

When opportunities to revitalise a community arise — for example, by placing an art and craft outlet in an unused railway station, or by opening a museum with a collection of memorabilia to a local hero, or by offering locally grown produce at functions hosted by a local tour operator — they may be undertaken by non-profit, community-based organisations. Events such as agricultural shows, fishing competitions and sporting fixtures begun generations earlier may be revitalised in the light of increased interest from domestic and international tourists. Some of these enterprises, which return the personal investment made by volunteers or underemployed locals, can generate funds to rejuvenate aspects of the community's infrastructure.

Expertise, finance, professionalism, time, energy, management and audience are often offered voluntarily by local people to assist in the creation of amenities such as festivals, heritage sites, museums, galleries and well-signposted loops and trails that highlight relevant themes and events in the district. These people recognise the incubator nature of such initiatives and hope that further investment by government or the private sector may transform these ideas into viable longer-term opportunities. Tourists are agents of change. Each community seeks to establish thresholds with which they are comfortable, so that they can manage the resources and the communal will appropriately. Increased SIT activity has significant implications for regional economic development.

Community leaders stress the opportunities in a given situation rather than the problems. This emphasis follows the direction taken by such commentators as the late Robert Theobold and David Suzuki, who advocate centralised investment in regional tourism infrastructure, as occurs in other areas of endeavour. They recognise the importance of using fundamental values such as honesty, responsibility, humility and cooperation, and favour a community-based approach to economic management, with most of the funds for those who need help being generated locally. People want to work on what matters most to them.

Table 1.2 *Simplified SIT product analysis*

STRENGTHS	WEAKNESSES	OPPORTUNITIES	THREATS
• Labour intensive; can generate employment opportunities through markets, studios, performance • Small-scale operations • Capitalise on educational, interpretative, participatory activity • Celebrate unique sense of place and community lifestyle choices • Explore built and natural heritage • Offer a variety of appealing landscapes and lifestyle choices • Capitalise on personal strengths, skills, experience of entrepreneurs • Investment in distinctive products and services	• Poor recognition of host region as a prime cultural tourism destination • Lack of data on tourism assets; need for research and audit of resources • Lack of cooperation between small businesses in regional promotion and industry development • Poor networking and cooperation between players • Lack of professional administrative, marketing and finance expertise • Ad hoc volunteer committees convene special community events without accountability, monitoring or evaluation • Elitist approach to providing some arts/cultural/heritage/community/public land management services • Seasonal limitations on tourist visits • Inadequate public transport service and infrastructure in regional areas • Inadeqate signage (e.g. a lack of internationally recognised symbols) • Degradation of existing heritage property, public amenities	• Answers some regional economic woes • Offers chances for authentic lifestyle sharing through personalised small-scale operations that involve mixing with and meeting local people • Can link with other promotions, such as ATC theme years, regional consortia marketing and specialist area collaboration • Increased protection and sustenance of lifestyle options • Cultural tourism can be placed at the centre of urban regeneration strategies, reanimate and rejuvenate existing cultural facilities, and attract investment — Mainstreet, Tidy Towns, civic design projects • Opportunities to capitalise on larger domestic markets through distinctive, uniform signage on main roads • Breaks the seasonal cycle of tourist visits by introducing special events or consolidating existing attractive elements of community calendar	• Commodification of cultural products — authenticity compromised • Artists struggle to make a living in a disorganised marketplace • Exploitation of natural resources through increased carrying capacity (e.g. for festivals and special events) degrading locations • Marginalisation of some host community activities as they fail to attract tourists • Lack of appropriate and adequate funding for specific projects • Lack of ability to locate sufficient investment • Competition from other (domestic and international) regions • Lack of cooperative information sharing

STRENGTHS	WEAKNESSES	OPPORTUNITIES	THREATS
	• Lack of appropriate venues for performance • Can become difficult to manage, monitor and redress, especially when Free Independent Travellers (FIT) involved with car hire and backpacking, rather than organised groups • Contact between host community and visitors can have poor social impacts, with numbers, range and scale of visits, and can cause ambivalence about tourism by locals; hostility towards tourists may increase • Small-scale operations are unlikely to be profitable. • Emphasis on yield could price product or service out of the market or lead to need to offer volume and mass tourism product	• Provides user-pays training programs for volunteer administrators; summer schools; artform classes; cooperative education programs with heritage and conservation agencies • Provides equipped workspaces for production and training of artists; incubator work places encouraging studio visits and retailing	

Source: *Adapted from Derrett (2000)*

1.8 MANAGING SIT

■ 1.8.1 Understanding *balance*

Minimising tourism's negative physical impacts presents challenges. Stakeholders at all levels are looking for balance. They are seeking to maximise the local economic and social benefits of tourism through sound and appropriate strategies, using approaches that integrate the environment into tourism policies and plans. This should ensure the application of appropriate management tools and techniques and the incorporation of training and education methods that empower, monitor and evaluate impact.

Partnerships for sustainable tourism involve business strategies allowing for the development of industry standards and accreditation, codes of good practice, voluntary actions and audits leading to environment-oriented management. The financing of sustainable tourism seeks to encourage initiatives in the public and private sectors. Linking supply and demand through innovative marketing strategies places greater emphasis on information sharing, collaborative projects, involvement of the media and the role of tourism boards and tour operators. Public participation in sustainable tourism will allow for greater sensitivity of development, response to visitor needs, encouragement of community-based initiatives and the empowerment of indigenous people. Government at all levels is being urged to take a greater role. The traditional top-down model of tourism development policy and planning had government and expert-driven activity steeped in entrepreneurial practices that smacked of neocolonialism. The bottom-up approach adopted in recent times, with its market orientation, suggests a more sustainable way forward.

■ 1.8.2 Impacts *on host communities*

Table 1.3 briefly identifies the changes that may take place over time in the resident community as a result of its interaction with tourism. While the framework is limited in its application, it needs to recognise the various opinions that may exist simultaneously in any community. It introduces the literature on tourism impacts that must be considered by students of SIT. The passive or active responses to tourism and favourable or unfavourable attitudes are addressed in the literature.

■ Table 1.3
Research into sociocultural impacts of tourism on communities

DOXEY (1975)	BUTLER (1974)	AP & CROMPTON (1993)	KRIPPENDORF (1984:46–7)	DOGAN (1989)
euphoria	active	embracement	direct, continuous contact; depend on tourism for income	resistance
apathy	passive	tolerance	beneficiaries of tourism businesses	retreatism
irritation	favourable	adjustment	direct, frequent contact; only partly derive from income from tourism	boundary maintenance
antagonism	unfavourable	withdrawal	locals have little contact with tourists; see them in passing	revitalisation
final level			politicians and political lobbyists	adoption

It is useful to examine the research upon which the observations in the table are made and reflect on the range of possible responses that community management, tourism planning and development, and government policy may make.

1.9 FUTURE TRENDS

The trends taking SIT into the twenty-first century have profound implications for all sectors of society. Corporate, government and community sectors will feel the impact of changes in the lives of individuals. The global marketplace will need to respond to new demands. Individuals are concerned for their safety, security and health, and issues concerning terrorism and crime may cause shrinking outbound markets — from the United States, for example. Despite these concerns, certain trends are becoming clear. Research conducted by *Travel & Tourism Analyst* (Cockerell 1999) shows evidence that international long-haul travel is growing faster than short-haul and that short breaks — especially city breaks — have urban tourism growing in appeal. Other growth sectors include the cruise business, adventure travel and health tourism. With an increase in demand for travel and related products from people of 60 years and over, the seniors market is also growing strongly.

Operators of SIT businesses bent on satisfying current and future needs will not only have to work more smartly in the operational climate, but also recognise the forces that concern individual needs, particularly in the areas of humanitarianism, familial responsibilities, law and order issues, personal health and education. Interestingly, the earlier commitment to sustainable, nature-based tourism, at the forefront of alternative tourism movements of the 1980s, now appears to attract less attention. Our natural capital — resources such as clean air and drinking water — appears to have been subsumed by the global industrial system. SIT's role in dealing with future environmental change is part of the complex evolution of any industrial landscape.

1.10 SUMMARY

This chapter has introduced the complex area of SIT through the forces shaping the phenomenon and its impacts. Practical, academic and case study approaches have been employed to explore what preferences SIT participants have, what they seek and how operators address this growing market for specifically tailored tourism products and services.

Subsequent chapters will identify how research into SIT has developed and will showcase how particular aspects of this sector of tourism have manifested themselves in the marketplace. One trend is that individuals with special interests they pursue 'at home' now take these interests 'on holiday'. There is a greater willingness to pursue novel and risky adventures while on holiday and a growing sensitivity to biophysical environments, host communities and sociocultural resources. These factors will influence tourist choice. Because SIT provides such diverse options to participants, it is difficult to gauge its precise impact on the overall tourism market. What can be determined is that SIT tourists will want to spend the major part of their holiday involved in a specific activity. Businesses entering this sector will have to address this need.

Questions

1.1 When the SIT entrepreneur has chosen the operation's business framework, what other mechanisms need to be put in place to effectively and efficiently conduct the business?

1.2 When tourists want 'a holiday with a difference', what is available to them? Outline three trends in consumer behaviour that are being catered for by the SIT sector.

1.3 Choose an SIT subclass and describe the product two enterprises provide for their target markets. How successful are they in meeting the specific expressed needs of their market?

1.4 'Mass tourism need not be uncontrolled, unplanned, short-term or unstable. Green tourism is not always and inevitably considerate, optimising, controlled, planned and under local control' (Butler 1990). Evaluate the relative merits of mass and alternative tourism, giving examples to substantiate your observations.

REFERENCES

Allenby, Guy. 2000. 'The Wheel World'. *Sydney Morning Herald*, Weekend 6, 12 August, Travel p. 1.

Ap, J. & Crompton, J. L. 1993. 'Residents' Strategies for Responding to Tourism Impacts'. *Journal of Travel Research*, Summer, pp. 47–50.

Brockensha, P. & Guldberg, H. 1992. *Cultural Tourism in Australia*. Canberra: Australian Government Publishing Service.

Brotherton, Bob. 1997. 'Beyond Destinations — Special Interest Tourism'. *Anatolia: An International Journal of Tourism and Hospitality Research*, 8 (3): 11–30.

Butler, R. W. 1990. 'Alternative Tourism: Pious Hope or Trojan Horse?'. *Journal of Travel Research*, Winter, p. 40.

Cockerell, N. 1999. 'Short-term Trends and Key Issues in the Tourism Industry'. *Travel and Tourism Analyst* 6: 65–79.

Cohen, E. 1972. 'Towards a Sociology of International Tourism'. *Social Research* 39: 164–82.

Cohen, E. 1989. 'Alternative Tourism — A Critique'. In Singh, Theuns & Co. (Eds.). *Towards Appropriate Tourism.* Frankfurt: Lang, pp. 27–42.

Craik, J. 1995. 'Is Cultural Tourism Viable?'. *Smarts* 2. Canberra Department of Communications and the Arts, pp. 6–7.

Crompton, J. L. 1979. 'Motivations for Pleasure Travel'. *Annals of Tourism Research* 6: 408–24.

Derrett, R. 2000. *NR Regional Cultural Tourism Plan.* Byron Bay: NR Regional Cultural Tourism Organisation.

Dickman, S. 1997. *Arts Marketing, the Pocket Guide.* Sydney: Centre for Professional Development and Australia Council.

Dogan, H. Z. 1989. 'Forms of Adjustment: Socio Cultural Impacts of Tourism'. *Annals of Tourism Research* 16 (2): 216–36.

Doxey, G. V. 1975. 'A Causation Theory of Visitor–Resident Irritants: Methodology and Research Inferences'. *Proceedings of the Travel Research Association.* Sixth Annual Conference, San Diego, California, 1975, pp. 195–8.

France, L. (Ed.). 1997. *The Earthscan Reader in Sustainable Tourism.* London: Earthscan Publications.

Hall, C. M. & Weiler, B. 1992. 'What's Special About Special Interest Tourism?'. In Hall & Weiler. *Special Interest Tourism.* London: Belhaven Press.

Krippendorf, J. 1984. *The Holiday Makers: Understanding the Impact of Leisure and Travel.* London: Heinemann.

Krippendorf, J. 1997. 'The Motives of the Mobile Leisureman: Travel Between Norm, Promise and Hope'. In France, L. (Ed.). *The Earthscan Reader in Sustainable Tourism.* London: Earthscan Publications, p. 38.

Lane, B. 1989. 'Modern Mass Tourism: A Critique'. *The Independent*, 13 May.

Manning, Ted. 1999. 'Indicators of Tourism Sustainability'. *Tourism Management* 20: 179–81.

Morgan, Roy & Ogilvy and Mather. 1997. Cited in Dickman, S. *Arts Marketing, the Pocket Guide.* Melbourne: Centre for Professional Development.

Naisbitt, J. 1990. *Megatrends 2000.* New York: William Morrow.

Nykiel, R. A. 1996. 'Ten Trends to the Millennium'. *Journal of Hospitality and Leisure Marketing* 4 (2): 77–80.

Oelrichs, I. & Prosser, G. (Eds.). 1992. *Endemic Tourism, A Profitable Industry in a Sustainable Environment.* Sydney: PATA.

Plog, S. C. 1974. 'Why Destination Areas Rise and Fall in Popularity'. *Cornell Hotel and Restaurant Administration Quarterly* 15: 55–8.

Poon, A. 1993. *Tourism, Technology and Competitive Strategies.* Wallingford, UK: CAB International.

Poon, A. 1997. 'Global Transformation: New Tourism Defined'. In France, L. (Ed.). *The Earthscan Reader in Sustainable Tourism.* London: Earthscan Publications.

Popcorn, Faith & Marigold, Lys. 1999. Cited in Kotler, P., Bowen, J. & Makens, J. *Marketing for Hospitality and Tourism.* Second Edition. New Jersey: Prentice Hall, p. 129.

Read, S. E. 1980. 'A Prime Force in the Expansion of Tourism in the Next Decade: Special Interest Travel'. In Hawkins, D. E., Shafer, E. L. & Rovelstad, J. M. (Eds.). *Tourism Marketing and Management Issues.* Washington, DC: George Washington University, pp. 193–202.

Ross, M. & Ross, T. 1990. *Big Marketing Ideas for Small Service Business.* Homewood, Illinois, USA: Dow Jones–Irwin.

Smith, V. (Ed.). 1989. *Hosts and Guests: The Anthropology of Tourism.* Second Edition. Philadelphia: University of Pennsylvania Press.

Stear, L. 1994. '"Special Interest Tourism": Publications in Review'. *Annals of Tourism Research* 22 (1): 238–40.

Stebbins, R. A. 1982. 'Serious Leisure: A Conceptual Statement'. *Pacific Sociological Review.* 25: 251–72.

Suzuki, D. T. 1999. *Naked Ape to Superspecies: A Personal Perspective on Humanity and the Global Eco-crisis.* St Leonards, NSW: Allen & Unwin.

Theobold, R. 1999. *We Do Have Future Choices: Strategies for Fundamentally Changing the 21st Century.* Lismore: Southern University Press.

Twining-Ward, L. 1999. 'Towards Sustainable Tourism Development: Observations from a Distance'. *Tourism Management* 20: 187–8.

Urry, J. 1990. *The Tourist Gaze: Leisure and Travel in Contemporary Societies.* London: Sage Publications.

WCED (World Commission on Environment and Development). 1987. *Our Common Future.* Oxford: Oxford University Press.

Weaver, D. & Oppermann, M. 1999. *Tourism Management.* Brisbane: John Wiley & Sons.

Wheeler, B. 1991. 'Alternative Tourism — A Deceptive Ploy'. *Progress in Tourism, Recreation & Hospitality Management* 5 (11). Chichester, UK: John Wiley & Sons.

Wheeler, B. 1992. 'Is Progressive Tourism Appropriate?'. *Tourism Management,* June, pp. 91–6.

Wheeler, B. 1997. 'Tourism's Troubled Times: Responsible Tourism Is Not the Answer'. In France, L. (Ed.). *The Earthscan Reader in Sustainable Tourism.* London: Earthscan Publications.

Wood, C. 1992. *Frameworks for Travellers.* Melbourne: Australians Studying Abroad.

Wood, C. 1993. 'Package Tourism and New Tourism Compared'. In *Proceedings from National Conference, Community Culture and Tourism,* July 1993, Melbourne, p. 11.

Sandrifter Safaris, Alice Springs, Australia:
Specialists in 4WD private charter

The landscape of Central Australia is distinctive. Its essential elements provide many unique attractions for visitors. The dynamic combination of climate, terrain, the scale of its iconic natural features and the history of human contact provides a variety of stimuli to engage domestic and international visitors. Sandrifter is one small business committed to providing quality information, interpretation and safari services, offering educational and professional tours for people who generally don't access mass tourism package tours. The personalised short tours allow the knowledgeable entrepreneurs to share specialised, secure experiences.

The company offers two specific products: an annual programme of three tours developed by the company and a private charter service. Tours in the annual programme are from 12 to 16 days and the company specialises in providing tour services for artists. An inclusive cost covers the provision of a themed tour, determined by the owners, through the region's stimulating and challenging landscapes.

Cruising the Mighty Murray offers artists a houseboat tour in summer. Participants cruise upstream past cliff faces, lagoons and quiet backwaters; they can paint or draw on one of the boat's three decks or on the riverbank. There are opportunities to go fishing and swimming and to learn of the natural and cultural heritage from experts. These tours are limited to ten passengers, who are required to bring their own art materials.

Practising artists can participate in a different camping tour each year designed to provide distinctive attractive locations. *Alice Art 2000*, for instance, allowed participants to stay for two weeks at one campsite in the spectacular Ruby Gap National Park. The geological formations and natural environment underpin tours to Arltunga Historical Reserve where the old Police Station and Gaol, Government House and Cemetery are explored. In some years the tours are more mobile. Each tour provides comfortable camping equipment and healthy cuisine.

The annual expedition is designed to explore different locations in Australia. *Expedition 2000* followed the Old Ghan Railway and Oodnadatta Track to Lake Eyre and the Flinders Ranges to Alice Springs. Meals, swags, stretchers and 4WD transport are included with visits to Aboriginal and European heritage sites.

The company's 25-year reputation for delivering safe, efficient tours ensures repeat business and effective word-of-mouth promotion. Consistent quality experiences are delivered because of the owners' experience and understanding of environmental conditions, the standard of equipment required and the knowledge of subcontracted authorities in particular fields.

Professional groups, family groups, incentive groups and special interest groups approach the company to design short or long tours to meet their specific needs. This private charter niche involves a negotiated price for services rendered. The owners' local knowledge and experience is backed up by tour guides and interpreters who accompany overseas guests wishing to explore the continent's centre. The average size of such groups is fifteen to twenty people, though much larger groups can be accommodated. The company also offers 4WD tag-along tours.

Figure 1.1 *Campers on a Sandrifter Safari take a break from the day's activity.*

Specialist groups have included motorbike enthusiasts, who come with instructors and who are led by Sandrifter through unique landscapes, orienteering specialists, experienced bushwalkers, corporate groups undertaking team-building exercises, geologists studying particular locations, and professional photographers.

Factors determining price and service levels include the number of participants, the duration of the tour and the distance to be travelled. Costings are made on resources required to deliver an acceptable standard. These may involve hire of boats, helicopters or extra vehicles, outsourcing for particular expertise, necessary fees and licences, particular foods and camping equipment.

Essentially three types of accommodation are offered. The first is a break camp overnight kit, which comprises a rain- and insect-proof swag (a large sheet of canvas wrapped around a mattress with sleeping bag, sleeping sheet and pillow supplied). The second includes a dome-shaped tent sleeping two people comfortably, and the third a large tent with stretchers and bedding for prolonged stays.

Most participants in a Sandrifter Safari know one another before they take up the tour. Word of mouth is a significant contributor to establishing a market. An attractive aspect of accessing such products is being in the company of like-minded people. These represent the key elements of the SIT market. They are mature people with adequate time and sufficient funds and interest to be flexible about accessing the tours. Visitors come from a shared interest group or are members of the same corporate, community or cultural group, or are family groups celebrating milestones or sharing an adventure.

Repeat business is important to this small company. Over 250 annual personal *Sandrifter Monitor* newsletters are distributed to past participants and suppliers. This maintains a personal connection between the owners and future tours. Contact with the Meetings Incentives Conferences and Exhibitions (MICE) sector in Alice Springs and globally allows conference attendees an inclusive Central Australia travel experience in their attendance fee, or access to an add-on excursion. A geology conference, for example, may require a tailor-made tour to satisfy specific interests. Interpreters may be organised by the hirer or by Sandrifter.

Personalised service, from the pick-up at airports or hotel, to meeting special dietary needs, to locating particular items that will enhance the visitor's experience, is part of the product. Discounts apply for repeat participants on a sliding scale — 15 per cent for three or more, 17.5 per cent for more than four and 20 per cent for more than five trips. One client has been on 11 different annual trips!

Promotion includes advertising in *Australian Artist* magazine for three months each year to publicise the art-based tours. Melbourne, for instance, has been targeted, as a demonstrable market exists among artists and TAFE arts students there. The company has found it viable to operate in Central Australia from April through October each year. This period is the most suitable for touring Australia's outback.

Gerry Gerrard started the business 26 years ago with the dream of being his own boss and working in an environment that he knew and loved with people who wanted to expand their horizons. As small business operators he and his partner have recognised the need to lease equipment required only during the season. Gerry's personal skills as a mechanic, panelbeater, plumber, cook, naturalist and natural historian support his interest in sharing the landscape with people willing to pay for his expertise. The company owns essential equipment and maintains it to a high standard. He has observed other operators come and go over the years.

The personal nature of the services offered and built up over time could mean difficulty in selling the company. The business deals with individual clients, other tour companies in Alice Springs and Sydney who may outsource extra work to Sandrifter Safaris at certain times, and domestic and international travel businesses requesting niche services.

For each partner in this fragmented sector of the tourism industry, detailed knowledge of consumers' needs, trends in the marketplace, competitors' product ranges and effective negotiating skills are called for. Understanding the challenging state and federal legislative environments means that owners need to keep abreast of policy and planning issues. Such matters as insurance, vehicle registrations, potential litigation in the adventure/ecotourism market provide challenges. They must watch for developments in equipment and technology that could be used to improve services; for example, solar panels, gas and solar refrigeration, food packaging for specific diets and new pumping installations.

Sandrifter Safaris recognises opportunities to collaborate with others in the tourism and hospitality industry. Owners of riverboats could market their boats and hire Sandrifter to conduct specific tours. Indigenous communities entering the tourism marketplace could add another dynamic to the products available to the company's clients. Owners must pay consistent attention to updating the content of the experience. There needs to be a balance between authenticity, special interest and the quality and entertainment expected by the participants.

Questions

1 What relationship does this company need to have with public land managers of sites to which they may wish to take their clients?

2 Often small companies do not have resources for mass marketing. What alternative marketing strategies could be employed by the owners?

3 Small operators tend to be individualistic in their approach to business. What are the benefits for small business of effective partnerships with others?

4 What are some of the risks characterising the economic profile of companies such as Sandrifter Safaris? How do such operations become sustainable?

5 What are the skills that the operators of such a business require to effectively deliver a quality product? How do tour companies best provide for participation, interpretation, interaction with the built and natural environment, quality service, value for money and a significant 'real' experience?

Robyn Bushell

CHAPTER 2

2 Practice,
provision and impacts

LEARNING OBJECTIVES

After reading this chapter, you will have an appreciation of:

- the potential impacts on natural and social environments of different types of special interest tourism (SIT)

- key concepts in the practice and provision of SIT

- the role and place of tourism as a tool for community development

- the issues of visitor impact management.

2.1 $\mathcal{I}$NTRODUCTION

Chapter 1 introduced the broad definitions and characteristics of **special interest tourism** (SIT). It covered a number of the issues, concerns and challenges of SIT and outlined the mechanisms needed to make SIT viable. Some of these issues relate directly to tourism operators and their goals, and some to visitors and their demands as more sophisticated and informed consumers with particular interests and specific expectations. But many of the issues and concerns centre on the local **host community**. In this chapter we will examine in more detail the issues relating to host communities and to the tourism destination, and the notion of impacts, both positive and negative, on the social and natural environments. We will discuss the role of tourism in community and community development; the idea of **quality of life**, what this concept means and how it can be applied in the planning and management of SIT. Sustainable development was introduced in chapter one. This discussion will be expanded within the context of biodiversity **conservation**, quality of life, health and tourism, and **sense of place**. These concerns will be explained and discussed with examples of policies and practices, both national and international, that have been developed to ensure tourism is better integrated into broader planning frameworks. Finally, we will discuss visitor impact management and the approaches and tools designed to assist in the monitoring and evaluation of the impacts of visitors on places and people.

2.2 $\mathcal{S}$IT AS A MORE SUSTAINABLE FORM OF TOURISM

In chapter 1 we defined SIT as 'the provision of customised leisure and recreational experiences driven by the specific expressed interests of individuals and groups' and established that it is undertaken for a distinct and specific reason. SIT tourists, we suggested, are seeking more 'authentic' experiences that enable closer interaction with the host community in a non-exploitative manner, along with more personalised service. This raises many questions. Is it that markets and options for tourists are now more sophisticated and SIT is merely meeting a market demand? What is authentic and what is appropriate? How should 'culture' be presented? Does the host community actually want close and meaningful interaction with the visitors/tourists? Might 'mass tourism' quarantined into 'tourism designated areas' in fact be more viable in the longer term for the host community and the natural environment? This raises the further issue of whether tourism is for the benefit of the tourist or of the local economy, and, hence, the local people. If tourism is part of community development and serves the same role as any other industry — providing employment and income — should it be managed in the same way as other industrial activities are managed, with special zones, particular services, rates and planning regulations? If confined, it would mean locals whose businesses do not relate to tourism, and who often consider tourists an intrusion, would be less affected by visitors in their midst. It would also greatly reduce environmental impacts and enable a greater user-pays approach, so that local ratepayers would not be paying for the services associated with tourism businesses and tourist facilities.

This then leads to ethical questions of rights of access to public goods. Do visitors who have a long and productive association with an area have fewer rights than a newly settled person? Who are visitors and who are tourists? Who are locals? What activities and services are tourism related? As SIT becomes more embedded within the local context and is more personalised, it attempts to move beyond the touristic experience into a host/guest relationship. Do the commercial realities of tourism allow this to happen?

Questions about culture and appropriate and sustainable use of social, cultural and natural resources have raised many criticisms of SIT. These suggest that its many forms, such as adventure tourism, rural tourism, indigenous tourism, ecotourism, wildlife tourism and so on, are as prone to creating negative social and environmental impacts as any other form of tourism. A good example may be drawn from the Himalayas. Before 1965 fewer than 10 000 tourists visited Nepal each year. By 1996 the number had increased to more than 250 000. In the nature sanctuary of Annapurna the tree line has risen hundreds of metres as a result of local residents harvesting firewood to sell to trekkers and lodge owners. Populations of certain species of fauna have declined, and litter and water pollution have increased. So although these visitors would consider themselves nature tourists, ultimately their presence has degraded or destroyed the natural resources (Ceballos-Lascuráin 1996).

The statement 'I am a traveller, you are a visitor, they are tourists' encapsulates the paradox of SIT. As tourists, we want to travel to exotic, wild and beautiful places but are outraged by the impact of large numbers of fellow humans doing likewise. Tourism is growing at a faster rate than other industries. This trend is likely to continue, but the challenge is for the growth to be managed in a sustainable way. The reality, however, is that we are threatening the very places we admire — the coastlines, the rainforests and the vast wilderness. While SIT encourages travel to places like Antarctica or into villages in remote places, it brings with it the social and ecological impacts of human activity, development and modernity. Ironically, we are 'loving these places to death' or, at the very least, radically changing them.

This is not the place to explore these complex ethical issues fully, but the reader is encouraged to consider the writings of MacCannell (1976); Urry (1990); Butler (1980); Smith (1989); Ceballos-Lascuráin (1996); Wall (1996) and Ringer (1998) as starting points for a deeper study of fundamental social and ecological issues related to tourism. These works will assist readers to form their own opinions about the guidelines proposed in chapter one to make SIT sustainable.

Cohen (1995) suggests that a consequence of the growing popularity of SIT and of initially small numbers of 'alternative tourists' exploring previously unvisited spaces — whether they be remote or urban, in developing or developed nations — is ultimately to open these spaces for mass tourism. The alternative tourist will then seek to penetrate even deeper into unspoiled places. SIT is often small-scale and locally based. It can be related to local character through rural tourism; to people through indigenous tourism; to heritage through cultural tourism; and to the natural environment through ecotourism. Each of these and other forms of SIT will be discussed in detail later in this book. In the remainder of this chapter we will consider the impacts of SIT.

2.3 WHAT IS SUSTAINABLE DEVELOPMENT?

In order to understand the impacts of SIT, a thorough understanding of the broader concept of sustainable development is essential. The concept of ecologically sustainable development (ESD), introduced in chapter one, is not a new one. However, a number of factors are increasing our awareness of the real costs of human activity and increases in our standard of living. These include increases in:

- industrialisation in all countries in the past several decades
- population
- urbanisation
- globalisation
- air and water pollution
- waste production
- soil erosion
- loss of wetlands and agricultural lands
- deforestation
- desertification and salt intrusion
- global warming and sea levels.

Mass tourism is one result of an improved lifestyle. Tourism is considered a relatively 'clean' industry compared with other forms of economic activity such as extractive industries. Nevertheless, it is largely responsible for the massive increase in international air travel and with it a great deal of development, often in the most fragile of ecosystems, such as coastlines, rivers and wetlands. A consequence is the displacement of open space, wildlife corridors and breeding grounds.

■ 2.3.1 A brief *history of ESD*

The concept of ESD was established at the United Nations Conference in Stockholm in 1972. In 1980 the International Union for the Conservation of Nature (IUCN), the United Nations Environment Program (UNEP) and the World Wide Fund for Nature (WWF) produced the *World Conservation Strategy*, subtitled *Living Resource Conservation for Sustainable Development*. This document set out the urgent need to protect our ecological systems if the Earth is to support future economic and social development (Commonwealth of Australia 1991). The World Health Organisation's (WHO) Ottawa

Charter in 1986 set the challenge to link health and the environment conceptually through a vision of a new, ecological public health.

The World Commission on Environment and Development report produced in 1987 under the title *Our Common Future* (also known as the Brundtland Report) stressed the need to reconcile economic development with the resource endowment of the natural world. The 1992 Rio Earth Summit in Brazil and the consequent 'Agenda 21' declaration placed ESD firmly on the agenda of national, state and local governments throughout the world. The challenge posed by the Brundtland Report was to achieve sustainable development, though this admirable objective has been clouded somewhat by the ambiguity of the term 'sustainable'. It took some time to recognise that **sustainability** is socially and politically constructed (McCool 1996) and that political and economic agendas differ considerably from place to place and can override the ecological agenda.

If tourism development is to be sustainable, it must be environmentally responsible by embracing a more ecological and balanced approach. This requires an understanding of biological processes, ecological principles and the sensitivities of the biological systems of which humans are a part. The wellbeing of humanity depends on maintaining the health and wellbeing of the biosphere's ecosystem. Ninety per cent of the negative ecological load caused by humans is due to industrial activities and the use of machines and vehicles driven by fossil fuels as part of our urban lifestyle (Boyden & Shirlow 1989).

Tourism usually encourages high, and unsustainable, energy usage in developing as well as developed areas. It demands high use of resources like water and prime agricultural land. It also creates awareness, expectations and demands for a western standard of living with its high resource consumption in the developing countries with their often massive populations. This alone is a good reason for tourism to strive to demonstrate truly sustainable development rather than promoting excesses of luxury and a hedonistic lifestyle.

As we move into the new millennium there is growing concern that the deep societal and economic changes required have not occurred. Indeed, the overall status of global environmental systems is worse now than in the early 1980s. A special session of the General Assembly of the United Nations in 1997, five years after 'Agenda 21' was adopted at the Earth Summit, acknowledged that 'a number of positive results have been achieved, but we are deeply concerned that the overall trends for sustainable development are worse today than they were in 1992' (Griffith 2000).

Many concepts have been well developed in the literature on sustainable tourism. These include:
• the notion of **carrying capacity**
• **limits of acceptable change** and acceptable use
• maintenance of *sense of place*
• host/guest relationships
• the debate on authenticity and commodification of culture and place
• the debate on the ethics of tourism, particularly in developing countries and areas where populations are more vulnerable and impressionable to the demonstration effects of visitors from wealthier nations
• the idea of the destination life cycle.

In all of these areas the debate centres on different principles of sustainable development; the tension between economic rationalism and other value systems; and the dialectic between spatial, temporal and ethical approaches to tourism planning and development. These approaches include supply versus demand, global versus local, small scale versus large scale and local versus imported (goods, services and labour). The challenge lies in utilising these concepts to help make the practice of tourism sustainable.

■ 2.3.2 Defining *sustainable tourism*

In 1995 the World Tourism Organisation, the World Travel and Tourism Council and the Earth Council adopted a joint declaration, 'Agenda 21 for the Travel and Tourism Industry: Towards Environmentally Sustainable Development'. This draft action program for the tourism industry includes the principles outlined below.

- Tourism should help people live a healthy and productive life in harmony with nature.
- Tourism should contribute to the conservation, protection and rehabilitation of ecosystems.
- Protection of the environment should be an integral component of tourism development.
- Tourism should be planned at the local level and allow for the participation of local people.
- Tourism should recognise and support the identity, culture and interests of indigenous peoples.
- International agreements to protect the environment should be respected by the tourism industry.

How can these principles be addressed? In the following sections of this chapter we will consider some of the impacts of tourism and ways to manage them.

2.4 *I*MPACTS OF TOURISM

■ 2.4.1 Social *impacts*

Most of the goals of tourism planning authorities are numeric and are measured in visitor numbers and yield, in terms of investment and spending. The underlying assumption that tourism will generate economic benefit is reasonable. But the extension that more visitors will necessarily result in greater gain is inherently flawed, since it does not consider the large amount of additional infrastructure required, such as roads, public transport, utilities, services and facilities. This creates considerable expense for local ratepayers and overburdens existing systems designed for steady population growth rather than massive seasonal influxes. Inconvenience, loss of amenity, crowding, congestion and other generally negative social impacts, including increases in crime and pollution, can be added to these.

Investors and employees are often not local; goods and services are often imported. This means the promised economic benefit frequently 'leaks out'. These pressures contribute to a sense of loss of control and loss of 'place' by residents of popular destinations, who do not necessarily see tangible benefits. What is the social *carrying capacity* of a community to cope with the constant pressure of visitors? The negative social effects are more marked in developing countries and regions with more traditional social and cultural values. Economic goals of ever increasing numbers of visitors can also lead to the trap of 'profitless volume'. This can affect an individual business in a variety of ways, such as incurring the expense of putting on a new bus and an additional driver to cater for only a marginal increase in visitor numbers. It can also affect whole areas by requiring massive new capital investment for basic infrastructure beyond the return, or infrastructure increases that create changes in patterns of normal life.

Despite the many benefits cited there is little research to demonstrate that 'nature based or cultural tourism' is socially, culturally or environmentally benign (Pearce 1992). Indeed, numerous studies suggest that even the most lightly trodden path of tourism can destroy fragile soils and flora and that fauna can be adversely affected merely by being watched (McElroy & de Albuquerque 1996). The 'take only photos, leave only footprints' ethic of ecotourism can be highly disruptive to the lives of many people who do not welcome the 'invasion' of visitors. This is particularly so when photographers are attracted to the most sacred of ceremonies and intrude on private lives, and when bushwalkers tramp over sacred sites. The popularity among visitors for climbing Uluru (Ayers Rock), and using the Sky Rail over the rainforest on the outskirts of Cairns, are two examples. As well as offending local custodians, this type of tourism can often set up conflict within communities, usually between those who object, and those who stand to profit, and therefore consider disruptive change to be acceptable.

These problems associated with tourism compromise sustainability, particularly in ecologically and culturally sensitive areas such as arid outback regions, remnant rainforests and small islands. The other main issue of sustainability concerns tourism's pervasive nature and the uncertainty of development over space and time (McElroy & de Albuquerque 1996; Pigram 1992). Once tourism development begins it usually prompts further development, each stage justifying and/or necessitating the next. This is one of the main concerns of SIT; it is seen as 'the thin edge of the wedge'. Tourism is highly competitive and very seasonal, so economic returns take precedence over ecological concerns such as the maintenance of biodiversity. The natural environment becomes increasingly vulnerable to short-term economic decision making.

The concept of carrying capacity was first developed in the 1940s in the fields of agriculture and wildlife management. In more recent years the idea has been a useful tool for tourism planning when considering ecological and social impacts (Inskeep 1991). Ecological carrying capacity in relation to tourism is the level of visitation beyond which unacceptable ecological impacts will occur. It relates to the environment's capacity to withstand use or activity. Social carrying capacity for the visitor is the level of visitation beyond which satisfaction is not achieved because of overcrowding, noise, aesthetic deterioration or limited access to services. For the host community, the social carrying capacity is the level of visitation beyond which unacceptable change occurs — this can be physical, cultural, economic, ecological or psychological. In each case, the carrying capacity will vary according to a range of factors such as season, weather conditions, type of activity, time of day and so on; it is very site and activity specific and highly subjective.

The carrying capacity model is attractive, but determining these limits scientifically, socially and politically is difficult. Everyone will be affected differently and will have a different idea about what is acceptable. The process of applying this model is also expensive, so usually the limits are never determined. However, nature does have limits, and tourism must be planned to recognise them. Tourism planning and development needs to be integrated into broader bioregional planning, rather than just local government or tourism region planning. It needs to utilise tools such as integrated resource management. Ongoing social and environmental impact assessment are necessary, since the impacts of tourism are cumulative and extend well beyond the immediate site (Bushell 1999a).

Tourism needs to be managed to maximise both visitor satisfaction and local distribution of benefits. The indicators of successful tourism need to be broadened well beyond the current economic indicators, so the goals reflect other values, and the various planning processes incorporate them. What are the other benefits to plan for? What benefits can be built in for biodiversity and heritage conservation? How can indigenous people benefit? How can local residents benefit?

The principles of ESD and sustainable development must be set within a local context. Neither will have practical application until grounded in the particular social organisation, economy, knowledge, customs, technology and environment in which it is to operate (Griffith 2000). As the Brundtland Report states, 'no single blueprint will be found, as economic and social systems and ecological conditions differ widely among countries. Each nation will have to work out its own concrete policy implications' (WCED 1987).

■ 2.4.2 Indigenous *people and tourism*

Together with issues concerning the host community are issues relating to the 'traditional use' of resources, land rights and ownership. We are coming to understand that indigenous knowledge is tied up with concepts of sustainable land use. Indigenous peoples have local laws about caring for the land that regulate human behaviour in harmony with nature's cycles. Throughout the world there are many examples of indigenous knowledge leading the way in ecological thinking (Cordell 1993).

In the struggles to save their forests, such as in the Amazon basin and Borneo, a number of indigenous peoples have looked to nature-based and cultural tourism as a means of regaining ownership, control and financial independence. The increasingly discerning ecotourism markets are very interested in supporting indigenous peoples. Careful and expert consideration is required in planning and developing tourism activities that involve traditional communities and their role and rights. The most successful models appear to be tourism operations that are indigenously owned and managed so the people and culture are not exploited. This topic is covered in greater detail in chapter 10.

■ 2.4.3 Protected *areas and tourism*

Designated 'protected' areas have been dedicated for the preservation and enjoyment of natural and cultural heritage, the conservation of biodiversity and the maintenance of ecological systems. National parks are the most common form of protected area. Increasingly, marine parks, like the Great Barrier Reef Marine Park, are being designated. However, we must remind ourselves that the concept of 'nature' is socially constructed. For example, many of the areas the western world considers wilderness have for centuries been home to indigenous people.

The idea of wilderness as an 'untouched or untamed land is an urban perception, the view of people who are far removed from the natural environment they depend upon' (Gomez-Pompa & Kaus 1992:273). A vast 'undisturbed' area, with unique wildlife species and spectacular scenery — the typical popular image associated with protected areas — represents different values to different people. The same area may be regarded by conservationists as an ideal habitat for rare species; by a biologist as having exceptional scientific merit; by a forester as representing high economic value; by a hunter as a great place to go shooting; and by an indigenous person as a site of significant spiritual meaning. Protected areas are a social space, socially conceived and preserved (Ghimire & Pimbert 1997:5). This 'construction of nature' varies in time according to cultural, political and social beliefs and economic status. This influences the values placed on nature, the priority given for its protection and what is considered acceptable use (Figgis 1999; Staiff, Kennedy & Bushell 1999). Nature-based tourism is but one of the contested forms of use for such places. Ecotourism attempts to respect the ecological, spiritual and cultural values of such places while still enabling economic development and enjoyment by a wide range of people.

Nature-based tourism and ecotourism in particular also importantly create the opportunity to provide incentive for conservation and the maintenance of protected areas. Nature-based tourism and outdoor recreation can help foster the notion of stewardship by making people more appreciative of nature and more attuned to the increasing loss of open space and the impacts of our current lifestyles on the natural environment.

■ 2.4.4 Environmental *impacts of tourism*

Tourism is an industry largely based on natural resources and so has an impact on air, land, water, flora and fauna. Also, its acute seasonal peaks in demand create pressure on infrastructure, such as water supply, sewerage systems, roads and community services, usually designed to cater for a much smaller population base. Seasonal demand can also concentrate pressure on natural resources, causing adverse impacts. General environmental impacts of tourism include those resulting from the development of tourism infrastructure and facilities, and those arising from tourists themselves. The impacts will vary according to the area, its features and the type of tourism activity and intensity of use.

Coastal zone tourism developments have resulted in beach and dune erosion, decreased diversity in native vegetation and loss of some species. Some ecosystems, such as wetlands, have been lost, with significant ramifications for biodiversity and for other economic sectors such as fishing and agriculture. Marine environments are affected by human intrusion and activities on nearby lands. Conservationists worry that ecotourism spreads the impact of tourism beyond urbanised areas.

Protected areas need especially careful consideration. Tourism already relies on protected areas and the experiences they offer the visitor. The growing trend towards nature-based tourism will intensify ecological pressures. Semi-arid and arid lands have become a drawcard for tourism. The increasing accessibility of outback areas has the potential to generate significant impacts. Ecosystems in semi-arid and arid regions may not be as resilient as ecosystems with higher rainfall and greater reserves of water. Alpine areas also attract many recreational activities, such as skiing in winter and bushwalking, fishing and horse riding in summer.

2.5 MAKING TOURISM SUSTAINABLE

The term 'sustainable tourism' has been widely adopted by the tourism industry, yet attitudes towards it can still be a cause for concern. Sustainable tourism should not be perceived simply as an approach to maintaining environmental assets for the future benefit of tourism, as it is so often described. To become a mature, responsible and ethical global industry, tourism must first acknowledge that most of the assets it exploits — natural, built, social and cultural — have their own intrinsic value beyond the economic. They are resources held in common, not the sole province of business. The tourism industry must recognise that it has a moral obligation to conserve them, and that economic activities should not damage or detract from these assets in order to profit from them.

It is self-evident that since tourism business depends so heavily on these assets, its future is limited without them. There has been a major shift within the global industry towards recognising the economic imperative to conserve the natural environment in order to maintain financial viability. However, until the industry, and society generally, concedes this relationship and makes the necessary attitudinal shift, the balance between economic needs and genuine long-term environmental and social values will remain elusive.

The value of SIT is that some, although certainly not all, forms aspire to such an ethic. For example, genuine ecotourism, as opposed to nature-based tourism, seeks to respect nature, to conserve, contribute and educate. One of the concerns about SIT is that the unscrupulous can use the ethical labels to marketing advantage without applying the principles. It is a promising sign to see a shift from economically rationalist thinking. However, anthropocentric views still pose a major threat to biodiversity and sustainable futures. **Tourism service providers** must make compromises that favour nature. Examples may include that:

- ecolodges are not placed in World Heritage Areas or near the breeding grounds of endangered species
- the aesthetics of scenic views are not converted to dollars by placing restaurants, accommodation or casinos on the edge of the 'million dollar view', but rather some distance from it
- wilderness is left undeveloped
- coastal belts are not hardened and mangroves are conserved
- realistic green corridors for wildlife are maintained so that habitats are not removed.

Tourism, like other forms of development, still has a long way to go before it can claim to be sustainable.

SPECIAL INTEREST INVESTIGATION
Nature-based tourism and protected areas

To be successful, nature-based tourism depends on high levels of environmental quality and suitable levels of consumer service. Much of the nature-based tourism available worldwide is in parks and other forms of protected areas (Eagles 1999). In the United States between 10 and 24 per cent of all visits in 1995 were directly related to protected areas (TWAC 1996).

The land area covered by the world's parks and protected areas has increased dramatically in the past 30 years. However, in many parts of the world protected areas are seen as marginal in the context of other areas of policy, such as economic development and agriculture. Protected areas need increased support (Sheppard 1999). The relationship between tourism and protected areas can be useful in this process. Increasingly, parks are being identified as major attractions for visitors, both domestic and foreign. Although tourism benefits associated with protected areas can be significant, it is important that tourism/visitor use is planned carefully and does not destroy the natural resource on which it is based. Despite plenty of examples of good practice, there are many cases around the world of high tourist use of protected areas coupled with poor planning, which have caused significant environmental degradation. A key future challenge is how to manage visitor use of protected areas in a more effective way, that allows appropriate use and enjoyment while not destroying natural values (Sheppard 1999).

(*continued*)

One of the social realities associated with this type of tourism is the priority given to economic values of nature. Nature-based tourism is increasingly important because of its potential to contribute to local and national economies. The economic benefits of park-based tourism can far exceed government expenditure on managing sites (Driml & Common 1995; Taskforce on Economic Benefits 1998).

NSW National Parks and Wildlife Services has completed a number of studies looking at the socioeconomic issues surrounding nature conservation, designed to foster better relationships with local government, community groups, other agencies and individuals and to ensure the wellbeing of these rural and regional areas. In assessing the economic benefits of protected areas for regional economies, input–output analysis has been used to measure the contribution of an area to gross regional output (business turnover), gross regional product (value-added activity), household income and employment. National parks contribute economically in several ways: through park management, which oversees the protection and conservation of natural and cultural heritage; through purchases of local goods and services, which stimulate local businesses and trade; through direct employment of local people in the parks, and through consumer spending by park staff and their families. Also, capital works utilise local contractors, goods and services in establishing and maintaining new park offices and visitor centres. Finally, visitors, attracted to the region by the national park, purchase accommodation, food and beverages, transport and motor vehicle services, and contribute to the regional economy through shopping and other related activities.

Nature-based tourism is an important element in the economic benefit that the park brings to the region. In the case of Minnamurra Rainforest Centre, for example, the park is 5700 hectares in size. It is dominated by subtropical and warm temperate rainforest vegetation providing habitat for 70 bird, 20 mammal and 11 reptile native species. It has a visitor centre, 1.6 kilometres of raised boardwalk with disabled access, a 2.6-kilometre return access route to the Minnamurra Falls, an outdoor classroom in the rainforest, a cafe, picnic/barbecue facilities and parking. Park visitation has increased from 72 000 in 1992 to 140 000 in 1995. Annual local expenditure by visitors to the rainforest centre is estimated to contribute over $4.1 million in gross regional output and $2 million in gross regional product, including $1.4 million in household income payments to the equivalent of 119 local people (Gillespie 1997; Conner 1999). Through ongoing research the Parks Service is identifying strategies for improved contribution to their local regional communities. Nature-based tourism will be an important element in this contribution.

The challenge for planners is to ensure that tourism becomes a tool of conservation management rather than having national parks used merely as sites of tourism business (Bushell 1999b).

2.6 THE PLACE OF TOURISM IN COMMUNITY DEVELOPMENT

Tourism literature frequently refers to host communities. These are the people who live and work in the places that tourists visit. For some in the host community tourism is a way of life. They work in the industry and derive their living from tourism-associated businesses. Others go about their normal routine often unaware of, and unaffected by, the proximity of tourism businesses and tourists. For others, tourism can be a source of considerable concern because of the impacts of development and changes to the natural and built character of a place. These can be associated with tourism infrastructure such as accommodation, parking and attractions or can relate to the loss of amenity, privacy and the sense of invasion that tourism can cause. For local government managers, tourism can demand constant attention as those in the industry call for improved services and planning approvals; visitors call for improved infrastructure such as public toilets, shade, signage and tourist information; and local ratepayers make contrary demands and complain that their rates are supporting private enterprises.

The relationship between tourism and community can be considered using a model identifying four different stakeholder groups concerned with tourism within any locale:

1. *government authorities*, who are responsible for the planning, resourcing and maintenance of basic municipal infrastructure
2. *the local business community*, who derive an income from the operation of commercial enterprises
3. *the local community*, who share their area with each other and with the visitors
4. *the visitors*, who make tourism viable (Bushell 1998).

None of these stakeholder groups is homogenous. Different members have different values, aspirations, levels of education, needs and desires. Neither are they static; new members come regularly as others leave. Often the same person will belong to more than one **stakeholder** group. It is important that the issues of tourism are seen in the broader context of the community and not in isolation, where only people who run tourism businesses feel they have the right to contribute to decisions that affect tourism. If it is a major component of the local economy, tourism affects everyone who lives or works in the community. Local rates are used for many projects specifically for the benefit of visitors and hence tourism businesses. Tourism operators often forget that they do not own, or have special rights over, the basic assets of their business. Likewise, community members often fail to see that improvements made for tourism bring many benefits to the local community. The integration of tourism into the broader social planning for an area will help to encourage all stakeholders to take an interest in tourism issues and address conflicts within the broader context of community development.

■ 2.6.1 Defining *community*

Generally we think of a community as those people who live and work together. Communities are dynamic and complex. In some countries, a community has traditionally been based on kinship; in others on common language or beliefs. In developed countries today, communities are constantly changing as the population grows, ages and migrates. Not all members of a community are necessarily interested in the long-term future of the area. What criteria establish someone as part of a particular community? Do they include someone who rents a home there so does not pay local taxes? Or someone who pays taxes as an absentee landlord but does not live there? Do they include someone who does not live locally, but who works there? What about someone who has great fondness for the area and visits it regularly over many years? These different perspectives may create tensions in loyalty or strong opinions on particular issues. This increasingly complicates the task of 'consulting the community'.

Communities organise themselves in order to share resources, manage these resources, and achieve common goals in relation to quality of life aspirations. This is true whether they are business groups, church groups, sporting groups or entire towns. Local government structures, community groups and businesses work together on environmental, physical, cultural, social and economic aspects of that community. The greatest contributions to the health and wellbeing of nations are made by local communities, not by the medical profession. Health is a state of physical, mental and social wellbeing that has many attributes, largely planned and managed at the local level. These aspects of community include living and working conditions (income, physical environment, public policies) and social support (caring communities, education, health services, family, friends, cultural, spiritual and recreational opportunities). A healthy community shares a broad vision of quality of life and health — the need for clean air and water, safety, open space, housing, a sense of pride and belonging and protection of the natural and social heritage, as well as the need for economic development.

■ 2.6.2 Community *development*

Each community is unique. Each has a specific history, physical environment (natural and built), population, culture, social pattern and economic structure. Community development centres on achieving a healthier community and encompasses people from all walks of life, ages and backgrounds working together. Sound community development recognises the need for a balance between environmental, social and economic needs.

A vital step in achieving sound development is for communities to define their own vision. Everyone needs to be encouraged to think about what they want collectively. As well as providing cohesion and direction, this can be the basis for addressing conflict. A planned development may offer economic benefits but at a cost of reduced open space or impaired air or water quality. The community vision helps to determine what is acceptable change and what is considered to be in the best long-term interests of the whole community. Development is a process involving change, but it does not always have to be physical change. It can be attitudinal or cultural change and it does not have to be measured only in economic terms. The attributes of a healthy community, according to the City of Toronto (1996), include:

- whether it meets the basic needs of its citizens (food, water, housing, safety, employment)
- the quality of the environment (natural and built)
- the vitality of the community's social fabric (including diversity, tolerance and commitment)
- its efficient use of material resources
- its cultural accomplishments
- the vitality, strength and integrity of its economy
- access to public and private services
- the involvement of its citizens in decisions that affect them
- the health and wellbeing of its citizens (physical, mental and social).

■ 2.6.3 Tourism *and community*

Specific policies, plans and actions are needed to achieve community goals. Tourism planning should be part of this process. Local government authorities influence these plans. They are responsible for the housing and accommodation types in a neighbourhood, the scale and style of development approved, the variety and location of recreational facilities, the streetscape and the type of commercial development. Together with a range of regional and state government agencies, which differ in role and name from one country to another but basically operate in a similar way, they provide essential services such as:

- safe drinking water
- public transport and transit
- roads and footpaths
- sewerage and garbage collection
- waste disposal
- electricity
- police and fire protection
- child-care centres and homes for the elderly
- hospitals
- libraries and museums
- parks and recreation facilities.

As well as being essential to a community, these services form the basis of all tourism enterprises. Together with state and national government departments, local governments also exercise regulatory control that influences lifestyle and development through taxation/rates, licensing, zoning and land use planning (City of Toronto 1996).

One of the axioms of sustainable tourism is the need to consult with communities as part of the tourism planning process. For the sorts of reasons already discussed, including the complexity of communities, plus all the time and cost constraints on the consultative process, consulting with communities is neither simple and readily achievable nor necessarily effective.

Some of the most vociferous local lobby groups have quite specific agendas, particularly in relation to tourism planning. These include groups who champion human use over nature conservation, industries and recreational groups who demand access to natural resources purely for human profit or pleasure, such as mining, logging, hunting, off-road vehicle enthusiasts and so on (Figgis 1999). Thus, while the involvement of a broad range of stakeholders in planning is commendable, it is neither straightforward nor guaranteed to achieve sustainable use objectives.

Planners and stakeholders need to develop a shared vision and common ground on the future development and nature of a place and on the role that tourism might play in this vision. Procedures that inform such planning processes should be inexpensive, technically simple and effective. Differences must be identified and aired in order to find working solutions. The goals of tourism planning should reflect a desire for the benefits to include less tangible but nonetheless important improvements to the quality of life for residents. These can include contributions to the conservation of cultural and natural heritage, raising awareness of local history, building a sense of pride and belonging, and helping to preserve open space. Such contributions need to be relevant to the local context and to be shared, discussed and regularly revised.

BREAKTHROUGH TOURISM
The Great River Walk

The Great River Walk (GRW) illustrates the connection between community wellbeing, individual wellness and the health of our environment. GRW is a special interest tourism project in its initial stages — the vision of the Hawkesbury Nepean Catchment Management Trust. It builds on the WHO concept of healthy tourism. For tourism to contribute to healthy lives, the ecological, social and economic needs of the host community, the visitor and the industry must be balanced; we need a sense and knowledge of place, pride in our heritage and a commitment to 'caring for our place'.

The notion of 'place' is important in the context of health. Work undertaken by the WHO Collaborating Centre for Environmental Health at the University of Western Sydney has developed a framework of Healthy Places. It involves continuously identifying and resolving issues of priority related to health, development and wellbeing by advocating, facilitating and enabling these issues to be addressed in partnerships among communities, organisations and agencies at local, national and regional levels. Within this framework is the idea of Healthy Tourism. Its aims are that tourism, recreation and leisure development should contribute to the environmental, social, cultural and economic welfare of people and places — that is, to fostering 'healthy people and healthy places'. The following is an example of a community working together for a healthy tourism and recreation outcome.

The Great River Walk will traverse the length of the Hawkesbury Nepean River, a distance of 570 kilometres, from its source south of Goulburn to its mouth at Broken Bay, Sydney. This visionary project will take many years to complete. It will be more than just a walking track. Those using it may travel by foot, bicycle, canoe or in some areas, where appropriate, by horseback.

It will take people through the living landscape of the river and its catchment, embracing its settlement and cultural heritage, both indigenous and non-indigenous. Natural bush, urban fringe and agricultural lands, with numerous loops and side trails, will help to illustrate the history of the area as well as the forces that are shaping its future.

Visitors will experience spectacular sandstone escarpments, productive and picturesque farmlands, dramatic river gorges, highland villages, bushland parks and reserves, quiet inlets and reaches. They will learn about Aboriginal culture, European exploration and history, the way the river system works and how the catchment is used.

The Great River Walk offers opportunities to conserve the resources upon which health, recreation and leisure depend; to promote the Hawkesbury Nepean River through its scenic, cultural and natural assets; and to support local and regional tourism, commerce and industry and provide a source of employment for local people. Employment initiatives will include skills development schemes in areas such as track building and maintenance; bush regeneration; development of interpretation; and tour guiding. These initiatives will work with local small businesses, youth and unemployment schemes and land care groups. The scheme will link into existing outdoor recreation facilities and businesses and is expected to create many new associations with existing cultural and historical groups, environmental initiatives and community health and welfare programs.

2.7 *Q*UALITY OF LIFE AND THE ROLE OF TOURISM

The World Tourism Organisation (1990) defines sustainable tourism as a 'form of economic development that is designed to improve the *quality of life* of the *host community* ...' (my italics). Quality of life, defined as the physical and social attractiveness of a place, is a very subjective yet very important factor in influencing people to move to, live in, visit, work or play in an area. Elements that make cities liveable, and contribute to quality of life include public safety, food costs, living space, housing standards, communications, educational opportunity, level of health, peace and quiet, traffic flow and clean air. Interestingly, the cities of the world that rank highest according to this criterion have the slowest rates of growth. Quality of life is concerned not only with availability of services and infrastructure, but also with access (Mercer 1994). Vitality is also important to the perception of quality of life. If communities feel disenfranchised or experience loss of control when outside investors and visitors seem to influence their lives, then the level of resentment towards the industry rises.

A common element that motivates people to travel and encourages communities to welcome tourists is the search for improvement in their quality of life. Health and wellbeing are clearly important attributes in attaining this goal. This aspect can distinguish SIT from other forms of tourism.

2.8 SENSE OF PLACE

Sense of place is a factor that deserves special consideration and should be an integral component when communities are developing land use plans, tourism strategies and guidelines for streetscapes. This is especially important in small towns and rural areas whose distinctive character sets them apart from each other and from larger urban centres. The dimensions that go into constructing a sense of place include:

- *physical factors* — of the built environment, such as buildings and architectural style, signage, landmarks, streetscapes, space, transport systems; and of the natural environment, such as landscape, vegetation, special features, wildlife
- *environmental factors* — climate, biodiversity, scenic values, heritage
- *cultural factors* — people, attitudes, lifestyle, traditions, customs, continuity, recreation, festivals and events, history and heritage, storytelling, occupations, crafts, foods and beverages
- *social factors* — leadership, civic pride, community cohesiveness, character
- *spiritual factors* — awareness of character and intrinsic values, connection to the past, religious significance, solitude, peace and quiet
- *economic factors* — prosperity, industry
- *psychological factors* — memory, history, symbols, friendliness, familiarity, attachment, relationships, intrigue, privacy, space, scale (Ambrosi et al. undated).

Sense of place heritage has tangible elements like buildings, streetscape and landscape, but it also has intangible elements such as history, sentiment, memory, familiarity, civic pride and emotions that together contribute to a place's identity. A sense of place comes from knowledge of, and commitment to, caring for our place. It needs to be a perception shared by all members of the community, even if this highlights contested values, histories and significance. It identifies the shared values and aspects that town planners, local governments, community organisations and businesses need to acknowledge, recognise and respect in any form of development. If tourism planning is able to preserve, conserve, enhance or contribute to attributes identified by the community as highly significant, it will mean tourism is truly working for the host community and the quality of life in that area. The process itself fuels civic pride. Equally, it is these attributes that make a place different and special that are the draw card for visitors (Ambrosi et al. undated).

For some places tourism may spell the demise of local traditions or customs, the commodification of culture and the destruction of valued places and spaces. The challenge for tourism is to be able to protect the values and needs of the place and the community and at the same time accommodate the needs of economic growth. SIT relies heavily on sense of place in many forms including cultural, nature-based and heritage tourism. Sense of place has an important role to play in the life of towns and can strengthen a community's quality of life. Projects should involve local participation and foster a sense of community ownership and commitment.

2.9 MANAGING VISITOR IMPACTS

Tourism unavoidably affects host communities, placing increased demand on services and amenities. This can cause tension between visitors and locals, especially during peak seasonal periods. Sometimes these pressures escalate into conflict, which can divide a community. Discord can find many forms of expression, including anti-tourism sentiment, the vilification of visitors and public protests. Seasonal influxes bring inconvenience, crowding, loss of amenity and other generally negative impacts. Findings of the Attitudes Survey in Toronto, Canada (Miller 1997), show that these pressures contribute to a deterioration in quality of life through a loss of control and of 'place' among residents. These conclusions support the ideas of Doxey (1976), who developed the Tourism Irritation Index based on observations of locals in Niagara township, Niagara Falls.

Tourism is usually seen in economic terms, but too often the cultural and social ramifications are either inadequately considered or simply ignored. The overall goal of tourism plans is to improve yield from tourism, but this must not focus only on the number of visitors. Successful tourism depends on effective partnerships between government, industry and community.

Over the past 40 years a number of visitor management models have been developed that seek to address the issues of visitor management. Most of them have their origins in natural resource management, mainly in the US and Canadian national parks services. A number of them have been tested in Australian national parks with only limited success. The main problem is in identifying the indicators that are sensitive to providing economic benefit and visitor satisfaction, and in effectively monitoring the social and ecological carrying capacity of a particular place, time and activity mix. The first of these models is the best known.

- Recreational Opportunity Spectrum (ROS) was developed in 1963. It still has some application in natural areas but limited ability to manage impacts.

- Carrying Capacity (CC) was adapted to recreation settings in 1965 to determine the level of use without unacceptable deterioration of the resource or the experience. Identifying precisely how many campers, for example, were acceptable proved impossible since the figure was influenced by constantly changing variables such as weather, season, behaviour, soil and vegetation type. The most common application of the concept is to limiting parking space available at a site.
- Limits of Acceptable Change (LAC) grew out of dissatisfaction with CC. LAC focuses on the resource rather than visitor management but lacks social and economic dimensions.
- Visitor Impact Management (VIM) evolved out of LAC in 1980. It focuses on negative impacts rather than the range of opportunities but is inflexible as it relies on fixed standards.
- Visitor Experience Resource Protection (VERP) was developed in 1991 to redress the balance between resource conservation and a high quality visitor experience, building on ROS and VIM. It has also proven rather inflexible.

- Visitor Activity Management Program (VAMP) was also developed in 1991 to help increase the level of integration of visitor management into protected area management, but VAMP is issue based rather than an ongoing management tool.

Tourism NSW is developing a process for use by local government and community groups that will identify tourism-related issues and address them in a way suited to the specific situation and resources within that community.

2.10 SUMMARY

This chapter has examined issues relating to host communities and the notion of impacts, both positive and negative. We have considered questions about appropriate and sustainable use of social, cultural and natural resources that have given rise to criticisms of SIT. Among these were claims that special interest forms such as adventure tourism, rural tourism, indigenous tourism, ecotourism and wildlife tourism may be just as prone to creating adverse social and environmental impacts as any other forms of tourism. We examined ecologically sustainable development within the context of tourism and biodiversity conservation, quality of life, health and sense of place. The role of tourism in community and community development was discussed, including the need for tourism planning to be better integrated into broader planning frameworks. We also introduced the principles that tourism should help people live healthy and productive lives; should contribute to the conservation, protection and rehabilitation of ecosystems; should be planned and allow for participation at the local level, and should recognise and support the identity, culture and interests of indigenous peoples.

The idea of community is familiar but difficult to define, being constantly dynamic. We considered community development, the process of striving to achieve a healthier community, with people from all walks of life, ages and backgrounds working together, and the attributes of a healthy community and the role of tourism in this process.

The concept of sense of place was suggested as one element that would assist tourism planning to preserve, enhance or contribute to attributes identified by locals as highly significant. We described sense of place as having tangible elements, like buildings, streetscape and landscape, but also intangible elements such as history, sentiment, memory, familiarity, civic pride and emotions that together contribute to a place's identity. It identifies the shared values and concerns that town planners, local governments, community organisations and businesses need to acknowledge and respect in any form of tourism development.

A number of visitor management models have been developed over the past 40 years, most with their origins in natural resource management. We discussed these as tools designed to assist in the monitoring and evaluation of the impacts of visitors on places and people. We outlined the concepts of carrying capacity and limits of acceptable change, attractive ideas that are nonetheless difficult to put into operation and manage.

Questions

2.1 Would the impact of multiple small-scale SIT operations be less, the same or greater than the impacts (both positive and negative) from fewer larger-scale tourism operations? What are these different impacts and how are they assessed?

2.2 Should an ecotourism or nature-based tourism operation be allowed to operate *within* a World Heritage Area; for example, using 4WD vehicles to access rainforests, or introducing exotic grasses in order to provide guests with manicured poolside lawns and gardens? What ethical and ecological issues does this involve?

2.3 How does SIT planning fit into broader community development planning? Who are the various stakeholders who should be consulted and involved?

2.4 Take an example of a SIT sector, such as heritage tours, and list the types of community groups and organisations that have a right to be involved. Consider the role each might play to ensure the tours are successful and deliver benefits to the community.

REFERENCES

Ambrosi, J., Marshall, N. & Wong, L. (undated). *Sense of Place in Small Towns.* Briefing notes. University of Calgary: Centre for Liveable Communities.

Bates, J. 1989. *Developing a Visitor Impact Management Tool for NSW.* Sydney: Tourism NSW.

Bates, J. 1999. *Planning for Tourism and Major Developments: Issues Affecting Local Government.* Sydney: NSW Tourism Commission.

Boyden, S. & Shirlow, M. 1989. 'Ecological Sustainability and the Quality of Life'. In Brown, V. (Ed.). *A Sustainable Healthy Future: Toward an Ecology of Health.* Melbourne: Oxford University Press, pp. 31–42.

Burgess, R. 1976. *Tourism in Manly: A Study by the Town Planning Dept.* Manly: Manly Municipal Council.

Burgess, R. 1983. *Planning for Tourism.* Town Planning Dept. Manly: Manly Municipal Council.

Bushell, R., Simmons, B. & Reizes, J. 1997. *Community, Environment & Tourism: Evaluation of Sustainable Development Practices in an Urban Coastal Council.* Tourism Research Building a Better Industry Conference Proceedings. Canberra: Bureau of Tourism Research.

Bushell, R. 1998. *The Health of the Host Community in Sustainable Tourism Planning.* Report for Centre for Research in Healthy Futures, University of Western Sydney.

Bushell, R. 1999a. *Global Issues for Protected Areas and Nature-based Tourism: Case Studies of Partnerships in Australia Addressing Some of These Issues.* Proceedings of the International Workshop on Sustainable Use of Biodiversity: The Example of Tourism. 11–14 November. Isle of Vilm, Germany: Federal Agency for Nature Conservation & International Academy for Nature Conservation.

Bushell, R. 1999b. *Development of Approaches and Practice for Sustainable Use of Biological Resources: Tourism.* Prepared on behalf of WCPA for the SBSTTA 4 (agenda item 4.8) meeting for the Convention on Biological Diversity, Montreal. 21–25 June. Gland, Switzerland: International Union for the Conservation of Nature.

Butler R. W. 1980. 'The Concept of a Tourist Area Cycle of Evolution: Implications for the Management of Resources'. *Canadian Geographer* 24: 5–10.

Ceballos-Lascuráin, H. 1996. *Tourism, Ecotourism and Protected Areas,* Gland, Switzerland: International Union for the Conservation of Nature.

City of Toronto, 1996. *Communities and Local Government Working Together: A Resource Manual of Strategies.* Toronto: City Clerks Dept.

Cohen, E. 1995. 'Contemporary Tourism — Trends and Challenges: Sustainable Authenticity or Contrived Post-Modernity?'. In Butler, R. W. & Pearce, D. G. (Eds.). *Change in Tourism: People, Places, Processes.* London: Routledge.

Commonwealth of Australia. 1991. *Ecologically Sustainable Development Working Groups Final Report: Tourism.* Canberra: Australian Government Printing Service.

Conner, N. 1999. *The Contribution of National Parks to Sustainable Rural and Regional Development.* Sydney: NSW National Parks and Wildlife Service.

Cordell, J. 1993. 'Who Owns the Land? Indigenous Involvement in Australian Protected Areas'. In Kempf, E. (Ed.). *The Law of the Mother: Protecting Indigenous People in Protected Areas.* USA: Sierra Book Club.

Doxey, G. V. 1976. 'When Enough's Enough: The Natives Are Getting Restless in Old Niagara'. *Heritage Canada* 2(2): 26–7.

Driml, S. & Common, M. 1995. 'Economic and Financial Benefits of Tourism in Major Protected Areas'. *Australian Journal of Environmental Management* 2 (2): 19–39.

Eagles, P. F. J. 1999. *International Trends in Park Tourism and Ecotourism.* Background paper for the Mediterranean Protected Areas: Status, Adequacy, Management and Training Needs Workshop, Cilento, Italy, 4–7 November 1999.

Figgis, P. 1999. *Australia's National Parks and Protected Areas: Future Directions: A Discussion Paper.* Occasional paper No. 8. Sydney: Australian Committee for IUCN.

Ghimire, K. B. & Pimbert, M. P. (Eds.). 1997. *Social Change and Conservation.* London: Earthscan Publications.

Gillespie, R. 1997. *Economic Value and Regional Economic Impact of Minnamurra Rainforest Centre, Budderoo N.P.* Sydney: NSW National Parks & Wildlife Service.

Gomez-Pompa, A. & Kaus, A. 1992. 'Taming the Wilderness Myth'. *Bioscience* 42 (4): 271–9.

Griffith, R. 2000. *Sustainable Development: Should We Read the Obituary?* Proceedings of the Sixth Internation Congress on Sustainable Development Research, Leeds.

Inskeep, E. 1991. *Tourism Planning: An Integrated and Sustainable Development Approach.* New York: Van Nostrand Reinhold.

MacCannell, D. 1976. 'Staged Authenticity'. In *The Tourist: A New Theory of the Leisure Class.* New York: Schocken Books, pp. 91–107.

Manly Municipal Council. 1999. *Community Annual Report 1998/1999;1997/1998.* Manly: Manly Municipal Council.

McCool, S. F. 1996. *Searching for Sustainability: A Difficult Course; an Uncertain Outcome.* Paper presented at the 1996 Global Congress on Coastal and Marine Tourism, Honolulu, Hawaii, 19–22 June.

McElroy, J. L. & de Albuquerque, K. 1996. 'Sustainable Alternative to Insular Mass Tourism: Recent Theory and Practice'. In Briguglio, L., Archer, B., Jafari, J. & Wall, G. (Eds.). *Sustainable Tourism in Islands and Small Island States.* New York: Pinter.

Mercer, C. 1994. *Urban and Regional Quality of Life Indicators.* Griffith University, Queensland: Institute for Cultural Policy Studies.

Miller, M. 1997. 'How Do We Know If Good Is Good?'. *Urban Quality Indicators* 1 (4): 1–3.

Pearce, D. G. 1992. 'Alternative Tourism: Concepts, Classifications, and Questions'. In Smith, V. L. & Eadington, W. R. (Eds.). *Tourism Alternatives: Potentials and Problems in the Development of Tourism.* Philadelphia: University of Pennsylvania Press.

Pigram, J. 1992. 'Alternative Tourism: Tourism and Sustainable Resource Management'. In Smith, V. L. & Eadington, W. R. (Eds.). *Tourism Alternatives: Potentials and Problems in the Development of Tourism.* Philadelphia: University of Pennsylvania Press.

Reizes, J. 1994. *Strategy for Ecologically Sustainable Development in the Suburbs.* Manly: Manly Municipal Council.

Ringer, G. (Ed.). 1998. *Destinations: Cultural Landscapes of Tourism*. London: Routledge.

Sheppard, D. 1999. *Nature Based Tourism and Protected Areas*. Paper presented to the Mediterranean Protected Areas: Status, Adequacy, Management and Training Needs Workshop, Cilento, Italy, 4–7 November 1999.

Smith, V. L. (Ed.). 1989. *Hosts and Guests: The Anthropology of Tourism*. Second Edition. Philadelphia: University of Pennsylvania Press.

Staiff, R., Kennedy, P. & Bushell, R. 1999. *From Museums to Parks: An Interpretative Leap*. Paper presented to the International Symposium on Society and Resource Management, August, Brisbane.

Taskforce on Economic Benefits of Protected Areas, of the World Commission on Protected Areas of IUCN, in collaboration with the Economic Service Unit of IUCN. 1998. *Economic Values of Protected Areas: Guidelines for Protected Area Managers*. Gland, Switzerland, and Cambridge: IUCN.

Tourism Marketing and Investment, John Larcombe & Assoc. & EDAW Pty Ltd. 1993. *Manly — Tourism Plan of Management*. Manly: Manly Municipal Council.

Tourism Works for American Council. 1996. *Annual Report*. Washington, DC: TWAC.

Urry, J. 1990. *The Tourist Gaze: Leisure and Travel in Contemporary Societies*. London: Sage Publications.

Wall, G. 1996. 'Rethinking Impacts of Tourism'. *Progress in Tourism & Hospitality Research* 2 (3): 207–16.

World Commission on Environment and Development. 1987. *Our Common Future*. New York: Oxford University Press.

World Tourism Organization. 1990. *Globe '90 Conference: Tourism Stream, Action Strategy*. Vancouver: WTO.

World Tourism Organization. 1995. *Agenda 21 for the Travel and Tourism Industry: Towards Environmentally Sustainable Development*. World Tourism Organization, World Travel and Tourism Council, and the Earth Council.

Tourism planning
in Manly

Manly, New South Wales, is a seaside resort and a symbol of tourism in Sydney. It boasts a scenic location at the northern head of Sydney Harbour and is an enjoyable 15-minute ferry ride from the heart of Sydney (see figure 2.1). The local tourism industry has long promoted this seaside suburb as 'Manly — 7 miles from Sydney and a thousand miles from care'. It has significant natural and built heritage and is home to many established festivals, such as the Manly Jazz Festival and the Manly Wine and Food Festival — each attracting between 60 000 and 80 000 visitors over two to three days — as well as surfing and lifesaving classics. The combination of these attributes makes it an attractive tourism destination and a suitable context for SIT.

Tourism has been the main economic activity of Manly since the 1850s with the establishment of the first ferry service between Circular Quay and Manly (Burgess 1976). Manly has a local population of around 36 000 (based on the 1996 ABS Census). Since the 1960s Manly Council and community have been concerned about tourism: on the one hand about its decline, and on the other about its impact on the local community (Burgess 1976; Reizes 1994). Special planning mechanisms have been introduced, such as the establishment of a special residential zoning or 'tourist zone' to allow a mix of residential buildings and hotels and motels. In the 1980s many low-cost rental 'boarding house beds' were converted to higher economic yield tourist accommodation, much of it high-rise holiday apartments or backpacker accommodation. More recently there has also been general concern about the impact of tourism-related activities on the natural environment (Bushell, Simmons & Reizes 1997). The most recent tourism strategy sought to position the entire destination as a site of ecotourism as a means to ensure that both the natural and social fabrics of Manly were better cared for by the operators, and that they attracted visitors who shared local concern for environmental protection.

Figure 2.1 *Manly's Development Control Plan seeks to encourage a sense of place. (Manly Visitor Information Centre)*

The most recent Tourism Plan produced for Manly Council in 1993 identified:

Goals for Tourism in Manly:

To make Manly attractive to residents and visitors; to develop a character and image that reflects the unique features of Manly; to build on strengths — natural environment, heritage, history, culture, people, lifestyle; to establish Manly as a leading ecotourism centre with world standard ecotourism product and services; to become a showpiece for environmental management, education and ecotourism. (TMI 1993)

The council recognised that tourism had always been and would always be a major element in the social, cultural, environmental and business life of Manly. The challenge was to balance the values of each and of the visitor. With this in mind, the Tourism Plan identified:

- a need to rename the Visitors Information Bureau (VIB) to the Visitor and Community Board and restructure it to strengthen and reflect the needs of the whole community
- the need to attract visitors who will be sympathetic to Manly's environment, especially long-stay visitors
- a desire to improve the attractiveness, amenities, social tone and safety of the 'Town Centre'; to preserve and enhance existing character and scale; to introduce urban design guidelines and civic improvement measures to improve attractiveness, including seating, shade, landscaping, paving and public facilities; and to address behaviour and safety issues in the Corso
- the need to improve the retail and cultural mix of the Town Centre area, and facilitate the development of a retail mix to attract residents and long-stay visitors
- a demand for more cultural activities
- a community desire for appropriate redevelopment — to create a development vision and mechanisms to encourage redevelopment consistent with the vision for Manly
- a need to improve the management of tourism and related issues (TMI 1993).

As with all development there are costs, and the changes introduced over the last twenty years through development in general and that aimed to reinvigorate tourism have led to a number of impacts on local residents. These have included increased congestion, parking problems, increased rubbish, noise and crime, a change to the mix of retail shopping and increased land values. Tourism continues to be the most significant economic activity in Manly; it attracts somewhere in the order of 6 million visitors each year. It brings visitors and jobs, but it also continues to create conflict in a small population. These issues require processes that address and balance different values, needs and views.

The *Manly Local Environmental Plan* (LEP) (1988) recognises that tourism is a major industry and employer in the Manly area, and aims to encourage its growth and continuing viability by:
- encouraging and concentrating tourist development in tourist areas
- encouraging tourism to coexist with local residents to their mutual advantage
- encouraging a diversity of commercial recreation activities suitable for adults as well as youth that will complement the tourist attractiveness of Manly.

The *Development Control Plan* (DCP) — Manly Business Zone (1989) emphasises townscape considerations, requiring that each development proposal takes into account how it will appear when viewed from and in conjunction with surrounding buildings spaces and streets.

Planning policies and practices aim to make Manly:

- a good place to live
- a good place to visit
- a place where cultural, heritage and environmental values are protected.

The *Regional Environmental Plan* (REP) and LEP both contribute towards the protection of the environmental, cultural and heritage attributes of Manly, such as the scenic foreshore protection areas, the Corso protection area and the waterways. Most of these attributes are accessible from the tourist zone. The DCP helps to protect, conserve and encourage a sense of place in Manly by ensuring that new developments complement and are sympathetic with the surrounding environment.

Tourism is a land use that can be very difficult to accommodate under a single land use definition or zone. LEPs and REPs address issues of land use, but tourism involves much more complex activity than just land use. Tourism creates movement of people in and out of an area. It requires marketing; it is a big user of public space; and it is dependent on a range of factors external to the block of land on which the development is situated (Bates 1989).

Questions

1 What likely effects would changing the name of a council committee from the 'Visitors Information Bureau' to the 'Visitor and Community Board' have on the planning and management of tourism?

2 What effect does the retail mix in a town's commercial centre have on the relationship between locals and visitors?

3 How might a local community go about attracting a particular type of tourist to ensure high yield and low social and environmental impact?

4 How do local environmental plans (LEPs) affect tourism businesses?

Nerilee Hing

CHAPTER 3

Entrepreneurship
and small
business

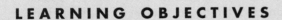

LEARNING OBJECTIVES

After reading this chapter, you will have an appreciation of:

- the economic, psychological, sociological and management perspectives on entrepreneurship

- the approaches to identifying and evaluating opportunities for small business entrepreneurship in special interest tourism (SIT)

- the purpose and typical contents of business plans for SIT ventures

- the central role of owner-managers in the performance of small SIT ventures

- the need for a strategic fit between the entrepreneur, the small firm and the emerging industry structure typical of SIT ventures

- the competitive advantages inherent in most small SIT ventures.

3.1 INTRODUCTION

Entrepreneurship has attracted unprecedented attention in the last few decades. Businesses have been urged to become more entrepreneurial in seizing opportunities to remain competitive into the twenty-first century. Entrepreneurship not only creates new employment and avenues for creativity and independence; it also acts on market opportunities that are increasingly suitable for small innovative businesses. These include the growing emergence of niche markets, rapid technological developments and shorter product life cycles driven by customer demand for better and different products and services (Industry Task Force on Leadership and Management Skills 1995).

SIT presents particular opportunities for entrepreneurship. It inherently caters for niche markets seeking specialised, innovative and often personalised customised experiences. The fact that SIT industries are a relatively recent innovation means small firms predominate and can use their adaptability, flexibility and quick decision making to **competitive advantage**. Thus potential and existing SIT operators can benefit from an understanding of entrepreneurship, and the process of identifying and evaluating venture opportunities, planning a new venture and managing it through start-up and growth.

3.2 UNDERSTANDING ENTREPRENEURSHIP

This section examines how the meanings of 'entrepreneurship' and 'entrepreneur' have evolved from economic, psychological, sociological and management perspectives. Each can contribute to an understanding of entrepreneurship, of the key players in this process — the entrepreneurs — and of the relationship between entrepreneurship and SIT.

3.2.1 An economic *perspective on entrepreneurship*

Much early interest in entrepreneurship stemmed from the field of economics. Economic theory is concerned with how a society creates and distributes wealth (Kirchhoff 1997:445). Economists have thus viewed entrepreneurship as a major mechanism for ensuring wealth creation and distribution.

Richard Cantillon is generally credited with giving the concept of entrepreneurship a central role in economics (Holt 1992:3). He described an entrepreneur as a person who pays a certain price for a product in order to then resell it at an uncertain price (Cantillon 1755). Thus, entrepreneurs consciously make decisions about resource allocation and so assume the risk of enterprise in seeking superior opportunities for using resources to yield the highest commercial benefit (Holt 1992:3).

Writing in the early 1800s, Jean Baptiste Say regarded economic development as the result of venture creation (Filion 1998:2). Although he agreed with Cantillon that entrepreneurs are *influenced by* market forces, Say also recognised that entrepreneurs *influence* society by creating new ventures (Holt 1992:4). Say drew a distinction between entrepreneurs and capitalists, viewing entrepreneurs as innovators and agents of change (Filion 1998:3).

The rise of neoclassical economics in the early twentieth century paid little attention to entrepreneurs. It assumed that capitalism distributes income equitably through the operation of market forces and ignored the role of entrepreneurs in creating new demand (Kirchhoff 1997:448–9). However, Joseph Schumpeter disagreed that the mechanism of wealth distribution was driven by competitive markets functioning to achieve equilibrium between supply and demand. Instead, he observed 'chaotic markets' driven by the regular entrance of entrepreneurs bringing innovations that challenge established suppliers. He called this process 'creative destruction', because entrepreneurs create new wealth through the process of destroying existing market structures (Kirchhoff 1997:450). Schumpeter observed that:

> The essence of entrepreneurship lies in the perception and exploitation of new opportunities in the realm of business...it always has to do with bringing about a different use of national resources in that they are withdrawn from their traditional employ and subjected to new conditions (Schumpeter 1928:483, in Filion 1998:3).

Because these innovations *create* new demand, entrepreneurs are central to wealth creation and distribution (Kirchhoff 1997:451). Schumpeter played a key role in launching the field of entrepreneurship by associating it clearly with *innovation* and by articulating the importance of entrepreneurs in explaining economic development (Filion 1998:3).

In summary, an economic perspective on entrepreneurship dominated the field from the 1700s to the mid-1900s. This perspective was concerned with what entrepreneurs do, or the role they play as the 'motor of the economic system' (Filion 1988:4). Thus, entrepreneurs were viewed as innovators, detectors of opportunities, creators of enterprises, risk-takers and coordinators of resources (Filion 1988:4). Not only did they satisfy market demand for new products and services, but they also created demand where none had previously existed. From this perspective, we can appreciate the role of entrepreneurship in SIT in contributing to economic development. The burgeoning of SIT, from gourmet tours to adventure tourism, has resulted from entrepreneurs conceiving innovative ideas, recognising opportunities for new products and services, creating market demand for those products and services, coordinating resources to establish ventures to meet that demand and assuming the risks involved.

BREAKTHROUGH TOURISM
Thomas Cook — from SIT to mass tourism

Although Thomas Cook contributed greatly to the emergence of mass tourism, he commenced operations by creating and catering for a market with particular travel needs and wants. The special interest of these tourists was religious development. Cook was a Baptist preacher concerned with the 'declining morals' of the English working class. He conceived the idea of chartering trains to take workers to temperance meetings and bible camps in the countryside, operating the first of these day trips in 1841. Cook's excursions gradually expanded, from one-day excursions to various English destinations, to international and round-the-world tours. For example, his 1851 excursion to the Great Exhibition in London attracted 160 000 participants. In 1863 Cook organised his first international excursion, and in 1872 his first round-the-world tour. Participants' motivations for these trips shifted almost entirely from spiritual purposes to sightseeing and pleasure. The attraction was that the tours were prepackaged, with participants paying an affordable, prepaid, one-fee ticket that included transportation, accommodation, guides, food and other goods and services for travel on an organised itinerary. This heralded the commencement of package tours, a major component of modern tourism industries (Weaver & Opperman 2000:64–5).

Cook was therefore an early entrepreneur in SIT. He conceived an innovative idea and recognised opportunities presented by communications and transportation innovations such as the railway, steamship and telegraph, utilised to increase his venture's efficiency. He coordinated the many necessary resources and applied industrial principles in order to offer standardised, precisely timed, commercialised, high-volume package tours. He reacted to growing demand for travel and created new demand. Cook both created and distributed new wealth by challenging existing market structures, contributing to the economic development of tourism industries and the regions and countries within which his company operated.

■ 3.2.2 A psychological *perspective on entrepreneurship*

From the 1960s, attention turned to a psychological view that attempted to explain the personal characteristics of entrepreneurs. Psychologists believed entrepreneurial success could be optimised if entrepreneurial behaviour could be described, explained and predicted by identifying its underlying needs, drives, attitudes, beliefs and values. Many personality factors have been associated with entrepreneurs. For example, Timmons (1994) identifies the following attitudes and behaviours of successful entrepreneurs:

- commitment, determination, perseverance, persistent problem solving
- high need for achievement, low need for status and power

- opportunity and goal oriented
- creativity, self-reliance and ability to adapt
- tolerance for stress, ambiguity and uncertainty, moderate risk-taking
- leadership
- high energy, health and emotional stability
- innovation
- high intelligence and conceptual ability
- vision and the capacity to inspire.

Considerable empirical research has been conducted into the psychology of the entrepreneur. While often yielding conflicting and inconclusive results, there is general agreement that entrepreneurs display:

- *a high need for achievement:* a desire to do well, not just for the sake of social recognition or prestige, but to attain an inner feeling of personal accomplishment. They prefer to be personally responsible for solving problems, setting goals and reaching these goals through personal effort.
- *an internal locus of control:* a belief that success is due to personal effort and skill rather than to other people, luck, chance or fate (external locus of control)
- *a propensity to take calculated risks:* preferring situations of intermediate risk where they can exercise some control over the outcome
- *a high tolerance of ambiguity:* as entrepreneurship encompasses various functions performed under conditions of uncertainty.

While these traits are common among entrepreneurs, they do not appear to distinguish entrepreneurs from successful executives. Nevertheless, longitudinal research in Australia has demonstrated that **small business** owner-managers with a high need for achievement, an internal locus of control, moderate risk-taking propensity and a high tolerance of ambiguity have a better business survival rate than those without these traits (Williams 1987).

In summary, empirical research into the psychology of entrepreneurs has been extensive but has failed to identify a set of psychological traits distinctive to entrepreneurs (Timmons 1990:161). However, the traits discussed above do have value in describing the entrepreneurial mind.

■ *3.2.3* **A sociological** *perspective on entrepreneurship*

With the failure of psychologists to provide a complete explanation for entrepreneurship, the concept first attracted attention from sociologists in the 1980s. Sociological perspectives on entrepreneurship are concerned with societal factors that affect the acceptance and value of entrepreneurship and that hinder or facilitate entrepreneurial activity, and social influences on the decisions of individuals to pursue an entrepreneurial career.

Societal factors influencing entrepreneurship

Although the environments within which new ventures are created show extensive variation, one only has to observe concentrated entrepreneurial activity in Silicon Valley in the United States or Byron Bay in Australia to appreciate that some features of these environments might make them particularly conducive to entrepreneurship. The personal characteristics of certain individuals may incline towards entrepreneurship, but the environment may determine whether those intentions are translated into action.

Bruno and Tyebjee (1982:293) identify the most frequently cited 'essential' environmental factors for new venture creation as:
- venture capital availability
- presence of experienced entrepreneurs
- technically skilled labour force
- accessibility of suppliers
- accessibility of customers or new markets
- favourable government policies
- proximity of universities
- availability of land or facilities
- accessibility to transportation
- receptive population
- availability of supporting services
- attractive living conditions.

An alternative set of environmental factors proposed as influencing entrepreneurship is shown in table 3.1.

■ **Table 3.1** *A framework for entrepreneurial environments*

ENVIRONMENT	FACTORS
Government policies and procedures	• Restrictions on imports and exports • Provision of bankruptcy laws • Entry barriers • Procedural requirements for registration and licensing • Number of institutions for entrepreneurs to report to • Rules and regulations governing entrepreneurial activities • Laws to protect proprietary rights
Socioeconomic conditions	• Public attitude to entrepreneurship • Presence of experienced entrepreneurs • Successful role models • Existence of persons with entrepreneurial characteristics • Recognition of exemplary entrepreneurial performance • Proportion of small firms in the population of firms • Diversity of economic activities • Extent of economic growth
Financial assistance	• Venture capital • Alternative sources of financing • Low-cost loans • Willingness of financial institutions to finance small entrepreneurs • Credit guarantee program for start-up enterprises • Competition among financial institutions

(continued)

Non-financial assistance	• Counselling and support services • Entrepreneurial networks • Incubator facilities • Government procurement programs for small businesses • Government support for research and development • Tax incentives and exemptions • Local and international information networks • Modern transport and communications facilities
Entrepreneurial and business skills	• Technical and vocational education • Business education • Entrepreneurial training programs • Technical and vocational training programs • Availability of information

Source: *Adapted from Gnyawali and Fogel (1994:45)*

SPECIAL INTEREST INVESTIGATION
Social factors encouraging special interest tourism in Byron Bay

Many conditions conducive to new venture creation exist in Byron Bay, a small coastal town in northern New South Wales. With a resident population of about 4000 people, the town is a vibrant centre dominated by small tourism and hospitality-related businesses, many of them established from new by their owner-operators. Byron Bay has around 100 food outlets, 12 backpacker hostels, dozens of motels, hotels and holiday units, more than 20 bed and breakfast establishments, as well as numerous SIT ventures, including Harley motorbike tours, health resorts, scuba diving, rainforest tours, charter boat operations, hang gliding and a diversity of special events, from rock concerts to writers' festivals.

The local environment has been particularly welcoming for new venture creation in SIT. The town abounds in experienced entrepreneurs providing role models for aspiring ones. Opportunities for new businesses are enhanced by the swarms of tourists and daytrippers who provide an accessible market. The local government has been largely pro-development and new business and retail space is continually created. The local community has been extremely vocal in opposing large-scale developments or those by multinational companies such as Club Med and McDonald's. 'Small is beautiful' when it comes to venture creation. The population is receptive to new businesses, particularly those offering something small-scale, innovative and catering to a niche market. The attractive living conditions in the area and its particular appeal to younger people mean there is a steady supply of employees who can gain ready access to additional training and education. Moreover, Byron Bay attracts tourists interested in alternative lifestyles, providing numerous opportunities for small businesses offering SIT products and services.

Social influences on the entrepreneurial decision

A second set of sociological factors relates to social influences on entrepreneurial career choices. Shapero and Sokol (1982:83) categorise these as life path changes, perceptions of desirability and perceptions of feasibility.

Life path changes

Decisions to make major changes in career paths can result from negative displacements, positive pulls or from finding oneself between careers. Research shows that individuals are more likely to establish new ventures because of negative displacements. These include forcible emigration or being fired, insulted, angered or bored at work, reaching middle age, or becoming divorced or widowed (Shapero & Sokol 1982:83). Positive pulls can come from a partner, mentor, colleague, investor or customer, and may include the offer of financial assistance, a contract from a potential customer or a partnership (Shapero & Sokol 1982:83). Others decide to embark on the entrepreneurial path when confronted with the need to make a major career decision, such as when they leave school, the army or prison, or perhaps when faced with an 'empty nest' (Shapero & Sokol 1982:83). However, the decision to establish a new venture also depends on individual perceptions of its desirability and feasibility.

Perceptions of desirability

The perceived desirability and credibility of an entrepreneurial career is largely a product of individual value systems, shaped primarily by culture, family, peers, colleagues and mentors (Shapero & Sokol 1982). For example, a disproportionate number of entrepreneurs have self-employed fathers (Shapero & Sokol 1982:84), while Handy (1999) reports that most entrepreneurs in his study experienced upbringings in which childhood curiosity and independence were encouraged, stimulated and unstifled. Peers, colleagues and mentors can reinforce an individual's self-belief and provide positive role models.

Perceptions of feasibility

Perceptions of feasibility are influenced by financial and other support, the demonstration effect from role models, and support from mentors, partners and significant others (Shapero & Sokol 1982:83). Most venture start-ups are financed from personal savings and borrowings, particularly from relatives (Shapero & Sokol 1982:86). Thus, availability of finance is a key determinant of how feasible a new venture is perceived. This is also shaped by the moral support, labour, skills, shared risks and companionship of a business partner, and by general support from family and friends.

In summary, a sociological perspective on entrepreneurship takes account of the social and cultural influences on the entrepreneurial decision, both at a general societal level and at the level of individual career choice. Importantly, it draws attention to ways in which entrepreneurship can be nurtured through the provision of environments conducive to new venture creation, through the exertion of positive pulls, and through influences that can modify perceptions of desirability and feasibility. We have already considered an example of how certain environments are conducive to the establishment of new ventures in SIT. Examples also abound of how social influences have been instrumental in people's decisions to establish SIT ventures. The personal passion of the entrepreneur for a particular interest, activity, sport or hobby, combined with supportive networks provided by family, friends and colleagues, have often been the driving forces behind new venture creation in SIT.

■ 3.2.4 A **management** *perspective on entrepreneurship*

Management scholars became interested in entrepreneurship around the same time as sociologists. They are interested in the *activities* performed in entrepreneurship, particularly in the process of creating a new enterprise. Some relevant questions on entrepreneurship from a management perspective include: What is involved in perceiving opportunities? What are key tasks in successfully establishing new organisations? How are these tasks different from those involved in managing ongoing organisations? and What are the entrepreneur's unique contributions to this process? (Bygrave & Hofer 1991:16).

The management perspective sees entrepreneurship as a process. Hisrich and Peters (1989:30) identify four distinct phases — identifying and evaluating the opportunity, developing the business plan, gathering necessary resources and managing the resulting enterprise. Similarly, Timmons (1990:5) defines entrepreneurship as:

> the process of creating or seizing an opportunity and pursuing it regardless of the resources currently controlled. Entrepreneurship involves the definition, creation, and distribution of value and benefits to individuals, groups, organizations, and society.

Management scholars therefore view entrepreneurship as a purposeful activity in which the chances of success can be enhanced through developing entrepreneurial and management skills. In the remainder of this chapter, we take a management or process approach to entrepreneurship. Having acknowledged that entrepreneurship has an important economic role, and that numerous psychological and sociological factors shape the entrepreneurial decision, we proceed to examine, in the context of SIT, how opportunities for small business entrepreneurship can be identified and evaluated, how to plan the new venture, and important considerations in the general and strategic management of entrepreneurial firms.

3.3 OPPORTUNITIES FOR SMALL BUSINESS ENTREPRENEURSHIP IN SIT

Every successful venture is underpinned by an attractive and well-defined opportunity. Thus, recognising and evaluating opportunities deserve particular attention in entrepreneurship.

■ 3.3.1 Opportunities *for new venture creation in SIT: the influence of industry structure*

Opportunities for entrepreneurship in SIT are plentiful, when compared with many other industries, including those catering for mass tourism. To understand why, it is useful to consider the typical structure of SIT industries and to identify characteristics that make them conducive to new venture creation. To this end, this section draws on a framework developed by Michael Porter, a renowned strategic management scholar.

According to Porter, the state of competition in any industry is the main determinant of how attractive that industry is for new entrants and existing businesses (1980). Porter (1980) defines competition more broadly than usual, identifying five types of competitive forces:

- existing industry competitors (intra-industry rivalry)
- threat of entry into the industry by new businesses
- bargaining power of buyers for the industry's products or services
- bargaining power of suppliers to the industry
- availability of substitute products for those produced by the industry.

For potential entrepreneurs, the attractiveness of the industry they are planning to enter should be a key factor in deciding whether or not to launch the new venture. Because entrepreneurship involves identifying and acting on business opportunities, the level of competition in an industry affects the availability of entrepreneurial opportunities in that industry. Potential entrepreneurs should therefore look for industries where competitive forces are weak. This tends to occur in emerging industries — those that are relatively new or those in which a technological breakthrough changes established industry structures. Figure 3.1 depicts how industries generally progress through their life cycle, from emergence through maturity and decline. According to Porter (1980), the five competitive forces are weakest in emerging industries and strongest in mature and decadent industries.

■ **Figure 3.1**
Industry life cycle model

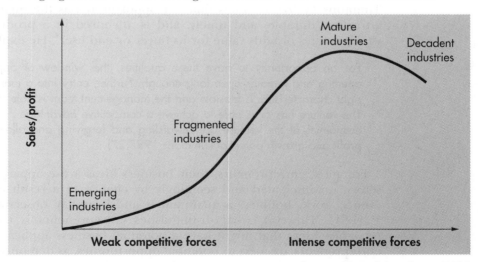

Source: *Derived from Porter (1980)*

Industries associated with SIT can be classed as emerging industries where Porter's five competitive forces are comparatively weak. For example, eco-resorts, bungy jumping operations, Aboriginal tours, gourmet and educational tours and adventure tourism generally have the characteristics outlined below.

- Intra-industry rivalry is low, since market demand generally outweighs supply of the product or service. And since most businesses in emerging industries are small, promotional activities, price-cutting and other competitive strategies are not usually extensive.
- Entry barriers are low, requiring little capital investment to establish a new venture, few economies of scale and unsophisticated distribution channels.
- Buyer power is weak, since most are first-time or relatively inexperienced buyers, who are likely to be less discerning and demanding, are less likely to shop around for a better deal and will be less loyal to particular brands.
- Supplier power is weak, since many of these industries offer services requiring few suppliers. Where supplies for the product or service are needed, these are generally sourced from small businesses whose bargaining power is weak.
- Substitute products are few, since these industries offer unique or special experiences.

Above we have identified some characteristics that make SIT industries conducive to entrepreneurial opportunities. The following sections discuss how a potential entrepreneur might identify and evaluate particular opportunities for new venture creation in SIT.

■ 3.3.2 **Towards** *innovation: identifying opportunities*

Timmons (1997:27) notes that 'an opportunity has the qualities of being attractive, durable, and timely, and is anchored in a product or service which creates or adds value for its buyer or end user'. He explains that:

> For an opportunity to have these qualities, the 'window of opportunity' is opening and remains open long enough. Further, entry into a market with the right characteristics is feasible and the management team is able to achieve it. The venture has or is able to achieve a competitive advantage ... Finally, the economics of the venture are rewarding and forgiving and allow significant profit and growth potential (Timmons 1997:27).

For most entrepreneurs, their business ideas arose apparently by themselves, unanticipated and seemingly by chance as a result of unforeseen events, work, hobbies, acquaintances and everyday observations (Vesper 1994:31). However, what distinguishes entrepreneurs is their ability to recognise ideas that might have a potential business application — that is, entrepreneurs are alert to potential opportunities, as demonstrated by Tony and Maureen Wheeler of Lonely Planet Publications.

BREAKTHROUGH TOURISM
Lonely Planet finds a niche

In the 1970s backpacking emerged as a kind of SIT pursued by travellers seeking an alternative to mass tourism. Pearce (1990:1) argues that five criteria distinguish backpackers from other travellers — a preference for budget accommodation, an emphasis on meeting other travellers, an independently organised and flexible travel schedule, longer rather than very brief holidays, and an emphasis on informal and participatory holiday activities. Since the 1970s backpacking has become much more industrialised as specialist accommodation, food and beverage outlets and other services have been established to cater for this niche market. A particularly strong influence on the development of the industry has been Lonely Planet Publications, started in 1972 by Tony and Maureen Wheeler. Their experiences, described below by Lewis (1996:217–8), provide an example of opportunity recognition in SIT.

> In 1972 a young and adventurous newly married English couple, Tony and Maureen Wheeler, then 26 and 22 years old respectively, walked, hitched and backpacked their way to Australia across Asia from England. They arrived in Sydney on Boxing Day with precisely 27 cents in their pockets. In order to survive, Tony pawned his camera and Maureen got a job in a milk bar.
>
> Soon the numerous 'how did you do it?' inquiries from friends inspired them to write down their travel experiences. With virtually no publishing knowledge (although Tony had worked on a university newspaper in his student days) and working from a kitchen table in the basement of a Sydney flat, they converted their meticulously kept travel notes into a publication — a cut and paste job they called *Across Asia on the Cheap*.

Tony Wheeler described those early days:

> 'We did everything. We wrote the books, we edited them, we sold them, and we delivered them. When *Across Asia* was published, I took a day off work in Sydney to come sell it in Melbourne. I loaded up a suitcase with books, flew to Melbourne, took a bus to the city, put the books in the left luggage office at the train station, went around the book shops and sold the books, went back to the station, picked up the suitcase and then delivered them.'
>
> *Across Asia on the Cheap* became an instant success, with the initial print run of 1500 copies becoming sold out in 10 days, it inspired thoughts of a second trip to Asia. Encouraged by their success and driven by their love of being 'on the road', they postponed their return to England and set out again for Southeast Asia.

(continued)

This trip resulted in *Southeast Asia on a Shoestring*. Cobbled together in a cheap Singapore hotel between fortnightly visits to the authorities to renew their visas, *Southeast Asia on a Shoestring* was published in 1973. Fifteen thousand copies were sold in Australia, New Zealand, Britain, the United States and Asia. Its meticulously researched information, communicated in a down-to-earth style, was to create an entirely new genre of travel-guide writing.

Tony Wheeler, reflecting on this early success, observed:

'Now I can look back and think that was a really clever idea, but at the time I didn't realise it. It was just a nice thing to do. As soon as we saw how well the first book went we thought, "Let's do another". We grew very slowly at first. It took us five years to get to ten titles.'

Today, Lonely Planet employs nearly 300 people. While it initially covered far-flung destinations for budget travellers, it now covers popular destinations worldwide and offers good-value options for travellers of all types seeking down-to-earth advice, accurate maps and enriching background information (http://press.lonelyplanet.com). Thus, the Wheelers' venture has been truly entrepreneurial, introducing an innovative product that has shaped the nature of the backpacking industry. An entry in Lonely Planet publications is keenly sought by many hostels, guesthouses, tour operations, attractions, cafes and bars in recognition of its pervading influence on travellers' choices. Lonely Planet's success has been derived from the Wheelers' ability to recognise an opportunity to capitalise on an emerging market niche by providing a specialist product.

The most common source of business ideas is prior employment, followed by hobbies and social encounters, respectively (Vesper 1994:31–2). In SIT, many business ideas arise from the entrepreneur's personal interest in a particular sport, hobby or pastime. However, individuals can also use various mechanisms to deliberately seek out ideas that represent a potential business opportunity.

Alizadeh (1999:55) suggests that posing the following questions can assist in overcoming creative barriers to idea generation:
- Is there a new way to do it?
- Can you borrow or adapt it?
- Can you give it a new twist?
- Do you merely need more of the same?
- Do you just need less of the same?
- Is there a substitute?
- Can the parts be rearranged?
- What if we do just the opposite?
- Can ideas be combined?

- Can we put it to other uses?
- What else could we make from this?
- Are there other markets for it?

Many new ventures in SIT have arisen in response to some of the questions above. Homestays and farmstays are examples of where enterprising people have found alternate uses for spare bedrooms and other facilities. Some existing businesses have adapted their facilities to become tourist attractions, such as sheep-shearing exhibitions, factory tours, culinary classes and wineries. Educational tourism is an example of where travelling and learning have been combined. In fact, by definition, SIT involves a combination of travel with a special interest.

◾ 3.3.3 Evaluating *ideas and opportunities*

Ideas should be carefully evaluated to determine whether the specific products or services will provide the returns needed for the required resources (Hisrich & Peters 1989:31–2). This may involve examining:
- what has created the opportunity
- whether the opportunity fits with the personal skills and goals of the entrepreneur
- what the risks and returns of the opportunity are.

What has created the opportunity?

Holt (1992) observes that entrepreneurs tend to be strategic thinkers who recognise changes and see opportunities where others do not. Further, Drucker (1994:25) contends that entrepreneurs see change as 'the norm' and as healthy. Usually they do not bring about the change themselves, but the entrepreneur always searches for change, responds to it and exploits it as an opportunity. Holt (1992:41–9) identifies six types of change from which opportunities for innovations or venture creation might arise:
- scientific knowledge, such as new inventions
- process innovations, or techniques and methods used to make knowledge or ideas useful
- industrial changes, through either natural or human events
- market changes, resulting in unmet demand
- demographic changes
- social and cultural changes.

Does the opportunity fit with the entrepreneur?

To represent an opportunity, an idea also needs to be attractive to the entrepreneur and consistent with his or her skills and goals. Technical capability is usually all-important (Vesper 1994:70), although additional aspects may include appropriate contacts, qualifications, training, experience and reputation. Further, venturing often requires that the work be performed exceptionally well, with passion, enthusiasm and commitment, particularly in SIT where the customer often interacts personally with the operator. The attractiveness of the opportunity to the entrepreneur therefore plays an important role in determining the ability to excel.

What are the risks and returns of the opportunity?

Van Slyke, Stevenson and Roberts (1992:82–4) identify five questions to help evaluate the risks and returns of an opportunity.

- What are the dimensions of the 'window of opportunity'?
- Is the profit potential of the opportunity adequate to provide a satisfactory return?
- Does the opportunity open up additional options for expansion, diversification or integration?
- Will the profit stream be durable in the face of probable obstacles?
- Does the product or service meet a real need?

If an opportunity can pass this initial evaluation, it is time to move to the next level of investigation — a more thorough screening. This is best achieved through developing a business plan for the new venture.

3.4 PLANNING THE SMALL ENTREPRENEURIAL VENTURE

Analysis of business failures reveals that entrepreneurs often launch a venture without undertaking a thorough and detailed study of its likely problems and prospects. Research indicates that many common causes of small business failure could have been avoided or minimised by sound business planning. Entrepreneurs should develop and use a comprehensive business plan to increase their chances of success.

Although there is no single 'correct' format for a business plan, a systematic approach is needed. Figure 3.2 identifies some common elements in business plans. The purpose is to draw attention to what is required, rather than provide a step-by-step guide. Many texts on small business management provide comprehensive guidelines for developing a business plan (for example, Hisrich & Peters 1992; Timmons 1994; English 1998). A particularly useful website is *The Business Plan: Roadmap to Success* (1997) (http://www.sba.gov/starting/businessplan.html).

It is clear from figure 3.2 that after developing a business plan, the entrepreneur will have clearly defined the business concept, tested its feasibility in the marketplace, identified how the product or service will be produced and marketed, decided on the venture's organisational structure and management team, identified tasks to be achieved prior to start-up, assessed critical risks and problems, developed contingency plans to overcome these, identified legal and financial requirements, and assessed the likely financial performance for the first few years of business operation. As such, developing a business plan should result in a thorough appraisal of the business opportunity and so reduce the risks involved.

1. Cover Page

2. Executive Summary

3. Overview of the Venture
   3.1 The Business's Mission or Overall Strategy
   3.2 Product
   3.3 Services
   3.4 Location and Size
   3.5 Founder or Company

4. Industry and Market Analysis
   4.1 Industry Outlook and Trends
   4.2 The Target Market
   4.3 Market Size and Trends
   4.4 Estimated Market Value
   4.5 Analysis of Competitors
   4.6 Market Share and Sales

5. Production Plan
   5.1 Production Process
   5.2 Facilities Requirements
   5.3 Inventory Control Measures

6. Marketing Plan
   6.1 Situation Analysis
   6.2 Marketing Goals or Objectives
   6.3 Marketing Strategies
   6.4 Promotional Budget

7. Organisational Plan
   7.1 The Organisational Structure
   7.2 The Management Team
   7.3 Roles and Responsibilities of Organisational Members
   7.4 Legal Structure

8. Schedule of Operations

9. Critical Risks and Problems
   9.1 Assessment of Risk
   9.2 Contingency Plans

10. Financial Plan
    10.1 Start-up Expenses
    10.2 Pro-Forma Monthly Income Statement Year 1
    10.3 Pro-Forma Income Statement 3 Year Summary
    10.4 Pro-Forma Monthly Cashflow Budget Year 1
    10.5 Pro-Forma Cashflow Budget 3 Year Summary
    10.6 Pro-Forma Balance Sheet 3 Year Summary
    10.7 Break-even Analysis

11. Appendices

Source: *Hing and Knox (2000:110–11)*

GENERAL MANAGEMENT IN THE SMALL ENTREPRENEURIAL VENTURE

Central to the performance of the small entrepreneurial firm is the entrepreneur. This section discusses the importance of owner-managers in small business management and how their roles change as the organisation grows and develops.

■ 3.5.1 The importance *of the owner-manager in small business*

The Australian Bureau of Statistics defines a small business as a manufacturing business with fewer than 100 employees or other non-agricultural business with fewer than 20 employees. Further, it is generally agreed that small businesses tend to:
* be independently owned and managed
* be closely controlled by owner-managers who contribute most or all of the operating capital
* have the principal decision-making functions resting with the owner-manager
* have operations, and sometimes markets, that tend to be locally based
* be small relative to the size of the largest firm in the industry — small firms generally do not have much market power (http://www.dewrsb. gov.au/group_osb/smallbus/research.htm).

Similarly, the Wiltshire Committee Report on small business in Australia has emphasised the importance of management characteristics. It defined a small business as one in which:

> one or two persons are required to make all the critical management decisions — finance, accounting, personnel, purchasing, processing or servicing, marketing, selling — without the aid of internal specialists and with specific knowledge in only one or two functional areas (cited in Johns, Dunlop & Sheehan 1989).

These typical characteristics emphasise the critical importance of owner-managers in small business success and failure. Table 3.2 summarises the results of a comprehensive study of small business failures in Australia (Williams 1987), with over 80 per cent attributable to management deficiencies. These data are somewhat dated but provide at least an indication of causes of small business failure in the absence of any official statistics (Australian Bureau of Statistics 1999:101).

■ 3.5.2 Changing *management roles in small business*

Given the importance of owner-managers to small business performance, it is instructive to examine how their role generally changes during typical organisational life cycle stages.

Table 3.2
Reasons given by owner-managers for small business failure in Australia

REASON	FREQUENCY %
Financial management and liquidity	32.0
Management incompetence and inexperience	14.6
Inflation and economic conditions	12.4
Poor books and records	12.3
Sales and marketing problems	10.8
Staffing problems	9.0
Union problems and 'interference'	6.2
Failure to seek and use external advice	2.7
	100.0

Source: *Williams (1987)*

Management roles in the start-up stage

The start-up stage in most small businesses usually covers the first few years, when sales tend to be slow and profits, if there are any, are relatively low. This early period is the most perilous stage: Williams (1987) found that nearly one-third of the 13 780 new small Australian ventures he studied failed in their first year. More than half had failed by their third year and nearly three-quarters by their fifth year in business, as shown in table 3.3. Further, as is illustrated in table 3.3, small business failure rates were highest in the first few years.

Table 3.3
Profile of small business failures in Australia

FAILURES WITHIN	PERCENTAGE	CUMULATIVE %
1st year	32.0	32.0
2nd year	16.5	48.5
3rd year	13.0	61.5
4th year	7.0	68.5
5th year	5.0	73.5

Source: *Williams (1987)*

The start-up stage is characterised by long work hours and enormous amounts of drive and determination, where true entrepreneurial traits such as innovation, dedication, vision and perseverance are active. The owner-manager will be totally responsible for all decisions and will usually exercise complete control over every aspect of the business, which will reflect a highly centralised organisational structure. With so much importance and power attributed to the entrepreneur, many organisational traits, such as culture, ethos and style, will reflect that individual's ideologies. The owner-manager's roles at this stage primarily involve innovating, initiating, organising and doing (English 1998).

MAJOR CAUSE ATTRIBUTED	1983–84 %	1996–97 %	1997–98 %	1998–99 %
Lack of capital	13.2	10.0	10.7	9.7
Lack of business ability	32.9	10.7	11.8	12.2
Failure to keep proper books	1.0	1.7	2.3	2.1
Economic conditions	23.6	14.5	14.7	14.7
Seasonal conditions	2.6	2.0	1.9	1.9
Excessive interest	4.4	7.4	10.7	6.8
Inability to collect debts	3.0	3.0	2.6	3.5
Excessive drawings	4.4	2.6	4.1	3.8
Gambling or speculation	0.5	0.5	1.9	1.8
Personal reasons	6.1	8.8	n.a.	n.a.
Other reasons or not stated	8.4	38.7	39.1	45.5

Source: *Australian Bureau of Statistics (1999:103)*

Management roles in the growth stage

This stage is often associated with rapid sales growth and delegation of some responsibility. This is a volatile period when the entrepreneur often has to relinquish some power and control over decision making. 'Entrepreneurial power' should be transformed into 'personal power,' with emphasis on managing, communicating and interacting with others on a larger scale, and with individuals employed for expertise in specific areas. The ability to 'step back', reflect and allow others to make major decisions contrasts markedly with the entrepreneur's role in the start-up stage. The entrepreneurial spirit is still present but team development should be nurtured. Emphasis shifts somewhat from the entrepreneur to the management team. More standardised operational procedures are usually evident and the organisation will increase in complexity. An important management role is to influence and manage others.

Management roles in the maturity stage

In this stage, sales tend to stabilise or sometimes decline as similar products become available and compete for market share. The owner-manager's role changes to one of managing managers, as the business requires more formalised systems. The entrepreneur needs to develop administrative and leadership skills, to steer the growing hierarchy of staff towards achieving the organisation's mission. Owner-managers should also take steps to prevent or delay a slowdown in sales. Before the organisation reaches maturity and decline, the entrepreneurial spirit will be looking to build, develop and promote other avenues to support current activities.

Strategic management is the process of using organisational resources to achieve long-term organisational goals under prevailing external conditions. It should be holistic, attempting to integrate organisational actions to achieve cohesion and synergy over the longer term. To achieve the business's mission, strategic management in small entrepreneurial firms should attain a 'fit' between:

- the entrepreneur
- the organisation and its resources
- the external environment (Morrison, Rimmington & Williams 1999:194).

■ 3.6.1 The role *of the entrepreneur in strategic management*

Strategies in small entrepreneurial firms generally differ from those in larger bureaucratic organisations in both content and process.

Strategy content

In small owner-managed firms, the entrepreneur's personal and business objectives are usually highly intertwined (Morrison, Rimmington & Williams 1999:193). The types of business strategies pursued, therefore, are usually the product of one person's mind — the entrepreneur's. While other organisational members may have some input, the entrepreneur generally dominates decision making, with **strategy** driven by his or her vision, intuition, judgement, experience and capabilities.

For example, many SIT operators establish their businesses for lifestyle reasons. They may simply use 'copycat' strategies, pricing products and services in line with competitors, introducing new products and services only when popular in competitors' businesses, and distributing and marketing them in conventional ways. They may have no desire to pursue strategies to increase market share, expand the business or diversify business activities. At the opposite extreme, other special tourism operators may pursue highly ambitious strategies, as Thomas Cook did.

Strategy process

The strategy process is often divided into three stages:

- *strategy formulation:* deciding what to do
- *strategy implementation:* doing it or achieving results
- *strategy evaluation:* assessing results against expectations.

However, these stages often overlap in the entrepreneurial firm. Strategy formulation may not involve a planned, conscious decision on 'what to do'; it may simply evolve over time as an extension of the entrepreneur's goals and vision. Strategy implementation, too, may not occur on a planned, step-by-step basis; it is more likely to occur ad hoc, the result of a series of operational decisions that gradually shape the business's direction and competitive positioning. Strategy is more likely to *emerge* in entrepreneurial firms than to be preplanned. Strategy evaluation may occur informally in the mind of the entrepreneur, who continually and intuitively adjusts the business's strategy. Formal evaluation against predetermined strategic objectives appears to be uncommon.

Thus, the entrepreneurial school of strategic management (Mintzberg 1990) regards strategy as formed through a visionary process, resulting from the leader's intuitive, semi-conscious perspective of the organisation's direction. Strategy formation relies exclusively on the single leader and his or her most innate mental states and processes — intuition, judgement, wisdom, experience, insight and vision. The organisation is considered subservient, responsive to the leader's dictates (Mintzberg 1990).

Further, strategy formation may precede *or* accompany strategy implementation, as the strategic vision is often malleable and the organisation small and so flexible and adaptable to change. The small firm often does not plan its strategies in advance and then implement them; rather, strategy generally evolves and is made 'on the run'. This is not necessarily ineffective; a distinct advantage of many small firms is that they can quickly change strategies to seize unexpected opportunities or avoid unanticipated threats. The leader maintains close personal control of strategy implementation as well as formulation of the strategic vision, and can change his or her mind at will. Therefore the organisational structure needs to be simple, responsive to the leader's directions.

■ 3.6.2 **The role** *of the internal environment in strategic management*

A second element central to strategic management is the organisation and its resources, or its internal environment. This comprises factors the business has some control over. The 7-S Framework (Waterman, Peters & Phillips 1980/1995) provides a useful way of identifying a business's internal resources. The seven S's refer to:

- *structure* — how labour is divided into tasks and how these tasks are then coordinated
- *systems* — such as budgeting, production, training, reward and appraisal systems that determine how things get done
- *style* — of management, including personality and priorities
- *staff* — a pool of resources to be nurtured, developed, guarded and allocated
- *skills* — or the organisation's dominating capabilities, its distinctive competence
- *superordinate goals* — guiding concepts, values, aspirations, ideology and culture
- *strategy*.

Waterman, Peters and Phillips (1980/1995:139–40) contend that the seven S's need to be interconnected and mutually supportive for effective strategic management. For example, a change in strategy is likely to require a change to some or all of the other six S's to support that strategy. A change in skills or style may require a change in strategy.

The entrepreneurial firm's internal environment therefore both influences and is influenced by strategy. The organisational structure is generally flat, with power and decision making concentrated in the entrepreneur. The firm has far fewer resources than large bureaucracies have. However, it has internal characteristics that can be used to advantage, such as a strong culture, the ability to make quick decisions, flexibility and high customer contact. These internal limitations and advantages need to be considered in strategic management.

■ 3.6.3 The role *of the external environment in strategic management*

Industries can be characterised by their stage in an industry life cycle. Entrepreneurial firms generally predominate in emerging industries, such as SIT, where key success factors include innovation, risk-taking and adaptability. Conversely, mature industry environments are generally unsuitable for small entrepreneurial firms, since key success factors include massive resources, formalised systems and economies of scale.

Porter (1980) identifies the following characteristics of the external environment facing emerging industries:

- *technological uncertainty:* about appropriate product or service configurations, production systems or distribution channels
- *strategic uncertainty:* about the 'best' strategies in terms of market positioning, marketing, pricing and servicing
- *high initial costs but steep cost reduction:* emanating from newness and initial small production volumes followed by rapid gains in productivity and economies of scale;
- *embryonic companies and spin-offs:* where most firms are small and newly formed
- *first-time buyers:* marketing should induce substitution and persuade buyers to purchase the new product or service
- *short time horizon:* where businesses deal with issues expediently, rather than through analysis of future conditions
- *subsidy:* from government and non-government sources, making the industry vulnerable to political decisions that can be quickly reversed or modified.

The entrepreneurial firm is particularly suited to these external conditions. As Porter (1980, in Porter 1995:236) explains:

> The nature of the early barriers is a key reason why we observe newly created companies in emerging industries. The typical early barriers stem less from the need to command massive resources than from the ability to bear risk, be creative technologically, and make forward-looking decisions to garner input supplies and distribution channels ...

Further, Mintzberg (1995:227) notes that the:

> entrepreneurial configuration is fostered by an external context that is both simple and dynamic. Simpler environments ... enable one person at the top to retain so much influence, while it is the dynamic environment that requires flexible structure, which in turn enables the organization to outmaneuver the bureaucracies. Entrepreneurial leaders are naturally attracted to such conditions.

Emerging industries such as SIT are therefore particularly suited to small entrepreneurial ventures. This is where a **strategic fit** between the entrepreneur, the small business and its external environment can be found.

■ 3.6.4 **Towards** *competitive advantage*

While the 'best' strategy is a fit between the entrepreneur and the venture's internal and external environments, these three factors vary substantially among ventures. However, some inherent competitive advantages of small entrepreneurial ventures provide clues to potentially effective strategies. Meredith (1988:28–31) summarises these as:
- personalised service
- flexibility and adaptability
- specialised and customised products
- quick decision making
- employer and employee motivation
- geographic specialisation.

In summarising the conventional wisdom on appropriate competitive strategies for small entrepreneurial firms, Cooper (1989:100–101) argues that they should choose a 'niche' and avoid direct competition with larger companies. Although direct competition is possible, small firms should concentrate on where they have a competitive advantage or where large firms are complacent or doing a poor job.
- Large firms usually concentrate on mass markets, so small firms should concentrate on specialised markets.
- Large firms are usually slow to react, so small firms should concentrate on opportunities arising from rapid market change.
- Large firms are usually organised around large production runs and standardised service; small firms can concentrate on short production runs, quick delivery and extra service.
- Large firms must be concerned about whether supplies, workforces, and manufacturing and personnel policies are suitable for large-volume operations; small firms can use scarce materials, locate in areas with small labour forces and utilise unique approaches.
- Large firms must be concerned about government regulatory attitudes and their visibility to communities and unions; small firms have a low profile, can move more quickly and be less concerned about reactions of such groups.

In summary, strategy management in small SIT ventures should aim for a strategic 'fit' between the entrepreneur, the organisation and its external environment. Thus, the goals and capabilities of the entrepreneur, the natural competitive advantages and disadvantages of small firms, and the characteristics of the emerging industry environment should all be considered in the venture's strategic management.

3.7 SUMMARY

In examining the role of entrepreneurship in SIT, this chapter firstly discussed entrepreneurship from the perspective of economic, psychological, sociological and management disciplines. Economists consider entrepreneurship in terms of its contribution to wealth creation and distribution, and view entrepreneurs as innovators, risk-takers, opportunists, resource-allocators and agents of change. Psychology also enhances our understanding of entrepreneurs by providing insights into the entrepreneurial mind, particularly those qualities of high need for achievement, internal locus of control, calculated risk-taking and ambiguity tolerance. The discipline of sociology provides a supplementary perspective. It assists in identifying environmental conditions that foster entrepreneurship and trigger the entrepreneurial career decision. Finally, a management perspective illuminates entrepreneurial activities, particularly the process of creating a new enterprise and managing it through start-up and growth.

Following a process approach to entrepreneurship, we then examined some ways to identify and evaluate opportunities for entrepreneurship in special interest tourism. Porter's 'five forces model' (1980) was applied to explain why the industry structure of many special tourism industries is conducive to entrepreneurial opportunities. We then examined some sources of innovative ideas and how to evaluate whether these constitute an opportunity that is timely and durable, that fits with the entrepreneur's skills and ambitions, and that will provide an adequate return for the risks involved. Developing a business plan more thoroughly screens the opportunity and its potential feasibility.

Once the new venture is launched, the entrepreneur then needs to manage the business from start-up through growth. We examined the central role of the entrepreneur in small business management and how this changes during the organisational life cycle. With most small business failures attributable to management deficiencies, entrepreneurs should develop the requisite management skills, from 'doing' to 'managing' to 'managing managers,' as the business matures.

Finally, we discussed the importance in small SIT ventures of achieving a strategic 'fit' between the entrepreneur, the organisation and its external environment. We explored the role of these elements in strategically managing small entrepreneurial firms and noted typical aspects of their internal and external environments that should be considered in attaining competitive advantage.

Questions

3.1 The goal of economic activity is assumed by economists to be the pursuit of profits. Discuss whether entrepreneurs are driven primarily by profit or by other motives.

3.2 Debate whether entrepreneurs are born or made. Support your debate with examples of SIT operators.

3.3 Visit the website at http://www.dewrsb.gov.au. Assess how well the Australian Federal Government appears to have addressed the concerns raised by the Small Business Deregulation Task Force (1996) and detailed at http://www.about.business.gov.au/bep/sbtf/keyfind.htm.

3.4 Using the questions that Alizadeh (1999:55) suggests can assist in overcoming creative barriers (see section 3.3.2), brainstorm ideas for new SIT products and services.

3.5 Write a case study on an entrepreneur in SIT that assesses his or her economic role and contribution and the psychological and sociological influences on that person's decision to start the venture. Describe the process undertaken by that person in establishing that venture.

3.6 'SIT is a distinctive industry comprising a similar set of business organisations serving a distinctive market, so its managers should adopt a particular approach when formulating and implementing strategy.' Discuss this statement by drawing on theoretical writings on management and strategy and on observations about SIT businesses.

3.7 Select a tourist destination and research the environmental factors facilitating and hindering new enterprise creation in SIT in that destination.

3.8 Interview some SIT entrepreneurs on whether and how their management roles have changed as their business has progressed from start-up through growth and maturity.

REFERENCES

Alizadeh, Y. 1999. *Concepts of Entrepreneurship: Study Guide.* Graduate College of Management. Lismore: Southern Cross University.

Australian Bureau of Statistics. 1999. *Small Business in Australia 1999.* Catalogue No. 1321.0. Canberra: Australian Government Publishing Service.

Bruno, A. V. & Tyebjee, T. T. 1982. 'The Environment for Entrepreneurship'. In Kent, C., Sexton, D. L., & Vesper, K. H. (Eds.). *Encyclopedia of Entrepreneurship.* New Jersey: Prentice Hall, pp. 288–307.

Bygrave, W. D. & Hofer, C. W. 1991. 'Theorizing about Entrepreneurship'. *Entrepreneurship Theory and Practice* 16 (2): 13–22.

Cantillon, R. 1755. *Essai sur la Nature du Commerce en General.* Translated by H. Higgs. 1931. London: Macmillan.

Cooper, A. C. 1989. 'Strategic Management: New Ventures and Small Business'. In Lloyd, B. (Ed.). *Entrepreneurship: Creating and Managing New Ventures.* Oxford, UK: Pergamon Press, pp. 97–103.

Department of Workplace Relations and Small Business. 1997. *Guide to the Government's Small Business Statement: More Time for Business.* http://www.dewrsb.gov.au

Drucker, P. 1994. *Innovation and Entrepreneurship.* Second Edition. Oxford, UK: Butterworth-Heinemann.

English, J. W. 1998. *How to Organise and Operate a Small Business in Australia.* Seventh Edition. Melbourne: Allen & Unwin.

Filion, J. 1998. 'From Entrepreneurship to Entreprenology: The Emergence of a New Discipline'. *Journal of Enterprising Culture* 6 (1): 1–23 (March).

Gnyawali, D. R. & Fogel, D. S. 1994. 'Environments for Entrepreneurship Development: Key Dimensions and Research Implications'. *Entrepreneurship Theory and Practice* 18 (4): 43–62 (Summer).

Handy, C. 1999. *The New Alchemists.* London: Hutchinson.

Hing, N. & Knox, K. 2000. *Entrepreneurship in Tourism and Hospitality: Study Guide.* Lismore: Southern Cross University.

Hisrich, R. D. & Peters, M. P. 1989. *Entrepreneurship: Starting, Developing, and Managing a New Enterprise.* Homewood, Illinois, USA: Irwin.

Holt, D. H. 1992. *Entrepreneurship: New Venture Creation.* New Jersey: Prentice Hall.

Industry Task Force on Leadership and Management Skills. 1995. *Enterprising Nation: Renewing Australia's Managers to Meet the Challenges of the Asia-Pacific Century.* Canberra: Australian Government Publishing Service.

Johns, B. L., Dunlop, W. C. & Sheehan, W. J. 1989. *Small Business in Australia: Problems and Prospects.* Sydney: Allen & Unwin.

Kirchhoff, B. A. 1997. 'Entrepreneurship Economics'. In Bygrave, W. D. (Ed.). *The Portable MBA in Entrepreneurship.* New York: John Wiley & Sons, pp.444–74.

Lewis, G. 1996. *Cases in Strategic Management: Australia and New Zealand.* Second Edition. Sydney: Prentice Hall.

Meredith, G. G. 1988. *Small Business Management in Australia.* Sydney: McGraw-Hill.

Mintzberg, H. 1990. 'Strategy Formation: Schools of Thought'. In Fredrickson, J. W. (Ed.). *Perspectives on Strategic Management.* New York: Harper and Row, pp. 105–235.

Mintzberg, H. 1995. 'The Entrepreneurial Organization'. In Mintzberg, H. & Quinn, J. B. (Eds.). *The Strategy Process.* Collegiate Edition. New Jersey: Prentice Hall, pp. 226–33.

Morrison, A., Rimmington, M. & Williams, C. 1999. *Entrepreneurship in the Hospitality, Tourism and Leisure Industries.* Oxford, UK: Butterworth-Heinemann.

Pearce, P. L. 1990. *The Backpacker Phenomenon: Preliminary Answers to Basic Questions.* Townsville, Qld: Department of Tourism, James Cook University.

Porter, M. 1980. *Competitive Strategy: Techniques for Analyzing Industries and Competitors.* New York: The Free Press.

Porter, M. 1995. 'Competitive Strategy in Emerging Industries'. In Mintzberg, H., Quinn, J. B. & Voyer, J. (Eds.). *The Strategy Process.* Collegiate Edition. New Jersey: Prentice Hall, pp. 234–37.

Shapero, A. & Sokol, L. 1982. 'The Social Dimensions of Entrepreneurship'. In Kent, C., Sexton, D. L. & Vesper, K. H. (Eds.). *Encyclopedia of Entrepreneurship.* New Jersey: Prentice Hall, pp. 72–90.

Timmons, J. A. 1990. *New Venture Creation: Entrepreneurship in the 1990s.* Third Edition. Homewood, Illinois, USA: Irwin.

Timmons, J. A. 1994. *New Venture Creation: Entrepreneurship for the 21st Century.* Fourth Edition. Burr Ridge, Illinois, USA: Irwin.

Timmons, J. A. 1997. 'Opportunity Recognition'. In Bygrave, W. D. (Ed.). *The Portable MBA in Entrepreneurship.* New York: John Wiley & Sons, pp. 27–53.

Van Slyke, J. R., Stevenson, H. H. & Roberts, M. J. 1992. 'The Start-Up Process'. In Sahlman, W. A. & Stevenson, H. H. (Eds.). *The Entrepreneurial Venture.* Boston: Harvard Business School Publications, pp. 81–97.

Vesper, K. H. 1994. *New Venture Experience.* Seattle: Vector Books.

Waterman, R. H., Peters, T. J. & Phillips, J. R. 1980/1995. 'The 7-S Framework'. In Mintzberg, H., Quinn, J. B. & Voyer, J. (Eds.). *The Strategy Process.* Collegiate Edition. New Jersey: Prentice Hall, pp. 139–44.

Weaver, D. & Opperman, M. 2000. *Tourism Management.* Brisbane: John Wiley & Sons.

Williams, A. J. 1987. The Characteristics and Performance of Small Business in Australia (1973–1985). Unpublished doctoral thesis. Newcastle: University of Newcastle.

Anangu Tours

Anangu Tours is a cultural tourism company employing Nyangatjatjara people that daily takes groups of tourists from around the world on educational and informative tours. Anangu Tours operates in the Uluru Kata Tjuta National Park. Uluru is the Anangu word for Ayers Rock, and Kata Tjuta is their name for The Olgas. The Park has two entries on the World Heritage listing because of its natural values and cultural values. The expertise of Anangu (the Aboriginal word meaning 'people') in cultural tourism has recently been recognised by UNESCO and Brolga Awards for excellence in tourism.

With Anangu Tours, tourists are able to discover the 'real Uluru' through small group tours guided by local Aboriginal people. Anangu guides tell creation stories thousands of generations old and demonstrate bush survival skills learned from their grandparents. All guides have grown up in Central Australia and have an intricate understanding of the environment, flora, fauna and desert survival. All tours are conducted in the guide's traditional language, with translation provided by experienced interpreters. This makes the tours very special. Visitors hear the ancient languages and know they are getting an authentic, quite extraordinary experience.

Tours include:

- *The Aboriginal Uluru Tour:* This four- to five-hour tour starts at sunrise with a short base tour of Uluru. Breakfast is served in the Cultural Centre before participants join the Aboriginal guide for the Liru Walk. The creation stories shown in the scars and features of Uluru are thousands of generations old. Visitors see how traditional tools, weapons and implements are made and used in daily life, learn how to make the oldest glue in the world and practise throwing spears.

- *The Kuniya Sunset Tour:* This half-day tour starts with a tour of the Cultural Centre, then, near the Mutitjulu Waterhole, the guide traces the creation story of the Kuniya Python Woman in the ripples and marks on Uluru. Tourists visit caves where the guide's ancestors left paintings in time-worn ochre, see a variety of local bush foods and hear tales of desert survival, before watching the sunset.

- *The Uluru Cultural Centre Tour:* This is a tour of the Uluru Kata Tjuta Cultural Centre, including an interpretation by a local Aboriginal guide of the magnificent dot paintings. The tour driver then takes tourists on a short base tour of Uluru.

Anangu Tours Pty Ltd is entirely Aboriginal owned, established in 1995 as a corporate vehicle for direct participation and involvement in Australian tourism industries. It aims to provide employment for local Anangu and profit for its Aboriginal community shareholders. It is one of the largest employers of Aboriginal people in the Central Desert region.

Anangu Tours is the tourism arm of Wana Ungkunytja Pty Ltd, established in 1993 to initiate and manage regional economic growth within the Nyangatjatjara region in the south-west of the Northern Territory. The Nyangatjatjara Aboriginal Corporation is the regional community development body for the area and is the beneficial owner of Wana Ungkunytja Pty Ltd and its subsidiary companies.

The mission of the Nyangatjatjara Aboriginal Corporation is to promote the aims and ideals and develop the commercial infrastructure of the Aboriginal community of Central Australia in the vicinity of Uluru. All adult Anangu people living in the three main communities are members of the Corporation.

The Nyangatjatjara Aboriginal Corporation was established to foster the survival and growth of Anangu culture and society by providing a vehicle for the common voice of its members and the achievement of common aspirations to benefit present and future generations. It is intended that Nyangatjatjara provide a coordinating role for the design and delivery of services throughout the region, from both government and non-government agencies, in order to achieve the maximum benefit from resource allocation and utilisation for its members. Nyangatjatjara is also entrusted with directly assisting improvement in the wellbeing and socioeconomic status of its members through fostering participation and growth of the economic and wealth-creating activities within the Nyangatjatjara region.

The objectives of Nyangatjatjara Aboriginal Corporation are to:

- facilitate identified social justice strategies and community development initiatives for cultural survival and growth
- provide regional resource planning, coordination and implementation
- integrate the planning, service capacities and responsibilities of service providers, within both government and independent agencies
- assist in the improvement of the economy, efficiency and effectiveness of all program activities
- design and supervise performance indicators for all service providers and the conduct of an annual service audit
- assist with the design, provision and maintenance of appropriate community infrastructure
- foster enterprise development and management through Nyangatjatjara's business trading company, Wana Ungkunytja Pty Ltd
- provide investment and trust account management
- foster employment creation for all adult Anangu
- provide land acquisition, development and management services
- provide appropriate regional management services for external agencies on a fee-for-service basis
- provide appropriate regional management services for internal organisations on a fee-for-service basis
- provide regional services for ATSIC as required
- develop and manage appropriate primary and secondary education services, as well as trade and occupational training, including the design and construction of facilities.

Nyangatjatjara Aboriginal Corporation has four major strategic thrusts.

- *Adult Education:* An Adult Education Centre, funded and designed by the Nyangatjatjara Corporation, was completed at the end of 1997.
- *Secondary Education:* Nyangatjatjara College, established in 1997, is only the second secondary school for Aboriginal people situated on Aboriginal land.
- *Employment Development:* Nyangatjatjara Corporation is working with existing employment development programs and enterprises for the local people. Anangu Tours is wholly owned and Nyangatjatjara is indirectly associated with a mud brick industry and Ayers Rock Resort Management. Dividends are being used to refurbish the local garage and petrol station, and develop a new roadhouse and tourist camping site. These enterprises mean further economic development.
- *Economic Development:* Tourism is central to the region's economic development, owing to the presence of Uluru, Kata Tjuta and the National Parks and Wildlife Commission. Visitor numbers to Uluru have increased from around 50 000 in 1973 to nearly 350 000 in 1995 (http://www.users.bigpond.com/LBANANGU).

Questions

1 Anangu Tours has identified and acted on an opportunity for entrepreneurship. What factors have helped to create this opportunity?

2 What are the apparent competitive advantages of Anangu Tours?

3 Discuss how Anangu Tours is contributing to the strategic economic and social objectives of the Nyangatjatjara Corporation.

4 Drawing on your wider knowledge of tourism and special interest tourism, discuss whether and how Anangu Tours appears to have achieved a strategic fit between its management, its internal resources and the opportunities arising from its external environments.

Gary Prosser

CHAPTER 4

Regional *tourism*

LEARNING OBJECTIVES

After reading this chapter, you will have an appreciation of:

■ why it is important to the tourism industry, regional communities and politicians to encourage tourists to move beyond the major international gateways

■ the different ways of defining regional tourism, and their implications

■ the economic, sociocultural and environmental impacts of tourism in regional Australia

■ the different potential for tourism development among regional locations and factors that might influence development potential

■ the opportunities and challenges facing governments and businesses wanting to develop tourism in regional locations.

4.1 INTRODUCTION

The preceding chapters have introduced concepts and discussions relating to, among many other things, who participates in special interest tourism (SIT), how the impacts can best be managed, and business principles for the SIT operator. This chapter looks at where the SIT experience commonly takes place. Much of the SIT product is found in regional areas, outside major urban centres. This is not to say that it does not happen in cities. Indeed, chapter 18 looks specifically at urban tourism. Many cultural, heritage, wine and food, educational and event SIT experiences are city based. This chapter explains the reasons why government and non-government organisations are increasingly investing energy and finance into developing **regional tourism** and the benefits this can bring to both the supply and demand sides of the industry.

4.2 THE CHANGING NATURE OF REGIONAL AREAS

Global social and economic change is placing pressure on rural and regional communities in most industrialised countries. The changing nature of regional economies and rural lifestyles is being driven by:
• more efficient agricultural practices
• new technologies
• free or less restricted trade
• decline of traditional industries
• widening gaps between rich and poor
• rising unemployment
• new and different employment opportunities
• changing population patterns
• faster and more comfortable transport
• growing conflict among competing land uses
• increased environmental awareness.

Regional areas are affected unevenly by these global forces and their impacts vary according to differing population patterns and social and political networks, variations in economic activity, and cultural and environmental diversity. These social and economic changes have led to pressure on governments to 'do something' about the declining fortunes of rural and regional areas.

The changing nature of regional areas poses fundamental challenges for residents, business operators, community leaders and governments concerned with maintaining economically strong, environmentally sustainable and socially vibrant regional communities. Regional economies need to diversify through new and innovative approaches to enterprise development. To address these issues, governments in Australia and in other countries are focusing increased attention on regional development. Many regional communities have skilled labour, space and other physical resources needed for enterprise development. Decentralised, service-based industries such as tourism offer the potential to diversify regional economic activity in the face of the changing global economy.

Regional tourism is a key issue not just because of governments' concern with economic policy. Other factors have stimulated interest from the tourism industry in regional Australia, particularly the weakening of Australia's key inbound markets following the Asian financial crisis in the late 1990s. A tourism industry that had become accustomed to strong growth in international tourism was reminded that domestic tourism still accounts for most of Australia's tourism activity and that most domestic visitor nights are spent outside the capital cities. A further important factor for the tourism industry is strong consumer demand for natural and cultural attractions in both the domestic and international markets and an interest in less packaged and more 'authentic' experiences. This search for authenticity has also been referred to as **REAL travel** — travel that is Rewarding, Enriching, Adventuresome and based on Learning experiences (Read 1980). Regional areas are well placed to cater for these market trends.

Both the tourism industry and governments are interested in finding ways to optimise tourism's economic and social contribution in regional areas. The 'Hutchison Report', *Tourism: Getting it Right for the Millennium* (Hutchison 1997), identifies regional tourism development and research as industry priorities, as do government policy statements.

4.3 WHAT IS 'REGIONAL' TOURISM?

In an academic context, defining a 'region' is merely a device for identifying a spatial unit for description and analysis. It is placing a notional boundary around part of a larger whole. For example, a region may be part of a metropolitan area, such as western Sydney; it may be part of a nation, such as Central Australia; or it may be part of the world, such as the Southeast Asian region. Sometimes regional boundaries will coincide with political or administrative boundaries, such as state borders, but this is not necessarily the case. Biogeographic characteristics may also be used to define a region in a way that does not reflect administrative boundaries. For example, the alpine region of Australia includes parts of New South Wales, Victoria and the Australian Capital Territory. Depending on the circumstances, 'Central Australia' may include parts of the Northern Territory, Western Australia, South Australia, New South Wales and Queensland. Economic, social or cultural links may be another way to define the boundaries of a region.

To confuse matters further, 'regional' has taken on a different meaning in popular and political debate. When politicians talk about 'regional Australia', they are usually talking about those parts of the country beyond the capital cities. This is not the same as talking about 'rural Australia'. Regional areas include densely populated industrial centres such as Newcastle, Wollongong and Geelong, as well as more sparsely populated parts of the country engaged in primary production.

In this chapter, regional tourism encompasses tourism in 'concentrated tourist areas', coastal resorts, towns and other urban settlements and the countryside, hinterland or coastline outside capital cities. It does not rely on particular activities or experiences; its character is determined by the places where tourism occurs. It may encompass rural tourism, nature-based tourism, ecotourism, cultural tourism, food and wine tourism, backpacker tourism, adventure tourism, industrial tourism, educational tourism and the like.

■ **Figure 4.1**
The components of regional tourism

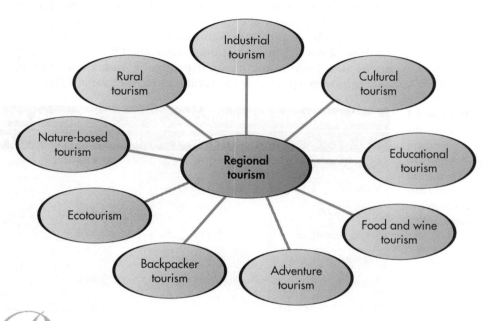

REGIONAL TOURISM IN AUSTRALIA — AN OVERVIEW

Tourism is increasingly recognised as a viable alternative to more traditional agricultural and resource-based industries. According to the Department of Industry, Science and Resources (2000), in 1996–97 tourism directly or indirectly accounted for more than 11 per cent of Australia's gross domestic product, and contributed approximately $17 billion in taxes to federal, state and local government. Tourism's direct contribution to GDP is greater than almost all national account industries with the exception of manufacturing, retail trade, construction and property services, and ownership. Against comparative export earnings, it is estimated that the value of international tourism exceeds manufacturing (excluding machinery and transport equipment), metal ores and minerals, coal, wool and grain. It accounts for 14.9 per cent of Australia's total exports and 61.7 per cent of all service exports. In relation to jobs, the DISR estimates that the Australian tourism industry directly employs more people than the construction industry or the agricultural, forestry, fishing, mining and communication industries combined. In 1996–97 tourism was directly responsible for the employment of more than 670 000 people (8 per cent of all people employed) and indirectly for a further 290 000 jobs (totalling 11.5 per cent of all people employed) (DISR 2000). Two-thirds of all tourism jobs during the period were full-time and 80 per cent were in **small business**.

Regional tourism accounts for a substantial proportion of this success, generating more than 60 per cent of all domestic and international visitor nights. The value of international tourism in regional Australia exceeds the value of other regional exports such as cereal grains.

The results of the 1998 National Visitor Survey highlight the significance of domestic tourism for regional Australia. Of more than 203 million nights spent away from home within Australia by Australian residents in 1998, 69.4 per cent were spent outside capital cities (see table 4.1).

■ Table 4.1
Domestic visitor nights in Australian capital cities and regional areas, 1998

STATE/TERRITORY	CAPITAL CITY	REGIONAL AREAS	
	NIGHTS (000)	NIGHTS (000)	PER CENT
New South Wales	26 118	68 744	72.5
Victoria	18 551	37 167	66.7
Queensland	15 220	54 438	78.2
South Australia	8 712	11 520	56.9
Western Australia	8 965	20 805	69.9
Tasmania	2 786	6 391	69.6
Northern Territory	3 110	4 573	59.4
ACT	5 253	0	0.0
Total	88 715	203 638	69.4

Source: *Bureau of Tourism Research (1998a)*

New South Wales had the highest number of nights spent in regional areas (68 million) when compared with other states and territories, although Queensland had the greatest proportion of nights (78 per cent) spent in regional areas. The relative importance of domestic tourism for regional Australia is clearly demonstrated by a comparison with the proportion of international visitor nights spent in regional areas. Only 29.9 per cent of international visitor nights were spent outside capital cities in 1998, compared with the 69.4 per cent of domestic visitor nights.

The most popular destinations for Australians travelling within their own country are the major capital cities of Sydney, Melbourne and Brisbane. This in part reflects the significant amount of business-related travel to these cities. Nevertheless, regional destinations feature prominently in the domestic travel market. National Visitor Survey data on visits and nights for the 20 most visited capital cities and regions in 1998, ranked by the number of visits, are provided in table 4.2.

■ Table 4.2
*The 20 most
visited
Australian
destinations
by domestic
travellers,
1998*

REGION VISITED*	RANK	VISITS (000)	%	RANK	NIGHTS (000)	%
Sydney, NSW	1	8250	11	1	26118	9
Melbourne, Vic.	2	6377	9	2	19151	7
Brisbane, Qld	3	4020	5	3	15220	5
Gold Coast, Qld	4	3150	4	4	14430	5
The Great Ocean Road, Vic.	5	2729	4	11	7386	3
South Coast, NSW	6	2593	4	5	10352	4
Bays & Peninsulas, Vic.	7	2513	3	13	6290	2
Hunter, NSW	8	2414	3	10	7636	3
Sunshine Coast, Qld	9	2404	3	6	9940	3
Adelaide, SA	10	2377	3	8	8712	3
Perth, WA	11	2233	3	7	8965	3
Central West, NSW	12	2186	3	15	5555	2
Mid North Coast, NSW	13	2112	3	9	8015	3
Goldfields, Vic.	14	2004	3	18	4391	1
Phillip Island & Gippsland, Vic.	15	1976	3	14	5588	2
Northern Rivers, NSW	16	1873	3	12	6829	2
Canberra, ACT	17	1873	3	17	5253	2
The Murray, Vic.	18	1777	2	16	5378	2
Goulburn Murray Waters, Vic.	19	1650	2	19	4357	1
Central Coast, NSW	20	1449	2	20	3921	1

* Tourism regions are defined by the relevant State or Territory
  tourism authority. Visitors may visit more than one region during their trip.

Source: *Bureau of Tourism Research (1998a)*

Queensland's Gold Coast was clearly the most popular destination in regional Australia in 1998, followed by the Great Ocean Road region in Victoria. While the Great Ocean Road ranked fifth in terms of visits, it dropped to eleventh in number of visitor nights. This reflects its role as a transit route, with a shorter average length of stay than destination resort areas such as the Gold Coast, the Sunshine Coast and even the South Coast of New South Wales. Of the 20 most visited regions by domestic travellers in 1998, 14 are outside capital cities and all of these are located in the eastern states of Queensland, New South Wales and Victoria.

The most popular destinations identified above are based on the number of travellers who spent at least one night in the region. Daytrippers to the region are excluded. Daytripping is a significant component of domestic travel. Data from the National Visitor Survey provide a measure of the extent of daytripping by Australian residents to regional areas of Australia (see table 4.3).

■ Table 4.3
Day visits by domestic travellers, 1998

STATE/TERRITORY	CAPITAL CITY	REGIONAL AREAS	
	VISITS (000)	VISITS (000)	PER CENT
New South Wales	19 206	33 240	63.4
Victoria	16 527	27 422	62.4
Queensland	7 801	17 551	69.2
South Australia	4 625	6 241	57.4
Western Australia	5 883	6 508	52.5
Tasmania	1 429	3 887	73.1
Northern Territory	434	393	47.5
ACT	1 927	0	0.0
Total	57 832	95 242	62.2

Source: *Bureau of Tourism Research (1998a)*

More than 95 million day visits were taken outside capital cities in 1998, 62.2 per cent of all day visits made by Australian residents in 1998. To a large extent, the number of day visits taken reflects the population density of different parts of the country. Queenslanders are most likely to venture beyond the capital city for day visits. It was mentioned above that only 29.9 per cent of international visitor nights were spent outside capital cities in 1998, compared with the 69.4 per cent of domestic visitor nights. These international visitor nights still represent an important component of regional tourism activity in Australia. Data from the 1998 International Visitor Survey reveal that more than 29 million international visitor nights were spent in regional locations outside the capital cities (see table 4.4).

The role of Sydney as Australia's premier international gateway is clearly demonstrated by these figures, with 67 per cent more international visitor nights spent in Sydney than in Melbourne, the next most visited city. Fewer than 17 per cent of international visitor nights in New South Wales are spent outside Sydney. The proportion of international visitor nights spent in regional Victoria is even lower, at 12 per cent. In Queensland, the impact of the Gold Coast and Tropical North Queensland on the distribution of inter-national visitors is reflected in more than 70 per cent of international visitor nights being spent outside Brisbane, the state's capital city. Similarly in the Northern Territory, a majority of visitor nights (66 per cent) are spent outside the capital Darwin, while nearly half of all international visitor nights in Tasmania are spent in regional areas.

■ Table 4.4
*International
visitor
nights in
Australian
capital cities
and regional
areas, 1998*

STATE/TERRITORY	CAPITAL CITY	REGIONAL AREAS	
	NIGHTS (000)	NIGHTS (000)	PER CENT
New South Wales	28 234	5 603	16.6
Victoria	16 934	2 407	12.4
Queensland	6 290	15 457	71.1
South Australia	3 605	829	18.7
Western Australia	9 129	2 369	20.6
Tasmania	1 028	623	37.7
Northern Territory	1 079	1 835	63.0
ACT	2 011	0	0.0
Total	68 310	29 123	29.9

Source: *Bureau of Tourism Research (1998b)*

The Bureau of Tourism Research estimates that 30 per cent of all Australian expenditure by international visitors in 1997 occurred in non-capital city regions (see table 4.5).

■ Table 4.5
*International
visitor
expenditure
in Australia,
1997*

STATE/TERRITORY	CAPITAL CITY	REGIONAL AREAS	
	$ MILLION	$ MILLION	% OF STATE
New South Wales	2475	286	10.4
Victoria	1131	90	7.3
Queensland	417	1458	77.8
South Australia	195	36	15.7
Western Australia	609	62	9.3
Tasmania	51	43	45.8
Northern Territory	46	141	75.6
ACT	120	0	0.0
Total	5043	2116	29.6

Source: *BTR Occasional Paper No. 29 (September 1999)*

Table 4.5 reveals an interesting phenomenon in the distribution of international visitor expenditure. It shows that the proportion of visitor expenditure in regional areas is slightly below the proportion of visitor nights spent by international visitors in New South Wales (10.4 per cent of expenditure and 18.3 per cent of visitor nights in 1997), Victoria (7.3 per cent and 13.3 per cent), South Australia (15.7 per cent and 18.9 per cent), Western Australia (9.3 per cent and 19.1 per cent) and Tasmania (45.8 per cent and 47 per cent). This is explained by the generally cheaper accommodation rates in regional areas and fewer opportunities for tourist shopping. However, in

Queensland and the Northern Territory, where a majority of visitor nights are spent outside the capital cities, the proportion of visitor expenditure exceeds the proportion of nights. In Queensland, regional destinations attract 77.8 per cent of expenditure and 71 per cent of nights, while in the Northern Territory 75.6 per cent of expenditure occurs outside Darwin, where 66 per cent of nights were spent during the same period in 1997.

The most popular destinations in Australia for international visitors are our two largest cities — Sydney and Melbourne. However, Queensland's major regional destinations, the Gold Coast and Tropical North Queensland, rank third and fourth respectively amongst the locations most visited by international tourists. International Visitor Survey data on visits and nights for the 20 most visited capital cities and regions in 1998, ranked by the number of visits, are provided in table 4.6.

■ **Table 4.6**
The 20 most visited Australian destinations by international visitors, 1998

REGION VISITED*	RANK	VISITS (000)	%	RANK	NIGHTS (000)	%
Sydney, NSW	1	2148.4	56.2	1	28 234	29.0
Melbourne, Vic.	2	983.3	25.7	2	16 934	17.4
Gold Coast, Qld	3	855.9	22.4	5	5 338	5.5
Tropical North Queensland, Qld	4	704.2	18.4	6	4 840	5.0
Brisbane, Qld	5	631.8	16.5	4	6 290	6.5
Perth, WA	6	487.2	12.7	3	9 129	9.4
Adelaide, SA	7	279.8	7.3	7	3 605	3.7
Petermann, NT	8	248.6	6.5	18	540	0.6
Canberra, ACT	9	207.8	5.4	8	2 011	2.1
Alice Springs, NT	10	204.8	5.4	14	753	0.8
Sunshine Coast, Qld	11	180.2	4.7	9	1 284	1.3
Whitsunday Islands, Qld	12	176.3	4.6	12	909	0.9
Hervey Bay/ Maryborough, Qld	13	158.2	4.1	17	602	0.6
Northern Rivers, NSW	14	167.2	4.4	11	1 029	1.1
Darwin, NT	15	158.2	4.1	10	1 079	1.1
Great Barrier Reef, Qld	16	153.1	4.0	16	625	0.6
Northern, Qld	17	128.5	3.4	13	818	0.8
Fitzroy, Qld	18	110.2	2.9	15	649	0.7
Western, Vic.	19	101.4	2.6	19	349	0.4
Blue Mountains, NSW	20	88.1	2.3	20	282	0.3

* *Tourism regions are defined by the relevant State or Territory tourism authority. Visitors typically visit more than one region during their trip.*

Source: *Bureau of Tourism Research (1998b)*

Of the top 20 areas visited by international visitors in 1998, 13 are outside capital cities. After the Gold Coast and Tropical North Queensland, the next most visited regional destinations are Petermann in the Northern Territory (which includes the iconic Uluru), Alice Springs and the Sunshine Coast, Whitsunday Islands and Hervey Bay in Queensland. Outside the Northern Territory and Queensland, the region most visited by international travellers is Northern Rivers in New South Wales, which includes Byron Bay, a popular destination for backpackers. The relatively long-staying backpackers make Northern Rivers the fourth-ranked regional destination in terms of international visitor nights after the Gold Coast, Tropical North Queensland and the Sunshine Coast.

In summary, data from the National and International Visitor Surveys conducted by the Bureau of Tourism Research reveal that more than 230 million visitor nights were spent in non-capital city regions of Australia in 1998, which accounts for approximately 60 per cent of all international and domestic visitor nights.

4.5 IMPACTS OF REGIONAL TOURISM

In the introduction to this chapter we discussed the changing nature of regional areas, and the challenges facing residents, business operators, community leaders and governments concerned with maintaining economically strong, environmentally sustainable and socially vibrant regional communities. Much of the interest in regional tourism is generated by the expectation that it can deliver net economic, environmental and social benefits to communities that at least match those potentially delivered by other forms of economic development. Therefore it is important to examine more closely the potential benefits and costs of regional tourism development.

4.5.1 Economic *impacts*

Tourism in regional Australia has the potential to drive **regional economic development** through:
- economic diversification
- new enterprise development
- creating income and employment in regional economies
- generating tax revenue
- creating opportunities for investment and infrastructure development.
  Each of these points is addressed below (see figure 4.2).

Economic diversification
Although economic characteristics vary significantly from one region to another, within a region local economies are often narrowly based. A narrow

economic base increases regional vulnerability to economic and social change, and economic structures at a regional level are changing rapidly in the modern global economy.

Diversification of regional economies will help sustain local communities affected by a decline in traditional industries. Tourism presents opportunities to diversify the economic base of regional areas and to stem the leakage of labour and capital. Tourism also frequently uses existing resources and, because of the wide range of activities involved, helps to support or establish other industries, further strengthening the economy. Wine and food tourism is a good example of how tourism can benefit traditional rural industries.

Tourism consumption is generated by *importing* customers to the product at its place of production rather than by *exporting* product to customers as most other industries do. To satisfy the needs of visitors, the tourism industry also draws on supplies of 'upstream' goods and services (food and other agricultural products, retail products, building and public works, transport, insurance and so on). In doing so, it provides leverage for other economic activities and promotes local production in a range of sectors. Tourists might even acquire new tastes for some of these products, helping to build demand and develop export markets. Again, the development of food and wine tourism in regional Australia is a good example of this.

Tourism may help to attract investment in other industries too. For example, the Gold Coast became a successful centre for light industry after it had developed as a popular tourist destination. Tourism attracts investment in commercial and residential property and creates work for the building and construction industries.

■ **Figure 4.2**
Economic impacts of regional tourism

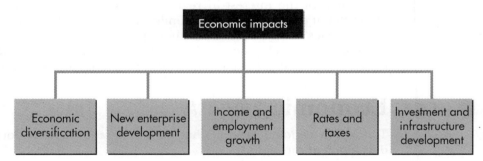

New enterprise development

Tourism creates new small business opportunities. Excellent opportunities for development of new tourism enterprises arise from low capital requirements and comparatively few barriers to entry for small businesses. The potential beneficiaries of tourism activity are spread across various sectors of the regional economy, as are opportunities for new enterprise development in the provision of services such as accommodation, cafes and restaurants, tours and local attractions. Almost 80 per cent of tourism-related employment in regional Australia is in small business.

Income and employment growth

Tourism activity will benefit regional economies through the demand created by visitors for local goods and services. Visitors spend money on a variety of goods and services including entertainment, transport, shopping for gifts and souvenirs, food and drink, petrol and accommodation. This direct expenditure by visitors has a positive impact on business profitability and employment growth in regional areas.

Employment in the services sector in developed countries such as Australia is rapidly increasing. As employment generated by primary and secondary industries stagnates or declines, tourism becomes one of the key opportunities to generate new jobs in regional Australia. Tourism is a labour-intensive industry in an age of great technological advancement and declining relative demand for labour. The tourism industry and those industries closely aligned with it provide many full-time and part-time job opportunities across a range of skill areas. This is particularly beneficial in regional economies.

From a public policy perspective, tourism is an efficient form of employment generation, since the average cost to public funds of creating full-time jobs in tourism is substantially lower than in most other industries (Witt 1987). Among major industries in Australia, tourism is relatively decentralised and provides jobs that keep people, particularly young people, in regional areas.

As well as creating jobs in businesses serving the needs of tourists, tourism has the potential to create employment opportunities in related service industries and more traditional rural industries. The list of potential employment opportunities is considerable and includes retail, food and wine production and processing, manufacturing, construction, banking, commerce, police services and health.

Tourism dollars are 'new dollars' injected into a regional economy that will have a **multiplier effect** in the local economy as they are spent and respent by employers and employees. The more money circulates within the economy, the larger the multiplier effect. Leakage occurs when money generated by tourism is spent outside the local economy. A region cannot usually provide all the goods and services visitors and residents will require; businesses may employ staff or have shareholders residing outside the region, and residents within regions also travel and spend money in other regions. Therefore money generated from tourism will eventually leave the regional economy. The size of the tourist multiplier will be affected by the size and diversity of the regional economy, the proportion of goods and services imported into the region for consumption by tourists, the availability of suitable local products and services and the patterns of purchasing behaviour by both tourists and residents.

Rates and taxes

Regional tourism generates income for businesses, for individuals in the form of wages and share earnings and for local government in the form of rates and levies. From a local government perspective, tourism has the potential to diversify and increase the rate base and inject money into the local economy by encouraging new businesses to start up and by bringing people into the area. Local government also benefits from income generated by visitor patronage of public golf courses, art galleries and other attractions; council-owned caravan parks; and events or services held in council-owned premises or on Crown land. This income contributes to the quality and quantity of local services and facilities provided for the benefit of both residents and visitors.

Investment and infrastructure development

Unlike many industries, tourism can be built utilising largely existing **infrastructure**. Carefully focused tourism development policy can also contribute to the costs of this infrastructure and maintaining other essential services. In this way, tourism can help to reverse the trend of diminishing facilities in regional Australia and may even act as a catalyst for increased investment in services and infrastructure such as transport, power and water supplies, environmental protection, sewerage, communication, health, education, police, fire and sporting facilities, as well as parks and recreation reserves.

Synopsis

Tourism has the potential to generate substantial economic benefits for regional Australia. It is labour intensive and decentralised, providing numerous job opportunities to keep people, particularly young people, in regional areas. It can assist in diversifying regional economies, may strengthen existing industries and even create opportunities for new industries. It utilises and contributes to the cost of existing infrastructure and can develop new infrastructure that will help to further stimulate investment, local commerce and industry.

The ability of tourism to realise its potential as a tool for regional development will depend on a broad range of economic, social and political factors. These factors include the region's natural and cultural attractions, its infrastructure and industrial base and the levels of community support. However, the distribution of economic benefits will tend to be uneven within and between regions. Some regions have limited tourism potential.

The distribution of benefits will be affected by the location of tourism attractions relative to major population centres and tourism routes, the recognised attractiveness of a region, the size and character of the regional economy, the degree of linkage among various economic sectors, the pattern of visitor expenditure as well as the extent of leakage from the regional economic system.

The benefits of tourism for regional economic development will be realised only through the coordinated efforts of local communities, government agencies and the tourism industry. This coordination became an important theme of the Government's Regional Australia Summit held in 1999 (see Special interest investigation).

SPECIAL INTEREST INVESTIGATION
Regional Australia Summit

The Regional Australia Strategy, announced in 1998, draws together Government initiatives that have an impact on regional Australia. Its foundation is a coordinated, 'whole of government' approach to achieving sustainable growth in regional Australia. A cornerstone of the Regional Australia Strategy is encouraging collaboration between government, business and communities to find realistic solutions to the challenges faced by regional, rural and remote communities. An important example of this collaborative approach was the Regional Australia Summit held in Canberra in October 1999. The summit called for the new partnership to be based on renewed respect for regional Australia on the part of urban Australians and between the different types of communities. Outcomes included those outlined below.

1. There are no easy solutions to the problems facing regional Australia. The problems are shared by many countries.

2. Community development will not happen without government, business and community stakeholders each making contributions towards locally developed plans within a regional context.

3. Communities that have reinvented themselves have identified and capitalised on their natural strengths, resources and self-interest to enhance their environmental assets and at the same time generate economic and social development.

4. Communities want to share responsibility with government for development of their regions. Communities don't want solutions imposed on them. One size does not fit all.

5. Government, industries and communities must invest significant ongoing resources in skilling, learning, education and training, and leadership to develop the human capacity of regional Australia. Distribution of these resources needs to be inclusive of all sectors of regional society.

6. Communities want to include and invest in their youth.

7. One of the most extraordinary assets of regional Australia is our unique natural environment, a natural heritage that is a rich and evocative element of our national identity. The summit recognised that mistakes have been made in the management of the natural resources that contribute so much to our current wealth and quality of life. All Australians share a responsibility to restore the productive capacity of our rural landscapes for the benefit of current and future Australians. Equally, the summit recognised the great economic and social opportunities our vast, unique rural landscapes offer us to develop new products, services and enterprises based on world-leading management of our natural resources.

(continued)

8. Governments, industries and communities must ensure affordable, reliable access to telecommunications. Professional advice must be available to maximise the community and economic opportunities provided by rapidly emerging developments in information technology.
9. Indigenous people are stakeholders in regional Australia.
10. Governments must accept responsibility for facilitating adequate provision and maintenance of basic infrastructure. People in all sectors of regional Australia need equitable standards and access to essential services, including telecommunications, power and energy, water, transport, health and education.
11. Creative ways of providing infrastructure need to be explored, without at the same time imposing unreasonable costs on regional industries or communities.
12. Governments, urban business and industry must become more responsive to the unique requirements of sectors and areas of regional Australia in designing and delivering programs and services.
13. The three tiers of government must remove unnecessary regulatory impediments that increase the cost of doing business and stifle innovation and action in regional Australia.
14. Governments must create a climate, including tax incentives, that encourages investment for rural enterprise and philanthropy.
15. Key business leaders expressed their support for the idea of partnerships but sought commitment from the Federal Government to 'take some risks' that would assist business rather than create barriers that serve to hinder private sector investment in regional Australia. Their view was that tax incentives were a crucial factor in attracting investment to areas outside the major metropolitan areas.

At the conclusion of the summit, the Government announced the establishment of the Regional Australia Summit Steering Committee to develop a plan for implementing outcomes from the summit. The steering committee is comprised of summit delegates and two members the Summit Reference Group, which was set up to guide the development of the summit.

Further details on the Regional Australia Summit may be found at http://www.dotrs.gov.au/regional/summit.

■ 4.5.2 Environmental *impacts*

Most of the attractions of regional Australia are inextricably linked with features of our natural and cultural environments. Recognising that the environment is a complex, multifaceted concept, in this section we deal principally with the biophysical environment; the sociocultural environment is the subject of the next section.

A positive aspect of tourism as an agent of regional economic and social development is that it may offer a more ecologically sustainable form of development than other traditional industries such as mining and agriculture. Regional tourism may also increase the environmental awareness of both visitors and regional communities and provide incentives to conserve important features of the natural and cultural environment for special interest markets wanting eco-, adventure-, heritage-, indigenous- and nature-based experiences (see figure 4.3).

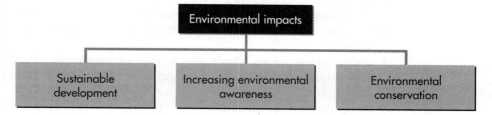

■ **Figure 4.3**
Environmental impacts of regional tourism

Sustainable development

Tourism claims a special relationship with the environment — a relationship that is mutually supportive and beneficial, contributing to the economic development of local communities while conserving natural and cultural environments and providing visitors with satisfying and enjoyable travel experiences. However, it is a relationship that cannot be taken for granted by governments, interest groups, local communities or the tourism industry, since it may be threatened by poorly planned tourism activity and by environmental degradation generated by other human activities. In Australia, most regional tourism is environmentally dependent, since facilities and infrastructure by themselves are usually not sufficient to attract visitors (Prosser et al. 2000).

Tourism has helped to stimulate community and political interest in environmental issues. Growing demand by visitors for nature-based experiences has served to increase awareness of the importance of natural environments in regional areas and the need for appropriate planning and land management policies to conserve those environments.

Increasing environmental awareness

There is evidence of growing consumer demand for nature-based experiences, heritage and cultural attractions, and environmental responsibility on the part of tourism operators driven by increasing interest in and concern about environmental issues. Regional tourism can be a major beneficiary of these market trends but must have its own house in order to do so. Appropriately planned and managed tourism development is essential if regional destinations are to satisfy environmentally aware customers.

Tourism also provides incentives for cleaning up built environments, which can therefore result in aesthetic improvements in regional cities, towns and villages and transport corridors. It has often prompted participation in Tidy Town and Main Street programs leading to beautification and revitalisation of local communities.

Environmental conservation

Tourism is an important justification for the establishment of national parks and other categories of protected areas. It provides not only the stimulus but increasingly also the financial resources needed for conservation management. According to the Australian Conservation Foundation, tourism's promotion of conservation knowledge and ethics, environmental protection and the preservation of indigenous knowledge provides benefits for natural and cultural conservation including:

- an incentive to expand protected areas
- an incentive for private land owners to conserve their lands
- the provision of funds to research, manage and restore natural lands and wildlife
- the provision of an alternative source of income for local communities who might otherwise use the land in a manner that is not ecologically sustainable
- the education and inspiration of visitors who will continue their commitment to the protection of the area and/or their respect for the culture after visitation
- the provision of ecologically sustainable employment (Prosser et al. 2000).

Synopsis

Tourism can increase community, industry and visitor awareness of the significance of the environment, leading to changes in individual and commercial behaviour. It generates financial and non-financial support for natural (and built) environments from residents, visitors, business operators and government. The relationship between tourism and the environment will vary from region to region and from site to site within a region. It will also change with time and in relation to broader economic, environmental and social concerns. A beneficial relationship between tourism and the environment should not be taken for granted but must result from ongoing cooperative efforts between regional communities, visitors, tourism operators and government.

■ 4.5.3 Sociocultural *impacts*

Tourism has the potential to transfer capital, income and employment from the cities to regional Australia. Spending power and wealth may be redistributed when urban incomes are spent on regional goods and services, significantly affecting the host region. In addition to being an economic issue, tourism is also a sociocultural issue, since residents share their local resources with tourists. Tourism changes local communities in ways that may influence established behaviour patterns, lifestyles and quality of life. A positive relationship between residents and visitors can contribute to the growth of regional tourism and make regional communities more diverse and interesting places to live; it can also build community pride (see figure 4.4). Alternatively, tourism can divide communities, alienate long-term residents and lead to crowding and diminished quality of life.

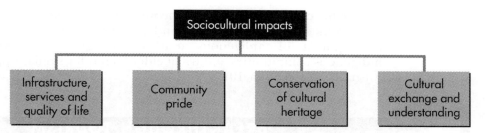

Infrastructure, services and quality of life

As the tourism industry grows, new and expanded services and facilities cater to both visitors and local residents. Services and facilities that are supported or introduced as a result of tourism include transport, visitor centres, galleries, attractions, restaurants, retail shops and entertainment opportunities. Regional tourism can also stimulate improvements in community infrastructure such as barbecue and toilet facilities in parks and gardens, health and sporting facilities, and new walking and cycling tracks.

Tourism can support a wider range and better quality of community services than the resident population. Research into the impacts of tourism on a regional Australian city has indicated that, combined with business opportunities, these benefits are rated as the most positive tourism impacts for a community (Ross 1992).

Community pride

Planned regional tourism requires a region to take stock of its assets and distinctive characteristics. Unplanned tourism forces regions to do the same. In both cases, the result may be an increase in residents' awareness of and interest in their region. Stimulating local pride may result in community celebration and the maintenance or revival of traditional cultural activities. Activities such as festivals and other public events foster community spirit and contribute to social cohesion within a region, making it a more interesting place to live in and visit.

Conservation of cultural heritage

Tourism acts as a major stimulus for conservation of important elements of the cultural heritage of an area. 'It is tourism that makes heritage economically viable . . . it plays a role in the heritage economy, which is largely a not-for-profit enterprise in the public interest' (Kirshenblatt-Gimblett 1996:30). It also increases community awareness and pride in local heritage and reinforces cultural identity. According to Carole Carpenter of the Ontario Folklife Centre, tourism is a contemporary imperative in heritage conservation and provides a means of giving living heritage a significant future (Carpenter 1996:17). This may result in conservation of historic sites, revitalisation of traditional arts, handicrafts, performances, festivals, folklore and lifestyles as well as financial assistance for maintaining other cultural assets such as museums and theatres. The Stockman's Hall of Fame in Longreach in Queensland has had a similar effect on local tourism and interest in Australia's bush heritage. This interest will be the focus of the Australian Year of the Outback in 2002 (see Breakthrough tourism).

In many countries, indigenous peoples are becoming involved in tourism to help meet their own goals of independence and cultural survival. The development of indigenous tourism strategies in consultation with indigenous communities and tribal elders can offer similar opportunities in Australia (see chapter 10).

BREAKTHROUGH TOURISM
Year of the Outback

Two thousand and two has been designated the Australian Year of the Outback, providing a significant platform for Australia to showcase the Australian Outback in the global marketplace. The Federal Government has agreed to fund a business plan for the year of celebrations that will provide rural and regional Australia with a great opportunity to promote 'the spirit, the uniqueness, the natural wonders and endless potential of the Outback'. Deputy Prime Minister John Anderson says the Year of the Outback will be a major celebration of Outback history, culture and achievements. He says the year-long event will generate awareness of how much rural, regional and remote areas have contributed to Australian life. The year of celebrations is expected to include music festivals, art shows and special award ceremonies.

The official launch of Outback 2002 took place at Longreach in November 1999. Outback 2002 has been endorsed by a wide range of national organisations, including the Australian Council of Agricultural Societies, with 600 shows nationwide attracting approximately 6 million people, the Local Government Association of Australia, the Australian Country Music Association, rural faculty of the Royal Australian College of General Practitioners and Tourism Council Australia, to name just a few. A gathering is planned in each state and territory to provide interested people with the opportunity to contribute their ideas about events, initiatives, projects and activities their regions and communities could develop for the Year of the Outback.

Year of the Outback 2002 is also the International Year of Ecotourism, providing opportunities to link these two initiatives and focus attention on the extraordinary landscapes and natural resources of the Outback. The *National Geographic Traveller* magazine, with its vast international readership, has identified Australia's Outback as one of the 'must see' places in the world. Organisers of Outback 2002 are promoting the key features outlined below as reasons for international tourists to visit Australia's Outback.

• The diversity of Outback accommodation available is the 'Australian Experience' tourists enjoy.

• The spring wildflowers are the most spectacular natural flower display in the world.

- National Parks and World Heritage areas cover much of the vast expanse of the Outback, providing extensive ecotourism opportunities.
- Rural and remote services include the Royal Flying Doctors and School of the Air.
- Stars fill the clear night sky from horizon to horizon and the peace of the open space regenerates the soul.

Bruce Campbell, chairman of Outback 2002 Ltd, explains:

> The Year of the Outback in 2002 is a target year for rural Australia to make initiatives happen, for towns to finish projects, for industries to highlight their ability in the global marketplace. Year of the Outback won't be just another Year — there is a massive commitment ensuring legacies are left, whether it be the continual flow of international tourists or a greater understanding between urban and rural Australians, accepting the different roles and appreciating that without each other neither is as effective. The Year of the Outback is a magnificent opportunity. It is now up to Australians to ensure it realises its full potential.

Further information on Year of the Outback 2002 is available at http://www.outback2002.com.

Cultural exchange and understanding, broader horizons and new ideas

Regional tourism provides an opportunity to experience different places and cultures, and to share different ideas and life experiences. This **cultural exchange** may lead to enhanced mutual understanding and respect for different value systems and traditions. Regional tourism can also increase the opportunities for social contact for people in isolated communities.

Synopsis

Communities reap social and cultural benefits from tourism. Tourism can provide new and improved services and facilities, create job opportunities, stimulate interest in and conservation of cultural heritage assets, and provide opportunities for new social contact and greater respect for different values and customs. All these factors may enhance the quality of life of regional communities.

The extent to which these benefits are achieved, if at all, will be determined by the number and type of visitors to a destination, the cultural differences between tourists and the regional communities they visit and the extent of disruption of local lifestyles caused by tourism activity. These factors are important when considering the role of tourism in regional economic and social development. Good planning is the key to achieving the best outcomes for a community.

The future of regional tourism in Australia has attracted the attention of researchers as well as politicians and communities. The Cooperative Research Centre for Sustainable Tourism, with Tourism Council Australia and Southern Cross University, has established the Centre for Regional Tourism Research to provide a foundation for the strategic development of regional tourism in Australia through a targeted research program. The research program aims to:

- review the role of tourism in regional social and economic development
- identify impediments to regional tourism development
- develop strategies for enhancing tourism's contribution to regional development and rural adjustment
- identify gaps in data available for destination planning, and mechanisms for improved data collection and analysis
- identify impediments to the development and distribution of regional tourism products
- evaluate the impact of tourism in regional areas
- assess the application of technology in regional areas, and examine public and private sector financing strategies for regional tourism infrastructure and **product development**.

To provide industry input to the development of its work program, the Centre for Regional Tourism Research conducted a regional tourism research scoping study during February and March 2000 based on focus group meetings in 10 regional locations. The focus groups identified nine principal issues confronting the tourism industry in regional Australia.

1. *Local and regional economic modelling:* There is a need to improve understanding of the contribution tourism makes to local and regional economies. Issues include identifying and describing regional economic value and linkages; sectoral impact studies; and improved data collection and analytical methods.

2. *Pricing, financing and business planning:* Business planning was identified as an important challenge at the Regional Australia Summit (see Special interest investigation). Business planning skills need to be improved and access to finance increased for many regional tourism operators. Issues that need to be addressed include pricing; access to finance; and business planning and management.

3. *Consumer behaviour, market research, marketing:* Tourism operators are searching for more and better information to assist them in identifying market trends and opportunities. Issues include market niche studies; analysis and forecasting; and marketing planning and brand development.

4. *Infrastructure, transport and information technology:* Many regional destinations are hampered by a lack of infrastructure (signage, transport, accommodation, convention and events venues), while some existing infrastructure (for example, rail) is underutilised. Information technology presents an important opportunity and challenge for regional

tourism operators. Issues include taking advantage of the potential benefits of information technology and improved transport infrastructure.

5. *Training and accreditation:* Many regions lack access or commitment (or both) to appropriate training for staff involved in both accommodation and tour operations. There is perceived to be a lack of industry leadership in some regions. Issues include leadership and management education; staff training; and industry accreditation.

6. *Destination development:* Protecting the natural and cultural assets that provide the product base for regional tourism is a widespread concern among operators. Ensuring the tourism industry has a strong and effective voice in regional and community development is a major challenge. Issues include destination planning and development; heritage conservation and management; and industry leadership and policy issues.

7. *Local and regional data collection:* There is almost universal concern that tourism operators and advocates do not have access to sufficient accurate and timely data on local tourism activity.

8. *Communication, extension and technology transfer:* Many regional tourism operators find it difficult to gain access to current research with potential relevance to the profitable and sustainable management of their business. It is essential that improvements are made in the communication of research outcomes to facilitate their uptake in regional Australia.

9. *Product development:* Developing the outstanding natural and cultural attractions of regional Australia into saleable tourism products remains a challenge. Issues include both product development and product packaging.

Ongoing research on these and other issues will deliver benefits to tourism operators in regional Australia; investors in tourism infrastructure; and local, state and federal government agencies responsible for tourism and regional development. Improved regional tourism research will ultimately benefit regional communities interested in **sustainable tourism development** that generates positive social and economic outcomes while protecting important features of the natural and cultural environment.

4.7 $\int$ UMMARY

More than 60 per cent of all international and domestic visitor nights in Australia are spent outside the capital cities, bringing a range of economic, sociocultural and environmental benefits to rural and regional communities. Spurred by declines in traditional rural industries, tourism is receiving increased attention as a tool for regional development in Australia and in many other countries around the world.

Tourism is dynamic and a powerful agent for change, but it also poses challenges. Tourism is not a universal solution to the ailments of regional

Australia and will not necessarily deliver benefits to the same extent in every region. Some regions have limited tourism potential and the investment of public funds to boost tourism could be wasteful. Even in areas that do possess the inherent or collective resources and capacities to attract tourists, not all forms of tourism are appropriate. Ensuring that the benefits of regional tourism are maximised and possible negative impacts are minimised may ultimately require limits to growth in certain regions.

Tourism will not solve all the problems of regional Australia, and not all locations have the same potential to attract tourists and develop a sustainable tourism industry.

Tourism may play an important role as part of a coordinated package of measures for sustainable regional economic and social development, but how can it be encouraged and what locations have the greatest potential? In the light of increased pressure on federal, state and local government to help regional areas to cope with the increasing pace of economic and social change, we need a better understanding of tourism's potential as a regional development tool.

Optimising the tourism industry's contribution to regional areas and ensuring that the benefits flow to all sectors of the communities requires an integrated approach to regional development. Appropriate tourism management structures must also be put into place. Cooperation and collaboration across all levels of government and industry are essential to overcome the diverse and often fragmented nature of regional tourism. Sustainable regional tourism also depends on the support of local communities, which can best be achieved by establishing clear processes for community involvement in planning and development. Community awareness of the benefits of regional tourism is critical to the successful outcome of these processes.

Questions

4.1 Why is it important to move tourists beyond the major international gateways — for the tourism industry? for regional communities? for politicians?

4.2 What is a 'tourism region'? How should regional boundaries be determined?

4.3 List some of the economic, sociocultural and environmental impacts (both positive and negative) of tourism in regional Australia.

4.4 Do all regional locations have the same potential for tourism development? If not, why not and is it possible to do anything about it?

4.5 Identify the single biggest opportunity and biggest challenge facing governments and businesses wanting to develop tourism in regional locations.

REFERENCES

Bureau of Tourism Research. 1998a. *National Visitor Survey*. Canberra: BTR.

Bureau of Tourism Research. 1998b. *International Visitor Survey*. Canberra: BTR.

Bureau of Tourism Research. 1999. *Tourism Expenditure by International Visitors in Regional Australia*. Occasional Paper No. 29. Canberra: BTR.

Carpenter, Carole H. 1996. 'Use It or Lose It: Conserving Traditions through Heritage Planning for Tourism'. In Davey, Gwenda Beed & Faine, Susan (Eds.). *Traditions and Tourism: The Good, the Bad and the Ugly*. Proceedings of the Sixth National Folklife Conference 1994. Monash University, Clayton: National Centre for Australian Studies, pp. 17–24.

Commonwealth Department of Industry, Science and Resources. 2000. *Impact*, July. Canberra: DISR.

Hutchison, Jon. 1997. *Tourism: Getting It Right for the Millennium*. Canberra: Office of National Tourism.

Kirshenblatt-Gimblett, Barbara. 1996. 'Tourism and Heritage'. In Davey, Gwenda Beed & Faine, Susan (Eds.). *Traditions and Tourism: The Good, the Bad and the Ugly*. Proceedings of the Sixth National Folklife Conference, 1994. Monash University, Clayton: National Centre for Australian Studies.

Prosser, G., Hunt, S., Braithwaite, R., Bonnett, G. & Rosemann, I. 2000. 'The Significance of Regional Tourism: A Preliminary Report'. Occasional Paper No. 2. Lismore: Centre for Regional Tourism Research.

Read, S. E. 1980. 'A Prime Force in the Expansion of Tourism in the Next Decade: Special Interest Travel'. In Hawkins, D. E., Shafer, E. L. and Rovelstad, J. M. (Eds.). *Tourism Marketing and Management Issues*. Washington, DC: George Washington University, pp. 193–202.

Ross, Glenn F. 1992. 'Resident Perceptions of the Impact of Tourism on an Australian City'. In *Journal of Travel Research* 30:13–17.

Witt, Stephen F. 1987. 'Economic Impact of Tourism on Wales'. In *Tourism Management* 8 (4): 306–16.

http://www.dotrs.gov/regional/summit

http://www.outback2002.com

Nundle

Nundle is a small town in a picturesque location in the Dungowan Valley at the foot of the Great Dividing Range, 60 kilometres from Tamworth in northern New South Wales. Located 26 kilometres from the New England Highway, Nundle is about five hours drive from Sydney and around six hours from Brisbane.

The district around Nundle was first settled by squatters taking advantage of the fertile soils for growing crops and raising sheep and cattle in the mid-nineteenth century. When gold was discovered in Swamp Creek in 1851 the town expanded rapidly; it boasted a local population of 12 000 (including 4000 Chinese), 16 pubs and a department store in its heyday. It has been estimated that between 1852 and 1856 alluvial gold to the value of over $1.5 million was extracted from the rivers and creeks around Nundle. One goldmine remains active today, but as commercial gold reserves declined, agriculture again became the principal source of income for the district, along with some forestry activity.

A few visitors explore the old mine workings and fossick for gold, crystals and semi-precious stones such as sapphires, zircons, jasper, prase, rhodonite and green crystal. However, Nundle is far enough from the New England Highway to deter casual visitors and tourism is a minor contributor to local economic activity.

Like other small towns around Australia, Nundle went into long-term and apparently terminal decline. A vicious cycle of business closures and reduced services set in, undermining the confidence and viability of those who remained. By the mid 1990s, the future looked bleak — that is, until the owners of a local cattle property, Judy and Peter Howarth, decided that they were going to 'do something for Nundle'. As the Howarths describe it, they were concerned that the decline of Nundle would make it increasingly difficult for them to attract and retain the number and quality of staff they needed to run their business interests in the district. So they decided to draw on their previous professional experience in real estate development and retail to invest in the future of Nundle. And the future they forecast had tourism as a central plank.

The Howarths' first move was to purchase some of the real estate that was for sale in the main street. They negotiated with the only remaining bank in Nundle to buy the attractive old bank building and the shop beside it. The bank realised its most valuable asset — the building — moved into the shop next door and was able to continue trading. Meanwhile the Howarths turned the restored original bank building into an upmarket guesthouse — the Jenkins Street Guest House, named after the main street of Nundle.

But the Howarths did not stop their real estate acquisitions with the old bank. They also purchased other property that was for sale including a motel, a petrol station and convenience store, the general store and the original garage. Peter Howarth's son has created backpacker accommodation and entertainment on a working sheep station — Dag Sheep Station — a short distance out of town.

Perhaps most significant in terms of its symbolism, the Howarths bought an old slab and iron building in the main street that served as the general store in the days of the gold rush. Their principal motive in buying this building was to conserve its heritage value. 'We bought it to save it.' Since it had no obvious commercial potential, the Howarths decided to lease the building — for the princely sum of $1 per annum — to a young couple to run as an art gallery. Not only is the building conserved; it is now made available to visitors to inspect, as well as providing an evocative setting for the display of artworks that attract visitors from near and far.

A feature of the Howarths' contribution to Nundle has been their encouragement of local tradespeople and suppliers, thereby helping to diversify the local economic base. For example, much of the furniture in the Jenkins Street Guest House was made by local craftspeople. According to Judy Howarth, 'It is amazing the talent you can squeeze out of a district'. Also significant is the supply of local produce to the excellent restaurant in the Jenkins Street Guest House. This includes organic fruit and vegetables grown locally, fresh and smoked trout produced by a local trout farm, pheasant, venison, rabbit and hare, as well as the beef for which the region is generally better known.

What has happened in Nundle over a relatively short period of time demonstrates that tourism in regional Australia can drive social and economic development in regional areas. Nundle is now reaping the benefits of economic diversification, new enterprise development, and new sources of income and employment in the local economy. In turn, this activity is providing benefits to local government and creating opportunities for investment and infrastructure development. Tourism development at Nundle is attracting people from the cities, who are spending their urban incomes on regional goods and services. As Anthony Dennis wrote in a *Sydney Morning Herald* review, 'Jenkins Street Guest House has finally provided those of us Sydneysiders who wish country and western music would just scoot with a reason to head Tamworth way' (*SMH*, 7 August 1999). Tourism is changing Nundle but in a mostly positive way that is making it a more diverse and interesting place in which to live. It is building community pride.

An essential feature of the Nundle experience is the economic and community leadership demonstrated by the Howarths. They have provided both a vision of what the future could be like and practical initiatives to work towards achieving that vision. But change is never easy. Although it is unlikely that any of the traditional residents of Nundle wanted to see their town die, that does not mean they necessarily welcomed the major and relatively sudden changes brought on by the Howarths. As Judy Howarth says, 'We've had a lot of support and a lot of opposition'. As people have grown accustomed to the new future of Nundle, there is little doubt that the overwhelming majority of locals are happy for the population to have increased to the point where the local school and its two teachers can continue to survive — as does the local police officer, the post office and the bank. Many similar towns in regional Australia have not been so lucky.

Questions

1 Why have the fortunes of Nundle changed when many other regional towns have struggled?

2 How could the multiplier effect of tourism in Nundle be enhanced?

3 What lessons can be learned from Nundle and applied to other towns in regional Australia?

4 What role can tourism play in addressing the challenges faced by regional Australia? Provide examples to illustrate your answer.

CHAPTER 5

Jennifer Craik

5 Cultural *tourism*

LEARNING OBJECTIVES

After reading this chapter, you will have an appreciation of:

- what is meant by the term cultural tourism and how it differs from other forms of tourism

- cultural tourists and how they differ from other categories of tourist

- the reasons for the popularity and growth of cultural tourism

- the central issues associated with cultural tourism concerning tourist culture, destination culture and cultural sustainability

- different approaches to cultural tourism and their likely outcomes

- why and how governments have become interested in promoting and developing cultural tourism.

5.1 INTRODUCTION

Cultural tourism has burgeoned in recent years, the term becoming something of a 'buzzword' conjuring up more meaningful tourist experiences. This chapter will introduce you to debates about cultural tourism to account for the rapid growth of cultural tourism in recent years and why it attracts ambivalent and contentious reactions. An obvious starting point is to say that cultural tourism concerns forms of tourism that relate to aspects of culture, whether profiling culture, involving cultural experiences, learning about culture or participating in culture. Looking through the list of chapter headings in this book, you will realise that cultural tourism overlaps many other forms of tourism, such as heritage tourism, rural tourism, educational tourism, adventure tourism, indigenous tourism, wine and food tourism, and festivals and special events tourism. Where do we draw the line? What makes cultural tourism different or specific?

5.2 WHAT IS CULTURAL TOURISM?

Cultural tourism refers to forms of tourism that highlight the cultural, heritage or artistic aspects of a destination or experiences and activities for the tourist — a kind of cultural immersion. Some people define themselves as cultural tourists because culture is the *primary* motivation for their travel. These are the pure or genuine cultural tourists; yet they are the minority. If we are referring solely to this group, then cultural tourism constitutes a *niche* or special interest form of travel. But other groups of tourists can also be classified as cultural tourists because they take advantage of cultural resources during their travel experience, which arises from other motivations (such as recreation, business, visiting friends or relatives, or sightseeing). For these tourists, culture is a *secondary*, ancillary or contingent motivation.

Cultural tourism has been defined in many ways, but a common theme of these definitions is the emphasis on learning about, experiencing or understanding cultural activities, resources and/or other cultures. Cultural tourism involves 'customised excursions into other cultures and places to learn about their people, lifestyle, heritage and arts in an informed way that genuinely represents those cultures and their historical contexts' (Craik 1995b). The emphasis here is on the *educational, experiential and communicative experience* and on the *authenticity, transparency* or *honesty* of such encounters. The former aspect reminds us of the educational and self-improvement motivations of Grand Tour travel popularised in Europe between 1600 and 1800 (Adler 1989; Hall & Zeppel 1990). The latter gives a more anthropological or ethnographic dimension to the experience; namely, that cultural tourism should achieve a level of interpersonal and intercultural communication that is absent from conventional tourist encounters (Blundell 1995–96).

The question remains: what counts as culture and what doesn't? Cultural tourism includes 'highbrow' forms of culture — that is, those associated with cultural improvement and development epitomised by the culture promoted by museums, galleries, historic houses and performing arts. It also includes historic and heritage tourism, including visiting sites and buildings of significance — indeed, this kind of tourism is distinctly more popular than 'highbrow' cultural tourism. Cultural tourism can also characterise tourist experiences of some forms of everyday culture, such as eating out or shopping; and some subcultural forms, such as going to the boxing in Bangkok or the running of the bulls in Spain. But where do we draw the line? Why is a visit to Paris inevitably regarded as a form of cultural tourism while a trip to Broken Hill is not? Is going to the soccer as valid a form of cultural tourism as a trip to the opera? As these examples suggest, where culture refers to sanctioned and official cultural forms, the definition is not too difficult. But when it comes to various kinds of everyday culture, living culture, popular culture and subcultures, it can be difficult to decide what counts and what does not. Even more vexed is the question of ethnic and indigenous culture: a visit to the Tjapukai Aboriginal Cultural Park or a multicultural festival counts as cultural tourism, but do visits to Bourke, Redfern or the western suburbs of Sydney count as cultural tourism?

Very often, cultural tourism is used to label 'romantic' notions of culture, especially those associated with the past and simpler times (a so-called golden age). Cultural tourism, then, presents culture packaged in pleasing ways that evoke widespread ideas about ways of life and other people. Well-intentioned though this kind of promotion may be, some commentators have argued that cultural tourism at best simply reinforces particular ideas visitors have and, at worst, justifies social hierarchies and past injustices.

To illustrate the nature of cultural tourism experiences — and their unintended consequences — Blundell cites the example of the Polar Bear Express in northern Ontario, Canada. Promoted as 'a trip through time and tradition', the excursion offers tourists a taste of various aspects of life in the early years of European settlement. The trip starts with a five-hour train ride to remote Moosonee, where tourists can see a reconstructed Hudson's Bay trading post, watch for Beluga whales, visit an old blacksmith's forge and then take a freighter across the Moose River to an Indian reserve to explore a tourist park. The park is physically separate from the residential section of the reserve and consists of reconstructed historic buildings, a cafe and a souvenir outlet. The highlight of the trip is a visit to a teepee where Native women cook traditional 'bannock' for tourists. After returning to Moosonee, most tourists depart that evening. Although the trip offers several samples of Canadian history, industries, ways of life and environment, the focus is clearly on sampling — or getting a taste of — indigenous culture. Blundell makes the point that the emphasis is on re-creating associations with traditional images of Cree people frozen in time, with no attention to their current lifestyle. Privileging activities that are no longer practised as authentic Cree culture is inappropriate, she argues.

Tourists may be discouraged from interpreting (other) contemporary Cree forms as (equally) authentic, and read them instead as signs of assimilation or cultural loss (as for example the permanent houses that they see just beyond the bannock tent). Therefore, while directing tourists towards 'traditional' forms such as the bannock tent may be an acceptable trade-off for those who wish to keep tourists at bay, such a strategy may well run the risk of reinforcing tendentious meanings about First Peoples (Blundell 1995–96:40).

Nonetheless, the Polar Bear Express typifies a popular approach to cultural tourism, namely the re-creation of ways of life that are regarded as 'traditional', 'typical' or 'iconic' — or, colloquially speaking, seeing how indigenous people live. In the case of North American First Peoples, imagery is fixed around conventions that developed in the 1930s when Indians began to be represented clad in feathered warbonnets and beaded buckskin outfits. The fact that such styles were confined only to the Plains Indian — and beading conventions typical of the Great Lakes Indians — was of no interest (Albers & James 1983). This iconic image of all North American Indians was reinforced by popular culture representations of cowboys and Indians in comics, toys, films and television (cf. Nicks 1999; Parezo 1999). Such conventions remain dominant and expected.

This pattern of symbolic representation is common. There are many stories of pressure from tourists forcing performers at cultural parks to 'dress' the part by abandoning everyday clothes and donning 'costumes' of the past, or ingrained representations of the past. As a result, most contemporary cultural parks fall in with visitors' preconceptions and adopt fancy dress. Examples include the Tjapukai Cultural Centre in Cairns, Sovereign Hill at Ballarat, Old Sydney Town, Colonial Williamsburg in Virginia, the Taiwan Aboriginal Culture Park in Formosa, Splendid China in Shenzhen, the Song Dynasty Village in Hangzou and Huis Ten Bosch in Japan (Larkin et al. 1999). These images are *sanitised* (into predictable and non-confronting stereotypes) and *commodified* (into easily experienced and consumed forms).

Cultural tourism gives tourists the opportunity to sample remnants, exemplars, replicas or fascsimiles of cultural life — past and/or present. This may occur in cultural precincts, theme parks, heritage sites or centres, museums, galleries, performing arts venues, festivals and even ordinary streetlife.

■ 5.2.1 **Staged sets,** *fronts and backs in cultural tourism*

The ideal of cultural tourism to provide authentic (i.e. genuine, trustworthy or reliable) cultural samples for tourists is necessarily unattainable, as indicated in the work of symbolic interactionists such as Erving Goffman and critical theorists such as Hans Magnus Enzensberger who have shown how communicative interchanges are always structured by role playing, symbolic performances, disguises and resistance to 'pure' communicative exchanges.

These ideas were applied to tourism by MacCannell (1973), who argued that the spaces in which tourist encounters occur are like '**staged sets**' in which different levels of 'staged authenticity' are performed.

MacCannell contrasts the *fronts* of tourist space (those areas deliberately set up for tourist display, sightseeing and consumption such as viewing platforms, museums or guided tours) and the *backs* of tourist space (areas that are private and off-limits to the public gaze such as private homes and gardens, restaurant kitchens or industrial factories). Tourism is organised around — indeed prides itself on — promoting its array of front attractions. A destination must have a minimum number and variety of 'fronts' before, for example, tour buses will stop there. Yet, as MacCannell argues, the motivations for the behaviour of tourists stem more from *wanting to get behind the fronts to experience the backs* — or rather, tourists *think* that is what they want to do! This explanation can be seen in expressions like 'getting off the beaten track', 'the great escape', and 'getting away from it all'.

In this sense, then, tourism is founded on a contradiction between its purported rationale (by the industry) to package the destination for visitors and the actual or imagined rationale (by the tourists) to experience another culture, try new activities or meet new people. Sometimes tourists contend that they want to experience the backs but in practice they still want the comforts and security of the fronts. An example is the desire of international tourists to see the Australian Outback: faced with the vast open spaces and forbidding terrain and climate, in fact most prefer managed and controlled samples of the 'Outback'. Examples include the Stockman's Hall of Fame in Longreach; organised tours of, and visitor centres in, national parks such as the 'Outback Undara experience' of lava tubes in Undara Volcanic National Park in Queensland; and organised indigenous cultural tours offered by companies like Desert Tracks (an educational ecotour owned by the Anganu Pitjantjatjara).

The implication is that although tourists may claim they want to experience gritty reality, generally they prefer a mediated experience. Evidence for this comes from surveys of visitor satisfaction. For example, marketing surveys found that visitors prefer the goldmining theme park Sovereign Hill to real pioneer villages because the latter were 'less historically "reliable"' (Evans 1991:149). Another advantage of this entirely manufactured historic village is that the site can be adapted as required. The park has consistently improved and extended its range of attractions based on historical research. It aims to achieve 'historical accuracy' rather than to create 'authentic reproductions' (Evans 1991; Peter Hiscock, interviewed on ABC 1997; Sovereign Hill Museums Association 2000). Since it also competes with theme parks such as Seaworld and Dreamworld, Sovereign Hill has upgraded its facilities (such as food outlets and toilets) to compete with these attractions. As this example shows, although one of the greatest preoccupations about cultural tourism is the search for 'authenticity', this quest is immaterial. Cultural tourism is inevitably about the production and consumption of simulacra, or products that make only a pretence to authenticity.

5.2.2 **Who** *is a cultural tourist?*

As we have seen, cultural tourism involves tourist experiences that focus on experiencing cultural resources, including arts and cultural production and expression, as well as heritage tourism, historical tourism and ethnic tourism (Zeppel & Hall 1991; cf. Foo & Rossetto 1998). As some analysts have noted, cultural tourists may be primary, incidental or accidental (Hughes 1987) or, as Bywater (1993) has termed them, *culturally motivated, culturally inspired* or *culturally attracted* tourists.

- *Culturally motivated tourists:* These tend to be better educated, mostly women and better off financially. Only this first category contains the genuine cultural tourist who is motivated specifically by the desire to see or experience certain specific cultural attractions and organises travel around cultural activities. They have more of what has been called *cultural capital* (see Richards 1996:267–8); that is, they possess a better than average knowledge of culture, are better educated and skilled and more articulate in expressing their views. However, they are not very numerous. Bywater (1993) estimates that only 5 per cent of the market is composed of culturally motivated tourists.
- *Culturally inspired tourists:* This type accounts for up to one-third of the market. They may be culturally inspired by a specific site (the Pompidou Centre; the Sistine Chapel; Sydney's Opera House) or event (a performance of Agatha Christie's *The Mousetrap* in the West End, London; the musical *Les Misérables; Opera in the Outback*). This group generally is likely to make only one visit to the icon of their dreams; they are unlikely to return. However, tourism promoters target this group with the hope of attracting them to new and special cultural events. Yet there is a downside to encouraging this type of cultural tourist. As Bywater (1993:44) points out, 'Culturally inspired tourists cause problems for tourist planners. They fill their day with as much as possible and frequently spend as little time and money as possible on a single destination'.
- *Culturally attracted tourists:* This term describes the majority of cultural tourists. They take advantage of the availability of a museum, historic site, concert, exhibition or other cultural event while on holiday for another reason. Often they only find out about cultural attractions once they reach the destination. This group of 'cultural daytrippers' creates problems because of the incidental, unplanned nature of their cultural consumption, which makes it hard for planners and site managers to predict tourist demand and cater for their needs. Nonetheless, numbering up to 60 per cent of tourists, this group is a potentially lucrative market share to snare.

5.2.3 **An alternative** *typology of cultural tourists*

Of course, these figures are guesstimates and vary. Silberberg (1995) has distinguished four degrees of consumer motivation for cultural tourism among residents and tourists: only 5 per cent of residents and 15 per cent of tourists are *greatly motivated* by cultural tourism; 15 per cent of residents and

30 per cent of tourists are *partly motivated*; 20 per cent of residents and 20 per cent of tourists have *adjunct motivations* (may include cultural attractions at a destination chosen for other reasons); and 20 per cent of residents and 20 per cent of tourists are *accidentally motivated* (unplanned, contingent cultural tourism; cf. Bywater's culturally attracted group). The remaining 40 per cent of residents and 15 per cent of tourists, according to Silberberg, are not interested in cultural tourism *'under any circumstances'* (my italics).

These figures and typologies are interesting because they suggest that much of the fanfare over cultural tourism may be wasted. That is, if cultural tourism is conceived of as the pursuit of highbrow cultural experiences, then there may be distinct limits to the potential for cultural tourism to grow based on existing levels of cultural capital possessed by different groups of tourists.

■ *5.2.4* **Why** *has cultural tourism become popular?*

Numerous explanations have been offered as to why cultural tourism has grown. Some relate its popularity to supply factors and some to demand. On the demand side, some analysts argue that tourists have become bored with conventional forms of tourism, especially those that rely on heavily packaged (or mediated) products; instead, they want something different that is apparently less packaged and more 'authentic'. In this sense, cultural tourism can be seen to be spearheading a *new phase of tourism product*, one that emphasises cultural products, experiences and communication. Others would argue — in a related way — that tourists are now seasoned travellers who are more mature, demanding and discriminating in their choice of travel. This more sophisticated group of tourists have been called 'inquisitive travellers' (Pozel, cited by Holgate 2000:16). Cultural tourism enables this type of tourist to engage in more intellectualised and specialised activities and contacts with destinations.

The third explanation relates to supply factors. From a destination point of view, cultural tourism is regarded as offering a new set of attractions to either replace or supplement tired existing forms; moreover, it is seen to have benefits for the promotion of the local sense of identity and bolster the cultural industries and cultural production. Fourth, cultural tourism is regarded as having less negative impacts than other forms of tourism, attracting a better class of visitors (wealthier, better educated and more responsible).

5.3 ISSUES IN CULTURAL TOURISM

The search for **cultural authenticity**, difference and new experiences apparently offered through 'genuine' brushes with culture and other people has exacerbated the contradiction between wanting 'backs' but preferring 'fronts' or mediated backs. Cultural tourists seek out the backs and contact with the local people in order to enhance their tourist experience. However, they may not realise that this can create a multitude of tensions and problems precisely because these spaces, activities and people are not geared up as fronts are to 'process', and accommodate the needs of tourists and the legacies of the visits.

Ironically, then, cultural tourism has been popularised because it is regarded as a more acceptable form of tourism for the three agents of tourist transactions: the tourist benefits because cultural tourists are people who genuinely want to learn about a destination; the local or resident benefits because they can showcase their specialities and identity; and governments and localities benefit because they generate economic activity, employment and kudos from promoting their distinctive culture and heritage. Yet cultural tourism also poses significant challenges in terms of its impacts and outcomes for the tourist experience, the local culture and governments. Above all, cultural tourism turns out to be more about the culture of tourists than about the culture of 'them' or the tourists' desire to learn about the destination culture (Crick 1989:328; cf. Craik 1997).

■ *5.3.1* Raw and cooked *tourism, cold and hot interpretation*

We may characterise the tensions in cultural tourism as a polarity between 'raw' and 'cooked' tourism and between 'cold' and 'hot' interpretation (Craik 1998). By this we mean that creating a cultural tourism product or experience requires translating a 'raw' entity into something that can be negotiated, understood, experienced and consumed by a tourist — in the 'cooked' version. The presentation of a historic cottage (using labels, guides, mannequin models and 'living' re-enactments of traditional activities) is an example of transforming the 'raw' material into a tourist product. In the process, cultural tourism emphasises codes and means for developing interpretations of the tourist product or experience. The traditional approach is to provide 'cold' interpretations via labels beside exhibits, catalogue entries or official tour spiels that are standardised and memorised.

Increasingly, cultural tourism is developing 'hot' interpretive strategies through which the visitor is encouraged to engage with the object or experience and make sense of it him- or herself. At Sovereign Hill, for example, schoolchildren can spend a day dressed in the clothes of the time and 'experience' the life of the school room of the 1850s — using chalk and boards, being disciplined, rote learning and so on. This first-hand experience of being a student in another age is arguably much more persuasive than a static re-creation of a 'typical' school room where one is fenced off and gazes at the static scene of furniture, furnishings and artefacts.

To achieve **hot interpretations**, an exhibit may counterpose a variety of objects that allude to a theme without explanation, thus requiring the visitor to use his or her own knowledge and interpretive skills to explain the juxtaposition and connections. The displays in the Museum of Sydney have adopted this approach by placing all kinds of objects in drawers that visitors are invited to search through. At Calthorpe's 1930s house in Canberra, the guides make ice and store it in the ice chest then offer visitors cool drinks. This demonstration of how an ice chest works sparks memories from the older generation and ignites interest in traditional technologies among younger visitors. In a similar way, a rendition by an enthusiastic guide on an old pianola creates far more vibrant experiences for visitors than simply looking at the pianola and reading the titles of its rolls ever could. Thus by juxtaposing objects, contexts and practices in a way that invites — or forces — interpretation by visitors, a range of explanations, responses and engagements can be achieved. Many cultural tourism products and experiences attempt a similar process.

■ 5.3.2 Tourist culture — *authenticity and commodification*

Much debate about cultural tourism has centred on the nature of the tourist culture that is produced. Three issues have dominated discussion of the nature of tourist culture. Often, commentators are preoccupied with whether — and, if so, to what extent — it is possible to achieve so-called authentic representations, re-creations and experiences of cultural phenomena. We have argued above that no matter how authentic the experience may seem, all tourist experiences are to some degree manufactured, artificial or manipulated; that is, they are 'fronts' of some sort and therefore are never authentic. At best they are simulacra or very plausible reproductions or re-creations. Moreover, the majority of tourists prefer — despite protestations — some type of moderated experience.

Even at '**living history**' venues, the aim is to engage visitors in the project of re-creating the ambience of the site or time or experience rather than simply exposing visitors to samples of the past. At Sovereign Hill, for example, the aim is 'to engage visitors, however fleetingly, in some discourse with our representation of the past, *to converse with visitors rather than talk at them*' (Evans 1991:150–1; my italics). Visitor reaction suggests that most visitors to Sovereign Hill appreciate this strategy. As one visitor put it:

> If you have everything behind glass cabinets, you don't really know because you can't touch it, there's no smell to it, and that sort of thing ... [Here they can] recreate the sort of smell. Even if they are phoney smells, you know people still have a more realistic viewpoint of it. I think it's a wonderful place (ABC 1997).

To this end, York's Jorvik Museum has recreated the somewhat putrid smells associated with Viking culture, while the medieval Hanseatic Museum in Bergen, Norway, relies on the natural odours from displayed dried fish to permeate the entire museum building (in fact the original factory, offices and lodgings) and create a rather overpowering backdrop to give visitors a sense of how the people lived and worked — in a huge, wooden, drafty, non-insulated building. In a similar way, chocolate factories, the Buderim Ginger Factory, the Castlemaine XXXX brewery and Bundaberg Rum distillery rely on the natural — and sweeter — smells of everyday factory production.

This raises the second concern about tourist culture — commodification. If tourism entails simulacra, then it also entails devising ways to transform the impetus for tourism into a tangible commodity. This involves creating a symbolic world of sense and meaning that can be deciphered as part of the tourist experience. A common form is souvenir culture, which consists of instantly recognisable and ubiquitous objects: postcards, T-shirts, key rings, fridge magnets, replicas and so on. Tourist culture has also produced distinctive types of tourist art, related to but different from other types of commercial art (Cohen 1992). Is commodification a desirable process? It is certainly inevitable in cultural tourism and could generally be argued to be benign, creating tourist products and experiences that tourists are usually relatively happy to consume, as well as mementos of the experience in various forms. These are permanent records or notations that serve as proof of their travel experiences.

The other concern is the modification of what is being manufactured for tourism, namely the art and craft work, performances and representations of the culture being sold. Does tourism inevitably result in debased and simplified versions of culture portrayed in usually crass formats? Although there are many examples that support this conclusion, other examples suggest that tourist culture can be a means of revitalising traditions and cultural forms, as well as creating new cultural forms. While some cultural forms may become extinct, other traditional forms may be transformed into new products: functional traditional; commercial traditional; souvenir novelty; reintegrated arts; assimilated fine arts; and popular arts (Graburn 1984). In other words, the issue of commodification may be more complex than first thought.

The Tjapukai Aboriginal Cultural Park in Cairns is an example of an evolving tourist culture that promises 'a magical, mystical world ... dedicated to preserving and presenting authentic Aboriginal culture with the aid of technology'. The complex includes 'five theatres, a museum, an art gallery and a traditional Aboriginal camp ... to give our visitors a complete and meaningful account of our rich and ancient culture'. The Tjapukai venture is indisputably a highly contrived re-creation of Aboriginal culture. At the same time, it is committed to enhancing the visibility and revitalisation of the Tjapukai language and Djabugay people as well as other indigenous people. For example, there is a Tjapukai language and culture program in several schools in the area. The park has won numerous tourism awards and takes credit for being the largest local private employer of indigenous people — 85 per cent of the 80 staff. It is involved in an employment training program and operates as an equity partnership between private shareholders (principally the founders, Judy and Don Freeman, a French Canadian and American respectively) and the Tjapukai, Yirrgandyji and Djabugay people. Use of indigenous artwork is a major feature of the park — including sales though a gallery and online

— and they have been working with the National Indigenous Arts Advocacy Association to develop a 'label of authenticity' for indigenous works and to regulate reproduction and copyright. Yet the artwork featured at Tjapukai is conventional and conservative, depicting realist portrayals of Aboriginal people (in the tradition of the 'noble savage') and commercial versions of 'typical' Aboriginal genres. Clearly, the Tjapukai venture has been very successful and popular with tourists as well as serving to assist a cultural revival program and generate employment for local indigenous people. Even so, it is hardly authentic and in many ways smacks of patronising and outdated representations of indigenous people and culture in the guise of entertainment.

Packaging a destination culture for the consumption of visitors raises many issues. Authenticity may be in the eye of the beholder and it is difficult to generalise about questions of commodification and standardisation. Many visitors are happy with a 'theme park' approach to presenting culture, while others would prefer a more 'authentic' experience. Such diverse attitudes influence the destination culture in varying ways but change certainly occurs.

■ 5.3.3 Cultural *sustainability*

Cultures may be transformed as a result of tourism, and this may or may not be beneficial. Although there are many examples of cultures being degraded — for example, as a result of sex tourism in Thailand and the Philippines — tourism can sometimes be used by local communities as a means to achieve **cultural sustainability**. An example is the Head-Smashed-In Buffalo Jump in Alberta, Canada. The site is 'where the foothills of the Rocky Mountains meet the great plains, the oldest, largest and best preserved buffalo jump' ('Head-Smashed-In Buffalo Jump' 2000). Head-Smashed-In was the scene of an annual buffalo hunt during which the local Blackfoot drove buffalo over a cliff to their death in order to process their meat, skins and bones. Legend has it that a young warrior wanted to watch the buffalo meet their death and stood under the cliff protected by an overhang. After the stampede was over, his tribe found him dead, his head crushed by the descending buffalo — hence the name of the site.

The construction of an interpretive centre at the site of a historic cultural event has enabled the local indigenous community to mobilise resources and participate in an exciting archaeological investigation. The centre relies on visitor participation and interpretation aided by interactive exhibits and indigenous guides. The interpretive centre successfully portrays the buffalo hunt and the way of life of the traditional and modern Blackfoot; visitors can appreciate the archaeological work at the site and learn about the ecology of the area. This example illustrates the importance of local cultural communities having a genuine degree of ownership over, and input into, a cultural tourism venture. Ownership, management, employment profiles, consultation and repatriation of profits are all close indicators of the sustainability of a cultural tourist venture and its acceptance by a community.

■ *5.3.4* **Cultural** *resistance*

This example shows how cultural tourism can be used as a positive, deliberative strategy to project heritage and contemporary identity and make links to other sectors. Communities frequently show considerable ingenuity in maintaining barriers between themselves and outsiders and protecting what they value most about the destination culture from the eyes of visitors. Boissevain (1996) outlines six strategies by which destination people protect their back regions. One example is the imposition of a *cordon sanitaire* — a no go area — to separate visitors from the locals. Boissevain cites the example of:

> a *cordon sanitaire* of more than six hundred tourist attractions — ranging from shops, museums, bus tours and pretzel factories to artificial homesteads — [that] keep the fifteen thousand Amish inhabitants in Lancaster County, Pennsylvania from being overrun by some five million annual visitors intent on photographing their archaic clothing and horse-drawn carriages and visiting their farms (1996:13).

Other examples are outlined below.

- *Covert resistance:* A variety of strategies may be adopted by individuals and service groups to respond to perceived rudeness, arrogance or inappropriate behaviour by tourists. These strategies may include ignoring visitors, refusing to reply, acting dumb, using rude nicknames for foreigners, sexually humiliating women and overcharging visitors.
- *Hiding:* Some aspects of a destination culture or celebrations associated with that culture may be held back from the tourist gaze by inviting only insiders, staging events outside holiday times and using local dialect (for example, the Sardinian term *sagra* rather than *festa* to refer to a celebration) (Boissevain 1996:17).
- *Fencing:* The fencing off of private local areas from tourist enclaves is increasingly common. Sometimes this can be deliberate and officially sanctioned (as in the case of Mauritius) and sometimes it can be informal and organic (as in the case of the Gold Coast or Long Island, New York).
- *Ritual:* Reinventing or inventing new rituals can confirm the identity of the locality in the face of the changes that tourist culture is bringing.
- *Organised protest:* When the impact of tourism or tourist culture sufficiently confronts locals, various forms of organised protest may occur; for example, campaigns to enforce modest dress codes, move icons of local significance away from the tourist gaze, oppose redevelopment and second-home ownership, and oppose tourist developments that are deemed inappropriate. In Byron Bay, local opposition to the construction of a Club Med resort was ultimately successful.
- *Aggression:* Sometimes other forms of resistance fail and conflict erupts, in the form of physical attacks on tourists and tourist facilities. In Malta, aggression frequently occurs when tourists 'invade' areas spotted with bird hides. The tourists are verbally abused and 'regularly menaced by hunters and bird trappers who object to foreigners invading territory they consider their domain. They feel that tourists threaten their hobby, since foreigners are usually critical of the large-scale shooting and trapping of migrating birds' (Boissevain 1996:20).

By using such strategies, communities can resist or deflect at least some of the impacts and consequences of tourism in order to shore up the local culture and sense of identity of locals. In his collection of studies of European reactions to mass tourism, Boissevain concludes that the residents of the communities studied were 'generally inventive and resilient' (1996:21). Undoubtedly, though, communities in third world countries who are less in control of the terms under which they become objects of the tourist gaze and pawns in the tourism industry have less ability to withstand impacts, determine their cultural integrity and maintain their cultural habits (Smith 1978).

SPECIAL INTEREST INVESTIGATION
The Amish as a cultural attraction

As the preceding section makes clear, the impact of cultural tourism depends on the nature of the destination culture. The following example concerns a closed community that has become a tourist attraction, the Amish people of Lancaster County, Pennsylvania, in the United States. The Amish are a strict religious sect who have retained their Swiss German dialect and who traditionally lived in closed and highly controlled communities. Dressed in distinctive 'folk' clothes and eschewing modern technology, the Amish unwittingly became a prime example of living American folk culture. The fact that this was their normal way of life — not staged for tourists — was not always appreciated. Boniface and Fowler cite the following observation of a miscommunication involving a tourist and an Amish:

> When a tourist from New York saw the Amish farmer, with his long beard, 18th century-style black hat and horse drawn plough, she removed the lens cap from the camera. 'Why don't you bring your horse over here, get off that plough and take a picture with me?' she said.
>
> As the farmer's faith preaches being a 'stranger and a pilgrim' in the world, he ignored the request and the tourist reported him to a Pennsylvania state trooper. 'She thought he was in costume to entertain her,' says Catherine Emerson, a museum educator in Lancaster County ... 'The Amish live this way all the time, whether tourists are around or not, but she just didn't get it' (Boniface & Fowler 1993:6).

At first, much of the Amish tourism was incidental to other heritage tours of the county. But soon the Amish became an attraction in their own right and bus tours would deposit curious tourists into the midst of Amish communities on a regular basis. This meant that tourists would wander around, poking into Amish houses, watching and photographing the Amish working, eating, gardening and so on. This led to strong complaints from the Amish leaders. However, as time went on the situation changed. Hovinen (1995) has asked why these conservative people became involved in tourism, and what effects this involvement is likely to have on their lifestyle, social structure and beliefs.

(*continued*)

The Amish involvement in tourism seems to have stemmed from a number of factors, including loss of opportunities in their traditional employment in agriculture; the trend for Amish women to seek paid work; the curiosity of young people about non-Amish ways of life; and the attempt to retain and revitalise Amish skills in woodwork and crafts by controlling and promoting the production and consumption of their culture. The result is that the Amish are now significantly involved in tourist enterprises. However, quite a lot of Amish tourism is still controlled by non-Amish people: actors dress up in costume; houses are reconstructed in the Amish style; there are inauthentic Amish souvenirs and tours and so on. Other evidence, such as the involvement of some young Amish in cocaine trafficking, suggests that drastic cultural changes are already occurring. The other major threat to Amish culture comes from another type of tourism developing in the county — discount outlet tourism. This growing activity is rivalling the importance of cultural tourism in the area.

Local governments and tourist bodies have been attempting to tackle these issues by introducing tighter planning and development approval practices along with a code of heritage and authenticity guidelines and listings (Lancaster Heritage Tourism 2000). This amounts to a belated attempt by public sector bodies to intervene in what has been rampant entrepreneurial private sector development.

This example illustrates how a special destination culture can become the object of cultural tourism and be fashioned into a specialised product. Changes to the destination culture inevitably occur as a result of contact with visitors, and such changes have the potential to undermine both the nature of the attraction itself and the dynamics of the destination culture. Whether the Amish would remain a tourist attraction if they all dressed in jeans, cooked in microwave ovens and drove cars is open to question. But should they keep dressing in traditional clothes and eschewing modern ways, transport and housing in order that the tourist industry remains viable? And is Amish tourism compatible with outlet tourism?

5.4 CULTURAL TOURISM IN AUSTRALIA

◼ 5.4.1 The development *of cultural tourism in Australia*

Cultural tourism is very, very important for Australia, but it is not about sophistication, it is about an Australian style which is something that we are defining which is unique to this country ... (Morse 1999).

These comments by the managing director of the Australian Tourist Commission confirm that cultural tourism is regarded as a key element of Australia's attractiveness as a tourist destination. In this sense, cultural tourism complements other attractions and puts a new spin on the Paul Hogan 'put another shrimp on the barbie' promotion of Australia as a laid-back place with lots of informal hospitality.

The earlier emphasis on Australia's unique fauna, flora and landscape is being downplayed in favour of an image of Australia as a modern nation — 'young, vibrant, stylish and colourful' (Morse 1999) — offering a range of attractions, activities and cultures. Above all, inbound visitors want 'this irreverence of attitude, this Australian sense of humour, the Australian people' (Morse 1999). These qualities are supposedly reflected in cultural activities and attractions such as wineries, cafes and restaurants, architecture, museums, galleries, trout fishing and Kakadu National Park. 'But above all, it's about authenticity, and that's what people love about this country. They love coming here because it's real; it's not fake' (Morse 1999).

Cultural tourism was recognised in the early 1990s as a special form of tourism with market potential, as reflected in studies by the Australia Council (on art and craft tourism and shopping) and a report by Brokensha and Guldberg (1992) commissioned by DASETT. But whereas these studies defined it as a specialist or niche form of tourism, more recent reports and statements view cultural tourism much more broadly, including any tourist who shows an interest in some aspect of Australian culture. Thus the Bureau of Tourism Research defines cultural tourism as visitors' attendance at:

- festivals or fairs (music, dance, comedy, visual arts, multi-arts and heritage)
- performing arts or concerts (theatre, opera, ballet, and classical and contemporary music)
- museums or art galleries
- historic or heritage buildings, sites or monuments
- art or craft workshops or studios
- Aboriginal sites and cultural displays (Foo & Rossetto 1998:7).

By using this inclusive definition, Foo and Rossetto (1998:18) calculate that 60 per cent of international tourists in 1996 sampled a cultural attraction during their Australian sojourn. Of these, 30 per cent visited a historic building, site or monument; 27 per cent visited a museum or art gallery; 15 per cent saw an Aboriginal site or cultural display; 12 per cent attended performing arts or concerts; 11 per cent visited art or craft workshops or studios; and 5 per cent attended a festival or fair (Foo & Rossetto 1998:19). A survey of inbound visitors who identified themselves as cultural tourists concluded that they accounted for 17 per cent of all inbound visitors (Foo & Rossetto 1998:60). This BTR paper has been used to promote the value of cultural tourism to Australia and argue that cultural attractions should be developed to broaden the appeal of Australia as a destination.

Further information about the growth of cultural attractions as a destination for inbound visitors is provided in figures of the most visited attractions. Instead of the Sydney Opera House and Uluru heading the list, 1997 inbound visitors most often visited the following attractions: Gold Coast theme parks (846 000), the Blue Mountains (832 000), the Great Barrier Reef (624 000), Fremantle (365 000), Phillip Island penguin parade (286 000), Parliament House, Canberra (192 000), Kakadu (106 000), Barossa Valley (102 000), and Port Arthur Historic Site (47 000) (ATC 2000). Although natural attractions and fauna still feature strongly (Blue Mountains, Great Barrier Reef, Phillip Island and Kakadu), also represented are cultural attractions covering a range of forms — artificial, cultural precincts, historic sites, cultural institutions and lifestyles.

Quoting figures such as 'one in two international visitors sought at least one cultural experience during their stay' (Foo & Rossetto 1998:4), governments have enthusiastically endorsed the rhetoric of cultural tourism as signalling a new phase in Australian inbound tourism.

In sum, cultural tourism has grown as a component of tourist activity and as a target of industry strategies. However, as we have seen, there has been a tendency to treat it as a way to re-badge mainstream tourism and diversify the appeal of Australia as a destination rather than to treat it as a niche, specialist form of tourism in a narrow sense.

■ 5.4.2 Cultural tourism, *cultural industries and the tourist industry*

While the Australian Tourist Commission does not include cultural tourism as a separate category in its expansive breakdown of SIT (ATC 2000), a number of its types could be grouped as cultural tourism, including Aboriginal, arts, Australiana, bed and breakfast, education, festivals, wine and food, historic, museum, shopping, theme park, and whale watching. Clearly, these categories overlap, and it is fair to ask: does there have to be a particular focus on the cultural or educational dimension of one of these types of SIT in order that it be counted as cultural tourism?

The tourist industry has boasted of the perceived 'quality' of cultural tourism while conveniently generalising the niche category. A similar process occurred with the term ecotourism, which began as a specialist niche form of enterprise and experience but became overgeneralised and eventually a marketing ploy hijacked by the mainstream industry. It can be plausibly argued that the same fate awaits cultural tourism. This 'cultural' recasting of tourism is evident in the Annual Report of the Department of Industry, Science, Resources and Tourism when it declares that:

> Australia's increasing recognition as a tourist destination with diverse, vibrant and sophisticated attractions, particularly the strong image of its unique and distinctive cultural attractions, provides opportunities for a wide range of involvement by [the cultural] industries (DIST 1998).

This incorporation of cultural tourism into mainstream tourism also occurs in other Australian government publications. With the 2000 Sydney Olympics, and citing the example of the Barcelona Olympics, pundits have predicted that cultural tourism has an unrealised growth potential to put Australia on the cultural map and consolidate new inbound markets and patterns of tourist activity; that is, less communing with nature and more indulgence in Australian cultural life (Holgate 2000).

Although this is the official government and industry approach to cultural tourism, attitudes and responses to this market development by the relevant cultural providers and cultural industries have varied widely. Whereas heritage tourism has had a longer and smoother relationship with the tourism industry, mutual suspicion has dominated relations between the cultural/arts industries and the tourism industry. Tourism industry promoters tend to downplay the importance of culture and the arts to their core business and have been slow to capitalise on opportunities.

Australian operators have only slowly recognised the potential of **indigenous cultural tourism**, despite significant interest from international tourists for some time. Now, however, indigenous tourism is recognised as a significant element of Australian inbound tourism and the linchpin of our future tourist appeal, because Australia 'is home to the single oldest continuous culture in the world. There is a desire to know who we are and how we live' (Morse 1999).

Generally, the arts industry has been reluctant to get involved in tourism. Many sectors of the arts community dismiss the tourist industry as crass and profit-driven. However, as funding sources for cultural activities have become more competitive and spending more accountable, the cultural industries — including galleries, museums, performing arts and festivals — have sought new avenues of activity and revenue-raising. Though ambivalence remains, tourism is acknowledged as a potential growth market.

To this end, some cultural institutions have adopted the 'blockbuster' strategy of mounting major exhibitions (such as the Asia Pacific Triennial), shows (*Cats*) and events (the Goodwill Games) to attract new audiences. Blockbusters tend to be characterised by sophisticated marketing and merchandising. Although a successful strategy, some sections of the cultural industries eschew blockbusters on the grounds that they attract the wrong kind of audience and take the focus away from their core concerns. Cultural industries have also experimented with other large-scale productions and exhibitions as part of an audience development strategy. For example, in 1998 Adelaide staged Wagner's *Ring* cycle at a cost of $8 million. The production reportedly 'injected $10 million into the South Australian economy', with 44 per cent of the audience being interstate and 12 per cent international (Holgate 2000:18).

Increasingly, cultural industries are recognising that they cannot afford to dismiss the potential of tourism to build audiences and generate revenue. Particular interest has been expressed in increasing their share of the international tourist market. For example, several cultural venues around Sydney's Circular Quay — the Museum of Contemporary Art (MCA), the Australian Centre for Craft and Design and the Sydney Opera House — have attempted to develop programs that attract more of the many tourists who wander around the precinct to become involved in their activities. The MCA has flirted with tourism because it receives little government subsidy and relies on income generation. It is currently devising a strategy to become a 'major tourist attraction' as well as a place with which locals identify (Cosic 2000).

While galleries and museums have led cultural institutions onto the tourist bandwagon, the performing arts have followed, although generally with less enthusiasm. One exception is the Sydney Opera House, which has developed a 'Discovering the Opera House' initiative that includes tours incorporating rehearsals of the Sydney Symphony Orchestra. So successful has this strategy been that the Opera House estimates that 25 per cent of its ticket buyers are tourists lured by having 'tasted' live performances. Other sectors have been more ambivalent. In a recent major inquiry into the deteriorating state of Australia's performing arts organisations, cultural tourism rated just one paragraph in the Discussion Paper and only passing reference in the Final Report (DoCITA 1999a, b), which did not identify tourism as part of the solution to the problem of rising costs and falling audiences in its recommendations. Thus, although cultural tourism is growing and some cultural industries have aligned themselves with the tourist industry to take advantage of this market, cultural tourism in Australia is generally embryonic and uneven in the range, quality and marketing of its products.

■ 5.4.3 Government *approaches to cultural tourism*

Despite much rhetoric about cultural tourism and the commissioning of various strategies at national, state, regional and local level — as well as at sector level, such as ATSI cultural tourism (ATSIC 1997; ATSIC & ONT 1997) — cultural tourism as a niche sector has not been effectively targeted as a specific or growth area. Although the Keating Government's publication *Creative Nation* (DoCA 1994) identified cultural tourism as an important area to focus on as a way of developing cultural production and export opportunities, the defeat of the Government before strategies could be implemented resulted in the shelving of this cultural policy. The general tenor of *Creative Nation* has been adopted by the Howard Government, but it has formed little more than a rhetorical substrata of government policy. Often it has been reduced to calculations of visitor expenditure on art and craft (e.g. Buchanan 1999).

The main federal initiative on cultural tourism stemmed from the previously mentioned 1998 BTR report. Observations and claims therein have been reproduced uncritically in other government publications, such as a Facts Sheet on Cultural Tourism distributed by the Department of Industry, Science, Resources and Tourism. Cultural tourism is touted as a way to promote Australian lifestyle, heritage, arts, industries and leisure pursuits. 'Cultural tourism encourages us to showcase those qualities and experiences that make us distinctly Australian and to demonstrate to the world our excellence in internationally recognised art forms' (DIST 1999).

The findings of the Department were enthusiastically endorsed — for example, in a joint statement by the Minister for Sport and Tourism, the Hon. Jackie Kelly, and the Minister for the Arts and the Centenary of Federation, the Hon. Peter McGauran.

With the report showing that around 60 per cent of all tourists to Australia visit our cultural attractions, our cultural sector will obviously benefit from continuing to develop a clear understanding of the cultural tourism market ... Cultural visitors spent more time in Australia than the average visitor, and on average, they spent $2230 — approximately $300 more than the average for all inbound visitors (Kelly & McGauran 1999).

Despite this enthusiasm, the main impediment to concerted, coordinated approaches to enhancing cultural tourism is the downgrading of tourism into a wide portfolio in the outer ministry as part of a hotchpotch of responsibilities (along with Science, Resources and Industry). Moreover, culture and the arts are now located in a different portfolio with Information Technology and Communications. This fragmentation of ministerial responsibility for cultural tourism has resulted in ministerial indifference towards this special interest area. The uneven government approach to the area at the federal level has minimised the likelihood of achieving sustained developmental strategies. This is true even in the area of indigenous cultural tourism, which has received more sustained attention. Although some sectors within the cultural industries have attempted to position themselves in the context of the cultural tourism market, the practice has been unpredictable and uneven. The divide between the activities of the tourism industry and cultural industries remains, as well as differences, or at least a lack of communication, between different tiers and agencies of governance. Ultimately, so long as cultural tourism is treated ambivalently it will continue to languish.

BREAKTHROUGH TOURISM
The case of the Tambo Teddies

This story demonstrates local initiative in establishing a small but sustainable niche product and subsequently using this success to develop a broader cultural tourism strategy. The case concerns Tambo, the oldest town in Queensland's central west and a town synonymous with sheep farming. In 1992 the 400-strong community of Tambo met to discuss responses to the declining local economy — wool prices were at a historic low and the wool stockpile overwhelming. The result was that the future of small remote traditional rural communities like Tambo was in jeopardy. The town sought ideas about how to revitalise the local economy. One result was Tambo Teddies, the initiative of three local women who saw the potential of manufacturing and marketing 'True Blue' Aussie sheepskin teddies filled with wool from the stockpile. These teddies have since been sold nationally and internationally ('Stockmen, Ringers and Bickie Bears' 1999).

(continued)

The teddies are unique; each is numbered and named after one of the properties in the Tambo district. There are two basic designs, Toby and Basil, but customers may choose a variety of shades of sheepskin and clothing colours and styles. The teddies are dressed in true blue Aussie outfits including moleskin pants, check shirts, plaited belts, 'bear-as-a-bone' coats, swags and leather hats. Annual limited edition jointed bears are manufactured and named after a local settler. About 20 000 teddies have been made and shipped to homes worldwide. Tambo Teddies provides part-time work for about 25 women who have made Tambo teddies 'a household name' (Jordan 1997), put Tambo on the tourist map and made Tambo internationally famous.

Visitors are directed by teddy street signs to the Shire Hall where the bears are produced and sold. Recently, the success of the Tambo Teddies has been taken up by the Federal Government's regional and community policymakers as an example of a local response to the crisis of the rural sector and regional Australia (Macdonald 1999; Alston 1999; Kenyon 1999).

The town of Tambo is now using the fame of its teddies to consolidate its tourist appeal by also marketing its historic sites and significance (old buildings, the world's unbroken shearing record and the historic Woolscour in nearby Blackall). The aim is to package Tambo and other towns on the Barcoo River as a unique taste of Queensland's Outback culture so visitors can 'experience the Australia of writers, poets, explorers, pioneers, stockmen, shearers and rogues' (Pollard 2000:41). Tambo has become recognised as one of the highlights of the Matilda Highway. This highway was named — after Banjo Paterson's unofficial national anthem — ten years ago as part of a strategy to unify and promote the area from the Queensland/New South Wales border to the Gulf of Carpentaria. Other tourist facilities include the Stockman's Hall of Fame in Longreach, the Australian Workers Heritage Centre in Barcaldine (the birthplace of the Queensland Labor Party), the Waltzing Matilda Centre in Winton and the Riversleigh Fossils Interpretive Centre in Mount Isa along with many places of natural beauty and significance. The appeal for tourists lies in the opportunity to experience the Outback, revel in its 'isolated, ancient territory' and 'follow in the footsteps of those great explorers — Landsborough, Leichhardt, Burke and Wills, discovering beauty beyond the beaten track' ('Travelling the Matilda Country' 1999). The success of the Matilda Highway has been remarkable; in just ten years, visitor numbers have grown to almost a quarter of a million.

In sum, Tambo Teddies has proved to be an unlikely but effective example of breakthrough tourism that has created and promoted a unique cultural product, put a tiny town on the international map, regenerated pride in local heritage and created a key attraction in a regional tourism destination. This case of cultural tourism has effectively served to integrate and balance the pitch of Outback tourism as a distinctive kind of tourist experience of Australia with a more benign and universally recognisable cultural experience.

Cultural tourism is tourism centred on cultural activities, sites or attractions that entail an experiential, communicative, educational or self-improvement component. Genuine cultural tourists organise a holiday with a cultural activity, site or attraction as the cornerstone of their experience, although other tourists may take advantage of cultural attractions while on holiday for other reasons. Cultural tourism is strictly a specialist or niche form of tourism, but it has been embraced by mainstream tourism as a way of diversifying the attractions of tourist destinations. Tourist culture refers to the contours and dynamics of what is offered to and consumed by tourists, and is characterised by debates about authenticity, commodification and standardisation. Impacts on destination culture refer to cultural changes brought by tourism development, while cultural sustainability refers to the ability of destinations to adapt to, resist or withstand tourist development, tourism impacts and tourist culture.

Questions

5.1 Why is authenticity such an important issue in cultural tourism?

5.2 What are the conditions under which cultural tourism can undermine or revitalise a destination culture?

5.3 Does cultural tourism development inevitably threaten cultural sustainability?

5.4 Is cultural tourism just a fad or marketing ploy?

5.5 Identify three examples of cultural activities or attractions that would not count as cultural tourism. Why not?

5.6 Identify the advantages and disadvantages of an artificial cultural tourism destination or attraction.

5.7 How does tourist art differ from other forms of art?

5.8 Why has 'living history' become so popular?

5.9 Contrast the terms 'raw' and 'cooked' and explain their importance in packaging cultural tourism.

5.10 What are the strengths and weaknesses of 'cold' versus 'hot' interpretation?

5.11 Contrast two examples of cultural tourism, one successful and one not. Account for their different fates.

5.12 Select a suitable destination or attraction for cultural tourism. Develop a cultural tourism strategy by undertaking a SWOT analysis; identifying existing and potential cultural attractions (scoping); developing appropriate government and industry incentives for cultural tourist development; and devising two examples of cultural enterprise initiative to promote particular cultural experiences or sites.

Aboriginal and Torres Strait Islander Commission. 1997. *National Aboriginal and Torres Strait Islander Cultural Industry Strategy.* Canberra: AGPS.

Aboriginal and Torres Strait Islander Commission & Office of National Tourism. 1997. *National Aboriginal and Torres Strait Islander Tourism Industry Strategy.* Canberra: AGPS.

Adler, J. 1989. 'Origins of Sightseeing'. *Annals of Tourism Research* 16 (1): 7–29.

Albers, P. & James, W. 1983. 'Tourism and the Changing Photographic Image of the Great Lakes Indians'. *Annals of Tourism Research* 10 (1): 123–48.

Alston, R. 1999. 'Empowering the Community Through Technology'. The Adelaide Biennial Summit: Economic, Social and Environmental Solutions for the New Millennium. Address by Senator the Hon. Richard Alston, Minister for Communications, Information Technology and the Arts, 7–9 April.

'An Update of International Visitors to Queensland — 1998'. 1999. *Trends* 18. Brisbane: Tourism Queensland. *http://www.tq.com.au/research/trends/issue18/update.htm*

Australian Broadcasting Corporation. 1997. *Wish You Were Here: Australian Tourism Studies.* Episode 6, 'Heritage Tourism'. Open Learning Australia Series and Radio National. Melbourne: Australian Broadcasting Corporation. *http://www.abc.net.au/ola/tourism/default.html*

Australian Tourist Commission. 1998. 'Special Interests'. *Facts Sheets.* Sydney: ATC.

Australian Tourist Commission. 2000. 'Inbound Tourism Statistics'. *Facts Sheets.* Sydney: ATC.

Black, A. 1996. 'Negotiating the Tourist Gaze. The Example of Malta'. In Boissevain, J. (Ed.). *Coping with Tourists. European Reactions to Mass Tourists.* Providence & Oxford: Berghahn Books, pp. 112–42.

Blackall Range Tourism Association. 1999. *The Blackall Range.* Promotional brochure. Montville: Blackall Range Tourism Association.

Blundell, V. 1995–96. 'Riding the Polar Bear Express: And Other Encounters Between Tourists and First Peoples in Canada'. *Journal of Canadian Studies* 30 (4): 28–51.

Boissevain, J. 1993. 'Some Problems with Cultural Tourism in Malta'. Paper presented to the International Conference on Sustainable Tourism in Islands and Small States. Foundation for International Studies, Malta, 18–20 November.

Boissevain, J. 1996. 'Introduction'. In Boissevain, J. (Ed.). *Coping with Tourists. European Reactions to Mass Tourists.* Providence & Oxford: Berghahn Books, pp. 1–26.

Boniface, P. & Fowler, P. 1993. *Heritage and Tourism in 'the Global Village'.* London & New York: Routledge.

Brokensha, P. & Guldberg, H. 1992. *Cultural Tourism in Australia.* Report to the Department of the Arts, Sport, the Environment and Territories. Canberra: AGPS.

Buchanan, I. 1999. *Cultural Tourism in Australia. Visual Art and Craft Shopping by International Visitors, 1997.* Canberra: DoCITA.

Bureau of Tourism Research. 1999. *Cultural Tourism in Australia. Visual Art & Craft Shopping by International Visitors, 1997.* Canberra: DoCITA.

Bywater, M. 1993. 'The Market for Cultural Tourism in Europe'. *EIU Travel and Tourism Analyst* 6: 30–46.

Cohen, E. 1992. 'Tourist Arts'. In Cooper, C. & Lockwood, A. (Eds.). *Progress in Tourism, Recreation and Hospitality Management.* London: Belhaven Press, pp. 3–31.

Commonwealth Department of Industry, Science, Resources and Tourism. 1998. *Annual Report 1996–97.* Canberra: DIST.

Commonwealth Department of Industry, Science, Resources and Tourism. 1999. 'Cultural Tourism'. *Facts Sheet*. Canberra: DIST.

Commonwealth Department of Tourism. 1994. *A Talent for Tourism*. Canberra: Commonwealth Department of Tourism.

Cosic, M. 2000. 'Art Attack'. *The Australian Magazine*, 18–19 March, pp. 28–31.

Craik, J. 1995a. 'Are There Cultural Limits to Tourism?' *Journal of Sustainable Tourism* 3 (2): 87–98.

Craik, J. 1995b. 'Is Cultural Tourism Viable?' *Smarts* 2: 6–7.

Craik, J. 1997. 'The Culture of Tourism'. In Rojek, C. & Urry, J. (Eds.). *Touring Cultures: Transformations of Travel and Theory*. London & New York: Routledge, pp. 103–36.

Craik, J. 1998. 'Interpretive Mismatch in Cultural Tourism'. *Tourism, Culture & Communication* 1 (2): 115–28.

Crick, M. 1989. 'Representations of International Tourism in the Social Sciences: Sun, Sex, Sights, Savings, and Servility'. *Annual Review of Anthropology* 18: 307–44.

Department of Communications and the Arts. 1994. *Creative Nation: Commonwealth Cultural Policy*. Canberra: AGPS.

Department of Communications, Information Technology and the Arts. 1999a. 'Securing the Future'. Major Performing Arts Inquiry Discussion Paper. Canberra: DoCITA.

Department of Communications, Information Technology and the Arts. 1999b. 'Securing the Future'. Major Performing Arts Inquiry Final Report. Canberra: DoCITA.

Eumundi and District Historical Association. 1999. *Eumundi Market*. Promotional Brochure. Eumundi: EHA.

Evans, M. 1991. 'Historical Interpretation at Sovereign Hill'. In Rickard, J. & Spearritt, P. (Eds.). *Packaging the Past? Public Histories*. Melbourne: Melbourne University Press, pp. 142–52.

Foo, L. M. & Rossetto, A. 1998. 'Cultural Tourism in Australia. Characteristics and Motivations'. Occasional Paper No. 27. Canberra: Bureau of Tourism Research.

Graburn, N. 1984. 'The Evolution of Tourist Arts'. *Annals of Tourism Research* 14 (1): 393–419.

Greenberg, K. E. 1991. 'Pilgrims Resist Progress'. *The European*, 11–13 January, p. 12. In Boniface, P. & Fowler, P. 1993. *Heritage and Tourism in 'the Global Village'*. London & New York: Routledge.

Gulf Savannah — Visitors Guide. 2000. http://www.gulf-savannah.com.au/tourism/welcome.html

Hall, M. & Zeppel, H. 1990. 'Cultural and Heritage Tourism: The New Grand Tour?' *Historic Environment* 7 (3): 86–98.

Head-Smashed-In Buffalo Jump. 2000. Head-Smashed-In Buffalo Jump Interpretive Centre. *http://www.head-smashed-in.com*

Holgate, B. 2000. 'Culture Vultures'. *The Weekend Australian Review*, 11–12 March, pp. 16–18.

Hovinen, G. 1995. 'Heritage Tourism in Urban Tourism: An Assessment of New Trends in Lancaster County'. *Tourism Management* 16 (5): 381–8.

Hughes, H. 1987. 'Culture as a Tourist Resource — A Theoretical Consideration'. *Tourism Management* 8 (3): 205–16.

Jordan, J. 1997. 'A Feast of Role Models: Good Practice in Local Government'. *Network News Journal* 1: 6–8.

Kelly, Hon. J. & McGauran, Hon. P. 1999. 'Cultural Tourism — A Drawcard to Australia'. Statement by the Hon. Jackie Kelly / the Hon. Peter McGauran, Minister for Sport and Tourism / Minister for the Arts and the Centenary of Federation, Media release, 19 March. Canberra: DIST.

Kenyon, P. 1999. 'Making It Happen in Outback Australia'. *ABC News Online.* 23 August, Australian Broadcasting Corporation. *http://www.abc.net.au/news/features/stories/kenyon.htm*

Lancaster Heritage Tourism. 2000. *Lancaster County Heritage.* County of Lancaster, Pennsylvania. *http://www.co.lancaster.pa.us/heritage.html*

Larkin, J., Tunistra, F., Stephens, J., Winterton, B. & Mutsuko, M. 1999. 'Themes for a Dream'. *Asiaweek* 25 (45). *http://www.cmn.com/ASIANOW/asiaweek/magazine/99/1112/disney_parks.html*

MacCannell, D. 1973. 'Staged Authenticity: Arrangements of Social Space in Tourist Settings'. *American Journal of Sociology* 79 (3): 589–603.

Macdonald, I. 1999. 'Overcoming Obstacles to Regional Growth'. Keynote Address, Infrastructure and Development Conference, Sydney, 30 July.

Marcello, A. 1995. 'Reclaiming the Outlook'. *In Focus. http://www.gn.apc.org/tourismconcern/magazine/australi.htm*

Morse, J. 1999. Telstra Address. Canberra: National Press Club. 12 October. *http://www.atc.net.au/media/npress2.htm*

Nicks, T. 1999. 'Indian Villages and Entertainments. Setting the Stage for Tourist Souvenir Sales'. In Phillips, R. & Steiner, C. (Eds.). *Unpacking Culture. Art and Commodity in Colonial and Postcolonial Worlds.* Berkeley, Los Angeles, London: University of California Press, pp. 301–15.

'Outback'. 1997. *Trends* 11 (June). Brisbane: Tourism Queensland.

Parezo, N. 1999. 'The Indian Fashion Show'. In Phillips, R. & Steiner, C. (Eds.). *Unpacking Culture. Art and Commodity in Colonial and Postcolonial Worlds.* Berkeley, Los Angeles, London: University of California Press: 243–63.

Pollard, D. 2000. 'Tambo to Isisford'. *The Road Ahead.* February/March. Brisbane: RACQ, p. 41.

'Queensland Visitor Survey'. 1998. *Trends* 17. Brisbane: Tourism Queensland. *http://www.tq.com.au/research/trends/199809/trends02.htm*

Richards, G. 1996. 'Production and Consumption of European Cultural Tourism'. *Annals of Tourism Research* 23 (2): 261–83.

Silberberg, T. 1995. 'Cultural Tourism and Business Opportunities for Museums and Heritage Sites'. *Tourism Management* 16 (5): 361–5.

Smith, V. (Ed.). 1978. *Hosts and Guests: The Anthropology of Tourism.* Oxford, UK: Blackwell.

Sovereign Hill Museums Association. 2000. *Sovereign Hill Ballarat Where History Comes Alive!* Ballarat: The Sovereign Hill Museums Association. *http://www.sovereignhill.austasia.net*

'Stockmen, Ringers and Bickie Bears'. 1999. *http://www.action-graphics.com.au/…y/html_pages/tambo/tamboteddies.html*

'Sunshine Coast'. 1998. *Queensland Snapshots.* September. Brisbane: Tourism Queensland. *http://www.tq.com.au/research/snapshots/sunshine.htm*

'Sunshine Coast Community Perceptions'. 1998. *Trends* 15. Brisbane: Tourism Queensland. *http://www.tq.com.au/research/trends/199809/trends04.htm*

'Sunshine Coast Image Evaluation'. 1999. *Trends* 18. Brisbane: Tourism Queensland. *http://www.tq.com.au/research/trends/issue18/sunshine.htm*

Tjapukai Aboriginal Cultural Park. 2000. *Tjapukai Aboriginal Cultural Park, Aboriginal Tours and Aboriginal Culture. http://www.tjapukai.com.au*

'Travelling the Matilda Country'. 1999. *http://www.action_graphics.com.au/…untry/html_pages/mintro.html*

Zeppel, H. & Hall, M. 1991. 'Selling Art and History: Cultural Heritage and Tourism'. *Journal of Tourism Studies* 2 (1): 29–45.

Cultural tourism *on the* *Sunshine Coast, Queensland*

This case study concerns a destination that is probably not usually associated with cultural tourism, for it does not offer the usual attractions of high culture or heritage. Nonetheless, I will argue that there are compelling reasons to identify this destination in terms of cultural tourism of a broader, more inclusive form that attracts a range of visitors and links dispersed and diverse localities in the region.

Located 100 kilometres north of Brisbane, the Sunshine Coast extends from Beerburrum to north of Noosa Heads and west to Kenilworth. Traditionally, the Sunshine Coast was a low-key, laid-back mecca for domestic holiday-makers, especially from Brisbane. Its main attractions were sun, sea, camping, bush-walking, fishing and boating — a quiet alternative to the bustle of the better-known Gold Coast. However, over the past decade the Sunshine Coast has been transformed into a destination for 'yuppies'. It has become a sought-after cosmopolitan holiday resort attracting significant numbers of interstate visitors, increasing numbers of international tourists and large numbers of holiday home owners and renters. The development of numerous luxury resorts (for example, Sheraton Noosa, Twin Waters, Hyatt Coolum, Netanya), a multitude of apartments and other kinds of accommodation have complemented the development of specialist shopping, cafes, restaurants and nightclubs to re-create the region as a site for conspicuous consumption of leisure, sport and recreation.

The visitor profile of the Sunshine Coast reveals that more than half of its almost 1.5 million visitors come from Queensland, about one-third from inter-state (half from New South Wales and over one-third from Victoria) and the rest from overseas (about 11 per cent). The IVS figures that also include staying with friends and relatives estimate an average annual growth rate of in excess of 17 per cent in international visitors to the Sunshine Coast, from 57 400 in 1990 to 150 800 in 1996 and 187 273 in 1998 (*Trends* September 1998; *Trends* 1999). While the Sunshine Coast ranks fourth in popularity as a Queensland destination, its strength lies in its mix of visitor types and growth in second-home owners.

Moreover, there is a good fit between the lifestyles and range of activities offered by the Sunshine Coast and the ideal holiday desired by visitors (*Trends* 18 1999). Visitors reported that the Sunshine Coast enabled them to 'experience a lifestyle instead of just a place', appreciate the diversity in landscape and enjoy a range of activities. 'You just become part of the whole thing' (*Trends* 18). This demonstration of visitor satisfaction has been important in the Sunshine Coast's development of an image of cultural tourism.

In addition to the so-called yuppie market, the Sunshine Coast has retained its appeal for families by developing a range of attractions and activities suitable for family groups, such as the Big Pineapple, Underwater World, The Ginger Factory, Forest Glen Deer Sanctuary, Super Bee, Ettamogah Pub, Aussie World, Bli Bli Castle, Australia Zoo and the Sunshine Plaza. Above all, however, the Sunshine Coast has capitalised on its relatively high incidence of alternative lifestyle residents and arts, crafts and cultural practitioners by establishing a vast network of cultural attractions, activities, studios, workshops and shopping outlets.

For example, the now internationally famous Saturday morning Eumundi Market offers more than 300 stalls selling handmade arts and crafts and home-grown foods. In addition to local produce and products, there is clothing, linen, jewellery, glass, wood, pottery, toys, homewares and knick-knacks.

It's a browsers' market — wide aisles wind around shady trees and quirky old buildings — and it's a fun market — you can get your face painted, your palm read, your feet massaged. Feast your eyes on artwork and your ears on everything from electronic didgeridoos to traditional bush poetry (Eumundi and District Historical Association 1999).

Considerable effort has gone into making the market the centrepiece of tourism in Eumundi complemented by other attractions (pubs, restaurants and arts and crafts outlets and studios) and heritage buildings. The success of the Eumundi Market (with an estimated million-dollar annual turnover) has increased the appeal of alternative, locally based shopping, looking and eating, and a number of other markets now operate in other towns and villages on the Sunshine Coast.

The promotion of the Blackall Range in the hinterland also illustrates how the area has diversified yet coordinated its cultural attractions as a distinctive destination (Blackall Range Tourism Association 1999). The Range is characterised by rich red soil, farming, rainforest and spectacular panoramas of the coast below. Numerous compact villages dot the hills. Perhaps the best known is Maleny. Described as 'an intriguing mix of rural life, commerce, the arts and cooperative ventures', the village epitomises how lifestyle and cultural production can be promoted. It was also the home of the annual folk festival before its relocation to Woodford. Nearby, Montville boasts more than a hundred arts and crafts facilities and eateries located in a lush, quaint and traditional village setting. According to the promotional brochure:

Montville is as close to an English village as you will ever find in Australia. First settled in 1887 by citrus growers, Montville has a village green between the local school and village hall, tiny timber churches, a three storey timber restaurant which was the original general store, and garden paths meandering through a maze of charming shops, potteries, restaurants and galleries (Blackall Range Tourism Association Inc 1999).

While the hinterland also offers spectacular scenery, national parks, adventure tourism, bushwalking, boating, and bed and breakfasting, its attractions physically overlook the attractions of the coastal strip, generally focusing on the beaches and sea but supplemented by built attractions. In the 40-kilometre stretch between Caloundra (the traditional destination on the Sunshine Coast) and Noosa (the contemporary holiday mecca with its heart in the promenade of Hastings Street), visitors can sample a vast range of forms of cultural and alternative tourism. The natural features and attractions of the area have been most successfully complemented by a diversified yet integrated array of cultural, artistic, gastronomic, sports, nature and educational activities. These have been showcased in a number of festivals and special events, including the Noosa Arts Festival, the Noosa Triathalon, the Hot and Chilly Food Festival, the Noosa Jazz Festival and the Noosa Film Festival.

This example illustrates how cultural tourism can be used to coordinate diverse cultural attractions and activities in order to build a coherent image of an area. In the case of the Sunshine Coast, culture mostly refers to contemporary forms with just a dash of heritage — but this freshness of appeal and orientation has proved popular with visitors wanting a change and a lifestyle holiday experience.

Questions

1 How would you define the use of the term cultural tourism in the case of the Sunshine Coast?

2 Contrast the tourist culture of the Sunshine Coast with that of the Gold Coast.

3 In what ways does a trip to an attraction like the Big Pineapple constitute a cultural tourist experience?

4 Account for the success of the Sunshine Coast as a cultural tourism destination.

5 Evaluate the advantages and disadvantages of relying on a 'lifestyle' basis of tourism promotion.

Robin Trotter

CHAPTER 6 Heritage *tourism*

LEARNING OBJECTIVES

After reading this chapter, you will have an appreciation of:

- the term 'heritage', the ways in which its meaning has changed and the ways in which heritage has been incorporated into a range of institutions, practices and activities

- the governmental, institutional, organisational and industry approaches to heritage and resultant conflicts over heritage

- the differing values associated with heritage and the implications these have for heritage tourism

- the problems associated with defining 'heritage tourism' as a special category of tourism

- the spread of stakeholders and the differing agendas that emerge around the notion of heritage as a tourist product

- the connections between notions of identity and place and how these might be enhanced or threatened by the development of heritage tourism

- policy and strategic guidelines developed to address problems that heritage tourism may entail

- practical responses to address some of the issues and problems that this chapter identifies.

6.1 INTRODUCTION

The term 'heritage' is broadly defined and means different things to different people. This chapter looks first at the term's historical development. The tourism industry takes heritage as a given. However, many of the issues relating to heritage tourism are embedded in a history of changing notions about heritage and what it might comprise. Heritage is also an emotive area with connotations of nationhood that link into personal, familial and localised values and histories. Consequently, when familiar and loved places or objects are opened up to strangers and to commercial activity it is not surprising that confrontation, or at least disquiet, often comes to the surface. Custodians of heritage also may have quite different agendas for the places and objects ostensibly 'in their care'. How these agendas are balanced with those of other stakeholders or interested parties is pertinent to any scrutiny of heritage tourism. Heritage today is disparate and diffuse, as the discussion on its history and characteristics reveals. We move on to examine issues of definition and content of heritage tourism, then explore some of the reasons why tourists might be interested in heritage. This leads to a study of the key issues for heritage tourism: authenticity, preservation versus access and **cultural sustainability**, and value-adding. Consideration of these issues opens up issues surrounding management of heritage tourism.

6.2 WHAT IS HERITAGE?

Before considering heritage tourism, we will explore the concept of heritage, ranging from its historical development and changes to its meaning over time, to a review of some contemporary notions of what comprises heritage in an ever-expanding field. Heritage, like culture, is increasingly being drawn into a globalised tourism industry that uses local and regional markers of uniqueness and identity. Like culture in its broader anthropological meaning, heritage is intimately linked to identity (personal, communal and national) and to core value systems; hence commodification of heritage as tourist 'product' is inevitably fraught with tensions. Moreover, the fabric of heritage in its tangible form is a non-renewable resource that is always in a state of decline and deterioration, albeit at varying rates depending on environmental conditions and the composition of the particular heritage object.

■ 6.2.1 Historical *development*

We first look to a British legacy for an understanding of heritage. An early usage of heritage related it to property that could be handed down. During the eighteenth and nineteenth centuries the concept of heritage as applicable to customs, traditions, language and intangible cultural elements became stronger and more direct.

As heritage became more entwined with culture and associated with the cultural rights and property of wider groups of people, so the concept of heritage became increasingly available to broader classes, races and social groups. This has entailed a movement from private heritage to public heritage, from material property to a more holistic embracing of the ideas and meanings around objects. 'In our time heritage has come to refer to things both more tangible, and more fragile, than the imperishable ideals of our ancestors (Davison 1991:1).

Contributing to this expansion of the field of heritage have been various intellectual and popular movements — particularly romanticism, nationalism and revolutionary democratic rhetoric. In the mid to late 1800s a preservation movement grew out of 'revulsion' to the growth of industry and manufacturing. Central to this romantic movement, which swept across western Europe at the end of the eighteenth and early nineteenth centuries in response to the transformation to an industrialised and urbanised society, was a desire to return to nature, to pre-industrial values and to pre-rationalist philosophies. As part of this movement, preservation of ancient edifices and monuments gave rise to the formation of organisations and the formulation of policy. In 1854 John Ruskin, artist, aesthete and social critic, submitted a proposal to the Society of Antiquaries that an association be formed to maintain an inventory of 'buildings of interest' under threat of demolition or restoration. Early conservation societies were established several decades later: the Commons Preservation Society in 1865, the Society for the Protection of Ancient Monuments in 1877 and the National Trust in 1895. In the 1860s legislation was passed to protect wildlife; in the 1870s and 1880s the British Government enacted bills to protect historical monuments, the Ancient Monuments Protection Act being passed in 1882. These societies were concerned not only with protection of property of historical value but also with ensuring public access to those properties and, in the case of the Commons Preservation Society and similar organisations, protecting a public interest in open spaces of the country for artists, walkers, the general public and even travellers (Bommes & Wright 1982:264–76 and 288–301; Wright 1985:48–56).

The intellectual pursuits of romanticism linked into strong nationalist ideologies and informed a range of folk preservation movements, nationalising strategies and national revivals. Numerous **folklore** societies formed to collect traditional stories, poems and songs and, at a more general and popular level, nationalist iconography and symbols were rediscovered and incorporated into every aspect of culture. Scholars and nationalists turned back to the past, to history, language and tradition. However, where these were found to be inadequate to particular objectives we find ancient materials being used to 'invent' new traditions, new constructions of the past, even historic continuities where none had existed before (Hobsbawm & Ranger 1983:1–14).

■ 6.2.2 **Natural** *and cultural heritage*

The connections between natural and cultural heritage are a legacy of the historical development of heritage. Sometimes the connections are tenuous, sometimes closely linked. In Australia a more clearly defined distinction was a product of the 1970s inquiry into the 'national estate', with the Hope Inquiry into natural and cultural heritage (1973) followed by the Pigott Inquiry into museums (1974). By the 1970s 'heritage' had become a 'shorthand for both the "built and natural remnants of the past"' (Davison 1991:3). Separated but also united, this position was confirmed when the **Australian Heritage Commission** defined its responsibilities in 1975 and described the **'National Estate'** as:

> those places, being components of the natural environment of Australia or the cultural environment of Australia, that have aesthetic, historic, scientific or social significance or other special value for future generations as well as for the present community (*Australian Heritage Commission Act*, 1975).

As the tourism industry looks to new strategies, new categories, new tourist segments, and as cultural tourism, with its broad encompassing of heritage, contemporary culture and indigenous attractions with geographical spaces and the environment, is increasingly promoted, so a new convergence between natural and cultural heritage is taking place.

■ *6.2.3* **Tangible** *and intangible heritage*

If natural and cultural heritage have undergone a form of separation for a period, there has also been an incorporation of intangible cultural elements into the notion of heritage. In a key address to the UNESCO Regional Seminar on Movable Cultural Property held in 1986 the heritage value of intangible or non-physical aspects of culture was recognised. 'A people's cultural heritage is also reflected in non-physical forms such as music, dance, drama, folklife, unwritten languages, scriptures, prose, poetry (Makagiansar 1989:9).

The work of international bodies and of national governments and non-government organisations, in particular the work of **UNESCO** on behalf of minority nations and peoples, has been instrumental in making heritage more relevant in both developed and developing nations and in promoting protection of natural heritage and cultural heritage in both tangible and **intangible** forms. Some important UNESCO recommendations that refer specifically to cultural rights also give more specific and selective definitions of cultural property and/or heritage as:

- 'the product and witness of the different traditions and the spiritual achievements of the past' (1968)
- property of national patrimony that 'on religious or secular grounds, is specifically designated by each State as being of importance for archaeology, history, literature, art or science' (1970)
- immovable items comprising 'monuments', 'groups of buildings' and 'sites' (1972)
- 'items in the categories of zoology, botany, geological specimens, archaeological objects, objects and documentation of ethnological interest, art and literature works, music, photography, cinematography, archives and documents' (1976).

Given such expanded notions of heritage, it is understandable that a National Heritage Conference in 1983 should define heritage simply as 'that which a past generation has preserved and handed on to the present and which a significant group of the population wishes to hand on to the future'. Moreover, this broadening of the notion and content of heritage reveals a shift from a predominant association with an aesthetic system to linking it to a way of life. However, in the late 1980s and 1990s there was another shift: now heritage is increasingly treated as a product. Nevertheless, each of the previous ways of thinking about heritage retains a currency while being incorporated into the latest paradigm.

SPECIAL INTEREST INVESTIGATION
Port Arthur, Tasmania

Port Arthur, the notorious penal settlement in Tasmania, was closed in 1877, and ever since authorities (at various levels and at different times) have made various attempts to obliterate the memory of its brutality. Immediately after closing, the site was partially demolished. In subsequent years fires gutted the remaining buildings. However, by 1913, with an interest in the historical significance of the site becoming evident, the state government acquired the remaining buildings and land and placed the acquisition under the control of the Scenery Preservation Board. At this time there were again suggestions that the convict buildings be demolished to provide scenic views of the bay. This was not done and the Board maintained control until the 1970s when, with a resurgence of interest in national parks and heritage, management was vested in Tasmania's National Parks and Wildlife Service. Over a long period the peninsula has been used as a site for general recreation, historical tourism having a subordinate role until recent decades. Apart from the Port Arthur complex the peninsula has been on the National Estate Register since 1980; however, little effort has gone into protecting the historical landscape or other heritage sites in the area.

In the late 1960s and 1970s a flood of material appeared that dealt with Port Arthur's history. This included books, pamphlets, tapes and educational material as well as a short documentary, *Lagged: The Story of a Convict*, an imaginative reconstruction of convict life. In addition, a Port Arthur Room was set up in the Tasmanian Museum and Art Gallery, one of the motives being to encourage visits to the site itself. These activities — the reproduction of Port Arthur in print, photographs, film and museum displays — became catalysts for 'setting the tourist into motion on his journey to find the true object' (MacCannell 1976:45).

Although the decision to preserve and restore Port Arthur was made during a renaissance of public interest in preserving Australia's cultural heritage, as Jim Allen points out, tourism was the 'fundamental determinant in the management plans of the National Parks and Wildlife Service' (Allen 1976:103).

By the 1970s tourism was already a significant income earner for the state and, although Port Arthur had long figured prominently in state promotions, by the 1970s the relationship between tourism and Port Arthur was 'so strong as to suggest that the vulnerability of the Tasmanian tourist industry rests in large measure upon the vulnerability of the Port Arthur ruins' (Allen 1976:103). The new management plans of the service included development as well as preservation and restoration. A motel, restaurant and souvenir shop already existed, so these were augmented with a car park, reception centre, on-site barbecue, picnic areas and toilet facilities — all central to developing the area as a recreational zone. The intention was 'to facilitate the appreciation of this historic site by giving it a mood of tranquility and quiet relations, matching the more serious aspects of its historical background' (Allen 1976:103). Facilities for interpreting the area were also part of the planning, with the provision of lecture areas, self-guiding equipment and activated displays.

Although various historians have criticised the historical accuracy of reconstructions of convict life offered at Port Arthur, the management and promotional material argues that the site presents a complex, multilayered landscape whose significance is exemplified in physical and documentary evidence dating from Aboriginal occupation to the penal period and up to the present day. Nevertheless, Allen has argued that a result of this project of preservation and restoration (to pre-1877 form) and development has been the construction of a new meaning. Whereas pre-1877 Port Arthur was a 'living hell designed to destroy men's souls', the process of rewriting the site as one for 'relaxation and quiet tranquility' has obliterated the message of a failed system of punishment and rehabilitation to which the ruined buildings had stood testimony for many years. The project of rebuilding not only raised issues of historical authenticity but also created 'a grotesque silhouette which does violence to the past and defrauds the future'.

Allen's focus on developments in the 1970s does, however, need some qualifying. The 1970s did bring a more organised and more profound restructuring, physically and iconically, but shifts in usage and meaning occurred much earlier. During the 1880s tourists began to visit the peninsula; a local resident even donned convict garb to pose for visitors. The level of visitation was such that a small cottage industry in souvenirs and a small private museum were established. Filming of *For the Term of His Natural Life* in the 1920s also brought Port Arthur to greater public prominence. So by 1930 Port Arthur was a well-known, well-patronised tourist attraction, and it continued to attract attention.

In 1995 more than 480 000 tourists contributed $800 million to the Tasmanian economy, the major tourist attraction of Port Arthur drawing up to 250 000 visitors each year. That was until 1996.

(continued)

In April 1996 the violent murder of 35 tourists in and around the Broad Arrow Cafe at Port Arthur resurrected images of brutality and horror. The Australian Tourist Commission, Tourism Tasmania and the Port Arthur Historic Site Management Authority were galvanised into action to ensure a tourism catastrophe did not follow on the steps of the human tragedy. There was also debate about the future of the cafe. Should it be retained as a monument, ceremonially destroyed to encourage a healing process or left to decay naturally? This debate, alongside that over the penal structures in their various decayed, restored and reconstructed states, illustrates the complexity of attitudes to heritage and also has implications for interpretive approaches and how these sites might be used by tourists.

6.3 $\mathcal{H}$ERITAGE TOURISM

This section looks first at a typology of tourism in order to locate heritage tourism within other tourist categories — categories that are, in the main, the product of tourism marketing activities and the search for destinations that will appeal to mass tourist markets or, increasingly, niche markets. We will then discuss what have been marked as heritage 'products' and examine some of the motivators for heritage tourism: the drives and forces that push or the magnets that draw tourists to heritage attractions.

■ 6.3.1 A typology *of tourism*

Heritage tourism is identified, in industry terms, as a subset of cultural tourism, and in fact the distinctions between these two categories are blurred. Moreover, other categories also fit within and between these forms of tourism.

Valene Smith's typology is a useful starting point for this discussion. Her categories of ethnic, cultural, historical (for this read heritage), environmental and recreational tourism are perceived as attracting a different quality and quantity of visitors, and these conclusions provide a critical framework for the concerns of those studying the impact of tourism on host communities. Smith argues that environmental and ethnic forms of tourism attract a 'tourist elite' with minimal host–guest impact. Recreational and cultural tourism, on the other hand, can involve maximal host–guest stresses (Smith 1989:4–6). Nelson Graburn also subscribes to this model but insists there is an interrelation of tourist types, each form of tourism having its own scale of values and hierarchy of special places where some forms are closer in function than are others. For example, ethnic tourism tends to combine cultural and nature tourism and historical (heritage) tourism, a subform of cultural tourism (Graburn 1989:32). Figure 6.1 illustrates this interrelationship between SIT forms.

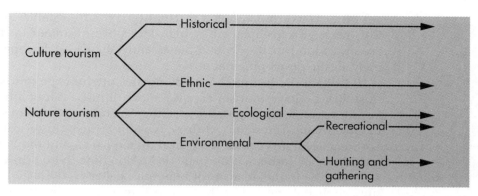

■ **Figure 6.1**
Typology of tourism

Culture tourism
— Historical ——————————→
— Ethnic ——————————→

Nature tourism
— Ecological ——————————→
— Environmental ——
— Recreational ———→
— Hunting and ———→ gathering

Source: *Smith (1989)*

The modern concept of heritage as a tourist destination is a legacy of the Grand Tour of seventeenth- and eighteenth-century Europe and is closely linked to the broader history of tourism — a history that documents changing motives for travel. From travelling abroad for the purposes of education and social advancement, the predominant motivation shifted towards sightseeing and a more generalised form of cultural tourism, thence to a 'scenic' form of tourism (Towner 1985). Subsequently, revolutions in transport and urbanisation, the regularisation of work life and greater availability of leisure time provided the conditions for mass tourism to take off. With heritage now marketed as a 'new' form of tourism that involves a special interest or educational theme and appeals to a narrower and more specialised tourist market than mass tourism, touring motives may have come full circle. Specialist tour operators are now offering special 'packages' for the heritage tourist.

■ *6.3.2* **Content** *of heritage tourism*

We are now ready to look at what heritage tourism might comprise: the places, objects and intangible elements that make up the totality of heritage tourism. From the traditions established by the Grand Tour, the visiting and viewing of historical monuments (such as the Pyramids, the Eiffel Tower or Notre Dame Cathedral) retain a high level of popularity among tourists. Cultural venues that hold and display objects of heritage value, such as museums, galleries and historic houses, also retain their popularity with tourists — especially those with an interest in heritage and/or history. Historic sites, historic precincts and villages, historical parks and theme parks are becoming increasingly popular as tourist destinations. And heritage activities — re-enactments, pageants and 'heritage' celebrations (especially those marking national events) — have multiplied. This phenomenon led, in the 1980s, to an ongoing debate about the 'heritage industry'. Although this debate has been conducted mostly in Britain, concerns are expressed more widely that excessive — even obsessive — attention is being given to heritage and its preservation. British critics have claimed that the whole country is becoming 'one big open air museum, and you just join it as you get off at Heathrow' (quoted in Hewison 1987:24). Similar preoccupations with heritage accompanied by high levels of investment in 'heritage sites' are also found in the United States and Canada, in Europe and, increasingly, in the developing nations.

In Britain, the historic house dominates the heritage tourism agenda. In Australia, heritage tourism entails a more diffused raft of attractions. Some key sites around the nation include the Australian Stockman's Hall of Fame in Queensland (museum), Sydney Town in Sydney (historical theme park), Sovereign Hill in Victoria (historical theme park), and the Port Arthur Historical Site in Tasmania (heritage site). Alongside these prime tourist attractions may be found an array of museums, galleries, heritage homes, historic sites, archaeological sites, historic precincts and villages, historical parks, theme parks and, increasingly, heritage trails. In Queensland, an injection of Centenary of Federation funding has seen $100 million invested in heritage sites around the state to create heritage trails and new venues or enhance existing heritage attractions.

The content of heritage in Australia can be grouped into various themes that are mobilised by tourism as frames for tourist products. The most popular themes are colonial pioneering (represented by a plethora of pioneer cottages, pioneer villages and pioneer artefacts), penal life and institutions, mining (represented by mine sites, mining towns and, in Victoria, a whole tourist region designated as the Victorian goldfields tourist region) and rural heritage (represented by sites dedicated to various rural industries and collections of rural memorabilia).

Another form of tourism especially popular with inbound tourists is indigenous or Aboriginal tourism (that is, tourism that involves viewing representations of, or experiencing, the culture of indigenous peoples. Also characteristic of Australian heritage tourism is a confusion and conflation between heritage and indigenous and/or cultural tourism. As the state increasingly appropriates Aboriginal culture and knits it into a notion of the nation's cultural resources, it becomes another object of heritage tourism. At the same time, many indigenous communities also see heritage or cultural tourism as a potential source of economic independence as well as a vehicle for reconciliation. Some communities, however, reject tourism; alternatively, the tourist products they offer are rejected by tourists and/or the industry. Aboriginal conceptions of culture — and heritage — differ from European positivist notions of culture. In Aboriginal culture, where past and present coexist in the Dreaming, heritage is inseparable from contemporary culture, so a European concept of heritage that centres on cultural artefacts has less meaning for many indigenous communities than has the ongoing observation of indigenous law and lived culture. Hence, the assertion of many indigenous people that their cultures are dynamic, living cultures, not dead systems requiring preservation and museums to contain cultural relics. Here intangible heritage — law expressed in relationships and values, and lore expressed in song, dance, ritual and lifestyles — is more important than material heritage, but at the same time it is more problematic as a tourism product.

Consequently, heritage tourism that involves indigenous cultural sites and activities may be fraught with contradictions. However, we will not undertake a comprehensive discussion of indigenous heritage tourism here. Use this chapter as only a starting point in studying indigenous tourism (see chapter 10 for a more substantive discussion).

■ 6.3.3 Motives *for heritage tourism*

This section considers some of the push/pull motives involved in heritage tourism and the visiting of heritage attractions. Heritage attractions form part of the mix of attractions on offer to all tourists. It is the selection of these attractions from the smorgasbord of offerings that identifies a heritage tourist. Obviously, the more heritage attractions a tourist includes in his or her itinerary, the more that tourist falls into the heritage tourist category. The difficulty is that tourists (and tourist packages) tend to include a mix of activities in their itineraries. Stakeholders of heritage properties also have a range of motives for promoting their sites as destinations. First, heritage — like history, popular memory, commemorations and national celebrations — links us as individuals and as groups into broader constituencies (the local community or the nation). Recognising and accepting the significance of heritage is part of identity making, of nostalgic remembering, of connecting with roots and origins, whether these are familial or national. Heritage tourism may involve a form of pilgrimage (Horne 1984). It may also involve the heritage of 'others', particularly indigenous 'others'.

Sightseeing

Dean MacCannell coined the notion of 'sacralised' tourist destinations. By this he was indicating that some places or objects acquire such a status and reputation that they exert a 'pull' on the tourist. This occurs when an object or place becomes denaturalised and separated out from its everyday existence because it has some special significance. Ultimately, it achieves such fame, or notoriety, that the tourist is enticed into a journey to locate and view the authentic object or place. Once the place or object reaches this stage, it is transformed from a lowly 'site' to an exalted 'sight' — something that the tourist 'must see' (MacCannell 1976:39–56). In Australia, Uluru and the Sydney Opera House have become sacralised 'sights' or icons that both international and domestic tourists feel they 'must see'.

The process of 'sight sacralisation' is not the sole result of tourism industry marking and marketing; it is also the product of the work of an array of conservation and preservation organisations and movements. The work of those early organisations noted above has in recent decades been augmented and built on by the National Trust movement and reconfirmed in government legislation such as, in Australia, the Australian Heritage Commission and, in Britain, Heritage England. In the 1970s Australia experienced the Green Bans, a political movement by various trade unions to protect cultural heritage sites from development. Local historical societies, preservation groups and friends' organisations have also mushroomed since the 1960s and 1970s. National celebrations (such as bicentennial commemorations) not only generate local interest in the past and the nation's heritage that encourages domestic heritage tourism, but also entice inbound visitors intent on participating in celebrations and in touring the pasts of 'others'. All these activities construct, and reconstruct, a frame of heritage around objects and places.

■ **Figure 6.2**
Sydney Opera House and Harbour Bridge: 'sacralised sights'?

Source: *Norman Douglas*

Education

Heritage organisations, the traditional custodians of the past, perceive one of their most important roles as education. Museums, for example, define themselves as non-profit institutions 'in the service of society' with the task of conserving, researching, communicating and exhibiting their collections for 'the purpose of study, education and enjoyment' (**ICOM** definition). This modern-day improving ethic is also manifest in the assertion that museums can offer visitors opportunities for 'elevating awareness' of aesthetic, historical, scientific and humanistic attributes and thereby fulfil three human needs: 'reverential experience, associational space and educational function' (Graburn, quoted in Griffin 1991:16). Theme parks, on the other hand, are distinguished by the specific goal of integrating entertainment with historical preservation, conservation, and public education (Roberts & Wall 1979). Although these objectives appear similar, the priorities given to each within the different forms of heritage — museums and theme parks — indicate different agendas; sometimes so different that certain museum administrators have been moved to disassociate their institutions from theme parks, from heritage and from tourism. However, in today's economic contexts few museums can afford to turn their backs on tourism, hence the recent interest from these institutions in cultural tourism. Suddenly museums are as ready as theme parks have always been to court the tourist and to enter partnerships with the tourism industry.

Engagement with the past

Figure 6.3 shows ways in which we access the past. Heritage, in its broadest application, can follow each of these routes — nostalgia, popular memory, mythos (symbolic/spiritual expressive elements produced by groups of people, ethnic groups or national groups), history and the historical sciences.

■ **Figure 6.3**
Routes to the past

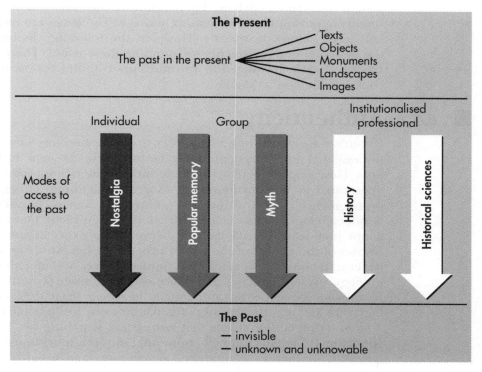

Source: *Trotter (1999)*

It is, however, through individual nostalgia or group popular memory and mythos that most people engage and interact with their past. This engagement may be driven by personal, familial, national and/or broad historical interests. The growing interest in genealogical studies has stimulated a curiosity in the past and has started many a tourist on a journey of discovery and search for family origins. Migration flows, the growth and consolidation of diasporas, and recognition and promotion of multicultural diversity — all encourage heritage pilgrimage. As David Lowenthal notes, 'Diasporas are notably heritage-hungry. Five out of six ancestry searches in Italy are made by Italian-Americans. Dublin is deluged with inquiries from Sons of Erin abroad' (Lowenthal 1998:9). Moreover, this quest for heritage from emigrés or their descendants can also re-energise an interest in heritage at the points of origin (Lowenthal 1998:9). Accessing the heritage of our 'indigenous pasts' is also being promoted to further reconciliation, to enrich our depth of heritage (as Australian Heritage Commission rhetoric asserts) and to develop an economic base for communities (as government rhetoric and some Aboriginal advisors argue).

Among the issues that bedevil tourism, the ones that are most relevant and problematic for heritage tourism are those around questions of authenticity and preservation versus access. The commodification of heritage is also an area of concern and debate. There is little accord over whether tourism represents opportunities or threats to heritage. The issues are indeed complex and, most often, site-specific. However, the following discussions explore the more general arguments surrounding these issues. The case study and special interest investigation provide opportunities for more site-specific consideration and evaluation.

■ 6.4.1 Authenticity

If tourists are drawn to heritage sites that have become 'sacralised', one of the essential attractions appears to be that these are 'real' rather than replicas. However, the extent to which **authenticity** is important to tourists is questioned in tourism literature. Moreover, defining authenticity is itself problematic for as Eric Cohen has pointed out, what is considered authentic is indeed relative and socially constructed (Cohen 1988). Questions also arise about how to achieve a balance between the expectations of tourists in respect of the totality of the tourist experience (an attraction's authenticity, its 'entertainment' value, and the tourist services and amenities that might impinge on authenticity) and those of the community and heritage professionals. Consequently, authenticity has long been debated in tourism literature and it is an issue of particular concern for heritage tourism.

Countering earlier claims that tourists are searching for 'pseudo events' (Boorstin 1971), MacCannell argues that modern tourists are pilgrims on a quest for 'authentic experiences, perceptions and insights'. He suggests, however, that this search is continually thwarted, especially by the construction of forms of 'staged authenticity' that leave the tourist trapped in a 'touristic space' (MacCannell 1976:100–106). Concerns about authenticity can be broken down into two areas: one relates to the product or object of heritage under consideration and evaluates its historical accuracy and integrity; the second is concerned with ways in which authenticity is discussed and debated in respect of the meanings constructed around heritage.

Authenticity of product

Site museums, historic buildings, and heritage sites — the major content of heritage tourism — purport to maintain historically accurate places and objects as evidence of cultural, social and historical characteristics of a place or its people. To ensure the historical authenticity and integrity of heritage buildings, Australia has drawn up the **Burra Charter** as the Australian version of the UNESCO agreement on best practices for the preservation of historical monuments. Articles 8, 9 and 10 of the charter state, respectively, that **conservation** requires the maintenance of an appropriate visual setting, that a building or work should remain in its historical location, and that removal of contents that form part of the **cultural heritage significance** of the place is unacceptable unless it is the sole means of ensuring their security and preservation. Removing heritage material and relocating it in historical villages, precincts and so on, and creating 'zoos' for obsolete buildings is, therefore, contentious and a source of tension between different groups working in the heritage area.

Although 'living history' and 'open air museums' were identified in the 1975 review of museums, also known as the Piggott Report, in Australia as having the potential to 'bring an awareness of the past to many thousands who would never enter a conventional museum or read an historical book' (Committee of Inquiry on Museums and National Collections 1975), these and historical theme parks, historic homes and heritage villages are destinations that typically draw criticism from historians and heritage professionals. Typical of this criticism are claims that these sites misrepresent history and/or that the history portrayed is inaccurate, sanitised, stereotypical and selective; that is, it ignores unsavoury, unpleasant or unhappy events, or tells the stories of some social groups and ignores those of more marginalised and less powerful people.

Authenticity is also a contentious issue in respect of indigenous cultural product, irrespective of whether this involves items of material culture, representations of Aboriginal culture or 'indigenous experiences' developed as tourist products. Product that represents a 'traditional' life can be quite contrary to contemporary Aboriginal life and hence it can, paradoxically, be claimed to be 'inauthentic' in that in implies a 'freezing' of indigenous culture and denies the dynamic and evolving nature of that culture. Items 'made' for the tourism industry could also be described as 'airport art' (that is, art made specifically for tourists). As well, the manufacture and marketing of certain products and designs might breach cultural protocols and the cultural rights of indigenous communities (see Janke 1998).

Authenticity of experience

The discussion so far has been concerned with the authenticity of a product in terms of historical accuracy and perceptions as to how 'real' the objects or place might seem to be, such assessments mainly coming from academics or professionals. There is another level of authenticity, or perception of authenticity, and this relates to the meanings that an object or place may represent, the messages that it conveys or that are conveyed through the object or place itself or the interpretive activities employed in relation to it. The conventional rhetoric of heritage tourism invites visitors to 'step back in time', to 'visit another era'. At Sovereign Hill (see the case study) costumed actors in the shops, cafe, printer's, bars and so on, interact with tourists in multiple roles as interpreters, craft workers and tradespeople. Visitors are drawn to actively participate in the life of the town, even though this is a 'pseudo' or replica town, only the cash exchanges being 'real'. What is being sought is an 'authentic experience' — a feeling that one can experience the past. It is in this context that perception becomes more critical than academic insight.

Perceptions can be shaped and constructed by heritage practices of contextualisation and interpretation. **Interpretation**, in particular, is increasingly a tool of tourism, especially heritage tourism. David Uzzell has suggested that interpretation has been hijacked by the tourism and leisure industries, that it is useful for 'pepping up tired tourist attractions and giving them a value-added component' (Uzzell 1989:3). More positively, Adrian Phillips suggests interpretation 'injects exciting new possibilities' and claims it has 'harnessed the pride of local people in their own surroundings, attracted new investment into old buildings and improved the green environment adjacent to built up areas' (Phillips 1989:131). In living history museums and theme parks, interpretation introduces a theatrical element that can inform, stimulate and interest people in the past. Interpretation transforms heritage tourism into experiential tourism. This may be an illusive experience; nevertheless, the fact that half a million tourists a year visit Sovereign Hill attests to its power.

Lowenthal has asserted that heritage and history are different routes to the past. History is about knowing the past, warts and all, while heritage is about celebrating the past and 'a profession of faith in a past tailored to present-day purposes' (Lowenthal 1998:x). Heritage, possibly more than any other of those routes to the past, is intimately linked with contemporary agendas, hence its appropriateness to tourism as a special interest category.

It would be taking a narrow view to consider these contemporary agendas as only economic. The case study will suggest other agendas.

■ 6.4.2 **Protection,** *conservation, access and exploitation*

Neil Cossons, director of the Science Museum in London, sums up the argument that heritage has to be treated as more than simply a tourist product.

> There is a popular misconception that museums and the heritage — as the national estate — exist for the purposes of tourism. The outstanding collections held in our great museums, archaeological sites maintained by the state, great country houses and enchanting landscapes cared for by the National Trust, are there to be consumed like any other commodity. This is not so. They are inalienable and irreplaceable and their use must satisfy more subtle, altruistic, and demanding criteria (1989:192).

Looking back to the 1970s, however, and to the re-emergence of 'cultural tourism' when it referred to the discovery of sites and monuments, this reshaping of tourism to be more appreciative of heritage was seen as a means of educating a broader public. It was hoped that by encouraging an appreciation of the cultural significance of such places public support for their ongoing preservation and protection might be won.

For some it would seem that the messages of the 1970s have been too successful; the public has been visiting heritage sites in such numbers that irretrievable damage is occurring. Vandalism and graffiti are obvious threats to heritage material, and examples abound. However, overuse causing excessive wear, vibration and erosion, changes in environment wrought by people pressure, exhaust fumes, and increased humidity and compaction can have more dramatic and drastic consequences for fragile historic sites, buildings and objects. As the complaint goes, heritage places are being loved to death. The famous Lascaux caves in France have had to be closed to the public because excessive numbers of tourists have damaged the delicate prehistoric artworks. There are numerous examples of indigenous rock art in Australia having to be protected behind steel cages to discourage not only deliberate vandalism but also physical contact by more 'appreciative' visitors. These are only two examples illustrating the destructive effects of heritage tourism on place sites.

Tom Griffith has documented the impact of heritage tourism on a community. Beechworth, a small town in rural Victoria, has undergone, over decades, transformation from a goldmining town to a tourist resort. With the decline well before the turn of the century, of its economic base, mining, the town turned early to tourism. From the 1950s the National Trust of Victoria became involved in preservation of the town. Beechworth was elevated to the status of a 'historic town' where the resurgence of wealth was to come not from gold but from tourists. In the process the town, which hosted a small museum, itself became a museum. Griffith describes the effects.

> So more tourists came, and they came just for a day. Townspeople felt the pressure of both these changes. But most of all they were affected by the new catalogue of sights that drew the post-war tourist. These modern visitors came not for the climate, lifestyle, or scenery advertised in earlier years, not for the 'beauty spots' so carefully carved out of the surrounding hills and gorges. Instead they were invited into the very town itself, to peer and snoop at people's veran-dahs. The townscape ... took centre stage. Residents and their homes came under scrutiny from the Trust, the Council and visitors alike. Tourists, the 'shy birds' of the 1920s, became the 'rubbernecks' of the 1970s and 80s (1987:86).

Critiques of heritage tourism, however, tend to ignore the positive impacts that such tourism can bring. Often, the tourist value of a place or site is the only capital that can sustain it when other values (economic use, social and cultural values) have declined, been lost or destroyed. Moreover, reuse of heritage buildings, industrial sites, rural structures or complexes as tourist attractions is, in many instances, one of the few options other than allowing such sites to fall into decay, to be demolished, modernised or replaced. Modernisation and urbanisation are as much threats to heritage as is tourism, and in some cases heritage tourism may offer the only future for heritage that is under threat from development.

Heritage tourism can be a vehicle for conservation and preservation of heritage; it can create interest and appreciation that may become a catalyst in its protection. Moreover, the interest of outsiders in heritage may also galvanise local residents to act to protect a place once they realise that the heritage has cultural or historical significance, or at least has proven it has economic value. The potential to reach wider audiences with heritage information and to convey to them 'messages' about heritage significance and conservation is another argument for heritage tourism. It is a means of providing access to people's own heritage and to the heritage of 'others' (where this is appropriate and is offered by the hosts). Heritage tourism may also encourage the development of cross-cultural relationships and exchanges of knowledge; understanding one's past and the past of others can be a pathway to understanding and reconciliation. Aboriginal heritage tourism is promoted by governments as well as indigenous supporters of tourism as a vehicle for reconciliation. However, some Aboriginal people are critical of tourism because tourism programs focus on traditional culture, tend to ignore cultural differences and construct a pan-Aboriginality in place of cultural diversity as well as acting as a form of exploitation.

◼ 6.4.3 Value-*adding*

At various points in this chapter we have alluded to the 'construction' of heritage and to the consequent adding of value. Although it is difficult to separate these two activities from the issues of conservation and authenticity, it is necessary to expand on these allusions and to draw the issues of heritage tourism together. First, heritage has no existence until it is produced or manufactured out of contemporary concerns, interests and practices that draw on the fragmentary remnants of the past that remain in existence in the present. A shard of pottery has no historical or aesthetic meaning until professionals have identified, measured and classified it and given it a 'story', a context and a 'place' in the past and in our hierarchy of cultural and artistic development. If the fragment of pottery remains in the archaeologist's drawer, it remains just that — a piece of processed clay. If, however, it is exhibited, its story related and given a meaning that can then be communicated to others, it acquires an aura of authority and connects viewers with that imagined and imaginary past.

Heritage is thus created through a number of processes and practices. Symbolic, historic, social values are also augmented by an economic value accrued by the professional work the item is subjected to, the ways in which it is framed, exhibited and presented, and by the desire of others to see the object and to know its story. So to lament the commodification of heritage is to ignore and misunderstand the nature of heritage, its production and its valuing. Second, and as a consequence of this 'manufacturing' process, different contributors in vastly different fields and social areas may produce the values that accrue around heritage. So we get entwined, but also contested, sets of values associated with specific items of heritage.

6.5 MANAGEMENT OF HERITAGE TOURISM

Given that heritage is at the heart of cultural tourism and (especially in its physical manifestation) is a resource that forces of nature and of modernity are continually depleting even while new heritage is being created, how that resource is managed is of concern to the stakeholders in both heritage and tourism. Several instruments of that management have already been noted: various UNESCO conventions, including the Burra Charter, and the Australian Heritage Commission Act. In this section we consider further heritage instruments and review some of the ways by which heritage tourism is being, or should be, managed to ensure a more sustainable industry.

■ 6.5.1 Adherence *to conventions, guidelines and instruments*

Consulting and honouring the various heritage instruments, which range from international standards and conventions to national, state and local government policies and regulations, have become increasingly important. In Australia, other key instruments include World Heritage legislation, Draft Guidelines for the Protection, Management and Use of Aboriginal and Torres Strait Islander Cultural Heritage Places, and commitment to the principles of international organisations such as UNESCO, **ICOMOS** and ICOM. Many of these bodies have specifically framed instruments for heritage tourism. Tourism industry organisations have also initiated industry-based guidelines and codes of practice such as Tourism Council Australia's Code of Sustainable Practice (1998). Two recent documents of particular interest for Australia are the Draft Heritage Tourism Guidelines Discussion Paper, 1999, and the 1998 Tshwane Declaration, a document setting out standards for tourism development of heritage resources in South Africa.

The Australian discussion paper sets out the global and national context informing the development of guidelines for 'best practice' for people involved in tourism and heritage places. The objective of the proposed guidelines is to achieve a balance between the needs of tourism and the heritage management sector. On one hand the industry looks for sustained profitability, development of markets, reduction of costs and overheads, and access to heritage resources to produce a tourist 'product' and satisfy tourist customers. On the other, the objective of heritage management is to protect and conserve the physical and intrinsic elements of heritage, to promote awareness and appreciation of heritage, and to provide access to heritage for educational, aesthetic and cultural purposes. Balancing the needs of tourism and heritage is complicated by the need also to balance the often conflicting objectives on each side of the divide. Nine heritage tourism principles are proposed in the draft guidelines:

- using Australia's heritage resources sustainably
- understanding the significance of place and setting
- achieving sustainable business practice
- investing in people, place and setting
- developing active partnerships
- marketing responsibly
- working with indigenous people
- offering service excellence
- establishing a process of continual improvement.

The guidelines provide the operational procedures and processes to ensure these principles will be achieved, thereby ensuring sustainable futures for heritage and heritage tourism.

The Tshwane Declaration is a socially informed document that focuses less on the mechanisms of industry and government and more on peoples and partnerships with its key guiding principles of equity, participation, empowerment and productivity. The document's preamble notes that, 'In the development of heritage tourism products and the presentation and interpretation of heritage resources of significance, the responsible agencies and visitors should respect the community values embedded in the heritage resource being used' (Galla 1998). The principles endorsed are described below.

- *Identity, image and profile:* This principle refers to diversity of cultures, cultural forms, imaging, cross-cultural communication and encouragement of imaging that addresses national, regional and local priorities.
- *Conservation:* This principle covers conservation of tangible and intangible heritage, authenticity of presentation and interpretation, observation of protocols and heritage regulations, conventions and so on, and recognition of the cultural and economic rights of the community.
- *Community participation:* This principle is about ensuring heritage tourism meets standards of community development and is grounded in the principles of the Reconstruction and Development program, respect for community norms and spiritual beliefs, the building capacity of local arts and craft workers and tourism managers, and community sharing of the economic benefits of heritage tourism.
- *Presentation and interpretation:* This principle refers to the integrity of interpretation, principles of training, access and recognition of community knowledge for the representation of cultural identities.
- *Heritage and tourism partnerships:* This last principle encourages partnerships between communities, public, industry and government to ensure quality practices, building capacity and responsible use of economic benefits.

■ 6.5.2 **Community** *consultation*

Although consultation and negotiation with communities (especially where Aboriginal culture is the focus of the tourist experience) is incorporated into the proposed Australian guidelines, they present a more managerialist set of practices than the Tshwane Declaration. The latter document is a model that stresses the role of the community in heritage tourism and promotes tourism as a vehicle for building capacity of communities (community development). There is a stronger sense here that heritage is vested in the communities rather than public property or a resource that requires managing. A push for stronger community engagement with tourism is not the prerogative of nations such as South Africa. Similar arguments are being heard around the globe, some even stimulated by globalisation itself. As Mike Teskey of Community First! Partners (Teskey 1996) states:

> Tourism becomes sustainable when communities:
> - collectively determine what heritage to develop and share with visitors
> - maintain quality in the tourism experience
> - create effective interpretation and tourist facilities
> - direct tourism travel flow
> - dedicate appropriate tourism revenue to care for resources
> - plan and maintain attractive overall environments.

■ 6.5.3 Addressing *vandalism and misuse*

While popularising heritage and making places and objects accessible to broader publics, heritage tourism can also expose heritage and make it more vulnerable to deliberate acts of vandalism. On the other hand, heritage tourism can also be a vehicle for lessening the threat of vandalism through increased surveillance by heritage protection managers as well as by other tourists. Along with broad public education, site-specific management planning is essential for the control of vandalism. For example, sites that are not staffed and are often in remote areas, such as rock art, will obviously require a different approach from that for a managed site. The strongest defence against vandalism is a sense of community ownership in heritage; it is a deterrent to vandals and ensures a more vigilant community with an interest in protecting and preserving its heritage.

■ 6.5.4 Addressing *overuse*

Large visitor numbers combine with other factors such as environmental pollution, vibration from traffic and natural disasters to accelerate natural deterioration; hence management of visitors and intervention to limit other causes of heritage decline and deterioration are called for in the conservation and preservation of heritage. Limiting or avoiding damage from visitor impacts and overcrowding also requires a managed approach informed by research into the impacts and carrying capacity as well as into visitor behaviour. Physical damage to heritage fabric can be compounded by impacts on the intrinsic values of heritage — changes in meaning or loss of aesthetic, religious or spiritual qualities. Communities with an interest in particular heritage may come to feel dispossessed and alienated from it because of a sense that it has been appropriated by strangers, by management bodies and/ or industry operators. Again, site-specific techniques and management strategies are called for that offer a range of approaches, depending on the particular heritage involved. Limiting hours of access, building boardwalks, charging entrance fees or manipulating them to reduce excessive levels of visitors in certain periods and routing visitor traffic to spread wear and tear are some management tools available for site management. **Management plans** that draw on the community of interest — indigenous or non-indigenous — for joint management and/or for site interpretation can contribute to the maintenance of heritage values. Implementing visitor 'protocols' can contribute to the preservation of the physical elements and also ensure that the intrinsic values are not lost or violated.

6.6 SUMMARY

Our lives are enriched by our heritage — natural and cultural, tangible and intangible. It is a source of identity and of sense of place. Heritage gives us pride and pleasure in the various pasts that have contributed to what we are today and explains, in some measure, who we are and where we come from. Heritage tourism draws on these attributes of heritage and knits them into the fabric of the tourist product. Destination sites become, in MacCannell's term, 'sacralised' by the mix of tangibles and intangibles that incite the tourist to travel and to visit such locations. On one hand, heritage tourism can pose a threat to the tangible and physical forms of heritage. On the other hand, it can be a means of ensuring the protection and preservation of heritage. However, it is the intangible heritage values that provide the real dilemma for heritage tourism. Images and meanings that accrue — and are created — around heritage destinations make these sites attractive to a wide range of audiences in ways that can undermine local ownership. Whose heritage values prevail becomes a problem for the ongoing sustainability of heritage within the framework of tourism. The challenge is to ensure that, in the transformation from heritage site to tourist sight, the physical attributes of heritage are not adversely affected or their deterioration accelerated, and that the heritage values are neither lost nor distorted.

Questions

6.1 It has often been said that Australia has no, or little, significant heritage. Would you agree? List your reasons for agreeing or disagreeing.

6.2 List tourist products that might be considered appropriate product for heritage tourism. Draw from the above question, but also look for other examples.

6.3 Look at a discrete location familiar to you (e.g., your suburb, a small town, a cell of suburban blocks or precinct) and identify items of heritage. Remember that there is no particular age, 'look' or 'style' that determines heritage. This will require you to ask questions about why something may be significant and for what constituency it may hold significance.

6.4 Cultural heritage and natural heritage are categories that are problematic from an indigenous perspective. Why might this be so?

6.5 Identify a potential heritage tourism site in your area and evaluate the heritage values of the site. Remember that this will involve asking questions about whose heritage values are involved.

6.6 Devise some strategies that will maximise the heritage values (as you have identified them) and also attract a range of different tourists. Give consideration to the interpretive strategies that might be appropriate for your heritage site.

6.7 Determine the risk potential to your heritage site that tourism activities might present and changes that might impinge on the heritage values. Summarise ways and means by which a management plan might minimise these risks while making maximum use of the site for tourist purposes.

REFERENCES

Allen, J. 1976. 'Port Arthur Site Museum, Australia: Its Preservation and Historical Perspectives'. *Museum* 28 (2).

Australian Heritage Commission and Tourism Council Australia. 1999. Draft Heritage Tourism Guidelines. Best Practice for People Involved in Tourism and Heritage Places. Canberra.

Bommes, M. & Wright, P. 1982. 'Charms of residence: The Public and the Past'. In Johnson, R. (Ed.). *Making Histories: Studies in History Writing and Politics.* London: Hutchinson.

Boniface, P. 1993. *Managing Quality Cultural Tourism.* London & New York: Routledge.

Boorstin, D. J. 1971. *The Image: Or What Happened to the American Dream?* New York: Athenaeum.

Cohen, E. 1988. 'Authenticity and Commoditisation in Tourism'. *Annals of Tourism Research.* 15 (3).

Committee of Inquiry into the National Estate. 1974. *Report on the National Estate.* (Also known as the Hope Report.) Canberra: AGPS.

Committee of Inquiry on Museums and National Collections. 1975. *Museums in Australia.* (Also known as the Pigott Report.) Canberra: AGPS.

Cossons, Neil. 1989. 'Heritage Tourism — Trends and Tribulations'. In *Tourism Management,* September, pp. 192–4.

Davison, G. 1988. 'The Use and Abuse of Australian History'. In *Australian Historical Studies* 23 (91): 55–76.

Davison, G. 1991. 'The Meaning of Heritage'. In Davison, G. & McConville, C. (Eds.). *A Heritage Handbook.* St. Leonards: Allen & Unwin.

Dunstan, K. 1997. 'Death as an Attraction'. In *The Bulletin,* 4 November, p. 40.

Evans, M. 1991. 'Historical Interpretation at Sovereign Hill'. In Rickard, J. & Spearrett, P. (Eds.). *Packaging the Past? Public Histories.* Special issue of *Australian Historical Studies.* Melbourne: Melbourne University Press, pp. 142–52.

Galla, A. 1998. *Tshwane Declaration.* Articles prepared for circulation at the ICOM 98 General Conference, ICOM Conservation Committee Session University and Heritage, International Forum UNESCO, Australia ICOMOS Cultural Tourism Symposium, October.

Graburn, N. 'Tourism: The Sacred Journey'. In Smith, V. L. (Ed.). *Hosts and Guests: The Anthropology of Tourism.* Second Edition. Philadelphia: University of Pennsylvania Press, pp. 21–36.

Griffin, D. 1991. 'What Is the Notion of Access in Museums All About'. In Tonkin, S. (Ed.). *Something for Everyone: Access to Museums.* Council of Australian Museums Associations, pp. 11–21.

Griffith, T. 1987. *Beechworth. An Australian Country Town and Its Pasts.* Richmond, Vic.: Greenhouse Publications.

Hewison, R. 1987. *The Heritage Industry: Britain in a Climate of Decline.* London: Methuen.

Hiscock, P. 1991. 'Interpreting Collections in an Outdoor Museum'. In *Australian Museums — Collecting and Presenting Australia.* CAMA, pp. 135–8.

Hobsbawm, E. & Ranger, T. 1993. *The Invention of Tradition.* Cambridge: Cambridge University Press.

Horne, D. 1984. *The Great Museum: The Re-presentation of History.* London: Pluto Press.

Janke, T. 1998. *Our Culture: Our Future — A Report on Australian Indigenous Cultural and Intellectual Property Rights.* Report prepared for the Australian Institute of Aboriginal and Torres Strait Islander Studies and the Aboriginal and Torres Strait Islander Commission, Canberra.

Lowenthal, D. 1985. *The Past Is a Foreign Country.* Cambridge: Cambridge University Press.

Lowenthal, D. 1998. *The Heritage Crusade and the Spoils of History.* Cambridge: University of Cambridge Press.

MacCannell, D. 1976. *The Tourist. A New Theory of the Leisure Class.* New York: Schocken Books.

Makagiansar, Makaminan. 1989. 'The Work of UNESCO: Protection or Plunder? Safeguarding the Future of Our Cultural Heritage'. In Prott, Lyndel V. & Specht, James (Eds.). Papers presented to the UNESCO Regional Seminar on Movable Cultural Property Convention, Brisbane.

Marquis-Kyle, P. & Walker, M. 1992. *The Illustrated Burra Charter.* Sydney: Australia ICOMOS and Australian Heritage Commission.

Phillips, A. 1989. 'Interpreting the Countryside and the Natural Environment'. In Uzzell, D. L. (Ed.). *Heritage Interpretation.* Volume 1. London: Belhaven Press, pp. 121–31.

Roberts, C. & Wall, G. 1979. 'Possible Impacts of Vaughan Theme Park'. In *Recreation Research Review* 7 (2): 11–14.

Smith, V. 1989 (first published 1977). *Hosts and Guests: The Anthropology of Tourism.* Second Edition. Philadelphia: University of Pennsylvania Press.

Teskey, K. 1996. *Sustainable Heritage Tourism. http.www.csn.net/~tesk*

Towner, J. 1985. 'The Grand Tour: A Key Phase in the History of Tourism'. In *Annals of Tourism Research* 12: 297–333.

Trotter, R. 1999. 'Nostalgia and Dreaming'. In *Journal of Australian Studies* 61: 19–26.

UNESCO. 1968. Recommendation Concerning the Preservation of Cultural Property Endangered by Public or Private Works. *http://www.unesco.org/culture/laws/works*

UNESCO. 1970. Convention on the Means of Prohibiting and Preventing the Illicit Import, Export or Transfer of Ownership of Cultural Property. *http://www.unesco.org/culture/laws/1970*

UNESCO. 1972. Recommendation Concerning the Protection, at a National Level, of the Cutural and Natural Heritage. *http://www.unesco.org/culture/laws/national*

UNESCO. 1976. Recommendation Concerning the International Exchange of Cultural Property. *http://www.unesco.org/culture/laws/exchange*

Uzzell, D. L. 1989. *Heritage Interpretation.* Volumes 1 and 2. London: Belhaven Press.

Wright, P. 1985. *On Living in an Old Country: The National Past in Contemporary Britain.* London: Verso.

Sovereign Hill

Ballarat is the home of one of Victoria's best-known tourist attractions, Sovereign Hill Historical Theme Park. The park is also a nucleus for the heritage-based tourist region known as the Victorian Goldfields. The park comprises an open-air living history museum-cum-theme park run by costumed staff and interpreters. The site incorporates a themed reconstruction of Sovereign Hill of the mid to late 1800s with town buildings (a mix of replicas, reconstructions and restorations), and a walk-in underground mine restored for demonstration. All buildings and facilities are 'working' sites; at the photographer's the visitor can don period costume for a 'period photograph', the theatre (one of the state's oldest) is fully operational with its own productions, the printer prints and sells personalised posters, and the wheel-making and coach-building operation repairs and makes wheeled vehicles for use on the site. The latest addition is an undertaker's establishment that interprets death in the nineteenth century for site visitors (Dunstan 1997:40). In recent years management has added an interpretive centre where visitors are 'inducted' into the history of the area and the activities of the park.

New attractions are always under development to keep the park up-to-date and to cater to return visitors. In 1992 a sound and light spectacular using the most modern technology was added as an after-dark attraction. *Blood on the Southern Cross* re-creates with sound and lights the battle at Eureka Stockade between the goldminers and soldiers and police. This show is marketed both as an add-on to the basic entry fee and as a separate entertainment package with options that include show, dinner and/or supper combinations; bookings can be made through travel agents.

In addition to these attractions, the site operates the Gold Museum and the Eureka Stockade Interpretive Centre. Sovereign Hill also conducts 'experiential activities' for local schoolchildren: school groups attend the park's historic schoolhouse for lessons and to gain insight into school life in the 1860s. On-site accommodation is one of the latest additions to the facilities on offer at Sovereign Hill.

The original conception of the park was as a memorial to the gold rush period of Ballarat's history, and when it opened in 1970 this was the focus of the interpretive approach. With a substantial majority of visitors to Sovereign Hill coming from Melbourne, it soon became evident that a concentration on the history of Ballarat as remembered by locals was untenable. Visitors were not interested in the history of Ballarat in particular; their interest was in the gold rushes in general and in an Australian story (Evans 1991:145).

Following the park's success with domestic tourists, various initiatives have been developed to encourage overseas visitors. One of the early buildings on the site was a Chinese joss house. Instead of reproducing this to the design of the joss house that had existed in the area — a mundane and unimpressive building — the new temple was designed from a postcard of an elaborate Macau temple (Evans 1991:143).

In recent years, special marketing programs have been undertaken to attract Chinese tourists with promotions in China and extension of interpretive programs that emphasise the history of Chinese people on the fields and with some programs catering specifically to Chinese tourists.

As a representation of a nineteenth-century goldfield, Sovereign Hill has been criticised as historically inaccurate and as a 'quieter, cleaner and more orderly' place than the original (Davison 1988:72). Historian Michael Evans has also argued that 'history at Sovereign Hill is not a simple presentation of research data, but a constructed representation of that history, highly loaded with the ideology of the present' (Evans 1991:148).

In response to criticisms of inaccuracy, the park's management insists attention to historical detail and sound historical research underpin the exhibitions. Criticisms of sanitisation or 'cleaning up' history to offer an unproblematised past are more difficult to counter. Nevertheless the director claims that his 'outdoor museum' has started to show 'not only diggers of high degree, but diggers and diggeresses of low degree', to include issues of work, women's roles, birth and death, and (through interpreters) to explore issues such as working conditions, wages and health. He accepts that outdoor museums may romanticise the past but also asserts they offer opportunities to present a process or an object contextually, and in many instances to ensure that it is 'dynamic' (Hiscock 1991:136).

Questions

1 What constraints do you think there might be on a theme park such as Sovereign Hill portraying a 'warts and all' history?

2 There are various approaches to using costumed interpreters in living history museums. In some venues interpreters are required to maintain a historical persona, to stay 'in character'; at other venues the interpretive role is more that of a guide or facilitator who engages not as an actor playing a historical character but as a contemporary commentator and guide, explaining the past to visitors. Consider the relative merits and/or problems with these approaches.

3 Sovereign Hill can trace its precursor as an open-air, outdoors museum back to Sweden in the late nineteenth century, when a model 'folk' village — Skansen — was opened in 1891. Here there were buildings that had been relocated from various Swedish provinces (including a Lapp encampment complete with Lapps, dogs and reindeer), farm livestock, a zoological garden, traditional Nordic flora landscaped around the buildings and, most importantly, displays of everyday life (work and leisure activities including traditional dance, music and art). It was a romantic park where nature and culture were brought together in a conservative endeavour to save that which was fast disappearing as Europe modernised. Might Sovereign Hill be seen as a similar reactive response to change, or might it be interpreted as a modernising move?

Les Killion

CHAPTER 7

Rural

tourism

LEARNING OBJECTIVES

After reading this chapter, you will have an appreciation of:

- the diverse nature of rural tourism and rural tourism products

- definitions of rural tourism, noting that these variously adopt geographic and demographic parameters, product-related parameters and tourist experience-related boundaries

- a general profile of rural tourists, noting the mix of domestic and international development.

The declining fortunes of the primary sector in advanced economies, confronting the impacts of globalisation, and the efforts of third world nations to gain a foothold on the ladder of economic and social development, have served to focus increasing attention on rural tourism. Although rural tourism in third world countries cannot be dismissed lightly, this chapter will focus mainly on the situation in advanced economies such as Australia. We begin by considering the diverse nature of rural tourism, its attractions and products. We outline the characteristics of those market segments attracted to rural destinations with reference to both domestic and international patterns. We discuss the extent to which tourism may contribute to the development of rural communities or compensate for the downturn in traditional means of gaining a livelihood. This discussion leads to an assessment of the role of government and public policy in the development of the rural tourism product, relating this to wider issues that influence the longevity of the rural sector under conditions of structural economic change. Finally, although rural tourism is certainly not confined to agriculture and farming, this chapter outlines some of the developments associated with farm tourism, again noting that even in this apparently singular form, rural tourism embraces a diversity of product and visitor experiences.

7.2   *W*HAT IS RURAL TOURISM? $\cdots\cdots\cdots\cdots$

Rural tourism is among the most polymorphous of all forms of SIT. The diversity of attractions included within rural tourism embrace indigenous and European heritage sites; aspects of culture (especially agriculture); industrial tourism (especially when related to farm practices); educational tourism; special events; ecological attractions; adventure tourism; and more recently established attractions within the built environment such as the Stockman's Hall of Fame at Longreach. More specific emergent special interest forms of tourism such as wine tourism also share boundaries with rural tourism.

The less tangible attractions that arise from the folkways of rural communities, and in some locations the special events that reflect local customs (popular culture's answer to the ancient harvest festival, but also agricultural shows, field days and industry-specific expositions), add further to the rural tourism product. Such diversity represents major opportunities for rural areas that have turned to tourism as a means of supplementing diminished incomes. However, diversity also presents a major challenge in developing a sufficiently differentiated rural tourism product that has the **drawing power** that will not only attract visitors out of urban settings but will steer them away from competing rural destinations that provide a range of similar product components.

■ *7.2.1* **Definitions** *of rural tourism*

Given the diverse nature of rural tourism and rural tourism products, it is not surprising that a single definition of this form of SIT is yet to emerge. Definitions currently employed tend to fall into one of three general categories.

Geographic and demographic definitions

These definitions emphasise the location of rural tourism outside urban areas and frequently employ an arbitrary population statistic to further clarify 'rurality'. In formulating the National Rural Tourism Strategy, the then Commonwealth Department of Tourism (DoT 1994) acknowledged the view of the Tourism Committee of the Organisation for Economic Cooperation and Development (OECD) that 'rurality as a concept ... [is] connected with low population densities and open space, and with small scale settlements, generally of fewer than 10 000 inhabitants [where] ... land use is dominated by farming, forestry and natural areas'. The definition subsequently developed by the Department of Tourism made allowance for Australian rural/urban definitions in seeing rural Australia as comprising 'those geographical areas which exclude the Capital City Statistical Divisions and the Statistical Divisions which surround other urban areas whose populations exceed 100 000' (DoT 1994:4). This then formed the basis for defining rural tourism as 'a multi-faceted activity that takes place in an environment outside heavily urbanised areas. It is an industry sector characterised by small scale tourism businesses, set in areas where land use is dominated by agricultural pursuits, forestry or natural areas' (DoT 1994:3).

Product-related definitions

This category places most emphasis on the range of attractions, activities and other components of the rural **destination mix**. Elsewhere in the National Rural Tourism Strategy, for example, the Commonwealth Department of Tourism (1994:4) suggested, within this approach, that the rural tourism product could be segmented to include such product components as rural attractions, rural adventure tours, nature-based tours, ecotourism tours, country towns, rural resorts and country-style accommodation, and farm and station holidays, together with festivals, events and agricultural education. The department (DoT 1994:4) further acknowledged a segmentation of product components based on location — island, coastal, hinterland, country, bush, Outback and remote. Product-related definitions present some difficulty given the diverse nature of rural tourism. However, the combination of product and location does provide a basis for the development of products tailored for identified niche markets.

Tourist experience-related definitions

These definitions can be equally broad, although they serve to remind us that within tourism there are demand-side as well as supply-side definitions to be considered. Within definitions of this type most emphasis is placed on what the rural tourist is seeking by way of a satisfying travel experience, be it a simple countryside picnic or the opportunity to participate actively in the operations of a working cattle station or to witness sheep shearing. Again, the National Rural Tourism Strategy attached importance to the experiential aspects of rural tourism in noting that 'rural tourism should be seen as offering a different range of experience to those offered in big cities' and that 'the emphasis in rural tourism is on the tourist's experience of the products and activities of rural Australia' (DoT 1994:3). Subsequently, the Australian Tourist Commission, in its study of 'Rural Travellers to Australia' (1995:2) sought to link location and tourist experience in suggesting that rural tourism is 'tourism taking place outside heavily urbanised or concentrated areas, which offers the tourist the experiences of society and heritage (indigenous and/or settlers), primary and secondary production, open space and/or contact with nature'.

Clearly, any definition of rural tourism will depend on the purposes for which it is being defined. These purposes may be to examine statistics for a destination area; to inventory the available rural tourism products; or to understand the experiences sought by rural tourism market segments.

7.3 WHO ARE THE RURAL TOURISTS? A PROFILE OF VISITORS AND MARKET TRENDS

7.3.1 A general *profile of rural visitors*

A review of the general status of rural tourism throughout the mid-1990s showed the industry was dominated by the domestic market. Rural destinations accounted for approximately 60 per cent of domestic visits while 20 per cent of international visitors visited rural areas (DoT 1994:10–11). The Bureau of Tourism Research surveys reviewed by O'Halloran (2000) indicated that more than one million inbound tourists visited rural regions, accounting for $1.1 billion of the total $7.8 billion estimated expenditure by inbound tourists. Some 43 million domestic visits were made to rural areas, accounting for an estimated $22 billion of the total $43 billion spent by domestic tourists.

The inbound tourist market trends appear to hold potential for the further development of rural tourism, particularly from Asian countries. However, there is reason for some caution here. It should be emphasised that because of their relatively short stays, competition from urban destinations and attractions, problems of distance and access, and the lack of rural tourism product knowledge, most inbound tourists tend to stay in only one region for the length of their visit and this region is usually the 'arrival gateway' (Australian Tourist Commission 1995:6). As shown in table 7.1, in New South Wales only about 16 per cent of international visitors travelled to rural areas, while only 14 per cent of such visitors visited rural Queensland.

■ Table 7.1
International visitors who visited rural areas per state and territory

STATE/TERRITORY	% OF TOTAL INTERNATIONAL VISITORS WHO VISITED RURAL AREAS
NSW rural	16.6
Vic. rural	17.1
Qld rural	14.2
SA rural	35.8
WA rural	26.9
Tas. rural	49.6
NT rural	88.3

Source: *Australian Tourist Commission (1995)*

It should also be emphasised that many of those inbound tourists visiting rural areas were close to urban arrival gateways and that 'remote areas must have a truly enticing product with a high international profile for international travellers to take the time and expense to travel there' (Australian Tourist Commission 1995:11). This was certainly the case in the Northern Territory, where more than 80 per cent of international visitors travelled to rural areas, drawn largely by the attractions of Kakadu and Uluru. The changing face of tourism and tourists nevertheless points to the potential of the international backpacker market segment in developing rural tourism.

The domestic rural tourism market has remained relatively stable over the past decade. New South Wales, Queensland and Victoria dominate the this market (see figure 7.1), although expansion in Western Australia and South Australia might be reasonably anticipated with the growth of such niche markets as wine tourism. O'Halloran (2000), however, reminds us that the true dimensions of the domestic rural tourism market are difficult to assess because of the nature of statistical definitions. The resultant data may well include an unknown number of tourists transiting rural areas whose primary destination is, in fact, an urban destination.

■ Figure 7.1
Percentage share of rural tourism expenditure

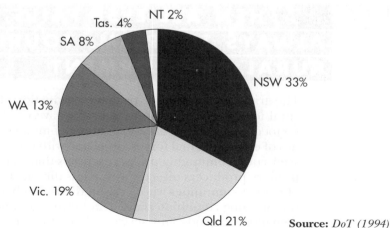

Tas. 4% NT 2% SA 8% WA 13% NSW 33% Vic. 19% Qld 21%

Source: *DoT (1994)*

■ 7.3.2 **Motives** *of the rural tourist*

Although his analysis is limited to the international market, O'Halloran (2000) provides important insights into the motives of those visiting rural destinations that may well reflect those of domestic visitors. Visiting friends and relatives in the region (a dominant reason for many domestic visits to any destination) and 'word of mouth recommendation' accounted for almost 50 per cent of the responses analysed. About 12 per cent of those surveyed had an interest in visiting rural or outback areas, with a slightly smaller percentage listing nature-based activities as their reason for visiting (about the same percentage of those visiting as part of a prepackaged tour). In terms of future growth potential, a number of O'Halloran's respondents reported being on a return visit. However, for these and other rural visitors improvements in shopping facilities and merchandise would enhance their visit (O'Halloran 2000).

Beeton (1999) has linked the motivations of rural tourists to the dominance of urbanisation in Australia. She argues that 'a motivating factor for tourists to visit rural areas is to experience, or at least view, what is still thought of as the "rural idyll"' (Beeton 1999:28). Such a focus has been a feature of both high and popular culture in Australia, reflected in art and literature, and further promoted through film and television. The search for the roots of longstanding folkways remains a powerful motive for domestic visitors, while images from *Crocodile Dundee, The Shiralee* and *A Town Like Alice* remain strong in the minds of domestic and international tourists alike.

The growth in demand for **REAL travel** (tourism that is **R**ewarding, **E**nriching, **A**dventuresome and provides an opportunity to **L**earn) noted by Read (1980) provides further opportunities for the development of rural tourism products as contemporary tourists become better educated and more discerning in their demands for a satisfying travel experience. Such tourists are also more interested in 'green' issues, more health conscious and have a greater interest in specialty food (OECD 1994, cited in Australian Tourist Commission 1995).

7.4 WHEN ALL ELSE FAILS, THERE'S ALWAYS TOURISM: TOURISM AND RURAL DEVELOPMENT

The traditional forms of primary production that have underpinned the rural idyll in Australia and elsewhere have experienced the full impacts of socioeconomic change. Globalisation, combined with the greater uncertainties of environmental forces associated with cycles of drought and flood, have seen rural commodity prices reach less-than-viable levels. This has affected primary producers directly, with a less direct, run-on impact on the viability of rural communities whose raison d'être has been as service centres for the surrounding rural hinterland. Diminished commodity values, and decreased demand for goods and services, have forced many rural communities to confront a period of contraction in service networks and a subsequent loss of population and economic base as residents migrate in search of employment. This process triggers a vicious circle: rural communities face a future of socioeconomic readjustment or become ghost towns.

Primary producers and rural communities have increasingly turned to tourism as an alternative means of achieving sustainable economic growth and development through restructuring, and greater diversification, of economic activity. Hall (1998), for example, has observed that 'tourism has emerged as one of the central means by which rural areas can adjust themselves economically, socially and politically to the new global environment'. Hall and Jenkins (1998) perceive the expansion of tourism in rural areas as designed to:

- sustain and create local incomes, employment and growth
- contribute to the costs of providing economic and social infrastructure
- encourage the development of other industrial sectors
- contribute to local resident amenities and services
- contribute to the conservation of environmental and cultural resources.

The potential of tourism to contribute to rural community development (in its broadest sense) provided a principal focus and rationale for the National Rural Tourism Strategy formulated in the mid-1990s (DoT 1994).

Some rural destinations have achieved a degree of success in using tourism as a tool for wider regional development. However, the success stories need to be weighed against the inherent difficulties that other rural destinations continue to face in seeking a position on the tourist map. These problems are outlined below.

- Rural areas that have been successful in developing tourism are most often those close to large urban centres (and hence potential domestic markets) and international arrival points. Developments in such areas as the Hunter Valley north of Sydney, the Bathurst–Mudgee area in western New South Wales and the township of Nundle close to Tamworth in north-western New South Wales reflect the advantages of shorter distances and travel times for both domestic and international visitors. The potential of tourism development in less accessible areas (often lacking attractions that have strong drawing power) has yet to be fully determined.
- Not all rural areas have a destination mix of sufficient drawing power to attract domestic, much less international, visitors. As Tonge (1992) put it so graphically, 'two snarling dogs and a discarded car body at the front gate of the rural property will not entice urban tourists to leave their cars'.
- Regardless of location, it must be recognised that the contribution of tourism to rural economic development depends upon the extent to which the goods and services demanded by visitors can be provided locally. As their economic base has been eroded, rural communities have come to rely increasingly on external sources of even basic commodities. In this context, the contribution of tourism may not be all that is hoped for, since such areas experience high levels of **leakage** as the income generated by tourism goes to pay for goods and services that must be imported. The real beneficiaries of rural tourism development could therefore be those living beyond the destination itself.
- While the growth of tourism is assumed to benefit rural communities, it should be noted that increased visitor numbers may also result in adverse

environmental, social and cultural impacts that, in the longer term, may destroy the very attractions that brought tourists into the area in the first place. The negative impacts that tourism development may make on the natural environment have been well documented. Less well understood in the context of rural communities are the social impacts that may undermine the attribute of the rural cultural idyll as lifestyle components are commercialised and marketised. The need for careful planning and ongoing monitoring of development is paramount.

- Finally, we would do well to heed the advice of the OECD (1994, cited in Australian Tourist Commission 1995:18) that:

  — not all areas are suitable for development
  — not all communities wish to be developed or are suitable for development
  — not all forms of tourism activity are acceptable in every location
  — there may have to be limits to growth in any one area
  — special visitor management techniques may have to be employed to prevent and/or repair environmental damage caused by visitor pressure.

BREAKTHROUGH TOURISM
Longreach taps into the tourist market

TOURISM BUSH BOOM INDUSTRY

By Frazer Pearce

Tourism in the bush is emerging as one of the boom industries of the next decade and Longreach [in Queensland] is leading the way.

Acting Prime Minister John Anderson said in Rockhampton last week that proactive country towns like Longreach were beginning to tap into a lucrative tourism market which had enormous growth potential.

Under the banner 'The Last Great Frontier', the Federal Government is planning to promote rural tourism to attract the six million Australians who did not leave home last year.

He used Longreach as a success story example of how important tourism was becoming to the bush.

He said last year the Longreach area had generated $48 million through tourism and $23 million by pastoral means.

Tourism Task Force chief executive Christopher Brown said tourism could be the economic saviour of rural Australia over the next decade.

He said the tourism push was a central part of the 10-year plan for rural and regional Australia being prepared by the federal government. He said the industry was delighted the government was recognising the key role of tourism in boosting rural economies.

'Mr Anderson is spot-on in identifying tourism as the key to sustainable economic development outside of metropolitan Australia,' he said in a statement.

'While primary and secondary industry has pursued a relentless historical drive to replace labour with technology, service industries such as tourism have taken up the slack in our cities.

'However, much more can be done to encourage a shift in the bush from economic dependence on traditional industries to tourism and related services.'

The Bureau of Tourism Research estimated that in 1997, international tourists spent $2.1 billion in regional Australia, which represented 30% of total expenditure by international visitors.

Mr Brown said for the full economic potential of tourism in the bush to be met, Australians had to be encouraged to travel in Australia again.

While inbound tourism was booming, there was little or no growth in the domestic market, which accounted for three-quarters of tourism business, he said.

Source: The Morning Bulletin, *Rockhampton, Capricornia Newspapers Pty Ltd (19 January 2000)*

THE ROLE OF GOVERNMENT POLICY PROVISIONS IN RURAL TOURISM DEVELOPMENT

The economic alternatives that tourism offers rural communities have prompted government focus increasingly on rural tourism development in order to generate wealth and employment in areas where traditional forms of primary production have ceased to be an option as the economic main-stay. Although such a policy shift may be viewed as a relatively recent development, in fact government policy decisions have long affected rural tourism.

As Beeton (1999) explains, this situation reflects the diffuse nature of tourism itself, which means that government policy activity over a wide range of portfolios affects the tourism industry either directly or indirectly. Even in the absence of a specific rural tourism policy, government decision making in such areas as transport, land and water resource management, heritage conservation, health and safety, indigenous land assignations and mineral development, among others, has implications for rural tourism. This is an important point since, as Beeton (1999) emphasises, policy decisions in one portfolio may well collide with decisions made in others. Within Australia's three-tier system of public administration, the situation is exacerbated by the fact that rural tourism is of policy interest to federal, state and local levels of government. Further, beyond the public sector there are many **stakeholders** interested in the nature and direction of tourism development whose views may have varying degrees of electoral significance.

To plot a path through the policy maze in order to develop a clear picture of rural policy is a far from simple task. However, as Hall and Jenkins (1998:24) emphasise, 'Rural tourism . . . [is] now invariably subject to government intervention. That intervention can restrict, create or maintain (at times simultaneously because government policies across sectors are not always coordinated or complementary) rural tourism and recreation opportunities'.

Leaving aside the complexities of the policy-making structures, Jenkins (1993) argues that 'tourism policies in rural Australia have been characterised by reactive responses to the need to find new incomes for rural communities in the hope that tourism will promote regional development and assist in restructuring rural communities'. In general terms, government policy has been directed more towards promotional activities than the further development of the rural tourism product. That is, the emphasis has been largely on the demand side of rural tourism, rather than the supply side. The Australian Tourist Commission's thematic approach that saw 1994 as the year to 'Discover the Great Australian Outdoors' and will see the declaration of the 'Year of the Outback' in 2002 exemplifies government's ongoing emphasis on promotion.

The National Rural Tourism Strategy (DoT 1994), an extension to the National Tourism Strategy released in 1992, was an important attempt by government to develop policies of a more proactive nature. Its aim was to lay the foundation for rural tourism development and capture the developmental potential of tourism for rural communities (Synapse Consulting 1992). The National Rural Tourism Strategy emphasised such issues as product development, accreditation and industry standards, education and training, market analysis, infrastructure development, and the role of local government authorities and industry leaders in further developing the rural tourism product. For this purpose the government of the day implemented the Rural Tourism Program (RTP) with funding amounting to $4 million over a four-year period.

While this program was destined to be short-lived, Hall and Page (1999) suggest that even had it continued, overall success in rural tourism development was likely to be limited. Much of the funding was directed at destinations and attractions in the rural–urban fringe and larger regional centres, rather than more remote areas where the need was arguably greater (http://www.dist.gov.au/tourism/publications/talkingtourism/june95.html). Related funding was also channelled through the Regional Tourism Development Program (RTDP).

In the event, the Rural Tourism Strategy and its associated funding provisions came to an end in 1996 with the election of the Howard Coalition Government. The Commonwealth Department of Tourism, which had been established by the Keating Labor Government, was replaced by the Office of National Tourism as a component of a multiple portfolio department. Hence, as Beeton (1999) points out, the Rural Tourism Strategy was effectively operational for a period of some fifteen months, rather than the five-year period envisaged at commencement.

This is not to suggest that the Coalition Government abandoned rural communities completely in their attempts to develop tourism. In 1997, for instance, the National Tourism Development Program was established with funding of $5.2 million for regional projects, although rural tourism was subsumed within a broader categorisation that saw funding available for 'major public tourism infrastructure; tourism projects that sustain the natural environment as a key attraction; the development of indigenous tourism; [and] projects that contribute to national industry coordination and leadership' (http://www.dist.gov.au/media/archive/aug97/279%2D97.html).

In the 1999–2000 federal budget, funding (amounting to $16 million over four years) allocated to the Regional Tourism Program aimed to 'help regional and rural Australia become more "tourism ready" by providing grants for new tourism products and attractions' (http://www.isr.gov.au/sport_tourism/publications/talktour/aug99/pg6.htm). These funding allocations and policy provisions again addressed rural tourism development from within the wider ambit of **regional tourism**, although Tourism Minister the Hon. Jackie Kelly noted that 'the initiatives in this year's Federal Budget confirm the Government's drive to ensure that regional and rural areas of Australia are ready and able to share in the benefits of this dynamic growth industry, particularly job creation'.

DOWN ON THE FARM: FARM TOURISM WITHIN THE RURAL TOURISM PRODUCT

While apparently a more straightforward concept, farm tourism displays the same polymorphic diversity that characterises rural tourism itself. Pizam and Pokela (1980), in describing the emergence of the 'vacation farm', saw it as an active or working property earning additional income through tourism. Attractive as this definition is in its simplicity, it makes little allowance for the growing complexity of the farm tourism sector. Farm tourism now includes a range of short- and long-stay accommodation on rural properties and in bed and breakfast establishments, with varying degrees of contact between the visitor and farm family. Similarly, farm tourism embraces a continuum of activities from active involvement in the day-to-day matters of cattle mustering, shearing, fruit picking, horse-riding and property inspections through to less participative activities where rural activities may be simply observed. Across this range further variations of levels of educational experience are provided to the visitor. Regardless of these variations, tourism is an *additional* activity on the family farm. This has important implications in terms of the time investment required by the farm family and the authenticity of the tourist experience that they deliver.

Essentially, farmers have entered tourism as a means of supplementing fluctuating property incomes. Fry's (1984) studies of farm families in Western Australia confirmed the economic motives identified by other researchers in explaining the emergence of farm tourism. However, the New Zealand studies reported by Pearce (1990) and Oppermann (1998) found that beyond the financial gains from tourism, farmers, and more especially farm women, identified the less tangible social benefits arising from the interactions between hosts and guests. Two important consequences flow from this. First, as Oppermann (1998) has pointed out, despite the initial anticipations of farm families, the profitability of farm tourism operations may not be immediately apparent, especially if the labour costs absorbed by members of the farm family are factored in. Second, the development of relationships between guests and their farm hosts may intrude on the daily schedule of farm operations, perhaps to the point where these become of secondary significance to tourism. This has implications for the delivery of an authentic farm tourism experience.

Farm tourism, well conducted, gives the tourist the opportunity to gain access to the 'back region' (MacCannell 1973). As Grolleau (1993) observes, 'rural tourism know-how is to a large extent imbued in the open-spiritedness of country people, namely their ability to communicate, through words, attitudes, décor and actions, with city-dwellers who have lost touch with the countryside and nature, for whom the countryside is a new source of exotic experiences, of the supreme luxury of the simple things in life'. It is well to note, however, that neither all farms nor all farm families are necessarily suited to tourism. Those farmers who intend to start a tourism operation as an additional economic activity must evaluate what their farm can actually offer the tourist, the area's attractiveness for tourism and the ability of the farm family to develop a rapport with guests. Pearce (1990) and Butler, Hall and Jenkins (1998) have emphasised the importance of the relationship between hosts and guests, the authenticity of the farm tourism experience and the importance of service transactions that will influence the supply side of tourism in the future.

■ **Figure 7.2**
Rural tourism in New Zealand benefits from spectacular scenery.

Source: *Norman Douglas*

In common with other special interest tourists, farm tourists are often drawn from high socioeconomic groups resident in metropolitan centres and travelling in family groups. Capturing the elements of the rural idyll through an authentic experience is the strongest motive for farm tourists. This motive is further consolidated in a society with a high level of urbanisation on the one hand and a cultural ethos steeped in rural traditions on the other. The prospect of budget accommodation in areas within short driving distances is another drawcard. The advantages of farm tourism are summed up well by Baker (1999):

> Almost four years down the track, I am now an unapologetic fan of farm holidays. They have many advantages over the more exotic vacation. They can be close to where you live so the travelling is far less tiring, are reasonably cheap in comparison to any other kind of holiday, and they introduce children to farm life in a relatively gentle and humane environment ... Farmstay venues also have a welcoming, home-away-from-home atmosphere and you should leave feeling that you've made friends. A farm holiday is ideal for a short break ... but it's not unusual for people to stay for anything up to a week ... But perhaps best of all is watching city children realise that their territory has miraculously expanded from its urban boundaries and they are free to roam and explore to their hearts' content.

The future success of the farm tourism sector requires a level of planning and coordination. This is the principal objective of the Australian Farm and Country Tourism Association, founded as a national organisation in 1987 (http://www.farmwide.com.au/nff/afact/AFACT.htm). Prior to this, separate state organisations existed in New South Wales, Queensland, South Australia, Western Australia and Victoria. AFACT has achieved some success in formulating a mission statement and strategic plan through to 2003 centred largely on an international marketing campaign, training and education, and product development. National membership of the organisation includes some 350 farms and stations. Although the true size of the farm tourism industry is difficult to determine, AFACT estimates that there are at least a further 1000 operators who are not affiliated.

SPECIAL INTEREST INVESTIGATION
Rural tourism in the rice paddies

TOURISM — COMPATIBLE WITH OTHER INDUSTRIES

The successful marketing of Leeton's produce has been good for both the people on the land and local industries. It has also put Leeton on the map for Japanese tourists.

Leeton is situated in the heart of the Murrumbidgee Irrigation Area in southern New South Wales. The rich irrigation environment, together with a wealth of agricultural products, gives the town a strong economic base.

Gus Dalitz was employed as tourism manager by Leeton Shire Council 16 years ago after it began to recognise the potential of rural tourism.

'In the early stages we promoted Leeton as an ideal base for group tours to the Murrumbidgee Irrigation Area and assisted schools and domestic tour operators in organising itineraries for the tours,' Gus said.

'We were fortunate that guided tours were available at rice and fruit processing plants at Leeton and we were able to build up a network of rice, fruit and vegetable farmers who were prepared to accept group tours on a fee-for-service basis.

'Leeton is viewed as Australia's rice capital. So, as interest in Australian rice increased, particularly from Japan, tour operators needed someone in Leeton to organise the itineraries. The Leeton Visitors Centre took on this role.

'The success of the tourism industry in Leeton has been in getting the tourism marketing mix right, packaging, marketing and coordinating products that already exist, including the farms, the rice and the fruit processing plants, and being able to sell them as the real rural experience.

'We have been particularly successful in selling rice-related group tours from Japan. Inbound rice-based tourism has exploded, with an increase in 1994 of 500 per cent over the previous year.

'We've had people from all levels of agriculture from the individual Japanese rice grower, right through to Japanese rice retailers and wholesalers.'

For rice growers it's an opportunity to promote the quality of their rice in the hope word gets back to Japanese officials about Leeton's disease-free, top quality product — particularly important given Japan is easing restrictions on imports.

(*continued*)

The tours take in the various agricultural points of Leeton. A typical two-day tour would include lunch at a local restaurant, followed by a technical visit to a farm or the Yanco Agricultural Institute. After spending a night in a local motel, the tourists are taken to the Rice Growers cooperative Visitors Centre at the Leeton rice mill which includes bilingual displays and videos as well as offering tastings of rice cooked in the traditional Japanese way.

To cater for the range of interests a number of product variations and options have been developed.

'The tour can be varied to suit the specific needs of the group. We might visit a vegetable farm, orchard or flower farm and as interest has broadened so has our ability to service these tours,' Gus said.

'I think the winning touch is in the people exchange which occurs during the visit. The highlight for the guests is when they go to a rice farm and meet with their Australian counterparts. The discussions which occur via the interpreter are always lively. I've never met a farmer yet who doesn't like talking about what they do.'

The thing that really sets rural tourism apart from all the other kinds of tourism is the unique interpersonal relationship. Margaret and Bruce Lang, who run a mixed farm with rice, sheep and cattle, accommodate some of the rice tours on their property.

'Farm tourism keeps us on our toes. The visitors, especially the Japanese tourists, can ask very technical questions,' Margaret Lang said.

'Social contacts with Japanese visitors are great. We're often the only contact they have with a real Australian farming family. We are their only real link with rural Australia.

'We've had people stay from all over the world and it's a great way for us to learn about other countries.

'The experience is good for other local farmers as well, because they meet the Japanese market and better understand their needs. We are all continually learning how to market our farms better as tourism ventures.

'A coordinated approach to rural tourism in Leeton has meant that more tourist dollars are distributed around the town.'

Source: *DIST, Cox Inall Communications (1996)*

7.7 ISSUES AND CHALLENGES: THE FUTURE OF RURAL TOURISM

Government at all levels has identified tourism's potential in developing and diversifying rural communities as a solution to the contemporary problems of economic restructuring. The realisation of this potential, however, will require both government and the tourism industry itself to address a range of complex issues and challenges. The most important are outlined below.

Geoffrey Blainey (1983) identified the 'tyranny of distance' as having exerted a profound impact on the human occupation of Australia, and this view is no less applicable to the development of rural tourism. Their remoteness is undoubtedly part of the attraction of rural areas for some tourists. For others, distance (both actual and perceived) has a notably dampening effect on tourism demand and the gravitational pull of rural attractions, especially among inbound visitors on relatively short stays and drawn to the more accessible attractions of urban arrival gateways.

The natural environments of rural locations provide a backdrop for the development of social and cultural attractions. While the natural environment is a major attraction for some rural visitors, others hold perceptions of an environment that is often harsh, dry, dusty and difficult, with considerable distances between attractions. Such images are not dispelled by necessary warnings provided to tourists concerning the need to carry water and to be prepared for a range of environmental hazards and possible vehicle failure in isolated areas on access routes of variable standard. The rural environment is often uncertain; drought and flooding are often very real prospects. While the experience of widespread flooding may have an identifiable drawing power, this soon dissipates among tourists who spend their vacation stranded in an isolated area waiting for floodwaters to subside.

Rural tourists are generally not mass tourists and this reduces pressures relating to carrying capacity; the natural environment can more easily sustain smaller visitor numbers. However, this is no reason to overlook the potential of tourism activities to exert detrimental impacts on environments, particularly in arid and semi-arid areas, that are no less fragile than coastal ecosystems.

The **carrying capacity** of infrastructure and the built environment require equal consideration. In rural areas and properties that may already be experiencing water shortages as a result of drought, providing water for drinking and bathing for even a small number of visitors may be quite difficult, particularly where tourists residing in better-serviced urban locations have developed a penchant for lengthy showers after a hot and dusty journey! Country road systems that are well able to carry local traffic may 'pothole' under the pressure of increased tourist flow. Issues of carrying capacity are of equal concern to local food outlets and accommodation, as well as to some attractions themselves.

The development of attractions, services and infrastructure in rural locations poses problems concerning available capital for investment purposes. It is worth repeating that individual property owners and rural communities alike have turned to tourism as a solution to their economic struggles. Despite a somewhat fanciful view that 'getting into tourism' is readily affordable by simply turning disued shearers' quarters into a thriving B&B, such development is far from cheap. The family's struggles to maintain a reasonable livelihood may have already eroded investment capital. In the absence of locally available capital, rural destinations are then exposed to external sources. Although these may well extend the range and quality of available products, such investment represents a further form of leakage as the financial, and sometimes job creation, benefits of tourism development flow to external investors and shareholders.

Rural areas offer a diverse product. Diversity can be considered a strength of rural destinations that are seen to offer 'something for everyone'.

However, diversity is also a source of considerable weakness. There is a lack of product specialisation to offer to identified niche markets among destinations that in many respects begin to exhibit a certain 'sameness'. Clearly, rural areas require a significantly 'different' or even 'unique' attraction before tourists will be motivated to visit.

Given the multifaceted nature of the rural tourism product, and the limitations that this places on drawing power, the future development of rural tourism will require more effective packaging to enhance drawing power if tourists are to be encouraged 'to stay an extra day'. Effective packaging itself depends on a level of cooperation between tourism operators and regional tourism authorities that has often been negated by parochial interests struggling to achieve market share.

The development of more specialised tourism products carries with it a potential loss of identity for rural tourism in its generic form as more specific niche markets open up for attractions that coincidentally occur in rural environments. Niche marketing, for example of wine tourism, environmental and ecotourism attractions and the like, undoubtedly serves to strengthen the drawing power of some rural destinations, but at the expense of those areas that lack this more specific product.

Rural tourism operates within an intensely competitive environment. The diversity of rural tourism products is the basis of a competitive battle between rural destinations. In turn, both separately and collectively, rural destinations must compete for a share of the domestic and inbound markets against urban destinations that enjoy a wider range of attractions, services and infrastructure bolstered by coastal locations that themselves have an entrenched position in the minds of visitors. Additionally, rural destinations are forced to compete against both rural and urban attractions overseas. Rural communities throughout Europe, Canada and the United States have been equally aware of the developmental potential of tourism. Nations in the third world also offer a growing range of rural tourism products that have the added appeal of cultural diversity and authenticity for those seeking REAL tourism.

Rural tourism has lacked strong industrial organisation. Industry groups such as AFACT and regional tourism authorities continue to recruit, but not all rural tourism operators are members of such organisations. This continues to have implications for the formulation and maintenance of appropriate industry standards; the development of comparable pricing structures and reservations systems; the resources available for industry promotion and the success of promotional strategies; and the ability of rural tourism operators to act as a significant pressure group able to influence government policy decisions.

A singular approach to government policy decision making is likely to prove inadequate given the multifaceted nature of rural tourism. While successive governments at all levels have enacted policies aimed at enhancing rural tourism development, they have frequently disregarded the fact that policy decisions in other portfolio areas may have equal or greater impacts on the future prospects of the industry. Competing and sometimes conflicting policy decisions in such areas as land, forestry, fisheries and water management, heritage protection, transport, taxation and regional economic development have at times been in conflict with rural tourism objectives that persist in their established focus on promotional activities.

The rural tourism industry remains in the hands of a large number of small business operators who often lack the expertise to operate a successful venture. Although government and industry groups have made moves to assist operators through advisory services both before and after the establishment of their businesses, much remains to be done at the fundamental level of effective tourism planning. Local government authorities that preside over most rural destinations themselves often lack the necessary planning expertise to achieve successful and sustainable tourism outcomes. At the level of individual operations, fundamental expertise in the provision of hospitality services is often lacking, or has been acquired only through trial and error. Hospitality is essential to a satisfying travel experience. It requires careful planning and consideration in order to ensure a balance between adequate service and the authenticity so important to rural tourists in their interactions with property owners, farm families and members of the host community.

7.8 SUMMARY

A definition of rural tourism may be based on geography and location, products supplied or tourism experiences. A product-oriented definition must encompass a broad range of destination mix components (cultural, heritage, environmental and so on) as rural tourism has come to share common boundaries with attractions that now have more specialised niche markets. Tourism experience–related definitions should extend to rural people as well as rural places, since it is the authenticity of the people as well as the places that attracts rural tourists. Both myth and reality attract these tourists, who in some cases have been motivated by rural images presented by the media of popular culture, and in others by a search for a rural idyll.

Effective rural tourism development relies on a clear recognition of the special needs of rural areas relative to the more heavily developed and promoted coastal tourism fringe. Apart from being the location of major gateways for the entry of inbound tourists, this coastal fringe is also the place of residence of the majority of the domestic rural tourism market. Rural destinations most likely to succeed in diversifying their economies through tourism development are those in close proximity to the coastal fringe, but they too must compete against these entrenched attractions. The distance between markets and rural attractions exerts a dampening influence on tourist demand unless the rural destination has outstanding features with their greater drawing power.

Governments and regional tourism authorities have a major role to play in the planning, development and marketing of rural destinations and their tourism products. Traditionally, these authorities have been more concerned with promotion than with product development. Regions and local communities that have turned to tourism as compensation for declining rural fortunes need community-specific research of tourism markets and the impacts associated with tourism development in order to develop a successful product. However, it is necessary to acknowledge that not all rural areas and their communities are suited to tourism. In planning the rural tourism destination mix, key considerations are remoteness of location, access issues, the need for rural capital and adequate labour to operate tourism ventures, the need to upgrade accommodation and infrastructure to cater for tourists and the need for adequate training in hospitality service delivery. These issues have specific ramifications for farm tourism operations, often more costly in time and money than first envisaged by the farming family, who are themselves a critical element in the delivery of an authentic tourist experience. The rural destination mix must be planned and developed in such a way as not to detract from the authenticity of the rural tourism experience sought by visitors in the search for REAL tourism.

At times contradictory government policies and inadequate resources and expertise are further impediments to the realisation of the potential of tourism growth for rural communities. However, increasing recognition of the need for rural tourism product development, provision of advice and financial incentives, together with the promotional activities of federal, state and regional tourism authorities and industry bodies themselves, gives some cause for optimism. Tourism may provide a restructured economic base for those rural communities that have few alternatives in the face of the forces of change.

Questions

7.1 Develop a statement that defines what you understand by 'rural tourism'. Critically review this statement. In terms of the three categories of definitions discussed in this chapter, is your statement geographic/demographic-related, product-related or tourist experience-related?

7.2 Discuss the view that rural tourism shares aspects of many other forms of special interest tourism. Relate your discussion to examples drawn from a rural destination with which you are familiar.

7.3 What factors might explain the relative dominance of the domestic market over the inbound market for rural tourism products?

7.4 Discuss the view that those destinations in close proximity to major urban centres are most likely to benefit from rural tourism development.

7.5 To what extent can rural tourism be regarded as a tool for rural economic, social and political development?

7.6 Working in a group of three, compile a listing of government policies and associated legislation that influence the nature and direction of rural tourism development. One member of the group should focus on federal government, another on state or territory government, and another on local government.
Comment on the policy aspects that overlap and those that may be seen as in conflict.

7.7 Using the material presented in the Leeton rice farm study in this chapter, discuss the view that economic returns may not be the only positive impacts associated with rural tourism development.

7.8 Visit a rural destination. Compile a list of the key issues and problems that would need to be resolved before the destination is able to realise its full potential in terms of rural tourism development. What approaches would you recommend for resolving the issues and problems you identify?

7.9 Log on to the AFACT website (http://www.farmwide.com.au/nff/afact/AFACT.htm). Critically review AFACT's mission statement. To what extent does this statement seek to address some of the major issues confronting rural tourism in general, and farm tourism in particular?

REFERENCES

Australian Tourist Commission. 1995. 'Rural Travellers to Australia'. Product Development. Woolloomooloo: Australian Tourist Commission.

Baker, C. 1999. 'Go Free Range'. *The Australian Magazine*, 4–5 December, pp. 41–5.

Beeton, S. 1999. 'Rural (Tourism) Policy: Cross-sectoral Land-use Regulation and Government Policy in Australia'. In Daugherty, C. M. (Ed.). *Proceedings of Sustaining Rural Environments: Issues in Globalization, Migration and Tourism.* Department of Geography and Public Planning. Flagstaff, Arizona: Northern Arizona University.

Blainey, G. 1983. *The Tyranny of Distance: How Distance Shaped Australia's History.* South Melbourne: Sun Books.

Butler, R., Hall, C. M. & Jenkins, J. (Eds.). 1998. *Tourism and Recreation in Rural Areas.* Chichester, UK: John Wiley & Sons.

Claremont Books. 1999. *Discover Queensland.* Melbourne: Penguin.

Commonwealth Department of Tourism. 1994. National Rural Tourism Strategy. Canberra: AGPS.

Commonwealth Department of Industry, Science and Tourism. 1996. *Cultivating Rural Tourism.* Cox Inall Communications Pty Ltd as an initiative under the Rural Tourism Program.

Dickman, S. 1989. *Tourism: An Introductory Text.* Caulfield: Edward Arnold.

Fry, M. 1984. 'Farm Tourism in Western Australia: A Report of a Pilot Study'. Perth: Rural and Allied Industries Council.

Grolleau, H. 1993. 'Marketing Quality Rural Tourism; Introduction — Putting Feelings First'. *Leader Magazine* 4, Autumn.

Hall, C. M. 1998. *Introduction to Tourism: Development, Dimensions and Issues.* Third Edition. South Melbourne: Addison Wesley Longman Australia.

Hall, C. M. & Jenkins, J. 1998. 'Rural Tourism and Recreation Policy Dimensions'. In Butler, R., Hall, C. M. & Jenkins, J. (Eds.). *Tourism and Recreation in Rural Areas.* Chichester, UK: John Wiley & Sons.

Hall, C. M. & Page, S. J. 1999. *The Geography of Tourism and Recreation: Environment, Place and Space.* London: Routledge.

Jenkins, J. M., 1993. 'Tourism Policy in Rural New South Wales: Policy and Research Priorities'. *GeoJournal* 29 (3): 281–90.

MacCannell, D. 1973. 'Staged Authenticity: Arrangements of Social Space in Tourist Settings'. *American Journal of Sociology* 79 (3): 357–61.

O'Halloran, M. 2000. 'Rural Tourism in Australia: An Expert Perspective'. Paper presented at CAUTHE Conference, School of Tourism and Hospitality, La Trobe University, Mt Buller.

Oppermann, M. 1998. 'Farm Tourism in New Zealand'. In Butler, R., Hall, C. M. & Jenkins, J. (Eds.). *Tourism and Recreation in Rural Areas.* Chichester, UK: John Wiley & Sons.

Pearce, P. 1990. 'Farm Tourism in New Zealand: A Social Situation Analysis'. *Annals of Tourism Research* 17: 337–52.

Pizam, A. & Pokela, J. 1980. 'The Vacation Farm: A New Form of Tourism Destination'. In Hawkins, D. E., Shafer, E. L. & Rovelstad, J. M. *Tourism Marketing and Management Issues.* Washington, DC: George Washington University.

Read, S. E. 1980. 'A Prime Force in the Expansion of Tourism in the Decade: Special Interest Travel'. In Hawkins, D. E., Shafer, E. L. & Rovelstad, J. M. *Tourism Marketing and Management Issues.* Washington, DC: George Washington University.

Synapse Consulting. 1992. *Australian Farm and Country Tourism Industry Workshop Proceedings.* Brisbane: Synapse Consulting.

Tonge, R. 1992. Rural Tourism Seminar, Monto, Queensland, 21 November.

Waltzing along the
Matilda Highway

A vivid profile of the diverse components of the destination mix that comprise the rural tourism product exists along the Matilda Highway through western Queensland. Completed in the mid-1990s, the Matilda Highway runs from the New South Wales border south of Cunnamulla through to Karumba on the Gulf of Carpentaria (see figure 7.3). The development of rural tourism along the Matilda Highway has involved a series of promotion and product-branding measures that began in 1987, when the separate regions of western Queensland joined forces to form the Outback Tourism Authority. This regional approach, supported by a product-branding strategy using a logo featuring the profile of a swagman carrying his 'matilda' (a blanket roll used for sleeping purposes), acknowledged that the Outback region lacked a major attraction with sufficient drawing power to pull in tourists. The Matilda Highway strategy reflects the importance of packaging in the development of rural tourism products. Supporting this development the then Queensland Tourist and Travel Corporation (now Tourism Queensland) and the Royal Automobile Club of Queensland released a special Matilda Highway motoring guide, and signs along the Highway (featuring the swagman logo) were upgraded. Figure 7.4 provides a generalised inventory of some of the rural products, together with travelling distances between the major centres located along the 1600-kilometre Matilda Highway.

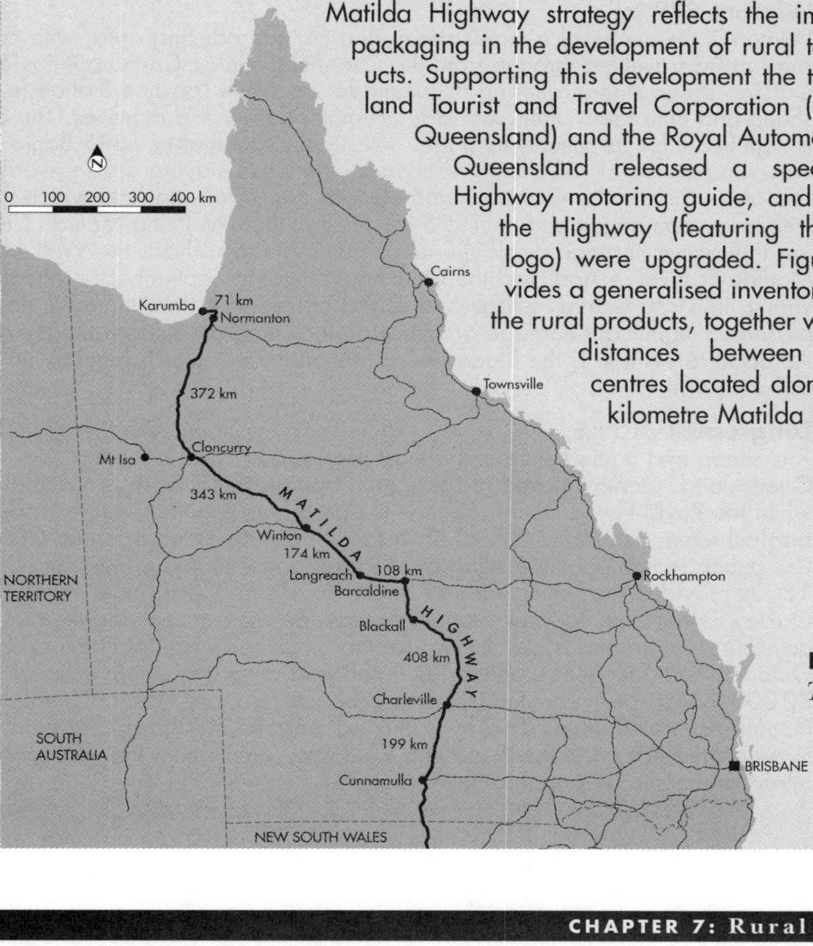

■ **Figure 7.3**
The Matilda Highway

■ **Figure 7.4** *From Karumba to Cunnamulla: a generalised inventory of rural products along the Matilda Highway*

Karumba: 1675 km
The centre of the Gulf prawning industry and barramundi fishing. A wetlands area with saltwater crocodiles and bird life including brolgas.

Normanton: 1604 km
The centre of Gulf Savannah and terminus of Normanton to Croydon railway. The *Gulflander* tourist train is a feature, as are abundant wildlife and bird watching opportunities. Dorunda Station (197 km NE) provides accommodation and fishing for barramundi and saratoga.

Cloncurry: 1232 km
A former mining town noted for copper reserves discovered by McKinlay in 1861 while searching for the explorers Burke and Wills. Cloncurry was Australia's largest copper mine in World War I, following which the cattle industry became more important. In 1920 Qantas established an air link between Cloncurry and Winton, and in 1928 Cloncurry became the first base for the Royal Flying Doctor Service (RFDS). About 118 km west of Cloncurry is Mount Isa, a major mining city. Recently, significant fossil finds have been made at Riversleigh.

Winton: 889 km
Winton is the centre of a major sheep and cattle producing area, with cattle road trains travelling through from the Channel Country. Carisbrooke is a working sheep station offering accommodation, while Lorraine Station (a sheep and emu farm) offers farmstay accommodation and activities. The area is significant for its cultural heritage, notably the fact that in 1895 Banjo Paterson penned his 'Waltzing Matilda' poem while staying on Dagworth Station — the nearby Combo waterhole was the 'billabong' into which the luckless swagman jumped. In 1998 the $3.3 million Waltzing Matilda Centre (an interactive heritage display) was opened. The town hosts the Waltzing Matilda Festival in April and the Outback Festival in September (in alternate years). In 1920 Qantas established its first office in Winton, the town has preserved significant heritage architecture, including an outdoor theatre. Adjacent to Winton is the Bladensberg National Park, which features a self-drive trail.

Longreach: 715 km
This sheep and cattle centre is the most prosperous town in western Queensland. Qantas moved to Longreach from its initial base in Winton, while the Royal Flying Doctor Service is based here together with a flying surgical team, as are the School of Distance Education and a former Cobb & Co. coach station. Cattle rustling by the bushranger Captain Starlight in the 1800s provided the setting for Rolf Boldrewood's *Robbery Under Arms*. Oakley Station and Toobrac Station provide farmstay accommodation and day tours. Longreach is best known for the Stockman's Hall of Fame and Outback Heritage Centre opened in 1988 and attracting approximately 70 000 tourists per year. Tourism now accounts for more than double the income generated in this area by traditional pastoral industries, and plans are in progress to develop the Australian Centre to complement the heritage attractions of the Stockman's Hall of Fame.

Barcaldine: 607 km
This pastoral and railway town was a former base for Cobb & Co. coach operations. It is best known as the site of the 'Tree of Knowledge', the focal point of the 1891 strike by shearers that was instrumental in the formation of the Australian Labor Party. Barcaldine contains the Australian Heritage Workers Centre. North Delta Station provides accommodation on a working Outback property.

Blackall: 500 km
The Wool Scour is a major heritage attraction and display illustrating the area's focus on pastoral activities.

Charleville: 199 km
Charleville is the terminus of the *Westlander* rail service and is located in the heart of 'mulga' country. It is a major sheep and cattle district within western Queensland.

Cunnamulla: 0 km
Cunnamulla is the starting point of the Matilda Highway journey. This area was explored by Mitchell in 1846 and Kennedy in 1847, and became a major centre of the Queensland sheep and wool industries. It is the largest wool-loading station on the Queensland railway network.

Source: *Details compiled from Claremont Books (1999)*

The celebration of 2002 as the Year of the Outback will contribute to a greater awareness of the tourism products that destinations along the Matilda Highway have to offer. The collective, packaged approach to tourism development throughout this area has served to strengthen regional drawing power. However, this will not in itself overcome the considerable distances to be travelled in order to enjoy the rural tourism experience of such areas.

Questions

1 Using the Matilda Highway as a case study, analyse the view that rural tourism is 'polymorphic'.

2 The destination mix comprises attractions, amenities, activities, access and accommodation (sometimes referred to as the 5 A's) (see, for example, Dickman 1989). How can the destination mix be applied to the Matilda Highway? What components of the destination mix provide the area with tourist drawing power? What components do you think might still be problematic for the development of tourism throughout this area?

Chris Wood

CHAPTER 8
Educational
tourism

LEARNING OBJECTIVES

After reading this chapter, you will have an appreciation of:

■ the definition of educational tourism based on the unique and essential qualities of education, and the way in which educational tourism views knowledge, perception, understanding and imagination

■ how commodity tourism differs from educational tourism

■ how educational tourism avoids stereotypes by exploring identity and enriches the meanings of monuments by showing their contexts

■ how many of the elements of commodity and educational tourism are embedded in the history of Eurocentric travel culture

■ how to enumerate the sources of cultural landscapes — location, human activity and the imagination — and identify their characteristics

■ how educational tourism's presentation of cultural landscapes differs from campus teaching of academic disciplines, and synthesises the knowledge and methodologies of these disciplines to create a new type of learning

■ how to apply what you have learned about approaches to cultural landscapes to writing tour descriptions, constructing thematic itineraries and describing how a tour lecturer should use these approaches on site visits

■ the potential of cultural landscapes for future tourism, for the study and teaching of traditional academic disciplines, and for destination presentation and interpretation.

This chapter aims to stimulate the discussion of educational tourism by exploring the following proposition: Educational tourism tells the stories of places in order to *enrich* the interactions of travellers with them. It blends discursive narrative with interdisciplinary, spatial investigation, and sets scholarly analysis of particular sites and events within global contexts or frameworks that deepen the world views of travellers. Educational travel increases people's capacity to learn about the world that surrounds them by teaching them how to decode places visually, how to see the relationships between places, and how to locate places in the evolution of society and culture.

Modern educational tourism evolved in the United States. American colleges and universities operate junior years or semesters abroad for undergraduates, and museum and alumni associations organise educational tours for their members. Most programs are based on partnerships between not-for-profit organisations and commercial tour companies, although an increasing number of tour companies have begun to specialise in this field. New types of thematic guidebooks responding to better-educated travellers' need for meaningful information have begun to replace traditional works, which were often little more than encyclopedias of dates, facts and statistics. Destinations have begun to tell their stories in more sophisticated ways to more receptive visitors.

Educational tourism organisations, publishers and destination interpreters, however, rarely enter professional or public deliberation about educational tourism's aims and methods. The potential of this field has received little attention in discussions of cultural tourism, heritage travel and ecotourism because it deals primarily with the perceptions of travellers, how they learn, and the nature and structure of knowledge rather than with the impact of tourism on natural and historic environments and regional cultures. It is uncommon, however, to see comparisons between educational tourism and sedentary education programs or conjectures about the capacity of educational tourism to enhance both tourism and education. The mainstream tourism industry, for its part, as yet shows little interest in the quality of tourists' perception and understanding, preferring to concentrate on marketing and infrastructure issues.

In attempting to create a theory of educational tourism, this chapter begins by isolating the unique and essential qualities of education, then goes on to suggest some of the ways in which educational tourism and mass-market tourism or 'commodity tourism' differ in their approach to knowledge and perception. I will submit reasons for these differences and explore the history of tourism in order to understand why and how particular attitudes to travellers and places have evolved. I will then propose that educational tourism investigate the cultural landscapes of places, and show how it uses the methods and objectives of scholarly disciplines along with traditional classroom learning, but how its approach also differs from such disciplines and learning.

■ 8.2.1 Definition *of education: its meaning for educational tourism*

Educational tourism is based on the concept of education. For education to take place the recipient must aspire to a deep understanding of that which is being learned. Education is broader than other types of learning because it relates elements of what is being learned to general principles, testing individual perceptions against universal ideas and values, which are in turn modified by particulars. Thus educational tourism uses information about specific places and events to enrich, amplify and modify travellers' views of the world and its history. This gives educational tourism breadth and scope.

In education, the acquisition of knowledge and understanding is valued and enjoyed for its own sake. Commercial gain may be a benefit of education but is not essential to it. Moreover, education is a process that has no manifest point of completion. We cannot, in this sense, 'become' educated because education leads us to anticipate and desire ever newer horizons of knowledge and understanding. Educational tourism acknowledges that teaching travellers is part of an ongoing process and so distrusts neat encapsulations of something as intricate as a society and its culture.

Education examines its own aims, processes and values philosophically. From this examination springs awareness and understanding of the relevance and meaning of knowledge. Educational tourism is distinguished by self-examination, and educational tour companies tend constantly to refine their programs' educational quality. An understanding of the history of travel, of the perceptions of past travellers and their interactions with places, aids and informs this process. A package tourism company feels little incentive to change a profitable product, except to garner greater profits.

■ 8.2.2 Definition *of commodity tourism: places and experiences as products*

Most travel experiences exist somewhere on a continuum between educational tourism and 'commodity tourism'. For the purposes of argument I shall characterise the latter in its most extreme form. As its name implies, commodity tourism commodifies knowledge, travel experiences and destinations, which it packages as a product for travellers whom it considers consumers. Any product for sale must be complete, for if it is not, consumers either cannot be enticed to buy it or will register dissatisfaction with it. This has far-reaching implications for the interaction of travellers with places. For example, a product cannot be complete without being finite and circumscribed. Because education is a continuous, limitless process, educational tourism can tolerate and enjoy the fact that societies are intricate and changeable and that viewing them is like looking through a multifaceted prism: minor alterations in viewpoint produce an infinite variety of representations. Commodity tourism, on the other hand, cannot tolerate the uncertainties such multiplicity causes, for this would compromise the validity of its product. Consumers, it seems to believe, must be presented with simplified, selective, stereotyped marketing images. Paul Hogan, for example, who once personified the Australian character, apparently still does so in the minds of many non-Australians. Such images entrap commodity tourism because customers' expectations must be fulfilled. Customers' perceptions of places must be managed with simplistic, standardised presentations. This, of course, is inimical to education.

8.3 EDUCATIONAL TOURISM VERSUS COMMODITY TOURISM: TWO EXEMPLARY DISTINCTIONS

8.3.1 People: *stereotyping versus exploring identity*

The inclination to stereotype people is a natural consequence of commodity tourism's need for simple classifications of people and places. Because educational tourism enjoys shifting perspectives — indeed, gains much pedagogical power from them — it can avoid stereotypes by exploring cultures through the beliefs people share and how they construct their communal identity. Communal identity derives not from community members' racial or genetic similarities but from the ability of individual community members to:

- share certain values (for example, Greek, Chinese and Scottish Australians all share what they believe to be 'Australian' values)
- imagine themselves to be part of a community (Greek, Chinese and Scottish Australians all imagine themselves to be Australian)
- be aware that others who share their values also imagine themselves to be part of this community (Greek Australians assume that Chinese and Scottish Australians also believe themselves to be Australian)
- presuppose that these other community members also assume that they share the community's values and that they imagine themselves as Australians (Greek Australians assume that Chinese and Scottish Australians assume that they themselves [the Greek Australians, that is] believe in the common values of Australians and also imagine themselves to be Australians)
- presuppose that the other community members know they are thinking this way.

We are, that is, what we think we are. This may seem bewildering but it is vital. How, for example, do Ladakhis living in secluded valleys of the Himalayas see themselves? Do they imagine themselves as part of the Indian nation? Possibly not, if they have never been to other parts of India and do not have television to tell them they are. Until the development of modern transport and mass media, the same could have applied to a Frenchman or an Italian. People, moreover, have multiple images of themselves depending upon the community to which, at any point in time, they are relating or with which they are interacting. An Australian might see himself or herself as a St Kilda football supporter when watching a match, a Melburnian when visiting Sydney, a Roman Catholic at church, a history student in lectures or an Australian while watching the Olympic Games. It is the sensitivity with which a traveller understands and can respond to these different communal values that distinguishes an educational tourism experience from one based on commodified, stereotyped caricatures of people (Anderson 1991).

The collective values and shared imaginings that constitute identity also constantly change. Russians, Czechs and Hungarians, for example, have begun to construct new national identities since the fall of the Soviet Union. A search for shared values can lead a nation to its past. Kemal Ataturk, who forged the modern nation state of Turkey from the ruins of the Ottoman Empire, sustained his quest for Turkish national identity by returning to the history of Turkish nomads who had entered the Middle East in the Middle Ages. Modern Czechs look back to Jan Hus, a fifteenth-century nationalist, religious reformer and father of the modern Czech language.

Travellers may discern assertions of identity everywhere. Scandinavian museums like those in Roskilde (Denmark) and Oslo not only display Viking material culture but also demonstrate how archaeology has revised outmoded historical judgements about the Scandinavians' forebears. The Vikings were once considered destructive transients because the only available literary descriptions of them were written by monks from the English monasteries they sacked. Archaeological finds like the Oseberg burial ship and its treasures have modified Scandinavians' identity by portraying the Vikings as great navigators and traders with a sophisticated, settled culture and technology.

■ 8.3.2 Monuments: *landmark statements versus contextual commentary*

Monuments like the Pyramids, the Parthenon and the Taj Mahal are of fundamental importance as pivotal destinations for world tourism; educational and commodity tourism present them in very different ways. Many tourists value a visit to the Eiffel Tower as a 'passage of life' but do not learn much of its historical context. Other, more inquisitive tourists regularly complain that professional tour guides frustrate them with trivia, combining unrelated, superficial minutiae such as the number of rivets in the Eiffel Tower with landmark statements about dimensions or relative size. Guides seldom give their facts and figures a broader, coheren, context. Listeners are left without a conceptual framework by which to integrate the Eiffel Tower into their understanding of Paris and its history. In contrast, an educational commentary would address issues like the tower's function as the centre-piece of the 1889 Paris Exhibition, aesthetic reactions to it, its place in the urbanism of Paris, and its later role as a symbol of the city and the nation. It might then flow seamlessly to broader issues, observing that Paris is a city of great monuments because it has a special status in French history that differentiates it from the capitals of other nations. Paris was the royal city of the kings of France, who forged their nation in a way that few other nations have been created by their monarchies. This example demonstrates how educational tourism creates contexts for places and relates these to universals by, for example, weaving the Eiffel Tower into its structural, aesthetic, political and social context. The narrative that achieves this is 'discursive', which means that it leaps from one associated idea to another rather than building an argument in a strictly linear and focused way as one does in an essay, article, book or traditional lecture. This constitutes a key difference between educational tourism and classroom teaching.

8.4 EDUCATIONAL TOURISM VERSUS COMMODITY TOURISM: WHY ARE THEY DIFFERENT?

8.4.1 Services *versus subject matter*

Commodity tourism has shown little inclination to nurture tourists' levels of understanding because it is concerned primarily with marketing, services and infrastructure. Educational tourism, on the other hand, is interested principally in the subject matter or content of travel. The text of a package tour itinerary usually catalogues the services a prospective traveller may expect. Its cursory description of the destination relies upon summary emotive adjectives like 'exotic', 'romantic', 'magnificent' or 'colourful'. Educational tour companies choose sites not for their landmark status but because they clarify and enrich the story being told by the tour program. Their itineraries describe and explain what is to be seen and place it in a broader thematic context.

8.4.2 Implications *of focusing exclusively upon services and infrastructure*

An emphasis upon services and product rather than content and perception compromises commodity tourism at many levels. Package tour companies compete with each other to provide superficial itineraries, such as a one-week 'Imperial Cities' tour of Morocco. Competition between identical tours using the same infrastructure leads to price cutting, minimisation of services, omission of interesting sites to avoid entry fees, inaccurate marketing and the debasement of travellers' experiences. Tourists with little pre-tour preparation are given a simplistic picture of the pattern of Moroccan history, culture and society and the significance and meaning of her monuments by tour guides who earn meagre salaries and therefore depend upon commissions from souvenir and carpet shops. Thus, site visits to monuments and museums become compressed episodes between long meals and shopping expeditions.

A focus on services to the detriment of content also creates anomalies. Before the explosion of international travel to Australia in the late 1980s the majority of travellers using accommodation and transport services were Australian holiday-makers. Many sought rest and recreation. They did not, like inbound tourists, require tourism to tell them the stories of Australian places. When Australia became an international destination its tourism industry quickly modified existing infrastructure for inbound tourists, but it ignored the tourism narratives that tell visitors what to see and do. International tourism to Australia in this sense developed back-to-front, so when Americans first began to inquire about visiting Victoria, for example, the state's tourism office in Los Angeles could offer only brochures selling hotel accommodation.

Australia seems still to be searching for tourism images and stories to tell to tourists. Tour companies in other countries show equal disregard for subject matter but most can draw upon pre-existing tourism narratives. This can itself distort cultures and places by blinkering operators and state tourism organisations. Egypt, for example, promotes Pharaonic monuments like the pyramids and ignores Cairo's mosques, madrasas (Koranic schools) and tombs, masterpieces from the Fattimid, Ayyubid and Mamluk periods. The bias towards Pharaonic monuments evolved to accommodate the tastes of nineteenth-century European travellers in search of ancient civilisations and has remained unchallenged by a tourism industry content to exploit tried formulae.

SPECIAL INTEREST INVESTIGATION
The American University in Cairo

In stark contrast to commodity tourism's focus upon Pharaonic Egypt is the work of the American University in Cairo, which has published a series of detailed maps of the Islamic monuments of Cairo; Caroline Williams' (1993) revisions of Richard Parker and Robin Sabin's *A Practical Guide to Islamic Monuments in Cairo*; and a number of histories, including Doris Behrens-Abouseif's *Islamic Architecture in Cairo, An Introduction* (1996). This groundbreaking work has been accompanied by recent private publishing initiatives such as Michael Haag's *Discovery Guide to Cairo: Including the Pyramids and Saqqara* (1990) and a partnership between a private tour company and the Egyptian tourism board to describe Islamic monuments on an Internet site (http://touregypt.net). This corpus of publications points to the fact that the development of educational tourism often begins with local university initiatives that originally may not have targeted tourists but rather their own or visiting students. Interpretive publications create the foundations and provide much-needed information for the development of better tourism interpretation and ultimately a more sophisticated tourism program. The American University, it should be noted, also teaches educational travel programs for the extremely successful US third-age educational tourism organisation Elderhostel.

HISTORICAL ROOTS OF MODERN TOURISM

The tourism industry's complexion and inclinations, tourism's subject matter, and tourists' perceptions of themselves and the places they visit have all been shaped by a Eurocentric culture of travel that has evolved since antiquity through interactions between images of travellers, styles of journeying, ways of perceiving and the places apprehended. The exceptional 'rites of passage' — often serendipitous experiences — of wandering pioneers have gradually been standardised and regulated to enable throngs of others to participate. Each epoch of travel has preserved, transformed or obscured the beliefs and practices of its predecessors, and contributed new elements to a steady accumulation of habits of experience that mould our impressions of places. Hierarchies of monuments, scenes, rituals and customs have evolved, determining what is worthy of attention. Since the Renaissance, for example, special significance has been attributed to the old and venerable. The importance of the antique in this Eurocentric tourism culture has led to a fascinating paradox in Melbourne. One of the most visited monuments is Melbourne's War Memorial, which speaks to Australians not only of the sacrifice of earlier generations but also of the opportunity the First World War gave the new Federation, founded in 1901, to act upon the world stage. This drama of sacrifice and identity formation would not have the same meaning for overseas visitors when they choose to visit the War Memorial. Stylistically, it is a hybrid combining the forms of the Parthenon and the Mausoleum of Halikarnassos (Bodrum, Turkey). Its style, not its story, gives it landmark value for travellers who have been taught by tourism culture that ancient monuments are worth visiting. Only when they enter its tomb-like interior, which evokes reverence, like some ancient sepulchre, would they come to understand its deep spiritual significance, whatever its story.

The shortcomings and inconsistencies of modern tourism stem partly from ignorance of the history of travel culture and of previous meanings of journeys. By understanding past interactions between travellers and places, we learn much about why we travel, where we choose to journey and how we perceive places. Many monuments, for example, owe their cultural status and meaning to travel; some were even created for travellers. This may be demonstrated by a short, very selective history of four periods and types of travel.

■ 8.5.1 Ancient *journeys and monuments*

Ancient narratives describe the travels of Gilgamesh, the Jews in the wilderness, the Greek Odysseus and the Trojan Aeneas as ordeals in which the wanderers searched for a place, often a home from which they had been torn (Leed 1991). Fabulous encounters, lengthy diversions and heroic acts often marked their voyages. Tales of adventure, exotic encounters and fantastic places have inspired European literature and travel culture ever since. Ancient epics associated passages of life, experiences of deep significance, with travel. Commodity tourism's use of landmarks constitutes the decay of this vital human legacy.

Herodotus (*c.* 484–420 BC), himself a wanderer, gave the mythic journey human scale. His history of a myriad peoples and places, based upon what he heard and saw in his journeys, taught travellers to be curious. Antiquity also invented the notion of the seven wonders of the world. The Greek traveller Pausanius (*c.* AD 120) described significant Greek monuments in what is arguably the earliest surviving guidebook. The majesty and theatricality of Roman public architecture, meantime, was intended to impress Imperial subjects, including travellers. Ever since, buildings have assumed a privileged status as objects of the tourist gaze.

■ 8.5.2 Medieval *pilgrimage*

By AD 1000 Europe's population, decimated five centuries earlier through imperial decline, barbarian invasion and war, was again increasing. Roman cities, with their majestic, scenographic architecture, were in ruins, but their memory still dominated the medieval imagination. Around 1000 pilgrimage, which had evolved since the third and fourth centuries, burgeoned into a mass movement. Martyrdom under emperors like Diocletian (284–305) had produced saints who could influence human destiny and absolve sin through their earthly remains, objects associated with their miracles and the instruments of their martyrdom. By the eleventh century thousands of pilgrims of all classes journeyed to the saints' shrines to give thanks for deliverance or good fortune, to beseech favours and, above all, to elicit forgiveness. Obsessed by sin and haunted by Matthew's and John the Evangelist's descriptions of the Last Judgement, penitents regarded their pilgrimages as journeys into the wilderness. They emulated the wanderings of Moses and his flock or Christ's tribulation in the desert, relinquished a stable existence for journeys without limits. They used neither maps nor printed itineraries, and many never returned.

Clerics and secular rulers realised the importance of this mass movement and gradually standardised it in order to increase their own power and amass wealth. They constructed majestic pilgrim churches of a grandeur appropriate to the status of the precious saintly relics displayed in them. These churches were often built not in response to pilgrims' demands to view relics but rather to attract these wanderers so as to gain profit. The classical ideal of venerable monuments was thereby transformed into the creation of attractions, prefiguring many modern governments' construction of tourism icons like London's Millennium Dome. Conflicts between the bishops and abbots of competing shrines were the forerunners of competition between modern tourism destinations. Pilgrims even wore insignia associated with their journeys — palms for the Holy Land, St Peter's keys for Rome — forerunners of modern souvenirs, mementos of passages of life, once mystical, today secularised.

BREAKTHROUGH TOURISM

From the politics of medieval pilgrimage to modern Spanish educational tourism

Medieval ecclesiastical and secular rulers who hoarded relics promoted pilgrimage for political ends. The immense popularity of the pilgrim shrine of Santiago in northwestern Spain derived from a ninth-century apocryphal story that angels had borne the Apostle James the Greater's decapitated body there after his martyrdom in the Holy Land (in the first century). Pilgrims returning from Santiago wore cockleshells picked up on the beach near his shrine to prove they had completed their pious journey. St James was depicted not as an Apostle but as a pilgrim, and his symbol became the cockleshell — eight hundred years after his death! Saints' symbols are invariably either the instruments of their martyrdom or objects associated with their lives. That St James should derive his image and symbol from his pilgrims reflects the strange fact that the pilgrim route itself, as much as his apocryphal remains, publicised what became the second most popular pilgrimage of western Europe.

Pilgrimage to Santiago was promoted by the small Christian kingdoms of León and Castile, Navarre and Aragón, who needed the support of a saintly hero to advance their territorial interests against the Muslims who controlled most of Iberia. James thus became the patron saint of Spain and was soon depicted as a soldier fighting the Muslims. The popularity of his shrine enabled the Spanish kingdoms to enmesh French armies in their dynastic pursuits and attracted French pilgrims to whom they gave incentives to settle in Christian frontier towns, for they needed to populate the vast, empty mesetas of Iberia in order to hold them against Muslim incursions.

St James' story, however, does not end with his pilgrimage. Recently, the Spanish government has revived the Santiago pilgrim route as an educational tourism corridor. It has identified and marked the original route with special sign posts and highly informative roadside displays, published detailed, informative thematic guidebooks, historical maps and archaeological surveys and restored many of its shrines in a careful, non-intrusive way. It has done so to attract educated tourists and modern pilgrims to northern Spain, providing an alternative to the debased holiday resorts of the Costa del Sol, and to link itself to its powerful neighbour, France (everywhere pilgrim route sign posts are accompanied by the symbol of the united Europe). It may also have developed this interpretation corridor, arguably the best documented of its type in Europe, to give its own disparate, separatist regional communities a common identity. Separatists, however, have graffitied many of the new roadside displays with their regionalist slogans (Wood 1998).

8.5.3 Cultural travel *from the Renaissance to the early nineteenth century*

Renaissance, Reformation and Enlightenment sceptics attacked the efficacy of relics and pilgrimage declined. Pilgrimage left its mark, however. It added a powerful mystical dimension to visiting monuments, which retained its psychological force in the eighteenth-century Grand Tour — a secular, cultural pilgrimage to the 'shrines' of Greek and Roman civilisation. This transformation from religious to secular pilgrimage gave monuments and artworks a new status. Medieval dynasts and ecclesiastics had collected relics, not art. The grand monuments and precious reliquaries that housed them, however, became associated with their mystical meaning. When medieval relic collections gave way to Renaissance art collections, this mystical meaning was aestheticised, which has led ultimately to the uninformed awe of many modern travellers in the presence of great buildings and artworks like Leonardo's *Mona Lisa*. Contexts developed by educational tourism may not only reinvest landmark monuments with meaning but also nourish discernment by revealing their original significance.

The sublime and the picturesque

Medieval pilgrims had feared the dangers of forests, mountains and rivers; their paradise, the Heavenly Jerusalem, was a city. Renaissance cartographers measured the world and subdued humans' terror of the unknown. With increased urbanisation the countryside became a source of pleasure and nostalgia, something to be 'managed' by gardening or a place of retreat from city cares. Landscape painting was invented to assuage a nostalgia for rural life. With eighteenth-century landscape gardening, civilisation appeared to triumph over nature. Romantic travellers reacted against this; they revered its counterpart, wilderness. To classical beauty, Edmund Burke added a new aesthetic category, the 'sublime', to describe places that inspired awe and terror. William Gilpin likewise coined the term 'picturesque' to denote asymmetrical, unmanaged beauty. These two aesthetic categories saturate modern tourism culture, often determining where people travel. 'Sublime' places include the European Alps, the Grand Canyon, Niagara Falls and Uluru. Their grandeur affirmed our more religious precursors' belief in the creative power of God (Sears 1989). More recently, commodity tourism has secularised them, subverting their original meanings, transforming them into 'three star' views, green strips and small rays on Michelin maps. Educational travel can reinvest them with dignity through understanding their past meanings. The 'picturesque', which also once had moral significance, has ultimately led to historically misleading folksy villages, craft markets and rustic festivals.

8.5.4 Modern tourism: *nineteenth and twentieth centuries*

Like pilgrimage, the Grand Tour became standardised. The travel book, a new literary genre, wrought this change. Early narratives of individuals' idiosyncratic reactions to places yielded to guidebooks that dictated the sites to be visited and even told travellers how to react to them. Meanwhile the Grand Tour became politicised by nineteenth-century British imperialists who appropriated an idealised model and the style and imagery of the Roman Empire; classical education was reinvigorated as a training for Imperial service. For Britons, Italy became by far the most significant place to visit. The status of many Italian landmarks and its choice of tourism narratives consequently derive largely from British tastes and concerns rather than Italian historical reality.

Much modern tourism relies on outmoded imperial propaganda and ceremonial like London's Changing of the Guard (Cannadine 1992). Nineteenth-century Britain, Germany and France also searched for images to underpin nationalism and invented fictions like 'merry olde England', more grist to modern tourism's mill (Schama 1995). Europeans, meanwhile, monopolised overseas travel, so non-European host countries like Egypt adopted images that reflected European tastes and preferences.

Since the nineteenth century, however, travel's function has undergone a fascinating change. Past journeys always took place from a stable, changeless home. Nineteenth-century industrialisation and urbanisation initiated a process of alienation in western society marked by two conditions of modern urban life, anonymity and unrelenting change. Once the attributes of travel, these conditions now determine our everyday lives. We now travel on quests for two seemingly opposed experiences. We seek changelessness and cultural continuity in venerable monuments or in non-industrial societies and yet our journeys also offer relief from the sameness of materialistic mass culture (Leed 1991).

8.6 MODERNITY, HISTORY, HERITAGE AND 'LIVING HISTORY'

■ 8.6.1 Inventing *the past versus telling its story*

People confronted by the constant changes of modern life lose their linkage to the past, their aptitude for identifying elements of the past in the present and, above all, their capacity to imagine the past. History cannot help, for history has moved from public view into professional academia. In its place we have 'heritage', an invention of the past (Lowenthal 1997). Heritage, while its motives are usually well-intentioned, often presents the past in over-restored buildings that are lifeless because the marks of their age have been removed. Alternatively, heritage presents the past in historical theme parks and historical re-enactments parading as 'living history', which are flawed because by presenting one past they obscure the continuum of change that links many pasts to the present. 'Living history' is also logically impossible because it attempts to represent a material, tangible, corporeal past in the present when the past by its very nature can only be imagined. In doing so it suffocates people's ability to imagine the past and compromises the pleasure this brings. This right is precious, because for many travellers the process of imagining the past is more fulfilling and enlightening than the attainment of historical reality.

■ **Figure 8.1**
Dr Amira Bennison of Cambridge talks to a study group at the Hassan Mosque, Rabat, Morocco

Source: *Chris Wood*

8.7 CULTURAL LANDSCAPES ....

Educational tourism, it has been suggested, may provide various solutions to problems encountered in commodity tourism, heritage restoration and reconstruction, and theme parks and historic re-enactments. The remainder of this chapter will characterise 'cultural landscapes' and discuss how they may be explored. 'Cultural landscapes' take two forms. They are physical expressions of the stories of places, such as agricultural or industrial regions, the countryside, rural scenes, cityscapes and townscapes, parklands or gardens; or creative evocations of the stories of places in text, image or tune.

■ 8.7.1 Three sources *of cultural landscapes*

Educational tourism can tell the stories of places by presenting travellers with their 'cultural landscapes' and teaching travellers how to decode them. Cultural landscapes evolve from interactions between people and their environment. From them we learn about human identity and the development of societies. Cultural landscapes result from:

• the influence of geology and topography upon the location, form and fortunes of human settlements and the quality and shape of human activity, be it religious, political, commercial, social or artistic

- changes wrought upon the environment by human activity in all its diversity
- creative interactions with the environment producing imagined landscapes, such as the settings of novels, the subject of paintings, the themes of musical compositions or the narratives of past travellers.

Cultural landscapes can be explored everywhere by travellers and can also enrich disciplines like history and geography (Matvejevic 1999).

■ 8.7.2 Methods *of exploring cultural landscapes*

How are cultural landscapes explored?

- They are perceived visually and spatially, which in turn enriches visual and spatial understanding. We may 'read' spaces just as we may analyse forms. A spatial understanding of a city, for example, would involve exploring the city's location and asking questions about its position; reading its plan and looking for reasons why its plan evolved in a particular way; analysing the locations, dimensions and shapes of its parks, squares and streets and the reasons for these. It may also involve locating and explaining the public 'nodes' of a city, the parts of it that are of particular importance to citizens.
- They require an interdisciplinary approach and show how academic disciplines may interrelate in new ways.
- They require that the past be seen as a continuum, not in discrete chronological units, and that it be approached through the present; this offers to the study of history new insights and broad perspectives.

Combined, these three modes of perception and comprehension enable educational tourism to:

- explore the interaction of space and time
- link specific information to universal ideas and values such as human identity
- nurture imagination in creative new ways.

■ 8.7.3 Visual *and spatial approach to cultural landscapes*

Travellers perceive the spaces, forms and activities that generate cultural landscapes visually rather than through texts, although texts obviously provide invaluable preparatory knowledge and understanding. Spatial investigation, therefore, can unlock different ways of understanding human society and propose new explanations for events. Various forms of academic history can provide knowledge and insight but often lack the visual orientation necessary to investigate cultural landscapes fully. Herbert Butterfield rightly observed: 'The task of the historian is to understand the people of the past better than they understood themselves' (Marwick 1970). Yet although past people may not have enjoyed the clarity of a historian's hindsight, they nevertheless perceived themselves and their culture spatially.

It is difficult enough for a scholar to imagine the spatial meanings of people's thoughts, actions and memories, let alone portray them to students on some faraway campus.

One of the greatest modern historians, Fernand Braudel, often adopted the role of traveller when analysing and describing the pasts of regions like the Mediterranean (1992). Spatial history, however, assumes its most compelling form in the study of Islamic society. Ibn Khaldûn (1332–1406), a great traveller, discussed in the first chapter of his masterpiece the *Muqqadimah* how climate and resources mould society (1989). In the vast arid sweep from the Atlantic coast of Morocco to Râjasthân in India, scarcity of water has shaped human consciousness, moulded social relations, dictated the locations of cities and inspired material culture. In Islam, paradise is a garden and hell is conceived as burning with thirst in the desert. Scarcity of water gave birth to nomadism, which contributed vitally to the nature of society and inspired many of Islam's greatest arts like poetry, music, textiles, jewellery and pottery. Ibn Khaldûn argued that the relationship between nomadism and urban life shaped the rhythm with which particular groups gained and lost power. Understanding Islamic history and culture therefore requires the spatial comprehension best offered by actual travel.

■ 8.7.4 Many-layered *cultural landscapes*

Cultural landscapes are like palimpsests, medieval parchments re-inscribed a number of times in which the ghosts of earlier texts may be discerned beneath their successors. The cultural landscape of modern Sicily is therefore made up of tombs of the Siculi and Sicani; Greek shrines; Roman and Byzantine villas; Islamic and European forms of Norman churches and palaces; Swabian fortresses; Catalan mansions; Baroque palaces, churches and monasteries, as well as enduring forms of local architecture such as peasants' huts. All contributed to modern Sicilian identity. Its people have developed customs that have mutated over centuries. Sicilian puppetry, for example, was imported from Naples in the early nineteenth century. The exploits of Charlemagne and his knights, performed in tiny puppet theatres in Palermo's backstreets, owe much to French Romantic drama. Their plots, however, may derive from ancient tales told by itinerant storytellers to Sicilian villagers since the Middle Ages. The storytellers have gone but their narratives remain, transmuted into the highly entertaining epic cycles played by tin-armoured marionettes.

■ 8.7.5 Travelling *through space and journeying through time*

The broad-brushed history engendered by the many layers of a cultural landscape encourages a traveller to explore the meaning of time, especially if physical landscapes are compared to imagined ones that invariably offer fresh perspectives and richer, deeper, more expansive meanings. Giuseppe Tomasi di Lampedusa's novel of nineteenth-century Sicily, *The Leopard*, evokes the cultural landscape of a decadent aristocracy and an island unable and unwilling to meet the challenges of the modern era. His tragic image of Sicily, her energies sapped by the unrelenting sun and by foreign dominion and exploitation, presents time's action upon a community in vivid images.

As each new element in a multilayered cultural landscape is encountered and its context understood, a traveller's historical imagination is constantly enriched. This is particularly so in a country like Iran, which has a vast, diverse topography of high mountains and steppelands that drop slowly to deserts at sea level, and an extraordinarily diverse material culture. Iranian history — and identity — have been shaped by the interaction of Persian civilisation, which emerged under ancient Persian empires between the sixth century BC and the seventh century AD, and the cultures of successive invaders, for the Iranian plateau occupies a strategic location between Central Asia, Anatolia, Iraq and Arabia. The most important invaders were the Arabs, who brought down the empire and Islamised Persia in the seventh century.

Encounters with ancient imperial cities like Persepolis; sculpted reliefs depicting emperors with their gods, processions of imperial subjects and courtly hunting scenes; Zoroastrian fire temples; exquisite miniature paintings, intricate carpets and priceless jewels in Tehran's museums; formal gardens near Yazd and Kerman (corporeal versions of scenes depicted in the miniatures and carpets), and multicoloured tiles, patterned brickwork and fine calligraphy in mosques, tombs and palaces — all augment a traveller's understanding of the endurance of Persian courtly culture with its love of rich colour and pattern. A mosaic of regional populations of Kurds, Turkomans, Azerbaijani, Lurs, Bakhtiaris, Qashqai, Gilaki, Mazanderani, Arabs and Persians, each with its own rituals, dress, vernacular architecture and cuisine, on the other hand, reflects the strategic position of the Iranian plateau and the constant movement of people across it. Everywhere, as a traveller makes a journey physically across space and imaginatively through time, the dynamic interaction between Persia's Aryan culture and its vigorous counterpart, Islam, manifests itself. Persia's distinctive language, Farsi, is written in Arabic script. The arching *iwans* of Zoroastrian fire temples, though, influenced Islamic architecture throughout Persia. Iran's great shrine cities — Mashad and Qom — and the massive new complex commemorating the Ayatollah Ruholla Khomeini remind travellers that the interaction of Persian culture with Islam contributed to the adoption of Shi'ism in the sixteenth century and ultimately the Iranian revolution of 1979. As travellers move across the Iranian plateau each of their myriad diverse encounters constitutes yet another intersection between space and time. These ultimately coalesce into a mental picture of Iran that exists simultaneously in space and time.

■ *8.7.6* **Interactions** *between cultural landscapes*

All places have multitudes of cultural landscapes that depend upon the perspective of those who perceive them and tell their stories. Landscapes of the imagination, for example, contribute to the formation of identity. The historian Franco Moretti has shown how the imagined local settings of Jane Austen's novels contributed to the growth of English nationalism (Moretti 1998). Sometimes imagined landscapes can be as palpable to their inhabitants as corporeal ones. The coloured flags with prayers printed upon them seen fading in the sun outside Tibetan and Ladakhi mountain monasteries are believed by Buddhist monks to be shedding their prayers, which soar down the great Himalayan valleys, across villages, stupas and walls of etched prayer stones to sanctify the Himalayan landscape. Travellers remark how Himalayan identity rests upon a special reverence for the environment.

Imagined landscapes can interact in a dynamic way with corporeal ones. This diversity enriches rather than confuses our understanding of identity. Venetian history demonstrates the interplay of the three factors that generate cultural landscapes — location, culture and imagination — in that the interaction of an extraordinary watery environment with a distinctive urban culture was enhanced by a unique conception of the status and prospects of the city. Heir to the visual opulence of Byzantium, the wealthy aristocratic republic of Venice so enriched itself visually that it resembled a precious jewel. The lustrous glimmer of St Mark's mosaics were echoed in the rich colours of Venetian palace facades, which in turn were reflected in shimmering images in its canals. Venice's visual bounty is prismatic and nebulous. Venetians created their city not by cutting waterways through existing land but by claiming terrain from marshlands. The city is built upon pylons driven deep to create individual islands that seem to sit on a reflecting plate of water. Each island reclaimed from the marshes evolved its own peculiar labyrinth of passages and piazzas so that the city coalesced from a number of ill-fitting precincts. Venice does not have the discernible spatial logic of Florence, whose core still retains the original grid street plan of a Roman *castrum*. Venetian space is fractured so we perceive the city in fragments.

This ethereal richness and intricacy is reflected in Antonio Canaletto's extraordinarily detailed paintings of Venice created for northern Grand Tourists. The multiplistic, microscopic realism of his panoramas hides the fact that he misrepresented the city. He 'personalised' these visual souvenirs for his aristocratic patrons by featuring the palaces they had rented in prominent, incorrect locations. Canaletto's deceptions reflect a theme in Venetian history. He created a mythic Venice, with all the multiplicity of a cosmos set apart from the outside world. His horizon is the city's profile, not the nearby Alps, which dominate the Veneto's northern horizon. His particular cultural landscapes reflect an imagery that had evolved in Venice over centuries. Italian cities flaunted their ancient pedigrees. Florence claimed high status from its founder Julius Caesar, Rome from Aeneas and Romulus. Siena celebrated Remus. Venice was a latecomer, founded not by the ancients but by medieval refugees from the barbarian invasions. To compensate for this deficit in ancestry, the Venetians stole the remains of St Mark from Alexandria, claiming that the Evangelist had received the message in a vision that Venice would be his final resting place. The Venetians continued to mythologise their city and to enrich it with imperial plunder, such as treasures carried off from the sack of Constantinople (1204). They called it 'La Serenissima', a precious emblem set apart from the world. Daniello Barbari's great map of 1516 presents the city isolated, jewel-like and multifaceted in its watery setting. Constant enrichment in fact and fancy ultimately fused myth and reality, so that by the time Canaletto's northern travellers arrived in the eighteenth and nineteenth centuries it was to ponder a fantastic world of past glory, an unreal, inimitable place.

■ 8.7.7 Cultural *landscapes and classroom learning*

The exploration of cultural landscapes differs from much scholarly research and many campus-based courses in two ways.

Transdisciplinary investigations

Reading cultural landscapes requires the interpretative skills of disciplines with strong visual orientations like art history. But the study of cultural land-scapes must also be transdisciplinary. Educational tourism must use the knowledge and methodologies of disparate disciplines — geography; geology; archaeology; intellectual, political, religious and social history; and the history of art and architecture, to name but a few — to tell the stories of landscapes, cityscapes, buildings, artworks, archaeological sites, agricultural activity and local markets, festivals and rituals. It must synthesise without losing the analytical rigour of each discipline. It must acknowledge each discipline's own internal logic and objectives but must use what each has to offer to tease out the stories of places.

The past in the present

Traditional history courses often teach history in discrete units like 'The Renaissance and Reformation'. Travellers, however, perceive the past in the present and must therefore understand the multiple layers contributed by different epochs to the landscapes they encounter. This approach and the insights it engenders, on the other hand, can provide thematic, broad-based, campus-based history courses with new insights and methodologies.

8.8 HOW EDUCATIONAL TOURISM MAY PRESENT AND INTERPRET CULTURAL LANDSCAPES

How may cultural landscapes be explored on tour programs? Introductions to tour itineraries and other preparatory material like pre-tour notes should paint a broad picture of a place, showing how its location, climate and topography interacted with human activity. A number of historical themes, discussed in the itinerary, should mould the choice and treatment of sites to be visited. Written itineraries and on-site commentaries should tease out and elaborate these themes and also suggest patterns of spatial development through visual analysis.

A city may be introduced with a talk using a city map to demonstrate how different periods moulded its growth in diverse ways. Located between the central ordered grid plan of Roman Florence and the river Arno are the winding streets of the medieval city, which required its water to manufacture woollen cloth. Beyond are the straight streets of the Renaissance city, their perspectives formed by rows of flanking patrician palaces. A nineteenth-century ring road surrounds this core, occupying the site of moribund defensive walls. Beyond lies the twentieth-century metropolis, its broad thoroughfares shaped for modern transport. By presenting the visual and spatial history of the city as a pattern, this introduction creates contexts for subsequent visits to precincts and buildings.

Site visits will refine and modify this basic introductory pattern. A tour lecturer must be ready for inconsistencies. Discrepancies will naturally appear and must be accommodated. Monuments from disparate periods may abut each other, newer edifices impairing the visual unity of older streetscapes. Empty spaces may reflect lost monuments. The present will constantly impinge upon the pattern of the past. It must not be ignored for it is part of the ongoing biography of the city and usually resonates with the past in special ways. Florentine Renaissance palaces, for example, now house chic shops and prestigious offices. They owe their prestige, however, to their original function. Their ground floors once housed shops, banks and warehouses, giving them capital value even in the fifteenth century. A lecturer may compare these well-kept establishments to the ruined aristocratic palaces of central Palermo, which had no commercial value and fell into rubble when the Sicilian aristocracy declined and Allied bombardment devastated the city's centre. The prestigious precincts of Sicilian cities are their modern suburbs. Tour lecturers must roam the world and its past to tease out such points.

8.9 SUMMARY

This chapter suggests that educational tourism may take on an important new role far beyond the activities of educational tour companies. This is based on the attributes of education — its wide-ranging, continuous quest for knowledge and meaning — and on a historical understanding of the relationship between travel, perception and imagination. Educational tourism's spatial readings of places through their cultural landscapes offer people living in an age of standardisation, commodification, anonymity and the uncertainty of constant, rapid change new ways of journeying through, and anchoring themselves in, the world. The world it offers, however, exists simultaneously in many places and times, on a space/time continuum perceived and imagined through the coexistence, in the present, of the many-layered pasts of places. Educational tourism can tell the stories of places by encouraging interactions between knowledge, perception, sensation and imagination only if its commentaries are allowed at times to meander in a discursive way. If this occurs, it can reveal unexpected connections and uncover patterns that academic discourse — constrained by its preoccupation with texts, its concern for linear argumentation and internal logic, and by the walls of distant campuses — may miss. This does not preclude analytical rigour; in good educational tourism broad understanding, precise knowledge, tight visual and spatial analysis and discursive exposition enrich each other. Yet discursive mental journeys and broad perspectives are peculiarly appropriate to, indeed exist in symbiosis with, the flood of fleeting impressions and wandering mental rhythms we experience while travelling.

Questions

8.1 This chapter attempts to build a theory of educational tourism dealing with human culture. What are its implications for other types of special interest tourism (e.g. ecotourism)?

8.2 How may this theory of educational tourism be used to change commodity tourism?

8.3 What are the implications of this theory for the on-site presentation of destinations?

8.4 How could 'cultural landscapes' enrich a traditional history or geography course?

8.5 Which novels you know have created vivid cultural landscapes? How are these used to portray human values?

REFERENCES

Anderson, B. 1991. *Imagined Communities, Reflections on the Origin and Spread of Nationalism.* London: Verso.

Behrens-Abouseif, D. 1996. *Islamic Architecture in Cairo, An Introduction.* Cairo: American University in Cairo Press.

Braudel, F. 1992. *The Mediterranean and the Mediterranean World in the Age of Phillip II.* (Transl. Reynolds, S., abridged Ollard, R.). London: HarperCollins.

Cannadine, D. 1992. 'The Context, Performance and Meaning of Ritual: The British Monarchy and "The Invention of Tradition". c. 1820–1977'. In Hobsbawm, E. & Ranger, T. (Eds). *The Invention of Tradition.* Cambridge, UK: Canto.

Haag, M. 1990. *Discovery Guide to Cairo: Including the Pyramids and Saqqara.* London: Michael Haag.

Ibn Khaldûn. 1989. *The Muqaddimah, An Introduction to History.* (Transl. Rosenthal, F; Ed. Dawood, N.). Princeton, New Jersey: Bollington Series.

Lampedusa, G. di. 1988. *The Leopard, with a Memory and Two Stories.* (Transl. Colquhuon, A.). London: Collins Harvell.

Leed, E. J. 1991. *The Mind of the Traveller: From Gilgamesh to Global Tourism.* USA: Basic Books.

Lowenthal, D. 1997. *The Heritage Crusade and the Spoils of History.* London: Viking.

Mackie, S. 1998. *The Iranians, Persia, Islam and the Soul of a Nation.* New York: Plume.

Marwick, A. 1970. *The Nature of History.* London: Macmillan.

Matvejevic, P. 1987. *Mediterranean, A Cultural Landscape.* (Transl. Heim, M. H.). 1999. Berkeley, Cal.: California University Press.

Moretti, F. 1998. *Atlas of the European Novel, 1800–1900.* London: Verso.

Rojek, C. & Urry, J. 1997. *Touring Cultures, Transformations of Travel and Theory.* London: Routledge.

Schama, S. 1995. *Landscape and Memory.* London: HarperCollins.

Sears, J. 1989. *Sacred Places: American Tourist Attractions in the Nineteenth Century.* New York: Oxford University Press.

Urry, J. 1995. *Consuming Places.* London: Routledge.

Williams, C. 1993. *Islamic Monuments in Cairo, A Practical Guide.* Cairo: American University in Cairo Press.

Wood, C. 1998. 'The Cult of St James: Pilgrimage and Power in Medieval Spain'. In McDonald, M. *Spain: A Historical and Cultural Guide.* Melbourne: Australians Studying Abroad.

Historic towns, *heritage precincts and cultural landscapes*

This case study discusses examples of three cities in which the built environment has been managed in two different ways: York, San Gimignano and Fés. It is deliberately argumentative. It then explores the implications of these differences for the Victorian Central Goldfields town of Clunes. The purpose of the case study is to invite you to consider the way in which Clunes' historic environment may be managed in the light of what you have read about educational tourism in this chapter.

The historic cores of York in northern England and San Gimignano in Tuscany have been transformed by the commodification of history for tourism. The restoration of York Cathedral was a necessary and laudable act. The cathedral's precinct and much of the city, however, have come to be dominated by what could be called 'commodified heritage', in which shops selling folksy 'historical' souvenirs, English porcelain, boutique jams and lavender bags sit alongside Devonshire Tea establishments. The painted signs on these premises seem just a little too picturesque to be true. Their paintwork is too shiny, lacking the patina of age in keeping with their 'traditional' content. Likewise, the central street of San Gimignano is now dominated by boutique wine cellars and shops selling Tuscan ceramics. It is becoming increasingly difficult for a local resident to buy milk, bread or vegetables in either place, or for tourists to encounter locals in them. These heritage precincts no longer belong to residents but are colonised by crowds of visitors on a vain search for history. For the histories of cities and towns resides in the memories local people invest in buildings and spaces. Even if old buildings are replaced, continuing local use of their successors constitutes a link to the past, for local residents see history as the changes that happen in their communities, not as the deliberate manufacture of an artificial, alienating past.

Fés, of all the cities in the world, probably best preserves its historic environment. Its life as a community has been nurtured rather than disrupted by the work of UNESCO, which has assisted in promoting the continuance of artisan activity in the city. The following description of Fés attempts to convey the vitality of its life in terms of its 'cultural landscape'.

At the centre of Fés el Bali (old Fés) is its venerable Qarawiyin mosque, which has been the religious focus of the city since its foundation in the seventh century AD. Nearby are two other types of important religious institutions: the tomb of Idris II, son of the leader who had Islamised Morocco, and a cluster of *madrasas* (Koranic schools), constructed in the sixteenth century.

The tomb is an important focus of Morocco's spiritual life. The *madrasas* had fallen into misuse but a number are being revived once again as Koranic schools. At the city's centre are also found markets for valuables such as silk, spices and books; this follows Islamic urban practice. In successive zones leading out from the city centre lie markets and artisanal districts dedicated to less valuable, more cumbersome products. For example, there are tanneries for Moroccan leather that have been in continuous use since the ninth century. Each commercial zone is served by a *funduuk*, an inn for visiting merchants. Each specialised neighbourhood of artisan communities, such as carpenters, tailors, metal workers, potters, dyers or weavers, has a communal oven for baking bread, a mosque that is a community centre as much as a place of prayer, and a *hamam* (public bath) used by both sexes, at strictly segregated times, as a place of genial sociability. The *hamam* is for women what the neighbourhood cafes are for the men. Just inside the city gates are the markets where food from the country is sold and outside them are the city's cemeteries, dotted with the tombs of holy men. These are of great spiritual importance as liminal zones between heaven and Earth.

Linking the centre of Fés to its gates are two wide thoroughfares. To either side, however, extend intricate networks of small streets that become progressively narrower as they enter deeper and deeper into domestic precincts. Insensitive foreigners who stray deep into these zones often find inhabitants less accommodating than in the major public thoroughfares, because these are private domains into which they are trespassing. The houses present only high, blank walls with few windows to these corridors. They look in on private courtyards, reflecting Islam's emphasis upon privacy.

Visiting tour members are guided through Fés in small groups. They are not allowed into mosques and generally are kept away from the more private areas of the city. Fés is a trading and artisan city. The objects available for sale are fundamentally the same as those made in the city for a millennium. They are sold in their respective specialised artisanal districts. Fés belongs to its residents and tourists feel very much like privileged guests.

The Central Victorian Goldfields town of Clunes was once a thriving centre for deep lead mining. The earliest photographs of Clunes show small temporary wooden buildings, few of which remain, surrounded by a landscape of bare mullock heaps. Clunes owed its existence to mining and all energy was spent on mining; few cared about the environmental devastation this wrought. From this first transient phase emerged a community that sought a permanent settlement. Substantial stone buildings, many of which still stand, began to appear. Churches, signifiers of civilisation, inflected the town's profile. Then the gold ran out and Clunes reinvented itself as an English village. The scars of its earlier existence, now seen only in its uneven topography, were disguised with English trees. Clunes compensated for loss of wealth by resorting to a venerable English idea — that sleepy villages and rural ways offer a more morally upright life than bustling cities. In the late nineteenth century it began to present itself in this way in the hope of attracting visitors. In the 1980s city dwellers in search of weekend escape and tourists began to discover the town.

Clunes now has various options. It can aggressively reinvent itself as a 'historic' town. This would be fundamentally different from its earlier transformation, which was effected by residents for themselves, not just for visitors. Clunes, therefore, made the transition from mining settlement to rural village in order to perpetuate, not put at risk, the life of its community. By reinventing Clunes as a historic town for tourists and arresting further development, heritage and tourism interests may actually destroy the local community's sense of its past — and future — and cloud Clunes' fascinating story. If this occurs it is even possible that tourists will lose interest, seeing it as artificial. A better alternative is to stabilise its built environment in a careful, non-invasive way, to allow further, sensitive development and to begin telling Clunes' story by interpreting what already exists through such vehicles as educational tours and pictorial exhibits of images of the town in different phases of its development.

Questions

1 Evaluate the arguments in this case study in the light of what you have read in this chapter. Can you identify similar examples of cities, towns and precincts in which history has been treated in radically different ways?

2 What are the key buildings and spaces that tell the story of a place you know well (e.g. your city, town or suburb)? What do they signify for local residents? What do local residents believe are the important stories they tell? How would you recount these stories to visitors?

Nigel Morpeth

CHAPTER 9

The renaissance of
cycle tourism

LEARNING OBJECTIVES

After reading this chapter, you will have an appreciation of:

- a special interest tourism form with alternative and sustainable tourism credentials
- the distinction between hard and soft forms of tourism
- how bicycle tourism, which has a historical lineage, has re-emerged as a popular tourism form
- the segmentation of bicycle tourism
- how to determine the diverse market segments for bicycle tourism
- the characteristics of small businesses involved in bicycle tourism, identifying lifestyle as well as commercial motivations
- the sustainable tourism credentials of bicycle tourism
- how the creation of bicycle tourism routes has stimulated new demand for bicycle tourism products, public sector infrastructure development, and community interest in and benefit from bicycle tourism.

INTRODUCTION

The search for implementable forms of sustainable tourism continues to be a topical issue, both within tourism literature and for tourism practitioners. This presents a challenge, not least for supply-side operators and policy makers, to find forms of tourism development that:

- are implementable
- respect the integrity of environmental, social and cultural resources
- are in a variety of geographical settings.

Adventure tourism is a form of activity-based tourism, with further distinctions between hard and soft tourism. There is a challenge in penetrating the 'blanketing of language' (Hoggarth 1995:157) and finding commonly agreed interpretations of 'catchall' terms, such as eco, green, environmentally sensitive and soft tourism. In this respect, Weaver notes how mountain trekkers may display characteristics of both adventure and ecotourism. The intrinsic motivation of risk taking associated with adventure tourism may seem to be the antithesis of nature-based tourism. However, these contradictory aspects may be made compatible with prudent planning and management (1998:23).

With the increasing popularity of activity tourism, especially adventure-based tourism, responsibility has been placed on supply-side operators to manage the motivational requirements of adventure tourists and be aware of the possible irreversible environmental impacts of certain activities. Adventure tourism incorporates hard and soft tourism, with a variety of motivational aspects underpinning a range of activities. This poses the following questions.

- What activity-based tourism forms have the flexibility to satisfy a broad range of motivational requirements of adventure tourists, from risk taking to more educational, knowledge-based and aesthetic motivations?
- Is it possible for these tourism forms to operate within the principles of sustainability?

This chapter investigates the contemporary applications of bicycle tourism, which has the flexibility to satisfy the motivational requirements of adventure tourism. Hard and soft dimensions of adventure tourism are considered and the soft adventure characteristics of bicycle tourism are reviewed within a global context.

CHOOSING ADVENTURE ACTIVITIES

On New Year's Eve, 1984, cousins Richard and Nicholas Crane cycled to the top of Kilimanjaro, Africa's highest mountain. In doing so, they raised £20 000 towards **Intermediate Technology** (I.T.), enabling the installation of a wind pump in a village in Zimbabwe. The Crane family are experienced adventure seekers who are partly motivated by an altruistic flair for fund raising for I.T. and other charitable concerns. Their search for suitable adventure experiences demonstrates the importance of finding the right chemistry between activity and location. The Crane family can be characterised as explorer or drifter travellers, driven by a complex amalgam of motivations, including a keen awareness of environmental, social and cultural considerations. They represent an elite band of international adventure seekers who epitomise high profile adventure travel that is beyond the grasp of the majority of travellers. In contrast is the more institutionalised travel market, where travel agents, from mainstream to niche operators, offer active holidays, in a variety of geographical and cultural locations.

Adventure tourism is viewed as part of the growing trend towards activity-based forms of leisure and tourism. This trend emerged at the start of the 1990s with the search for more energetic forms of tourism (Hall and Weiler 1992; Leisure Consultants 1997).

9.3 HARD AND SOFT ADVENTURE TOURISM

■ 9.3.1 Hard *adventure tourism*

The historical lineage of hard adventure tourism conjures up images of early forms of mountain exploration in nineteenth-century Europe and Oceania (Johnston 1992). However, its more contemporary and commercialised manifestations have, from the 1970s onwards, seen a proliferation of equipment providers, magazines and journals promoting adventure recreation and tourism in Australasia and North America (Hall 1992). In defining adventure tourism, Hall recognises that this form of tourism brings tourists into contact with natural outdoor settings, outside of their home environments, where they can engage in a variety of activities that have varying degrees of risk. The role of risk is a recurring theme in the literature on adventure tourism. Johnston highlights 'risk thresholds'. Participants will gain positive feelings from risk seeking if they stay below the risk threshold. However, exceeding it will lead to negative feelings towards particular activities. In citing Allen's (1980) structure of risk, as a continuum of risk, Johnston demonstrates that participants will determine the level of risk to pursue, with controlled support from operators and fellow participants.

Within the wider concern of the environmental impact of adventure tourism activities, a key role for the adventure tourism operator is to provide the adventure tourist with managed activities. These activities should occur in the most appropriate locations for the tourist to gain psychological benefits from confronting a challenge (Hall). Citing the work of Kearsley (1985:133), Johnston notes that in New Zealand there is a history of adventure recreation and tourism, which emphasises that confronting the challenge of the great outdoors is part of the collective psyche of New Zealanders. There is also an emphasis on the diverse motivations for travelling to mountain environments, which include sightseeing and educational travel.

■ 9.3.2 **Soft** *adventure tourism*

Educational motivations often underpin softer forms of adventure tourism. This is highlighted by Lee (1995), who profiles the work of Australis, an Australian nature tourism travel company. Australis promotes soft adventure natural history tours in the urban and rural environs of Melbourne. The emphasis is on educational discovery through natural and cultural interpretation provided by tour guides.

Pearce (1994) notes how in Munsterland, Germany, bicycle tourism was adopted as a form of soft tourism development. In the 1980s, the concept of soft tourism, or *sanfter Tourismus*, was particularly applied to European alpine regions. The focus was on environmentally sensitive policies related to tourism development. However, in citing the work of Broggi (1985:286), Pearce emphasises a broader definition provided by the 1984 Chur Declaration of the *Commission Internationale pour la Protection des Regions Alpines* (CIPRA). This focuses on the importance of retaining community and cultural priorities in development proposals, as well as considering the environmental impact of tourism activities. Soft tourism was contrasted with more large-scale, mainstream and commercial forms of hard tourism. Importantly, while Pearce identifies that these forms of tourism can be cast as opposites, there might be variations in the mainstream and intermediate cases (1994:19).

Table 9.1 summarises and contrasts the main characteristics of hard and soft adventure tourism.

■ Table 9.1
Main characteristics of hard and soft adventure tourism

HARD TOURISM	SOFT TOURISM
• Presents the tourist with challenging environments	• Education is the tourist's motivation
• Risk taking is the key motivation	• Environmental and cultural appreciation important aspect of the experience
	• Often includes guided tours

■ 9.3.3 **Managing** *the motivations of adventure tourists*

The concept of adventure tourism embraces a broad range of motivational characteristics, from the pursuit of risk and excitement to educational and aesthetic appreciation. This provides a challenge for tourism operators who act as intermediaries between the user and the resource, managing tourist motivations and satisfactions (Tabata 1992). This management function goes beyond inducing and controlling levels of risk and opportunities for discovery. It incorporates an understanding of how these adventure activities impact on the natural and cultural environment. This raises the wider issue of the long-term sustainability of resources for adventure tourism and places a responsibility on operators to manage resources sensitively, combining the ephemeral tourist experiences with the long-term maintenance of the environmental, social and cultural integrity of resources. Additionally, there is an onus on public sector agencies to apply legislative frameworks and planning acumen to the stewardship of environments for adventure tourism. This raises a question as to what forms of adventure tourism would be most appropriately managed within particular locations.

A list of 23 adventure tourism activities cited by Hall, ranging from mountaineering to white-water rafting and backpacking, also includes bicycle touring. With an upsurge in commercial interest and policy agendas for bicycle tourism, it has the flexibility to offer a range of diverse products which correspond to the principles of sustainable tourism. Before reviewing the role of bicycle tourism and its adventure tourism applications, contemporary methods of marketing adventure tourism should be considered.

■ *9.3.4* **Marketing** *adventure activities:*
the Adventure Guide

Contemporary initiatives in matching operators of adventure products with customer requirements are demonstrated through Web-based adventure tourism product brokers who focus largely on the element of risk taking, but also highlight softer forms of ecotourism-based adventure tourism. The Web-based Adventure Guide (http://www.adventureguide.com/start.htm) offers the opportunity to search for 'your special adventure', matching countries and regions with 45 selected adventures. This matching process of effectively linking adventure activities within specific locations is aimed at simplifying the search for special adventure linked to travel-related services. The Adventure Guide has special sections for business travellers, single women and active seniors which are based on inclusive group tours and marketed as multi-adventure holidays, catering for all ranges of experience and abilities. Bicycle tourism is highlighted as one of the 45 adventure tourist products in the guide, with the choice of on- and off-road cycling in a range of locations. Bicycle tourism will now be investigated as the main focus of the chapter.

9.4 DEFINING BICYCLE TOURISM ....

While bicycle tourism as a tourist activity has received relatively limited academic attention, a number of academics have taken the lead in producing contemporary studies that provide important insights into the market characteristics of bicycle tourism. In particular, Lumsdon (1995), Beioley (1995), Simonsen and Jorgensen (1996) and Ritchie (1998) have identified the demand characteristics of bicycle tourism. Bicycle tourism is essentially an activity that requires some degree of physical commitment, but it does not necessarily involve high levels of exertion and skill acquisition. It has the capacity, therefore, to attract a broad range of participants, who are not necessarily seeking improved physical fitness.

The wider debate about definitions of special interest tourism is pertinent to the analysis of bicycle tourism definitions. Ritchie distinguishes between those tourists who use their bicycles as the exclusive form of transport on holiday (the central hub of the tourist activity) and those who use mixed modes of transportation, with cycling used as a peripheral tourist pursuit. Simonsen and Jorgensen characterise a continuum of bicycle tourists, ranging from 'occasional cyclists' to 'cycling enthusiasts'. The implication is that the former category of cyclists might use the bicycle as one of many transport modes on holiday, while the cycling enthusiasts 'live their holiday' through the bicycle. In observing the work of Simonsen and Jorgensen, Ritchie estimates that the majority of bicycle tourists lie somewhere between these two poles on the continuum.

In line with Johnston's analysis of adventure tourists and the potential changing career motivations of adventure tourists, bicycle tourists are viewed as having the capacity to shift motivations towards different forms of bicycle tourism. In his definition of bicycle tourism, Lumsdon adopts an inclusive definition that incorporates both tourists and excursionists, stating that:

> cycle tourism encompasses recreational cycling activities ranging from a day to a long distance touring holiday. The fundamental ingredient is that cycling is perceived by the visitor as an integral part of an excursion or holiday, i.e. a positive way of enhancing leisure time.

■ **Figure 9.1**
Defining bicycle tourism

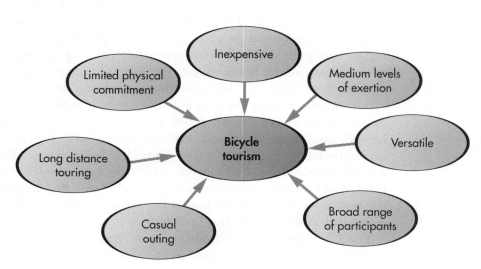

Lumsdon highlights the segmentation of the recreational cycling market into the following broad categories:
- types of bicycle tourist:
  - independent day cyclist
  - day bicycle hirer
  - short break tourer

- independent holiday
- group holiday
- solo mountain biker.

These categories may be broken into further subsegments.

■ 9.4.1 **Early origins** *of bicycle tourism*

Analysing the origins of bicycle tourism provides a broader perspective on the emergence of market segments for bicycle tourism and its requirements. Bicycle tourism is a SIT form with great versatility. While it is characterised as a contemporary form of tourism, it has an established historical pedigree as an early form of popular tourism in regions like the United Kingdom. It has survived and been adapted by changes in tourist trends and fashions, and metamorphosed into a number of forms of cycling. As a particular transport mode, the bicycle has enabled tourists with limited financial means to explore and discover natural landscapes outside of industrialised and urban environments.

The creation of leisure-based cycling clubs in the United Kingdom was stimulated, in part, by the formation of the national organisation the Cyclists Touring Club (CTC) in 1878. Similar to the pioneering nature of mountaineering as an early form of adventure tourism in New Zealand (Johnston), the CTC provided the impetus for cyclists to go on journeys of discovery, beyond urban boundaries, to explore the countryside of the United Kingdom. The CTC reached the zenith of its popularity in 1899, with more than 60 000 members. The bicycle played a role in 'renewing the urban acquaintance with the countryside', with continuing popularity into the early part of the twentieth century, despite the 'growing ubiquity of the car'(Patmore 1983:34). With continuing interest in recreational cycling within pre-war Britain, the guarantee of a week's holiday with pay (enabled by the *Holiday with Pay Act* 1938) gave cyclists extended leisure time to bicycle into rural areas and take advantage of affordable, rural-based accommodation, provided by the Youth Hostel Association. Bicycle tourism was an affordable form of tourism, which allowed 'escape' beyond the confines of industrialised regions into the rural hinterland. In post-war Britain, the use of 'cyclist trains' extended the scope for bicycle clubs to travel en masse into rural areas, beyond rail hubs.

The CTC continues to stimulate participation in cycling, and has been instrumental in creating a national network of CTC clubs within the United Kingdom. Additionally, there is a complementary network of independent cycling clubs that promote cycling for people involved in competitive, sporting, leisure-based and touring cycling.

Together with CTC members, club cyclists have established a discernible leisure subculture and traits of recreation specialisation (Bryan 1977). With identified club and amateur commitment (Stebbins 1979), certain market segments might be extending recreation specialisation into tourism choice.

■ *9.4.2* **Recreation** *specialisation*

McIntyre (1991), in citing the work of Bryan, identifies that recreation specialisation can be measured through the following observational criteria:

- ownership of equipment
- prior experience
- levels of skills acquisition
- club membership
- specialist literature readership
- choice of leisure setting.

This matches the criteria outlined by Hall in recognising the growth in adventure-based recreation and tourism. McIntyre emphasises that observational criteria may be more an indication of conspicuous consumption than the affective attachment that an individual has for a particular recreation or tourism activity. However, in the absence of detailed research related to the affective attachment of bicycle tourists, observational criteria can provide clues to recreation specialisation in bicycle tourists.

An annual expression of the recreation specialisation and subculture of cycling in the United Kingdom is the international CTC rally in the city of York, which attracts more than 10 000 cyclists for a weekend of camping and bicycle-based events. The events components are emblematic of recreation specialisation, with international and domestic participants engaging in a range of bicycle-related activities. Bicycle literature, trade stands, cycling memorabilia, auctions, slide shows, competitions, social rides and a cyclists' church service at York Minster are an example of bicycle tourism as recreation specialisation. This mass leisure tourism event has a comparable event in Australia in the Big Ride, which routinely attracts numbers of club cyclists similar to the CTC event. The Big Ride is purported to be the biggest mass leisure event in Australia, with the event shifting between different areas each year.

In addition to the CTC and independent bicycle club membership is more specialised club participation, including the Rough Stuff Fellowship, which predates the off-road cycling boom of mountain biking. Rough Stuff Fellowship cyclists epitomise cycling as adventure tourism, with intrepid cyclists going to great lengths to bicycle to inaccessible and remote countryside locations, demonstrating the highly specialised nature of bicycle tourism.

It is clear that the recreation specialisation of cyclists is an area for future research. However, it is possible to detect a solid base of recreational and tourist interest that has established the longevity of this activity. Beyond the homogenous qualities of this type of cyclist is the broader heterogeneity of cyclists, who receive particular attention from a range of supply-side operators.

■ *9.4.3* **Bicycle tourism** *operators: from hard to soft adventure*

The contemporary commercialisation of bicycle tourism involves intermediaries packaging bicycle tourism holidays. This is in contrast to the intrepid and adventure-based holidays of the early pioneering days of bicycle tourism, when the main emphasis was on independently organised trips. Post-war tourism within the United Kingdom and other westernised countries has witnessed increasing car-borne tourism and destinations accessed exclusively by aircraft. However, in the 1990s, bicycle tourism enjoyed a renaissance. The 1999 United Kingdom Day Visit Survey revealed that 71.4 million bicycle trips were taken by United Kingdom residents, making up two per cent of leisure trips. Within a tourism context, the United Kingdom Tourism Survey (1994) (UKTS) estimated that 500 000 mainly independent bicycle tourism holidays were taken by United Kingdom residents. On a wider global level, the research of Ritchie (1998:569) highlights the growing significance of bicycle tourism as a special interest tourism form by plotting the growing number of bicycle tourism holidays emerging within the speciality travel index.

Lumsdon and Ritchie emphasise that the stimulation of the latent demand for bicycle tourism products is attributable to a combination of factors. These include:
- considerable expansion in route development
- improvements in safety
- the applications of new forms of cycling technology, enabling cyclists to have easier access to testing and challenging environments.

In particular, the popularity of mountain biking has melded off-road adventure with youth culture and fashion, and has heralded a new generation of cyclists seeking new forms of adventure in testing mountain environments. The shifting image of contemporary cycling is characterised as 'wicker baskets, cycle clips and plastic capes, replaced by figure hugging lycra' (Beioley:17).

Bicycle tourism as hard adventure tourism

The commercialisation of hard, adventure-based bicycle tourism, which exemplifies the fusion of fashion and thrill seeking, is evidenced through the Adventure Guide, which includes a range of Northern and Southern hemisphere bicycle tours. Canadian Trails Adventure Tours (www.canadian-trails.com/icefields_parkway_tour.htm) offer a choice of all-inclusive group tours, providing the tourist with a list of 'Top 20' road and off-road bicycle tours. The choice is enlivened by an interactive Internet map to aid road and off-road route selection. Promoting some of the great mountain rides in the world, bicycle tourists are invited to choose from 1500 kilometres of mountain wilderness trails and roads over eight spectacular mountain ranges in the Canadian Rockies.

An example of the wider promotion of activity-based holidays that tap into a national profile of activity-based tourism is the Adventure Guide Website 100% Pure New Zealand–Thrill Zone, which promotes New Zealand as the ultimate outdoor adventure playground of untouched wilderness. This includes an invitation to 'venture into the New Zealand wilderness and discover the ultimate outdoor adventure playground' (www.purenz.com/thrillzone.cfm). Typical of these 'adrenaline rush' holidays are heli-mountain biking in the Southern Alps, with a helicopter ascent and 1300 vertical metres mountain bike ride down high country farm tracks. Wild Earth Adventures offers fully supported mountain biking trips in the Otago region for thrill seekers, as well as softer forms of adventure tourism, which combine slower, environmentally friendly rides with an opportunity to socialise with local communities. The CTC argue that, in addition to cycling being characterised as satisfying fitness, sporting competitiveness and thrill seeking, there is evidence that bicycle tourism provides an awareness of green and environment-based tourism, which exemplifies principles of soft tourism.

Bicycle tourism and versatile forms of soft adventure tourism

From the broad range of market segments identified by Lumsdon, it is apparent that bicycle tourism has many facets that will appeal to a wide spectrum of occasional cyclists and cycling enthusiasts. While bicycle tourism might be the hub around which tourist experiences are built (Hall & Weiler), there is tremendous scope for this core tourism experience to be augmented with other distinct interests. For example, Gausden notes how cycling combines well with a range of hobbies and emphasises that it is complementary to the enjoyment of nature and sightseeing, generally at a slow pace (1994:5). Morpeth (2000) establishes links between wine tourism and bicycle tourism, highlighting the existence of travel companies that offer a combination of cycling and winery visitation, emphasising the educational and social dimension of guided tours. From a public policy perspective in the European context, there is developing infrastructure provision for a proposed 3600-kilometre wine and gourmet route, from Nantes in France to Constanta in Romania. The route follows three major European rivers, the Loire, the Danube and the Rhine, and provides considerable opportunities for winery visitation. The type of trail development is part of a wider initiative of Euro Velo bicycle routes described on the following page.

The special interest product range for bicycle tourism incorporating soft adventure was epitomised in the 1970s by Cycling for Softies, with cycling holidays initially based in France. The packages offered non-strenuous cycling, with a luggage courier service between comfortable hotel accommodation.

Research by Thomas (1994) into the management of small firms shows that owners of tourism and hospitality businesses can be motivated by both commercial and lifestyle considerations. This was confirmed by Shaw and Williams (1994, cited in Thomas), in their study of small firms in Cornwall. The study focused on this taxonomy of ownership, identifying the entrepreneurial qualities of small firm owners as consumers as well as producers, the implication being that they consume the lifestyle benefits of running a business. This wider philosophy of business objectives suggests that small firms such as the Alternative Travel Group value principles of sustainable tourism as well as commercial imperatives. Operators such as these may have important insights into users and the resources on which their tourism products are based and therefore influence the potential interaction between them. In the new millennium, two companies in tune with promoting products underpinned with the principles of environmental, community and cultural considerations, outlined by the CIPRA declaration on soft tourism, are the Alternative Travel Group and Bicycle Beano.

A cutting edge policy initiative for cycle tourism trail development is emerging through the work of the European Cyclists Federation in conjunction with Sustrans, which has provided the impetus for the development of a European cycling network — Euro Velo. The central aspect of this initiative is the physical linkage of national routes, providing the capacity for bicycle tourists to move easily across national borders and combine soft adventure with other tourist experiences. Cyclists embarking on the developing European North Sea Cycle Route will be able to combine the cultural and landscape mixes of Norway, Sweden, Denmark, Germany, the Netherlands, England and Scotland. This will be a fully signposted route with local government and tourist facility and amenity support. For route development to occur political and policy support at a national and regional level are required. Resources for infrastructure development for cycling, with manifest benefits for the development of cycle tourism, must be committed. To this end, a working group of the European Cyclists Federation (ECF) put forward a proposal for funding from the European Community to create 12 European routes. In cycling terms, the design of high quality routes created across all European borders will act as a demonstration project to encourage non-cyclists to use new route infrastructure. In minimising the environmental impact of inbound travel and extending the economic benefit of bicycle tourism, the ECF identify bicycle tourism as a quintessential form of sustainable tourism.

Construction of the network will involve the creation of signed routes, specific segregated cycling-friendly trails, the coordination of cycling-friendly accommodation and support services. The ECF have created a combination of a central organising bureau and a consortia of separate local authorities and constituent organisations to coordinate the development of the route.

Although Euro Velo aims to create new infrastructure for cycling and bicycle tourism, the European Cycle Federation emphasises the rich legacy of existing route development. Typical of the quality infrastructure for bicycle tourism in Europe envisaged by Euro Velo is a network of cycle routes within Austria, which, since 1987, has seen the creation of 30 long distance routes covering 4000 kilometres.

A number of Euro Velo routes emphasise the cultural assets of bicycle route design. The emerging North Sea Circuit is a 6000-kilometre route that incorporates the cross-cultural benefits of cycling through Norway, Sweden, Denmark, Germany, the Netherlands, England and Scotland. A proposed 5000-kilometre European western seaboard Green Atlantis route incorporates the Isle of Skye (within Scotland's Western Isles), mainland Scotland, Portugal and Spain, emphasising the rich cultural heritage that cyclists can enjoy at a slow pace.

The Alternative Travel Group

The Alternative Travel Group, a United Kingdom–based travel company, offers specialist guided and independent cycling and walking holidays throughout Europe. Existing signed cycling and walking trails are used in addition to customised routes. Their managing director, Christopher Whinney, explains how the company 'was founded in 1979, based on principles of conservation and sustainable tourism, long before these concepts became fashionable' (2000:2). Guides and managers are given environmental training and 10 per cent of profits are committed to conservation projects in areas visited. Although holidays are facilitated by route managers, the accent is on clients 'discovering and enjoying' each area in their own time. The emphasis is on promoting the cultural, landscape and gastronomic aspects of the regions visited. Luggage is ferried between accommodation stops. Cycling has been introduced as a diversification from core walking products. The main aspect of these holidays is oriented towards soft adventure, emphasising educational and aesthetic appreciation. Marketing incorporates direct mailing of brochures to clients and word of mouth. A particular issue for the company, in respect of targeting appropriate market segments, is to balance the needs of people who enjoy activity based holidays but require cultural stimulation.

Bicycle Beano

Beioley identifies that within the United Kingdom there are approximately 350 bicycle tourism businesses. Perhaps typical of these businesses, and conforming to Thomas's taxonomy of lifestyle motivations for business development, is Bicycle Beano, founded in the early 1980s as a two-person business. As serious cycling participants, they shared a passionate interest in bicycle tourism. Described by one of their clients as 'an eating holiday interrupted by a bit of cycling', the emphasis is on relaxation and vegetarian cuisine, but a series of routes are created for cyclists, with the owners riding with the group (http://www.bicycle-beano.co.uk). All rides are based on a series of communal food stops at pubs, cafes and local houses, and visits to churches and other places of interest are built into itineraries. Routes do not follow established signed bicycle routes, but are derived from local knowledge of landscapes and points of interest. Holidays are aimed at a broad mix of cyclists, from the cycling enthusiast to the occasional cyclist, including family groups and with an even split of gender participation.

It is possible to speculate that the bottom line for this type of company is not commercial goals, but that it is more focused on lifestyle considerations. The success of holiday experiences is inextricably linked to the personal input and hands-on approach of the two owners, who 'live' the holiday experience with clients. The company has resisted the opportunity to create a 'cyclist's hotel' in one location, and has opted to use existing accommodation outlets. As with the operation of ecotourism firms in Australia noted by Lee, Bicycle Beano might have to compete with larger operators, who adopt a more hard line commercial edge to selling bicycle tourism holidays. However, Bicycle Beano's success is in the personal level of service offered and the melding of appreciation of landscape, cultural and community aspects of cycling holidays. Marketing involves direct mailing former clients and Web-based information.

SUPPLY-SIDE POLICY CONSIDERATIONS

In addition to commercial support for bicycle tourism is the support of public sector agencies for bicycle tourism development. The emergence of improved cycling infrastructure, with multifaceted applications for utilitarian, recreational and tourist use, has an international currency, with urban bicycle network development and trail development occurring in Australasia, North America and Europe. The European arena for bicycle tourism highlights the political and policy commitment to route development at a European, national and local level. Within a United Kingdom context, the development of utilitarian cycling and recreational and bicycle tourism has been spearheaded by Sustrans, a sustainable transport charity and the architects of the National Cycle Network in the United Kingdom. The East of England Tourist Board (EETB) has invested research and development in promoting bicycle tourism as a key special interest tourism product (see Special interest investigation). The case study of the Coast to Coast (C2C) bicycle trail emphasises the benefit of collaborative policy networks (Colebatch 1998), creating route infrastructure for bicycle tourism with positive community and tourist benefit.

■ 9.5.1 Utilitarian *bicycle development: an Australian perspective*

Developing route networks for cycling at a local level can be instrumental in encouraging multi-use of such networks, not only for riding to work or school but also as a prelude to stimulating recreational and tourist use. The New South Wales government has committed substantial funds over the first 10 years of this millennium to establish a statewide cycleway network, in recognition of the growing interest in pedalling for leisure. There are options for on- and off-road cycling for the 2000 bicycle owners in the State (Allenby 2000). The Roads and Traffic Authority New South Wales issues maps and encourages enthusiasts to ensure they have detailed instructions, adequate fitness and the right equipment, particularly for rides through prime scenic locations like national parks which are within reasonable distance of the Sydney metropolitan area.

■ **Figure 9.2** *Local governments in Australia are supporting off-road cycling.*

Source: *Graphiti Design/CC Photography*

Established in 1987 and operating as a bicycle unit within the Western Australia Department of Transport, Bikewest has successfully facilitated bicycle projects within Perth and its environs. It has taken advantage of statutory planning powers and works as a multiplier agency, attracting leverage funding for cycling infrastructure initiatives. The aim of the unit is to develop 'safe and convenient routes for cyclists, to travel to major destinations' (Bikewest 1995:1). It has primarily developed the scope for utilitarian cycling, supporting the development of a bicycle infrastructure in more than 30 local authority areas and coordinating the Perth Bicycle Network, which has recreational and tourist applications. Bikewest has also created a template for bicycle infrastructure development throughout Australia, providing an excellent model of political and policy support for bicycle network development.

SPECIAL INTEREST INVESTIGATION
The East of England Tourist Board

The East of England Tourist Board has become one of the most proactive regional tourist boards within the United Kingdom involved in the strategic development and promotion of bicycle tourism. Within their overall portfolio of product development and promotion, bicycle tourism has been given a high profile. As part of their strategy to target the diverse elements of the bicycle tourism market, the Board has conducted several major pieces of market research, with the profiling of bicycle tourists complementary to the academic profiling of bicycle tourism. The work of the EETB provides an invaluable insight as to how a supply-side tourism organisation identifies the bicycle tourism market as part of the process of planning and developing cycle tourism products. The EETB identified the development of bicycle routes and trails, which capitalise on the National Cycle Network, as a key product development (EETB 1996). In dubbing the East of England 'England's Cycling Country', they have launched a United Kingdom advertising campaign and promotions at overseas travel trade exhibitions and have established a cycling holiday operators network. The EETB aim to develop cycling holidays and short break products in conjunction with bicycle holiday operators and have been instrumental in initiating a 'cyclists welcome scheme' at attractions and accommodation establishments.

Research activities have enabled the Board to understand:

- the main types of cycling tourism activities in which people take part
- how the market can most usefully be segmented
- the interest of different cycling tourist segments in the different types of cycling tourism activity
- the key product requirements of each segment (EETB 1999:7).

(continued)

The EETB has categorised the main types of bicycle tourism and market segments as:
1. potential cyclists non/novice cyclists.
2. occasional leisure cyclists.
3. frequent cyclists.
4. cycling enthusiasts (adapted from EETB 1999:8,9).

One of the conclusions from the EETB research is that there will be some overlap in distinguishing between market segments and that bicycle tourists might 'move' between categories. Nevertheless, they conclude that there is a likely correlation between the frequency of leisure cycling and the choice of holiday products with the corresponding distance that people will bicycle on the holiday. The east of England does not include wilderness landscapes and is not viewed as attracting market segments that are attracted to challenge and risk-taking. The emphasis is on cyclists enjoying softer forms of adventure tourism that encompass heritage and cultural tourism, with the historic cathedral cities of Lincoln and Cambridge included in route itineraries.

9.6 *S*UMMARY

Adventure tourism is a manifestation of activity-based tourism. It includes soft and hard forms.

Hard forms of adventure tourism present the tourist with challenging environments. Risk taking is a key motivation. Matching activities and environments for hard forms of tourism has implications for tourism operators to manage both the tourist experience (risk management) and environment. Public sector agencies have an important role in establishing legislative frameworks that may improve adventure-based activities within specific geographical locations.

Soft adventure expresses a wider range of tourist motivations, which feed positively off the environmental, community and cultural resource base, in line with the principles for soft tourism established by CIPRA. These motivations relate more to educational and aesthetic appreciation, particularly expressed through nature-based tourism. However, tourism forms should not be typecast to specific nomenclatures, when in reality there is an overlap of tourist typologies. An example is the blurring of distinction between forms of adventure and ecotourism.

Bicycle tourism may incorporate manifestations of hard and soft tourism. Definitions and the profiling of market segments for bicycle tourism reveal a broad range of bicycle tourists, from occasional day riders to cycling enthusiasts, with potentially different product needs. The concept of recreational specialisation links utilitarian and recreational cycling and illustrates how these different forms of bicycling might lead to bicycle tourism participation. Bicycle tourism is an inclusive form of tourism, which attracts genders and groups diverse in age and lifestyle.

The response of supply-side operators incorporates the wider principles of sustainable tourism within products on offer. Small tourism businesses promote wider lifestyle elements as well as commercial considerations. From a supply-side perspective, bicycle tourism has gained a high profile politically through the endorsement of cycling infrastructure and as a tourism activity. Local government and national and international bodies support the development of cycling and bicycle tourism by providing route information and developing bicycle ways.

Developments in cycling and bicycle tourism provide evidence of the progress made in promoting their sustainable qualities. This special interest tourism form exemplifies how sustainable tourism can move beyond the symbolic policy level to demonstrate how policy can be implemented.

The renaissance of cycle tourism is a continuing process and future research will reveal its multidimensional qualities, not least as a soft form of adventure tourism.

Questions

9.1 Discuss how strategies for sustainable tourism might incorporate bicycle tourism as an implementable form of sustainable tourism.

9.2 (a) Is it possible for adventure tourism operators to effectively manage the motivations of adventure tourists and provide safeguards for fragile resource bases for adventure tourism?

(b) Can public sector agencies assist in this process?

9.3 How are motivations for soft adventure tourism distinct from motivations for hard adventure tourism?

9.4 Are specific market segments of bicycle tourism more likely to be attracted by motivations for soft adventure tourism?

9.5 (a) Contact coastal local authorities within your State and establish to what extent a coastal bicycle way for the State has been established.

(b) What barriers to the implementation of such a project can you identify? What benefits would be derived for utilitarian, recreational and bicycle tourism usage?

(c) How might residents from hosting local authorities benefit?

9.6 What specific infrastructure requirements and amenity support are required for recreational and tourist cyclists to overcome the tyranny of distance within Australia?

(*continued*)

9.7 (a) Identify and contact a bicycle tourism business and assess the extent to which business objectives are driven by commercial or lifestyle considerations.

(b) Does a commitment to lifestyle considerations benefit the tourist and offer wider environmental benefits? Does such a commitment expose businesses to uncertain financial futures?

9.8 (a) Identify the range of policy makers at the local, state and national level and analyse their commitment to different forms of cycling.

(b) Do strategies recognise links between utilitarian, recreational and tourism forms of cycling?

(c) Does soft adventure tourism feature as part of these strategies?

9.9 'Bicycle tourism is a part of the passing trend towards green tourism and is unlikely to be sustained as a viable form of special interest tourism.' Discuss.

REFERENCES

Allen, S. 1980. 'Risk Recreation: A Literature Review and Conceptual Model'. In Meier, J. F., Morash, W. T., Welton, G. E. (Eds.). *High Adventure Outdoor Pursuits: Organization and Leadership*. Utah: Brighton Publishing Company.

Allenby, Guy. 2000. 'The Wheel World'. *Sydney Morning Herald*, 12 August, Weekend 6, Travel p. 1.

Alternative Travel Group. 2000. *Footlose 2000: Independent Walking and Cycling*. Oxford, UK: Alternative Travel Group, pp. 1–2.

Beioley, S. 1995. 'On Yer Bike — Cycling and Tourism'. *Insights*, September: B17–31.

BikeWest, 1995. *Annual Report 1994–95*. Fremantle: Department of Transport.

Broggi, M. F. (Ed.). 1985. *Sanfter Tourismus: Schlagwort oder Chance fur den Alpenraum?* Vaduz: Commission Internationale pour las Protection des Regions Alpines (CIPRA).

Bryan, H. 1977. 'Leisure Value Systems and Recreation Specialisation: The Case of Trout Fishermen'. *Journal of Leisure Research* 9 (3): 174–87.

Colebatch, H. K. 1998. *Policy*. Buckingham: Open University Press.

Coleman, Robert. Unpublished address at Euro Velo Launch Conference, Logrono, Spain, 21 November 1997.

Cope, A., Doxford, D. & Hill, T. 1998. 'Monitoring Tourism on the UK's First Long-Distance Cycle Route'. *Journal of Sustainable Tourism* 6 (3): 210–23.

East of England Tourist Board. 1996. *England's Cycling Country: A Cycling Tourism Strategy for the East of England 1996–99*. East of England Tourist Board: Hadleigh, Suffolk, pp. i–iv.

East of England's Cycling Country. 1999. *England's Cycling Country: Understanding the Cycling Tourism Market*. East of England Tourist Board: Hadleigh, Suffolk, UK.

Gausden, C. 1994. *Weekend Cycling*. Leicester: The Promotional Reprint Company, p. 5.

Hall, C. M. 1992. 'Adventure, Sport and Health Tourism'. In Hall, C. M., & Weiler, B. *Special Interest Tourism*. London: Belhaven Press, pp. 141–58.

Hall, C. M. & Weiler, B. 1992. 'What's Special About Special Interest Tourism?'. In Weiler, B. & Hall, C. M. *Special Interest Tourism*. London: Belhaven Press.

Hoggarth, R. 1995. *The Way We Live Now.* London: Pimlico, p. 157.

Jackson, G. & Morpeth, N. 1999. 'Local Agenda 21 and Community Participation in Tourism in Tourism Policy and Planning: Future or Fallacy'. *Current Issues in Tourism* 1.

Johnston, M. E. 1992. 'Facing the Challenges: Adventure in the Mountains'. In Weiler, B. & Hall, C. M. (Eds.). *Special Interest Tourism*. London: Belhaven Press, pp. 159–70.

Kearsley, G. 'Wilderness Images and National Parks Management'. In Marks, D. F. & Russell, D. G. (Eds.). *Imagery 1, Proceedings of the First International Imagery Conference*. 1983, Dunedin: Human Performance Associates.

Lee, T. 1995. 'Australis: Soft Adventure Natural History Tours'. In Harris, R. & Leiper, N. (Eds.). *Sustainable Tourism: An Australian Perspective*. Sydney: Butterworth-Heinemann.

Leisure Consultants. 1997. 'Leisure Forecasts 1997–2001'. *Leisure Away from Home*. Sudbury: Leisure Consultants.

Lumsdon, L. 1995. 'Cycle Tourism a Growth Market'. Conference for Cycle Tourism: A Growth Market. Staffordshire University, 24 February.

McIntyre, N. 1991. 'Recreation Specialisation Re-examined: The Case of 4WD Campers'. Proceedings of the World Leisure and Recreation Association Congress, Sydney, 16–19 July.

Morpeth, N. 2000. 'Diversifying Wine Tourism Products: An Evaluation of Linkages Between Wine and Cycle Tourism'. In Hall, C. M., Sharples, E. & Macionis, N. (Eds.). *Wine and Tourism Around the World: Development, Management and Markets*, Oxford, UK: Butterworth-Heinemann, pp. 272–82.

Patmore, J. A. 1983. *Leisure Patterns and Leisure Places*. Oxford, UK: Blackwell, p. 34.

Pearce, D. 1994. 'Alternative Tourism: Concepts, Classifications and Questions' In Smith, V. & Eadington, W. (Eds.). *Tourism Alternatives: Potentials and Problems in the Development of Tourism*. Chichester, UK: John Wiley & Sons.

Ritchie, B. 1998. 'Bicycle Tourism in the South Island of New Zealand: Planning and Management Issues'. *Tourism Management* 19: 567–82.

Roads and Traffic Authority, New South Wales. 2000. *http://www.rta.nsw.gov.au*

Simonsen, P. & Jorgensen, B. 1996. Cycling Tourism: Environmental and Economic Sustainability? Unpublished paper. Bonholm Research Centre, Denmark.

Stebbins, R. A. 1979. *Amateurs: On the Margin Between Work and Leisure*. California: Sage, pp. 169–75.

Sustrans. 1995. 'The National Cycle Network': Update One. Bristol, UK: Sustrans.

Sustrans. 1997. *European Cycle Routes: A Report on National and International Developments*. Bristol, UK: Sustrans.

Tabata, R. S. 1992. 'Scuba Diving Holidays'. In Weiler, B. & Hall, C. M. (Eds.). *Special Interest Tourism*, Chichester, UK: Belhaven Press.

Weaver, D. 1998. *Ecotourism in the Less Developed World*. Oxford: CAB International, pp. 11–12.

Williams, A. M., Shaw, G. & Greenwood, J. 1989. 'From Tourist to Entrepreneur, from Consumption to Production: Evidence from Cornwall, England'. In Thomas, C. *Environment and Planning A* 21:1639–53.

The C2C Cycle Trail

The C2C Trail was opened in 1995 and was one of the first UK-based bicycle routes to be popularised by the television travel program *Wish You Were Here*. It was awarded the Tourism for Tomorrow Global Award. Within days of the program being screened, several thousand enquiries about details of the route were made to Sustrans, the architects of the route. It signified a latent demand for cycling holidays and the challenge of cycling across the high Pennine Hills, dubbed 'the roof of England', one of the remotest rural areas in the United Kingdom. This demand was not exclusively among existing cyclists, but included a widening group of special interest tourists.

This 140 mile coast-to-coast route incorporates two urban regions of industrial decline at the start and the end. The greater part of the route traverses rural areas, which traditionally have been peripheral, as well as satellite tourist areas to the dominant tourist area of the Lake District National Park, which cyclists travel through on the first part of the route. Part of the attraction of the rural landscape are the industrial heritage attractions, such as the former lead mining sites. Commissioned sculptural projects are found along the route.

Symbolically, cyclists dip their tyres in the Irish Sea on the west coast and in the North Sea at their journey's end. The route was a significant marker in the evolution of the National Cycle Network and re-oriented the focus from principally utilitarian cycling to the leisure and tourism potential of route development.

The C2C became the focus for academic scrutiny to determine the popularity of the bicycle trails. Cope, Doxford and Hill (1998), from the University of Sunderland in the United Kingdom, undertook surveys in 1996 and 1997. They adopted a number of survey methods, including automatic field counters, field interviews and telephone interviews. In 1996, between 12 000 and 15 000 people used the route, spending between £1.07 and £1.85 million. In 1997, 11 000 used the route.

The initiative is an exemplar of how tourism and its associated benefits can be generated for economically marginal and touristically under-developed areas, while minimising negative impacts. The economic benefits to communities in the area have been significant. Accommodation and hospitality outlets have benefited. In terms of the policy dimension of a commitment to bicycle tourism as a special interest tourism form, the C2C is an impressive example of a range of local authorities and supporting agencies and organisations coordinating and funding route development in conjunction with Sustrans. Fifteen local authorities have contributed to route development, in conjunction with the Lake District National Park and the North Pennines Tourism Partnerships. Cope noted, however, that cyclists were critical of the quality of signage and that there was a need for the various stakeholders associated with the route to be part of a management group. On balance, however, there is tangible evidence of the route capturing the imagination of communities through which it passes and the ability of special interest tourism to transform the tourist receipts of peripheral tourist regions.

A small sample of cyclists who completed the route in September 1998 were used to establish a profile of cyclists using the route. The sample of riders comprised a group of five professionally employed males aged 40 to 43 years. They travelled 300 hundred miles from Banbury in Oxfordshire and booked four nights accommodation before and en route. They can be characterised as occasional cyclists, who on average bicycle recreationally together once a week. All of the party had been on bicycle tourism holidays.

The group completed the route in three days, which is the average length of time. All members of the group surveyed were male. In 1996 and 1997, 73 per cent of cyclists were male. The Cyclists' Touring Club highlight the increasing number of short breaks and second and third holidays being filled by bicycle tourism short holidays. The evidence from this sample of cyclists confirms that the C2C is a supplementary holiday for bicycle tourists, with two cyclists going on three or more holidays. Each cyclist profiled went on a main holiday abroad during the year of their C2C bicycle ride and each rider suggested that after completing this route they would be interested in going on more bicycle holidays. A key motivation for choosing the route choice was that it was a challenge, but was also fun. The social aspect of the group was viewed as important.

Questions

1 Devise a marketing strategy to attract new cycle tourists to cycle a trail similar to the C2C route. What specific features of the trail would you promote?

2 Where is the nearest long distance bicycle trail to your home?
   (a) Who is responsible for funding route development and the overall management of the route?
   (b) Identify existing survey work which monitors the number of bicycle tourists using the route. If you are unable to identify an existing survey, devise your own to monitor the number of bicycle tourists using the route.
   (c) Using existing methodologies, identify how economic, environmental, community and cultural benefits of bicycle tourism can be assessed.

Heather Zeppel

CHAPTER 10

Aboriginal cultures *and* indigenous tourism

LEARNING OBJECTIVES

After reading this chapter, you will have an appreciation of:

- how indigenous cultures and peoples are involved in the tourism industry
- indigenous cultural tourism and diversified indigenous tourism sectors
- the variety of indigenous tourism enterprises operating in Australia
- key issues involved in developing and managing indigenous tourism ventures.

*I*NTRODUCTION

Worldwide, indigenous peoples are becoming more involved in the tourism industry. Tourism enterprises controlled by indigenous people include cultural attractions, nature-based tours and other tourist-oriented facilities or services. This chapter examines indigenous involvement in tourism through indigenous operators and providers of tourism experiences, with the main focus on Aboriginal tourism in Australia.

This chapter begins by defining indigenous peoples and indigenous tourism and considers that select indigenous groups are progressing from ethnic to indigenous tourism. The chapter then reviews Aboriginal tourism in Australia, including recent Aboriginal tourism strategies, tourist promotion of Aboriginal culture and research on Aboriginal tourism. Critical issues for developing Aboriginal tourism businesses are discussed and the chapter concludes that, in Australia, Aboriginal groups are advancing from ethnic to indigenous tourism; from being exotic tourist attractions to controlling tourism on Aboriginal lands and owning tourism enterprises.

■ 10.1.1 Key aspects *of indigenous tourism*

Indigenous tourism evolves when indigenous people operate tours and cultural centres, provide visitor facilities and control tourist access to cultural events and homelands.

Indigenous tourist attractions include native museums and cultural villages, indigenous festivals or special events and indigenous arts. Cultural, environmental and spiritual aspects of indigenous heritage and traditions feature in indigenous tourism. These indigenous tourism ventures are largely a response to the spread of tourism into rural and remote areas, including national parks, reserves and homelands that are traditional living areas for many indigenous groups. Native lands and urban areas in developed countries are also a growing focus for indigenous tourism (Lew & Van Otten 1998). The growing tourist demand for an indigenous cultural experience is matched by the need of indigenous people to derive income from land, cultural resources and new economic ventures.

During the 1990s, indigenous tourism developed into a new visitor market segment marked by indigenous ownership and management of cultural attractions and tours (Getz & Jamieson 1997; Zeppel 1998a, 1998b). Many of these indigenous tourism ventures are community-based, developed by native bands, tribal groups, or entrepreneurs living in a native community. Unique aspects of indigenous history and cultural traditions are included in both cultural and heritage tourism. Indigenous ties to the land and the use of natural resources are part of nature-based tourism (Miller 1996; Scheyvens 1999). Ceremonial aspects of indigenous cultures also feature in native festivals and special events.

Indigenous cultures are frequently the special interest or main motivating factor for tourist travel to exotic destinations, regions, attractions and events. However, indigenous tourism enterprises are often located in rural or remote regions, with limited infrastructure and access to tourist markets (Getz & Jamieson 1997). Hence, indigenous tourism also relates to:

- community-based tourism
- cultural tourism
- heritage tourism
- nature-based tourism
- festivals and events
- regional tourism.

■ 10.1.2 Defining *indigenous peoples and indigenous tourism*

Indigenous peoples are generally regarded as tribal or native groups still living in their homeland areas. They are considered to be original or first peoples, with unique cultural beliefs and practices closely linked to local ecosystems and the use of natural resources (Furze, De Lacey & Birckhead 1996). Different terms used to describe indigenous groups include ethnic minorities (China), tribes (Africa, South America), native or Indian (North and South America), Aboriginal (Australia), and First Nations (Canada). As an overall term, 'indigenous people is used to describe races of people who are endemic or native to a destination region' (Hinch & Butler 1996:9). These indigenous groups may either be the majority group (e.g. Papua New Guinea) or a minority group in the destination, particularly in colonised countries such as North America, Australia and New Zealand. Indigenous people themselves may also be tourists visiting indigenous cultural attractions or events outside of their local area.

Indigenous tourism is referred to as Aboriginal or indigenous tourism in Australia; aboriginal, native or First Nations tourism in Canada; and Indian or Native American tourism in the United States. It is also referred to as anthropological tourism or tribal tourism. In Canada, Parker (1993:400) defines aboriginal tourism as 'any tourism product or service which is owned and operated by aboriginal people'. Similarly, among the Kuna Indians of Panama, Swain (1989:85) considers indigenous tourism is 'tourism based on the group's land and cultural identity and controlled from within by the group'. For Smith (1996a:299), tribal tourism at Acoma Pueblo, New Mexico (USA), involves 'small scale enterprises that are labour intensive for an owner, a family, or a small tribe'. Indigenous tourism typically involves small businesses based on the inherited knowledge of culture and nature.

Indigenous tourism has also been called ethnic tourism (Smith 1989; de Burlo 1996; Moscardo & Pearce 1999). Ethnic tourism always involves some form of direct contact with host cultures and their environment. For Smith (1989), ethnic tourism typically occurs in remote areas that experience limited numbers of visitors, although 100 000 visitors a year now go trekking among the hill tribes of northern Thailand. Ethnic tourism also implies direct contact with immigrant groups who may not be native or indigenous to a destination.

This chapter uses the term indigenous tourism, with a key focus on indigenous-owned tourism ventures. Therefore, 'indigenous tourism refers to tourism activity in which indigenous people are directly involved, either through control and/or by having their culture serve as the essence of the attraction' (Hinch & Butler 1996:9). According to Smith (1996b:287), the four 'Hs' of habitat, heritage, history and handicrafts define indigenous tourism as 'a culture-bounded visitor experience'. Hence, indigenous tourism includes 'that segment of the visitor industry which directly involves native peoples whose ethnicity is a tourist attraction' (Smith 1996b:283). This includes personal tourism businesses with direct contact between indigenous hosts and visitors, and indirect businesses involving the production and sale of native handicrafts or manufactured 'aboriginal' products. Indigenous involvement and control are key factors defining indigenous tourism, as set out in figure 10.1.

■ **Figure 10.1**
Key features of indigenous tourism

INDIGENOUS TOURISM

Also referred to as cultural tourism, ethnic tourism, tribal tourism and anthropological tourism

- ■ connected with indigenous culture, values and traditions
- ■ tourism products owned and operated by indigenous people
- ■ based on indigenous land and cultural identity, controlled from within by indigenous groups
- ■ includes indigenous habitat, heritage, history and handicrafts
- ■ typically involves small tourism businesses owned by tribes or families
- ■ focuses on indigenous knowledge of culture and nature.

Source: *Based on Swain (1989); Parker (1993); Hinch & Butler (1996); Smith (1996a, 1996b)*

■ *10.1.3* **Indigenous** *cultural tourism and diversified indigenous tourism*

Hinch and Butler (1996) distinguish between indigenous controlled and indigenous themed tourism. Attractions based on indigenous culture that are owned and operated by indigenous people represent 'culture controlled' or **indigenous cultural tourism**. Other tourism ventures controlled by indigenous people that do not have indigenous culture as a main theme represent **diversified indigenous tourism**. Diversified tourist attractions and facilities owned by indigenous groups include resorts, boat cruises, road-houses, campgrounds and other visitor services. In the United States and Canada, native-owned casinos on reserve lands are a lucrative form of diversified indigenous tourism (Lew & Van Otten 1998). In the western United States, tourism on native reservations began in the 1960s (Browne & Nolan 1989). However, indigenous ownership of tourism and the expansion from culture-based to service-based indigenous tourism ventures has for the most part occurred during the 1990s.

An increasing number of indigenous special events such as dance and music festivals, powwows, rodeos, historical pageants and rituals, fairs and sports events, are also offered to tourists (Browne & Nolan 1989; Hinch & Delamere 1993; Zeppel 1999a). This chapter now examines the diversity of Aboriginal tourism ventures in Australia.

10.2 ABORIGINAL TOURISM IN AUSTRALIA

Aboriginal-owned tourism ventures are a growing segment of the Australian tourism industry, mainly since the 1990s (Commonwealth Department of Tourism 1994; Sykes 1995; Miller 1996; ATSIC 1997; Pitcher, van Oosterzee & Palmer 1999; Zeppel 1998a, 1999a). Aboriginal culture has mainly been promoted in the Northern Territory, but other states, such as New South Wales, Queensland, South Australia, Victoria and Western Australia, are also developing Aboriginal tourism products and cultural attractions. According to the South Australian Tourism Commission (1995:5), **Aboriginal tourism** in Australia can be defined as 'a tourism product which is either: Aboriginal owned or operated, employs Aboriginal people, or provides consenting contact with Aboriginal people, culture or land'.

The range of Aboriginal-owned tourism products includes cultural tours, art and craft galleries, cultural centres, accommodation, boat cruises and other visitor facilities (see table 10.1 on page 238). Aboriginal National Parks, such as Uluru and Kakadu (Northern Territory) and Mutawintji (New South Wales), jointly managed with Aboriginal custodians, also provide a variety of Aboriginal-owned tours. Well-known Aboriginal tourist ventures include the Tjapukai Aboriginal Cultural Park in Cairns (Queensland), which is 50 per cent owned by the local Djabugay people; and Tiwi Tours on Bathurst and Melville Islands in the Northern Territory (Moscardo & Pearce 1989), fully owned by the Tiwi Tourism Authority since 1995. Most indigenous tourist attractions in Australia involve mainland Aboriginal cultures, although Torres Strait Islander culture is also promoted as a tourist attraction in Queensland.

While many Aboriginal-owned tours and attractions focus on presenting Aboriginal culture, indigenous involvement in other mainstream tourism enterprises, such as accommodation or visitor service facilities (e.g. road-houses), is growing. This expansion from culture-based to service-based business ventures is termed 'diversified indigenous' tourism (Hinch & Butler 1996:10). In this broader view, 'indigenous tourism can be defined as any form of participation by indigenous people in the tourism industry, in either a direct or indirect way' (Office of Northern Development 1993:7). In the Northern Territory, Aboriginal land owners derive income from licensing, leasing, rent and tourism concessions operating on Aboriginal lands (Sykes 1995; Pitcher et al. 1999). In the remote Kimberley region of Western Australia, Aboriginal communities on the Dampier Peninsula charge access fees for tour groups and private vehicles.

■ *10.2.1* **Visitor** *interest in Aboriginal culture*

Aboriginal people are increasingly presenting their own cultures as a tourist attraction in Australia. There are around 200 indigenous tourism businesses in Australia, with an estimated value for Aboriginal cultural tourism of $5 million a year (ATSIC 1997). These Aboriginal-owned tourism enterprises are challenging the Aboriginal-based or Aboriginal-themed attractions or tours offered by non-Aboriginal operators (Office of Northern Development 1993; Zeppel 1998a, 1999a). There is a growing visitor demand for indigenous culture, with these experiences increasingly provided by Aboriginal communities. 'Around 557 000 international visitors, or 15 per cent of the total, visited indigenous sites and attractions in 1996, up by more than 45 per cent from 380 000 in 1995' (Office of National Tourism 1998). According to the 1998 international visitor survey, tourists who visit Aboriginal sites and cultural displays in Australia are mainly from Germany (48 per cent), other Europe (34 per cent), United Kingdom (24 per cent), United States (23 per cent) and Canada (21 per cent). Tourists with a high level of interest in Aboriginal culture include international backpackers, holidayers, educated professionals and females (SATC 1998). Whether these tourists prefer to visit tours and attractions owned by Aboriginal people is not known.

■ *10.2.2* **Economic** *value of Aboriginal tourism*

The estimated income from Aboriginal cultural tourism is $5 million a year, while diversified Aboriginal tourism enterprises generate $20 to $30 million (ATSIC 1997). For the majority of visitors, however, the encounter with Aboriginal culture involves buying Aboriginal art or viewing rock art sites. The current income from selling Aboriginal art, crafts and souvenir products is $200 million per annum, with half of this amount estimated from tourist sales (ATSIC 1997; Office of National Tourism 1998). Tourists alone spend $50 million each year on Northern Territory Aboriginal arts and crafts sold in galleries around Australia. The Northern Territory Tourist Commission found that 56 per cent of Aboriginal art sales in the Northern Territory are to young (20 to 24 years old) international visitors. Didgeridoos are a very popular tourist item, particularly with backpackers (see Special interest investigation on pages 239–40). Aboriginal art tours fly visitors directly to Aboriginal communities in Arnhem Land, East Kimberley and the Western Desert region to purchase paintings from well-known Aboriginal artists.

Tourist contact with rural Aboriginal communities is also increasing, with four-wheel-drive vehicles visiting remote areas in the Kimberley (Western Australia), Northern Territory and Cape York Peninsula (Queensland). There is a growing contrast between elite forms of Aboriginal tourism involving costly travel to remote areas and more accessible Aboriginal tours in national parks and urban centres.

■ Table 10.1
*Aboriginal-
owned
tourism
ventures in
Australia,
1995–99*

TYPE OF VENTURE	EXAMPLES

Indigenous cultural tourism

Aboriginal cultural centres	*Queensland*: Tjapukai Aboriginal Cultural Park, Cairns; Dreamtime Cultural Centre, Rockhampton *Victoria*: Galeena Beek Living Cultural Centre, Melbourne; Brambuk Living Cultural Centre, The Grampians (Gariwerd) *New South Wales*: Gavala Aboriginal Cultural Centre, Sydney; Brewarrina Aboriginal Cultural Museum, Brewarrina
Aboriginal cultural tours	*Northern Territory*: Tiwi Tours, Bathurst and Melville Islands, Tiwi Tourism Authority; Manyallaluk Tours, Katherine; Anangu Tours, Uluru *Queensland*: Native Guide Safari Tours, Port Douglas *South Australia*: Desert Tracks, Pitjantjatjara Lands *New South Wales*: Umbarra Cultural Tours, Narooma
Aboriginal art galleries	*Northern Territory*: Aboriginal Art and Culture Centre, Alice Springs *New South Wales*: Tobwabba Art, Forster

Diversified indigenous tourism

Tourist accommodation	*Northern Territory*: Gagudju Crocodile Hotel and Gagudju Lodge Cooinda, Gagudju Association, Kakadu; Munupi Lodge, Tiwi Tourism Authority; Glen Helen Lodge, West MacDonnell Ranges; Kings Canyon Resort, Watarrka (Kings Canyon) National Park; Wallace Rockhole Camping Ground and Caravan Park *Western Australia*: Darlngunaya Backpackers, Fitzroy Crossing, Kimberley; Kooljaman at Cape Leveque, Kimberley *Queensland*: Pajinka Wilderness Lodge, Injinoo Community, Cape York
Boat cruises	*Northern Territory*: Nitmiluk Tours, Katherine Gorge; Guluyambi Cruise, Kakadu *Western Australia*: Darngku Heritage Cruise, Geike Gorge, Kimberley *New South Wales*: Harbour Dreaming Cruise, Sydney Harbour
Visitor services and attractions	*Northern Territory*: Ininti Store Souvenirs and Cafe, Uluru *Western Australia*: Mimbi Caves, Fitzroy Crossing *South Australia*: Whale Watching, Yalata Aboriginal Lands, Nullarbor *Queensland*: Cherbourg Emu Farm *Victoria*: Snowy River Houseboats New South Wales: Brandybrook Lavender Farm, Clybucca

Note:
*Selected examples given for Aboriginal cultural tours and
art galleries, since there are now many in each State.*

Currently there is a worldwide fad for playing the didgeridoo (Neuenfeldt 1997; Zeppel 1999a:205–10). Aboriginal shops, galleries and tourist enterprises throughout Australia cater to this demand. Queues at Australian airports now regularly include backpackers with their didgeridoos. Aboriginal tourism businesses in Byron Bay (New South Wales), Queensland and the Northern Territory offer packages where visitors, often backpackers, make and learn to play their own didgeridoo. Daily didgeridoo demonstrations and talks are also presented at Aboriginal cultural centres around Australia. The Aboriginal Art and Culture Centre in Alice Springs provides didgeridoo classes at their 'didgeridoo university' and information about didgeridoos on their website (http://www.aboriginalart.com.au/didgeridoo). Didgeridoos are made and sold by both Aboriginal and non-Aboriginal people and painted or burnt with Aboriginal designs including cross-hatching, dot-art, animal figures and contemporary styles. Books and videos on how to play the didgeridoo and CDs of didgeridoo music are also sold.

Aboriginal enterprises have responded to the booming tourist demand for didgeridoos in various ways. For example, the Gavala Aboriginal Art Centre in Sydney place signs on their didgeridoos asking female tourists not to play these in the shop as this was against traditional Aboriginal custom. It is widely believed that only Aboriginal men are permitted to play the didgeridoo. However, some Aboriginal women do play the didgeridoo informally and southern Aboriginal groups, in rediscovering their Aboriginality, are adopting new age spiritual values in regard to playing the didgeridoo. An informal survey of 10 Aboriginal art galleries in Darwin (three Aboriginal-owned) found that none request female tourists to refrain from playing the didgeridoo. In Byron Bay and Alice Springs, Aboriginal men lead didgeridoo classes for both male and female tourists.

The didgeridoo derives from Arnhem Land and is used to accompany Aboriginal songs, chants and dance performances. The Maningrida Arts Centre in Arnhem Land receives e-mail requests worldwide from people wanting to buy didgeridoos or learn didgeridoo playing from an Aboriginal master player. In 1999, the Yolngu people in Arnhem Land held a yidaki (didgeridoo) masterclass for 10 international students at $1000 each. A statement on the appropriate use of didgeridoos was also prepared.

Didgeridoos are widely portrayed in tourist marketing of Aboriginal culture. As a result, tourists expect to see Aboriginal people playing the didgeridoo. Not all Aboriginal groups acknowledge the didgeridoo is traditional to Arnhem Land.

(continued)

Aboriginal people are concerned that non-indigenous people also collect wood, paint designs and sell didgeridoos in tourist outlets. This includes overcutting of didgeridoo wood in north Queensland and the Northern Territory, backpackers painting Aboriginal-style art on didgeridoos, decoration with dot-art desert designs and the mass production of didgeridoos in Australia and Indonesia (Schulz 1999). The Jawoyn people around Katherine in the Northern Territory are evaluating commercial wood collection for didgeridoos in their homelands. They aim to ensure a sustainable harvest with authentic didgeridoos collected and crafted by Aboriginal people.

■ **Figure 10.2** *An Aboriginal musician gives visitors instructions in didgeridoo playing.*

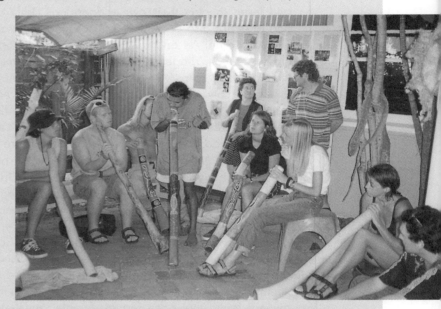

Source:
Heather Zeppel

■ *10.2.3* **Aboriginal** *tourism strategies*

Since 1995, federal and state government policies have supported the development of Aboriginal tourism in Australia, mainly as a means of achieving economic independence for Aboriginal communities (see table 10.2). The national Aboriginal and Torres Strait Islander tourism industry strategy (ATSIC 1997) is the main strategy for advancing Aboriginal tourism. It addresses the cultural, financial and business strategies required for developing Aboriginal tourism in Australia. This strategy arose from the 1991 Royal Commission into Aboriginal Deaths in Custody that identified tourism, cultural and rural industries as potential economic growth areas. Conflicts between Aboriginal cultural values and the commercial aspects of tourism business ventures were also highlighted in this strategy. A 1996 survey by the Office of National Tourism found that tourist visitation to Aboriginal cultural centres 'often reduced their use by community members' (ATSIC 1997:20). During 1999, a code of conduct for tourists visiting indigenous communities was developed. At the Office of National Tourism, indigenous tourism is part of the SIT products sector, along with ecotourism, cultural tourism, wine tourism, backpackers and tourist shopping. Aboriginal Tourism Australia also provides input to reports and policies on Aboriginal tourism. It is affiliated with the Tourism Council Australia and is based in Melbourne. In 1999, the Australian Tourism Commission appointed their first Aboriginal tourism product manager.

■ **Table 10.2** *Government strategies for developing Aboriginal tourism in Australia*

STRATEGY	AGENCY	YEAR
Tourism strategies		
Aboriginal tourism strategy	South Australian Tourism Commission	1995
Aboriginal tourism strategy	Northern Territory Tourist Commission	1996
Kimberley Aboriginal cultural tourism strategy	Kimberley Aboriginal Tourism Association	1996
Indigenous tourism product development principles	Tourism New South Wales	1997
National Aboriginal and Torres Strait Islander Tourism Industry strategy	ATSIC[1] and the Office of National Tourism	1997
Aboriginal tourism industry plan	Tourism Victoria	1998
Cultural tourism strategies		
Queensland cultural tourism	The Arts Office and QTTC[2]	1996
The cultural landscape: a cultural tourism action plan for Western Australia 1996–98	Western Australian Tourism Commission and Arts Western Australia	1996
Cultural tourism opportunities for South Australia	South Australian Tourism Commission	1996
Nature-based and ecotourism strategies		
Queensland ecotourism plan	Queensland Department of Tourism, Small Business and Industry	1997
Nature-based tourism strategy for WA	Western Australia Tourism Commission	1997
Economic development strategies		
Aboriginal economic development in WA	Department of Commerce and Trade	1997
Koori Business Network (Vic.)	Aboriginal Affairs Victoria	1999
Aboriginal Business Network (NSW)	State and Regional Development	1999

[1] *ATSIC — Aboriginal and Torres Strait Islander Commission*
[2] *QTTC — Queensland Tourist and Travel Corporation*

Aboriginal tourism strategies have also been prepared for South Australia, the Northern Territory, the Kimberley region in Western Australia and for Victoria. The strategies aim to improve the economic viability of Aboriginal tourism enterprises and promote Aboriginal cultural products to the tourist market. The provision of marketing advice and developing Aboriginal skills in business and tourism were key objectives of the Northern Territory and Victorian strategies. In 1999, Koori or

Aboriginal business networks were established in Victoria and New South Wales to assist Aboriginal business people, including those involved in tourism. Koori tourism ventures in Victoria include One Dream Time (Bendigo), Mia Mia Gallery (Melbourne), Narana Creations (Geelong) and Snowy River Houseboats (Abate 1999).

Cultural tourism and ecotourism strategies

The Kimberley Aboriginal cultural tourism strategy focused on community-based Aboriginal tourism through controlling tourist access to Aboriginal land and the interpretation of Aboriginal culture. In New South Wales, the indigenous tourism product development principles addressed Aboriginal cultural protocols and advised on business dealings with Aboriginal people in tourism. Aboriginal culture is also included as a special segment or area in cultural tourism plans (South Australia, Queensland, Western Australia) and ecotourism strategies (Queensland, Western Australia) developed by state tourism agencies.

The South Australian report on cultural tourism identified areas of market demand for Aboriginal cultural products such as Aboriginal souvenirs, arts and crafts, cultural displays and Aboriginal guided cultural tours. In Queensland, Aboriginal and Torres Strait Islander cultural products such as art, music and stories were linked with regional and local tourism development. In Western Australia, a cultural tourism pilot plan for Broome identified the development of an Aboriginal cultural centre, support for the Stompen Ground Aboriginal music festival and the promotion of Aboriginal art.

The Queensland ecotourism plan recognised opportunities for indigenous ecotours on Aboriginal lands and national park areas. This indigenous involvement in ecotourism included roles such as tour operators, trainers, educators, interpreters, resource managers, regulatory authorities, conservationists, interested local communities and visitors. The benefits of Aboriginal ecotourism were also recognised in the nature-based tourism strategy for Western Australia. However, methods for incorporating Western Australian Aboriginal people in nature-based tourism were not outlined. A report on Aboriginal economic development in Western Australia further reinforced state government support for Aboriginal tourism businesses, with a concentrated effort and focus on the Kimberley.

Implementing Aboriginal tourism strategies

Government strategies support the development of Aboriginal tourism in Australia. However, there has been limited government funding for implementation of the national Aboriginal and Torres Strait Islander tourism industry strategy (ATSIC 1997). The Aboriginal tourism strategies devised by state agencies are market-led and responsive to the commercial needs of the tourism industry. Aboriginal cultural and community concerns with tourism are little addressed. Aboriginal culture has a minor role in other cultural and ecotourism plans devised by state tourism agencies. Implementation of these Aboriginal tourism strategies largely depends on state funding and Aboriginal tourism coordinators.

During the 1990s, many state tourism and commerce agencies developed Aboriginal tourism positions. The Northern Territory Tourist Commission was the first state tourism agency to appoint an officer responsible for Aboriginal tourism in 1984 (Burchett 1992). Non-Aboriginal staff with responsibility for Aboriginal tourism were based in Alice Springs and Darwin. In 1998 these positions ended and Aboriginal tourism became part of overall tourism promotion in the Northern Territory. The influential Northern, Tiwi and Central Land Councils play a key role in negotiating Northern Territory Aboriginal tourism enterprises. Other Aboriginal tourism positions are filled by Aboriginal people in the following state government agencies:

- Queensland Tourist and Travel Corporation (since 1992)
- Tourism New South Wales (since 1996)
- Tourism Victoria (Koorie Tourism Unit 1990–91, 1996–98)
- South Australia Department of Industry and Trade (since 1996)
- Western Australia Tourism Commission, Broome (1995–98)
- Western Australia Department of Commerce and Trade, Derby.

Australian states increasingly compete with each other to attract tourists interested in indigenous culture. As a result, Aboriginal tourism is seen as part of state and regional economic development, as well as a means to revitalise aspects of Aboriginal culture (e.g. art, dance, music, Dreaming stories, bush lore) with the most tourist appeal.

■ 10.2.4 Promoting *Aboriginal tourism*

Aboriginal tourism brochures are produced by the Northern Territory, Queensland and South Australian state tourism agencies. Previous research by Zeppel (1998a, 1998c) analysed the tourist marketing of Aboriginal spirituality or the 'Dreamtime', the representation of an Aboriginal 'voice', Aboriginal ownership of tourism ventures and visitor access to Aboriginal cultures in these tourism brochures. These themes were based on key Aboriginal concerns with the impacts of tourism on Aboriginal culture (Ross 1991).

The main Aboriginal tourism brochure for the Northern Territory, for most of the 1990s was *Come Share Our Culture*. Until 1994, this brochure represented the only state tourism literature in Australia dedicated to marketing Aboriginal tourism 'products'. Through words and images, this brochure conveyed the message that tourists in the Northern Territory would achieve personal contact with Aboriginal people, hands-on experience of Aboriginal crafts and participation in Aboriginal cultural traditions. The latest Northern Australian Aboriginal tourism brochure is *Experience Aboriginal Culture in Australia's Northern Territory*. With a strong focus on visiting Aboriginal lands, the new Aboriginal tourism theme is 'come share our country'. Aboriginal people now own 50 per cent of land in the Northern Territory, achieved through the *Aboriginal Land Rights (NT) Act 1976*, giving many Aboriginal groups a new economic role in tourism as land managers and leaseholders.

The Queensland indigenous tourism brochure, *A Guide to Experiencing Aboriginal and Torres Strait Islander Culture*, was first produced in 1994. This brochure is part of the popular Sunlover Holidays product range marketed nationally by the Queensland Tourist and Travel Corporation (QTTC, now Tourism Queensland). Indigenous tours and attractions are listed for south-east, central and north Queensland, as well as Torres Strait and Cape York. The guide states that 'businesses listed in this brochure are owned and operated by Aboriginal organisations, and/or employ Aboriginal people'. However, five non-Aboriginal tour operators are included. The second indigenous tourism brochure, produced in 1996, was *Aboriginal and Torres Strait Islander Holiday Experiences*. 'Culture' had been replaced by 'holiday experiences'. Tourism Queensland is broadening the appeal of Aboriginal culture in order to attract the mass tourism market.

The South Australian Aboriginal Tourism Experience brochure was launched in May 1996. Approximately 20 Aboriginal tours are described in this brochure, covering five regions of South Australia. The tourism ventures owned by Aboriginal people include Camp Coorong, operated by the Ngarrindjeri people, Yalata Aboriginal lands on the west coast and Desert Tracks, owned by the Pitjantjatjara community. Other tours or boat cruises listed in the brochure include only a guide to Aboriginal sites.

In Western Australia, a *Guide to Kimberley Aboriginal Product Experiences* was produced in 1999. The Western Australia guide listed Aboriginal tours, accommodation, arts and crafts outlets, self-drive tours to Aboriginal communities (including access fees and visitor facilities), camel safaris, Magabala Books and Goolarri Media (Broome) and Mimbi Caves. The Aboriginal status or ownership was clearly listed for each Aboriginal tourism venture.

Aboriginal tours on television travel programs

Aboriginal tourism ventures also feature on *Getaway* and *The Great Outdoors*, two popular television travel programs screened nationally in Australia. *The Great Outdoors* is hosted by Ernie Dingo, a well-known Aboriginal actor. In 1996–97, Ernie presented travel stories on Tjapukai Aboriginal Cultural Park in Cairns and Anangu Tours at Uluru. *Getaway* has screened Aboriginal travel stories about Pajinka Wilderness Lodge (Cape York, Queensland); the Ku-Ring-Gai Dreamtime Walk in Sydney, New South Wales; Umorrduk Safaris in Arnhem Land and Magela Tours in Kakadu, Manyallaluk, the Tiwi Islands and Uluru (Northern Territory); and Kooljaman resort at Cape Leveque (Western Australia). These television travel shows and popular newspaper or travel magazine articles (Zeppel 2000) promote Aboriginal cultural tourism as a new travel experience in Australia. In 1999, Lonely Planet received a $100 000 federal tourism grant to produce *Guide to Aboriginal Australia and the Torres Strait Islands*.

■ *10.2.5* **Research** *on Aboriginal tourism*

Through the 1990s, there was diverse academic and industry research on Aboriginal tourism. This tourism research has mainly evaluated the impacts of tourism on Aboriginal culture and also visitor demand for Aboriginal tourism products (see figure 10.3). Industry perspectives on developing and marketing Aboriginal tourism ventures have also been addressed, including the opinions of Aboriginal people and communities involved in tourism (Office of Northern Development 1993; Miller 1996). To date, there has been limited application of this research to aiding Aboriginal involvement in tourism (Schuler, Aderdeen & Dyer 1999).

Contentious issues in Aboriginal tourism include:

- copyright and authenticity in Aboriginal art (Janke 1998)
- conflicting viewpoints within Aboriginal communities on the benefits of tourism (Finlayson 1991; ATSIC 1997; Zeppel 1998d; Pitcher et al. 1999)
- the tourist marketing of stereotyped images of traditional Aboriginal culture (Hollinshead 1996; Zeppel 1998a, 1998c, 2000; Waitt 1999).

While acknowledging these social and cultural impacts, this chapter focuses on Aboriginal tourism businesses as a special interest tourist attraction. Aboriginal cultural centres are new tourist attractions in Australia, having only recently become popular. These cultural centres are reviewed in the case study.

■ **Figure 10.3**
Research on Aboriginal tourism in Australia

INDIGENOUS TOURISM

- Various Aboriginal cultural tourism enterprises (Finlayson 1991; Zeppel 1998a, 1998d, 1999a)

- the sustainable development of Aboriginal tourism (Burchett 1992; Altman & Finlayson 1993; Miller 1996; Zeppel 1998b; Pitcher, van Oosterzee & Palmer 1999)

- the impacts of tourism on Aboriginal communities (Ross 1991; Schuler et al. 1999)

- visitor interest in Northern Territory Aboriginal tourism (Moscardo & Pearce 1989; Ryan & Huyton 1999)

- Aboriginal tourism at Lake Condah and Brambuk in West Victoria (Finlayson & Madden 1994)

- the controversial National Aboriginal Cultural Centre in Sydney (Zeppel 1999b)

- authenticity at the Dreamtime Cultural Centre in Rockhampton (Griffin & Shelley 1993)

- Aboriginal tourism in Uluru and Kakadu national parks (Mercer 1994)

- tourist marketing of Aboriginal culture (Wells 1996; Zeppel 1998a, 1998c, 2000; Waitt 1999)

- copyright and authenticity in Aboriginal art and culture used for tourism (Janke 1998)

- visitor satisfaction with Tjapukai Aboriginal Cultural Park (Moscardo & Pearce 1999)

- the positive impacts of the Tjapukai Dance Theatre in Kuranda (Finlayson 1995).

10.3 ABORIGINAL TOURISM BUSINESS DEVELOPMENT

There are several key factors limiting the development of Aboriginal tourism businesses. These are presented in figure 10.4 below. These factors include:

- difficulty in obtaining business finance
- continued reliance on government funding, particularly ATSIC and the CDEP program
- remoteness
- a lack of infrastructure for regional ventures
- newness of the enterprises
- a low tourist market profile (ATSIC 1997).

■ **Figure 10.4** *Key issues for developing Aboriginal tourism businesses in Australia*

INDIGENOUS TOURISM

Ownership	**Finances**
Communal land and resources	Communal projects hard to fund
Social/cultural goals versus profits	Lack of personal capital
External costs of businesses	Reliance on government grants
Private entrepreneurs and families	Lack of corporate sponsors
Little infrastructure in remote areas	Limited use of business shares
Tourism joint ventures	Loss of community control
Training	**Product**
Lack of tourism training	Deliverable tour products
Limited business management skills	Large Aboriginal attractions
Industry-based training providers	Competing cultural centres
High staff turnover	Develop diverse attractions
Marketing	**Partnerships**
Joint tourism organisations	Links with government agencies
Agreements with tour operators	Limited links with business sector
Marketing on websites Commercial print advertising	Few links with the public (e.g. membership, sponsorship)
Media advertising (radio & television)	Links with education providers
	Links with Aboriginal attractions

Source: *Modified from Getz & Jamieson (1997)*

There is little financial support for individual and family enterprises in tourism, since funding from ATSIC is directed to incorporated Aboriginal communities. Aboriginal communal lands also cannot be sold, mortgaged or used as collateral for business loans. Other factors include limited integration of Aboriginal tourism businesses with regional and state tourism networks and the need to develop indigenous skills in business and tourism management.

Funding for large-scale Aboriginal tourism ventures (e.g. Tjapukai Park) is provided by the Aboriginal and Torres Strait Islander Commercial Development Corporation. Other funding and support for Aboriginal tourism enterprise development, training and marketing differs in each state.

Government agencies assisting Aboriginal tourism operators include Aboriginal Affairs Victoria, New South Wales Department of State and Regional Development, Department of Commerce and Trade (Kimberley, WA), and the Department of Industry and Trade (SA). Aboriginal tourism coordinators in the Northern Territory, Western Australia, South Australia, New South Wales and Queensland also assist indigenous tour operators.

Most indigenous tourism enterprises focus on cultural revival and maintenance, learning about the tourism industry, and planning and organising for tourism. Only select indigenous operators are achieving viability, dealing with tour wholesalers and being export-ready for the inbound tourism market (ATSIC 1997).

There is limited utilisation of business shares and virtually no corporate sponsorship of Aboriginal tourism ventures. In late 1999, Aboriginal Australia offered a public float of shares to raise $5 million for their e-commerce art enterprise, the first from an Aboriginal business (http://www.aboriginalaustralia.com.au).

■ 10.3.1 **Aboriginal** *tourism training*

Training for Aboriginal people in tourism has generally been provided at technical and further education (TAFE) colleges, meeting the needs of Aboriginal students in areas of regional demand (e.g. Western New South Wales, Sydney; Pilbara and Kimberley, WA; North Queensland; Gippsland, Vic.). In Adelaide, the Tauondi Aboriginal Community College provides training for Aboriginal tour guides and arranges their work placements as guides at Adelaide Zoo, Cleland Wildlife Park and the Tandanya Institute. The Institute for Aboriginal Development in Alice Springs provides tourism training with the Aboriginal Art and Culture Centre, which established an Aboriginal tourism training centre in 1997 to train indigenous staff in tourism, business management and retailing. Aboriginal operators such as Sydney Aboriginal Discoveries and Kakadu Tourism (NT) provide other industry-based training courses.

Aboriginal business skills are aided by Koori/Aboriginal business networks (Vic./NSW) and the involvement of young Aboriginal tourism operators in business mentoring programs. The ATSIC Community Development Employment Program (CDEP), or 'work for the dole' scheme, supports most Aboriginal community ventures in tourism, but government changes now limit the 'employment' offered through this program.

■ *10.3.2* **Key issues** *for developing Aboriginal tourism*

Government support is mainly provided for established Aboriginal tourism ventures. Such enterprises are expected to become commercially viable and self-sustaining. There is limited funding for ongoing establishment and operating costs. Consequently, high capital cost ventures such as cultural centres are now diversifying into accommodation and convention services. Other government-funded centres, such as Galeena Beek in Melbourne, have been tendered for their commercial tourist operation.

Aboriginal ventures based on arts and crafts have tended to be more successful than Aboriginal tour operations in regional areas. Arts and crafts products can be licensed or sold through a variety of retail outlets, including the Internet, while cultural tours require trained Aboriginal guides, vehicles, access to Aboriginal sites and extensive marketing to attract tourists. New craft outlets are often based in town centres, while Aboriginal art cooperatives have established retail galleries in key tourist areas, such as Maruku Arts at Uluru and Desart in Sydney. Aboriginal tourism ventures are increasingly located in urban areas.

BREAKTHROUGH TOURISM
Aboriginal tourism in urban areas

An increasing number of Aboriginal cultural enterprises are located in capital cities and other key tourist centres around Australia. These urban areas are the main destination for both domestic and international visitors in Australia.

In Sydney, the Gavala Art Centre was established in 1995 by two Aboriginal artists with a $5000 investment. Initially located in the historic Rocks area, Gavala relocated to Darling Harbour with backing from Harbourside to establish a 100 per cent Aboriginal-owned and operated cultural centre. In 1999, Gavala opened a new retail gallery and performance space with daily free talks on Aboriginal art. Gavala also markets its own jewellery and giftware and provides Aboriginal cultural products for meetings and conventions in Sydney. In contrast, the National Aboriginal Cultural Centre, funded by 27 non-Aboriginal business investors for $2 million, targeted mass tourists and only operated for six months at Darling Harbour (Zeppel 1999b).

Sydney Aboriginal Discoveries provides walking tours and a Dreaming cruise of Sydney Harbour, describing the Eora Aboriginal culture. Other tourism initiatives are a new display on Aboriginal heroes at the Aboriginal 'Day of Mourning' building in downtown Sydney, coordinated by the National Aboriginal History and Heritage Council.

In 1999, the Central Desert art cooperative, Desart, opened a retail gallery in Sydney, with a second art gallery at the new Fox Studios. The Aboriginal design company, Balarinji, also relocated from Adelaide to Sydney in 1997, with Balarinji clothing styles sold at airport stores.

At Botany Bay, the La Perouse community sells Aboriginal artefacts and operates a bush tucker walkway. At Katoomba, in the Blue Mountains, the Western Sydney Aboriginal Corporation operates a Dreamtime Cafe and Arts and Crafts complex near the popular tourist lookout at the Three Sisters. In Adelaide, Aboriginal cultural tours are conducted at Tandanya, the Botanic Gardens and Cleland Wildlife Park. These Aboriginal guides are trained and coordinated by the Tauondi Aboriginal Community College. A $1.45 million Living Kaurna Cultural Centre was also constructed in Adelaide during 2000, with the first five years of operating costs met by the Marion City Council. In Melbourne, a new Aboriginal heritage walk is conducted in the Royal Botanic Gardens. There are also Aboriginal-owned galleries in Alice Springs, Darwin, Cairns, Geelong, Perth and Broome. In Cairns, an Aboriginal entrepreneur established a new gallery, Jama Dreaming, near major tourist resorts at Palm Cove.

Locating Aboriginal-owned enterprises at popular tourist destinations increases their chance of success. The Tjapukai Aboriginal Cultural Park in Cairns and the Aboriginal Art and Culture Centre in Alice Springs are examples. Aboriginal tourism in urban areas can tap into key tourist markets and also utilise existing cultural attractions. There is further scope for Aboriginal guides to interpret the major Aboriginal collections at state museums and art galleries.

Aboriginal tourism operators are also forming new business partnerships with other commercial travel enterprises. Examples include Anangu Tours with Ayers Rock Resort at Uluru; the Aboriginal Art and Culture Centre with accommodation properties and a transport company in Alice Springs; and Tobwabba Art with licensed souvenir companies. Consortia of Aboriginal enterprises are increasing marketing, such as Northern Territory and New South Wales Aboriginal tour operators at the Australian Tourism Exchange and the 'Aboriginal Connection' group trade stand of New South Wales Aboriginal artists at the Reed Gift Fair in Darling Harbour, Sydney. In New South Wales, the Aboriginal Traders Alliance has a website listing a range of Aboriginal tours, attractions, cultural products and services (http://www.abtrade.com.au). The Internet is becoming increasingly important as a marketing tool and e-commerce site for both larger Aboriginal cultural enterprises (e.g. Tobwabba Art, http://www.tobwabba.com.au) and smaller Aboriginal craft producers (e.g. Red Earth Gallery, New South Wales: http://www.crt.net.au/~lewis). The majority of Internet sales relate to arts and crafts rather than on-line tour bookings.

With growth in Aboriginal tourism, there is increased competition between Aboriginal cultural attractions, craft producers and tour providers. For example, the Aboriginal-owned and operated Gavala Centre was, for six months, in direct competition with the corporate-funded National Aboriginal Cultural Centre in Darling Harbour, Sydney (Zeppel 1999b).

The Tandanya Institute in Adelaide has positioned itself as a living arts centre in contrast to the 'theme park' approach adopted by the Tjapukai Cultural Park in Cairns (Parker 1999). Tjapukai Park also has an agreement that limits other cultural presentations for tourists by Djabugay community members (Schuler in Zeppel 1998d). In Byron Bay, two Aboriginal enterprises, Dreamtime Journey and Jalum Baygal, sell Aboriginal arts and crafts and offer didgeridoo-making workshops.

Visitor demand in popular tourist areas may well sustain multiple Aboriginal tourist ventures, but this still remains uncertain. The retail distribution of Aboriginal arts and crafts also creates further market competition. For example, exclusive installations of Balarinji products at duty free stores limit the distribution of other Aboriginal retailers like Tobwabba Art. However, Balarinji targets fashion design while Tobwabba mainly produces licensed souvenir merchandise. The positive outcome is that Aboriginal enterprises and communities are benefiting from Aboriginal tourism.

10.5 SUMMARY

Worldwide, there is growing indigenous involvement with tourism. Tourist demand for contact with indigenous peoples corresponds with the indigenous need for deriving income from land, cultural resources and new economic ventures, including tourism. Indigenous tourism involves indigenous ownership and control of tourism ventures in tribal homelands and in urban areas. These indigenous tourism enterprises include both cultural attractions and tours and also diversified visitor facilities. Instead of remaining exotic or ethnic tourist attractions, indigenous groups are taking control of tourism. For indigenous peoples in developed countries, legal recognition of land rights and resource ownership, together with the current trend for cultural revival, provides the main impetus for developing tourism.

Aboriginal groups in Australia operate a wide range of tourist enterprises, from large cultural centres such as Tjapukai to cultural tours and craft producers in remote and regional areas. The estimated market value for Aboriginal tourism is $200 million for Aboriginal arts and crafts, $20–30 million for diversified tourism enterprises and $5 million for Aboriginal cultural tourism. Aboriginal-owned and operated tourism has mainly developed in the 1990s, supported by state and federal tourism strategies and the appointment of Aboriginal tourism coordinators. Key areas of tourism demand include didgeridoos, Aboriginal cultural centres and Aboriginal tourism in urban areas. For many Aboriginal people in Australia today, 'the question is not whether to accept or reject tourism, but how to make it work better for them' (Pitcher et al. 1999:38).

Successful indigenous tourism ventures rely on government funding and support for community-based tourism and operators developing viable links with the commercial tourism industry. Most indigenous tourism enterprises are still in the establishment phase and are yet to record a strong commercial performance. Indigenous partnerships with the mainstream Australian tourism industry are crucial for success. Further development of indigenous skills in business and tourism management is also required. Other key goals are indigenous cultural maintenance and revival and the employment of community members. Competition between Aboriginal tourism enterprises is increasing with operators targeting niche markets. While Aboriginal groups are 'rich with legends' and cultural resources, the provision of Aboriginal tourist products involves new expertise in the business of tourism. In Australia, select Aboriginal groups are moving from ethnic tourism, or an exotic cultural attraction, to indigenous tourism with growing Aboriginal ownership of tourism ventures.

Questions

10.1 Explain the key differences between indigenous cultural tourism and diversified indigenous tourism enterprises.

10.2 How do Australian tourism strategies support the development of Aboriginal tourism?

10.3 What sources of government funding are used by Aboriginal tourism ventures?

10.4 Identify the key locations for indigenous tourism ventures in Australia. Consider urban areas, national parks and rural regions.

10.5 Examine the Internet site of one indigenous cultural attraction. How is tourism promoted? Look at the representation of people, cultural traditions, beliefs, crafts and tourist activities.

10.6 Contact or visit your local visitor information centre. What Aboriginal cultural attractions or Aboriginal tours are promoted? Are these tourism ventures Aboriginal-owned and operated?

10.7 Provide a definition of Aboriginal tourism and describe the main types of Aboriginal tourism enterprises operating in Australia.

10.8 What are the key barriers limiting the development of Aboriginal tourism businesses?

10.9 How do indigenous people present their art, culture, stories and traditions in tourism? Compare the marketing for indigenous tours, cultural centres and Aboriginal crafts.

10.10 To what extent do indigenous tourism ventures present unique regional aspects of Aboriginal cultures rather than stereotyped images of 'traditional' Aboriginal culture?

REFERENCES ···

Abate, A. 1999. *Open for Business: Experiences of Koori Business People in Victoria.* Melbourne: Koori Business Network, Aboriginal Affairs Victoria.

Altman, J. & Finlayson, J. 1993. 'Aborigines and Sustainable Development'. *Journal of Tourism Studies* 4 (1): 38–50.

ATSIC (Aboriginal and Torres Strait Islander Commission). 1997. *National Aboriginal and Torres Strait Islander Tourism Strategy.* Canberra: ATSIC & Office of National Tourism.

Browne, R. & Nolan, M. 1989. 'Western Indian Reservation Tourism Development'. *Annals of Tourism Research* 16 (3): 360–76.

Burchett, C. 1992. 'Ecologically Sustainable Development and its Relationship to Aboriginal Tourism in the Northern Territory'. In Weiler, B. (Ed.). *Ecotourism Incorporating the Global Classroom.* Canberra: Bureau of Tourism Research, pp. 70–4.

Commonwealth Department of Tourism. 1994. *A Talent for Tourism: Stories About Indigenous People in Tourism.* Canberra: Commonwealth Department of Tourism. *http://www.dist.gov.au/tourism/publications/talent/start.html*

De Burlo, C. 1996. 'Cultural Resistance and Ethnic Tourism on South Pentecost, Vanuatu'. In Butler, R. & Hinch, T. (Eds.). *Indigenous People and Tourism.* London: International Thomson Business Press, pp. 255–77.

Finlayson, J. 1991. 'Australian Aborigines and Cultural Tourism: Case Studies of Aboriginal Involvement in the Tourist Industry'. Working Papers on Multiculturalism No. 15. Wollongong: Centre for Multicultural Studies, University of Wollongong.

Finlayson, J. 1995. 'Aboriginal Employment, Native Title and Regionalism'. *CAEPR Discussion Paper No. 87.* Canberra: Centre for Aboriginal Economic Policy Research.

Finlayson, J. & Madden, R. 1994. 'Regional Tourism Case Studies: Indigenous Participation in Tourism in Victoria. In Faulkner, B., Fagence, M., Davidson, M. & Craig-Smith, S. (Eds.). *Tourism Research and Education in Australia.* Canberra: Bureau of Tourism Research, pp. 269–75.

Furze, B., De Lacy, T. & Birckhead, J. 1996. 'Indigenous People'. In *Culture, Conservation and Biodiversity.* Chichester, UK: John Wiley & Sons, pp. 126–45.

Getz, D. & Jamieson, W. 1997. 'Rural Tourism in Canada: Issues, Opportunities and Entrepreneurship in Aboriginal Tourism in Alberta'. In Page, S. J. & Getz, D. (Eds.). *The Business of Rural Tourism: International Perspectives.* London: International Thomson Business Press, pp. 93–107.

Griffin, G. & Shelley, R. 1993. 'Dreamtime in a Cow Town: The Dreamtime Cultural Centre in Rockhampton, Queensland'. *Culture and Policy* 5: 157–76.

Hinch, T. & Butler, R. 1996. 'Indigenous Tourism: A Common Ground for Discussion'. In Butler, R. & Hinch, T. (Eds.). *Tourism and Indigenous Peoples.* London: International Thomson Business Press, pp. 3–19.

Hinch, T. & Delamere, T. 1993. 'Aboriginal Festivals as Tourism Attractions: A Community Challenge'. *Journal of Applied Recreation Research* 18 (2).

Hollinshead, K. 1996. 'Marketing and Metaphysical Realism: The Disidentification of Aboriginal Life and Traditions Through Tourism'. In Butler, R. & Hinch, T. (Eds.). *Tourism and Indigenous Peoples.* London: International Thomson Business Press, pp. 308–48.

Janke, T. 1998. *Our Culture: Our Future: Report on Australian Indigenous Cultural and Intellectual Property Rights.* Canberra: Cultural Industries Section, ATSIC. *http://www.icip.lawnet.com.au*

Lew, A. A. & Van Otten, G. A. (Eds.). 1998. *Tourism and Gaming on American Indian Lands.* New York: Cognizant Communication Corporation.

Mercer, D. 1994. 'Native Peoples and Tourism: Conflict and Compromise'. In Theobald, F. (Ed.). *Global Tourism: The Next Decade.* Boston, USA: Butterworth–Heinemann, pp. 124–45.

Miller, G. 1996. 'Indigenous Tourism — A Queensland Perspective'. In Richins, H., Richardson, J. & Crabtree, A. *Ecotourism and Nature-based Tourism: Taking the Next Steps.* Brisbane: Ecotourism Association of Australia, pp. 45–57.

Moscardo, G. M. & Pearce, P. L. 1989. 'Ethnic Tourism: Understand the Tourist's Perspective'. In *Travel Research: Globilization, the Pacific Rim and Beyond.* Salt Lake City: Graduate School of Business, University of Utah, pp. 387–94.

Moscardo, G. M. & Pearce, P. L. 1999. 'Understanding Ethnic Tourists'. *Annals of Tourism Research* 26 (2): 416–34.

Neuenfeldt, K. (Ed.). 1997. *The Didjeridu: From Arnhem Land to Internet.* Sydney: John Libbey.

Office of National Tourism. 1998. 'Aboriginal and Torres Strait Islander Tourism'. *Tourism Facts No. 10.* Canberra: Department of Industry, Science and Tourism. *http://www.isr.gov.au/tourism/factsandfigures/abandtorrestourism.html*

Office of Northern Development. (Ed.). 1993. *Indigenous Australians and Tourism: A Focus on Northern Australia.* Darwin: ATSIC & Office of Northern Development.

Parker, B. 1993. 'Developing Aboriginal Tourism — Opportunities and Threats'. *Tourism Management* 14 (3): 400–4.

Parker, K. 1999. 'Tandanya Ten Years on'. *Australian Indigenous Art News* 1 (2): 20–1.

Pitcher, M., van Oosterzee, P. & Palmer, L. 1999. *'Choice and Control': The Development of Indigenous Tourism in Australia.* Darwin: Centre for Indigenous Natural & Cultural Resource Management & CRC Tourism.

Ross, H. 1991. 'Controlling Access to Environment and Self: Aboriginal Perspectives on Tourism'. *Australian Psychologist* 26 (3): 176–82.

Ryan, C. & Huyton, J. 1999. 'Aboriginal Tourism — A Linear Structural Relations Analysis of Domestic and International Tourism Demand'. *International Journal of Tourism Research* 5: 1–15.

SATC (South Australian Tourism Commission). 1995. *Aboriginal Tourism Strategy.* Adelaide: South Australian Tourism Commission.

SATC. 1998. *Indigenous Tourism: Background Research on the Demand for Indigenous Tourism Product in South Australia.* Adelaide: SATC.

Scheyvens, R. 1999. 'Ecotourism and the Empowerment of Local Communities'. *Tourism Management* 20 (2): 245–9.

Schuler, S., Aberdeen, L. & Dyer, P. 1999. 'Sensitivity to Cultural Difference in Tourism Research: Contingency in Research Design'. *Tourism Management* 20 (1): 59–70.

Schulz, D. 1999. 'Didgeridoo Fraud Prompts Copyright Call'. *The Age,* 20 December. *http://www.theage.com.au/news/19991220/A47324-1999Dec19.html*

Smith, V. L. 1989. 'Introduction'. In Smith, V. L. (Ed.). *Hosts and Guests: The Anthropology of Tourism.* Second Edition. Philadelphia: University of Pennsylvania Press, pp. 1–17.

Smith, V. L. 1996a. 'Indigenous Tourism: The Four Hs'. In Butler, R. & Hinch, T. (Eds). *Tourism and Indigenous Peoples.* London: International Thomson Business Press, pp. 283–307.

Smith, V. L. 1996b. 'The Four Hs of Tribal Tourism: Acoma — A Pueblo Case Study'. *Progress in Tourism and Hospitality Research* 2: 295–306.

Southgate, L. 1999. 'Tjapukai Dancers Step to Success'. *The Weekend Australian.* 4–5, September, p. 5.

Swain, M. B. 1989. 'Gender Roles in Indigenous Tourism: Kuna Mola, Kuna Yala, and Cultural Survival, In Smith, V. L. (Ed.). *Hosts and Guests: The Anthropology of Tourism.* Second Edition. Philadelphia: University of Pennsylvania Press, pp. 83–104.

Sykes, L. 1995. 'Welcome to Our Land'. *The Geographical Magazine* 67 (10): 22–5.

Waitt, G. 1999. 'Naturalizing the "Primitive": A Critique of Marketing Australia's Indigenous Peoples as "Hunter-Gatherers" '. *Tourism Geographies* 1 (2): 142–63.

Wells, J. 1996. 'Marketing Indigenous Heritage: A Case Study of Uluru National Park'. In Hall, C. M., & McArthur, S. (Eds.). *Heritage Management in Australia and New Zealand.* Melbourne: Oxford University Press, pp. 222–30.

Zeppel, H. 1998a. 'Selling the Dreamtime: Aboriginal Culture in Australian Tourism'. In Rowe, D. & Lawrence, G. (Eds.). *Tourism, Leisure, Sport: Critical Perspectives,* Sydney: Hodder Headline, pp. 23–38.

Zeppel, H. 1998b. 'Land and Culture: Sustainable Tourism and Indigenous Peoples'. In Hall, C. M. & Lew, A. (Eds.). *Sustainable Tourism: A Geographical Perspective.* London: Addison Wesley Longman, pp. 60–74.

Zeppel, H. 1998c. ' "Come Share our Culture": Marketing Aboriginal Tourism in Australia'. *Pacific Tourism Review* 2 (1): 67–81.

Zeppel, H. 1998d. 'Tourism and Aboriginal Australia'. *Tourism Management* 19 (5): 485–8.

Zeppel, H. 1999a. 'Aboriginal Tourism in Australia: A Research Bibliography'. *CRC Tourism Research Report Series: Report 2.* Gold Coast: CRC for Sustainable Tourism, pp. 210–26.

Zeppel, H. 1999b. 'Dreamtime in the City: The National Aboriginal Cultural Centre, Sydney'. In Molloy, J. & Davies, J. (Eds.). *Tourism and Hospitality: Delighting the Senses, Part One.* Canberra: Bureau of Tourism Research, pp. 131–40.

Zeppel, H. 2000. 'Touring Aboriginal Cultures: Encounters with Aboriginal People in Australian Travelogues'. *Tourism, Culture & Communication* 2 (2).

Aboriginal cultural centres
in Australia

Aboriginal cultural centres:
- include historical exhibitions about local Aboriginal cultures
- make and/or sell Aboriginal artefacts
- provide visitor services such as cultural tours, didgeridoo playing or bush tucker walks.

There are about 30 Aboriginal cultural centres in Australia. These include the Dreamtime Cultural Centre in Rockhampton, the Tandanya National Aboriginal Cultural Institute in Adelaide and the $9 million Tjapukai Aboriginal Cultural Park in Cairns, North Queensland, which replaced the popular Tjapukai Dance Theatre in Kuranda. Other Aboriginal cultural centres are located in national parks such as Uluru and Kakadu (NT), and Brambuk Living Cultural Centre in the Grampians, Victoria. The majority of these Aboriginal cultural centres have only been developed since the Bicentenary of Australia in 1988 (e.g. Dreamtime Cultural Centre, Brewarrina Aboriginal Cultural Museum). Most of the larger cultural centres are located in urban centres (e.g. Adelaide, Alice Springs, Cairns, Rockhampton, Sydney), although many smaller cultural centres are in regional destinations, particularly in New South Wales and Victoria (see table 10.3). Aboriginal Keeping Places, such as Krowathunkoolong in Bairnsdale, Victoria, feature a collection of Aboriginal artefacts returned to local communities.

Aboriginal communities around Australia are constructing an increasing number of cultural centres, with 20 new centres opened during the 1990s. Centres opened in the 1980s include the Dharnya Cultural Centre, Barmah Forest (Vic.), Camp Coorong (SA), Minjungbal Centre (NSW) and Kalkadoon Tribal Centre (Mt Isa, Qld). Aboriginal-owned and operated tourist enterprises include Tjapukai Cultural Park in Cairns (50 per cent Aboriginal-owned), the Aboriginal Art and Culture Centre in Alice Springs (owned by the Pwerte Marnte Marnte Aboriginal Corporation) and Gavala Aboriginal Cultural Centre in Sydney (privately owned by Aboriginal entrepreneurs). These cultural centres typically represent a particular Aboriginal group or cultural region. The Tandanya Institute, however, features Aboriginal people, artwork, crafts and dances from diverse areas of Australia. The Dreamtime Cultural Centre in Rockhampton also includes Torres Strait Islander culture. The Dreamtime Centre has an Aboriginal director and all 28 staff are indigenous.

■ **Table 10.3** *Aboriginal cultural centres in Australia*

CULTURAL CENTRE	LOCATION	YEAR OPENED
Aboriginal Art & Culture Centre http://www.aboriginalart.com.au	Alice Springs, NT	1996
Amaroo Aboriginal Museum and Cultural Centre http://www.austmus.gov.au/ahu/keep/keep06.htm	Walcha, NSW	1995
Brambuk Living Cultural Centre http://www.isr.gov.au/sport5F/tourism/publications/talent/brambuk.html	Halls Gap, The Grampians, Vic.	1991
Brewarrina Aboriginal Cultural Museum	Brewarrina, NSW	1988
Dreamtime Cultural Centre http://www.isr.gov.au/sport%5F/tourism/publications/talent/dreamtime.html	Rockhampton, Qld	1988
Galeena Beek Living Cultural Centre http://www.galeenabeek.com.au/galeena3.html	Melbourne, Vic.	1996
Gavala Aboriginal Cultural Centre http://www.gavala.com.au/main.htm	Darling Harbour, Sydney, NSW	1996
Minjungbal Aboriginal Cultural Centre	South Tweed Heads, NSW	1984
Tandanya National Aboriginal Cultural IInstitute http://www.tandanya.on.net	Adelaide, SA	1989
Tjapukai Aboriginal Cultural Park http://www.tjapukai.com.au	Cairns, Qld	1996

Many regional cultural centres are developed and managed by Aboriginal Corporations and Land Councils. The Western Sydney Aboriginal Corporation operates the Dreamtime Cafe and Arts and Crafts Gallery at Katoomba (NSW). Other centres have recently returned to Aboriginal control. In Tasmania, the Tiagarra Cultural Centre was returned to the Mersey Leven Aboriginal Corporation in 1995. The Tandanya Cultural Institute appointed its first Aboriginal Director at the end of 1997. Tandanya repaid a South Australia state government assistance loan in 1996 and has received funding from the Australia Council to develop its multicultural audience (Parker 1999). Many other Aboriginal art galleries also sell and exhibit Aboriginal paintings, art and crafts. Tobwabba Arts, based in Forster, New South Wales, has a retail art gallery and sells licensed souvenir products with Tobwabba designs in more than 400 retail outlets around Australia, including Aboriginal galleries. Tobwabba Art utilises CDEP (Community Development Employment Program) to employ 20 Aboriginal artists.

Most of these Aboriginal cultural centres depend on various forms of government funding (e.g. ATSIC, DETYA Jobskills programs, CDEP or 'work for the dole', state Aboriginal affairs and arts grants; Australia Council) for their development and continued operation. The failed Warrama Living History Centre, which opened and closed in Cairns during the latter half of 1990, absorbed $2.5 million in federal government funding (Finlayson 1991). Yet the Tjapukai Cultural Park, on the same site in Cairns, has an annual turnover of $7 million and received 250 000 visitors in 1999 (Southgate 1999). The Galeena Beek Living Cultural Centre in Melbourne was constructed in 1996 at a cost of $1.8 million. Yet in September 1999, the Coranderrk Koori Co-operative sought a commercial tourism operator to manage and further develop Galeena Beek as an indigenous tourist attraction. Without government grants or corporate support, many Aboriginal groups are unable to provide ongoing finance for operating cultural centres.

Visitor activities at Aboriginal cultural centres

These new Aboriginal cultural centres, which largely focus on selling Aboriginal-made goods, are established as a tourist drawcard and to fulfil community or family needs for economic and cultural development. Most of these centres make and/or sell Aboriginal arts and crafts (e.g. paintings, artefacts, didgeridoos, souvenirs, clothing and giftware with Aboriginal designs), provide Aboriginal employment and assist in maintaining local Aboriginal cultures (Finlayson 1995; ATSIC 1997). Various Aboriginal products, cultural activities or visitor services are provided at these cultural centres (see table 10.4). The Aboriginal Art and Culture Centre (Alice Springs, NT) exports Aboriginal products to 75 countries. The Centre also has an award-winning website (10 000 'visits' daily) with information on Aboriginal history, culture and tourism. New products include books, CD-ROMs and videos produced by Aboriginal people about their culture, including bush foods, Aboriginal history and life stories. Many centres also offer interactive tourist activities such as spear and boomerang throwing or ochre painting. Other centres, such as Minjungbal (NSW) and Tandanya (SA), now include Aboriginal dance performances and didgeridoo playing to enhance their tourist appeal. Other tourist activities at Tandanya include special art exhibitions, guided tours, Aboriginal music and theatre shows (Parker 1999).

Tandanya, Brambuk and the Yarrawarra Cultural Centre (Corindi, NSW) also include a bush tucker cafe. Other visitor facilities at Yarrawarra include a camping ground, dormitory accommodation, barbeque and picnic area, and a plant nursery selling bush tucker and medicinal plants. The Brambuk cooperative also operates a guest house and backpackers hostel at Halls Gap in the Grampians, Victoria. The Wigay Aboriginal Culture Park in Kempsey (NSW) includes food trees and bush tucker lunches, along with gumleaf playing and bullroarer demonstrations.

■ **Table 10.4** *Tourist features at Aboriginal cultural centres in Australia*

ABORIGINAL PRODUCTS	CULTURAL ACTIVITIES	VISITOR SERVICES
Arts and crafts	Aboriginal dances	Bush tucker cafe
Artefacts	Cultural talks	Barbecue picnic area
Culture exhibitions	Bush tucker walks	Camping ground
Books and videos	Didgeridoo performances	Plant nursery
Souvenirs	Boomerang and spear throwing	Guided tours
Art exhibitions	Ochre painting	Meetings and conventions
Clothing and giftware	Aboriginal storytellers	Visitor accommodation
Music CDs/tapes	Talks about Aboriginal art	School/educational tour

Other established cultural centres also offer diversified visitor services and facilities. The Dreamtime Cultural Centre opened a convention centre in August 1994, while the Tjapukai Park offers special cultural packages and performances for meetings, conventions and incentive travel groups in Cairns. The American international education or 'school excursion' market is a growth market for Tjapukai (Southgate 1999). These tourism initiatives involve new business partnerships with international and local tour operators, park boards (e.g. Brambuk, Vic.), tourist resorts, education providers, government funding agencies and private investors.

Visitor satisfaction with Tjapukai Aboriginal Cultural Park

A survey of 1556 visitors at Tjapukai Cultural Park found 70 per cent were international visitors, largely from Europe and North America, and 30 per cent were Australian visitors. The main types of visitors were couples and organised tour groups. Of this group, 25 per cent had seen Aboriginal dance performances, 49 per cent had visited an Aboriginal art gallery and 12 per cent had been on an Aboriginal tour (Moscardo & Pearce 1999). The visitors were mainly interested in local indigenous history, traditional lifestyles and contemporary ways of living, followed by contact with indigenous people, arts and crafts and dance performances. Based on their level of interest in indigenous culture, the main groups of visitors were the ethnic tourism connection group (36 per cent), the passive cultural learning group (24 per cent), the ethnic products and activities group (18 per cent), and the low ethnic interest group (18 per cent). The first two groups valued direct contact with indigenous people or cultural learning through Indigenous tourism experiences. All four groups of visitors were highly satisfied with their Tjapukai experience, by selecting cultural activities that met their interests or desire for interaction/learning from indigenous staff. Visitors were least satisfied with the amount of contact with Aboriginal people, but overall had an enjoyable encounter at Tjapukai Park.

Questions

1 What are the main tourist markets for Aboriginal cultural centres in urban and rural areas?

2 What types of cultural product or activity are provided at Aboriginal cultural centres?

3 How is the development and operation of Aboriginal cultural centres funded in Australia?

4 To what extent do cultural centres market stereotyped images of traditional Aboriginal culture (e.g. men in traditional costume, dot-art, didgeridoos) to attract non-indigenous visitors?

Ngaire Douglas

11

Travelling for health:
spa and health resorts

LEARNING OBJECTIVES

After reading this chapter, you will have an appreciation of:

- the concepts of health and health tourism in the twenty-first century
- the role of spas in the historical development of tourism
- the different categories of spas and health resorts
- the differences among spas and health resorts in Europe, the United States and Australia
- the changes in consumer demand and motivation
- future directions in growth in this sector of tourism.

11.1 INTRODUCTION

People's desire to improve their health has been a major motivation in the historical development of tourism for more than two millennia. Although the Romans are usually thought to have initiated the health tourism experience (see section 11.5), there is evidence that people of the Neolithic period (*c.* 4000–3000 BC) were aware of the value of certain natural environments to their sense of wellbeing. In more recent times, developments that specifically addressed the health motivations of tourists took place on land, with the growth of spa towns, and at sea with the British Medical Association's recommendation in the 1870s of a cruise as a way to improve people's health (Douglas & Douglas 1996).

With the increasingly frenetic pace of everyday life in the twenty-first century, the desire to use leisure time to pursue activities that positively contribute to health and wellbeing will probably increase, opening opportunities for entrepreneurs, both large and small, to value-add to existing products or design new products to meet the demand. Broadly speaking, participants in a variety of tourist experiences could be motivated by health reasons. The tourist seeking a wilderness or nature-based holiday might be hoping for a refreshed and recharged outlook on life. The soft adventure or cycling tourist might be hoping for a healthier body. The tourist seeking a cultural, heritage or indigenous travel package might be hoping for a broadened (or healthier) mind. This chapter examines one particular sector of the health tourism industry, the spa and health resort. We follow a discussion about what constitutes health tourism with a brief history of one of the oldest forms of tourism. We outline the differences in the concept between Europe, the United States and Australia and the current state of the spa and resort sector in each area. We concluded by discussing implications for future development.

11.2 WHAT IS HEALTH?

Health is commonly viewed in negative terms — as the absence of illness and disease (Naidoo & Wills 1994, Edlin & Golanty 1998). But the World Health Organisation (WTO), describes health as a state of complete mental, physical and social wellbeing, not merely the absence of disease or infirmity (WTO 1946, cited in Naidoo & Wills 1994). Health reflects a person's integrated wellbeing. Edlin and Golanty (1988) describe a holistic approach to health as one in which people attempt to balance the inter-related physical, social, psychological, emotional, spiritual and environmental factors that influence their lives in order to achieve a harmonious existence. Holistic medicine is concerned with the creation and maintenance of health, not the cure of illness, and this concept is the driving force behind the growing demand for the spa and health resort experience.

■ 11.2.1 What *is health tourism?*

As with other areas of tourism, establishing a widely accepted and applied definition of health tourism can be problematic. Definitions of health tourism may include references to:

- the provision of health facilities utilising the natural resources of the country, in particular mineral water and climate (IOUTO 1973, cited in Hall 1992)
- the attempt on the part of a tourist facility or destination to attract tourists by deliberately promoting its health-care services and facilities in addition to its regular tourist amenities (Goodrich & Goodrich 1987)
- the principal travel motivation being for health reasons, such as seeking a different climate or taking a cruise (Van Sleipen, cited in Hall 1992)
- travel to specific locations for a complete spa experience (Van Sleipen, cited in Hall 1992)
- travel for specific medical reasons (Van Sleipen, cited in Hall 1992)
- 'diet resorts', usually located in a desirable climatic area, where people go to lose weight and regain physical vitality (Inskeep 1991)
- reducing ranches for overweight middle-aged women (Gee et al. 1989)
- 'get away from it all' destinations in the country or mountains whose aim is to calm the nerves of anxious businessmen (Gee et al. 1989)
- 'environmentally friendly' medical treatment as an alternative to taking chemically based drugs (Bywater 1990)
- survival-related needs and 'cathartic' travel (for example, escape from stress), which tie into Maslow's hierarchy of needs (Holloway & Plant 1988).

■ **Figure 11.1**
Conceptual framework of the motivations and activities of participants in adventure, sport and health tourism

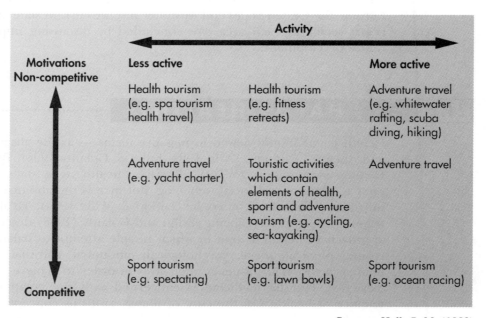

Source: *Hall, C. M. (1992)*

■ *11.2.2* **What** *do health tourists do?*

Hall (1992) and Bywater (1990) suggest that there is a continuum along which the health-motivated tourist moves. Younger travellers may satisfy their health-related needs by seeking out adventure and sports tourism destinations. As they grow older they will look for less demanding ways to meet these needs.

By making choices that involve travel to particular locations where participation in certain activities will contribute to at least one of the areas listed below, a person can be said to be participating in health tourism. The list does not claim to be a definitive one but suggests broad areas in which people seek to improve their lives. These include:
- improved fitness and/or physical skills
- loss of weight
- the willpower to quit smoking
- better digestion and circulation
- physical flexibility
- mental and physical relaxation
- better social interaction
- a more positive outlook on life
- body reshaping and/or cosmetic surgery
- stress management.

11.3 *D*EFINITIONS OF 'SPA'

The dictionary definition of the word *spa* is 'a mineral spring or a place or resort where such a spring is found' and this is the sense in which the traditional European industry uses the word. The European Spas Association (ESPA) has adopted this definition. Thermal springs arise in one of two ways: either from considerable depths through fissures in the rock or as a result of volcanic activity that forces water to the surface in the form of geysers and hot springs. Most thermal water contains minerals in solution. Water containing iron, for example, is said to cure anaemia, while carbonated salt springs are claimed to help rheumatic and neuralgic conditions and radioactive springs are put forward as a treatment for depression. The word *spa* comes from the town of the same name near Liège in Belgium, where there is a mineral spring. In Europe and Britain 'spa' refers to both a town where a natural mineral spring exists and an enterprise or group of enterprises that offer health treatments based on that source. Historically, spas have been situated in surroundings where air quality and climate are good. They also tend to feature grandiose architecture. Accurately or not, these mineral springs are held to have medicinal properties important in the treatment of certain diseases.

It is not only the waters that are considered beneficial. Thermalism, another term to describe spa treatment (Cockerell 1996), can rely on mud, herbs and climate as well. Spring and mud treatments are called hydrotherapy; balneotherapy is based on tap-water, so practitioners are not restricted to particular locations. Kneip therapy uses cold water hydrotherapy.

An unusual aspect of the French spa scene is the development of thalasso-therapy centres, which first arose in 1964 at Quiberon in Brittany. Thalasso-therapy involves a range of treatments using seawater; it is a tradition that goes back to the ancient Greeks and Romans. The theory behind thalassotherapy is that the 92 supposedly therapeutic oligo-elements that occur in seawater can find their way into the body via warm seawater baths and showers. Exponents claim the treatment is good for stress, cellulite and weight control, and post-natal problems. Bona fide centres must have a qualified doctor as well as specialist staff. Thalassotherapy centres generally fit into the **destination spa** category; that is, guests choose to travel to them specifically to experience the health programs offered. A few, however, have the character of resort spas, in which thalassotherapy is only one of a range of amenities available.

Traditionally, attendance at spas in Europe has been by referral for treatment of specific medical conditions. In countries like Germany, Italy and France costs have been covered either by the state or by private medical insurance companies. While this is still the most common way to get into a spa, recent economic measures by governments and reassessment by the insurers have had impacts that Smith and Jenner (2000) have described in considerable detail. These have included reduced length of stays and a growth in self-funded clients. Some 90 per cent of spas in Germany are state owned and managed and citizens are entitled to visit them for three weeks every four years. In northern Italy there has been a surge in spa development and the Italian Tourist Office actively promotes attendance as a way of reducing absenteeism and helping to maintain a healthy labour force (Bacon 1998).

■ 11.3.1 Spa *types*

Monteson and Singer (1992a) describe two distinct types of health tourism facilities. The first is the spa resort or destination spa. This type of establishment has a single purpose, which is the spa experience itself. Other distractions are minimal. Clients come to participate in a full program for a designated period. Many offer group programs focusing on stress management for corporations (see the Camp Eden case study, page 279). The experience is rarely cheap and in the early part of a week-long program guests are known to question their decision to attend. 'Why am I paying all this money to suffer like this!' According to industry sources, however, by the end of the program most clients depart feeling rejuvenated and considerably healthier.

Accommodation ranges from the spartan to the luxurious, meals from simple vegetarian to a full menu of gourmet delights. Programs, too, range from the vigorous and intense to the gentle and relaxing (Monteson & Singer 1992b). The European models fall within this type, even though their primary purpose is often quite different. They focus on providing 'cures' to people with illnesses of some sort. Clients of American and Australian spas, on the other hand, are generally healthy when they arrive and healthier when they depart.

At a resort spa, the spa experience is just one of a range of recreational activities available to guests. Monteson and Singer also call this an **amenity spa**. Many of the major hotel groups have added spas to their amenities. Resort and hotel guests use as few or as many of the health facilities as they have the time for, and interest in. The leisure, pleasure and recreation traveller may indulge daily in a variety of services including massages, aromatherapy, body wraps and pedicures, while the business traveller may visit the gym, the lap pool or the jogging track between appointments. Stress release is a major reason given for using spa facilities in this type of resort. Amenity spas have spawned a new type of spa-hopper — conference delegates and their partners. Monteson and Singer (1992b) believe that this group presents excellent opportunities for resorts that have a 60 per cent or higher group market.

BREAKTHROUGH TOURISM
Wellness at sea

In the twenty-first century, Renaissance Cruises is taking seriously the nineteenth-century British Medical Association's endorsement of the health benefits of the sea cruise. The company has contracted the internationally renowned Johns Hopkins Medical, a large US health care provider, to help plan the comprehensive wellness program on board its ships. Renaissance Cruises holds a number of 'firsts' in the cruise business. It was the first cruise company to conduct its marketing almost exclusively by direct mail; the first to charter luxury airliners to link clients to their port of departure; and it was the first to market a fleet of eight interchangeable ships. Thus, it has a reputation for benchmarking and this new venture is likely to continue the tradition. The small, exclusive ships attract well-travelled couples between age 20 and 50 seeking soft adventure tourism experiences cushioned by a private club atmosphere, which is actively promoted by Renaissance. Itineraries are destination driven, the shallow draft of the ships allowing them to slip in and out of places that most ships of comparable size must necessarily avoid.

The 'wellness at sea' program includes totally smoke-free ships, professionally staffed health centres, healthy food and consultation with Johns Hopkins staff through a 'telemedicine' link. This service is available 24 hours a day via a high-tech satellite video link. Management claims that this access to the best quality medical care is what distinguishes its program from other spas at sea. Johns Hopkins staff have been involved with the concept since the design phase of the ships, advising on medical facilities, equipment, medical policies and protocols.

Renaissance aims to establish the highest quality medical care on its R-class ships in keeping with Johns Hopkins' international reputation for service standards. But it will not be all doctors and nurses, medicines and consultations. The Spa and Fitness Centre offers the more traditional massages, seaweed wraps (fresh product perhaps!) and thalassotherapy whirlpool treatment. Personal trainers are available to design fitness programs to last the whole voyage. To fill the time between travelling and toning, the chefs on board offer a wide variety of healthy cuisine on the menus of all four dining rooms. The floating spa resort has the potential to become one of the most popular cruise products.

More information about Renaissance Cruises can be found on their website at http://www.renaissancecruises.com.

■ 11.3.2 Spa *associations*

To be a member of the European Spa Association (ESPA), spas must comply with the requirements by offering strictly controlled curative services. The British Spas Federation (BSF), however, is reviewing its guidelines for membership, which consists of the municipal authorities of spa towns. The BSF says that enterprises that do not meet the statutory definition could nevertheless be admitted if they offer a range of ancillary services contributing to the spa experience relating, for exmaple, to air quality, architecture and, of course, the efficacy of treatments. Other associations, especially in the United States, take a less rigid view of what constitutes a spa. For the US-based International Spa and Fitness Association (ISPFA), no natural mineral spring is required; ISPFA defines a spa simply as 'a place where active and sustained use of natural therapeutic agents and health-giving elements are applied within an hospitable environment over a period of time'. The International Spa Association (ISPA), also based in the US, has an even wider definition. It promotes and defines the spa experience as 'your time to relax, reflect, revitalise and rejoice'. At present there are no industry associations in Australia.

The collection of definitions adopted by ISPA (cited in Smith & Jenner 2000) allow for the inclusion of a variety of spa and health resort experiences in this discussion of health tourism. These include:

- *the club spa:* a facility whose primary purpose is fitness and that offers a variety of professionally administered spa services on a daily-use basis
- *the cruise ship spa:* a spa on board a cruise ship providing professionally administered spa services and healthy cuisine
- *the day spa:* a spa offering a variety of professionally administered spa services to clients on a daily-use basis
- *the destination spa:* a spa whose sole purpose is to provide guests with lifestyle improvement and health enhancement through professionally administered spa services, physical fitness and training courses on a full-board, live-in basis
- *the medical spa:* a spa set up by an individual or group of medical and spa professionals, and whose primary purpose is to provide comprehensive medical and wellness care in an environment that integrates spa services, conventional and complementary therapies and treatments
- *the mineral springs spa:* a spa that offers an on-site source of natural mineral, thermal or sea water for use in hydrotherapy treatments
- *the resort/hotel spa:* a spa located within a resort or hotel, providing professionally administered spa services, fitness and wellness programs and spa cuisine menu choices.

11.4 DATA COLLECTION

Collecting reliable data on participation, expenditure and development in this sector is very difficult. Because of a lack of agreement on what actually constitutes health tourism there is very little consistency in available statistics. Even in Australia, which has a sophisticated tourism data collection system managed by the Bureau of Tourism Research and other industry bodies, no recognition is given to health as a primary reason for travel, although a number of official categories have obvious health associations. National and regional tourist offices and the industry federations provide some information, but the former can rarely extract specific detail on spa and health activity participation from general tourism statistics, while the latter rely on data supplied by their members. ISPA, which has members in 38 countries and represents some 1300 health and wellness facilities and providers, can be a useful source. ISPA claims that it is 'committed to forming and maintaining alliances that will educate, set standards, provide resources, influence policy and build coalitions for the industry'.

A review of academic research publications indicates that in the past twenty years by far the majority of articles on health tourism have focused on European destinations and spa development. Country-specific research includes studies in France (Chaspoul 1995), Romania (Cooper et al. 1995), Spain (Harlfinger 1991) and Turkey (Kahraman 1991). Wider implications for Eastern Europe are discussed by Hall (1991) and for western Europe by Cockerell (1996). Publications on the health and spa scene in the United Kingdom primarily address the historical development of the seaside resort and places like Bath (Hembry 1997). Outside Europe some work has been done on spas and health tourism in Japan (Shimomura 1993), the Caribbean (Goodrich & Uysal 1994) and Israel (Bar-On 1989).

What becomes immediately obvious in a literature search is that very little material specifically on health tourism is available, and even less that is recent. The health tourism sector is discussed in many recent books on general tourism developments, but usually in a brief and somewhat disjointed way. This could reflect the difficulties in obtaining reliable and accurate data referred to earlier. In 1993 Frechtling reviewed 147 publications on health and tourism. He found that most of the articles were devoted to the history and development of spas and health resorts. Also the research was primarily focused on the supply side, with very little interest shown in the demand side of health tourism. Frechtling argued that there was a need for research into the desire for improved health as a motivation for travel. To date there has been little advance in this area.

11.5 THE HISTORICAL DEVELOPMENT OF HEALTH TOURISM

Visiting spas is one of the earliest forms of tourism. Archaeological evidence from the Neolithic and Bronze ages suggests that the water sources at Grisy and St Sauveur in France, Forlì in Italy and St Moritz in Switzerland were used in a ritual or sacred way (Smith & Jenner 2000). Historical evidence suggests that travel for medical and climate reasons started around the sixth century BC in India, Greece and Persia. Hippocrates (*c.* 460–370 BC), the Greek physician commonly regarded as the father of medicine, espoused the therapeutic values of particular environments (Kevan 1993).

The Romans were particular advocates of the pleasures and values of mineral baths and founded such famous spas as Bath in England, Baden-Baden in Germany and Vichy in France. These are still popular places to visit, though less to take the waters than to see where the waters were taken in earlier times. Bath plans to redevelop its thermal facilities, which are currently not in use. By the medieval period, the idea that thermal springs could have medicinal properties was widely accepted. The Inquisition Register for the Bishop of Pamiers for 1318–25 reveals that the sulphur baths at Aix-les-Thermes, France (still a spa today), were believed to cure a range of skin diseases including ringworm, scabies and leprosy. No doubt in those less hygienic times immersion in any water would have been beneficial to some extent! Holy wells acted as a magnet for the sick, and royal patronage was guaranteed to boost the reputation and desirability of a location.

Other patronage also helped build reputations. In 1858 at Lourdes, in southern France, the appearance of the Virgin Mary to a 16-year-old girl, to whom the curative powers of the waters was demonstrated, gave rise to Europe's most famous pilgrimage site. Many thousands of people still visit Lourdes annually seeking cures for everything from total paralysis to a broken heart.

■ 11.5.1 Taking *the waters*

During the eighteenth and nineteenth centuries, 'taking the waters' became a fashionable pastime for Europe's leisured classes. Spa centres adapted their town plans to meet the visitors' requirements. Promenades were laid out, botanical gardens planted and hotels and restaurants built to accommodate the influx of prosperous visitors. Places like Menton on the French Riviera, where the climate was thought to be the cure, hosted delegations of European and British royalty and gentry, who built grand palaces and residences in which they could live comfortably while seeking cures for their ailments. A stroll through the Menton cemetery is like reading a who's who of nineteenth-century notables for whom a cure proved elusive — or was sought too late. The Riviera was, in fact, a British invention. Dr Tobias Smollett, an Englishman suffering from both mental and physical illnesses, went to Nice in 1763. Impressed with the mild climate, the scenery and the hospitable people, he wrote copious letters home describing the area's virtues. Within 50 years there was a string of British and European homes and hospices along the eastern Riviera accompanied by English and Russian churches, grand salons, dressmakers, perfumeries, schools and milliners.

Pump rooms became places to see and be seen. These were rather like grand lounge bars that specialised in glasses of mineral-loaded water, thought to be vital for the body, both inside and out. The Pump House in Bath was built in 1706 following a visit by Queen Anne in 1702. The town flourished under the entrepreneurship of Richard Nash, who recognised that spas could be remodelled to attract and retain wealthy people. He introduced strict codes of dress, behaviour and routine to enforce genteel standards of etiquette and manners (Craik 1991). A typical day's schedule went as follows (Craig-Smith & French 1994).

8.00 a.m.	Breakfast at one's lodgings
9.00 a.m.	Taking the waters at the pump room — minimum three glasses
11.00 a.m.	Morning prayers at the Abbey
12 noon	Horse riding, walking or window shopping
2.00 p.m.	Dinner
3.00 p.m.	Further visit to the pump room
5.00 p.m.	Tea
7.00 p.m.	Ball, concert, theatre or gaming rooms

These early spas were the forerunners of what became known as 'health farms', still the preserve of the affluent. Such places do not necessarily have natural resources; rather, they emphasise the benefits of fitness and good diet. Champneys is probably the most famous health farm in Britain. Founded in 1926 when there was a belief that hardships such as fasting were beneficial, its initial, austere philosophy has since given way to a kinder regime. Today Champneys is a serious destination spa — that is, a retreat for people seeking mental and physical rejuvenation.

The traditional spa industry in Britain has been virtually defunct for years. There is a brine bath at Droitwich, attached to the town's hospital, and a Turkish bath at Harrogate. Currently there are 11 spa towns in the United Kingdom, most designated as Spa Heritage Towns. No one has actually bathed in the waters at what is probably the country's most famous spa, Bath, since 1978, owing to a withdrawal of National Health Service support for the medical spa and uncertainty over the purity of the water source. In fact, various attempts — five in the 1980s and 1990s — were made by the local council and by business concerns to reopen the baths, all of which ended in failure when it became clear that the capital cost of restoration was too great to allow profitable operation. But it seems there is about to be a renaissance in historic medical and mineral springs spas. In November 1997 the Millennium Commission — a charity funded by the country's national lottery — awarded an £8 million grant for the reopening of the spa at Bath. If this project proves successful, it is likely to encourage development in several other spa towns. The total cost of the Bath spa restoration and building project is put at £16 526 500 (Smith & Jenner 2000).

Bacon (1998) compares the economic systems of Britain and Europe and their different impacts on spa developments. He concludes that one of the primary reasons for the decline of the British spa is because it was a private-sector initiative; its entrepreneurs worked within a business environment dominated by market forces and the search for a short-term return on their investment that compared favourably with what could be achieved in any other economic sector. By contrast, in Europe, because of the strong public funding base, the process of development was not left entirely to market forces but rather was directed by state and professional planners who sought to regulate and control development in ways that would enhance the social and economic environments for everybody. It remains to be seen if renewed public interest and attempts to revive the British spa will benefit from hindsight.

The British Spas Federation (BSF), which until October 1999 was largely confined to the local authorities of spa towns, has now been opened to the wider spa industry. Champneys is described by the federation as 'a health resort that offers a true spa experience'. The BSF has said that although a natural water source will no longer be considered essential, spas that do not meet its standards on architecture, air quality and therapeutic treatments will continue to be excluded.

11.6 VISITS TO MEDICAL SPAS AND MINERAL SPRINGS IN EUROPE

According to figures from ESPA, each year around 20 million people in Europe (including Russia) visit spas, spending more than 120 million bed nights at them — an average of six nights per guest per visit. Visitors to German and the Finnish spas seem to be the most serious, staying about 10 nights, while in Spain the average is just over eight nights and in Italy seven nights. In Switzerland the average figure is just under four nights, while in Iceland the average stay is said to be more than three weeks. As indicated earlier, each member country has its own way of collecting figures, so comparisons are not easily made and data are not necessarily reliable. The British figure of 1.3 million guests relates to the number of overnight visitors at 10 spa towns and does not reflect wider interest in taking spa treatments wherever they are available. Similarly, figures for Germany cover only visitors to spa towns. Statistics for France are even more unrepresentative, including only those people actually taking treatment and excluding those visiting spa towns, who are far more numerous. Nor do ESPA figures generally include those places that do not have a natural source (or a lake or the sea). In other words, they tend to reflect the medical and mineral springs spas and to exclude the more recent day spas, destination spas and resort spas. The ESPA figures of 20 million people and 120 million bed nights, therefore, have to be treated cautiously.

What they do indicate is that spas provide significant business for the travel and tourism industry. Unlike a hospital, a medical spa may draw its clientele from all over the country (although rarely from overseas); in many cases, clients stay in hotels rather than in the treatment centre. Of course, most clients also enjoy other entertainments and diversions in the town and are therefore no different from other kinds of tourists. Table 11.1 shows the number of health spas in European countries in 1998.

COUNTRY	NO. OF SPAS	COUNTRY	NO. OF SPAS	COUNTRY	NO. OF SPAS
Austria	81	Greece	45	Poland	42
Belgium	3	Hungary	32	Russia	4519
Czech. Rep.	34	Iceland	1	Slovenia	15
Finland	50	Italy	300	Spain	128
France	104	Luxembourg	1	Switzerland	21
Germany	330	Netherlands	4	UK	12

Source: *Adapted from Smith & Jenner (2000)*

■ 11.6.1 **Profile** *of European spa clients*

Germans are Europe's most enthusiastic spa users. More than 1.4 million Germans attend spas regularly and 13 million are occasional users (Cockerell 1996). Participation by women slightly outnumbers that by men and figures show a steady increase in the over-60 age group. Although the government tried to curtail subsidised spa attendance in 1996, by 1998 it had reassessed its decision as a result of industry lobbying, which described the negative effects this was having on other sectors of the tourism industry such as accommodation, retail shopping and other businesses in spa towns. In 1998 13.5 per cent of guests in spa towns were subsidised by the government, which equates to 1.26 million visitors. Subsidised clients stay longer than non-subsidised clients.

Austrians have a similar enthusiasm for spas and their medicinal qualities, with state funding encouraging high participation. In France about 70 per cent of spa clients are state-funded. Government belt-tightening similar to that in Germany has caused a slight overall decline in the sector. Thalassotherapy remains popular, even though state subsidies ceased in 1998. The Accor hotel group has established the Thalassa International brand, with 10 domestic locations as well as one each in Portugal and Morocco. About 60 per cent of French spa clients are women and 70 per cent of all clients are over 50 years of age. The Swiss are also very fond of thalassotherapy and represent a very good market for French centres. In summary, although detailed data are sparse the most common profile of a spa client in Europe is female and over 60, staying more than two weeks on a state-funded package at a specific, medically referred destination.

■ 11.6.2 **Future** *growth area for European spas*

Europe will not necessarily mirror trends in the United States (see section 11.7) because of its long tradition of spa-going of a different kind. However, it is certain that Europe will see a growth in spas on the US pattern while the traditional sector fights to maintain its existing figures. What will Europe's private, new-style spa-goers be looking for? There are conflicting views within the industry.

Some believe they will seek the kind of serious approach taken by Champneys. They will look to the latest development in the US spa market of the so-called 'wellness centre', which has a medical and preventive health orientation rather than a preoccupation with beauty treatments. Others believe that the real growth will come from the leisure rather than the health side of the industry.

11.7 THE AMERICAN BLUEPRINT

The US industry uses a slightly different terminology from that used by ISPA; the phrase destination spa, for example, embraces the medical and mineral springs spa. When *Travel & Tourism Analyst* examined health and spa tourism in North America in 1998 it reported that the number of hotel or resort spas had grown from 80 in 1987 to 120 in 1997 and that day spas had increased in number from just 30 to 600. Additionally, hotels with amenity spas, which did not exist in 1987, totalled 110 in 1997. Another survey, by *Spa Management Journal* (cited in *T&TA* 2000), suggests an even faster rate of growth in day spas — from 20 to 25 in 1980, to 150 to 200 in 1990 and 3000 in 1997 (with 300 in Canada). Results from a 1999 survey of ISPA members in the United States reveal that day spas, hotel/resort spas and destination spas are all enjoying rapid growth. Members with turnover in the US$1 to US$5 million range reported a 47 per cent growth in earnings in 1999, up from 41 per cent in 1998. Nearly one-third of spas reported a sales volume of US$5 to US$10 million in 1999. These figures suggest that the US market is becoming more leisure-oriented than the spa and health resorts of Europe.

■ 11.7.1 Profiles *of US spa clients*

The most important point to grasp, perhaps, is that the typical US spa client does not consider himself or herself to be ill. According to the 1999 US survey referred to above, the majority of both day spa clients and resort/destination/cruise spa clients consider themselves to be in good or excellent health. Nevertheless, they have health concerns, including diet and exercise. Two-thirds of those who took part in the survey said they took vitamins, and nearly as many sought to limit the amount of fat they ate, yet the main motive of US respondents for going to a spa was relaxation. This was the primary motivation of 43 per cent of day spa participants and 61 per cent of resort/destination/cruise. Pampering and stress reduction, weight loss, health reasons, and exercise and fitness, while figuring well in the survey, are not rated so importantly.

The representation of men among US spa clients has been steadily increasing. Indeed, 68 per cent of ISPA spas offer treatments specifically designed for men, although they are less likely to visit day spas. The 34 to 52 age group makes up around half of the spa market, but the 20 to 30 age group is on the increase. Spa clients are 85 per cent female, whereas resort/destination/cruise spa-goers are only 65 per cent female. Otherwise, profiles are very similar in terms of education, marital status, income and age. Word of mouth and travel agents are the most commonly used sources of recommendation.

■ Table 11.2
*Comparison
of day spa-
goers and
resort/
destination/
cruise spa-
goers in the
United
States, 1999*

VARIABLE	DAY SPA CLIENTS	RESORT/DESTINATION/ CRUISE SPA CLIENTS
Sex	85% female 15% male	65% female 35% male
Education	39% college graduates	39% college graduates
Marital status	63% married	66% married
Income	26% US$35 000 or less 32% US$45 000–$79 999	27% US$35 000 or less 31% US$45 000–$74 999
Age	47% aged 34–52	54% aged 34–52

Source: *ISPA (cited in Smith & Jenner 2000)*

11.8 SPA AND HEALTH RESORTS IN AUSTRALIA

Australia has followed the US model in developing spa and health resorts, but that is where the similarity ends. It is virtually impossible to acquire any reliable domestic statistical information; there are no industry organisations of operators setting codes of practice or collating data. Australians have always headed for the beach and the bush for their holidays, even though public sea bathing was not condoned until 1903. The Hepburn Spa Resort in Victoria, opened in 1870, and the Hydro Majestic in Medlow Bath, New South Wales, opened in 1904, were among Australia's first attempts to develop traditional spa retreats. Although the former still operates as Australia's only mineral bath facility offering spa couches, areospas and flotation tanks (http://www.hepburnspa.com.au), the latter has undergone many changes and is currently promoting itself along nostalgic lines (http://www.hydromajestic.com.au). The Hydro Majestic was opened by retailer Mark Foy following his experience of hydropathic treatment in Matlock Bath, England. However, its therapeutic services were not as popular as he had hoped and he soon abandoned the spa idea and converted it into a family hotel.

The modern era of spa development began in the 1980s; a landmark event in 1989 was the opening of the Hyatt Regency Coolum, Queensland. At the time the president of Hyatt International, Bernd Chorengel, claimed the spa resort would become a model to be exported internationally, thus reversing the trend of hotel chains bringing new concepts *into* Australia (Stewart 1989). The resort, however, had been based on the much older La Costa health spa in San Diego, California. Health management, said Chorengel, 'was a concept which had only a five year history and was a result of people's changing attitudes and lifestyles'. The resort targeted the 'creative achievers aged 35 plus' and was described as 'the thinking person's hideaway' (Stewart 1989). More than a decade later the resort is still a leader in its field.

By 2000 there had been a flurry of development across the product spectrum. Products range from the five-star 'complete sensory experience' offered by the Hilton on the Park, Melbourne, the luxury boutique Crystal

Creek Rainforest Retreat near Murwillumbah, northern New South Wales, which offers 'the ultimate getaway from busy city life', and P&O Australian Resorts' Spa of Peace and Plenty on Dunk Island to the explosion in day spas and beauty shops offering massages, foot therapy and facials.

SPECIAL INTEREST INVESTIGATION
The Phoenician Spa Retreat, Gold Coast

The Phoenician Spa Retreat was originally opened by the Raptis Group as part of the Phoenician Spa and Health Resort at Broadbeach on the Gold Coast, Queensland. In 1998 it was sold as a separate business when the resort changed hands. It is luxurious and opulent with a marble entrance and fine columned Roman bath. A peaceful ambience is immediately established by the hushed atmosphere and fragrant burning oils. Staff are efficient and friendly. The spa's philosophy is to offer a complete experience, not just a 'quick fix'. In areas like the Gold Coast there is 'pretty much a masseuse on every corner, with beauty salons, aromatherapists and naturopaths all offering massages with their other services, to say nothing of people who just offer massages', the acting manager pointed out. The Phoenician incorporates such services as stress relief and toxin cleansing into its programs and available 'experiences', which last from two hours to five days in a 'Rest and Rejuvenation' treatment in which clients use the neighbouring Phoenician Resort facilities. Many clients come in for a full-day program, which includes a Roman bath, hydrotherapy bath, aromatherapy salt glow, body wrap, lunch, facial, pedispa and hand therapy. The client profile is 60 per cent female and 40 per cent male. Women prefer the total experience packages while men are conservative, with 85 per cent mainly settling for a massage and the remaining 15 per cent a facial or pedicure. The male demographic has been steadily increasing as men find it more socially acceptable to visit such places. This trend is also seen in the increasing numbers of males willing to go into what were traditionally seen as women's hairdressing salons. At the Phoenician 60 per cent of clients are holiday-makers, which is not surprising given its Gold Coast location. The balance, while classified as 'locals', come from a wide catchment area that includes Brisbane, a one-hour drive to the north. A Phoenician client usually fits into the 20s to mid 50s age groups. (Their youngest client was a nine-year-old sent in by her mother for a facial for her birthday.)

Management foresees increasing division between the operators who specialise in surgical and chemical health and beauty treatments and those who offer a natural product–based sensory experience. This will mean a growth in services designed to maintain the work done by cosmetic surgery while the growth area for the latter category of operators will be based on people seeking a better lifestyle. The stresses of the 1990s are certain to carry into and perhaps increase in the 2000s.

■ *11.8.1* **The Australian** *experience*

> Start with a morning walk in the rainforest and tropical breakfast. Decide between a horse ride, shiatsu massage and ocean swim, or some meditation and yoga. Feel your mind and body unwinding as one. Australia's health farms and spa resorts offer facilities and services to satisfy all tastes, in idyllic settings from our picturesque bush valleys to golden beaches and tropical islands . . .

So reads the Australian Tourism Commission's consumer website (http://www.australia.com). The site then offers two links — one to health resorts and one to spas. The former lists a number of links to actual resorts; the latter has even more links. These are not definitive lists of the products available in Australia, neither can they be taken as totally reliable. Operators choose to add their own links and categorise themselves. For example, one link is to a bed-and-breakfast establishment that has a spa bath. This highlights a widely held misconception. Ask most Australians what a spa is and they will probably describe a spa bath or a small pool with water jets found beside many backyard swimming pools. The total experience concept is not widely appreciated except by people who have actually spent time in a health resort or at least know someone who has. The popular perceptions of health resorts among people who have at least heard of them is that they are very expensive, they make you eat vegetarian food (Australians are numbered among the world's biggest meat eaters) and they are only for highly paid executives or wealthy, jaded society wives. The case study on one of the longest running health resorts in Australia gives a profile of clients that reveals broader market segments.

11.9 FUTURE DIRECTIONS

The leisure side of the spa and health resort business has greatest potential for growth. Although Europeans are increasingly inclined towards private medicine, most still look towards the state to provide, which is where the European market differs from the US and Australian markets. Australians have never been sent to spas at government expense. One of the problems for traditional European spas in the development of new markets is that 'healthy' clients interested in being pampered and in relaxation and beauty treatments will not happily holiday alongside people who have serious medical conditions. Moreover, although many traditional spas are worried about curbs on government spending, the client volumes they still enjoy are sufficient to rule out the need for serious new marketing initiatives. Indeed, many spas have never had to compete for business and do not have the necessary management and personnel skills in place to do so. The traditional European spas, then, will probably continue much as they are now. The growth will come from the destination and resort spas where the emphasis is on relaxation, fitness, stress reduction and beauty.

One US survey showed that 80 per cent of visitors to resort spas did not actually use the spa; nevertheless, some kind of spa has become an essential facility for every good hotel and resort. Specialisation is also emerging. Already in the United States there are 'golf spas' and 'ski spas', and the concept is also working in well with cruise tourism. For example, all of Carnival Cruise Lines' 'Fun Ships' offer gyms, aerobics, saunas, steam rooms, whirlpools, massage, aromatherapy and facials. Celebrity Cruises offers hydrotherapy, including thalassotherapy, aboard every ship, as well as the usual fitness facilities. Costa Cruises has its Pompeii Spa, which can be prebooked in half- to six-day packages. Crystal Cruises offers the Crystal Spa on board *Harmony* and *Symphony*. Indeed, spa facilities have become an essential part of ship design.

For the wider travel industry, the message is that some kind of spa facility — however much it may fall short of the ESPA or British Spas Federation definitions — will be increasingly viewed as an essential feature in resorts and resort hotels, and especially in established spa towns. With increasing demand for experiential holidays, the spa experience is likely to become more popular as a way of escaping the stresses and demands of twenty-first-century living.

11.10 SUMMARY

This chapter has focused on one particular aspect of health tourism — spas and health resorts. We began by discussing the broad concepts of health tourism, with reference to articles that have tried to define this somewhat elusive tourism sector. We then examined the spa experience and the different types of spa and health resort products. Because health reasons have been identified as one of the earliest motivations for people to travel, we then briefly outlined the history of this form of travel. We attempted to compare the different types of spa and health resort development and participation rates in Europe, the United States and Australia. Fundamentally, Europeans go to health resorts because they are sick; Americans and Australians go because they are healthy and want to stay that way. Finally, the case study that follows will examine one of Australia's health retreats.

It could be argued that a wide range of tourism experiences are health related. Surely the busy person who takes a two-week holiday in a resort just to lie around the pool and sip funny-coloured drinks, hoping to return to work feeling relaxed and recharged, is also participating in health tourism. This chapter, however, has focused on those people who make conscious destination choices that will satisfy health and wellbeing needs, either because they are instructed to do so by their doctor, as is the most common experience in Europe, or because they are aware of the potential benefits of the spa experience, as is the case in the United States and Australia.

Questions

11.1 Name five characteristics of European spas and their clients.

11.2 What is the fundamental difference between spa clients in Europe and those in the United States?

11.3 Describe the motivations of people in the twenty-first century who participate in health tourism in the United States, and Australia and increasingly in Europe.

11.4 How could a spa resort manager capitalise on those motivations when planning new products and marketing programs?

11.5 Find out where health resorts and spas in Australia advertise. Do these platforms suggest any particular markets they feel are most appropriate for their product? What are they?

11.6 Locate and compare at least six websites promoting spa resort experiences.

11.7 Discuss why Australia needs to develop a professional association for people who own and/or operate spa resorts. You should consider the implications for both the supply side and demand side of this tourism sector.

REFERENCES

Bacon, W. 1998. 'Economic Systems and Their Impact on Tourist Resort Development: The Case of the Spa in Europe'. *Tourism Economics* 4 (1): 21–32.

Bar-On, R. 1989. 'Cost–benefit Considerations for Spa Treatments, Illustrated by the Dead Sea and Arad, Israel'. *Revue de Tourisme* 44 (4): 12–15.

Bywater, M. 1990. 'Spas and Health Resorts in the European Community'. *EIU Travel & Tourism Analyst* 6: 56–67.

Chaspoul, C. 1995. 'Health Tourism: Spa Bathing and Seawater Therapy'. *Cahiers-d'Espaces* 43.

Cockerell, N. 1996. 'Spas and Health Resorts in Europe'. *EIU Travel & Tourism Analyst* 1: 53–77.

Cooper, C. P., Fletcher, J., Noble, A. & Westlake, J. N. 1995. 'Changing Tourism Demand in Central Europe: The Case of Romanian Tourist Spas'. *Journal of Tourism Studies* 6 (2): 30–44.

Craig-Smith, S. & French, C. 1994. *Learning to Live with Tourism.* Melbourne: Pitman.

Craik, J. 1991. *Resorting to Tourism.* Sydney: Allen & Unwin.

Douglas N. & Douglas, N. 1996. 'P&O's Pacific'. *Journal of Tourism Studies* 7 (2): 2–14.

Edlin, G. & Golanty, E. 1988. *Health and Wellness.* Boston, USA: Jones Bartlet.

Frechtling, D. 1993. *Annotated Bibliography on Health and Tourism Issues.* USA: Pan American Health Organisation.

Gee, C, Makens, J. C. & Choy, D. J. L. 1989. *The Travel Industry*. Second Edition. New York: Van Nostrand Reinhold.

Goodrich, J. N. & Goodrich, G. E. 1987. 'Health-care Tourism — An Exploratory Study'. *Tourism Management* 8: 217–22.

Goodrich, J. N. & Uysal, M. 1994. 'Health Tourism: A New Positioning Strategy for Tourist Destinations'. In Uysal, M. (Ed.). *Global Tourist Behaviour*. Birmingham: International Business Press, pp. 227–38.

Hall, C. M. 1992. 'Adventure, Sport and Health Tourism'. In Weiler, B. & Hall, C. M. (Eds.). *Special Interest Tourism*. London: Belhaven Press, pp. 141–58.

Hall, D. R. 1991. *Tourism and Economic Development in Eastern Europe and the Soviet Union*. London: Belhaven Press.

Harlfinger, O. 1991. 'Holiday Bioclimatology: A Study of Palma de Majorca, Spain'. *Geojournal* 25 (4): 377–81.

Hembry, P. 1989. *The English Spa 1560–1815: A Social History*. London: Athlone Press.

Hembry, P., Cowie, L. W. & Cowie, E. E. 1997. *British Spas from 1815 to the Present: A Social History*. London: Athlone Press.

Holloway. J. & Plant, T. R. 1988. *Marketing for Tourism*. London: Pitman.

Inskeep, E. 1991. *Tourism Planning — An Integrated and Sustainable Development Approach*. New York: Van Nostrand Reinhold.

IOUTO. 1973. *Health Tourism*. Geneva: United Nations.

Kahraman, N. 1991. 'The Importance of Thermal Springs in the Area of Health Tourism'. *Anatolia* 2 (15/16): 10–12.

Kevan, S. M. 1993. 'Quest for Cures: A History of Tourism for Climate and Health'. *International Journal of Biometeorology* 37 (3): 113–24.

Monteson, P. A. & Singer, J. 1992a. 'Turn Your Spa into a Winner'. *Cornell Hotel & Restaurant Quarterly* 33 (3): 37–44.

Monteson P. A. & Singer, J. 1992b. 'The Spa Who Loved Me'. *Lodging Hospitality*, February, pp. 46–8.

Naidoo, J. & Wills, J. 1994. *Health Promotions — Foundations for Practice*. London: Bailliere Tindall.

Shimomura, A. 1993. 'Studies on the Space Composition of the Hot Spring Resort in Japan'. *Bulletin of the Tokyo University Forests* 90: 23–9.

Smith C. & Jenner, P. 2000. 'Health Tourism in Europe'. *EIU Travel & Tourism Analyst* 1: 41–59.

Stewart, A. 1989. 'Coolum Introduces the Spa Resort'. *Business Review Weekly*, 3 February, p. 56.

Camp Eden
The business

Camp Eden claims to be Australia's leading holistic health retreat. Set in the lush tropical rainforest of the Gold Coast hinterland, just north of the New South Wales border with Mount Cougal National Park to the west, the 120-hectare property is an 'ideal getaway where guests can enjoy a week or two of pure health and relaxation. It is the ideal place to unwind, be pampered, shape up, have fun and discover a renewed sense of wellbeing' (http://www.campeden.com.au). Camp Eden's reputation has grown over the last 16 years from its commitment to giving each guest the ultimate rejuvenating holiday. Guests are offered healthy gourmet meals, exercise to individual levels of fitness and pampering treatments for total indulgence and relaxation. Guests also learn stress management techniques that include meditation, tai chi, yoga and some 'good old fashioned belly laughing'. Management claims that the most valuable gains a stay at Camp Eden can offer are the skills and knowledge people take with them to improve their lifestyle. The whole experience is often a life-changing one. Guests leave Camp Eden with a sense of clarity and direction, a feeling of well-being and a desire to make positive, permanent changes in their lives.

■ **Figure 11.2**
Workouts at Camp Eden, on Queensland's Gold Coast, can be rigorous.

Source: *Camp Eden Health Retreat*

Camp Eden's facilities include two tennis courts, a heated salt-water pool, sauna and steam rooms, a fully equipped gymnasium and many kilometres of tropical rainforest bushwalks. It boasts a challenging Outdoor Adventure circuit that includes Australia's longest flying fox, abseiling, rock climbing, and a power pole and high ropes course. Every human being would benefit from a week at Camp Eden, says manager, Steve Canning.

The staff

It was founded in 1984 by two Australians who operated women-only facilities in Asia and who recognised a need for a total package facility. Camp Eden's purpose, according to one of its policy statements, is 'to encourage as many people as possible to achieve optimum health in mind, body and spirit'. This philosophy applies to staff as much as it does to guests. After 16 years both directors and many of the original staff remain, a testimony to satisfaction and success in business and staff development. There are currently 65 people employed on both full-time and casual rosters. These include masseurs, physical education instructors, naturopaths, beauticians, housekeepers, kitchen staff, groundspeople, salespeople, administrators and management. Two-thirds of staff are involved in massage, physical education and beauty therapy. Six work experience staff are on site at all times; they are brought in to experience the complete program as guests for the first week and then continue on staff for a set period. Many come back to repeat the experience. Their enthusiasm and knowledge is enhanced by their first week's treatment; management considers it a 'win-win situation'.

The clients

Participation in the health resort experience peaked in the mid-1990s when many companies used their obligatory tax training levies to send executives for stress relief. Since the abolition of the levy, the profile has changed to include more individuals, couples and pairs of friends (usually two women); the resort hosts an average of 30 clients a week. Couples are not common on a week's retreat, but one person who has stayed at Camp Eden will frequently send her or his partner to stay at a later date. In 2000 it cost $1650 plus GST for a week-long program.

The Camp is normally a 'child free zone' except for specially designated weeks throughout the year. An adventure camp directed at confidence building is offered to 13- to 17-year-olds twice a year. Management also supports a Sydney-based project for the underprivileged by raising money to bring 36 children up for a camp once a year. A dozen past guests are invited back to help during this week. In 1999 they raised $50 000 towards this goal. Other special weeks include the Reach Within Spiritual Journey, described as 'a journey of self-discovery'; and the Ultimate Whitsunday Experience, when 10 guests join the 82-foot yacht *Iluka* to sail around the Great Barrier Reef. Staff in attendance provide massages along with all the usual adventure activities such as scuba diving and bushwalking. Two executive health and management program weeks include daily tutorials in leadership, company culture and vision among the other more physical activities.

The 30 to 50 age group represents some 44 per cent of all guests at Camp Eden. Sixty per cent of guests are women, but this figure is declining as men become more comfortable with this sort of experience; 40 per cent are married. Nearly 40 per cent classify themselves as filling managerial roles, 30 per cent as professional and 30 per cent as skilled people. About 50 per cent of all guests have a college or university education. Weight management is the motivation of some 20 per cent of clients while increased fitness motivates 10 per cent. Enhanced lifestyle skills, including stress management, accounts for another 30 per cent. When asked to describe their experience, 57 per cent choose the words 'fantastic/ great/pleasurable/wonderful' and 37 per cent indicate an intention to return.

Marketing

By far the most valuable form of marketing has proven to be word of mouth to friends and family. Camp Eden management has chosen not to invest heavily in marketing to date — the Yellow Pages of the telephone book are the only paid advertising they participate in. Complimentary experiences are provided to journalists from a very select group of magazines such as *marie claire* and *Vogue Living*. Management has such confidence in the product and the experience that they believe this is the best way to get their message across to potential guests. The introduction of an Internet site at http://www.campeden.com.au is attracting a small but increasing number of new participants (about 2 per cent in 1999). Brochures describing the special programs are available from the administration.

New directions

There are plans to build a number of luxury lodges on the property that buyers will then lease back to Camp Eden. Strong interest has been shown in this project by past clients. A new special product is being directed at sporting teams wishing to build both fitness and team skills.

A TYPICAL DAY

6.00 a.m.	tai chi and morning walk
7.00 a.m.	breakfast
8.30 a.m.	more morning exercises
9.30 a.m.	choice of five special programs — balance/recharge/time out/ indulgence/awakenings
12 noon	lunch (coffee, tea, chocolate and cigarettes are absolutely forbidden on the property)
2.00 p.m.	fun and games (includes volleyball, abseiling, water polo, tennis etc.)
6.30 p.m.	dinner followed by evening staff talks/presentations

(Go back to the daily activity description for Bath in the eighteenth century to see how the spa business has changed!)

Questions

1 How does the profile of clients at Camp Eden compare with those who attend spas in Europe and the United States?

2 What might be the marketing implications of having weeks designated for special programs?

3 Go to the Australian Tourism Commission website referred to earlier and compare Camp Eden with two other health resorts listed there. What are the similarities and differences?

Ross Dowling

CHAPTER 12

12
Environmental
tourism

LEARNING OBJECTIVES

After reading this chapter, you will have an appreciation of:

- the environment and its relationship to tourism
- the greening of the tourism industry
- the characteristics of environmental tourism
- what nature-based tourism is and how it is carried out
- examples of wildlife tourism
- ecotourism and its special role within the tourism industry
- the characteristics of Australian ecotourists
- how ecotourism is being developed in Queensland.

12.1 INTRODUCTION

The second half of the 1980s gave rise to two very different international phenomena. A growing concern for the conservation of our natural resources led to the rise of environmentalism as a mass movement. At the same time the proliferation of jumbo jets accelerated the rise of mass tourism. With the unparalleled growth of the two it was inevitable that one day they would come to interact. The intersection of concern for the environment and tourism gave rise to environmental tourism. This type of special interest tourism (SIT) may take many forms, among which the commonest are probably nature-based tourism, wildlife tourism and ecotourism.

Environmental tourism in natural areas has the potential for both beneficial and adverse environmental and sociocultural impacts. Thus, there are two streams of thought regarding the environment–tourism relationship. The first is that the natural environment is necessarily harmed by tourism, hence the two are fundamentally in conflict. The second is that environmentalism and tourism have the potential to work together in a symbiotic relationship in which each benefits the other. The key to the successful growth of the environmental tourism industry lies in the implementation of sustainable tourism planning and development. When this occurs environmental tourism can foster conservation of the biophysical environment, enhance the sociocultural wellbeing of communities and generate economic benefits to regions.

12.2 THE ENVIRONMENT

The term *environment* is open to many interpretations. Gilpin (1990:65) defines it as 'a concept which includes: all aspects of the surroundings of humanity, affecting individuals and social groupings. Environmental investigations are concerned, therefore, with people and their present and future activities in the surrounding atmosphere, water bodies and landscape.' The two most common perspectives on the environment are grounded in the human-centred or anthropocentric worldview and the life-centred or ecocentric worldview.

■ 12.2.1 The environment *as a resource*

Key principles of the human-centred worldview include that humans are the planet's most important species, set apart from, and in control of, the rest of nature. Adherents act on the assumption that the Earth has an unlimited supply of resources that are accessed by humans through science and technology. The human-centred approach to the environment prevails in most industrial societies today. According to this view, humans, as the planet's dominant species, can and should manage the planet mostly for their own benefit. Other species have only an instrumental value; that is, their value depends on whether or not they are useful to humans. Despite this, the human-centered approach to the environment often advocates the principle of *stewardship* by which humans have an ethical responsibility to manage and care for the Earth.

This dominant western environmental paradigm has underpinned the view of the natural environment as a resource. Thus, environmental tourism development can be viewed as following on naturally from the traditional development of the Earth's primary resources in farming, forestry, mining and fishing.

■ *12.2.2* **The environment** *as an attribute*

The alternate view regards the environment as an attribute — that is, it has certain intrinsic values, whether or not they are ascribed as having value to humanity. This view of the environment suggests that even our stewardship is unsustainable. Advocates suggest the need for us to change the way we think in order to recognise the inherent or intrinsic value of all forms of life — a value quite apart from their potential or actual use to us. This life-centred or ecocentric approach recognises biodiversity as vital for all life, understanding that the environment, as an attribute, is not a resource and that nature exists for all the Earth's species. By extension, humans are not viewed as being apart from, or superior to, the rest of nature. Some forms of economic growth are beneficial and some are harmful; our goal should be to design economic and political systems that encourage sustainable forms of growth and discourage or prohibit forms that cause ecological degradation or pollution. Underpinning such an approach to the environment is the view that a healthy economy depends on a healthy environment.

Major principles underlying the ecocentric or earth-centred approach include interconnectedness, intrinsic value, sustainability, conservation, intergenerational equity and individual responsibility. The principle of interconnectedness holds that humans are the equal of but not superior to other species. Every living thing has intrinsic value; it has a right to live simply because it exists. The principle of intrinsic value includes the notion that it is wrong for humans to cause the premature extinction of any wild species or the elimination or degradation of their habitats and focuses on the need for the preservation of wildlife and the principle of biodiversity. Sustainability concerns the maintenance of the Earth's life-support systems for humans and other species. Conservation promotes the wise use of the environment; and intergenerational equity addresses the notion that each generation should leave the Earth to the following generation in as good a condition as that in which they themselves inherited it.

12.2 **T**OURISM

Tourism is the fastest growing industry in the world and one of its fastest growing components is ecotourism. According to the World Travel and Tourism Council (WTTC), tourism is now the world's largest industry, generating 6 per cent of global gross national product and employing one in 15 workers worldwide. The World Tourism Organization's (WTO 1999) study 'Tourism: 2020 Vision', predicts that 1.6 billion tourists will visit foreign countries annually by the year 2020, spending more than US$2 trillion, or US$5 billion every day. Tourist arrivals are predicted to grow by an average 4.3 per cent a year over the next two decades, while receipts from international tourism will climb by 6.7 per cent a year. Tourism in the twenty-first century will not only be the world's biggest industry; it will be by far the largest that the world has ever seen. With its phenomenal size and growth, the tourism industry will also have to take greater responsibility for its extensive impacts — not only its economic impact, but also its environmental, social and cultural repercussions.

At the Ministerial Conference on Oceans and New Tourism Dimensions, held in connection with the Expo '98 World Fair in Lisbon, Portugal, the WTO secretary general, Francesco Frangialli, identified the emergence of products that will dominate the tourism market in the new millennium (WTO 1998a). These emerging tourism features include 'nature and ecotourism products, cruises, water sports, and tourism in the polar regions, the deserts and the great tropical forests' (WTO 1998a:1). The WTO reports that environmental tourism now holds one-fifth of the global market, accounts for approximately 20 per cent of total international travel and is worth US$20 billion a year (WTO 1998b).

12.4 THE ENVIRONMENT AND TOURISM

The environment–tourism relationship may be viewed from the standpoint of conflict or of symbiosis. Either point of view can be defended. However, in this chapter we will argue that, in either case, the way to reduce conflict and increase compatibility is through understanding, planning and management based on environmental principles that allow for sustainable development. The relationship between the environment and tourism should be grounded in the concepts of the sustainable use of natural resources established by the World Conservation Strategy (IUCN 1980) and the sustainable development strategy of the World Commission on Environment and Development (WCED 1987). This environment–development link often uses tourism as a bridge. The base of the partnership is resource sustainability. Tourism must be fully integrated into the resource management process, which will require the adoption of resource conservation values as well as the more traditional development goals. The achievement of resource sustainability requires an understanding that environmental protection and enhancement are prerequisites to the realisation of tourism potential. Therefore our journey of discovery into the field of ecotourism begins with the environment and our need to understand it.

The relationship between the environment and tourism has evolved through several phases over the latter half of the twentieth century

(Hudman 1991). In the 1950s it was viewed as being based on *coexistence* (Zierer 1952). However, with the advent of mass tourism in the 1960s increasing pressure was put on natural areas by tourism developments. This trend, together with the growth of environmental awareness in the early 1970s, led to a relationship increasingly perceived as one of *conflict* (Akoglu 1971). During the following decade this perspective was widely discussed in the literature (e.g. Cohen 1978; OECD 1980; Mathieson & Wall 1982). At the same time an argument was emerging that the relationship could be based on a *symbiosis* beneficial to both the environment and tourism (e.g. Budowski 1976; Pigram 1980; Romeril 1985).

At the beginning of the 1980s the relationship had potential for either conflict or symbiosis. This orientation is referred to as *integration* (Dowling 1990, 1992). It differs from the symbiotic view, with its inherent idealism, by recognising the potential for environmental conflicts caused by natural area tourism developments. Thus, according to the integrated view of the environment–tourism relationship, environmentally compatible tourism developments may be achieved by fostering sustainable development (Romeril 1989a; Farrell & Runyan 1991) through environmentally appropriate tourism planning (Murphy 1985; Gunn 1988; Inskeep 1991).

Indications of an environmentally responsible, 'integrated' tourism industry must be tempered by the knowledge that the relationship is still one of conflict in many parts of the world. Yet here, too, it is only through their integration that conflicts can be minimised and symbiotic possibilities advanced. This balance was addressed by the IUOTO (the predecessor to the WTO) in the 1960s, Haulot and Krippendorf in the 1970s, Romeril in the 1980s and Dowling in the 1990s and is the basis of the current drive for sustainable development.

The emerging view is that continued tourism development will only be sustained by the recognition of the interdependencies that exist among environmental and economic issues and policies. The concept of sustainable development is recognised by both those who describe the conflicts (Smith & Jenner 1989) and those who advocate a symbiotic approach (Romeril 1989a,b). Farrell and McLellan (1987:13) argue that 'an aware and completely changed industry can sustain tourism. In terms of modern thinking and ecodevelopment, if tourism is sustained significant steps have then been taken toward maintaining environmental integrity. A healthy environmental integrity means the possibility of successful tourism, which, when managed properly, becomes a resource in its own right.'

■ *12.4.1* **The need** *for planning*

Many writers have discussed the strong environment–tourism link in the context of both an increase in demand for natural area tourism (Bosselman 1978; Romeril 1989a; Smith & Jenner 1989) and an increase in tourism's role in advancing conservation (Budowski 1976; Phillips 1985; Murphy 1986). A summary of the literature indicates that, while it usually describes an exchange based on either conflict or symbiosis, neither view is exclusive; many writers recognise that to minimise conflicts and foster symbiosis requires an integrated approach to environmentally compatible tourism planning. This embraces environmental, social, economic, political, psychological, anthropological and technological factors. Tourism planning is also concerned with the past, present and future (Rose 1984). Therefore, like its objectives and structures, the methods and techniques of planning are diverse.

Planning involves people and so relies heavily on values. Community values are critical to planning and include spatial and temporal dimensions. Spatial factors important in planning include the scale (site, local, regional, national or international), concentration of use versus dispersal, land tenure and use as well as carrying capacity. Temporal factors incorporate both static views, such as 'a snapshot in time' approach, and dynamic views, by which planning is regarded as an ongoing process.

■ 12.4.2 The greening *of tourism*

Wight (1993) argues that the marketplace is becoming 'greener', or more environmentally sensitive, both in terms of awareness and in its desire to contribute through its efforts to a more sensitive approach to numerous activities and purchases. She notes that 85 per cent of the industrialised world's citizens rate the environment as the number one public issue and that the individual tourist has a significant influence over the nature of the tour operations and their environmental impact. The greening of the tourism industry is illustrated by the adoption of such practices as 'recycling and reductions in resource use, the introduction of codes of ethics and the establishment of facilitating intercorporate organisations such as Green Globe' (Weaver & Oppermann 2000:380).

12.5 ENVIRONMENTAL TOURISM ·················

Tourism may be defined as either mass tourism or alternative tourism. The former is characterised by large numbers of people seeking replication of their own culture in institutionalised settings, with little cultural or environmental interaction in authentic settings. Alternative tourism or SIT, however, places greater emphasis on contact and understanding between hosts and guests as well as between tourists and the environment (Smith & Eadington 1992).

The great explosion in special interest options began in the early 1980s. Influenced by the negative attitudes towards mass tourism, this new perspective tended to operate on the logic that large-scale tourism was problematic and that in most cases small-scale alternatives were therefore more desirable. The associated options, generalised under the umbrella term of alternative tourism, were thus primarily conceived as alternatives to mass tourism specifically (Weaver & Oppermann 2000:366–7). 'Alternative tourism can be broadly defined as forms of tourism that set out to be consistent with natural, social and community values and which allow both hosts and guests to enjoy positive and worthwhile interaction and shared experiences' (Wearing & Neil 1999:3).

Environmental tourism embraces tourism in the biophysical environment (see figure 12.1). Examples include nature-based tourism, in which viewing nature is the primary objective, and wildlife tourism, in which the focus is on the viewing of wildlife. Thus, environmental tourism is a general term for tourism in natural settings in which an emphasis is placed on the understanding and conservation of the natural environment. Essentially, it is tourism underpinned by an ecocentric philosophy. It excludes a number of other forms of tourism such as adventure tourism, in which the emphasis is on the activity rather than the environment; rural tourism, which generally occurs in human-altered landscapes; and indigenous tourism, the central feature of which is the native culture and/or heritage. Environmental tourism embraces the characteristics of ecologically sustainable tourism, which fosters a long-term view of the environment. It also embodies the principle of 'responsible tourism'. Harrison and Husbands (1996) describe responsible tourism not as a tourism type or product but rather as an approach to tourism that delivers benefits to tourists, host populations and governments.

■ **Figure 12.1**
An overview of tourism

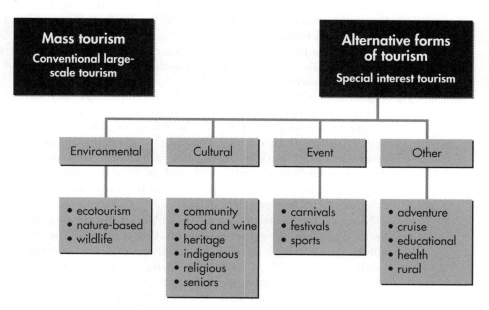

McLaren (1998) uses the term 'ecotravel' to encompass all forms of environmental tourism, conservation-focused tourism and other types of nature travel. She suggests that the number of tourists who travel solely to view nature or wildlife is actually quite modest. Most travellers also want an opportunity to experience a culture different from their own. Cultural activities and lifestyles are featured prominently in travel brochures. McLaren points out that environmental tourism covers a wide range of experiences — from spartan backpacking in special conservation zones to a purely hedonistic luxury vacation at a typical resort. However, they all offer a participatory experience in the natural environment.

At its best, environmental tourism promotes conservation, international understanding and cooperation, political and economic empowerment of local populations and cultural preservation. When it fulfils its mission, it not only has a minimal negative impact, but the local environment and community actually benefit from the experience; indeed, they may even own or control it. At its worst, however, as McLaren notes, environmental tourism is ecologically destructive, economically exploitative, culturally insensitive, 'greenwashed' travel (McLaren 1998:97).

■ 12.5.1 Nature-based *tourism*

As we have noted, there are a number of dimensions to tourism in the natural environment, which is categorised according to the relationship between specific tourism activities and nature. Wearing and Neil (1999:4) observe that they include activities or experiences for which the natural setting is incidental, those that are dependent on nature and those that are enhanced by nature. These three dimensions of natural area tourism equate to the environmental equivalents of education — *in*, *about* and *for* the environment (Dowling 1977, 1979). Thus, it is possible to characterise natural area tourism as:

- tourism *in* the environment — for example, adventure tourism
- tourism *about* the environment — for example, nature-based tourism and wildlife tourism
- tourism *for* the environment — for example, ecotourism.

Not all forms of tourism in the natural environment meet our definition of environmental tourism. If the focus of adventure tourism is on the activity rather than on its environment, then it does not strictly qualify as environmental tourism. And while adventure tourism may occur in the natural environment, unless it embraces a pro-conservation, sustainable, responsible and educative approach to the environment it fails to meet the criteria of environmental tourism.

Nature-based tourism is tourism in which the viewing of nature is the primary objective. The focus is upon the study and/or observation of the abiotic (non-living) part of the environment (for example, the rocks and landforms) as well as its biotic (living) component (fauna and flora). It therefore has a broader, more holistic focus than wildlife tourism. Despite a bias towards the small-scale, it can also take the form of mass or incipient mass tourism in many national parks (for example, in Yosemite in California). It is sometimes perceived as synonymous with ecotourism, since one of its aims is to protect natural areas, but it also differs from ecotourism in its lack of overt environmental interpretation and/or education.

■ 12.5.2 Wildlife *tourism*

Often it is the quality or variety of a natural area's living or biotic element — that is, its fauna and flora — that plays the primary role in attracting tourists. Wildlife tourists seek an experience that will enable them to observe and explore, no matter for how short a time, an ecosystem and all its inhabitants. Some tourists are lifelong wildlife enthusiasts; others merely take day-trips to a wilderness area from a luxury hotel base. Some seek to be informed and educated, while others wish primarily to be entertained.

There are many different kinds of wildlife-watching holidays — from a luxury, hotel-based safari in Kenya to wilderness backpacking in the Rockies to an Antarctic cruise to watch penguins and killer whales (Shackley 1996).

The rise in popularity of wildlife viewing in recent years has been phenomenal (Ceballos-Lascuráin 1998). In the United States more than 75 million people watch wildlife each year: it is now the country's number one outdoor recreational activity. In response to this trend, a national group of government agencies and conservation organisations created the Watchable Wildlife Initiative in 1990. Its goals are to promote wildlife viewing, conserve biodiversity, foster environmental education and generate economic opportunities based on ecotourism.

California's 'Watchable Wildlife Program' was established five years ago and is now the largest and most successful such program through its promotion of 'six steps to sustainable success' (Garrison 1997). These steps include selecting sites based on regional diversity, biological sustainability and quality viewing as well as ensuring that each site provides adequate visitor services and resource protection. Another key goal is to provide 'seamless' recreational and educational opportunities focusing on quality products and statewide programs of visibility shared between all agencies. Other objectives include establishing partnerships, identifying market segments and developing cooperative market strategies.

SPECIAL INTEREST INVESTIGATION
Dolphin viewing at Shark Bay, Western Australia

Shark Bay is located on the eastern edge of the Indian Ocean at the most westerly point of the Australian continent. The bay is the largest enclosed marine embayment in Australia, covering 22 000 square kilometres of which 66 per cent is marine. The bay straddles the tropical and temperate climatic boundary. Its unique features are its marine fauna and flora; it contains a wide range of large marine mammals including sharks, whales, dolphins and manta rays. Shark Bay also provides a habitat for the world's largest herd of dugongs, which graze on vast seagrass beds covering 400 square kilometres of the bay. In 1991 Shark Bay was added to the World Heritage List; it was then one of only 11 (out of approximately 400) World Heritage Sites to be declared on the basis of meeting all four natural criteria for listing (CALM 1994).

The bay is also home to a pod of wild bottlenose dolphins that have been swimming into a beach at Monkey Mia to interact with people since the early 1960s (see figure 12.2). A recreation reserve has been created at Monkey Mia to regulate the development and use of the area (CALM 1993). The main goals of the reserve are to protect the dolphin population and its habitat, enhance visitor experiences with the dolphins, increase visitor awareness of the conservation values of the area, and maintain the area's conservation values while providing and encouraging recreation and tourism activities.

(continued)

The dolphins are the prime attraction for visitors to the area, contributing substantially to the region's economy. In the early 1990s more than 100 000 tourists visited the dolphins each year. Although visitor numbers fluctuate they appear to have stabilised at around 80 000 a year with July, the most popular month, bringing approximately 15 500 visitors or 500 each day. The tourism industry is a rapidly growing component of the Shark Bay economy. A resort has been built at Monkey Mia and marine tour ventures include two catamarans offering marine wildlife tours, a glass-bottomed boat that visits a nearby pearl farm, other boats for hire along with ground and aerial tours.

Most (58 per cent) of Shark Bay's tourists are Western Australians (Dowling 1991), with 29 per cent interstate and 13 per cent international tourists. The most popular form of tourist accommodation in the area is in caravan parks (43 per cent). Perth people travel to the area principally by private car (a smaller number visit by commercial bus or by air), whereas interstate and international visitors usually visit by coach or rental vehicle.

A management plan for the area has been prepared, its major focus to maintain the interactive experience between humans and dolphins. A review of dolphin management introduced regular beach feeding and a number of education, interpretation and research programs. Over the next few years the resort proposes to increase its capacity from 550 to 1375 visitors. This increase will place even greater pressure on dolphin–human interaction. However, a study undertaken to review future development at Monkey Mia has suggested that the dolphin interaction area could cater for approximately 700 people per day, 200 more than the present peak of 500 a day (O'Brien Planning Consultants 1995).

■ **Figure 12.2**
Human–dolphin interaction at Monkey Mia, Shark Bay, WA

Source: *Ross Dowling*

The permanent population of Shark Bay is about 1500 and a survey of residents indicates that tourism generates more money (69 per cent) for the local people than other commercial activities, suggesting that it distributes economic benefits more evenly than commercial fishing, mining or pastoralism (Dowling 1996). As tourism in the area increases, so does the influx of outsiders who come to invest or work in the industry.

The World Heritage Area strategy, which makes several provisions for nature-based tourism in the area, recognises the need to provide a range of tourism and visitor opportunities. The primary tourism development strategy is to ensure that conservation values are protected while providing a range of tourism development opportunities. Environmental tourism will provide a sustainable future for the Shark Bay region so long as it is well planned to ensure that environmental and community goals are not displaced by economic imperatives.

■ *12.5.3* Ecotourism

People are often confused between the terms 'nature-based tourism' and 'ecotourism'. Ceballos-Lascuráin (1998) warns that ecotourism should not be equated with nature-based tourism since the latter refers to any tourism activity practised in a natural setting. Such tourism may or may not be environmentally friendly. Drumm (1998:197) points out that while both take place in natural areas, ecotourism also 'implies conservation, education, responsibility and active community participation'. In his landmark book on ecotourism Fennell (1999) does not propose that ecotourism is some form of 'pure' tourism that will in the long term challenge mainstream tourism; rather, he suggests that it is a niche form of tourism comprising a segment of SIT. Thus, ecotourism is environmental tourism that generally incorporates ecologically sustainable activities, conservation measures at the local level, active interpretation and/or education about the region and the involvement of the local community.

The Canadian Environmental Advisory Council (1991:25) suggests that ecotourism should embrace the following characteristics.
1. It must promote positive environmental ethics.
2. It does not degrade the resource.
3. It concentrates on intrinsic rather than extrinsic values. Facilities never become attractions in their own right.
4. It is ecocentric rather than anthropocentric in orientation.
5. It must benefit the wildlife and the environment (socially, economically, scientifically, managerially or politically).
6. It is a first-hand experience with the natural environment.
7. It includes a component of education and/or appreciation.
8. It has a high cognitive and affective experiential dimension.

These criteria are reiterated in papers by Butler (1991) and Wight (1994). The advisory council adds that, theoretically, such ecotourism experiences will encourage environmental protection by developing awareness, insight, knowledge, understanding, appreciation and respect of the local environment among participants. However, as noted by Ballantine and Eagles (1994), meeting these extensive criteria, is difficult. What is certain is the sharp contrast to more conventional forms of tourism in ecotourism's unique ecocentric focus and the emphasis on environmental education, personal growth and other intrinsic values underlying travel motivation (Wearing & Neil 1999).

The US-based Ecotourism Society (TES) defines ecotourism as purposeful travel to natural areas to understand the cultural and natural history of the environment, taking care not to alter the integrity of the ecosystem while producing economic opportunities that make the conservation of natural resources financially beneficial to local citizens (TES 1993). It places emphasis on responsible travel to natural areas, conservation of the environment and the wellbeing of local people. The Australian National Ecotourism Strategy defines ecotourism as:

> nature-based tourism that involves education and interpretation of the natural environment and is managed to be ecologically sustainable. The definition recognises that 'natural environment' includes cultural components and that 'ecologically sustainable' involves an appropriate return to the local community and long-term conservation of the resource (Australian Department of Tourism 1994:17).

The IUCN (World Conservation Union) defines ecotourism as 'environmentally responsible travel and visitation to relatively undisturbed natural areas, in order to enjoy and appreciate nature (and any accompanying cultural features — both past and present) that promotes conservation, has low visitor negative impact and provides for beneficially active socio-economic involvement of local populations' (Ceballos-Lascuráin 1996). Taking the above into account there appear to be a number of key ecotourism characteristics.

The prefix 'eco' affirms that ecotourism should be an ecologically responsible form of tourism. Indeed, if this is not the case then the natural attributes upon which the tourism is based will suffer degradation to the point that tourists will no longer be attracted to it. At the same time the scale of such ecotourism activities must limit tourist numbers and consequently supporting facilities can be kept to a minimum and will be less intrusive. Cater (1994:72) argues that ecotourism, with its connotations of sound environmental management and consequent maintenance of environmental capital, should in theory provide a viable economic alternative to exploitation of the environment. Ecotourism can be divided into two types — hard and soft. The first category encompasses a form of self-reliant tourism in natural areas where tourists seek wilderness-type experiences. The second category is characterised by short trips often organised as part of a package deal.

The educative aspect of ecotourism is a key characteristic distinguishing it from other forms of nature-based tourism. Environmental education and interpretation (see figure 12.3) are important tools in creating an enjoyable and meaningful ecotourism experience. Interpretation — helping people to learn about the environment — is a central tenet of ecotourism (Weiler & Davis 1993). 'It is a complex activity that goes beyond making the communication of information enjoyable. Best practice interpretation requires a thorough understanding and integration of audience, message and technique' (McArthur 1998:83).

■ **Figure 12.3**
Environmental education is a central characteristic of ecotourism

Source: *Ross Dowling*

Ecotourism attracts people who wish to interact with the environment in order to develop their knowledge, awareness and appreciation of it. By extension, ecotourism should ideally lead to positive action for the environment by fostering enhanced conservation awareness. Ecotourism education can influence tourist, community and industry behaviour and assist in the longer-term sustainability of tourist activity in natural areas. Education can also be useful as a management tool in relation to natural areas. Interpretation helps tourists see the big picture concerning the environment. It acknowledges the natural and cultural values of the area visited as well as other issues such as resource management. Ecotourism may be best summed up as a form of tourism that has the four E's. It is:

- environmentally based
- ecologically sound
- educative
- ethical.

Ecotourists expect high levels of ecological information. The quality of the environment and the visibility of its flora and fauna are essential features of their experience. They also demand conservation (Chalker 1994:91). Clear statements of the nature and aims of ecotourism need to be incorporated into the literature and publicity material to educate and encourage active participation by stakeholders as well as by the tourists themselves (Hall & Kinnaird 1994). Lawrence et al. (1997) note that a dominant purpose of ecotourism is for tourists to learn about and appreciate the natural environment in order to advance the cause of conservation.

The involvement of local communities not only benefits the community and the environment but also improves the quality of the tourist experience for all participants. Local communities can become involved in ecotourism operations in the provision of knowledge, services, facilities and products. The benefits should outweigh the costs of ecotourism both to the host community and in relation to the environment. In addition to social and cultural benefits ecotourism can generate income badly needed for resource conservation management. This contribution may be directly financial, with part of the cost of the tour helping to subsidise a conservation project; alternatively, it may consist of practical help in the field, with the tourists themselves being involved in environmental data collection and/or analysis. Drumm (1998) points out that local communities may regard ecotourism as an accessible development alternative that will enable them to improve their living standards without having to sell off their natural resources or compromise their culture. In the absence of other sustainable alternatives, participation in ecotourism is often perceived as the best option open to local communities for achieving their aspiration of sustainable development.

Ecotourism provides a context for local incentives for conservation and protection. Norris (1992) has argued that ecotourism should integrate the protection of resources with the provision of local economic benefits. For example, in the Annapurna Conservation Area Project of Nepal local people are actively encouraged to take a leading role in conservation and development activities, expressing their needs and concerns in open forums (Gurung & De Coursey 1994). These writers contend that conservation and development are complementary rather than opposing forces and argue that for either to be sustainable, both must be coordinated with the same main objective, the long-term welfare of the people and the environment. Ceballos-Lascuráin (1998) notes that ecotourism is now beginning to produce positive benefits in the fields of conservation and sustainable development. The implementation of ecotourism as an exemplar for sustainable development stems largely from its potential to generate economic benefits (Lindberg 1998). These benefits include generating revenue for management of natural areas and the creation of employment opportunities for the local population.

The satisfaction of visitors with the ecotourism experience is essential to the long-term viability of the ecotourism industry. Information provided about ecotourism opportunities should accurately represent the opportunities offered at particular ecotourism destinations. The ecotourism experience should match or exceed the realistic expectations of the visitor. As a priority, the provision of high-quality client services and satisfaction should come second only to the conservation and protection of the environments they visit.

BREAKTHROUGH TOURISM
Australian ecotourists

A number of major studies on ecotourism have been carried out in Australia (e.g. Blamey 1995). A national survey conducted in 1997 determined the factors that influenced people to participate in ecotourism activities and tours, the length of tours taken, activities undertaken while on the tour, tour expenditure, satisfaction determinants, information used to find out about the tour and transport used on tour (Blamey & Hatch 1998). Nature-based tourists were defined as national park visitors or participants in snorkelling or scuba diving, whale watching, horse riding, rock climbing or mountaineering, bushwalking or outback safari or 4WD tours.

Visitors aged 20 to 29 years accounted for the largest share of ecotourists (36.4 per cent). They were also most likely to participate in nature-based activities, with just under half (48.7 per cent) of all visitors undertaking at least one such activity. Asian visitors accounted for the majority of international participants in ecotourism activities, although this reflected the fact that Asian visitors account for the majority of all international visitors to Australia. Scandinavian visitors accounted for fewer than 3 per cent of all ecotourists but they had the greatest participation rate, with 72.1 per cent undertaking at least one nature-based activity during their stay in Australia. Participation rates for ecotourists from other countries included those from 'Other Europe' (58.6 per cent), the United Kingdom and Ireland (52 per cent), and the Americas (48.9 per cent).

Professional people formed the largest demographic group among all eco-tourists; viewing the natural beauty of the sites visited was the most important factor for most visitors. However, the opportunities to see or to experience something new, to see wildlife close up and to be close to nature were also regarded as important.

Most ecotourists ranked 'a different or unique way of experiencing nature' as a very important motivation. Most visitors (69.5 per cent) also stated that an educational or learning experience was important. They included observing animals, plants and landscapes, being provided with information about the biology or ecology of a species or region, learning about the cultural and/or historical aspects of the area and being provided with information about the geology or landscapes of the area.

Ecotourists found their tours predominantly through word-of-mouth information. Activities undertaken by international ecotourists in Australia in 1995 included bushwalking, scuba diving and snorkelling, rock climbing and mountaineering, horse riding and trail riding, outback safari tours and wildflower viewing. The number of visitors to national parks has grown at an annual average of 17 per cent. This growth was exceeded only by that for visitation to Aboriginal sites, which grew by 30 per cent per annum.

Generally, ecotourists to Australia were most satisfied by the quality of the sites visited, the number of guides on the tour, the measures taken to minimise the environmental impacts of the tour and the information provided about the natural environment. They were least satisfied with the size of tours, time spent at sites and the food provided.

■ *12.5.4* **The magnitude** *of ecotourism*

Estimates on the scale of ecotourism vary dramatically. The US-based Specialty Travel Index suggests that ecotourism accounted for between 1.5 and 2.5 per cent of all tourism in the late 1980s (Whelan 1991). In contrast, Hawkins (cited in Giannecchini 1993) proposes a figure of 20 to 25 per cent of all leisure travel, while the Ecotourism Society (TES 1998) cites sources that suggest 20 to 40 per cent of all international tourists travel for wildlife-related purposes. Clearly, the first estimate applies a stricter definition of ecotourism, while the second and third are more inclusive, embracing the entire hard-to-soft spectrum and extending ecotourism into the realm of mass tourism (Weaver & Oppermann 2000:370).

Hvenegaard (1994) notes that ecotourism activities generate considerable economic impacts on a global, national and local scale. Ecotourism and wildlife-related tourism may account for up to US$1 trillion a year. Khan and Hawkins (1997) observe that, with consumers' increased ecological awareness and the need for sustainable tourism development, it is not surprising that ecotourism is on the rise. Reports show that 8 million adult US travellers have taken an ecotour and 35 million are likely to take an ecotour in the next few years. The potential ecotourism market, according to a study conducted by the United States Travel Data Center (1992), is 43 million. Ecotourism visitors are expected to grow 10 to 15 per cent annually.

In a more recent study, Honey (1999) suggests that many countries around the world have now embraced ecotourism. They include countries such as Bhutan and Myanmar (which once were wary of tourism), nations of the former Soviet Union and eastern Europe, China and Vietnam (which once tightly controlled tourism) and South Africa and Cuba (previously international outcasts). Some entire countries, such as Costa Rica and Belize, are billed as ecotourism destinations. Elsewhere, wilderness pockets are promoted, such as the Galapagos Islands, owned by Ecuador; the habitat of the mountain gorillas in Uganda; and Fiordland in New Zealand. In 1998 the WTO predicted that developing countries would continue to gain from the tourism boom and that international travellers would remain 'interested in visiting and maintaining environmentally sound destinations' (Jaura 1998, cited in Honey 1999:18).

According to the WTO, ecotourism is one of the fastest-growing sectors within the more than US$425 billion worldwide tourism industry. It has been promoted as a way for developing countries to achieve self-sufficiency without losing autonomy (Nixon 1999). Thus, ecotourism is here to stay and will be of undoubted future significance to developing nations (Cater 1994).

With such statements and predictions emanating from the industry, governments and researchers, it could be argued that environmental tourism has moved, or is fast moving, from a small, narrow niche market into mainstream tourism. However, the case appears to be overstated; environmental tourism to natural areas, including nature-based tourism, wildlife tourism and ecotourism, collectively still represents a relatively small segment of the overall industry. Nevertheless, the truth remains that the future of environmental tourism is predicated on there being a pristine environment capable of sustaining ever-increasing numbers of interested visitors. The key to retaining these natural areas is to encourage appropriate and adequate environmental safeguards in the planning, development and management of environmental tourism.

The natural environment is viewed from a number of different perspectives. The two most common perspectives are the human-centred (anthropocentric) view, which regards the environment as a resource, and the life-centred (ecocentric) view, in which the environment is seen as an attribute. Environmental tourism embraces the latter view and at its simplest can be described as tourism *for* the environment rather than merely *in* the environment.

Three major types of environmental tourism are nature-based tourism, wildlife tourism and ecotourism. In nature-based tourism the viewing of nature is the primary objective and the focus is upon the study and/or observation of flora, fauna and/or landscape. Wildlife tourism addresses the living organisms of the environment and often focuses on one component such as bird watching, or even on one population only — for example, whale watching. Ecotourism embraces aspects of both nature-based tourism and wildlife tourism but also includes elements of conservation, education, responsibility and community participation. It is best thought of as a form of tourism that is environmentally based, ecologically sound, educative and ethical (the four E's).

Ecotourism can be divided into two types — hard and soft. Hard ecotourism is a form of self-reliant tourism in which tourists seek wilderness-type experiences requiring a high degree of challenge. Soft ecotourism is characterised by short trips that are usually organised as part of a package deal and accompanied by a high level of service and facility provision.

The peak tourism industry body, the World Tourism Organization, estimates that environmental tourism now comprises 20 per cent of the global tourism market, accounts for approximately 20 per cent of total international travel and is worth US$20 billion a year. This form of SIT is obviously already large and the predictions are that it will continue to grow in the new millennium.

···

Questions

12.1 What are the two main perspectives on the environment and how are they expressed in practice? Clearly delineate the difference between an environmental attribute and a resource.

12.2 Define the difference between mass tourism and alternative forms of tourism.

12.3 What do you think will happen in Shark Bay if the dolphins no longer swim in to the beach each day? Will tourism survive there?

12.4 What worldview gave rise to the national park movement?

(continued)

12.5 Obtain a range of brochures from a number of travel agents and/ or information centres on environmental tours in your region. Write a report on your findings taking into consideration the following points.

(a) How are the tours marketed? What features do they highlight?

(b) What type of environmental tourism are they?

(c) What environmentally friendly activities do they outline as part of their tour?

(d) Do they claim to be certified as part of the National Ecotourism Accreditation Program? If so, to what level — nature tourism, ecotourism or advanced ecotourism accreditation?

(e) What conclusion can you draw about the nature of environmental tourism in your community?

(f) As a class, compare and contrast your results.

12.6 Imagine that you are about to set up an environmental tour of your region. Prepare an itinerary for the tour after carefully examining the area's natural resources.

(a) What will be the main feature of the tour? What differentiates it from other existing tours, if any are already on offer?

(b) What type of environmental tourism will it offer?

(c) What will be the maximum number of people on each tour?

(d) What is a suitable name for your tour company?

(e) Where will you get your information about the attractions in order to share this knowledge with your clients?

(f) What environmental activities should be included on the tour?

(g) Make up a suitable brochure in order to market the tours.

12.7 What is meant by the term intergenerational equity? Why is it important for the environment? Describe appropriate activities that you can undertake now in order to fulfil the spirit of this goal.

12.8 It is suggested that environmental tourism has underpinned the greening of tourism. Why is this the case? Find out ways in which businesses in your region are becoming more environmentally aware and active.

12.9 Compare and contrast nature-based tourism, wildlife tourism and ecotourism.

12.10 What phases has the environment–tourism relationship evolved through?

12.11 Are definitions of ecotourism the same in Canada, the United States and Australia? What are the common elements and what is different about the definitions?

12.12 Do you agree with the World Tourism Organization's assessment that one in five global tourists is an environmental tourist?

REFERENCES

Akoglu, T. 1971. 'Tourism and the Problem of Environment'. *Tourist Review* 26: 18–20.

Australian Department of Tourism. 1994. *National Ecotourism Strategy.* Canberra: Commonwealth Government Publishing Service.

Ballantine, J. & Eagles, P. 1994. 'Defining Canadian Ecotourists'. *Journal of Sustainable Tourism* 2 (4): 210–4.

Blamey, R. 1995. *The Nature of Ecotourism.* BTR Occasional Paper No. 21. Canberra: Bureau of Tourism Research.

Blamey, R. & Hatch, D. 1998. *Profiles and Motivations of Nature-Based Tourists Visiting Australia.* BTR Occasional Paper No. 25. Canberra: Bureau of Tourism Research.

Bosselman, F. P. 1978. *In the Wake of the Tourist: Managing Special Places in Eight Countries.* Washington, DC: The Conservation Foundation.

Budowski, G. 1976. 'Tourism and Environmental Conservation: Conflict, Coexistence, or Symbiosis?'. *Environmental Conservation* 3 (1): 27–31.

Butler, R. W. 1991. 'Tourism, Environment, and Sustainable Development'. *Environmental Conservation* 18 (3): 201–9.

CALM. 1993. *Monkey Mia Reserve: Draft Management Plan.* Perth: WA Department of Conservation and Land Management.

CALM. 1994. *Shark Bay World Heritage Area.* Perth: WA Department of Conservation and Land Management.

Canadian Environmental Advisory Council. 1991. *A Protected Areas Vision for Canada.* Ottawa: Minister of Supply and Services.

Cater, E. 1994. 'Ecotourism in the Third World — Problems and Prospects for Sustainability'. In Cater, E. & Lowman, G. (Eds.). *Ecotourism: A Sustainable Option?* Chichester, UK: John Wiley & Sons, pp. 69–86.

Cater, E. & Lowman, G. (Eds.). 1994. *Ecotourism: A Sustainable Option.* Chichester, UK: John Wiley & Sons.

Ceballos-Lascuráin, H. 1996. *Tourism, Ecotourism and Protected Areas.* Gland, Switzerland: IUCN (The World Conservation Union).

Ceballos-Lascuráin, H. 1998. 'Introduction'. In Lindberg, K., Epler Wood, M. & Engeldrum, D. (Eds.). *Ecotourism: A Guide for Planners & Managers.* Volume 2. Vermont, USA: The Ecotourism Society, pp. 7–10.

Chalker, B. 1994. 'Ecotourism: On the Trail of Destruction or Sustainability? A Minister's View'. In Cater, E. & Lowman, G. (Eds.). *Ecotourism: A Sustainable Option?* Chichester, UK: John Wiley & Sons, pp. 87–99.

Cohen, E. 1978. 'The Impact of Tourism on the Physical Environment'. *Annals of Tourism Research* 5 (2): 215–37.

Dowling, R. K. 1977. 'Environmental Education'. *New Zealand Environment* 16: 24–6.

Dowling, R. K. (Ed.). 1979. *Environmental Education Handbook: For New Zealand Secondary Schools.* Christchurch: Canterbury Environment Centre Publication, p. 215.

Dowling, R. K. 1990. 'Integrating Tourism and Conservation'. In Verma, S. R., Singh, S. & Kumar, S. (Eds.). *Environmental Protection — A Movement.* Delhi, India: Nature Conservators, pp. 5–25.

Dowling, R. K. 1991. 'Tourism and the Natural Environment: Shark Bay, Western Australia'. *Tourism Recreation Research* 16 (2): 44–8.

Dowling, R. K. 1992. 'Tourism and Environmental Integration: The Journey from Idealism to Realism'. In Cooper, C. P. & Lockwood, A. (Eds.). *Progress in Tourism, Recreation and Hospitality Management.* Volume 4. London: Belhaven Press, pp. 33–46.

Dowling, R. K. 1996. 'Visitor Management in Shark Bay, Western Australia'. In Hall, C. M. & McArthur, S. (Eds.). *Heritage Management in Australia and New Zealand: The Human Dimension.* Second Edition. Melbourne: Oxford University Press, pp. 160–9.

Dowling, R. K. & Charters, T. 2000. 'The Planning and Development of Ecotourism in Queensland'. In Charters, T. & Law, K. (Eds.). *Best Practice Ecotourism in Queensland.* Brisbane: Tourism Queensland, pp. 1–16.

Drumm, A. 1998. 'New Approaches to Community-based Ecotourism Management'. In Lindberg, K., Epler Wood, M. & Engeldrum, D. (Eds.). *Ecotourism: A Guide for Planners & Managers.* Volume 2. Vermont, USA: The Ecotourism Society, pp. 197–213.

Farrell, B. H. & McLellan, R. W. 1987. 'Tourism and Physical Environment Research'. *Annals of Tourism Research* 14 (1): 1–16.

Farrell, B. H. & Runyan, D. 1991. 'Ecology and Tourism'. *Annals of Tourism Research* 18 (1): 41–56.

Fennell, D. 1999. *Ecotourism: An Introduction.* London: Routledge.

Garrison R. W. 1997. 'Sustainable Nature Tourism: California's Regional Approach'. In *World Ecotour '97 Abstracts Volume.* Rio de Janeiro, Brazil: BIOSFERA, pp. 180–2.

Giannecchini, J. 1993. 'Ecotourism: New Partners, New Relationships'. *Conservation Biology* 7 (2): 429–32.

Gilpin, A. 1990. *An Australian Dictionary of Environment and Planning.* Melbourne: Oxford University Press.

Gunn, C. A. 1988. *Tourism Planning.* Second Edition. New York: Taylor and Francis.

Gurung, C. P. & De Coursey, M. 1994. 'The Annapurna Conservation Area Project: A Pioneering Example of Sustainable Tourism'. In Cater, E. & Lowman, G. (Eds.). *Ecotourism: A Sustainable Option?* Chichester, UK: John Wiley & Sons, pp. 177–94.

Hall, D. & Kinnaird, V. 1994. 'Ecotourism in Eastern Europe'. In Cater, E. & Lowman, G. (Eds.). *Ecotourism: A Sustainable Option?*, Chichester, UK: John Wiley & Sons, pp. 111–36.

Hanlot, A. 1974. *Tourisme et Environnement: La Recherche d'un Equilibre.* Verviers, Belgium: Marabout Monde Moderne.

Harrison, L. C. & Husbands, W. (Eds.). 1996. *Practising Responsible Tourism: International Case Studies in Tourism Planning, Policy and Development.* New York: John Wiley & Sons.

Honey, M. 1999. *Ecotourism and Sustainable Development: Who Owns Paradise?* Washington, DC: Island Press.

Hudman, L. E. 1991. 'Tourist Impacts: The Need for Regional Planning'. *The Tourist Review* 4/91: 17–21.

Hvenegaard, G. 1994. 'Ecotourism: A Status Report and Conceptual Framework'. *Journal of Tourism Studies* 5 (2): 24–34.

Inskeep, E. 1991. *Tourism Planning: An Integrated and Sustainable Development Approach.* New York: Van Nostrand Reinhold.

IUCN. 1980. *World Conservation Strategy.* Gland, Switzerland: IUCN.

IUOTO. 1971. 'Study on Human Environment'. Paper presented at the International Union of Official Travel Organizations General Assembly, Ankara, Turkey.

Khan, M. & Hawkins, D. 1997. 'American Ecotourists: An Empirical Evaluation of Their Characteristics'. *The Evolution of Tourism: Adapting to Change.* Proceedings of the 28th Annual Travel and Tourism Association Conference, Lexington, USA: TTRA, pp. 388–95.

Krippendorf, J. 1975. *Die Landschaftsfresser.* Berne, Switzerland: Hallwag Verlag.

Law, K. 2000. 'Environmental Tourism Audit: How We Are Tracking'. *Tourism Queensland News* 1: 12.

Lawrence, T., Wickins, D. & Phillips, N. 1997. 'Managing Legitimacy in Ecotourism'. *Tourism Management* 18 (5): 307–16.

Lindberg, K. 1998. 'Economic Aspects of Ecotourism'. In Lindberg, K., Epler Wood, M. & Engeldrum, D. (Eds.). *Ecotourism: A Guide for Planners & Managers.* Volume 2. Vermont, USA: The Ecotourism Society, pp. 87–117.

Mathieson, A. & Wall, G. 1982. *Tourism: Economic, Physical and Social Impacts.* Harlow, UK: Longman Scientific and Technical.

McArthur, S. 1998. 'Introducing the Undercapitalized World of Interpretation'. In Lindberg, K., Epler Wood, M. & Engeldrum, D. (Eds.). *Ecotourism: A Guide for Planners & Managers.* Volume 2. Vermont, USA: The Ecotourism Society, pp. 63–85.

McLaren, D. 1998. *Rethinking Tourism and Ecotravel: The Paving of Paradise and What You Can Do to Stop It.* Connecticut, USA: Kumarian Press.

Murphy, P. E. 1985. *Tourism: A Community Approach.* New York: Methuen.

Murphy, P. E. 1986. 'Tourism as an Agent for Landscape Conservation: An Assessment'. *The Science of the Total Environment* 55: 387–95.

Nixon, R. 1999. 'Green Travel'. *Hispanic* 12 (5): 43–6.

Norris, R. 1992. 'Can Ecotourism Save Natural Areas?' *Parks,* January/February: 31–4.

O'Brien Planning Consultants. 1995. *Monkey Mia Outline Development Plan.* Prepared for the Western Australian Planning Commission. Perth: WAPC.

OECD. 1980. *The Impact of Tourism on the Environment.* Paris: Organisation for Economic Cooperation and Development.

Phillips, A. 1985. 'Opening Address'. In *Tourism, Recreation and Conservation in National Parks and Equivalent Reserves.* A European Heritage Landscapes Conference, Peak National Park Centre. Derbyshire, UK: Peak Park Joint Planning Board, pp. 9–14.

Pigram, J. J. 1980. 'Environmental Implications of Tourism Development'. *Annals of Tourism Research* 7 (4): 554–83.

Queensland Government. 1997. *Queensland Ecotourism Plan.* Brisbane: Queensland Department of Tourism, Small Business and Industry.

Queensland Tourist and Travel Corporation. 1998. A Survey of Ecotourism Operators in Queensland. Unpublished study. Brisbane: Queensland Tourist and Travel Corporation.

Romeril, M. 1985. 'Tourism and the Environment — Towards a Symbiotic Relationship (Introductory Paper)'. *International Journal of Environmental Studies* 25 (4): 215–8.

Romeril, M. 1989a. 'Tourism and the Environment — Accord or Discord?' *Tourism Management* 10 (3): 204–8.

Romeril, M. 1989b. 'Tourism — the Environmental Dimension'. In Cooper, C. P. (Ed.). *Progress in Tourism, Recreation and Hospitality Management*. London: Belhaven Press, pp. 103–13.

Rose, E. A. 1984. 'Philosophy and Purpose in Planning'. In Bruton, M. J. (Ed.). *The Spirit and Purpose of Planning*. Second Edition. London: Hutchinson, pp. 31–65.

Shackley, M. 1996. *Wildlife Tourism*. London: International Thomson Business Press.

Smith, V. L. & Eadington, W. R. (Eds.). 1992. *Tourism Alternatives: Potentials and Problems in the Development of Tourism*. International Academy for the Study of Tourism. Philadelphia, USA: University of Pennsylvania Press.

Smith, C. & Jenner, P. 1989. 'Tourism and the Environment'. Occasional Studies. *EIU Travel and Tourism Analyst* 5: 68–86.

TES. 1993. *Ecotourism Guidelines: For Nature Tour Operators*. Vermont, USA: The Ecotourism Society.

TES. 1998. *Ecotourism Statistical Fact Sheet*. Vermont, USA: The Ecotourism Society.

Tolhurst, C. 1998. 'Sound the Retreat; It's Time to Go Bush'. *The Weekend Australian Financial Review*, 11–12 July.

US Travel Data Center. 1992. *Discover America: Tourism and the Environment — a Guide to Challenges and Opportunities for Travel Industry Businesses*. Washington, DC: Travel Industry Association of America.

WCED. 1987. *Our Common Future*. Report of the World Commission on Environment and Development (the Brundtland Commission). Oxford, UK: Oxford University Press.

Wearing, S. & Neil, J. 1999. *Ecotourism Impacts, Potentials and Possibilities*. Melbourne: Butterworth-Heinemann.

Weaver, D. & Oppermann, M. 2000. *Tourism Management*. Brisbane: John Wiley & Sons.

Weiler, B. & Davis, D. 1993. 'An Exploratory Investigation into the Roles of the Nature-based Tour Leader'. *Tourism Management* 14 (2): 91–8.

Whelan, T. (Ed.). 1991. *Nature Tourism: Managing for the Environment*. Washington, DC: Island Press.

Wight, P. 1993. 'Ecotourism: Ethics or Eco-Sell?' *Journal of Travel Research* 31 (3): 3–9.

Wight, P. 1994. 'Environmentally Responsible Marketing of Tourism'. In Cater, E. & Lowman, G. (Eds.). *Ecotourism: A Sustainable Option?* Chichester, UK: John Wiley & Sons, 39–55.

WTO. 1998a. 'Protection: From the Amazon to Antarctica'. *World Tourism Organisation News*. July–August, pp. 10–11.

WTO. 1998b. 'Ecotourism — Now One-Fifth of Market'. *World Tourism Organization News*, January–February, p. 6.

WTO. 1999. *Tourism: 2020 Vision*. Madrid: World Tourism Organization.

Zierer, C. M. 1952. 'Tourism and Recreation in the West'. *Geographical Review* 42: 462–81.

Environmental tourism
in Queensland

Tourism is Australia's fastest growing industry and much of its growth is occurring in natural areas. Queensland is a major tourism destination primarily owing to its abundance of natural resources. Five of Australia's 13 World Heritage Areas are in Queensland. They are the Great Barrier Reef, the Wet Tropics, Fraser Island, the Central Eastern Rainforests and the Riversleigh Fossil Fields. In 1997 a plan was implemented to promote the development of environmental tourism in the state.

Queensland's environmental tourism operations can be broadly separated into three categories — accommodation, tours and attractions. Within each of these categories there is a very wide spread of operations, from small-scale, owner-operator businesses (for example, the Daintree Ecolodge in Far North Queensland) to large-scale operations involving the investment of tens of millions of dollars (for example, the 350-bed Couran Cove Resort, South Stradbroke Island, on the Gold Coast [Tolhurst 1998]).

Participants in Queensland's environmental tourism vary significantly across the state. In the Cairns and Gold Coast regions overseas tourist numbers are significantly higher than in many other areas owing to the international profile of these destinations and their overseas air access. Other significant sites such as Fraser Island also receive large numbers of international visitors as a result of their strong profile. In a recent study of 14 environmental tourism accommodation sites in Queensland, the profile of visitors revealed that 57 per cent of visitors were from professional, administrative or clerical occupations, 50 per cent had tertiary qualifications, and 34 per cent had a family income above $60 000 (Queensland Tourist and Travel Corporation 1998).

The Queensland Ecotourism Plan (QEP), released in June 1997, outlined the vision for the future of environmental tourism in Queensland. Its aim was to provide a framework for planning, developing, managing, operating and marketing Queensland's environmental tourism (Queensland Government 1997). The implementation of the plan is now the responsibility of Tourism Queensland through its Environmental Tourism Unit. The core aim of the plan is for environmental tourism opportunities to be made available within representative areas of each of Queensland's 18 biogeographical regions, distributed over a wider variety of land tenure types than is currently the case and encouraged on freehold and leasehold properties. The plan has four key objectives: environmental protection and management, along with industry, infrastructure and community development.

The aim of the environmental protection and management objective is to protect the natural and associated cultural values that underpin environmental tourism in Queensland through research, planning, monitoring and control. Industry development is helping to create the systems and regulatory environment that support the development of environmental tourism opportunities. The development of infrastructure provides the measures necessary to protect and present natural and associated cultural resource values consistent with the principles of environmental tourism. Finally, community development is required to ensure local people and the wider community benefits from environmental tourism and to develop greater environmental awareness.

The implementation of the plan in its first three years is well in advance of the established targets. However, while the development of environmental tourism in Queensland holds considerable promise, there are a number of issues that require further investigation. They include a susceptability to adverse impacts on both the natural and cultural environments, the accurate identification of emerging market segments and the supply of environmental tourism attractions and accommodation. In early 2000 Tourism Queensland sampled 300 operators to identify the core issues influencing the development and operation of environmental tourism and to benchmark the growth of the industry in the state.

When all of the above issues are considered in total, the outlook for environmental tourism in Queensland is very positive (Dowling & Charters 2000). Now other states and territories are beginning to promote environmental tourism development as a result of the perception that it is a high-yielding component of the industry. Given this nationwide growth, it will be interesting to see whether other states allow Queensland to steal a march on environmental tourism or whether they respond with viable alternative strategies and initiatives.

Questions

1 What are Queensland's advantages when it comes to environmental tourism?

2 Prepare a brochure promoting Queensland's environmental attractions.

C. Michael Hall
and
Richard Mitchell

CHAPTER 13
Wine and food *tourism*

LEARNING OBJECTIVES

After reading this chapter, you will have an appreciation of:

- the concept of wine and food tourism, and the difficulties in defining this concept
- the way in which tourism both contributes to and is influenced by cuisine
- how wine, food and tourism all contribute to place identity and destination promotion
- the nature of the growth of the wine tourism market in Australia and New Zealand
- the different motivations associated with wine tourism
- how different wine regions, while showing certain similarities in the demographic and psychographic profiles of winery visitors, may also illustrate significant differences
- the manner in which government has contributed to wine tourism development in Australia
- the potential positive and negative contributions of wine tourism to individual business and regional development.

Wine, food and tourism have long been closely related. For example, eating out is a major tourism activity. However, it is only recently that the roles that wine and food play in attracting tourists to a destination have come to be explicitly recognised by governments, researchers and by the wine, food and tourism industries. Food has become recognised as:

• part of the local culture which tourists consume
• part of tourism promotion
• a potential component of local agricultural and economic development
• something at the local level that is affected by the consumption patterns and perceived preferences of tourists.

For the tourism industry, wine and food are an important component of the attractiveness and image of a destination and can be a major motivating factor for visitors. For the wine and food industries, tourism is a very important way of establishing relationships with customers who can experience wine and food production first-hand. Visitors also have the opportunity to meet many of the producers themselves. For many smaller businesses direct selling to visitors is often an essential component of their business.

This chapter identifies important roles that wine and food play in tourism development and the reciprocal roles that tourism plays in the development of specialist wine and food businesses. It also examines the extent to which wine and food affect place identity, thereby contributing significantly to destination promotion and marketing. Substantial attention is given to the characteristics and development of wine tourism, because of the size of the sector and the concentration of research in the area. The chapter concludes with a discussion of the advantages and disadvantages of wine and food tourism in both a business and regional context.

13.2 DEFINING WINE AND FOOD TOURISM ·····················

Wine tourism can be defined as visitation to vineyards, wineries, wine festivals and wine shows for which grape wine tasting and/or experiencing the attributes of a grape wine region are the prime motivating factors for visitors (Hall 1996; Macionis 1996). Macionis (1996) proposed a model of wine tourism based around a special interest in wine, motivated by the destination (wine region) and/or the activity (wine tasting). However, tourism in general, including day-tripping and excursions, is important for providing many wineries with the opportunity to sell wine either directly to visitors through cellar sales or to place such customers on a direct mail order list.

The above approach to wine tourism may also be applied to defining food tourism. Food tourism is visitation to primary and secondary food producers, food festivals, restaurants and specific locations for which food tasting and/or experiencing the attributes of a specialist food production region are the primary motivating factors for travel. This definition does not mean that any trip to a restaurant is food tourism, rather, the desire to experience a particular type of food, the produce of a specific region, or even to taste the dishes of a particular chef must be the major motivation for the travel. Indeed, if food is a primary influencing travel behaviour and decision making, special interest travel, wine and food tourism can be viewed as gourmet or cuisine tourism. This is because 'foodies' regard their interest in wine and food as a form of 'serious leisure'.

Johnson (1998) argued that the above definition of wine tourism seems to suggest that all visitors to wineries have wine-related motivations. Instead, visitors to wineries and wine regions differ in their interest in and expertise on wine. An example of this is the story of a church group who booked a tour of a vineyard, only to inform the winery guide on arrival that they did not drink wine, but were nonetheless interested in how it was made. Johnson (1998) correctly observed that the attributes of a grape wine region that appeal to those visiting a wine region (such as the scenic landscape) may be quite unrelated to consuming wine, and raised the question that as grape wine regions are almost always rural areas, at what point does rural tourism become wine tourism? At what point therefore does a visitor to a wine region become a wine tourist? These are questions which apply equally to food tourism. As Hall et al. (2000a:4) argue, 'such questions are not merely academic as the increasing focus on wine and tourism interrelationships by government and industry heightens the need for good data collection on which sound business decisions can be made. Indeed, one of the great problems in tourism is the propensity to overestimate its economic and development benefits in relation to other industries'. Nevertheless, as recent research has demonstrated (Mitchell et al. 2000), the regional landscape, the **winescape** or '*terroir* of tourism' does provide a set of aesthetic and regional attributes that appear to be attractive to visitors in its own right.

13.3 CUISINE AND TRAVEL

The development of wine and food tourism is closely related to the growth of small-scale and specialist wine and food producers in Australia. In the wine sector, this is closely related to the development of small-scale 'boutique' wine producers, which have very small levels of production and which, initially at least, will not be the sole source of employment for the winery owner. In the case of food production, the last 20 years has also witnessed the growth of specialty food producers. For example, specialist cheeses, oils, and fruit and vegetable produce are no longer the preserve of specific ethnic groups but have become a part of mainstream Australian cuisine. Indeed, it is testimony to the growth of interest in wine and food in Australia that we can now even talk about the possibility of there being an Australian cuisine (e.g. Symons 1993).

Nevertheless, there is now a diverse range of publications on the Australianness of cuisine including 'bush tucker' (e.g. Bruneteau 1996), which uses indigenous foods, the migrant origins of much contemporary Australian cooking (e.g. Newton 1996), and the new fusion cooking that is regarded as indicative of Australian and Pacific Rim cuisine (e.g. Saunders 1999). Tourism has both contributed to and benefited from the development of Australian and fusion styles of cooking. Despite debates on the authenticity of cuisine that occur from within a static perception of culture and diet, regional and local cuisines are changing, particularly under the influence of globalisation and localisation. Hall and Mitchell (1999) described the changes that have occurred with respect to cuisine and food preference within the framework of 'waves of change', which are related to broader processes of economic and cultural globalisation. These waves can broadly be described as:

- the mercantile wave of the fifteenth to eighteenth centuries, when European traders transferred plants and animals between the new and old worlds
- the migration wave of the eighteenth to mid-twentieth centuries, in which large numbers of European settlers, and to a lesser extent Asian settlers, took their **foodways** with them as part of the large-scale nineteenth- and early twentieth-century migrations
- the communication/technology wave of the twentieth and twenty-first centuries. Rapid improvements in transport technology have enabled the large-scale transport of food products around the world as well as mass tourism. The communications revolution supports global marketing of food products, place promotion on an international scale, and the heightened role of the media in promoting and creating cuisines (for example, through food programs) in areas quite culturally distant from the cuisine's place of origin.

In this third wave, tourism, cuisine and food preferences have become closely entwined as places seek competitive advantage in the international marketplace. This is achieved through the promotion of cuisine, which increases demand and leads to corresponding influences on the production and consumption of wine and food, and where international travel has itself allowed for the transfer of culinary skills and ideas, and changes in consumer demands. Food and travel have become entwined in contemporary lifestyles with magazines devoted to the links between the two, for example *Australian Gourmet Traveller, Cuisine, Vogue Travel and Entertaining*. Numerous television and radio programs focus on food and cooking, typically with reference to the food's origin (Hall & Mitchell 1999).

Tables 13.1 to 13.3 provide a content analysis of the 'marketplace' section of the December issue of *Australian Gourmet Traveller* from 1992 to 1999, to illustrate some of the products and places advertised in the magazine.

■ Table 13.1
Guest houses, hotels and villas advertised in Australian Gourmet Traveller, *December 1992–99*

	1992	1993	1994	1995	1996	1997	1998	1999
Australia								
NSW	4	4	3	8	3	9	4	7
Qld		2		1	3	7	4	1
SA					1	1		
Tas.			1	1				
Vic.		4	1	2				1
WA	1	1				2	1	
New Zealand	1							
Europe (general)			2	3	2	1		
France		1	1	2	1	1		
Italy				2				

■ Table 13.2
Travel and tours advertised in the Australian Gourmet Traveller, *December 1992–99*

	1992	1993	1994	1995	1996	1997	1998	1999	TOTAL
Australia					1	1			2
NSW		1	1	1	3	3			9
Qld					1	1	2	3	7
Tas.					1				1
Vic.			1			2			3
WA						2		2	4
Europe (general)	2	3		3	3	4	1	2	18
Africa	1				1	3	3	1	9
Greece	1								1
International		1		2		2	3	6	14
Hong Kong		1							1
India		1							1
UK		1			1	1		1	4
France			1	2	6	4	8	6	27
Austria			1						1
Italy			1	1	10	6	11	7	36
Vietnam			1					1	2
Caribbean			1		1				2
Antarctica				1					1
USA				1					1
Fiji					1	1	1	1	4
Argentina					1				1
Chile					1				1
Spain					1	1	1	2	5
Portugal					1	1	1	1	4
Morocco					1	2	2	1	6
Thailand						1	1		2
Middle East						1			1
Turkey							1	1	2
South America							1		1
Arctic							1		1
Mexico							1		1
New Zealand								1	1
Maldives								1	1
Mauritius								1	1

■ Table 13.3
Cooking
school
advertising
in the
Australian
Gourmet
Traveller,
December
1992–99

	1992	1993	1994	1995	1996	1997	1998	1999
NSW	1	1	2	2	2	3	2	1
Qld			1	1		1		1
Vic.	1		2					
Ireland								1
Italy				1				1

Australia's migrant population has been a significant factor in the production of specialty foods. However, it is the temporary migration of many Australians as part of their overseas experience that has also proven a catalyst for the development of a wider appreciation of wine and food and an international profile for Australian wine and food. Australian and New Zealand chefs who have travelled to Europe, Asia and the Americas have combined techniques and flavours from their 'home' country with products, dishes and techniques from the countries they visited (e.g. Judelson 1997; Webb & Whittington 1997). At the same time there has been a steady flow inwards of overseas chefs, particularly from Europe, who have contributed to this increasing maturity and diversity.

13.4 WINE AND FOOD TOURISM AND PLACE IDENTITY AND PROMOTION

Wine and food are of increasing significance to the way in which Australia and other countries are perceived overseas. This occurs through the profile of produce in the marketplace and increasingly through the profile of Australian chefs in the United Kingdom and North America, and of Australian winemakers in Europe and North America, the so-called 'flying winemakers'. Such a profile also has significant implications for tourism as wine and food, like tourism, are often branded by place. Wine is often referred to by its regional origins, for example Hunter Valley, Margaret River and Barossa. Similarly, food products such as cheese have distinct place references, for example Cheshire, Wensleydale and Cheddar. Such place connections are important not only for branding but also for representing the effect of local conditions on what is produced. For example, the concept of *terroir* is extremely important in **viticulture**. No precise English equivalent exists for the term. However, major elements are climate (from macro-through to micro-climate), sunlight, topography, pedo-geomorphology and hydrology. The concept of *terroir* is important because it underlies the notion of **appellation** control. This is a legal geographical delimitation that seeks to establish a distinctive identity for the wine produced within a specified region or place. Ideas of place or *terroir* associated with wine are also related to notions of cultural and regional identity. Local food production practices may be linked with the development of distinct cultural landscapes and the perpetuation of regional traditions (de Blij 1983).

It is this cultural landscape, de Blij argues, that gives identity to a region. Wine and food can therefore express regional culture as well as a regional environment. Such a relationship is extremely significant for tourism. It provides possibilities for using wine and the associated vineyard landscape to establish a strong regional identity in the tourism marketplace, as well as to convey the notion that tourists will have authentic experiences when they visit a region. Indeed, Cambourne et al. (2000) extend the definition of wine tourism beyond the location of vineyards and wineries, to encompass tourism influenced by and occurring within the regional *terroir* or appellation. That is, **wine tourism** is influenced by the physical, social and cultural dimensions of the winescape and its components. According to Cambourne et al. (2000), conceptualising wine tourism in a non-wine specific context such as simply purchasing a bottle of regional wine in a restaurant, cycling or walking through wine country, or eating regional cuisine broadens both the market and wine tourism practitioner base. In doing so, it not only expands backward economic linkages, but also recognises the importance of social and environmental linkages that may encourage stakeholders to identify their roles, responsibilities and opportunities for further development.

Therefore, this relationship between cuisine, place and visitor experience is increasingly important for tourism as well as for the enthusiastic gourmet. Indeed, the significance of this relationship for tourism is demonstrated by the extent to which television food programs are often sponsored by national and regional tourism associations. Wine is becoming a significant dimension both in promoting a regional image and representing a focal point of tourist interest. In a globalised economy wine is traded internationally, and along with the trading of wine goes the trading of brands and regional images, which are particularly important characteristics of wine promotion.

Consequently, there are substantial place promotion synergies to be made through joint marketing of wine and food with tourism. Wine and food export and tourism are ideal partners for joint marketing activities because they target consumers with a high discretionary income (Dodd 1995), use similar brand statements based on clean, green and healthy lifestyle images and reflect and promote the distinctiveness of regions (Australian Wine Foundation 1996). Such is the importance of regional names in product branding that in order for Australian wine to have greater market access in the European Union (EU), Australia has agreed to phase out the use of European regional names that have been in general wine industry use; for example champagne, burgundy and claret. In addition, Australia is now developing a series of geographical indicators that refer to specific Australian zones, regions and sub-regions. As at 25 August 1999, some 65 geographical indicators had been registered and submitted to the European Union on an interim list (Taylor 2000).

The wine and food connection has been used extensively to promote New Zealand. For example, the New Zealand Tourism Board (NZTB) entered a joint marketing program with Air New Zealand and Silver Fern Holidays to capitalise on the export success of New Zealand wine to Canada (New Zealand Tourism News [NZTN], 1994). The NZTB combined demographic information with consumer profiles of New Zealand product sales to target key markets in urban centres through the Canadian travel magazine *Latitudes*. The issue featured New Zealand, its wines, wine regions and wine heritage and included a recipe insert called *A Taste of New Zealand*. Similar campaigns have also been held in conjunction with food exporters. A 1997 NZTB marketing campaign in four of its key markets involved both tourism wholesalers and two non-tourism partners Zespri (New Zealand kiwifruit brand) and ENZA (export division of the New Zealand Apple and Pear Marketing Board). The Australian campaign promoted a broader range of products than previously, including 'fine wine and food' (NZTN 1997). One advertisement stated 'We're not ones to brag, but our wines are winning awards, even in France' (NZTN 1997:6).

BREAKTHROUGH TOURISM
New Zealand Way

Recognising the importance of the relationship between images of food exports and tourism, the NZTB and TradeNZ now jointly market products under the 'New Zealand Way' brand and 'Fern' logo. Launched in 1993, New Zealand Way is an international branding exercise that identifies, positions and markets quality New Zealand products. It was developed after it was recognised that New Zealand did not have a high international profile and while generally positive images existed they lacked clarity and consistency. Research showed that while New Zealand was generally regarded as a distant and friendly country, with a strong 'clean and green' association, this was usually a vague understanding and did not translate into competitive advantage. In some developing markets, customers had little or no perception of New Zealand at all (New Zealand Way 1998a).

The brand and logo has now been registered in 44 countries across the globe. New Zealand Way uses a range of events, advertising, promotional activities and imaginative public relations exercises developed around themes such as 'Fresh The New Zealand Way', 'Taste The New Zealand Way' (both associated with wine and food products) and 'Experience The New Zealand Way' (associated with tourism activities). New Zealand Way's 170 'Brand Partners' jointly account for 20 per cent of New Zealand's foreign exchange earnings (NZ$4 billion) and represent the top 20 per cent of New Zealand companies (New Zealand Way 1998a). Some of the more well known Brand Partners include: A. J. Hackett Bungy (Queenstown) Ltd; Helicopter Line; Air New Zealand; Quality Hotels Ltd, Corbans Wines, Wine Institute of New Zealand (WINZ), Steinlager, ENZA, Anchor, Fernleaf and Cervena (New Zealand Way 1998b).

Little research on food tourism is publicly available, in contrast to research on the consumption of food products and the activities of tourists. However, in recent years research has been undertaken on visitation to wineries. This section examines the profile that has been developed for consumers of this significant wine tourism product and the overall economic impact of wine tourism.

The Winemakers Federation of Australia estimated the total Australian wine tourism figures to be in the order of 5.3 million visits, worth $428 million in 1995 (Winemakers' Federation of Australia 1996 in Hall & Macionis 1998). The value of wine tourism is expected to grow to $1100 million by 2025 (Australian Wine Foundation 1996). According to the Bureau of Tourism Research, almost 1 in 11 international visitors (9 per cent) to Australia in 1994 visited wineries during their stay, and 1 in 10 international visitors (10 per cent) purchased wine to take home, with 45 per cent of all international visitors to South Australia in 1995 visiting the State's wineries (Ruberto 1996).

The regional impact of wine tourism may also be substantial. For example, in South Australia, the McLaren Vale Winemakers estimated that the annual value of the region's wine tourism industry was in excess of $50 million, of which $8.7 million was attributable to wine sales alone. Tourism New South Wales estimated that approximately 1.5 million domestic and international tourists will visit a winery in that State (Macionis 1996). The Hunter Valley Vineyards Association estimated annual visitation to the region's vineyards to be in excess of 500 000 visitors. Based on an average expenditure of $246 per visitor, the total tourist expenditure generated by the wine industry is estimated at $123 million per annum, with additional indirect expenditure of approximately $158 million per annum (Committee of Inquiry into the Winegrape and Wine Industry 1995).

The Victorian Wineries Tourism Council (VWTC) reported that visits to Victorian wineries increased from 1.6 million to over two million in the period 1995 to 1998. The VWTC estimated that in 1998 there was approximately $200 million of tourism expenditure in Victorian wine regions, with cellar door sales accounting for around $40 million and the balance spent on food, accommodation, fuel, and other goods and services. Indeed, it is estimated that for every $1 spent at the cellar door of a Victorian winery, another $3 to $4 is spent regionally (King 1998; Shelmerdine 1999). Similarly, in the Margaret River region of Western Australia, the presence of a wine industry is seen as a major reason for tourist visits to the area (Committee of Inquiry into the Winegrape and Wine Industry 1995).

In New Zealand, the economic impact is also regarded as significant. Hall and Johnson (1998) estimated that the aggregate contribution measured in terms of products and services sold at wineries was approximately NZ$127 million for 1997. In a survey of New Zealand wineries, 75 per cent of respondents described cellar door sales as being highly or extremely important to their business, representing approximately 20 per cent of the wineries' total sales. Cellar door sales were ranked second in importance behind other domestic wine sales in the composition of total winery sales (Hall & Johnson 1998a).

■ 13.5.1 **Characteristics** *of wine tourists*

In order to understand the phenomenon of wine tourism it is important that a profile of the consumer (wine tourist) is developed. Until the end of the 1990s there was little published research on the characteristics of wine consumers, let alone wine tourists, with the available market segmentations tending to be product-focused. However, such a product-focused approach ignores the experiential and recreational motivations that may be of significance to wine consumers, and more specifically to wine tourists (Macionis 1997).

While market segmentations for wine and food consumers are available, how such segments relate to wine and food tourists is unclear. Dodd and Biggotte (1995) found no significant difference between those who did and those who did not purchase wine at the winery on the basis of their average consumption of wine and how much they spent on it. Understanding why wine consumers (or people generally) choose not to visit wineries is at least of equal interest to wine producers; however, there is also a lack of information on this.

Early descriptions of the characteristics of wine tourists bordered on the stereotypical, including 'wine connoisseurs', 'the passing tourist who thinks a "winery crawl" is just a good holiday', and 'mobile drunks' (Macionis & Cambourne 1998). However, wine tourism is not the sole preserve of wine connoisseurs. Neither is wine tourism for drunkards. Indeed, wineries take special care to ensure that alcohol is not abused by their visitors.

An analysis of research on wine tourism by Macionis and Cambourne (1998) suggested the majority of winery visitors are likely to be:
- mature (30–50 years old)
- employed full-time and in the moderate to high income bracket
- from within the State or regional catchment area
- regular consumers of wine
- in possession of an intermediate to advanced knowledge of wine
- visitors to wineries or wine regions several times a year.

Details such as gender, age, income and origin all provide a useful insight into identifying wine tourists. However, Mitchell et al. (2000) emphasise that this information has been gathered for a relatively small number of wine regions, mainly from Australasia, and is usually of limited geographical extent and with relatively small sample sizes. Nevertheless, there does appear to be a degree of consistency across the studies, which reflects the observations of Macionis and Cambourne and allows for some generalisations to be made, although each region, winery and festival will have its own set of visitor characteristics (see Mitchell et al. 2000 for a detailed overview of this research).

For example, in terms of their understanding of wine, around half of the visitors to Victorian (55 per cent) and New Zealand (50.5 per cent) wineries reported that they had an intermediate knowledge of wine, 40 per cent basic knowledge and less than 10 per cent advanced knowledge. Wineries' perceptions of visitor knowledge, however, may be less flattering. Canberra wineries ascribe basic knowledge to 62 per cent, intermediate to 31 per cent and only 7 per cent advanced (Macionis 1996), while New Zealand wineries ascribed 27 per cent, 80 per cent and 17 per cent respectively (The total does not equal 100 per cent as 16 per cent of respondents selected more than one segment to typify the 'majority' of their visitors.) (Mitchell et al. 2000). In a study of winery visitors in the Margaret River region of Western Australia King and Morris (1997) reported that 52 per cent of respondents rated themselves as knowledgeable/highly knowledgeable in wines. Cellar door visits and tastings, guided tours and wine and food festivals are among the means by which people experience and learn about wine.

■ **Figure 13.1**
Visitors in the extensive estate of Domaine Chandon in Victoria

Source: *Norman Douglas*

From an industry perspective, wine education plays a 'fundamental role' in the growth of the wine industry with an educated and well informed marketplace translating to better sales of premium wine (Hills 1998). In Australia and New Zealand, where wine drinking is only in its infancy as an established part of the way of life, wine tourism may serve a very important role in introducing customers to wine and the development of their wine knowledge and appreciation in a friendly, social and unthreatening atmosphere (Mitchell et al. 2000). Mitchell et al. suggest that, for many, wine tasting and learning about wine and winemaking is a way to 'minimise risk' when purchasing wine (that is, by increasing their experience and knowledge they are able to make more informed decisions about wine). Similarly, further examination of a day out and relaxation as motives reveals a widespread need for escape from city life. Visitors who were motivated by meeting the wine maker or owner were concerned with such things as the believability and passion associated with the wine interpretation presented and therefore raised issues of authenticity.

Motivational information provides an extremely useful basis for marketers and winery managers to more effectively target potential visitors and wine consumers. However, further visitor market research is required to establish a detailed profile of wine tourists and wine tourist segments, and to ascertain how wine tourism relates to other forms of tourist activity. Indeed, recent New Zealand research indicates that there are significant differences in winery visitors between wine regions within a country let alone between countries (see Hall et al. 2000b). Such an observation is extremely important as it highlights the fact that profiles of wine tourists within a particular region or winery should not automatically be assumed to be the same as in another. Despite the lack of a detailed understanding of the demographic and motivational profile of wine tourists in many regions, government and regional tourist organisations have maintained substantial interest in developing wine tourism.

13.6 GOVERNMENT POLICIES AND WINE TOURISM

A number of Australian state and federal governments have undertaken various initiatives encouraging the development of wine tourism (see table 13.4). The state with the longest involvement is Victoria. In 1984, the Victorian Government's Economic and Budget Review Committee commissioned a Report on the Wine Industry in Victoria. Among other issues, the report provided for an evaluation of the wine industry's involvement in marketing and tourism, and an examination of Victoria's position relative to other States in terms of the wine industry's tourism potential (Victorian Parliament Economic Budget Review Committee 1985). The Committee reported that while around 86 per cent of wineries participating in the inquiry 'allow and encourage the general public to visit', there was no consistent policy regarding opening times which could frustrate intended tourist visits. It went on to record that 'tourist facilities are relatively restricted at both small and intermediate wineries. Sales facilities, picnic areas and separate tasting rooms are the most frequently reported' (1985:183).

In addition, the Committee of Inquiry expressed a concern that 'many small and intermediate wineries had not realised the potential of winery-based tourist facilities', and that if wineries are to attract visitors 'one way is to increase the range of facilities available — both sales facilities and special features. This would encourage not only increased private and family patronage, but also coach tours to those wineries with suitable facilities. Such developments would benefit the winery directly, and contribute to the growth of tourist-related services in the region itself' (1985:186).

However, the inquiry also indicated that assessment of visitation to Victorian wineries was difficult because 'in some cases it was clear that the winery had little, if any, idea of the breakdown of cellar door sales by wine type or of the number of visitors to the winery' (1985:113). Nevertheless, the report concluded that 'the committee believes that there is scope to develop a tourism policy for the Victorian wine industry and integrate this policy with state and regional tourism strategies' (1985:181). The momentum generated by the report and the recognition of tourism as a component in winery business and rural regional development, meant that in 1993 the Victorian State Government established the Victorian Wineries Tourism Council to take advantage of Victoria's growing reputation as a wine tourism destination.

Other States soon followed the leadership of the Victorian wine industry. The South Australian Government established the South Australian Wine

Tourism Council in 1996. Similarly, the marketing opportunities of wine promotion were seen as having great potential in increasing the benefits of regional tourism in New South Wales.

■ **Table 13.4** *Mission and aims of the Victorian, South Australian and New South Wales State wine tourism bodies*

ORGAN-ISATION/ STRATEGY	VICTORIAN WINERIES TOURISM COUNCIL	SOUTH AUSTRALIAN WINERIES TOURISM COUNCIL	TOURISM NEW SOUTH WALES 'FOOD AND TOURISM' PLAN
Year formed	1993	1996	1996
Mission	To increase the economic contribution to Victoria by increasing the number of visitors to Victoria's wineries and wine regions	Raising the profile and championing wine tourism in South Australia	To weave food and wine into every part of the tourist experience and its promotion
Priority aims	1. Product development and regional tourism promotion through: (a) Promotion of Victorian Wines (b) Industry communication 2. Identify impediments to and opportunities for Victorian wine tourism	1. Product development and infrastructure 2. Promotional activities 3. Research 4. Develop attractions within wine agricultural and tourism industries	1. To package and market food as an integral part of the tourism experience 2. Encourage the delivery of food and wine experiences 3. Foster greater coordination and cooperation between the food, wine and tourism industries

Source: *After Hall and Macionis (1998)*

According to the NSW Tourism Minister, Brian Langton, 'NSW will embrace wine and food as an integral part of the visitor experience and the focus on wine and food will broaden the destinational appeal of NSW, and encourage more first time visitors to come back for seconds' (Langton 1996:3). Tourism New South Wales launched a strategy document on wine and food tourism in November 1996. In addition, since 1997 the governments of Queensland, Western Australian, and the Australian Capital Territory have contributed funds to the development of wine tourism strategies and/or projects that seek to assist the further development of the wine industry through wine tourism (Macionis & Cambourne 2000).

The Federal Government supported regional wine tourism development through the Rural Tourism Development Program and the Regional Tourism Development Program in the early 1990s. According to Hall and Macionis (1998) projects funded included:
- the development of wine and food trails (Albury–Wodonga, NSW and Geelong, Vic.)
- the building of wine interpretive and visitor centres (Barossa Valley and McLaren Vale, SA)
- the provision of signage systems for vineyard areas (Cessnock, NSW)
- the development of food, wine and cultural tourism strategies (Barossa Valley, SA; Hunter Valley, NSW; Augusta–Margaret River, WA).

More recently the Commonwealth has supported the development of a National Wine Tourism Strategy. The Australian wine industry's 30-year development plan, 'Strategy 2025' identified wine tourism as priority strategy for 'improving the profitability for Australian winemakers' (Winemakers' Federation of Australia 1996). Central to this was the development and implementation of a National Wine Tourism Strategy (Sutton 1999). In 1997, the Federal Government's Office of National Tourism (ONT) provided the Winemakers' Federation of Australia with a grant under the National Tourism Development Program to develop a National Wine Tourism Strategy (NWTS). The objectives of the project included:

- raising the awareness and understanding of tourism in the wine industry
- establishing wine tourism industry standards and increasing the skill levels of wine tourism practitioners and employees
- fostering links between wine, food and Australian lifestyle (Office of National Tourism 1997).

One of the outcomes of the development of the strategy is the creation of a National Wine Tourism Council (NWTC), composed of representatives of peak state wine industry bodies, State wine tourism councils or tourism authorities, the Australian Tourist Commission, the Australian Wine Export Council and the Winemakers' Federation of Australia, which will seek to implement the new strategy (Macionis & Cambourne 2000). However, one of the issues that the strategy and the NWTC will have to address is the extent to which the institutional arrangements for wine tourism supports small wineries and businesses, rather than the larger companies, which are geared towards the wine export market or international tourism.

13.7 WINE AND FOOD TOURISM AND REGIONAL DEVELOPMENT

In Australia, many regional areas are aiming to build on the production of regional foods and wines in order to market new travel and destinational experiences. Wine tourism has therefore emerged as a strong and growing area of special interest tourism in Australia, and has become an increasingly significant component of the Australian regional tourism product.

During the last 20 years in particular, rural areas have experienced numerous, often far-reaching economic, social and political/institutional changes which have had profound effects. In many New World wine regions and, increasingly, traditional wine-growing areas in Europe, wine tourism is seen as a means to combat the effects of rural restructuring. Boutique wineries are the archetypal small business in rural economies where small-scale businesses dominate and are most affected by economic restructuring. Wine-related tourism is therefore a significant factor in sustainable rural development, most obviously through the creation of jobs, the sale of local merchandise and the potential for creating linkages with other local businesses.

From the perspective of winery business development, wine tourism can be part of the core business activities for many boutique wineries, especially those which have chosen winemaking as a lifestyle option. Newly established small-scale wineries tend to sell most of their wine at the cellar door, and gain an essential source of cash-flow in these early stages of business development, particularly as they experience greater per bottle returns from the cellar door than by selling through retail outlets. In addition, cellar door sales provide an opportunity to develop a mailing-list of customers which can then be used for direct-marketing. Some wineries also produce a newsletter and/or website as a means of maintaining customer relationships. One difficulty of cellar-door sales for some small wineries, however, is that serving customers may take time away from other viticultural activities, particularly during harvest. In addition, the small-scale production of many boutique wineries means that they may have to close the cellar door to visitors for some periods of the year if they have run out of stock.

For established wineries, visitors provide a test-bed for new products. Wine tourism also facilitates producer–consumer interaction and involves education about and experience of wine products and wine regions, including local cultures and winescapes. For both large- and small-scale wineries, wine tourism can be very important in terms of brand development. However, wine tourism needs to be seen as part of the overall development of a wine business rather than necessarily an end in itself. The manner in which wine tourism is used as a component of the business mix will therefore depend on the stage of business development, overall business goals, location, and target markets (Dodd & Biggotte 1995; Hall et al. 2000c). To summarise, the advantages of wine tourism for small wineries include:

- increased consumer exposure — to the product and increased opportunities to sample the product
- brand awareness and loyalty — built through establishing links between producer and consumer, and purchase of company branded merchandise
- relationships with customers — the opportunity to meet winery staff and to see 'behind the scenes' can lead to positive relationships with consumers, which may lead to both direct sales and indirect sales through positive 'word of mouth' advertising
- increased margins — through direct sale to consumer, where the absence of distributor costs is not carried over entirely to the consumer
- an additional sales outlet — or, for smaller wine producers who cannot guarantee volume or constancy of supply, the only feasible sales outlet
- marketing intelligence on products — wine producers can gain instant and valuable feedback on the consumer reaction to their existing products, and are able to trial new additions to their product range

(continued)

- marketing intelligence on customers — visitors to the winery can be added to a mailing list, which can be developed as a customer database to both target and inform customers
- educational opportunities — visits to wineries help create awareness and appreciation of wine and the wine industry, and the knowledge and interest generated by this can be expected to result in increased consumption

Some of the disadvantages of wine tourism for small wineries are:

- increased costs and management time — the operation of a tasting room may be costly, particularly when it requires paid staff. While the profitability gap is higher on direct sales to the consumer, profit may be reduced if wineries do not charge for tastings.
- capital required — suitable facilities for hosting visitors may be prohibitively expensive for some small wineries, especially as winemaking is a capital-intensive business
- inability to substantially increase sales — the number of visitors a winery can attract is limited and if a winery cannot sell all of its stock, it will eventually need to use other distribution outlets
- opportunity costs — investments in tasting rooms and tourist facilities means that capital is not available for other investments.

Viticulture also has the capacity to provide sustainable land use in previously uneconomic agricultural areas, while tourism can help support the viability of agricultural diversification and maximise the returns on existing viticulture. Also, wine and food tourism can contribute to tourists' perception of an authentic visitor experience. Being based on a working industry and a 'living' culture, wine tourism thus has the potential to change and be sustained by that change. Nevertheless, some problems may emerge unless wine tourism is managed in a regional context.

Rural areas are increasingly popular 'playgrounds for urban dwellers'. This presents many opportunities for wine tourism but perhaps paradoxically may threaten viticulture, and thus ultimately wine tourism as well. Rural tourism may be a major force for change in rural areas contributing to permanent in-migration and increased second home ownership. For example, in the Nelson area, in the north of New Zealand's South Island, the price of suitable land for wine growing is inflated by high demand from 'lifestylers' migrating from urban centres (Hall & Johnson 1998b). In addition, viticultural practices may not be welcomed by second home owners attracted in their purchasing behaviour by tranquil images of vineyards in pleasant rural areas. For example, in order to deter birds that may peck at grapes on the vine, potentially causing substantial damage, many vineyards will use bird scarers such as loud air guns. Similarly, helicopters are sometimes used in order to prevent frosts from damaging tender grape buds. However, opposition to the noise from such activities in some grape-growing areas has resulted in limitations being imposed on helicopter use.

Concerns may sometimes be expressed over the spray programs applied on some vineyards. In some instances, wine tourism must also compete with existing farming practices. Any sustainable development of wine tourism will thus have to balance these competing demands on resources. However, rural holidays will impact on the everyday lifestyle of urban tourists when they return home, including changes to their mind set on rural concerns. Wine tourism may therefore also be an ally in retaining the 'right to farm' (Hall et al. 2000d).

13.8 SUMMARY

This chapter has highlighted the important role that wine and food play in travel and tourism. Tourism has both influenced the consumption of different types of cuisine and affected their production. Moreover, an interest in wine and food is now a significant component of contemporary lifestyles. Wine and food is also closely linked with place identity and destination promotion. The geographical influences on the production of some foods and especially wine mean that they are branded by the place they come from. This has created opportunities for destinations to link themselves with the profile of their food.

An example of wine tourism was used to show the nature of the wine tourism market and the demographic and psychographic profile of visitors. However, it was also emphasised that different places will have different profiles although some similarities were noted. The growth in wine tourism has also meant that government has shown increased interest and support for wine and food tourism in recent years with substantial support given for the development of wine tourism strategies at the national and state levels. The interest by government is generated, at least in part, by the potential contribution that wine and food tourism can make to economic development and employment generation in rural regions that have been affected by restructuring. However, wine and food tourism, like any other form of tourism, has advantages and disadvantages which need to be recognised both at the business level and within regions as a whole.

Questions

13.1 What are the main difficulties in defining a wine and food tourist?

13.2 When does wine tourism become rural tourism?

13.3 How might wine and food tourism contribute to the maintenance of regional identity?

13.4 What is the usual profile of winery visitors?

13.5 How has government assisted the development of wine and food tourism?

13.6 To what extent might wine and food tourism contribute to regional development?

REFERENCES ·

Australian Wine Foundation. 1996. *Strategy 2025: the Australian Wine Industry.* Adelaide: Winemakers' Federation of Australia.

Bruneteau, J. 1996. *Tukka: Real Australian Food.* Sydney: HarperCollins Publishers.

Cambourne, B., Hall, C. M., Johnson, G., Macionis, N., Mitchell, R. & Sharples, L. 2000. 'The Future of Wine Tourism'. In Hall, C. M., Sharples, E., Cambourne, B. & Macionis, N. (Eds.). *Wine Tourism Around the World: Development, Management and Markets.* Oxford, UK: Butterworth-Heinemann, pp. 297–320.

Committee of Inquiry into the Winegrape and Wine Industry. 1995. *Winegrape and Wine Industry in Australia* (Final Report). Canberra: AGPS.

de Blij, H. J. 1983. *Wine: A Geographic Appreciation.* Totowa: Rowman & Allanheld.

Dodd, T. H. 1995. 'Opportunities and Pitfalls of Tourism in a Developing Wine Industry'. *International Journal of Wine Marketing* 7 (1): 15–16.

Dodd, T. H. & Bigotte, V. 1995. *Visitors to Texas Wineries: Their Demographic Characteristics and Purchasing Behavior.* Lubbock, Texas: Texas Wine Marketing Research Institute.

Hall, C. M. 1996. 'Wine Tourism in New Zealand'. In *Proceedings of Tourism Down Under II: A Tourism Research Conference.* Dunedin: University of Otago, pp. 109–119.

Hall, C. M. & Johnson, G. 1997, 'Wine Tourism in New Zealand: Larger Bottles or Better Relationships?' In Higham J. (Ed.). *Trails, Tourism and Regional Development Conference Proceedings.* Dunedin: Centre for Tourism, University of Otago, pp. 73–86.

Hall, C. M. & Johnson, G. 1998a. 'Wine Tourism: An Imbalanced Partnership'. In Dowling, R. & Carlsen, J. (Eds.). *Wine Tourism — Perfect Partners, Proceedings of the first Australian Wine Tourism Conference, Margaret River, Western Australia, May 1998.* Canberra: Bureau of Tourism Research, pp. 51–72.

Hall, C. M. & Johnson, G. 1998b. 'Wine and Food Tourism in New Zealand: Difficulties in the Creation of Sustainable Tourism Business Networks', In Hall, D. & O'Hanlon, L. (Eds.). *Rural Tourism Management: Sustainable Options.* Auchenvyre: Scottish Agricultural College, pp. 21–38.

Hall, C. M. Johnson, G., Cambourne, B., Macionis, N., Mitchell, R. & Sharples, L. 2000a.'Wine Tourism: An Introduction'. In Hall, C. M., Sharples, E., Cambourne, B. & Macionis N. (Eds.). *Wine Tourism Around the World: Development, Management and Markets.* Oxford, UK: Butterworth-Heinemann, pp. 1–23.

Hall, C. M., Johnson, G. & Mitchell, R. 2000d. 'Wine Tourism and Regional Development'. In Hall, C. M., Sharples, E., Cambourne, B. & Macionis, N. (Eds.). *Wine Tourism Around the World: Development, Management and Markets,* Oxford. UK: Butterworth-Heinemann, pp. 196–225.

Hall, C. M., Longo, A. M., Mitchell, R. & Johnson, G. 2000b. 'Wine Tourism in New Zealand'. In Hall, C. M., Sharples, E., Cambourne, B. & Macionis, N. (Eds.). *Wine Tourism Around the World: Development, Management and Markets.* Oxford, UK: Butterworth-Heinemann, pp. 150–74.

Hall, C. M. & Macionis, N. 1998. 'Wine Tourism in Australia and New Zealand'. In Butler, R. W., Hall, C. M. & Jenkins, J. (Eds.). *Tourism and Recreation in Rural Areas.* Chichester. UK: John Wiley & Sons, pp. 267–98.

Hall, C. M. & Mitchell, R. 1999. 'We Are What We Eat: Food, Tourism and Globalisation'. *Tourism, Culture and Communication.* Volume 2.

Hall, C. M., Sharples, E., Cambourne, B. & Macionis, N. (Eds.). 2000c. *Wine Tourism Around the World: Development, Management and Markets.* Oxford, UK: Butterworth-Heinemann.

Hills, C. 1998. 'Quenching the Thirst for Knowledge'. *Australian and New Zealand Wine Industry Journal* 13 (1): 66–7.

Innes, S. 1996. 'Pacesetting SA Wineries, the Toast of Tourism'. *SA Advertiser,* 6 March, p. 5.

Johnson, G. 1998. Wine Tourism in New Zealand — A National Survey of Wineries. Unpublished Dip Tour Dissertation, University of Otago, Dunedin.

Judelson, S. 1997. 'Introduction: What is East–West Food?'. In Judelson, S. (Ed.). *East–West Food: Food from the Pacific Rim and Beyond, with 10 of the World's Hottest Chefs.* London: Hamlyn, pp. 7–11.

King, C. & Morris, R. 1997, 'Wine Tourism: A Western Australian Case Study', *Australian and New Zealand Wine Industry Journal* 12 (3): 246–9.

King, J. 1998. 'National Wine Tourism Strategy Green Paper'. Unpublished discussion paper. National Wine Tourism Strategy Task Force.

Langton, B. 1996. 'News'. *Tourism NSW Newsletter,* Spring.

Macionis, N. 1996. 'Wine Tourism in Australia'. In *Proceedings of Tourism Down Under II: A Tourism Research Conference.* Dunedin: University of Otago, pp. 264–86.

Macionis, N. 1997. Wine Tourism in Australia: Emergence, Development and Critical Issues. Unpublished Masters Thesis. Belconnen: University of Canberra.

Macionis, N. & Cambourne, B. 1998. 'Wine Tourism: Just What Is It All About?' *The Australian and New Zealand Wine Industry Journal* 13 (1): 41–7.

Macionis, N. & Cambourne, B. 2000. 'Towards a National Wine Tourism Plan: Wine Tourism Organizations and Development in Australia'. In Hall, C. M., Sharples, E., Cambourne, B. & Macionis, N. (Eds.). *Wine Tourism Around the World: Development, Management and Markets.* Oxford, UK: Butterworth-Heinemann, pp. 226–52.

Mitchell, R., Hall, C. M. & McIntosh, A. 2000. 'Wine Tourism and Consumer Behaviour'. In Hall, C. M., Sharples, E., Cambourne, B. & Macionis, N. (Eds.). *Wine Tourism Around the World: Development, Management and Markets.* Oxford, UK: Butterworth-Heinemann, pp. 115–35.

Newton, J. 1996. *Wogfood: An Oral History with Recipes.* Milsons Point, Sydney: Random House.

New Zealand Tourism News (NZTN). 1994. 'New Zealand's Wines Attract Canadian Visitors'. *New Zealand Tourism News,* February, p. 8.

New Zealand Tourism News (NZTN). 1997. 'Increasing Focus on Destination Marketing'. *New Zealand Tourism News,* December, pp. 6–7.

New Zealand Way. 1998a. *Re-imaging New Zealand. http://www.nzway.co.nz/contents.html*

New Zealand Way. 1998b. *Brand Partners and Associates of The New Zealand Way. http://www.nzway.co.nz/contents.html*

Office of National Tourism. 1997. *Information Sheet National Tourism Development Program Category D: National Industry Development and Coordination.* Canberra: Office of National Tourism.

Ruberto, A. 1996. 'Visitors to Wine Regions'. *BTR Tourism Update,* Summer, p. 4.

Saunders, A. 1999. *Australian Food: A Celebration of the New Cuisine with Recipes for Home Cooking by Leading Chefs and Writers.* Sydney: Landsdowne Press.

Shelmerdine, S. 1999. 'The Victorian Wineries Tourism Council', In Dowling, R. & Carlsen, J. (Eds.). *Wine Tourism: Perfect Partners, Proceedings of the First Australian Wine Tourism Conference, Margaret River, Western Australia, May 1998.* Canberra: Bureau of Tourism Research, pp. 159–62.

Sutton, I. 1999. 'National Wine Tourism Strategy — Introduction and Overview'. In Dowling, R. & Carlsen, J. (Eds.). *Wine Tourism: Perfect Partners, Proceedings of the First Australian Wine Tourism Conference, Margaret River, Western Australia, May 1998.* Canberra: Bureau of Tourism Research, pp. 267–76.

Symons, M. 1993. *The Shared Table: Ideas for Australian Cuisine.* Canberra: Office of Multicultural Affairs, AGPS.

Taylor, W. 2000. 'Soothing the Growing Pains: Protection of Geographical Indications and Traditional Expressions'. *Wine Industry Journal* 15 (1): 33–41.

Victorian Parliament Economic Budget Review Committee. 1985. *Report on the Wine Industry in Victoria.* Melbourne: Parliament of Victoria.

Webb, M. & Whittington, R. 1997. *Fusions: A New Look at Australian Cooking,* London: Ebury Press.

Winemakers Federation of Australia. 1996. 'Strategy 2025'. *Australian and New Zealand Wine Industry Journal* 11 (3): 196–211.

CASE STUDY ···

The James Winery
Experience

The James Winery is a small boutique winery that has been established in a cool climate wine district 40 kilometres from X, a city of several hundred thousand people. It is now ten years since the owners purchased the property. The 25 hectare property was initially purchased as part of a lifestyle decision by the husband and wife owners to move to the country. Several options had been evaluated for potential, including olives, nut trees, truffles, free-range chickens, grapes and organic horticulture. As the owners have a long-standing interest in wine they eventually decided to develop a small vineyard after discussions with a viticultural consultant, who reported that the site had a suitable micro-climate for grapes. They also decided to maintain some olive and nut trees as they felt it might also diversify their product base as well as contribute to the 'Mediterranean feel' they wanted on their property.

Because of the substantial start-up costs of developing the property as a working vineyard, the owners continued to work in the city. Four hectares of pinot noir vines were initially planted as these were likely to bring high initial returns. Since it cost about NZ$25 000 per hectare to plant the vineyard and no commercial size crop would be expected for three years, a good financial yield was important. Fortunately, they were able to enter an agreement with a neighbouring established vineyard and winery to help manage their grapes and, just as importantly, purchase their crop for years three to six of its development. However, their dream was to be able to sell their own wine and the owners were committed to developing the property further.

After further consideration they decided to plant more grapes and build a small on-site winery and cellar. Because of the site characteristics and changing market trends, they then planted four hectares of riesling and six more of pinot gris. They also decided to develop a small experimental vineyard of other grape varieties to determine what might be developed on the site in the longer term. However, after developing the new blocks of vines, they realised that they were in great danger of overextending themselves financially if they tried to develop a fully-operational winery. Fortunately, the area they had set aside as the winery was situated beside the old farmstead in which they lived and they decided instead to modify their building plans and have a cellar and tasting room only and contract the wine-making out to the winery that had already contracted to purchase their fruit. In order to pay for the building, the couple had to continue working in the city. Their lifestyle choice meant that they were actually working longer hours per week than they had been prior to purchasing the block and planting the vines.

By the end of the sixth year they had to make their income from their vines themselves, rather than being able to rely on neighbours purchasing the fruit. They knew their fruit was of good quality as the neighbours had produced silver medal wine with it at the district's wine show. They now had to pay their neighbour's wine maker to make their wine for them. Fortunately, they had favourable conditions for their first harvest as independent producers and they were able to get the grapes to the winemaker in peak condition. However, they still had to sell their wine.

Given the development of several wineries in the district, the local government body had assisted in the development of a signed wine trail in the district that also had a number of arts and crafts businesses on the trail. At weekends a small wine tour business also operated. After talking with the local visitor centre and the wine tour operator they found that they were able to become part of the trail as well as the tour. They quickly ensured that their tasting room was ready for visitors. They had their wines on display as well as a range of other produce from their property, as they had found that visitors also wanted to buy some of the olives and walnuts they had planted along the driveway to the house.

Some of the visitors who were interested in their wines and had brought friends with them asked if they could bring picnics on the next visit and have lunch on the lawns of the homestead. Soon the owners realised that they had some important business decisions to make. Should they invest their money into developing their own winery or further develop the tourist side of the business? After careful consideration they decided on the latter. To develop a fully operational winery would cost them another NZ$500 000. To build a commercial kitchen and offer lunches would cost them only NZ$8000. They also realised that for another NZ$5000 they could renovate the old shearer's cottage and offer vineyard accommodation. It was a difficult decision, but they realised that to have the lifestyle they wanted they should not continue to try expanding wine production. Instead, they should concentrate on producing high-value quality wine as well as deriving financial returns from the tourist component of the operation.

By their ninth year, the wife was able to give up her job in the city and the James Winery was selling 40 per cent of its wine directly from the cellar door to visitors. A further 30 per cent was sold from their mail order list, and this was likely to increase. Some of their original customers were more like old friends, regularly visiting from the city to have lunch and sample wines, even if they had sampled them only two months previously! Lunches were now available six days a week rather than only on the weekend, and they had employed a daughter of one of their neighbours to help in the kitchen. They had been approached by one of the large bus companies to take tour groups of around 40 people, but they declined. Although they could have accommodated this number for lunch, they decided it would ruin the feel of the experience provided. They remembered that when they used to visit wineries before buying their own property, they would continue driving if they saw a tour bus in a vineyard they had hoped to visit! Furthermore, their dog didn't like large tour buses and she had become one of the most important parts of their vineyard, always going up to greet customers and being called by name!

In the tenth year, they were still mortgaged to the bank but were now earning enough from the vineyard to enable the husband to give up his lecturing job at the university, although he continued to teach part-time. The shearer's house was rented out for about 60 per cent of the time, while the farmstay down the road was only rented out on weekends. This was apparently because their guests liked the 'romance' of staying on a vineyard.

They had also started to feature dinners and events in their wine cellar, with local foods including goat's cheese and meats from one of the neighbours, olives and artichokes from a small holding about a kilometre away, and sourdough breads from the specialist bakers in the nearby village.

Many in the local community had been sceptical about the 'trendy' bakers that seemed to cater mainly to city-dwellers who had moved into the district in the past ten years, and to day-trippers and weekenders from the city. But they were nonetheless pleased as the previous bakers had closed down 15 years earlier when the supermarket opened.

Most pleasing to the husband and wife team was that both their pinot gris and riesling had won awards at the Easter wine show. The publicity had meant that their wine was more in demand than ever and they could afford to charge a little more for their product. About 10 per cent of their production was now being shipped to the United Kingdom and the United States at a premium and, thanks to the interest of one of their visitors, also to Norway and Sweden.

However, they found their success in the wine industry more than a little amusing. They had what visitors regarded as a very successful winery. Yet, although they grew the grapes, they still had to contract a winemaker to make the wine.

The wine was only stored in the casks in the cellar after it had been carefully transported from their neighbour's winery. Even the bottling was done by a portable unit on a semi-trailer which worked its way through the region. When it came through they closed the vineyard to visitors because they didn't want the romantic perceptions of the vineyard to be affected.

Almost 40 per cent of the returns on the property came from the kitchen, the accommodation and from other purchases by visitors, including T-shirts and picnic baskets. Without the tourism aspect, however, they knew they would never have had the capital to build up such a well-managed vineyard and enjoy so many sales over the counter and through mail order. They were finally in a situation where they were working only a few more hours than they had been before they changed their lifestyles.

They could have expanded further, but like so many boutique vineyards in the region, they decided against it since it would require investing yet more capital and more labour. Instead they realised that they had finally come close to what they had wanted. The focus now would be on improving the quality of their wines and the overall experience that their lifestyle provided, not simply on increasing the volume of sales.

Questions

1 Why might the potential wine tourist be interested in the James Winery even though the wine isn't made there?

2 What is the James Winery's core business?

3 To what extent do you think its true to say that wine tourists are able to take their memories home in a bottle?

4 As other wineries develop in their region to what extent might they distract from the James Winery's competitive position?

5 Identify a winery or food producer that allows visitors.

(a) To what extent is it visitor friendly?

(b) How is tourism used to sell its product and create relationships with their customers?

(c) Do they realise that they are in the business of tourism?

Norman Douglas
and
Ngaire Douglas

The cruise
experience

LEARNING OBJECTIVES

After reading this chapter, you will have an appreciation of:

- the essential terminology of cruising
- the historical growth of cruising
- the economic impacts of the cruise industry
- the differences between large cruise lines and other types of cruising
- the marketing imagery employed by cruise lines
- the motivations of people who choose to cruise
- the geography of cruising
- the significance of cruise ships in the Asia–Pacific region.

Cruising has become one of the fastest growing sectors within tourism. A holiday on a cruise ship is generally portrayed as a special experience and because of all the inclusions usually offered by cruise companies, such as meals, activities, entertainment and varied destinations, a cruise is promoted as the best example of the 'one-stop holiday shop'. Interest in all types of cruising has become so widespread that cruise imagery is borrowed by other travel sectors. A Sydney-based air tours company calls itself AirCruising Australia, while an advertisement for the trans-Australia rail service, Indian Pacific, depicts the train as an ocean liner, 'the only cruise ship in the world where the staterooms [cabins] have a view of the outback' (Indian Pacific 2000) (see below for further discussion of cruise imagery). All this may make cruising appear a mainstream tourist activity, but in fact it remains a specialised form of travel.

Even in its largest growth area, the United States, it remains a niche market, albeit an ever-expanding niche. In other parts of the world, Australia and New Zealand for example, it accounts for only a very small percentage of travellers. Indeed, it may be argued that the international cruise business is in reality a collection of special interest markets (Dwyer & Forsyth 1996:41, see below). Many countries are still quite unaffected by the apparent boom in cruising, which is often ignored completely in detailed reports of tourist activity.

This chapter examines some of the essential terminology of cruising and its historical growth. We outline the motivations of people who choose to cruise and show the methods used to estimate the economic impact of a cruise ship's arrival in port. We describe the development of the cruise business in the Asia–Pacific region, providing examples from Australia. We then illustrate and discuss the recurring imagery used by cruise marketers and explain the different types of cruise operations. Finally, the case study focuses on a Fiji company that has been one of the most successful operators of special interest cruises in the region for many years, having grown from the most modest of beginnings.

14.2 **CRUISE TERMINOLOGY** ·

We begin our discussion of cruise tourism by defining some of the terms used by the industry. A **cruise** is a voyage on a ship undertaken wholly for reasons of leisure and recreation. A **line voyage** is a sea trip taken with the express purpose of getting from port A to port B. Since the advent of affordable air travel for the masses in the early 1960s, the line voyage has largely fallen into disuse. In the early twentieth century business people in London with appointments in New York had to allow at least five days for an Atlantic crossing. By the end of the century they could catch a super-sonic jet and arrive in a few hours. These days the concept of line voyages is sometimes applied to long sections of a world cruise — London to Sydney, for example. In an illustration of the use of nostalgia in today's cruise ship marketing, Cunard and P&O promote long legs on round-the-world itineraries as line voyages. It should also be said that in 'cruisespeak' the word *crossing* refers only to a trans-Atlantic voyage, usually from Britain to North America or vice versa. A **positioning voyage**, by which a company temporarily locates a ship in another part of the world for a short season, is sometimes referred to as a line voyage. However, given that the great majority of passengers are on board for holiday purposes, intending either to fly home directly from their destination or to take a short post-cruise trip from the destination, this is a misuse of the term.

Cruising has two fundamental categories. The first is the *round trip*, in which the ship leaves embarkation port A for a certain number of days, visits several other ports of call along the way and returns to port A, where its passengers disembark. The few traditionalists left within the industry still insist that this is the only 'true' cruise. The second is the *fly/cruise*, in which the ship leaves port A, visits various ports of call and upon its arrival at port X, the passengers disembark and fly home. A new complement of passengers, who have flown to pick up the ship in port X, now join and the ship sails on to other ports, thus beginning another cruise. A number of companies offer round-the-world cruises taking several months. Many passengers stay on for the whole trip, while others will purchase shorter fly/cruise segments.

The distinction between a *port of call* and a *port of embarkation/disembarkation* is also important. A ship usually spends about eight to ten hours at its port of call, arriving early in the morning and sailing in late afternoon or early evening. Because of high port charges and the need to maintain strict schedules, ships rarely stay in ports of call overnight. One notable exception within the region is Ho Chi Minh City (Saigon) in Vietnam, a river port, where it takes about four hours to cover the distance from the river's entrance to the ship's berth, and where arrival/departure times are determined strictly by tide. Ports of embarkation or disembarkation, such as Singapore and Sydney, may be further distinguished by the local suppliers and the services they provide for both ships and passengers.

14.3 THE LITERATURE

Academic research on cruising is in its infancy compared with other areas of tourism, although there are numerous popular accounts, ranging from detailed examinations of individual vessels to extensive company histories. Most academic publications focus on the Caribbean and the American cruise sector (Hobson 1993; Showalter 1994; Bull 1996; Dale & Robinson 1998). This is hardly surprising given that Americans constitute more than 80 per cent of cruise passengers and the Caribbean hosts 50 per cent of all cruises. The emergence of the Asia–Pacific region as both destination and hub is explained by Douglas and Douglas (1996), Dwyer and Forsyth (1996), Peisley (1999) and Singh (1999). Although most studies concentrate on the ships, a few have focused on the passengers. Studies of cruise passenger behaviour (Douglas & Douglas 1999b), passenger types

(Morrison et al. 1996; Moscardo et al. 1996) and passenger satisfaction (Teye & Leclerc 1998) have appeared only recently. The Cruise Lines International Association (CLIA) and the quarterly releases of the *International Cruise Monitor* provide the most up-to-date statistics, trends and regional reports, as do the Internet sites of a number of individual cruise companies.

14.4 A BRIEF HISTORY OF OCEAN CRUISING

The introduction of ocean cruising is credited to Arthur Anderson, co-founder of the great Peninsular and Oriental Steam Navigation Company, popularly known as P&O. In 1844 Anderson's dream of several years was realised when P&O started selling round-trip tickets on its ships servicing the Mediterranean. From chilly England passengers sailed to warmer ports like Cairo, Athens and Constantinople, where they took organised shore excursions. P&O can also claim credit for establishing the role of the sponsored travel writer by subsidising popular writers of the time who, in exchange for a free trip, published accounts of their adventures in exotic locations, not forgetting to describe enthusiastically the delights of a sea voyage. These were cruises on ships intended primarily for transporting cargo; passengers were usually people going out to other countries as government officers, missionaries, scientists or traders. Facilities were basic. However, in 1881, inspired by a *British Medical Journal* report on the health benefits of a sea cruise, the Oceanic Yachting Company purchased the *SS Ceylon* from P&O and converted it into the world's first 'cruising yacht' (Howarth & Howarth 1986).

A German company, Hamburg-Amerika, is credited with launching the first custom-built cruise ship, the *Prinzessin Victoria Luise*, in 1900. It was small, luxurious and intended for the very rich. One hundred years later companies like Silversea Cruises continue the tradition. Hamburg-Amerika also pioneered the all-white cruise ship to symbolise summer cruising. Today white is still the preferred colour for cruise ships' paintwork. Until the Great Depression of the 1930s, cruising generally meant long trips that only the very wealthy could afford in both time and expense. Several companies converted their ships to accommodate first-class passengers for trips to warmer climates during seasons when the weather on line voyage routes was inclement.

The temperance movement, a significant factor in the growth of the legendary Thomas Cook travel company, was also a major reason for the shift to popular cruising. During the prohibition era in the United States, big companies like Cunard and White Star began to operate 'booze cruises', short, cheap overnight trips to nowhere out of New York during which people could partake of the alcohol forbidden them on shore. As demand grew, so did the length of these special interest cruises, which began to put into the Caribbean, still the most popular destination for the American cruise market (McAuley 1997). The short cruise to nowhere is still used by companies hoping to give new markets a taste for the cruise experience.

In the 1920s and 1930s cruising boomed. Ports in the Mediterranean, the Caribbean, the Norwegian Fjords and, less frequently, Asia and the South Pacific all greeted hordes of passengers who swarmed down gangways, overwhelmed local shopkeepers, rushed out to accessible natural and built attractions, colonised beaches and bars and then sailed off into the evening. In many parts of the world, cruise passengers were the first tourists. With each new ship built designers fought to outdo each other in style, size, luxury and facilities. The Italians introduced the 'floating resort' concept in 1932 when they turned the outdoor 'Lido' deck space into a replica of a beach resort. Early cruise ships presented magnificent challenges to the traditional grand hotels. Beach umbrellas and sand around the pool were popular features.

After World War II a number of developments, while appearing to have little to do with cruising for pleasure, had major impacts on how shipping companies operated. In the late 1940s and 1950s there was a migration boom similar to the one that had occurred in the last two decades of the nineteenth century, when millions of Europeans boarded ships for the New World. The ships that brought British and European migrants to Australia and New Zealand began to offer short cruise seasons within the region. When a ship berthed in Sydney thousands of nervous newcomers would venture cautiously down the gangway after a gruelling six-week trip in regimented conditions. The next day hundreds of eager holiday-makers would crowd the rails as the same ship sailed under Sydney Harbour Bridge en route for a three-week trip to Pacific destinations such as Tonga, Fiji and Tahiti. Upon its return to Sydney a boatload of eager young antipodeans would board for the six-week voyage to London. In the 1960s increasingly affordable air travel forced shipping lines to reassess their product. While line voyages were seriously affected by this development, cruise operators were able to promote fly/cruise packages, thus extending their product and range of activities. The world fuel crisis of the early 1970s caused further reassessment. In the preceding years ships accommodating over 1000 passengers were popular. But big ships also meant big fuel consumption. Smaller ships were now preferred. Smaller ships and fewer passengers also opened up previously inaccessible ports of call, and itinerary planners became more adventurous. The last decade of the twentieth century saw a strong reversal of this trend.

14.5 THEME CRUISES AND EXTRA SPECIAL INTERESTS

Within the special interest world of cruising, interests are becoming further specialised as more and more cruises cater for very specific tastes. Special interest cruising probably began with the 'booze cruises' of the prohibition era, but the range has broadened spectacularly within the last few years. 'Theme cruises', featuring special interests such as jazz, opera, chamber music, gardening, art appreciation, photography, flower arranging, golf, cookery, wine tasting, bridge, line dancing and so on, are now regular occurrences, providing progams of a quality and intensity to rival those experienced by land-based devotees. Renaissance Cruises, for example, offers in association with Johns Hopkins Medical a 'Wellness at Sea' program that includes almost every feature offered by health resorts on land (http://www.porthole.com/newsletter). 'Swingers' cruises' are a popular option for some. Gay and/or lesbian cruises have an increasing number of enthusiastic subscribers and may exclude heterosexuals, although standard heterosexual cruises may not exclude gays and lesbians. Nude cruises — 'the latest wrinkle', according to one specialist — have been promoted and 'nude shore excursions are also scheduled on certain sailings' (Slater & Basch 1997:58). No, they are not necessarily for dedicated naturists. A combination of the last two special interests is surely not far away. Dialysis cruises (featuring 'assisted living') are already a reality.

If state-of-the-art 'floating resorts' don't appeal, 'small ship cruising' on well-appointed ocean-going vessels carrying about 100 passengers or fewer provide a popular alternative, especially in the US. Then there are 'freighter cruises', which may last for months and on which passengers are accommodated in what used to be officers' quarters. The cruises follow the standard freighter routes, hence the long duration of many. With computerised cargo vessels now requiring fewer officers, the companies involved are selling the usually well-appointed and spacious accommodation to people who seek a different cruise experience. Generally, no individual sectors are sold; passengers need to have a great deal of time available. Port schedules are relatively flexible compared with the regular cruise ships. No special activities or entertainments are provided for passengers, either aboard or ashore, although some ships may have small swimming pools and libraries, also intended primarily for officers. Passengers take their meals with and eat the same food as the officers. Passenger numbers are very low, generally between two and 12, depending on space, but this form of alternative cruising is so popular with special interest cruisers — usually people of mature years — that accommodation is often booked out many months in advance. Passengers seeking a cheap vacation should look elsewhere. The 'unique' nature of the experience means that the carriers can charge top prices, often the equivalent of the better-known cruise ships, for which intense competition tends to result in frequent discounting.

There are also river cruises — sometimes on traditionally styled paddle-wheelers — from the Mississippi to the Murray, lake cruises, harbour cruises, barge cruises, canal boat cruises, motor yacht cruises, sailing ship cruises and cruises on such vessels as *Club Med II*, which combines the last two features. In early 2000 one Internet site was promoting cruises on Kastaway Island, 'the kind of experience you often dream about, but rarely encounter'. Kastaway Island was 'the first cruise ship that, with the creative use of paint and fibreglass, will be renovated to look like a lush tropical island floating along the water' (http://www.kastawayisland.com). The ship did not actually exist at the time pre-paid holiday packages were being advertised; they appeared to be based on a time-share principle. The history of cruising is full of rare encounters, creative usages and promised ships that failed to materialise. In almost all instances, advance bookings had been sold.

The numbers of vessels engaged in cruising of one sort or another are enormous. The variety involved in ocean cruising alone makes nonsense of the claim that 'a cruise on sea is a trip on a ship *purposefully styled as a swimming leisure environment*' (Ritter & Schaffer 1998, emphasis added). A container vessel is hardly a 'purposefully styled swimming leisure environment'; many lesser but still functioning cruise ships once saw service as ferries. Some of the smaller expeditionary vessels have only token swimming pools and some inter-island and short-range cruise vessels have none.

SPECIAL INTEREST INVESTIGATION
Cruising and the environment

The days when cruise ships routinely dumped waste overboard are over, although isolated instances are still reported. Large cruise lines such as P&O are keen to publicise their concern for the environment, while a number of smaller companies, whose reputations are built on their interaction with relatively remote and 'unspoiled' destinations, are taking an active part in the conservation of those destinations.

Since 1979 Lindblad Expeditions has been providing small ship adventure cruises to destinations around the world, including Antarctica, the Arctic, Central and South America, Europe, North America, North Africa and the South Pacific. The company now caters for up to 12 000 passengers annually. Tours to the Galapagos Islands account for more than 20 per cent of Lindblad's overall business. The company conducts 5 per cent of all tourist trade to the islands. Last year, more than 3000 guests were introduced to the Galapagos on 45 expeditions on board the 80-passenger *Polaris*. Through the creation of the Galapagos Conservation Fund, Lindblad Expeditions has pioneered an approach that has raised more than US$500 000 since 1997, an average of US$4000 a week, in support of conservation projects in the Galapagos Islands. Lindblad guests have contributed US$250 000 annually to the GCF. By comparison, the annual operating budget after salaries of the Galapagos National Park is approximately US$600 000.

Since 1997 the company has experienced a 54 per cent increase in the number of guests travelling to the Galapagos. The Galapagos trips have helped to account for a 5 per cent increase in Lindblad's business worldwide. According to Michael Seltzer, the New York–based director of Business Enterprises for Sustainable Travel (BEST):

> Lindblad Expeditions has created an important philanthropic model that preserves the natural assets of one of its most vital destinations while providing environmental education to its customers and building positive relationships with local government officials who set the terms for the business regulatory environment.

The Galapagos Conservation Fund is not a legal entity. Contributions are administered by the Charles Darwin Foundation, an international non-profit organisation based in Washington, DC. Lindblad covers all administrative overheads for the Galapagos Conservation Fund, ensuring that 100 per cent of donated funds go to support projects on the ground. Supported projects include the eradication of feral pigs from the island of Santiago, support for the Galapagos National Park's only patrol boat combating illegal commercial fishing and the introduction of environmental education for local residents.

Lindblad has won recognition for its environmentally aware policies, including awards from the *Smithsonian Magazine*, the Audubon Society and *Condé Nast Traveler* and public service commendations from the US Coast Guard. The company also sponsors other programs aimed at education and sustainability in travel and tourism, including the Baja California guide training program, graduates of which are given internships on Lindblad vessels. Since 1991 Lindblad has contributed extensively to the efforts of organisations involved in conservation education and the preservation of tropical environments.

Sources: *BEST: media release, 8 June 2000; Lindblad Expeditions: http://www.expeditions.com*

14.6 THE ROMANCE OF THE SEA: CRUISE IMAGERY

It's more than a cruise. It's the Love Boat (Princess Cruises advertising slogan).

Luxury has become the most universal language and imagery in the world and Silversea [Cruises] is committed to providing the ultimate ultra-luxury travel experience (Pedelaborde 1997).

Just remember — living well is the best revenge (Bratton 1996).

If travel in any form may be regarded as an escape from the reality of one's day-to-day existence, cruising represents the ultimate escape, or at least so its publicity would have us believe. Most holiday travel places us in a space/time dimension different from the one in which we normally exist. Cruising, especially ocean cruising, goes a step further by removing us from land entirely — except for brief, sometimes almost incidental port visits — and placing us in a self-contained world from which space appears limitless and time seems of no consequence at all, ship's clocks and meal hours notwithstanding. 'The last thing you'll be aware of is travelling', says one cruise brochure (P&O 1993). This sense of unreality is heightened by the advertising claims made for cruising, which may seem limitless, but are dominated by a few frequently repeated concepts — romance, luxury, exotica and nostalgia. Almost from the beginnings of cruising as a travel experience, these concepts have been in the forefront of cruise imagery, both visual and verbal.

Notions of romance, which imbued much of the early fictional literature of the sea, were rapidly reduced to clichés and incorporated into cruise promotion. Evidence of this tendency, whose roots stretch back as far as the early twentieth century, now leaps out from almost every cruise brochure or poster and is reflected in the descriptions or even the names of the vessels. Princess Cruises established its reputation largely through the popular 1970s television series *The Love Boat*, a tag the company now applies to all its ships, in spite of the fact that almost no aspect of the ship shown in the series resembles the current vessels. The massive Carnival Corporation, with interests in six well-known cruise brand names, takes an even blunter approach to marketing 'romance'. Ships of its own brand bear names such as *Fantasy, Elation, Sensation* and *Ecstasy*. Carnival quite literally likes to spell out the appeal of its cruises for people who might be in danger of missing the point. This is a far cry from the days when companies gave their ships names that emphasised their size or regal aspect, such as *Titanic* or *Majestic* or the many Queens, Empresses and Princesses.

In 1999 the US trade magazine *Porthole* conducted a poll in which cruisers were invited to nominate their favourite 'places for onboard intimacy'. Possibilities included 'by the pool', 'in a lifeboat', 'in the casino', 'in the gym' and 'in the galley'. The most popular location, 'in the cabin', suggested a fundamentally conservative attitude among most romantics, but a few voted for something more bizarre: 'the infirmary [hospital]' and the 'empty kids playroom' were two choices (http://www.porthole.com). It is worth noting also that the film *Titanic*, which depicts one of the greatest maritime disasters of the twentieth century, is credited by industry sources with stimulating an increased interest in cruising, because for many film-goers the love affair between the two principals was far more significant than the ship's fate. The irony in this hardly needs comment but serves as another illustration of an apparently indestructible cruise myth. The perception that cruising equals romance equals sexual licence leads to regular excesses on 'schoolie' cruises, whose passengers are predominantly high-school students in their late teens. A late 1999 example on P&O's *Fair Princess* was described as '11 days and 10 nights of testosterone and vomit' (Bearup 1999). Perhaps the company should not be too surprised by these developments. One finding of a 1999 *Fair Princess* passenger survey was that cruising was seen 'as sexier than other holiday experiences' (P&O 1999).

The term *luxury* is so freely applied that it has become almost inseparable from 'cruise' itself, turning up incongruously in reference to vessels with one- and two-star classifications, in which the facilities could more accurately be described as rudimentary. Operators of higher rated vessels are thus obliged to grope for even greater superlatives, resorting to 'ultimate luxury' or 'unsurpassed luxury'. In the limited vocabulary of cruise marketing the term *exotic* also occurs with predictable regularity and seems to be used vaguely in the sense of 'a bit different' rather than its more precise meanings of 'foreign' or 'bizarre'. It generally serves to describe ports of call so familiar and so frequently visited these days that the application of the term to them is meaningless, although a century ago, when cruising itself was relatively novel and destinations were not glutted with regular invasions of visitors, it had greater significance.

For all the evocation of the exotic, however, there are times when a simple appeal to patriotic instincts works best. 'You're in good hands with our British officers', reads a picture caption in a P&O brochure. Patriotism may also underpin mealtimes and passenger activities: 'Do you favour a full English breakfast?' asks the same brochure, and later: 'To remind you that we're British, we offer bridge tournaments and, of course, traditional afternoon tea' (P&O 1993). Security and the comfort of the familiar are thus guaranteed. P&O (UK based), which also operates Princess Cruises (US based), prefers as a matter of policy to keep its British and American markets fairly distinct from each other, since the expectations of its passengers differ depending on their national origins.

Related to this rather old-world stance are the continual attempts by cruise marketers to evoke an earlier era, a misty time generally referred to as the 'golden age of travel', which might refer to the turn of the (nineteenth) century or to the supposed heyday of cruising, the 1920s. 'If the past is a foreign country', writes Lowenthal, 'nostalgia has made it the foreign country with the healthiest tourist trade of all' (Lowenthal 1985:4). Nostalgia as a marketing tool is better illustrated in cruising than in any other form of travel. We might note the repeated use of the term 'classic' by the now defunct Royal Viking Line (Royal Viking 1994); the use of colourful luggage labels that recall the 1920s in P&O and Cunard brochures; the interior decor of the motor/sail cruise ship *Club Med II*; and posters and brochure covers that abandon photography in favour of a return to the art design of many decades ago, with illustrations of the towering bow of *Queen Elizabeth 2* or some unnamed vessel, and that consciously recall much earlier representations of ships such as *Normandie* or *Queen Mary* (Cunard 1999; Infinity Cruises 1993).

Just as there is comfort in knowing that your officers, food and diversions are all familiarly British, so there is evidently a feeling of security in travelling in a kind of time capsule in an era that unreliable memory assures us was much safer than the present. Passenger perceptions of security, after all, play a major part in the appeal of cruising. However, if nostalgic contrivance doesn't fully convince, then the long-term players in this very competitive game are anxious to assert their own historical credentials. 'P&O, the company that invented cruising', reads that group's website. 'Cunard — advancing civilisation since 1840', claims a newspaper advertisement for that cruise line (Cunard 2000). P&O, perhaps more skilled at this exercise than most others, even offers to its passengers for lunch 'a *legendary* P&O curry' (P&O 1993, emphasis added).

■ **Figure 14.1**
*Cunard's
brochure for
its 2001
World Cruise
uses the
imagery of
an earlier
time.*

Source: *Courtesy Cunard Asia Pacific*

14.7 A CRUISE INDUSTRY OVERVIEW ......

The world cruise sector has grown at a remarkable rate in the past 20 years with 8.5 million passengers anticipated in 2000 and 11.5 million by 2005. The 1980s averaged 10 per cent annual growth; the 1990s slowed somewhat to about 7 per cent. Although North America now accounts for almost 80 per cent of total cruise passengers, this dominance is expected to decline as other markets mature. International cruise revenue is estimated at US$17 billion a year (Young 1999). The Caribbean is likely to maintain its position as the most popular cruise destination in the world because of the increasing preference for shorter cruises and an ever-younger market. The two- to five-day cruise accounts for some 37 per cent of the total product. The Southeast Asian markets grew significantly in the 1990s with the establishment of two Asian-owned cruise lines — Star Cruises and Sun Cruises — and the opening of dedicated cruise terminals in Singapore and Port Klang, Malaysia. Sun Cruises ceased business following the sinking of its ship in the Straits of Malacca in May 1999. In Europe, Britain, Germany, Italy and France are the most significant contributors to cruise passenger statistics.

A small number of operators dominate the cruise market and in light of recent takeovers and mergers this group is likely to become even more select. The Carnival Corporation is by far the largest. Royal Caribbean International and P&O Princess Cruises vie for second place. *Fielding's Worldwide Cruises* (Slater & Basch 1997) profiles 61 cruise lines, but there are many more. Some operate in very limited areas, many have only a single ship and others accommodate very specialist markets. Ships in the 500- to 1500-berth capacities account for 63 per cent of total berths. Newly launched ships are considerably larger. In the next few years some 60 ships currently on order will be seeking to fill their cabins, leading to speculation about oversupply and aggressive competition. Royal Caribbean International's (RCI) *Voyager of the Seas*, launched in 1999, is the biggest cruise ship ever built at 142 000 **gross registered tonnes** (**GRT**). It is 30 per cent larger than the previous title-holder, P&O Princess Cruises' *Grand Princess*, launched in 1998 at 109 000 GRT. *Voyager* accommodates 3000 passengers, who can experience rock climbing, ice-skating and a floating television station. Some 'floating resorts' have golf driving ranges and jogging tracks; they rival — some would say exceed — any land-based resort in facilities, fixtures and fittings. Other shipping lines are installing cyber cafes, cigar lounges and international museum–standard art collections. With a usual passenger to crew ratio of almost 2 to 1, ships like *Voyager* must be able to sustain up to 4500 people at any one time perhaps for several days before resupplying is possible.

There is strong competition to provide the biggest, the best, the most luxurious, the most exclusive or the most diverse facilities. The size of many new ships, however, also dictates their cruising routes: they are simply too big to pass through the Panama Canal into the Pacific and are therefore restricted to the Caribbean and Mediterranean 'ponds'. They have flatter hulls than their predecessors and this, coupled with increasingly tall superstructures, means they are unsuitable for dealing with oceans and seas in those regions of the world that experience severe winds and currents. The South Pacific is one such example.

Building bigger ships is a deliberate move on the part of cruise lines for whom economies of scale and the need to replace aging small ships drive the design. 'After all', one **cruise director** told the authors, 'the captain is the highest paid person on board and you only need one whether you have 200 or 2000 passengers!' The next development is to be floating condominiums. The concept has been around for several years but it is expected to become a reality in December 2001 with the launch of *The World of the Residensea*. With 110 privately owned residences, the 40 000 GRT, 12-deck vessel will operate on a continuous round-the-world itinerary. The idea of living at sea is not entirely new in the cruise business. Most of the big companies can point to examples of passengers who have taken one or two suites or cabins, decorated them according to their own taste and occupied them for many months, sometimes several years, as the ship sails on. With all the facilities and services ships provide, including fully equipped hospitals with excellent medical staff, this can be an interesting, if expensive, alternative to a possibly lonely life on land.

14.8 WHO CRUISES? A CONSUMER PROFILE

The profile of a cruise passenger shows someone over 45 years and most often female, who is well educated, married and retired; who invests considerable time in planning and preparation for the trip; who frequently uses on-board sports and gym facilities; who anticipates romance and elegance from the experience; and who prefers escorted tours and puts a strong emphasis on the safety and organisation that the cruise cocoon offers (Moscardo et al. 1996). Many cruise frequently. Overall satisfaction with the cruise experience is very high, with 89 per cent of passengers claiming they would cruise again. Younger passengers cruise for the party atmosphere provided by companies such as Carnival and P&O Australia, both of which have identified 'fun ships' for this market. The environment is rowdy and boisterous but tightly controlled by vigilant staff. Since it is life on board that matters to this market, the ports of call are often irrelevant. Older passengers are often more interested in the port experience. On board they play bridge, attend informative lectures, learn new skills such as investment or yoga, or quietly read on deck. They have the time and money to take longer cruises (Douglas & Douglas 1999b). On the Asian ships a high percentage of passengers cruise in order to access gambling facilities that are not readily — or legally — available in their home countries, while the ships provide many activities to occupy their families. The fastest growing segment is the very short two- to five-day cruise, although the six- to eight-day package remains the largest. The 25 to 40 age group is the fastest growing element of the market.

14.9 ECONOMIC IMPACTS OF CRUISE SHIPS

Having observed the apparently spectacular growth of cruise tourism during the past 20 years, a number of regions are keen to maximise the economic potential of this booming sector. Australia's National Cruise Shipping Strategy (Commonwealth Department of Tourism 1995), although criticised for its lack of specific direction (Douglas & Douglas 1999), represents one of the steps being taken to develop an efficient and viable cruise sector. Dwyer and Forsyth (1998) stress that policies that will achieve this goal depend on a full understanding of both benefits and costs. There must be a clear distinction between *impacts* and relevant *benefits and costs*. It is possible that a full analysis would conclude that cruising costs the economy rather more than it contributes in net benefits. Factors to be considered include the degree of foreign ownership of ships, the percentage of international passengers, the available infrastructure to service the requirements of both ships and passengers, and the role of ports on any schedule, whether ports of embarkation/disembarkation or ports of call. The distribution of benefits and costs regionally or nationally is also significant.

Expenditure on cruising falls into two categories (see table 14.1). Any analysis must take into account variables such as direct leakages resulting from the demand for imported goods and services; flow-on effects of wages paid to local crews; stimulated production resulting from higher demand for local goods and services; and impacts on other areas of the regional economy that may be quite unrelated to the cruise industry. Thus, both direct and indirect costs and benefits need to be identified.

■ Table 14.1
Cruise related expenditure

PASSENGER EXPENDITURE	OPERATOR EXPENDITURE	CREW EXPENDITURE
Airfares to/from base country Internal travel **Add-on expenditure:** Accommodation Meals Shopping Excursions **Port expenditure:** Meals Excursions and travel Shopping	**Port expenditures:** Government charges Port charges (include terminal) Towage **Provedoring** Stores and provedoring Bunkering Services (waste disposal, water)	Local crew Port expenditure by foreign crew Ship maintenance Marketing in base country **Taxes:** Income tax Customs duties Departure taxes

Source: *Adapted from Dwyer and Forsyth (1998)*

It has been estimated that stopover passengers on an international cruise spend $A206 on a single day's visit to an Australian port. Fly/cruise passengers on an Australia-only cruise spend $A859. Fly/cruise passengers joining a foreign cruise at an Australian port spend $A426. A number of ports outside the Sydney hub have been developing their own strategies to maximise cruising to their state. Port authorities in Victoria, for example, estimate that cruising contributes $A1.2 million to the local economy per cruise ship visit. Norwegian Capricorn Line (NCL) claimed it contributed $A47 million annually to the national economy while maintaining that this figure excluded passenger expenditure in port. The divergence in these figures indicates how important it is to incorporate a wide range of variables into an economic analysis of cruising.

The Caribbean, accounting for 50 per cent of capacity in 1999, is the most popular cruise ship destination. Its convenient proximity to North America makes it an easily accessible 'pleasure periphery' for that market. Miami has ensured its place as the major hub from which most ships into the region operate, with up to 30 departures a week. Other major destinations include the Mediterranean (15 per cent), Alaska (8 per cent) trans–Panama Canal (6 per cent), west Mexico (5 per cent) and northern Europe (4 per cent). The length of the cruise season in these locations, however, is determined by climatic conditions. Alaska and northern Europe, for example, are very much northern summer destinations. During the northern winter off-season several companies direct their ships to the South Pacific for the southern summer. Unfortunately, this is not the best time to cruise in the Pacific because of the likelihood of storms and accompanying rough seas.

14.11 ASIA–PACIFIC CRUISE DEVELOPMENTS ···················

The strong growth during the 1990s of the Asian cruise industry, particularly for Asian passengers, has interested industry watchers, especially in light of the widespread Asian financial crisis of the late 1990s and the recurring political unrest in the region. The Asia–Pacific region attracts 13.5 per cent of the world's cruise passengers. Britain, Australia and the United States are being targeted with fly/cruise packages to Asian waters, particularly with the introduction of week-long fly/cruise packages by Star. Significant investment in infrastructure prompted by strong growth (see table 14.2) has ensured that Singapore will remain the hub for Asian cruise operators. It processes more than 32 per cent of the region's passenger share; Hong Kong and Sydney each account for 4 per cent. However, it should be noted that these official statistics include those who use the very short gambling cruises, which distorts the picture somewhat. The Port of Singapore Authority (PSA) has announced plans for further upgrading and expansion early in the new millennium, which will certainly help to maintain significant contributions to the local economy by cruise ships and their passengers (Peisley 1999).

■ Table 14.2
Growth of Singapore Port

YEAR	SHIPS VISITINGS	NUMBER OF CALLS	PASSENGERS HANDLED	SHIPS HOMEPORTED
1991	29	276	131 491	1
1998	54	1691	1 050 000	10

Source: *Adapted from Singh (1999)*

■14.11.1 Star Cruises

Star Cruises has been one of the great success stories in recent Asian tourism development. It was founded in 1993 by the Genting International Group, a Malaysian consortium whose primary interests are in property and gaming; Malaysian interests still retain majority ownership. The gaming connection also helps to explain the rapid growth of the company. In the early years the principal product was short cruises out of Singapore primarily to allow Singaporeans and other Asians to access the on-board gaming facilities. However, Star rapidly outgrew that market, which is well catered to by a variety of small companies that purchase ships other companies are retiring and convert them to floating casinos. Star has also allocated two of its ships specifically to the MICE (Meetings, Incentives, Conventions and Events) market, including catering to the demands of corporations and their timetables.

Despite dire predictions of failure, Star has excelled in opening up the cruise experience to people from ASEAN (Association of South East Asian Nations) countries, which provide 50 per cent of its market. It has also needed to invest substantially in appropriate regional infrastructure. Cargo carriers and cruise ships do not mix well; while there were abundant facilities for the former, the latter had to severely compromise the comfort and safety of passengers when using the same berthing facilities. Star responded by spending US$40 million at Port Klang, the port for Kuala Lumpur, Malaysia, and US$12 million at Langkawi, Malaysia. Further developments are also planned for Phuket, Thailand (Peisley 1999:6). In March 2000 Star Cruises acquired Norwegian Cruise Line and its subsidiary Orient Line, bringing its total fleet to twenty ships. Predictions are for continued strong growth in demand for Asian cruises by Asian cruisers. The emergence of a large middle class with disposable income in both China and India presents great opportunities to increase target markets. Star has seized upon the opportunities to tailor the cruise product to meet the specific requirements of the various segments within the Asian market and the increased maturity of these segments. The all-inclusive pricing structure of a cruise holiday has great appeal among people whose currencies were so devalued in the late 1990s and will also assist intraregional cruising to continue its growth pattern.

The Japanese market remains elusive. Traditionally, the Japanese have preferred to cruise on Japanese-owned and -operated ships and, unlike the growing preference for the cruise experience in other Asian markets, Japanese interest has remained more or less static since the mid 1990s, resting at about 200 000 passengers annually. In contrast, Koreans have taken to cruising enthusiastically, although they too prefer nationally owned and operated ships. As a move towards political cooperation, the Hyundai company's joint cruise venture with the North Korean Asia Pacific Peace Committee must rate very highly. Using Star ships and expertise, the Korean cruises travel from Tonghae in South Korea to Mt Keumgang in North Korea, a traditionally sacred area for all Koreans where extensive tourist facilities are being developed. While the company has plans to sail beyond Korean waters, the specific cultural requirements of the Koreans themselves may determine the success of such expansion (Peisley 1999:13–15).

The Australian cruise sector has the potential to grow from its currently quite small base. Australia hosts 1.5 per cent of international cruise passengers; 3 per cent of Australian holiday-makers choose to cruise (some 100 000 Australians have cruised at some time) and the industry is worth about $200 million a year (Young 1999). The biggest obstacle to growth is Australia's distance from major cruise markets. Asia is close but indications to date are that the Asian market prefers its own product. North American passengers of fly/cruise options initially face a long flight and the psychological barrier to that needs to be overcome. Northern Europeans, including Britons, have an equally long flight although they may have family or friends in Australia with whom their stay can be extended.

P&O Cruises has monopolised the Australian market since 1988 when it purchased the famous *Fairstar*. The previous owner, Sitmar, had been operating year-long cruises out of Sydney into the South Pacific since 1974. *Fairstar* was finally retired in 1997. The legendary 'fun ship', a nickname that helps to explain its reputation, was replaced by the equally venerable *Fair Princess*.

■ **Figure 14.2** *P&O's veteran* Fair Princess *at its most popular port of call, Vila in Vanuatu*

Source: *Norman Douglas*

In November 2000 another replacement, the younger *Sky Princess*, renamed *Pacific Sky*, became P&O's southern flagship. Although the company has tried hard to shed its 'fun ship' reputation, this has proved more difficult than expected. Stories still abound of young men expecting to embark with only the T-shirt and shorts they were wearing and a carton of beer as their luggage. P&O sources say that the ambience of *Fairstar* will be revived on *Sky Princess*. A challenge to P&O's monopoly was taken up in Sydney in December 1998. Norwegian Capricorn Line, an Australian initiative, arrived with

Norwegian Star to begin a year-long cruise program that sought to include more Australian ports and venture into Indonesian ports to enlarge the Australian cruise atlas. The company set its sights on an upmarket passenger profile but did not attract enough international cruisers to maintain this position. The question of whether the Australian market could sustain two ships permanently based in Australia was answered in March 2000 when, after a change in the ownership of Norwegian Capricorn's parent company, the new owners, Star Cruises, decided to terminate the Australia-based company and reposition the ship, a decision that took effect in October of that year.

BREAKTHROUGH TOURISM
Cruising Victoria

From the post–World War II period until the 1960s Station Pier, Melbourne, regularly welcomed European migrants arriving to start a new life in Australia. Then followed two decades during which a passenger ship was a rare sight in Melbourne, with no more than three or four visits a year. However, in 1997–98 the number of visits jumped to a record 19, bringing an estimated 20 000 cruise tourists (passengers and crew) to the state.

Those responsible for developing the cruise market in Victoria say that this growth was a reflection of the global activity by shipping operators actively seeking out new ports of call to broaden their product base. During the 1998–99 season, 26 ships called with some 35 000 tourists. With cruise companies organising itineraries with a lead time of up to two years, Melbourne continues to attract annual visits from more than 20 ships. Since visits are estimated to inject, on average, more than $1 million into the state's economy, the benefits are obvious. The cruise season in Victoria coincides with the southern hemisphere summer and a number of major events in Melbourne. The season begins in November, and the first ship arrives in time for the Spring Racing Carnival. It continues through January, with the Australian Tennis Open, to March, with the Australian Grand Prix, and ends in April or May.

Visiting cruise ships fall into two main categories: large cruise liners (1200 or more passengers and 500 or more crew) and boutique cruise vessels (800 or fewer passengers and 300 or fewer crew). Passengers tend to be mature-aged travellers, generally from Europe and the United States, visiting this region during the northern hemisphere winter. A lesser-known type of visit is that by vessels of the Royal Australian Navy (RAN) and other navies. These visits, which often coincide with Melbourne's major events and public holidays, also contribute significantly to the state's economy. About 28 navy ships visit Victoria each year. While cruise ships usually stay only one day, navy ship stays average between three and five days. An economic evaluation undertaken by the RAN for one vessel revealed a direct spending figure of approximately $900 000, based on bunkering, provedoring and crew expenditure.

(continued)

In early 1997, following major reforms and the restructuring of Victoria's ports, the responsibility for overall coordination and management of the cruise support business was transferred to the Department of Infrastructure. This department subsequently convened the Melbourne Cruise Ship Committee, which has taken up the role of coordinating the efforts of the industry, service providers and government agencies. Together they launched the Victorian Cruise Shipping Strategy in February 1999. The broad aim of the strategy is to increase the number of cruise ships and passengers visiting Victoria for the economic benefit of the state. Five broad areas of action include improving the infrastructure required by both ships and passengers; increasing the efficiency and competitiveness of services; developing a marketing strategy that emphasises Melbourne's strengths; implementing continual monitoring of the cruise industry, both internationally and nationally, in order to anticipate its needs; and, finally, capitalising on new opportunities such as extending the cruise season and opening up new itineraries.

Source: *Cruising Victoria: The Victorian Cruise Shipping Strategy 1998–99 to 2000–01. Melbourne: Victoria Department of Infrastructure.*

14.13 SUMMARY

Cruising is a complex phenomenon that, while representing tourism's most dynamic growth sector, remains essentially a special interest. This quality is illustrated by the varieties of very specific activity that fall into the general category of 'cruising'. The growth of ocean cruising can be traced back to the 1840s and the pioneer efforts of P&O. The slump in cruising that took place in the 1960s, following the rapid development of large-bodied long distance aircraft, was overcome by new management and operational practices that saw the emergence of the 'floating resort' concept in cruise vessels. This trend led eventually to the mega-cruisers of the late twentieth and early twenty-first centuries. However, it also led to a reaction among cruise enthusiasts against the impersonal nature of such vessels. As a result, demand has increased for alternative types of cruise experience such as small ship ocean cruising, expeditionary vessels, freighter cruises and so on. Demand has increased also for theme cruises that cater to the needs of very specific interest groups.

The typical cruise passenger is a middle-aged female, well educated and financially secure. Perceptions of security, comfort and romance play a large part in decision making among cruise passengers and are dominant features of the marketing programs of cruise companies, large and small. These perceptions are evidently corroborated by the cruise experience, since a great majority of passengers say they would cruise again. Although academic research on cruising is not extensive, the available literature provides valuable insights into such aspects as cruise history, economic impacts and consumer behaviour and motivations.

The geographical spread of cruising is limited by the size of the new 'mega-ships' and their inability to call at ports lacking the necessary infrastructure to accommodate their bulk or the numbers of passengers they carry. However, this presents opportunities for smaller ship cruise companies and expeditionary vessels of limited size. In the East Asia region Singapore and Hong Kong remain the major cruising hubs, while in Australia and the South Pacific Sydney, because of its convenient location and its improved facilities, is likely to continue as the centre of interest for both permanently based and seasonally operated vessels.

Questions

14.1 Obtain three cruise brochures/catalogues from your local travel agent and examine them for content. Comment on such features as the use of language and the selection of images to describe both the ship and the ports of call.

14.2 What are the aspects of cruising that might persuade/dissuade people from going on a cruise?

14.3 Discuss the major differences between an ocean cruise and a typical land-based tour package of similar duration.

14.4 What problems are faced by Australia-based operators of (a) ocean cruises and (b) river cruises?

14.5 What factors might limit the growth of cruising in the Asia–Pacific region?

14.6 Several cruise lines and agencies have Internet sites that post 'employment opportunities'. Examine one or more of these and discuss whether or not you would be attracted by the prospect of working on a cruise ship, giving reasons for your decision.

14.7 How would you estimate the economic impacts of the arrival of a cruise ship in (a) a small Pacific island, (b) Sydney and (c) Singapore?

REFERENCES

Bearup, G. 1999. 'Terror on the Good Ship Schoolie'. *Sydney Morning Herald*, 8 December, p. 3.

Bratton, S. (Ed.). 1996. *Cunard Newsletter*, 5 November, p. 2.

Bull, A. 1996. 'The Economics of Cruising: An Application to the Short Ocean Cruise Market'. *Journal of Tourism Studies* 7 (2): 28–35.

Commonwealth Department of Tourism. 1995. *National Cruise Shipping Strategy.* Canberra: Commonwealth Department of Tourism.

Cruise Lines International Association. 1995. *The Cruise Industry: An Overview.* New York: Cruise Lines International Association.

Cunard. 1999. *QE2 Transatlantic.* December, cover.

Cunard. 2000. *Sydney Morning Herald,* 5 February.

Dale, C & Robinson, N. 1998. 'Bermuda, Tourism and the Visiting Cruise Sector: Strategies for Sustained Growth'. *Journal of Vacation Marketing* 5 (4): 333–9.

Dickinson B. & Vladimir, A. 1997. *Selling the Sea: An Inside Look at the Cruise Industry.* New York: John Wiley & Sons.

Douglas, N. & Douglas, N. 1997. 'P&O's Pacific'. *Journal of Tourism Studies* 7 (2): 2–14.

Douglas, N. & Douglas, N. 1999a. 'The Australian National Cruise Shipping Strategy 1995: A Rowboat Sent to Guide the Liners?' In Heung, V., Ap, J. & Wong, K. (Eds.). *Tourism 2000: Asia Pacific's Role in the New Millennium.* Conference Proceedings, Asia Pacific Tourism Association. Volume 2. Hong Kong, 23–25 August, pp. 800–9.

Douglas, N. & Douglas, N. 1999b. 'Cruise Consumer Behaviour: A Comparative Study'. In Pizam, A. & Mansfeld, Y. (Eds.). *Consumer Behaviour in Travel and Tourism.* New York: Haworth Hospitality Press, pp. 369–92.

Douglas, N. & Douglas, N. 2000. 'Internet Tourism Sites: Cruising'. *International Journal of Tourism Research* 2: 1–2.

Dwyer, L. & Forsyth, P. 1996. 'Economic Impacts of Cruise Tourism in Australia'. *Journal of Tourism Studies* 7 (2): 36–43.

Dwyer, L. & Forsyth, P. 1998. 'Economic Significance of Cruise Tourism'. *Annals of Tourism Research* 25 (2): 393–415.

Hobson, J. S. P. 1993. 'Analysis of the US Cruise Line Industry'. *Tourism Management* 14 (4): 453–62.

Howarth, D. & Howarth, S. 1986. *The Story of P&O.* London: Weidenfeld & Nicolson.

Indian Pacific. 2000. Good Weekend Magazine, *Sydney Morning Herald,* 19 February, p. 49.

Infinity Cruises. 1993. *The Cruise Book,* cover.

Lowenthal, D. 1985. *The Past is a Foreign Country.* Cambridge, UK: Cambridge University Press.

McAuley, R. 1997. *The Liners: A Voyage of Discovery.* London: Boxtree.

Morrison, A. M., Yang, C.-H., O'Leary, J. T. & Nadkarni, N. 1996. 'Comparative Profiles of Travellers on Cruises and Land-based Resort Vacations'. *Journal of Tourism Studies* 7 (2): 15–27.

Moscardo, G., Morrison, A. M., Cai, L., Nadkarni, N. & O'Leary, J. T. 1996. 'Tourist Perspectives on Cruising: Multi-dimensional Scaling Analyses of Cruising and Other Holiday Types'. *Journal of Tourism Studies* 7 (2): 54–63.

Pedelaborde, D. 1997. 'Anatomy of a Global Cruise Industry: Ultra-luxury Cruising for the "Been There, Done That" Crowd'. In *Seatrade Pacific Cruise Convention Conference Papers,* 3–5 November.

Peisley, T. 1999. 'The Cruise Business in Asia Pacific'. *Travel and Tourism Analyst* 2: 1–20.

P&O. 1993. *P&O World Voyages.* Sydney: P&O Holidays.

P&O. 1999. *Fair Princess Facts* (http://www.fairprincess.com.au).

Ritter, W. & Schaffer, C. 1998. 'Cruise-tourism: A Chance of Sustainability'. *Tourism Recreation Research* 23 (1): 65–71.

Royal Viking Line. 1994. *Royal Viking Line Cruise Atlas.* Coral Gables: Royal Viking Line.

Showalter, G. R. 1994. 'Cruise Ships and Private Islands in the Caribbean'. *Journal of Travel and Tourism Marketing* 3 (4): 117–8.

Singh, A. 1999. 'Growth and Development of the Cruise Line Industry in Southeast Asia'. *Asia Pacific Journal of Tourism Research* 3 (2): 24–31.

Slater, S. & Basch, H. 1997. *Fielding's Worldwide Cruises 1997.* Redondo Beach, USA: Fielding Worldwide Inc.

Teye, V. & Leclerc, D. 1998. 'Product and Service Delivery Satisfaction among North American Cruise Passengers'. *Tourism Management* 19 (2): 153–60.

Wood, R. E. 2000. 'Caribbean Cruise Tourism: Globalisation at Sea'. *Annals of Tourism Research* 27 (2): 345–70.

Young, P. 1999. 'Cruise: Continuing the Dynamic Growth'. In *Proceedings of the 1999 Cruise Industry Conference.* Sydney, 16–17 August, np.

http://www.bluelagooncruises.com

http://www.expeditions.com

http://www.fairprincess.com.au

http://www.kastawayisland.com

http://www.porthole.com

....

Blue Lagoon Cruises

The Fiji-based company Blue Lagoon Cruises is an outstanding regional example of successful small ship, special interest cruising, catering for visitors who seek an experience of smaller Pacific islands and their inhabitants. The company was founded in 1950 by Trevor Withers, a young New Zealander. With his friend Harold Gatty, an Australian aviator, Withers had come to Fiji some years earlier hoping to establish a tuna fishing industry. Fiji, then a British Crown Colony, had relatively little tourism. Visitors generally transited Fiji on their way to somewhere else, either by air or by sea.

Withers and Gatty set up headquarters in Suva and began to assess the potential for tuna fishing using two small boats. Fijian protocol and tradition demanded that they make a special visit to the islands to pay their respects to the local chiefs before proceeding with their venture. At Yalobi village on the island of Waya in the Yasawa Group, Withers found that the chief and his people could speak neither English nor a dialect understood by his crew. On the nearby island of Waya Lailai they enlisted a young villager as an interpreter. With his help, Withers obtained the full support of the Yasawa people for his fishing venture and established firm friendships with the chiefs and the people of the Yasawa Islands. Later this became crucial to Blue Lagoon Cruises.

Four years later Withers and Gatty were obliged to admit that their hopes of establishing a tuna fishing industry in Fiji had come to nothing. But both had become fond of Fiji and decided to remain. Gatty went on to establish Fiji Airways, the forerunner to Fiji's national airline, Air Pacific. Withers began to consider taking visitors on cruises through the Yasawa Islands. His enthusiasm for the new project was not shared by many. Tourists were still few. Determined to realise his aim, Withers returned to the Yasawa Islands to request again the support of the chief and his people. To his delight, they met his cruise proposal with promises of cooperation. Pondering a suitable name, Withers recalled his association with the original version of *Blue Lagoon* filmed partly on location in the Yasawa Islands in 1948. He had lent a hand on the set and had met the English star, Jean Simmons. The name 'Blue Lagoon' seemed totally appropriate for the enterprise he envisaged.

Withers purchased his first boat from the New Zealand Civil Aviation Authorities in Fiji and christened it *Turaga Levu* ('Great Chief', Withers' local nickname). The reconfigured boat was launched in Suva's Walu Bay. The first cruise date was scheduled and advertised — and brought a complete lack of response. As the hour of its first departure drew near it appeared that *Turaga Levu* would sail empty. Withers, though tempted to cancel, was reluctant to disappoint the islanders awaiting its arrival. He invited six Fijian men on the wharf who had previously assisted him to become *Turaga Levu*'s first cruise passengers. For the first month, Withers sailed every Monday, often carrying Fijians to their Yasawa villages but still without any paying passengers. Ten days into his second month of operation he secured his first charter.

During the following three months, however, only 27 passengers were carried on the cruise. Facing bankruptcy, Withers made a final gamble. After obtaining an agreement with airlines flying the Pacific to undertake a joint promotion in North America, he sold his possessions for £7000 to finance a whirlwind visit to travel agents in the United States and Canada. The gamble succeeded. By 1966 Blue Lagoon Cruises had established an international reputation and Withers, by then suffering poor health, retired after selling the business. He died in 1981, by which time Blue Lagoon had changed hands at least twice and its vessels were being purpose built.

As do other tourism enterprises in the area, Blue Lagoon supports the Yasawa Islands community financially, contributing to the island children's education and development projects, including the construction of schools and assistance with school fees and necessary books, uniforms and medical clinics. The company is an important factor in the cash economy of the Yasawas, providing the opportunity for the people of the islands to earn revenue through the company's payments to access beaches and visit villages for performances of traditional Fijian entertainment and for the sale of shells and artefacts. The company also assists freely in times of hurricanes, maritime accidents and medical emergencies.

In 1986 the company enlarged its investments, purchasing freehold title to a 23.5 hectare plantation on the island of Nanuya Lailai in the Yasawas, as well as a commercial property adjoining the company's Lautoka headquarters. By 1990 the company's facilities had become too small to support its corporate needs effectively. Construction of a new F$3 million headquarters complex in Lautoka commenced in 1991. Formally opened in 1993, it houses a passenger pre-boarding lounge, a small cafe, a bar, a boutique, executive offices, engineering workshops, stores and refrigeration facilities, shore galley, staff association office and training rooms.

In early 2000 the Blue Lagoon fleet consisted of four vessels with a total passenger capacity of 230. The largest, *Mystique Princess*, has a capacity of 72. The company reports that its passenger base continues to grow at a rate of about 10 per cent annually but declines to provide actual figures. Company staff total 176, most of them Fijians. Regular in-house training is given and food and beverage training is continuous. Other training courses include upgrades in engineering, international safety management practices, first aid, firefighting and cooking. Employees also participate in courses conducted by the Fiji National Training Council, which range from those concerning seamanship to aspects of hotel catering. With company support, the company's seamen and engineers study at the Fiji Marine College.

Blue Lagoon Cruises depart from Lautoka, Fiji's second major port, to cruise the Mamanuca and Yasawa groups of islands. Itineraries depend on the duration of cruises, which varies between 3 days/2 nights and 7 days/6 nights, and like all cruises may be modified owing to weather or even social factors, although certain islands — the large Naviti, for example, or the company-owned Nanuya Lailai — are more frequently visited. Vessels are of small ship 'state of the art' quality.

Passengers reflect the company's international promotion policy. A typical cruise might include Americans, Canadians, varied Europeans, New Zealanders and Australians, the latter still representing Fiji's largest single market. Weddings may be conducted on board, but not spontaneously — advance notice is required and special tariffs apply. Shore activities for passengers (generally included in the fare) are leisurely and may include visits to villages, shell and artefact markets, beach barbecues, swimming/snorkelling and crew versus passenger volleyball, which Fijians play with robust determination. The vessels cruise overnight so that passengers may maximise their time ashore during the day. Evening entertainment on board is provided by members of the crew or by village *meke* (dance) groups.

Sources: *Blue Lagoon Cruises; Fiji Visitors Bureau*

Questions

1 What factors contributed to the apparent success of Blue Lagoon Cruises?

2 What operational or management difficulties might such an enterprise face?

3 How does the enterprise benefit the wider community?

4 Compare and contrast Blue Lagoon Cruises with another small ship cruise company of your choice, in Australia or elsewhere, drawing particular attention to such aspects as management practices, marketing methods and environmental policies.

Kay Dimmock
and
Margaret Tiyce

CHAPTER 15

Festivals and events: *celebrating special interest tourism*

LEARNING OBJECTIVES

After reading this chapter, you will have an appreciation of:

- the terms festival and event and the community-based festival or event
- why communities choose to host festivals and events
- how festivals and events are linked to special interest tourism (SIT)
- why people attend festivals and events
- the impacts festivals and events can have on communities
- who festival and event stakeholders are
- some of the management challenges of hosting festivals and events.

15.1 INTRODUCTION

Festivals and events are important contributors to the wellbeing of communities. They are also an important sector of SIT. This chapter discusses the character and role of festivals and events, particularly community-based festivals and events. The chapter is designed to assist you to define the terms *festival* and *event* and provide an understanding of the links with SIT. We examine the reasons why a community might elect to host a festival or event and why people are motivated to attend. As you read through this chapter you will also gain an appreciation of the benefits and costs that festivals and events can bring to a community, as well as a realistic view of the challenges that confront event organisers.

15.2 WHAT ARE FESTIVALS AND EVENTS?

Historically, we know there have always been reasons for people to come together to celebrate, to demonstrate, to worship, to honour, to remember, to socialise, to relive. The desire to participate in festivals and events is not new or specific to any particular culture, religion or community group. However, academic interest and research on festivals and events has grown considerably in the last fifteen years (Schneider & Backman 1996), most likely because of the number of public celebrations held and the social and economic contribution that events can make to society.

The literature defines festivals as *themed public celebrations* (Getz 1993:945). They can include celebrations of sporting pursuits, such as a swimming carnival, football match or gymkhana. Alternatively, the celebration may involve a display of fine art that brings people together to honour the work of an individual. Whatever the activity or theme, collective celebration is a key element.

What is also common to definitions of festivals and events is that they are of *limited duration*; that is, they are not continuous. They may differ in size, volume and impact, and the rationale for hosting them might be different, but they are all of limited duration. The limited duration consolidates and focuses the complete bundle of experiences and celebrations into a limited time frame. It may take a year's work, for example, to prepare for a celebration that lasts a week, a few days or even a few hours. The New Year's Eve fireworks displays in Australia's capital cities and other regional centres are examples.

More specific terms define particular types of festivals and events. **Special events** are one-time or infrequently occurring events (McDonnell, Allen & O'Toole 1999). Special events can include both *mega* and **hallmark events** that are recognised by their large size and scale. *Mega events* may affect entire communities, countries or continents. They often require enormous resources, particularly financial and human resources. Examples of mega events include the Olympic Games and world fairs. Somewhat smaller in scale, *hallmark events*, have special significance for a community or region. They may be defined as major one-time or recurring events of limited duration often developed primarily to enhance awareness, appeal and the profitability of a tourism destination over the short term (McDonnell et al. 1999). Examples of hallmark events include the Sydney Gay and Lesbian Mardi Gras, the Foster's Australasian Country Music Festival at Tamworth and capital city festivals, such as the Sydney Festival and the festivals of Melbourne and Adelaide.

Other events occur more regularly than the large extravaganzas of mega and hallmark events; they may be much smaller, and appeal to a much smaller **market segment**. They may not be called a festival or event. Instead, they may be known as a carnival, tournament, contest, competition, exhibition, fete or fiesta. This type of *community-based event* will be the focus of this chapter.

Community-based festivals and events (also called *local events*) originate, as the name suggests, within a sector of the community that has a need or desire to celebrate features of its way of life or history. They, too, are of limited duration but are generally held more regularly than special events. The event may be held annually to coincide with a crop harvest or floral bloom, such as the Rose and Garden Festival in Manawatu, New Zealand (Ryan 1995). Alternatively, the event may be held more often, such as an honouring of the changing solar and lunar patterns. In this instance we identify with celebrations surrounding the summer and winter solstice or the full moon celebrations in Kho Panghan, Thailand, which are now popular internationally. Similarly, the Grafton Jacaranda Festival and the Alstonville Tibouchina Festival in northern New South Wales are examples of how the cycle of the seasons and the celebration of flowerings can become a focus for celebrating community life (Dunstan 1994).

■ Table 15.1
Typology of events

TYPE	FEATURES	EXAMPLE
Mega	• Affects entire communities, countries and continents • Limited duration • Requires enormous resources	• Olympic Games
Hallmark	• Large in size and scale • Significant for community or region • One time or recurring • Limited duration • Enhances awareness, appeal and profitability of a destination over the short term	• Sydney Gay and Lesbian Mardi Gras • Foster's Australasian Country Music Festival at Tamworth • Festivals of Sydney, Melbourne and Adelaide
Community-based (local)	• Smaller in scale and size • Limited duration • Held more regularly than mega or hallmark events • Celebrates features of a community's way of life	• Grafton Jacaranda Festival • Kho Panghan Full Moon Festival • Lygon Street Festa, Melbourne • Madcat Women's International Film and Video Festival, San Francisco

Many events will be spontaneous celebrations, such as art exhibitions, music festivals or community fundraising ventures. A cooperative approach may lead to an annual calendar of local events providing ongoing and complementary reasons to celebrate the features and talents of a community.

Community based festivals and events may be defined as themed public occasions designed to occur for a limited duration that celebrate valued aspects of a community's way of life.

15.3 WHY COMMUNITIES HOST FESTIVALS AND EVENTS

There are many tangible and intangible reasons why communities host festivals and events (Backman et al. 1995). These can extend to social, political, cultural, economic or environmental motivations. Often a number of reasons are important (Frisby & Getz 1989; Getz 1993).

A festival or event may be organised for any of the following reasons:
- celebration and identity
- external revenue generation
- internal revenue generation
- recreation or socialisation
- agriculture
- natural resources
- tourism
- culture and education (Mayfield & Crompton 1995; Dunstan 1994).

One overt reason is to generate revenue. Local organisations may seek to enhance the quality of life of the community through fundraising ventures aimed at improving local facilities and resources. Events that attract tourists can provide additional economic opportunities. External income generated in the host economy may contribute substantially through increased visitor expenditures, length of stay, increased taxes collected and local employment (Backman et al. 1995; Getz 1991). However, most events are organised by non-profit or governmental groups and this suggests other important reasons.

Celebration of the traditions, cultures and way of life of the community is a very strong motivator. Festivals can celebrate identity, both personal and social, and reinforce community pride (Dunstan 1994; Frisby & Getz 1989). They provide the context and process for forging and reinforcing bonds between community members. Events provide strong sociocultural benefits and psychological experiences, which may be the driving force behind the event development.

Showcasing special community features such as agriculture, arts, sport or the natural environment are examples of celebration of community or individual achievement, uniqueness and identity. Consider the local agricultural show that takes place annually in most towns across Australia. Or think of the abundance of arts festivals, such as the Madcat Women's International

Film and Video Festival, in San Francisco, which highlights dedication and commitment to art and performance (Erickson 2000). Each event publicly and collectively celebrates personal and community achievement, identity and pride.

Celebrations may also be intended to educate participants and thereby preserve and enhance the culture, society or natural environment (Uysal, Gahan & Martin 1993). One good example of this is Groote Eylandt's Inter-tribal Festival, in the Gulf of Carpentaria, where nearly 1000 Aborigines gather regularly to celebrate traditional dance, song and story. Participants come from as far afield as the desert regions of Western Australia, the Northern Territory, Cape York Peninsula and Bathurst and Melville islands. This event is not only an important celebration of Aboriginal culture and identity, but also an attempt to preserve and enhance it (Hancock 1993).

Similarly, in Montana in the United States a three-day Powwow and Cultural Rendezvous attracts up to 4000 visitors for a celebration of the culture of indigenous Americans and western settlers. The event is based on the traditional theme of powwows and is a celebration of culture and of bringing people together. Traditional rituals and activities are presented and visitor participation encouraged. Although the essence of this event is to help to establish and develop the cultural themes being celebrated, it also provides revenue for local businesses and awareness and education of traditions (Anon 1998).

Festivals and events provide communities with opportunities to celebrate their way of life and their identity. Where these festivals are socially, culturally or environmentally unique, they may have added appeal to special interest tourists.

15.4 FESTIVALS, EVENTS AND SIT — THE LINK

A contemporary theme is the role of festivals and events as a form of SIT. Community festivals and events are primarily held by communities for communities. However, they are becoming increasingly popular as a form of SIT (Getz in Uysal, Gahan & Martin 1993). Festivals and events have the potential to provide SIT experiences because of the strong:

- use of novel and unique themes and activities
- emphasis on authentic forms of culture and history
- integration of elements including participation and education (Hall 1993).

Features of festivals and events that may make them appealing include:

- *satisfying multiple roles:* such as tourism, heritage, community development, urban renewal or cultural awareness
- *satisfying basic needs:* physical, interpersonal and psychological needs can be satisfied along with leisure and travel needs

- *festival spirit:* sharing values, developing a sense of belonging, enhancing joyfulness, ambience and revelry through interaction and the unpredictable
- *uniqueness:* the creation of unique sights and experiences
- *authenticity:* of indigenous or historical cultural values and processes
- *tradition:* a celebration of history or past ways of life
- *hospitality:* sharing of values and cultures
- *tangibility:* the physical structures and activities of the event
- *symbolism:* honouring cultural rituals and their special significance
- *convenience:* provide spontaneous, often unplanned leisure opportunities
- *theming:* spirit, tradition, cultural values or branding
- *flexibility:* accommodate market and environmental needs (Getz 1991).

Attention to these features can produce an event that caters successfully for special interest tourists and locals. An emerging feature is the opportunity for special interest tourists to follow a circuit of festivals on a particular theme and hosted across different parts of the country. This fulfils a special interest and the desire to travel. It provides economic, social and cultural benefits for host communities. An example is the Cowboy Poetry gatherings held across the United States. Based on traditional folk festivals, these events present the culture of traditional cowboys and ranch life documented through rudimentary forms of poetry. This form of SIT is particularly attractive to the niche market of contemporary cowboy subculture (Walle 1994).

15.5 WHY DO PEOPLE ATTEND FESTIVALS AND EVENTS?

Festivals and events have wide appeal among both locals and visitors, particularly given the wide range of experiences events can provide. Opportunities for leisure, entertainment, relaxation and socialising with others are common motivations for attending (Schneider & Backman 1996). For special interest tourists, the opportunity to learn about and participate in unique activities and environments is also important (Hall 1993). It is often the very uniqueness of community festivals and events that make then so appealing.

Pursuit of *leisure, relaxation and recreation* is a major reason for attending. Leisure is a subjective state — that is, it is different for each of us (Samdahl 1992). It could mean participating in the annual City to Surf marathon in Sydney, or enjoying the theatre and music of the Festival of Sydney. Each provides opportunities to enjoy leisurely and relaxing experiences beyond our everyday lives (Haggard & Williams 1992).

Escape from routine and pressures of everyday life is another well-recognised reason. It may be a festival in the local community or another town that allows participants to step outside their routine at least for a short while. Whether sailing in the Sydney to Hobart yacht race, visiting Birdsville for the annual races or visiting the local community market on a Sunday afternoon, escape is an integral part of attending festivals and events.

Observation of and *participation* in the way of life of others is a strong motivation for attending events. The opportunity to witness different cultures, traditions, crafts, environments or lives is a feature driving the popularity of both community festivals and SIT. For a short time tourists become part of another community or culture. They do what the locals do with relative ease and minimal involvement or commitment. It may mean witnessing displays of physical ability, such as a woodchopping contest at the local agricultural show, or visiting Nimbin during the annual Mardi Grass festival to witness an alternative culture. In confirming an interest in seeing or participating in aspects of the event, visitors are supporting the values of the host community, its culture and way of life.

Socialising is an important human need. People attend festivals and events to be part of a group, enhance family togetherness, meet with friends, extend social contacts and be with others who are enjoying themselves (Mohr et al. 1993). Festival and event marketing should promote opportunities for socialisation, relaxation and leisure. Participants attending the six-day Fraser Island Fishing Expo, in Queensland, enjoy extensive relaxation and leisure time and confirm that the greatest motivation for attending the event is to socialise outside their own group (Raybould 1998).

Opportunities to *learn* are important, especially for special interest tourists (Hall 1993). They may wish to increase their awareness and understanding of alternative cultures or learn new skills through participating in seminars and workshops. The annual Woodford Folk Festival in south-east Queensland provides an opportunity both to relax and be entertained and to participate in a wide range of workshops and learning situations that allow visitors enriched learning experiences. Visitors enjoy wide choices including education, recreation, social and cultural experiences (McDonnell et al. 1999).

Nostalgia is a theme in many festivals and events. Celebrating or reliving a feature of the past reinforces community bonds and links modern lives with memories or family stories. These events may have few common threads with the historical happenings they celebrate. The Easter Bonnet Parade at the local public school or Australia Day fireworks displays appear to have little in common with the religious or historical origins of the events they celebrate. Other celebrations, however, are strongly driven by nostalgia and a faithful recreation of the past. In fact, festivals can facilitate the preservation of aspects of the community's heritage such as old crafts, skills, buildings or traditions. Attendees might listen to bush poetry at the Tenterfield Oracles of the Bush or travel to Alice Springs to witness the running of the Camel Cup, which recognises the contribution of Afghani camel drivers and their animals to the settlement of inland Australia.

One of the many pleasures of attending festivals is the opportunity to experience the unique *atmosphere* of collective celebration. The Lantern Parade and Fire Event at the close of the Lismore Folk Festival is steeped in traditional dance, music, ritual and symbolism. It is a unique and theatrical spectacle of light and dark, fire and water, good and evil that is not readily manifested or experienced in other areas of everyday life. Opportunities for visitors simultaneously to have fun, to be entertained and surprised and to be emotionally stirred by the exotic, the surreal and the spiritual are important in creating an exciting festival atmosphere. An intangible element, atmosphere can be difficult to create but is often absolutely essential for the success of a festival.

SPECIAL INTEREST INVESTIGATION
The Birdsville Races

Birdsville, in far western Queensland, sits on the edge of the Diamantina River in the Simpson Desert, 1585 kilometres west of Brisbane.

The small depot emerged as a customs point for stock and supplies entering South Australia and grew through cattle droving, with supplies being transported on camels, and later through access to railways and pastoral activity. Before Federation, Birdsville was a thriving community of 270 residents, three hotels, two general stores and other businesses. Today, this isolated community boasts one hotel, an inland mission hospital, a caravan park, an airport, a police station and one store.

The town's annual Picnic Race Carnival began in 1882. The event is held over the first weekend each September and has captured the imagination of metropolitan Australia. In recent years pilgrimages to the Birdsville Races have become an iconic example of outback tourism. The town's present population of around 100 people comes to life during the four days of the Birdsville Picnic Race Carnival, when between 5000 and 8000 visitors arrive to taste life in the Outback.

The event is attractive for reasons other than horses and sweepstakes. It is an opportunity to experience the region's culture, celebrate traditions that are being upheld. For those with a special interest in experiencing and learning about the people of the area and the way of life they have experienced, it provides a meeting place for host–guest interaction and sharing.

The Birdsville Hotel becomes the focus of celebration, story telling, new unions and reunions. The pub, built two years after the races began, is a storehouse of more than 50 years of stockmen's memorabilia, hats, photographs and souvenirs of the Birdsville Races.

The festivities commence on Friday night with the Ringers Dance and continue on Saturday night with the Birdsville Races Grand Ball. Meanwhile Fred Brophy's Boxing Troupe provides evening entertainment from Wednesday through to Sunday night. The troupe sets up in the centre of town, across from the pub. The experience extends to side-shows, stalls and bull-riding.

Local mayor David Brooks believes the Races are valuable to the host community in providing locals with a chance to experience a change in their usual lives while enabling them to mix with a different, unfamiliar society. The outcome is a greater sense of belonging and community involvement.

The event generates certain revenues for the local economy, sustaining local businesses, charitable organisations, schools and medical staff for a considerable time. Organisers are obliged to bring in from outside resources that are required for the event. Profit earned from staging the event is given to the Royal Flying Doctors Service, the local hospital and the resident nurse. Between $40 000 and $60 000 was raised for the service in 1998. Revenue raised from recycling the thousands of beer cans emptied during the event is donated every year to the local school.

The event has dramatically increased tourism to the region. Event revenue has improved visitor and resident amenities; for example, a tourism information centre is planned and a local library has been established. The event provides an opportunity for visitors travelling from their (usually) urban environment to access a sharply contrasting, distinctive, desolate and remote landscape.

Source: *Adapted from Stickens, Howle and Lucock (1998)*

People participate in events for any or all of the above reasons. These celebrations fulfil a number of basic human needs, especially those of socialisation, esteem and self-actualisation (Maslow, cited in Kotler et al. 1994).

Considering the range of attributes and variety of appeal, it is understandable that festival markets contain substantial variation; festival and event attendees are far from being a homogenous group (Formica & Uysal 1996). Different groups will be attracted to a festival in order to satisfy different personal needs. In fact, community-based festivals and events often appeal to niche markets within SIT. Organisers try to focus their aims and objectives to satisfy the needs and experiences of each market segment. Research is important in achieving this. For example, research shows that consumers of arts festivals in Alberta, Canada, are predominantly young, highly educated people with discretionary income to spend on attending the arts (Grant & Paliwoda 1998). This information assists festival organisers to satisfy visitor needs and to attract ongoing interest in the festival.

For attendees and hosts, there are expectations of positive experiences and outcomes. An examination of event impacts, both positive and negative, is important to understand a festival's value and sustainability.

■ **Figure 15.1**
Event satisfaction

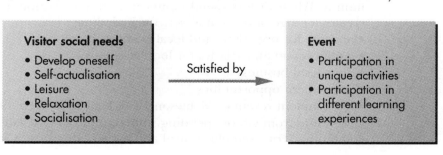

THE IMPACTS OF FESTIVALS AND EVENTS

Festivals and events are increasingly promoted as important contributors to the economic, social and cultural wellbeing of communities (Hall 1993; Getz 1997). Indeed, Australian authorities actively encourage them for the perceived economic boost they provide. However, hosting events, especially those that attract large numbers of tourists, can have substantial impacts on a community (Mathieson & Wall 1982; McDonnell et al. 1999).

Festivals have impacts on the social, cultural, political and economic wellbeing of society. The natural and built environment will be affected, while those involved in tourism may experience quite different impacts. Some of these positive and negative impacts are listed in table 15.1.

An important role of organisers and managers is to monitor and evaluate the impacts of the festival or event on the local environment and community. The aim should be to maximise benefits (positive impacts) and to ensure that costs (negative impacts) are minimised. This is not an easy task! Impacts are not evenly distributed throughout the community. Organisers and sponsors will often receive greater economic benefit than others in the community. Conversely, local residents, particularly those with no interest in the event, can be unfairly burdened by the social costs of congested streets and shopping centres, lack of parking, littering and property damage. Festival and event promotion will generally focus on the positive benefits (usually economic and cultural) and disregard social or environmental costs. Check your local newspaper for articles and promotional advertising.

■ 15.6.1 Economic *impacts*

The potential economic benefits of festivals and events are often emphasised over other impacts, particularly by local authorities and investors. Indeed, the success of a festival or event is commonly measured in terms of its economic contribution to event stakeholders, the community and the region. Certainly, financial viability is a major concern for organisers and investors, since the economic outcome may be a deciding factor for continuing the event in future (Goldblatt 1997).

In recent times, much of the focus of festivals and events has been on attracting tourists for the additional economic benefits they bring to the community. When visitors spend money in a town or region, their expenditure creates a range of economic benefits including:
- income for organisers and local businesses
- employment and salaries for local residents
- increased business
- investment opportunities
- government revenue (Mableson 1995; Hall 1993; Getz 1991).

Revenue from visitor spending will continue to circulate throughout the community. For example, a meal and a beer bought by a festival visitor at a local hotel will provide income for hotel owners and their employees, and result in extra business for food producers and suppliers, transport companies and breweries. In turn, this will stimulate extra business for other related businesses. This additional induced expenditure is known as the **multiplier effect** (Getz 1991; McDonnell et al. 1999). Although economic impacts can be relatively easy to calculate, multiplier benefits are more difficult to trace. For instance, **leakage** may occur when money is extracted from the local economy, especially for goods and services brought in from outside. Monitoring the flow of benefits and strategies to keep economic benefits in the community should be intrinsic to festival and event planning (Long & Perdue 1990). After all, events should be profitable not only for organisers and investors but for the community as a whole.

Events can have numerous negative economic impacts on the host community. Local residents may have to live with increased prices, driven up by event patrons' willingness to pay higher prices for goods and services. There can be substantial **opportunity cost** from hosting events, if resources are directed into infrastructure for the event at the expense of services and facilities needed by the community.

Many community events use large numbers of unskilled volunteers and an ad hoc approach to management, which, coupled with the events' intermittent nature, means investment may be difficult to attract and the risks of financial failure great. Unprofessional management can result in poor accountability and the misallocation of funds (McDonnell et al. 1999). The economic success of events can be tenuous. Imagine hosting an outdoor music festival in the pouring rain! Crowd attendance and revenue from the gate could be affected considerably.

■ *15.6.2* **Impacts** *on the natural environment*

Community events can degrade natural environments. Environmental damage can take the form of destruction of soils, plants and animals through trampling, erosion, vandalism, pollution of land and water and destruction of habitat (Murphy 1985). A loss in recreational opportunities and amenities for local people can result. Further, the degradation of unique heritage areas valuable to the local community and society can occur.

If the event is held in a public place, like a park or town centre, impacts on the environment may be even greater because of the concentrations of people in both time and space. Environmental impacts can be minimised if the event is held in site-hardened, purpose-built areas, such as stadiums or entertainment centres. However, effectively planning and managing the movement of concentrated numbers of people through the event environment is critical, as is efficient management of waste.

Although it is common to focus on the negative impacts people can have on natural environments, festivals and events can also have positive impacts. Growing concern for the natural environment has prompted development of best practice environmental standards and guidelines that address issues such as recycling, effective waste management and crowd control. An environmental impact assessment (EIA) is now an accepted requirement in Australia for gaining approval for festivals that incorporate natural areas. Consultation with local authorities and natural resource managers is an important part of minimising adverse impacts on the natural environment. For example, close cooperation between event managers and local government authorities in Lismore, New South Wales, has improved the management of waste at local events.

Importantly, festivals and events provide opportunities for increased awareness and education of the value of natural environments. This can lead to conservation and protection of unique natural areas in parks and reserves. The 1973 Aquarius Festival, held in Nimbin, northern New South Wales, highlighted for participants the ecological and conservation value of the nearby Terania Creek Basin. Subsequently, after a great deal of protest action and public support, Terania Creek and surrounds were designated the Nightcap National Park in 1979 and World Heritage listed in 1986.

Events can also be a catalyst for improvements in outdoor recreational facilities, providing greater amenity and enjoyment for visitors and locals. These facilities remain long after the event and provide improved outdoor places and spaces. Effective planning and cooperation with land managers is the key to ensuring natural environments are protected and enhanced.

■ **Table 15.2**
Impacts of festivals and events

DOMAIN	BENEFITS	COSTS
Economic	Business income Personal income Investment and sponsorship Tax revenue Employment and training Increased business opportunities Improved standard of living	Inflated prices Opportunity costs High risk of failure Poor accountability Misallocation of funds
Natural environment	Conservation and protection Development of best practice Education and awareness Increased recreational facilities Improved amenity	Degradation of natural resources Pollution Erosion of heritage values Loss of recreational opportunities Decreased amenity
Built environment	Improved infrastructure Transport Communications Recycling and waste management Urban development and renewal Increased social services	Vandalisation of public facilities Built heritage destruction
Cultural	Revitalisation of traditions Development of arts and crafts Greater intercultural understanding	Commoditisation of culture Destruction of cultural heritage

DOMAIN	BENEFITS	COSTS
Social	Shared celebration Sense of community pride Skills development Enhanced sense of place and identity Increased community participation Validation of community groups Exchange of skills and ideologies	People and traffic congestion Bad behaviour Noise pollution Substance abuse Crime — theft, property damage, prostitution Erosion of local language Disruption to residents' way of life Challenges to morals and values Loss of identity Social instability Community alienation Outmigration
Political	Improved profile International prestige Regulatory and social change	Legitimisation of ideology Propaganda Loss of community ownership and control
Tourism	Improved destination image Increased marketing Increased visitor numbers Extended length of stay Higher yield	Exploitation Loss of authenticity Demonstration effects

Sources: *McDonnell, Allen & O'Toole (1999); Hall (1993); Murphy (1985).*

■ 15.6.3 Impacts *on the built environment*

A festival can be a catalyst for infrastructure improvements, such as road networks, transport, communication systems and other services in the community. Improved amenities, parks, gardens, playgrounds and seating enhance the visual aesthetics and use value of public places. Conversely, staging events can result in vandalism and destruction of facilities and public places, and degrading scenery, obstructed through signage and buildings (Jurowski 1996).

Events have been a catalyst for revitalising neglected and run-down urban areas. In Fremantle, Western Australia, many older buildings of the city were restored and rejuvenated, thereby enhancing the architectural heritage of the city, in preparation for the 1986–87 America's Cup (Hall 1993). Brisbane's Southbank is now a major urban recreational area and tourist attraction, providing recreational opportunities close to the city centre. The 1988 World Expo was an international event that caused redevelopment of that site, a run-down business precinct, and provided impetus for development of recreational space in the area (Hall 1993).

However, when precincts undergo revitalisation the alterations to buildings and public places may not be popular with residents who experience a loss in their established way of life. At least 70 properties and 130 people were displaced to make way for the development at the Brisbane Expo site (Minnikin 1987). Furthermore, development has changed the nature of the precinct and surrounding business and residential areas, undoubtedly displacing people who cannot afford the higher costs of residing in this now fashionable area.

■ 15.6.4 The cultural *impacts of festivals and events*

Festivals and events are primarily celebrations (Dunstan 1994). Creativity, expressions of cultural uniqueness and local talents, customs and lifestyles are intrinsic components of the celebration. They provide opportunities to learn about other cultures, customs and ways of life, and encourage greater understanding and tolerance of cultural diversity (Hall 1993; Smith 1989). They encourage retention and revitalisation of unique cultures and traditions.

If not carefully managed, however, **commoditisation** of cultures can be a major issue. Commoditisation occurs when community activities are altered to meet the needs and expectations of tourists, thus eroding the integrity, authenticity and traditional value of the culture. Himalayan masked dance festivals are regular religious festivals held in the Himalayas, Tibet and Nepal. Although primarily local events at which visitors are tolerated but seldom welcomed, some popular festivals are being altered for the convenience of tourists (Shackley, Robinson & Boniface 1999). The concern is that the traditions, uniqueness and real significance of these festivals for local people is sacrificed through their commercialisation.

Another traditional cultural ceremony, the Bun Bang-Fai or Skyrocket Festival, is held in north-east Thailand. As promotion of the festival as a major tourist attraction increases, it is being transformed to meet the needs of tourists. There is decreasing emphasis on the cultural significance and meaning for local communities (Rabibhadana 1992).

Australian Aboriginal corroborees are unique and spectacular events steeped in ritual and custom. However, modification of corroborees for tourist consumption can result in little more than a degrading spectacle for visitors and locals alike (Hawke 1990). Thus, not only may the community lose an important part of its heritage to the needs of tourists, but tourists themselves may view the spectacle as inauthentic and contrived and no longer find it attractive. This is a major issue in planning and managing cultural tourism experiences.

Tourists should be encouraged to appreciate and admire culture and cultural festivals and attractions in their original form. Indeed, the uniqueness and authenticity of festivals are their primary attraction. Tourism can be used as a vehicle to preserve local cultures and cultural heritage; however, careful planning and management are essential to avoid the incremental creep towards commoditisation. To achieve this, cultural integrity must take priority over economic gain or satisfying tourists' needs.

■ 15.6.5 The social *impacts of festivals and events*

Social impacts can include changes in a host community's collective and individual value systems, behaviour patterns, community structures, lifestyle and quality of life (Hall 1993). Events can have a positive impact on a way of life through providing opportunities for celebration that enhance a community's identity, sense of place and community pride. They can entertain, broaden the mind and promote the exchange of skills and ideologies (Hall 1993; Smith 1989). They can validate the role of community groups, encourage greater community participation and improve the community's quality of life.

However, if not managed with the community in mind, events can have negative impacts on the social structure and way of life. Disruption to daily activities, traffic congestion, restricted parking and crowding in shopping areas or other community places causes inconvenience and irritation towards visitors and the event (Doxey 1975; Ap & Crompton 1993). Those living and working close to the event location and those in small communities who can't escape are most negatively affected. When festivals and events attract tourists, impacts are amplified. Litter and noise pollution can affect local residents, as may criminal activity and bad behaviour, vandalism, substance abuse, prostitution, theft and property damage (Getz 1997; Hall 1993; Murphy 1985).

For local community members, decreasing levels of safety and increasing social instability can result. Changes in residents' normal way of life, challenges to their values and morals, and reshaping the image of the location can cause social instability, loss of identity and even displacement and out-migration from the area (Hall 1993; Murphy 1985). In a study of the social impacts on local residents of the Gold Coast Indy, Fredline and Faulkner (1998) found that, although residents supported the event, they were faced with substantial negative impacts. Excessive noise levels, traffic congestion, overcrowding and disruption to their normal lifestyle were reported. Meanwhile, other enterprising residents benefited financially by relocating during the race and securing exorbitant rentals during their absence.

■ 15.6.6 Political *impacts*

Some events have political motives that introduce different political perspectives and challenge attitudes and established societal norms. The Sydney Gay and Lesbian Mardi Gras and the Nimbin Mardi Grass are two examples of politically motivated festivals. Both challenge societal norms and established laws. The Sydney Mardi Gras seeks to change society's attitudes and the legal framework relating to homosexuality. Similarly, the Nimbin Mardi Grass aims to bring about cannabis law reform. Such celebrations inform communities' attitudes towards presumed foreign ideologies.

Events have been used by politicians to improve the political profile and image and bring prestige to a destination (McDonnell et al. 1999). This can encourage the use of propaganda and result in a loss of community control over resources. Additionally, negative impacts arise in the form of opportunity costs, when resources are channeled into the event at the expense of other community needs (Murphy 1985; Hall 1993).

When Melbourne won the opportunity to host the Australian Formula One Grand Prix in 1996, the decision was hailed as a coup by the then Victorian government. Located in the city centre adjacent to populated residential areas, one of Melbourne's most historically important and popular parks, Albert Park Reserve, was taken over for the event. The Victorian government had passed the Australian Grand Prix Act in 1994 to fast-track development and bypass public consultation, EIA and cost–benefit analysis. Not surprisingly, the community outcry was substantial. Not only have residents been affected by lack of access, congestion and inconvenience, but there has been a substantial loss to Melbourne's historic, environmental and recreational features. With expenditure on event infrastructure alone totalling in excess of $55 million, the opportunity costs to the rest of the community have been substantial (Littewood & Ward 1998).

■ *15.6.7* **Impacts** *on the tourism environment*

Festivals emit strong imagery that can position a destination in the market and provide strong competitive advantage (McDonnell et al. 1999). They can be the feature of destination marketing, brochures and tourist information that increases visitation, visitor spending and length of stay. They can help overcome the effects of seasonality.

Festivals and events are important to the SIT market. However, the scale of tourism can compound adverse impacts, particularly on host communities, through:
- **demonstration effects**
- commoditisation of products
- inherent exploitation (when tourists have limited commitment to the destination).

Planners and managers should be cautious of tourism and its perceived benefits.

Community festivals and events provide considerable benefits for event stakeholders, host communities and the wider public. The economic benefits are particularly attractive. However, festivals and events can have negative impacts on natural and built environments and particularly on the social fabric of host communities. It is important that event planning and management include monitoring and evaluating the positive and negative impacts of festivals or events. This is critical if the event is to remain sustainable and provide benefits to all of the community.

15.7 FESTIVAL AND EVENT STAKEHOLDERS

An ongoing challenge for management is the need to satisfy all stakeholders. Stakeholders are the groups, organisations and individuals with an interest or investment in the successful outcome of the event. From a manager's point of view, stakeholders become partners of the event organisers for the event duration, since they share a common goal — a successful event.

Stakeholders may include:

- staff and volunteers
- investors and sponsors
- authorities and resource managers
- festival attendees
- the host community
- event organisers
- interested others.

■ 15.7.1 Staff *and volunteers*

Community events require the contribution of many people. **Volunteers** provide significant input (Williams, Dossa & Tompkins 1995). The ratio of paid staff to unpaid staff is often very low in community events. For example, in New South Wales and Victoria, local government-funded programs, such as the Main Street program, are often managed by a small number of paid local government staff with much of the work organised and carried out by volunteer community members.

Williams et al. (1995) identify the motivation to volunteer towards the management of an event as a desire for association or belongingness. Altruism is also recognised as an important volunteer characteristic (McCleary 1995). Volunteer contributions are valuable, not only to satisfy staffing demands, but for other important reasons. The contribution provides local support for the event and the benefits of extra skills or employment for the individual concerned.

■ 15.7.2 Investors *and sponsors*

Investment and sponsorship provide a contribution that alleviates financial burdens and constraints. For the community event, sponsorship can mean the difference between financial success and failure. It often involves promoting the company name in return for a financial contribution. Alternatively, the **sponsor** may offer free goods and/or services (known as **in–kind support** or sponsorship). Whichever form it takes, the sponsor will anticipate some benefit or gain from the transaction.

■ 15.7.3 Authorities *and resource managers*

Government authorities and resource managers often control public resources important for the operation of the event. Their cooperation and support can be critical. They will have their own policies and guidelines (and agendas) for the use of resources. It is important, therefore, to ensure a cooperative approach with adequate planning and management to ensure public resources are appropriately accessed, managed and protected.

■ 15.7.4 **Festival** *attendees*

Satisfying visitor needs is a major objective for organisers. Goldblatt (1997) recommends incorporating into event planning all of the five senses — touch, smell, taste, sight and hearing — to satisfy visitor needs. Visitors will have particular expectations, so researching these expectations provides useful and beneficial direction. However, a balance between community expectations and visitor needs may need to be found. In managing community events there is a danger of spreading resources too thin or trying to be everything to everyone.

■ 15.7.5 **The host** *community*

While often overlooked, the host community has an important stake in festivals and events held in their town or city. The local community provide many of the businesses, public places and hospitality services used by visitors. Staff, volunteers and a great many resources come from the local community. Opportunities for residents to share their views on aspects of the festival through consultation or community forums that bring issues and views together are important. Involving the broader community ensures fewer problems and greater community acceptance than if only the business community, or others from outside the community, are involved (McCleary 1995).

■ **Figure 15.2**
Event
stakeholders

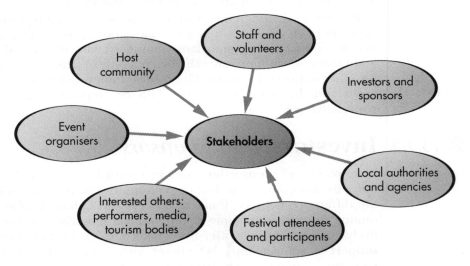

■ 15.7.6 **Event** *organisers*

Community events are often founded and organised by strong community leaders. The leaders create the dream that attracts the support needed to host the event (Dunstan 1994). Undertaking the leadership role means creating a vision of the event, ensuring strategies and goals are set and inspiring others to follow that vision. Leaders need the ability to inspire and motivate others and excellent communication skills. They have to influence the actions of others. Creative leaders can empower people to seek opportunities, make decisions, take responsibility, focus on goals and results and remain flexible. However, because of the enormous scope for creativity, the reliance on volunteers and the diverse interests involved, events are prone to idiosyncratic leadership.

Let's consider the different leadership styles apparent in event management (Mintzberg, cited in Getz 1997:73).

1. *Charismatic leaders:* These leaders have an attractive appearance and personality that motivates staff and volunteers to do as asked. However, the event organisation is vulnerable to collapse should this type of leader leave.
2. *Visionary leaders:* Such leaders have vision, seeing the event and all its possibilities, but sometimes have trouble finding the way to get there. They need a multi-skilled and talented team to support them.
3. *Autocratic leaders:* They make all the important decisions and expect to be obeyed. This can lead to revolt in the team.
4. *Democratic leaders:* They want to hold a vote on every decision. However, this can lead to actions not being carried out and objectives not being achieved.
5. *Bureaucratic leaders:* They believe in forming subcommittees to examine the implications and options available for every task; as a result, tasks often do not get done or they take too long.
6. *Inspirational leaders:* They inspire others to get things done. They are not concerned with knowing all the details or having the last word. These leaders are well liked and often very effective, but there can be a lack of coordination.
7. *Artistic leaders:* These leaders want to be creative with the event program, leaving the operational aspects to someone else; as a result, they need a colleague with business and management skills to manage the event.
8. *Technocratic leaders:* They are concerned with the detail of the event. They have little or no creativity and need the assistance of a creative person to ensure balance.
9. *Entrepreneurial leaders:* They know how to make money but want all decisions to reflect their impact on the 'bottom line', which sometimes leads to conflict.

Leaders have an important role in the success and sustainability of events. However, they function best when part of an organising team that contains complementary skills and leadership styles. Both creative and visionary people and pragmatic people who focus on the details of operation and processes are essential.

■ *15.7.7* **Interested** *others*

This eclectic group includes performers who will provide entertainment and the ambience for the event, those who provide facilities and infrastructure to create the event, the media and local tourism bodies. These people often include members of the local community such as musicians and artists. Similarly, local engineering firms and businesses seek opportunities to improve revenue from an event. Local tourism bodies have a tourism interest in any event and the media are always valuable. Also, not-for-profit groups can benefit from educational opportunities offered by representation at community events.

By now you can appreciate that festival and event planners and managers are confronted with a huge challenge — not only must they manage for a successful event, but they also have a range of responsibilities to the various stakeholders involved. To be successful a festival should reflect the character of its host community, provide a unique and attractive product and meet the needs of its citizens and visitors (Schofield 1995). Not an easy task!

Effective organisation and management are critical. Surprisingly, however, the practicalities of planning and hosting community events mean they are often informally managed (Getz 1993). There may be some strategic planning, but many organising groups remain small and flexible and have an ad hoc approach to management (Backman et al. 1995).

The management of festivals and events can vary from informal to professional (Getz 1993). The formalisation of festival organisations over time can be depicted in the following stages:
1. Origin
2. Informal organisation
3. Emergence of leadership
4. Formal organisation
5. Professionalism (Katz 1981, cited in Getz 1993:13).

While professional educational qualifications are becoming more readily available in this area, there remains ample opportunity for the organisation and provision of non-profit community-based festivals and events (Getz & Wicks 1994). Many volunteer-based organisations never reach the last two stages of festival development outlined above. A need for a professional approach to managing community festivals and events is, however, important.

A professional approach to festival and event management requires a considered approach to managing the range of tasks and responsibilities involved. To accommodate these tasks and responsibilities, Goldblatt (1997) believes successful event management should involve the following five important stages:
1. *research:* to determine market demand, market profile, community tolerance and other hidden issues, and to meet visitor needs
2. *design:* to mould the event and identify realistic strengths and weaknesses
3. *planning:* to ensure a clear picture of the tasks, processes and outcomes
4. *coordination:* to link the different elements
5. *evaluation:* to improve future events and ensure pragmatic outcomes (Goldblatt 1997).

Research

A critical issue for organisers is providing the right type of festival or event for a community. This has implications for host community impacts and visitor satisfaction. Research can be important in determining desired and appropriate events and the level of community tolerance (Goldblatt 1997). The more information organisers have about visitors, the greater the chance of meeting expectations and satisfying visitor needs (Mohr et al. 1993).

Design

What does the festival aim to achieve? This stage requires developing the project around the aim of the festival. This is not the time to focus on bringing money to the community, since this is actually an outcome of the event. Rather, an artistic or creative objective should be the focus. The research stage has identified what needs (or demand) might exist within a community. Now creativity, artistic expression and the input of festival committee members should be marshalled to determine the theme and objectives of the festival.

Planning

The planning stage clarifies the tasks and processes needed to achieve successful event outcomes. Input from staff and volunteers is important so that realistic goals are achieved. Committees should meet regularly to consolidate outcomes and document planning, communications and decisions to avoid discrepancies. As timelines and strategies are refined objectives and the festival vision should be revisited. Following the KISS principle (Keep It Supremely Simple) ensures efficiency of resource use and procedures.

Coordination

The person responsible for coordination will require excellent communication skills and an understanding of project management. Time management issues can be challenged as the event opening approaches. Each division of the organisation will look to the coordinator for direction and assurance if problems arise. Realistically, the coordinator is often the only person familiar with all aspects of the event. This role requires keeping people informed of process and progress.

Evaluation

Once the celebration is complete and everyone has gone home, it is a common oversight to forget evaluation. Often, minor problems can be rectified in future events if an evaluation occur at this stage. Gathering the organising team to brainstorm issues, successes and challenges is a useful exercise. The results should be recorded, along with proposed actions to overcome future problems.

■ **Figure 15.3**
Event influence on community

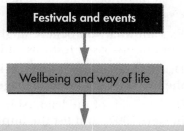

As a popular form of SIT, community-based festivals and events are themed public occasions designed to occur for a limited duration and celebrate valued aspects of a community's way of life. The reasons communities host festivals and events are numerous. Celebration, reaffirming identity, revenue raising, socialisation and recreation, tourism, and promoting the natural and cultural environment may be important contributors. Events provide opportunities to pursue SIT, offering themed, unique, authentic, participatory and learning experiences. People also attend events to satisfy their need for leisure, relaxation, socialisation and an escape from their normal lives.

Festivals and events are important contributors to the wellbeing and way of life of communities. However, there may be both positive and negative impacts on event stakeholders and the host community. These can include social, cultural, economic, political and environmental benefits and costs. Research and effective planning and management are critical in managing event impacts for positive outcomes.

Organisers must also satisfy the needs of numerous stakeholder groups, including volunteers and staff, investors and sponsors, local authorities and the local community. Effective management will assist the development and accomplishment of a successful event for all involved.

Questions

Identify three community-based festivals or events in your area or that you have visited.

15.1 What appear to be the main reasons for hosting these events? Are they economic, cultural, social, political or environmental reasons?

15.2 What do you believe are the features of these events that might make them appealing to special interest tourists?

15.3 What benefits might these events have for their host communities? Examine the negative impacts they might have on the environment or host community.

15.4 Identify the stakeholders of each event. How important is each to the success of these events?

15.5 What might be some of challenges faced by the organisers of each event?

15.6 Explain what you believe might limit the continued popularity of community-based festivals and events as a form of SIT.

15.7 Discuss how an event that you know well might be managed utilising the five stages of event management identified by Goldblatt (1997).

15.8 Review each of the leadership styles identified by Mintzberg (cited in Getz 1997) and list the implications of each style when planning and managing a community-based event.

REFERENCES ....

Allen, L., Long, P., Perdue, R. & Kieselbach, S. 1988. 'The Impact of Tourism Development on Residents' Perception of Community'. *Journal of Travel Research* 27 (1): 16–21.

Altmann, C. 2000. 'Living High off the Hog'. *Weekend Australian*, 5 February, p. 24.

Anon. 1998. 'The United Peoples Powwow and Cultural Rendezvous: A Cultural Event'. *Montana Business Quarterly*, Summer, p. 17.

Ap, J. & Crompton, J. L. 1993. 'Residents' Strategies for Responding to Tourism Impacts'. *Journal of Travel Research*, Summer, pp. 47–50.

Backman, K. F., Backman, S. J., Uysal, M. & Sunshine, K. M. 1995. 'Event Tourism: An Examination of Motivations and Activities'. *Festival Management & Event Tourism* 3: 15–24.

Doxey, G. V. 1975. 'A Causation Theory of Visitor–Resident Irritants, Methodology and Research Inferences'. *The Impact of Tourism*. Sixth Annual Conference Proceedings of the Travel Research Association, San Diego.

Dunstan, G. 1975. In Smith, C. & Crossley, R. (Eds.). *The Way Out: Radical Alternatives in Australia*. Melbourne: Lansdowne Press.

Dunstan, G. 1994. Becoming Coastwise: The Path of Festivals and Cultural Tourism. Unpublished paper prepared for the Coastwise Project – Landscape and Lifestyle Choices for the Northern Rivers Region of NSW. Lismore: Southern Cross University.

Erickson, L. 2000. 'State of the Alternative Festival'. *Afterimage* 27 (5): 1–7.

Formica, S. & Uysal, M. 1996. 'A Market Segmentation of Festival Visitors: Umbria Jazz Festival in Italy'. *Festival Management & Event Tourism* 3: 175–83.

Fredline, E. & Faulkner, B. 1998. 'Resident Reaction to a Major Tourist Event: The Gold Coast Indy Car Race'. *Festival Management & Event Tourism* 5 (4): 185–205.

Frisby, W. & Getz, D. 1989. 'Festival Management: A Case Study Perspective'. *Journal of Travel Research*, Summer, pp. 7–11.

Getz, D. 1991. *Festivals, Special Events and Tourism*. New York: Van Nostrand Reinhold.

Getz, D. 1993. 'Corporate Culture in Not-for-profit Festival Organisations: Concepts and Potential Applications'. *Festival Management & Event Tourism* 1: 11–17.

Getz, D. 1997. *Event Management and Event Tourism*. New York: Cognizant Communication Corporation.

Getz, D. & Wicks, B. 1994. 'Professionalism and Certification for Festivals and Event Practitioners: Trends and Issues'. *Festival Management & Event Tourism* 2: 103–9.

Goldblatt, J. J. 1997. *Special Events: Best Practices in Modern Event Management*. Second Edition. New York: Van Nostrand Reinhold.

Grant, D. & Paliwoda, S. 1998. 'Segmenting Alberta Arts and Festival Consumers: Part 1: Overview of the Arts Consumer'. *Festival Management & Event Tourism* 5: 207–20.

Haggard, L. M. & Williams, D. R. 1992. 'Identity Affirmation Through Leisure Activities: Leisure Symbols of the Self'. *Journal of Leisure Research* 24 (1): 1–18.

Hall, C. M. 1993. *Hallmark Tourist Events: Impacts Management and Planning*. London: Belhaven Press.

Hancock, D. 1993. 'Groote Eylandt's Inter-tribal Festival'. *Good Weekend*, 1 May, pp. 13–17.

Hawke, S. 1990. 'Diary: A Personal Note'. *The Independent Monthly*, May, p. 3.

Ickis, M. 1964. *The Book of Festival Holidays*. New York: Dodd, Mead and Company.

Jurowski, C. 1996. 'Tourism Means More than Money to the Host Community'. *Parks and Recreation* 31 (9): 110–18.

Kotler, P., Chandler, P., Brown, L. & Adam, S. 1994. *Marketing: Australia and New Zealand*. New York: Prentice Hall.

Krippendorf, J. 1987. *The Holiday Makers: Understanding the Impacts of Leisure and Travel*. London: Heinemann.

Littlewood, D. & Ward, H. 1998. 'The Save Albert Park Campaign: Opposing the Use of Inner City Public Parkland for the Melbourne Grand Prix'. *Festival Management & Event Tourism*. 5: 159–65.

Long, P. T. & Perdue, R. R. 1990. 'The Economic Impact of Rural Festivals and Special Events'. *Journal of Travel Research*, Spring, pp. 10–14.

Mableson, R. 1995. 'Measuring the Impact of Festivals'. *SMARTS* 4, December, pp. 5–6.

Mathieson, A. & Wall, G. 1982. *Tourism: Economic, Physical and Social Impacts*. London: Longman.

Mayfield, T. L. & Crompton, J. L. 1995. 'Development of an Instrument for Identifying Community Reasons for Staging a Festival'. *Journal of Travel Research*, Winter, pp. 37–44.

McCleary, K. W. 1995. 'Applying Internal Marketing Techniques for Better Festival Organisation and Management'. *Festival Management & Event Tourism* 3: 1–7.

McDonnell, I., Allen, J. & O'Toole, W. 1999. *Festival and Special Event Management*. Brisbane: John Wiley & Sons.

Minnikin, R. 1987. 'World Expo 88: An Economic Impact Study'. In *The Effects of Hallmark Events on Cities*. Centre of Urban Research, University of Western Australia.

Mohr, K., Backman, K., Gahan, L., & Backman, S. 1993. 'An Investigation of Festival Motivations and Event Satisfaction by Visitor Type'. *Festival Management & Event Tourism* 1: 89–97.

Murphy, P. E. 1985. *Tourism: A Community Approach*. London: Methuen.

Rabibhadana, A. 1992. 'Tourism and Culture: Bang-Fai Festival in Esan'. The 1992 Year-End Conference: Thailand's Economic Structure: Towards Balanced Development? 12–13 December, 1992, Chon Buri, Thailand.

Raybould, M. 1998. 'Participant Motivation in a Remote Fishing Village'. *Festival Management & Event Tourism* 5: 231–41.

Ryan, C. 1995. 'Finance, Flowers and Festivals — A Case Study of Little Economic Impact'. *Tourism Economics* 1 (2): 183–19.

Samdahl, D. M. 1992. 'Leisure in Our Lives: Exploring the Common Leisure Occasion'. *Journal of Leisure Research* 24 (1): 19–32.

Schneider, I. & Backman, S. J. 1996. 'Cross-cultural Equivalence in Festival Motivations: A Study in Jordan'. *Festival Management & Event Tourism* 4: 139–44.

Schofield, L. 1995. 'On Making and Marketing a Festival'. *SMARTS* 4, December, pp. 7–8.

Shackley, M., Robinson, M. & Boniface, P. 1999. 'Managing the Cultural Impacts of Religious Tourism in the Himalayas, Tibet and Nepal'. In *Tourism and Cultural Conflicts*. Wallingford, UK: CAB International.

Smith, V. (Ed.). 1989. *Hosts and Guests: The Anthropology of Tourism*. Second Edition. Philadelphia: University of Pennsylvania.

Stickens, A., Howle, L. & Lucock, A. 1998. The Birdsville Races. Unpublished student paper. Lismore: Southern Cross University.

Uysal, M., Gahan, L. & Martin, B. 1993. 'An Examination of Event Motivations: A Case Study'. *Festival Management & Event Tourism* 1: 5–10.

Walle, A. H. 1994. 'The Festival Life Cycle and Tourism Strategies: The Case of the Cowboy Poetry Gathering'. *Festival Management & Event Tourism* 2: 85–94.

Williams, P., Dossa, K. & Tompkins, L. 1995. 'Volunteerism and Special Event Management: A Case Study of Whistler's Men's World Cup of Skiing. *Festival Management & Event Tourism* 3: 83–95.

Aquarius to Mardi Grass

Ours is a cultural celebration, a colourful gathering of people
in a spirit of freedom, seeking truth and clarity
and a future world free from injustice (Dunstan 1994).

Nimbin is a small rural village located in northern New South Wales, 46 kilometres north of Lismore. From the arrival of white settlers in the 1880s, Nimbin's
economy was based on agriculture, predominantly dairying and bananas. A
shift away from agriculture began in the 1960s for many rural Australian communities. Nimbin was an early casualty, with a previously strong dairy industry
falling into steep decline. But for a group of students seeking a conducive environment to hold a major youth festival in the early 1970s, Nimbin was ideal. Lots
of infrastructure was in place, many shops were empty and the community was
eager for economic revitalisation.

The Aquarius Festival was held in the village in 1973. A vision for the festival
was created and enacted through a guiding document known as the May
Manifesto. Organisers were driven by a desire to celebrate and encourage
alternative options to traditional structures, processes and lifestyles through the
media of music, art, discussion and creativity.

After the festival many celebrants stayed in Nimbin, buying properties and
businesses. There were vast differences between the traditional farmers and the
new settlers. Their attitudes towards the environment, for example, were radically opposed. In 1978 the new settlers challenged the logging of the Terania
Creek Basin, which eventually resulted in its designation as Nightcap National
Park in 1979.

In this social climate the first Mardi Grass Festival was held in 1989. The
Mardi Grass is a political law reform rally aimed at changing laws prohibiting
cannabis use through a celebration of the values and lifestyles of Nimbin's alternative culture. The abundant artistic spirit in the area fuels a political protest
and a cultural celebration held on the first weekend in May each year. The celebration includes education about the positive uses of cannabis, as medicine,
fibre, fuel, food and social drug. Elements of the festival include displays, music,
spirituality, recreational activities, alternative foods and spectacular dress and
performance.

The three-day festival features the Harvest Ball, Cannabis Cup, Hemp Expo,
Pickers Ball, Pot Poetry & Yarndi Yarns, Hemp Comedy Club, Pot Art, the Kombi
Konvoy, Hemp Olympix and Mardi Grass Markets. These activities culminate in
the Mardi Grass Law Reform Rally and Parade through the main street of the
village. The Parade features the Big Joint, Peace Bus, Ganja Faeries and a
colourful array of supporters.

While the use of cannabis remains illegal in Australia, Mardi Grass protests this illegality in a forum designed to inform the community and celebrate the unique culture and identity of Nimbin. The mood is peaceful and non-threatening, one of celebration more than protest. For visitors, Mardi Grass offers the opportunity to protest, observe or participate in an alternative culture in a non-threatening, festive environment.

The Mardi Grass Festival attracts between 5000 and 10 000 visitors each year and contributes more than $350 000 to the local economy. In a village of only 600 people, this represents a substantial impact both on community resources and on the local economy. Visitors come predominantly from the local north coast region and from the urban areas of south-east Queensland, curious about alternative lifestyles and seeking interesting, fun and different experiences.

Although a small community event organised by community volunteers on an ad hoc basis, Mardi Grass is a highly successful festival. It attracts substantial numbers of visitors and fulfils organisers' goals of gaining widespread media and public attention. While its focus is highly controversial, the festival takes place in an atmosphere of cooperation and celebration of community values and identity.

However, the festival is not problem free. One is the increasing tension between festival organisers and others in the community. As the festival continues to develop, many in the community are becoming strongly opposed to the festival. A series of community forums held in the village highlighted the attitudes and concerns of local community groups. Community attitudes are becoming increasingly polarised. At one extreme the festival is perceived as causing unacceptable negative impacts on residents of the village; at the other, the festival is seen as a positive event that provides a great many benefits, notably in attracting tourists.

Mardi Grass supporters regard the social impacts of the festival as positive. They point out that visitors spend much-needed money in the village and support the development of local arts and crafts. The event provides visitors with an opportunity to learn about and experience the benefits of alternative lifestyles. Supporters see the festival as an opportunity for the community to come together and celebrate the good things about their village and way of life. They refer to the revitalisation of businesses and increased employment and training for local people.

However, those opposed to the festival believe the social costs are increasing and are now unacceptable for local residents, particularly those living close to festival activities. Congestion in the village centre and main street makes vehicular access to local businesses and areas beyond difficult during the festival and impossible for the duration of the parade. Emergency access and provisions for the disabled and elderly are believed to be inadequate. The intrusion by visitors on private property and vandalism of public places are also concerns. With limited tourism infrastructure either to accommodate visitors or to direct them away from the village centre, visitors party in the streets, camp on residents' front lawns and generally consume the social amenity of the town with little concern for local resources and sensitivities. Some residents feel intimidated, fearful and annoyed at the disruption to their town and their lives.

While event organisers argue for the use of the village showground to minimise impacts, traditional farmers are unwilling to provide access to this land. Members of the local Chamber of Commerce have decided not to trade during Mardi Grass. The strength of opposition to the festival by more conservative Nimbin residents is such that they are actively obstructing the festival by withholding resources. They want organisers to take the event to another location away from their village. The increasing opposition to the festival comes not only because of its physical impacts on local people; many of these could be resolved through consultation and improved practices. The opposition is also a result of intrinsic differences in beliefs and values between more conservative members of the community and Mardi Grass supporters. They believe Mardi Grass is a catalyst for escalating drug and health problems in the town. Meanwhile, Mardi Grass supporters focus on their agenda of changing what they perceive as unjust and unnecessary laws, which they claim only aggravate the existing drug problems for their community and society as a whole.

Nimbin and the Mardi Grass Festival have certainly developed a reputation as a destination for tolerance of illicit drug consumption and alternative lifestyles. This has brought increasing numbers of tourists to the village each year. Some come to drop out of mainstream society and live an alternative lifestyle for a while, some indulge in the drug culture and some experience the unique culture of Nimbin, its picturesque landscapes, locally produced arts and crafts and unique atmosphere. The social structure of Nimbin has experienced enormous change since the 1973 Aquarius Festival and continues to be shaped by both those who live there and those who visit.

■ **Figure 15.4** *Revellers at Nimbin's Mardi Grass*

Source: *Peter Derrett*

Questions

1 List and explain the impacts of the Mardi Grass Festival on the Nimbin community.

2 Describe the style of leadership that might best suit the management of this festival. Why?

3 Who are the stakeholders in the festival? What might be the investment of each?

4 What are the ethical issues in this case? Explain how they might be different for each of the stakeholders involved.

5 What might be the appeal of this festivals for special interest tourists?

6 Examine the future challenges for the Mardi Grass organisers. How might they be overcome?

CHAPTER 16

16

Sex
tourism

Chris Ryan

LEARNING OBJECTIVES

After reading this chapter, you will have an appreciation of:

■ the historical antecedents of both tourism and prostitution
■ the parameters of sex tourism
■ some of the issues surrounding sex tourism in an Australian context
■ sex tourism as a tourism product.

16.1 INTRODUCTION ·····································

This chapter examines sex tourism from a number of perspectives. It begins by briefly describing current attitudes towards prostitution and tourism as consequences of modernisation in the nineteenth century. It then seeks to establish what sex tourism is. The definition of sex tourism adopted in this chapter is based in social mores and concerns. Therefore, an example of a product based on a celebration of sex — the Sydney Gay and Lesbian Mardi Gras — is examined. It is important to state that the juxtaposition of gay and lesbian celebration with issues of crime and prostitution arises only as a consequence of the conceptualisation of sex tourism advanced early in this chapter. No direct relationship is otherwise implied. However, because of the success and economic significance of the Sydney Gay and Lesbian Mardi Gras, it would be odd to omit such an important event. It is not possible to explore all the nuances of such a complex and controversial subject as sex tourism in one chapter. The topics discussed therefore are, to some extent, an eclectic selection of the points discussed by different writers and significant omissions exist. For example, the views of a writer like Katherine Barry (1995) have not been examined. Although the major emphasis of this chapter is on consensual sex between adults, more controversial aspects of sex tourism are also discussed.

16.2 SEX TOURISM AND SEX TOURISTS

To understand sex tourism you must consider the tourist's behaviour within broad societal trends. Sex tourism engages liminal people; that is, people occupying space on the edges of society. By simply existing, sex tourism denies and plays with concepts such as monogamy within marriages, reinforces notions of hedonism at its most basic and offers insights into exploitations based on attitudes to females, child labour and homosexuality. It operationalises notions of fantasy, creates meanings wherein individuals come to accept their own bodies and sexuality and raises issues of morality and ethics.

Given this 'messy' nature, it is not surprising that sex tourism is difficult to define. Is sex tourism solely about commercial sex between tourists and sex workers? What about visitors to red light districts drawn by the reputation of these places, but who do not actually engage in sex? Are they sex tourists? Is the businessperson away from home who visits a striptease club a sex tourist? Is this tourist more reprehensible than the 'schoolie' (senior school student who has usually just completed final examinations) who visits Queensland's Gold Coast with every intention to 'score' during schoolies' week? Are people who attend the Sydney Gay and Lesbian Mardi Gras, with its obvious displays of sexuality, not partly drawn by sex? What about the people who went on the Love Bus tours (organised by the Eros Foundation) of Canberra's adult shops and massage parlours? Are they sex tourists?

Sex tourism can:
• be an education
• have implications for wellbeing

- challenge the conventional culture of Judaeo-Christian traditions
- have important economic and social implications.

There are links with the concepts defined in the chapters on cultural, education and health tourism in this book. Its tentacles extend into the body politic, as shown by sex scandals and police corruption in Australia, yet those very scandals arose from the body politic that wants to deny, yet legislate, the sex industry.

16.3 HISTORICAL ANTECEDENTS OF TOURISM AND THE SEX INDUSTRY

Ryan and Hall (2001) argue that a strong historical relationship exists between tourism and the sex industry. The antecedents of both, in their current form, lay in the western society that emerged from the industrial revolution of the nineteenth century. The holiday was a modern consequence of industrialisation in western economies. The notion of the tourist using periods of non-work specifically to relax developed. The growth of industry created a managerial class that sought to copy the manners of the aristocracy with visits to the cultural centres of the world, albeit in more time-constrained periods. The working classes created alternative escapes, aided by the growth of cheap rail travel and steamers. Places of organised pleasure, such as Coney Island in the United States and Luna Park in Sydney, developed. These areas used new technical wonders like electricity for light-hearted entertainment.

After World War II, cheap air travel to mass-developed Mediterranean resorts became available for people living in Europe, while at the same time the foundations of Queensland's Gold Coast were being laid. Modernisation produced a temporary **liminal person** who enjoyed a sanctioned escape from the work ethic of nineteenth-century Christianity. The processes of relaxation and holidaying were subjected to industrialisation, commercialisation, marketing and branding. In other words, the very means of escape became characterised by the same processes from which people sought escape. Mass tourism was born.

At the same time, these processes helped to define further the 'scarlet woman' — a woman beyond respectable society. Following the example of the United Kingdom, in the nineteenth century various Australian states enacted contagious diseases Acts. For example, in 1868 the Queensland legislature passed the *Contagious Diseases Act*, arguing that it was necessary to contain outbreaks of syphilis due to a:

> tide of immigration that set to in this colony about 1864 and subsequent years ... [As a result] a large number of loose women were landed in Brisbane, whose gross conduct and behaviour in the public streets in broad daylight, betokened that they had not come to this colony to earn their livelihood by honest toil, but on the contrary, to lead lives of vice and prostitution (Queensland Parliament 1879:1389–95).

This Act was not repealed until 1971. While application of the Act was uneven for those women who fell within its purvey, the result was one of labelling, debasing and positioning the woman outside 'polite society' (Evans 1984). The concept of 'whore' was not new, but whereas some eighteenth-century literature depicted her as an independent, resourceful woman like Moll Flanders, in the nineteenth and earlier twentieth centuries the threat posed by the prostitute as an independent woman meeting 'male needs' was legislated into confinement. Acts like the Western Australian *Police Act 1892*, the *Police Offences Act 1891* (Vic.) and the *Health Act 1911* (Qld) all sought to control, suppress and make illicit prostitution. Such Acts perpetuated the modern notion of clinical definition and categorisation of symptoms. Today the same process continues, at least to some degree, as evidenced by legislation in various Australian states where sex workers cannot use drivers to take them to hotels, or group together to work in a common house, both of which would increase their safety. Thus, argue Ryan and Hall, by the end of the modern period there existed two groups of liminal person, the socially condoned tourist and the socially condemned sex worker. To these groups can be added the socially condemned/condoned homosexual.

There were other themes pertinent to the emergence of modern sex tourism. Said (1978) has drawn attention to the racism inherent in 'orientalism'. Bishop and Robinson (1998) have traced the themes of Anna Leonowens' publications on the harem of King Mongkut of Siam to the images of pliant, sexually free and available women of the *soi* (streets) of Patpong. The shadows cast by the nineteenth century have lasted to the twenty-first; women of South-East Asia are seen as both sexually active and demure, albeit today further marginalised through the contracting of AIDS. In an Australian context it has been contended that:

> The anti-trafficking campaigns actually have a detrimental effect on [sex] workers and increase discrimination as they perpetuate the stereotype of Asian workers as passive and diseased. Clients are encouraged to think of Asian workers as helpless victims who are unable to resist, so may be more likely to violate the rights of these workers. The campaigns also encourage racism towards Asian workers within the industry ... and in the general community where Asian workers form an ostracized new 'underclass' without equal rights (Murray, 1998:58).

16.4 PARAMETERS OF SEX TOURISM

How, then, is sex tourism defined? Oppermann (1999) identified a number of parameters, as shown in figure 16.1. He noted that 'monetary exchange is only one side of the spectrum' (Oppermann:255) and that tourist intentions and actual behaviours may shift as the holiday progresses. In various studies of the travel behaviours of young people, significant incidences of sex with someone other than their usual partner have been discovered (e.g. Ford & Eiser 1996). Business travellers have also been identified as having similar incidences of sexual encounters when travelling (e.g. Hawkes et al. 1994). Oppermann asked whether such travellers would have described themselves as 'sex tourists' and concluded that it is unlikely. He also noted that significant amounts of travel are undertaken by sex workers in search of work and this, too, can be defined as part of sex tourism.

■ **Figure 16.1**
Parameters of sex tourism

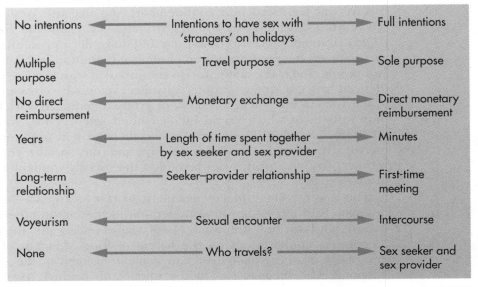

Source: *Oppermann (1999:255)*

Ryan (2000) approached the question of sex tourism in a slightly different way by trying to establish relationships between the different parameters. He suggested the model shown in figure 16.2. Here he suggested that sex tourism can be identified along three continua. The first was whether the relationship entered into was one that was voluntary or exploitative. The second was whether it was commercial or non-commercial and the third was whether the relationship confirmed or negated a sense of integrity or self-worth. Using these dimensions, Ryan argued that it was possible to locate the various forms of relationships found in sex tourism. In doing this, he showed the complex nature of the phenomenon. Therefore, a relationship between students who willingly had sexual intercourse while on a backpacking holiday would be different from one in which a male schoolie took advantage of a female schoolie who had had too much to drink and, as a consequence, felt 'dirty' and 'exploited'. In terms of figure 16.2, such an event would be non-commercial, but from a female perspective would be exploitative and negate her sense of self-worth. Similarly, the model permits an understanding of how women might become sex workers because of economic necessity and yet find that they gained personal strength and a reconfirmation of their worth, as is described by some writers like Bell (1994) or Kruhse-Mount Burton (1996). Figure 16.2 also shows where the different forms of sex tourism may appear on these continua.

■ **Figure 16.2**
Sex tourism
paradigms

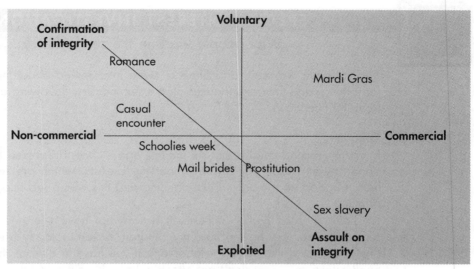

Source: *Ryan (2000)*

Hence, from a simple perspective, sex tourism can be defined as travel associated with sex, whether involving intercourse, voyeurism or observation. Sex tourism represents a complex phenomenon that is contextualised and marginalised by its surrounding society in many ways. Geographically, sex tourism may be demarcated by 'red light' areas, like Darlinghurst in Sydney, or the west end of Hindley Street in Adelaide, each of which have adult shops and strip bars. Canberra also has massage parlours; a quick check on the Internet revealed 31 in the capital. Those who engage in commercial sex while away from home often do not regard themselves as sex tourists and indeed may deny the term, even where sex has loomed large in both their intentions and behaviour. This last comes about because, at least in non-Australian contexts, the practice of buying gifts and giving presents creates a 'veil' over the commercial nature of the transaction (e.g. Günther 1998; Albuquerque 1998).

16.5 REASONS FOR BECOMING A SEX WORKER

The motives for entering the sex industry are many and varied, but a basic theme is the need for money on the part of the strippers and prostitutes. In their study of strippers and tourists in Darwin, Ryan and Martin (2001) cite examples of women who turned to stripping and prostitution essentially for economic reasons. However, there are other motivations, some of which are positive. For example, two Gold Coast strippers entered the profession not simply for money and because of a lack of other qualifications, but also because of the need for greater self-esteem, a fondness for dancing and a belief that stripping is a 'glamorous' profession. One of the women came from a Baptist missionary family (see the Special interest investigation).

Two strippers, Roxanne and Sheena, were interviewed about their reasons for joining, and their experiences of, the sex industry. Following are excerpts from the interviews.

Roxanne

I had my second child about six months ago — was depressed and critical about myself, about my figure, about my breasts, which are important to men. I had to earn money. I like dancing and this was a job I could do with dancing.

I have a much higher self-esteem now; what have I learnt? Not to be afraid of men ... I haven't told my children, haven't told my friends — no-one knows ... I like talking to people, but you have to give all the time — I need affection — you don't get affection here. It's giving all the time!

You have to pay a fine of $15 for being late — you pay $90 for the dress — but at least you don't having to pay for new clothes all the time — shoes — yes you have to buy shoes — high heels — how can you be comfortable having to wear high heels all the time! [From the fantasy fee income] we pay [to management] $70–$30 — it used to be $60–$40 but there is high turn-over of staff — so the management changed it so we can keep more money. They were losing too many clients. They are all tourists here, but they aren't spending enough — it's very slow sometimes.

I like it — it's given me a lot of confidence. I'm 34, 1 don't feel too old ... you just take one day at a time — just like any other job really.

Sheena

I've been 29 now for a couple of years and been stripping for about nine years! I've an interesting history in that my parents were and still are Baptist Ministers — in fact they are missionaries in the Solomon Islands at the moment. I certainly respect their beliefs and of course was brought up with them and while I don't call myself a Christian I certainly share many of their beliefs ... I actually began stripping while I was still living with them.... I started dancing because I like dancing and because I thought strippers were glamorous. I had been working in retail but was interested in stripping, so went to this club and while very nervous and not knowing much, I got up and did a dance for the manager and she thought I had potential and taught me some moves and so here I am still doing it.

I think one reason why so many strippers have such poor relationships and experiences with men is because of the nature of the industry. I met my boyfriend because he lived over a club and so often came down for a drink — but he was into drugs and was snorting cocaine up to 20 times a day ... eventually he was imprisoned for selling drugs ...

> [When her mother found out] my mum was upset but took it quite well, but of course I was more concerned about my father with him being a respected minister of the church ... but he was very good, very supportive.
>
> I didn't have any problem with getting up and stripping in terms of my beliefs — it didn't seem to be an issue for me ... and as I said, it seemed glamorous. I know many of the girls here have become men haters, but I have always talked to them and treat them as individuals ... I went out with one older man and he used to buy me presents. He didn't have a lot of money but he would say what would you like, and he would put it on lay-by and every time we went out for a meal he would pay a bit extra. He was a regular and the older women who had worked at the club said he was quite safe to go with. So I was being paid in a way — but there was no sex. But for some of the men it's a fantasy thing ...
>
> I think in some ways it is more difficult these days. Before lap dancing you could put on a real show. I have lots of costumes, but of course here you have to wear the uniform and the revolving stage makes it more difficult. You can make reasonable money, but it's uneven ... However, I enjoy it. You are very much in charge here.

The examples in the Special interest investigation illustrate themes inherent in sex work from the viewpoint of the participants. It is glamorous but seedy; self-confirming, but carries the risk of social disapproval, even from loved ones. Sex work pays the bills and pays better than alternative work for females with few skills, but it does not provide longer term financial security as there is no sick pay or superannuation. It offers independent working and companionship, but is subject to the whim of managers. And, as Ryan and Martin point out, it offers the paradox that sex workers fulfil male fantasies as sexual objects, but often have poor relationships with men because of the hours they work.

Another feature of the Australian sex industry in some tourist locations is the relationship between the industry and crime. The relationship between tourism and crime has been the subject of significant discussion in the literature. For example, Prideaux (1996), in the context of Australia, has identified different levels of crime with different types of tourist location. He found that 'hedonistic' locations like Queensland's Gold Coast have higher levels of crime than more family-oriented destinations like the Sunshine Coast. Prideaux links crime rates with the tourist destination life cycle. The existence of strip clubs and the services of sex workers marketed through 'small ads' is a commonplace feature of hedonistic tourist locations. For example, while brothels are illegal on the Gold Coast, the services of sex workers may be easily accessed through newspaper advertisements, the escort services listed in the Yellow Pages of the local telephone directory and, increasingly, over the Internet.

Ryan and Kinder (1996a, 1996b) have argued that sex tourism involving the services of sex workers is like many other forms of tourism in that it meets the same needs as many other holidays. It offers:

- escape from routine
- relaxation
- social stimulation with often pleasant company
- the engagement of fantasy
- the enacting of roles different from those usually engaged in.

Additionally, having sex is not unique to the commercial transaction with a sex worker. As stated earlier, sex with someone other than the usual partner is a component of other forms of holidaying that have closer or more distant relationships with prostitution. Holiday locations also provide advantages in terms of anonymity to the client. Ryan and Kinder (1996b) argue that social inhibitions are reduced for many clients while on holiday (see figures 16.3 and 16.4). They also argue that many red light districts are organised in a way that reinforces notions of anonymity for both client and sex worker, with back entrances to massage parlours, or entrances to rooms from within otherwise legal bars.

Figure 16.3 shows that the sex tourist formulates a predisposition towards sex with another person. This predisposition is based on factors such as personality, background and value system and assesses the likelihood of being able to achieve this as an opportunity arises. Figure 16.4 continues from figure 16.3 in that it represents the choice of venue and the considerations that arise with reference to that choice.

A number of observations about this model can be made. First, the selection of the words 'worthy' or 'unworthy' are value-laden. The model says little about the perspective or processes by which these acts of sex become characterised in this way. This process of self-justification is examined elsewhere (see, for example, Ryan and Hall in their adaptation of the social psychological theories of writers like Brierley (1984) and Stoller (1975)). The second observation is that the conceptualisation is similar to the motivational theories of writers like Fishbein (1967), whereby behaviours are related to attitudes, the importance attributed to them and the possible consequences of any given behaviour. Third, it can be argued that the modelling is so general that it can be applied to almost any tourist behaviour. For example, Kruse (1983) provides five reasons for wilderness based tourism, namely sporting and playful activities not possible at home, fascination with the wilderness, wilderness as a refuge from everyday life, as a place where natural heritage may be felt and as a source of personal satisfaction. By replacing 'wilderness' with 'sexual activity', similar motivations can be applied as reasons for the activity. Furthermore, figures 16.3 and 16.4 can be applied with little amendment to a wilderness experience — the existence of predisposition, presentation of opportunity and seeking an appropriate location. Perhaps the major difference is that of anonymity, but even this might apply to some individuals. In models of adventure tourism that discuss the role of the guide, the role of the sex worker might be inserted in lieu of the guide.

■ **Figure 16.3**
*Initial
involvement
model*

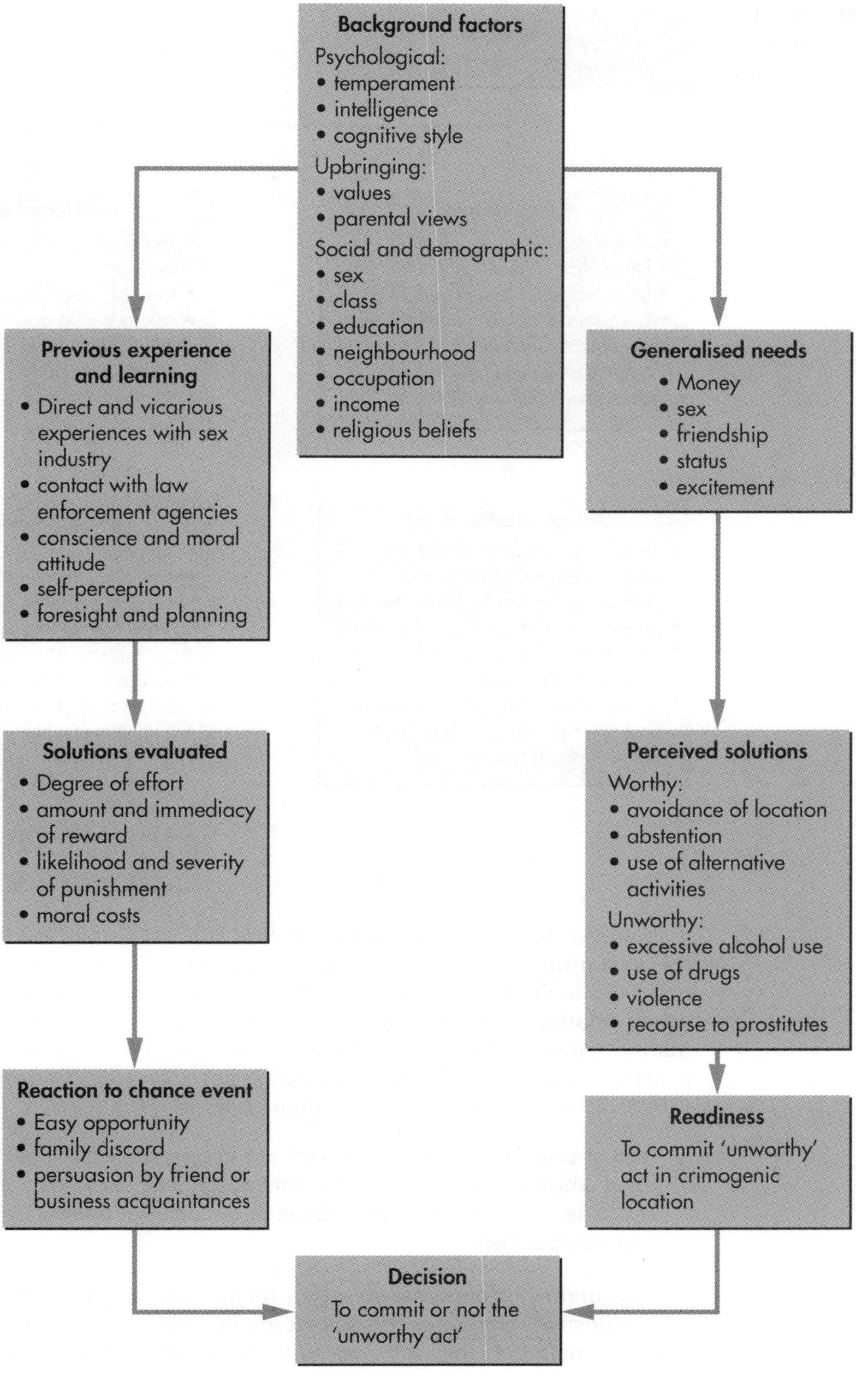

Background factors
Psychological:
• temperament
• intelligence
• cognitive style
Upbringing:
• values
• parental views
Social and demographic:
• sex
• class
• education
• neighbourhood
• occupation
• income
• religious beliefs

**Previous experience
and learning**
• Direct and vicarious
experiences with sex
industry
• contact with law
enforcement agencies
• conscience and moral
attitude
• self-perception
• foresight and planning

Generalised needs
• Money
• sex
• friendship
• status
• excitement

Solutions evaluated
• Degree of effort
• amount and immediacy
of reward
• likelihood and severity
of punishment
• moral costs

Perceived solutions
Worthy:
• avoidance of location
• abstention
• use of alternative
activities
Unworthy:
• excessive alcohol use
• use of drugs
• violence
• recourse to prostitutes

Reaction to chance event
• Easy opportunity
• family discord
• persuasion by friend or
business acquaintances

Readiness
To commit 'unworthy'
act in crimogenic
location

Decision
To commit or not the
'unworthy act'

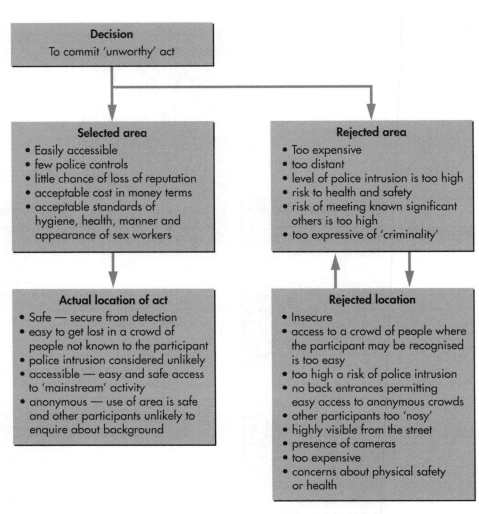

Decision
To commit 'unworthy' act

Selected area
- Easily accessible
- few police controls
- little chance of loss of reputation
- acceptable cost in money terms
- acceptable standards of hygiene, health, manner and appearance of sex workers

Rejected area
- Too expensive
- too distant
- level of police intrusion is too high
- risk to health and safety
- risk of meeting known significant others is too high
- too expressive of 'criminality'

Actual location of act
- Safe — secure from detection
- easy to get lost in a crowd of people not known to the participant
- police intrusion considered unlikely
- accessible — easy and safe access to 'mainstream' activity
- anonymous — use of area is safe and other participants unlikely to enquire about background

Rejected location
- Insecure
- access to a crowd of people where the participant may be recognised is too easy
- too high a risk of police intrusion
- no back entrances permitting easy access to anonymous crowds
- other participants too 'nosy'
- highly visible from the street
- presence of cameras
- too expensive
- concerns about physical safety or health

However, many people would say that the sex tourist is very different to the adventure tourist. This makes assumptions about the sex tourist, who may be perceived as seedy, (usually) a man who has difficulties in sexual or other relationships with people and is lacking in psychological maturity. Many writers would have us believe that this is an apt description of the prostitute's client and the sex tourist. For example, O'Connell Davidson (1998:173–4) argued that male clients possess an:

> idea of sexuality so utterly objectified and so completely alienated from self that I find it bizarre … It seems to me that through their sex tourism they also possess a sense of inclusion and prestige in a masculine community which otherwise escapes them.

She distinguishes between the often furtive use of a prostitute at home with the collective character of sex tourism she has observed in Bangkok whereby male bonding is based on boasts of sexual conquest.

There seems to be a lot of truth in this. Any review of the pages of the *World Sex Guide* provides ample evidence of objectification of women in terms of their body parts. Yet, when one talks to sex workers a common response is just how nice the majority of their clients are and how representative of men in general they are. To say that any perception of men by a prostitute comes from a skewed perspective is to fall into the danger of equally classifying sex workers as deviant. A lot of research shows them to be women seeking to cope with life and family responsibilities, although some are indeed abused, others achieve fulfilment, and yet others fit prostitution around 'normal' lifestyles (see the works of Jordan 1991, Silver 1994, Macey 1996). In Australia one of the largest studies of male clients of sex workers was that of Kruhse-Mount Burton. In a study of 301 clients she concluded that:

> Clients of call girl prostitution ... were in many ways typical of the male population. Single men and divorcees were over-represented, indicating that the institution provides an important outlet for men without partners ... The men varied enormously in physical presentation, ideal weight and general fitness, but their average score is a reflection of the relative youth [mean age was 32] of the sample. They were better educated and more likely to be self-employed or in management than the average Australian male, indicating that the cost of the service is a consideration (p. 113).

In terms of sociodemographics, apart from a bias towards higher income and education, there was nothing specific to demarcate her client group. In terms of emotional state, 51 per cent were categorised as being positive, four per cent were demanding and aggressive, and three individuals were feeling suicidal. The remainder confessed to varying degrees of emotional concern. Forty per cent expressed some anxiety about their relationships with women, but these ran through a continuum of concerns from worry about being alienated from their wives, through upset over the loss of partners, to wishing to escape from the constraints of marriage. There is, therefore, evidence for complementary and simultaneously different expressions of male thought and behaviour towards sex workers and women. Any theories of male and female identity need to recognise these factors:

> The normality of the client profile, and of their behaviour within the commercial encounter, is indicative of the inadequacy of explanations which insisted that the primary role of prostitution is to cater to the aberrant and psychologically maladjusted. (Kruhse-Mount Burton:114).

16.7 SEX WORK, CRIME AND TOURISM

In Australia, the most public revelations relating to crime, corruption and the sex industry were probably those of the Fitzgerald Inquiry of 1987. This report was large and complex and its reverberations still affect Queensland politics. The State and the rest of Australia were shocked, titillated and astonished as revelations concerning prostitutes, organised crime, drugs, smuggling and corruption were reported. The revelations resulted in a number of changes, including legislation that banned brothels in Queensland. Griffith (1992:1) commented that 'Queensland is set to become the capital of suburban prostitution, solo operations and escort agencies' with all the attendant problems:

> Without a legal alternative, sex workers will have little choice other than to work alone, a situation that will render them vulnerable to the 'Mr Bigs' who will move to control solo operations. Further, these prostitutes will face the increased physical danger of working alone, especially those housed in rented high-rise apartments invisible to authorities and far from help.

Cynics might also say that the 1997 case of the Federal Member of Parliament, Tony Smith, who was questioned by police for his visit to a Brisbane brothel, indicated how different procedures exist for people who work in brothels and those who visit them. Mr Smith was not charged with any crime; on the other hand, the police regard raids on brothels as being a legitimate exercise.

What is the relationship between these events and tourism? Ryan (1991) noted many reasons why a link between crime and tourism might exist, particularly in places of mass tourism like the Gold Coast. Among these are the high volume of people and the lack of a stable population that makes tracing the movements of individuals more difficult. Associated with these factors are a large number of transactions, many fairly small in value and involving cash. These circumstances also make it more difficult to trace records, creating opportunities for money laundering. Businesses involved in such transactions might be set up as front businesses for organised crime (businesses that have been used as fronts by organised crime include travel agencies, hotels, wine bars and a *bureau de change*). Additionally, the demand from tourists for sexual favours or entertainment based upon sex helps sustain a 'respectable' front end for an industry that can attract attention from organised crime for more nefarious ends.

16.8 SOCIAL IMPACTS OF SEX TOURISM — THE SYDNEY GAY AND LESBIAN MARDI GRAS

As shown in figures 16.1 and 16.2, not all sex tourism is associated with heterosexual intercourse and crime. Indeed, if the wider perspectives of sex tourism encapsulated in these diagrams are to be taken into account, comparatively little sex tourism in Australia involves heterosexual and criminal activities. An example of sex tourism that has had significant beneficial results is the Sydney Gay and Lesbian Mardi Gras. In 2001 the festival celebrates its twenty-third anniversary. Born out of controversy, the event has continued to arouse passions and pose challenges. For example, in 1998, at the official opening of the festival, the Reverend Dr Dorothy McRae McMahon stated:

> We are not defined by our sexuality alone. We are spiritual and loving people. We claim with pride that we are people who have the right to love. Most of us would also claim that we are spiritual beings. We are people of body, mind, heart and soul — full and free human beings.

However, such a clerical presence was not without controversy within Christian circles and the previous year the New South Wales Synod General had been presented with a petition to not enter a float in the carnival. The Synod and the Uniting Church, after serious debate, persuaded those who moved the petition to withdraw it, but made a distinction between the wider community and the support provided by Eastside Parish to the organising group. In short, the Uniting Church sought to show Christian support for people as human beings, while recognising that the event caused concern and offence to many Christians.

That the event does cause offence is easily demonstrated. For example, Goldsmith, a female commentator of the political right, cites her objection to the homosexual displays of Sydney's Gay and Lesbian Mardi Gras on the basis that

> Some drag queens are an undisguised and vicious parody of womanhood: their grotesque make-up and clothing and their grossly exaggerated breasts and mannerisms turn women into a joke ... Again, some of the bondage in the Mardi Gras is a worry, when it displays, for example, men leading women along by chokers around their necks. In a society where women are demonstrably less than equal and are subject to domestic and sexual violence, such images reinforce negative stereotypes and show violence against women as acceptable (1996:78).

This tourism event encapsulates the point that sex tourism has the potential to provoke serious discussion and examination of conventional social mores.

16.9 AN ASSESSMENT OF SEX TOURISM

It was stated at the beginning of this chapter that many aspects of sex tourism were omitted, and therefore any assessment of sex tourism will, by necessity, also be incomplete. The chapter has not, for example, discussed sex tourism in such well known locations as Patpong in Thailand. The issues of child protection have been illustrated only briefly (see Breakthrough tourism and figure 16.5). The discussion has primarily been within an Australian context, but even within an Australian context, this chapter has largely ignored the role played by Australians as sex tourists.

The topic of sex tourism generally is one of comparatively little actual research, which given the industry's size and its social and economic implications, is itself noteworthy. It reflects both the marginalisation of the actors and the consequent difficulty of obtaining data. From a research perspective it raises significant issues of methodology and approaches (for example, see the discussion by Ryan and Martin). Much of what has been written on the issue has concentrated upon third world environments. Even in the wider literature, much of the reported research has been based upon 'headline' locations like Thailand, the Caribbean (including Cuba) and not upon, for example, African countries.

There is a very real problem and denial of basic social justice to many who are the victims of the trafficking of slaves, which is associated with the sex industry in places as diverse as Europe, the Arabian Gulf countries and elsewhere. For example, Bindman (1998) refers to the desperate conditions of debt-bonded women in Taiwan's sex industry.

■ **Figure 16.5**
ECPAT's brochure confronts another aspect of sex tourism (ECPAT)

The organisation ECPAT (End Child Prostitution, Pornography and Trafficking) was formed in the 1980s as a response to increasing international concern over child prostitution, especially in Asia (the letters AT in the acronym originally stood for Asian Tourism). ECPAT claims that 'more Australians are prosecuted overseas for the sexual exploitation of children than nationals from any other country'. The following extract is from the organisation's publication *Child Wise Tourism*.

The prostitution of children in tourism destinations, commonly called child sex tourism, is definitely a tourism industry issue. We know that tourism is not the cause of child exploitation but it does provide potential abusers the anonymity and the environment to seek out vulnerable children. The abusers are not always leisure tourists, they can be business travellers or expatriates. Local people are often involved.

Child sex tourism is a phenomenon that affects children all over the world. The prostitution and exploitation of children is internationally condemned and should not be tolerated under any circumstance ... The problem for most hotels, tour guides, travel agencies and airlines is that they do not have the specialist knowledge to deal appropriately with child sex tourism. They think it won't involve their clients or staff and they become reluctant to interfere.

ECPAT believes that all travel and hospitality businesses should know about child sex tourism and what to do about it. The tourism industry can help to put an end to child sex tourism.

Child Wise Tourism Training is a training program that provides information and teacher training on the prevention of child sex tourism. It provides information on policy development and practical guidelines. It connects the tourism industry to community based organisations to promote corporate–community partnerships in combating child sex tourism. It recognises that information materials alone are not sufficient to develop sustainable training programs. The issue of child sex tourism is so sensitive in some communities that it requires a process of consultation and the nurturing of support from key industry bodies and government authorities.

The Child Wise Tourism concept recognises the importance of:
• a 'working together' approach
• promotion of good practice models
• the development of specialist knowledge.

In 1999 ECPAT Australia worked together with the travel industry and travel educators in Thailand and Vietnam to pilot the Child Wise Tourism training concept in Asia. This pilot was supported and endorsed by PATA (the Pacific Asia Travel Association) ...

(continued)

ECPAT Australia has worked closely with the tourism industry forging successful links with local and regional partners. It has produced resources which have been used extensively by the tourism industry and for tourism training.

... [A]t an international level ... ECPAT [has developed] close working relationships with world tourism bodies. These ... include:

- the World Tourism Organization
- The Universal Federation of Travel Agents Associations (UFTAA)
- The International Air Transport Association (IATA)
- The International Hotels & Restaurant Association (IHRA)
- The International Federation of Women's Travel Organisations (IFWTO).

In 1995 ECPAT Australia was awarded the Australian Federation of Travel Agents award for the most significant contribution to the travel industry. In 1996 ECPAT Australia was successful in encouraging the Australian Federation of Travel Agents (AFTA) to include condemnation of child sex tourism in their industry code of ethics. [Other awards ECPAT has received include those from the Australian Human Rights Commission and the Australian Council for Overseas Aid.]

Source: *ECPAT Australia (1999)*

This last section concentrates on the 'visible' component of sex tourism within an Australian context alone. Furthermore, it is solely concerned with sex tourism as a form of special interest tourism from the perspectives of the models described earlier.

Craik (1997), writing of cultural tourism, observed that:

the commercialisation of culture and cultural products; the restructuring of cultural production into the cultural industries ... These trends have — to some degree — converged in the development of cultural tourism, but this convergence is more a convenience than a genuine conversion to the benefits of culture and cultural capital (pp. 113–4).

She argued that cultural tourism has been packaged, commercialised, commodified and thus becomes simply yet another example of consumerism. In undergoing this process, products perhaps lose something and become bland and acceptable. The drive for differentiation therefore leads entrepreneurs into new extremes, which in turn become commodified. It may have always been like this, but the difference today is that the speed of the process has increased. Tourism is part of this process and like many other things, the process has both a positive and a negative component. In the case of indigenous peoples, tourism has offered opportunities for an otherwise marginalised group to gain not only economic benefits, but also political recognition. For example, the New Zealand Tourism Board has a Maori subcommittee and tourism looms large in discussions of economic development for Maori. Might the same happen for the sex industry and sex tourism? The significance of a product like the Love Bus is that it commodifies and confers a degree of respectability upon that which is commodified. It becomes a commercial transaction, just like other tourism enterprises. It permits the sex industry to talk of the economic benefits it brings, the people it employs and establishes a linkage with a respectable industry like tourism. Ironically, the very success of the Love Bus led to its discontinuance in Canberra because it was threatening to take time away from the main functions of the Eros Foundation, but plans exist to revive it in Canberra as well as Melbourne.

The process of commodification, which is often viewed as a negative process, has other positive benefits. For example, Ryan and Hall discuss what it means for those who work in the sex industry and the way in which they perceive themselves:

> Utilising the dimensions ... of the SERVQUAL model (Parasuraman et al. 1988), namely 'tangibles', 'reliability', 'responsiveness', empathy' and 'assurance', the brothel seeks to perform 'excellent service' like some bank. By commodifying it normalises, and by commodification the sex worker assumes a professional pride. It inserts codes of professionalism between the emotional trauma and economic truths of inequality of power. Sex work becomes but work, like any other. Behind this approach lies a functionalist rationalisation of sex work, but it possesses for its adherents the advantages of removing stigmas of victimisation.

On the other hand, commodification poses problems for some sex tourism products. For example, for some gay people the success of the Sydney Gay and Lesbian Mardi Gras is a mixed blessing. On the one hand it has led to a much greater acceptance of gay people. An example is the number of Web pages of Sydney hotels that state that the hotel is 'gay friendly'. On the other hand, as the event attracts increasing numbers of 'straight' tourists, there exists a concern that the nature of the event might change. The Web pages associated with the event relate concerns that, whereas in the past bisexuals were not permitted to join certain organisations, 'straights' could do so by simply ticking a column that they were 'gay'. Hughes (1997:6) wrote that:

> Tourism and being gay are inextricably linked. Because of social disapproval of homosexuality many gay men are forced to find gay space (the 'push'); the ability to establish and confirm identity usually necessitates relationships with other gay men. Gay space is limited ...

As tourism commodifies gay spaces there exists a danger that the tourist product of gay locations becomes yet another 'authentic' experience to be purchased by non-gay tourists. Having experienced the Greek taverna, the real outback, the Aboriginal corroboree, the Maori hangi, why not add the gay space?

Tourism represents a means of escape, so it carries within it the danger of having to be 'extra-real' and uncommon. Paradoxically, by selling the uncommon, tourism makes it commonplace and ordinary. The souvenir of the bungee jump becomes a T-shirt with a video to take home to show friends, to join all the other T-shirts and holiday movies. The gay pubs of the Princess and Whitworth Street areas of Manchester are now finding that their current chic as gay locations attracts a broader clientele. Tourism and leisure therefore legitimise what was once a fringe activity, but intrude upon the gay space required to confirm identity to its members. By making the uncommon common, the challenges of alternatives to 'mainstream' society are forced to further redefine their relationships with that society. The space, whether psychological, social or geographical, is further redrawn.

16.10 SUMMARY

Sex tourism exists in a continuous state of tension between the acceptable, the condonable, the rejected and, when discussing sex trafficking, that which is immoral compared to that which is moral. For many tourists, holidays have many purposes and they engage in many behaviours. Experiences are therefore 'messy', chaotic, fun or repellent. In this regard sex tourism is no different from other forms of tourism. It is closely related to other forms of tourism, it uses the organisational systems of the tourism industry and, equally, like all forms of tourism, it both confirms and challenges the social contexts within which it exists.

Questions

16.1 What is sex tourism?

16.2 What is the role of sex tourism in contemporary society?

16.3 Can sex tourism be legitimately defined as simply another form of 'special interest tourism'?

REFERENCES

Albuquerque, K. de. 1998. 'Sex, Beach Boys and Female Tourists in the Caribbean'. *Sexuality and Culture* 2: 87–111.

Barry, K. 1995. *The Prostitution of Sexuality.* New York. New York University Press.

Bell, S. 1994. *Reading, Writing and Rewriting the Prostitute Body.* Bloomington & Indianopolis: Indiana University Press.

Bindman, J. 'An International Perspective on Slavery in the Sex Industry'. In Kempadoo, K. & Doezema, J. (Eds.). 1998. *Global Sex Workers: Rights, Resistance and Redefinition.* London: Routledge, pp. 65–8.

Bishop, R. & Robinson, L. S. 1998. *Night Market: Sexual Cultures and the Thai Economic Miracle.* London: Routledge.

Brierley, H. 1984. 'Gender Identity and Sexual Behaviour'. In Howells, K. (Ed.). *The Psychology of Sexual Diversity*. Oxford, UK: Basil Blackwell, pp 63–88.

Craik, J. 1997. 'The Culture of Tourism'. In Rojek, C. & Urry, J. (Eds.). *Touring Cultures: Transformations of Travel and Theory*. London: Routledge, pp. 113–37.

ECPAT Australia. 1999. *Child Wise Tourism*. Melbourne: ECPAT.

Evans, S. 1984. '"Soiled Doves": Prostitution in Colonial Queensland'. In Daniels, K. (Ed.). *So Much Hard Work: Women and Prostitution in Australian History*. Sydney: Fontana/Collins, pp. 127–61.

Felson, M. 1986. Linking Criminal Choices, Routine Activities, Informal Control, and Criminal Outcomes. In Cornish, D. B. & Clarke, R. V. (Eds.). *The Reasoning Criminal — Rational Choice Perspectives on Offending*. New York: Springer-Verlag.

Fishbein, M. 1967. *Readings in Attitude Theory and Measurement*. New York: John Wiley & Sons.

Ford, N. & Eiser, J. R. 1996. 'Risk and Liminality: the HIV-related Socio-sexual Interaction of Young Tourists'. In Clift, S. & Page, S. J. (Eds.). *Health and the International Tourist*. London: Routledge, pp. 152–78.

Goldsmith, M. 1996. *Political Incorrectness — Defying the Thought Police*. Rydalmere, NSW: Hodder and Stoughton.

Griffith, C. 1992. 'Prostitution Policy is Fraught with Pitfalls. *Sun-Herald*, 1 November.

Günther, A. 1998. 'Sex Tourism without Sex Tourists'. In Oppermann, M. (Ed.). *Sex Tourism and Prostitution: Aspects of Leisure, Recreation and Work*. New York: Cognizant Communication Corporation, pp. 71–80.

Hawkes, S. J., Hart, G. J., Johnson, A. M., Shergold, C., Ross, E., Herbert, K. M., Parry, J. V. & Mabey, D. 1994. 'Risk Behavior and HIV Prevalence in International Travellers'. *AIDS* 8: 247–52.

Hughes, H. 1997. Holidays and Homosexual Identity'. *Tourism Management* 18 (1): 3–8.

Jordan, J. 1991. *Working Girls: Women in the New Zealand Sex Industry Talk to Jan Jordan*. Auckland: Penguin.

Kruhse-Mount Burton, S. 1996. The Contemporary Client of Prostitution in Darwin, Australia. PhD thesis, Griffith University, Nathan, Queensland.

Kruse, L. 1983. 'Katastrophe und Erholung — Die Natur in der umweltpsychologischen Forschung [Disaster and Recreation — Nature Within the Context of Environmental Psychology]'. In Grossklaus, G. & Oldemeyer, E. 1983. *Natur als Gegenwelt, Beitraege zur Kulturgeschichte der Natur [Nature as the Opposite World — Contributions towards the Cultural History of Nature]*. Karlsruhe, Germany: Loeper Verlag.

Lyon, T. 1999. 'Making Special Events Special'. *The Cyber-Journal of Sport Marketing*. October. *http://www.cjsm.com/default.htm*

Macey, M. 1996. *Working Sex: An Odyssey into Our Cultural Underworld*. New York: Carroll and Graf Publishers Inc.

Murray, A. 1998. 'Debt-Bondage and Trafficking: Don't Believe the Hype'. In Kempadoo, K. & Doezema, J. (Eds.). *Global Sex Workers: Rights, Resistance and Redefinition*. London: Routledge, pp. 51–64.

O'Connell Davidson, J. 1998. *Prostitution, Power and Freedom*. London: Routledge.

Oppermann, M. 1999. 'Sex Tourism'. *Annals of Tourism Research* 26 (2): 251–66.

Parasuraman, A. Zeithaml, V. A. & Berry, L. L. 1988. 'SERVQUAL: A Multiple-item Scale for Measuring Consumer Perceptions of Service Quality Research'. *Journal of Retailing* 64 (Spring): 12–37.

Prideaux, B. 1996. 'The Tourism Crime Cycle: A Beach Destination Case Study'. In Pizam, A. & Mansfeld, Y. (Eds.). *Tourism, Crime and International Security Issues.* Chichester, UK: John Wiley & Sons, pp. 59–76.

Queensland Parliament. 1879. *Legislative Council Journals* 28.

Ryan, C. 1991. 'Tourism, Terrorism and Violence — the Risks of Wider World Travel'. *Conflict Study* 244. London: Research Institute for the Study of Conflict and Terrorism.

Ryan, C. 2000. 'Sex Tourism: Paradigms of Confusion'. In Carter, S. & Clift, S. (Eds.). *Tourism and Sex: Culture, Commerce and Coercion.* London: Cassell, pp. 35–71.

Ryan, C. & Kinder, R. 1996a. 'Sex, Tourism and Sex Tourism: Fulfilling Similar Needs?' *Tourism Management* 17 (7): 507–18.

Ryan, C. & Kinder, R. 1996b. 'The Deviant Tourist and the Crimogenic Place'. In Pizam, A. & Mansfeld, Y. (Eds.). *Tourism Crime and International Security Issues.* Chichester, UK: John Wiley & Sons, pp. 23–36.

Ryan, C. & Hall, C. M. 2001. *Sex Tourism, Marginalities and Liminal People.* London: Routledge.

Ryan, C. & Martin, A. 2001. 'Tourists and Strippers: Liminal Theater'. *Annals of Tourism Research* 28 (1): 140–63.

Said, E. 1978. *Orientalism.* New York: Pantheon–Random House.

Seebohm, K. 1991. A Historical Geography of a Symbolic Landscape: the Sydney Mardi Gras. MA thesis, University of Sydney.

Silver, R. 1994. *The Girl in Scarlet Heels.* London: Arrow Books Limited.

Stoller, R. J. 1975. *Perversion: The Erotic Form of Hatred.* New York: Pantheon Books.

The Sydney Gay and Lesbian Mardi Gras: *sex tourism or celebration of sexuality?*

The Sydney Gay and Lesbian Mardi Gras tradition started on 24 June 1978, when a group of approximately 1000 people moved down Oxford Street, celebrating International Gay Solidarity (Seebohm 1991). The event ended with a police blockade, riots and many arrests. These sparked a campaign for the right of gay men and lesbians to march. More marches followed, resulting in a growing gay presence. The Sydney Gay and Lesbian Mardi Gras began as an annual commemoration of these events and a restatement of gay and lesbian rights. Today, the event is a month long and features art, culture, sports, film, theatre, concerts, parties and fundraising activities. The Queer Film Festival, held within the structure of the festival, is the fourth largest film festival in the world.

The event has both a serious and frivolous purpose. It hosts public forums on issues like AIDS, discrimination, racial intolerance, gay and lesbian parenting and gay bashing, among other topics. On the fun side, it has given rise to Frocks at Fox, The Gay and Lesbian Swim Carnival, Wet Girls Beach Picnic Day and, of course, the famous parade. It is estimated that 600 000 to 700 000 people watch the carnival from the streets and it is followed by an all-night party for more than 20 000 gay and lesbian revellers. Dawn is marked by a new form of partying, recovery parties. The event draws about 5000 gay and lesbian tourists from outside the region.

Following the event, which attracts a number of overseas visitors, locally based gay and lesbian tour operators have created a number of tours to well-known Australian tourism icons, including Uluru and Alice Springs. The latter enjoys some notoriety among the gay community as it featured in the film *Priscilla, Queen of the Desert*, with its memorable line about a cock in a frock on a rock. As an example of 'add-on' tourism marketing, the Tropical Daze — A Mardi Gras Recovery Week, based in Palm Cove (a suburb of Cairns) represents a successful venture. One highlight of this tour is the night dance at Turtle Cove.

Many specialised products and tour operations have been created around the Sydney Gay and Lesbian Mardi Gras, some with international links. For example, for a time in the late 1990s, the Hero Parade in Auckland, New Zealand, was jointly packaged with the Sydney Gay and Lesbian Mardi Gras for overseas travellers. The festival also attracts industry support. For example, in 1998 the Australian Tourist Commission organised a visiting gay journalists familiarisation tour for the festival. On its Web pages, Telstra announces that it is proud to be a sponsor and that it also supports the New South Wales Gay and Lesbian Counselling Service, VIC Switchboard Counselling Service and The Adelaide GT Gay and Lesbian Community Awards. The festival has helped in the process of legitimising gay demands for recognition.

Apart from its social significance, the Sydney Gay and Lesbian Mardi Gras also represents the purchasing power of the 'pink purse'. Lyon (1999) cites research that estimated the economic impact of the event in 1993 as $12 million. An industry has been based upon the festival — specialist tour operators and travel agents exist to provide sales to gay and lesbian tourists. Mardi Gras Travel is one such company. It does not provide brochures, but relies on Internet traffic. It is estimated that 69 per cent of its 13 000 clients are regular users of the Internet. In 1998 the International Gay and Lesbian Travel Association established its first international office in Sydney. Between 1998 and 2000, its membership of travel companies grew from 25 to 120. Mainstream tourism information suppliers have recognised the gay market. For example, travel.com.au includes specific gay and lesbian information and a weekly travel newsletter for members. Much of this expertise was built upon the success of the Sydney festival.

Product development is also occurring in Sydney. For example, there are walks based upon the homosexual experience in the colonial and convict periods. The sodomites walk visits sites associated with events such as the trial of William Williams in 1842 for engaging in 'un-natural acts'.

Questions

1 Do you regard the Sydney Gay and Lesbian Mardi Gras to be a form of sex tourism?

2 As a form of special interest tourism, does the Mardi Gras raise issues of power and legitimacy that parallel other forms of special interest tourism?

3 Why is the festival successful?

Hein Ruys
and
Sherrie Wei

CHAPTER 17

17
Senior
tourism

LEARNING OBJECTIVES

After reading this chapter, you will have an appreciation of:

■ the impact of demographic changes, particularly the increasing older population, on tourism in economies such as those of Australia and New Zealand

■ the ageing process and how people perceive ageing

■ the incentives and disincentives for older people to travel

■ product development for the seniors tourist market.

17.1 INTRODUCTION

In previous chapters you have gained an appreciation of a variety of tourism activities associated with individual tourism preferences and motivations. This chapter focuses on the older person as tourist and considers how tourism service providers can better serve this segment of the market.

The statement 'There is no such thing as old, just older!' is used by the Commonwealth Government to make all Australians aware that thinking of people dismissively as 'old' is no longer acceptable. The United Nations nominated 1999 as the International Year of Older Persons. For this occasion the Australian state and territory governments, as part of the National Healthy Ageing Strategy, introduced initiatives to build awareness in the broader community and, more specifically, to improve tourism operators' understanding of this increasingly important segment of the Australian tourism market. Governments now believe that leisure activities benefit peoples' health as well as their psychological wellbeing. Instead of being reactive in aged care, they now incorporate leisure in a proactive manner for older people.

In this chapter we discuss the changing phenomenon and perceptions of ageing, travel patterns of older people and services of tourism providers in the context of **senior tourism**. We first examine the demographic changes that have made the older person an important market segment for the tourism industry and present an overview of their needs and wants. An outline of government policies towards tourism for **seniors** is also presented. We go on to discuss the services of tourism service providers in the context of senior tourism. While our findings are based on research concerning the Australian senior tourist, they may also benefit the large numbers of international older tourists who visit Australia and New Zealand in the future.

17.2 WHAT'S IN A NAME?

How do we define being 'older' or 'senior'? Social convention defines the elderly as those aged 65 (the age of retirement in Australia and many other countries) and older. Current demographic data still rely on that arbitrary number. But Bernice Neugarten, a highly respected gerontologist, called the age of 65 'irrelevant'. She was ahead of her time when she argued that chronological age was becoming a poorer and poorer indicator of the way people live (Hall 1980).

The term 'third age' is sometimes used to describe the older age group without specifying a number of years. This classification relates to the view that the human life span is divided into three distinct ages, the first devoted to learning, the second to intense employment and the third to progressive withdrawal from employment. Associations organised for the benefit of older persons tend to define older or senior at an earlier age. For example, the National Seniors Association, which is the largest such organisation in Australia, consists of those aged 50 and over.

Terms such as 'older', 'aged', 'golden' and 'greying' are popularly applied to the same group of people. Terms that are perceived as negative, such as 'pensioners', 'old age pensioners' or 'retirees', are slowly declining in use. Two points are worth emphasising. First, chronological age is neither a reliable indicator of physical function nor, it appears, a good predictor of consumer behaviour. Second, each successive cohort is likely to be different with respect to lifestyles and perceptions of ageing, because ageing is inherently multidimensional, depending on a wide variability in attitudes, behaviours and abilities. In order to reach a group as heterogeneous as the seniors market, a business should match its offerings with the needs of the subgroups of that market (Moschis 1992).

17.3 THE AGEING OF THE POPULATION

While the low fertility of the population is the major factor, lifestyle changes have also had a significant impact on the ageing population. People live longer owing to better medical services, a lower risk of acute and infectious diseases, better hygiene, healthier lifestyles and better nutrition. Many older people use preventative medications, exercise regularly and avoid smoking and alcohol. Healthier lifestyles include stimulating environments and enriching experiences such as travel. The United Nations, on the occasion of the Year of Older Persons, called attention to the fact that one out of ten people is now aged 60 or over, and by the year 2050 one out of five people will be in this age group. The median age in 1960 was 23 years; the median age in 2050 is predicted to be 37 years (UN Population Division 1999). Table 17.1 illustrates the ageing world population.

■ Table 17.1
World population by age

AGE	1995 (%)	2025 (%)	2075 (%)	2125 (%)
0–14	31	23	19	18
15–59	58	60	49	52
60 +	10	15	26	30
80 +	1	2	6	10

Source: *United Nations Population Division, http://www.un.org (December 1999)*

The seniors market segment of the Australian population is expected to grow from 3 million to 4 million by 2007, and to more than 7 million by 2051, by which year it will represent approximately 32 per cent of the population. On the other hand, the 15 to 44 age group is not expected to grow in the next 50 years. The population growth of the seniors segment is illustrated in figure 17.1.

■ **Figure 17.1**
Projected population growth of seniors, 2001–2051

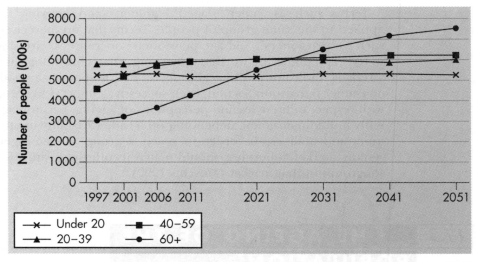

Source: *Australian Bureau of Statistics (1997)*

As the older market grows and the younger market declines, many industries, including tourism, could benefit from recognising the consumer potential that the seniors segment offers. Creating new products and adapting existing products and services are among the challenges that industry needs to face. To do this effectively, an understanding of the ageing process and how older people are perceived is important.

■ 17.3.1 **Perceptions** *of ageing*

The stereotype has it that as people age they become more and more like one another (in terms of likes, wants and needs toward travel). In truth they become less and less alike. If you look at people's lives, they are like the spreading of a fan. The longer people live, the greater the differences (in terms of needs and wants) between them (Hall 1980:80).

Different cultures have different perceptions of ageing. In Aboriginal and other traditional cultures, the 'elders', or older members of the community, are accorded respect and authority. They are honoured by the younger members and receive recognition for their wisdom (Berndt & Berndt 1984). In western cultures, on the other hand, it is often believed that the older a person, the less socially attractive he or she is (Dychtwald & Flower 1989). Although this view is changing, it is not uncommon for older people to be perceived as being not as bright as younger people, unproductive, unattractive and sexless. Sometimes they are seen by the young as 'funny old people' who behave inappropriately; at other times, they are cute, bright, productive and active, like clever children (Rowland 1991:3). People are increasingly seeing themselves as much younger than their parents did at the same age. Furthermore, as the quality of life improves, increased life expectancy is accompanied by increased expectations from life. However, perceptions of ageing have not as yet fully accommodated these changes.

17.4 THE OLDER PERSON AND LEISURE ACTIVITIES

The essence of leisure and recreation is freedom of choice — being free to do what one wants, where and with whom one wants. For many older people leisure is possibly the last frontier of their autonomy and the sole source through which the self-esteem, dignity and independence they strive for can be achieved (Barwick 1984). The active participation of older people in leisure activities is likely to mean that they will enjoy a healthier life.

In general, older persons have more time available for leisure activities than younger people, who are more likely to be still in the workforce. And it is probably safe to predict that in future the older person is generally likely to become even more leisure oriented. Leisure patterns will change, with the younger group of the older Australians possibly devoting a larger proportion of their time to leisure than their older counterparts.

■ 17.4.1 Propensity *to travel*

Where travel is concerned, older Australians appear to be prepared to change the duration of their holidays or the class of their accommodation rather than to defer or abandon the trip. Changes in levels of disposable income tend to influence a person's **propensity to travel** (Small 1986). In one study, older Australians were asked which expenses they would reduce if they were forced to economise. Most respondents would choose to better control their spending by making fewer impulse purchases and by adhering more strictly to a holiday budget. On the other hand, reducing holiday expenditure was acceptable to only 22 per cent of the 50 to 64 age group and 15 per cent of the 65 and over age group. Because holidays are important for older Australians, economies in this area are not a popular means of reducing expenses (Leinberger 1992). As shown in figure 17.2 on the next page, couples aged 55 to 64 spend the highest percentage of their recreational budget on travel; this group is followed by couples aged 65 and over.

The older traveller may also be considered a 'new tourist' — that is, more experienced, flexible, independent and quality conscious and 'harder to please' than the more traditional tourist (Poon 1994). Older consumers' previous travel experience is one of the most important factors likely to change tourism demand. Seniors will be more discerning and will demand higher quality services, as well as a greater degree of choice and flexibility in their travel and tourism consumption. However, it should be remembered that a significant percentage of older persons do not and will not have sufficient health or resources to travel.

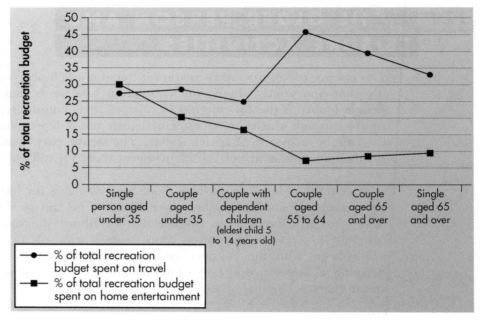

■ **Figure 17.2** *Choosing to travel: allocation of recreation budget, segmented by age and recreation type*

Source: *Australian Bureau of Statistics (1997)*

■ *17.4.2* **Reasons** *for travel and non-travel*

Travel barriers that older people consider important are well documented in the literature. They include lack of time, lack of companionship, cost, professional obligations, health limitations, family circumstances, lack of interest and safety concerns (McIntosh & Goeldner 1986; Blazey 1987; Environmetrics 1991). We now discuss the major issues of income, health and gender for the seniors market.

Income issues and the seniors market

Income is a key factor influencing the travel decision-making process for seniors, both in determining whether or not to travel for holidays and in the choice of destination. The discretionary income of the older Australian is proportionally higher than that of the average Australian. More than 4 million older Australian consumers control 75 per cent of Australia's assets and have $30 billion per year to spend on discretionary purchases. Figure 17.3 on the top right shows the projected travel expenditure by seniors increasing steadily over the next decades.

Many older people consider their current financial situation to be 'comfortable'. The income of most people peaks in their fifties and does not diminish until retirement. On retirement, cash income drops but most retired seniors have assets such as private savings. Although they have a lower disposable income, they also have fewer financial commitments in the form of mortgages, loans, school fees, cars and other outgoings. As we have indicated, for most older people travel is such a lifestyle priority that they are willing to pay for it on a regular basis.

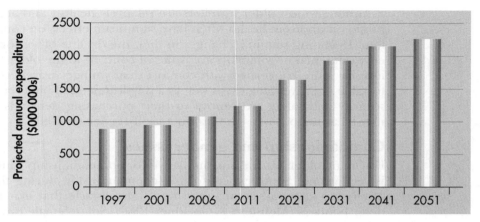

Source: *Australian Bureau of Statistics (1997)*

However, the future economic health of the seniors market is not easy to measure. Many older people depend on economic activities that are not age specific. Labour force and retirement trends, including redundancy, can have an impact on the frequency with which older people travel. Some older Australians depend on income from under-performing assets to fund their retirement. As a result, the issue of quality and price-value is becoming increasingly important (Harris & West 1995). For the same reasons, some older persons do not go on holidays at all and others limit both the frequency and style of their holidays, particularly when physical constraints would force them to select expensive accommodation. On the other hand, when older travellers feel that a product (for example, accommodation) is of good value, they will resist climbing the price ladder for the sake of a few extra amenities. Their life experiences have created a 'down to earth' group that is not impressed by frills, luxury and crafty marketing. They look for value for money, quality products and good, honest service. Many tourism service providers have recognised this and offer **discounted services** to older tourists. The older traveller is discovering the advantages of special rates and incentive programs (McInerney 1992).

Health issues

While ageing and health concerns may begin to influence the behaviour of older travellers, most activity limitations and serious health concerns relate to those in the group aged 80 and older (Pederson 1994). For many older persons, the fear of failing health is part of their lives and can act as a spur to 'do it while you can'. For many, ill health does not appear to be a major deterrent to taking a holiday. Recuperation from illness or recovery after major surgery is often a stimulus to travel. Blazey (1987) found that 25.6 per cent of travel constraints for seniors were related to 'health' issues, 19.6 per cent were related to disability and 9 per cent to a lack of energy for travel. Only 3 per cent of respondents felt that they were too old to take part. Some chose to ignore ill health and ageing in order to indulge in the travel experience (Environmetrics 1991).

Although most older travellers are relatively healthy and active, however, subtle variations in health often have significant effects on consumer behaviour. Declining stamina, changes in diet, the decline of sensory ability, and environmental negotiability are issues of concern to the older traveller. Seniors are more concerned with comfort than younger travellers. Being comfortable is a psychological as well as a physical need of older consumers and security and safety are central to their purchasing demands. Accessibility may be as important as the product itself (Pederson 1994).

Companionship and gender issues

For many older Australians the desire for companionship while holidaying is very strong. Some expect to find companionship during their holidays; others see a lack of companionship as an obstacle that may lead them to defer holidays (McIntosh & Goeldner 1986). Some female travellers dismiss this as a problem; they travel alone and are 'proud of it'.

Gender has an impact on income and therefore on travel. Females now have greater equality in the workforce and have expanded their role in management, politics and ownership of enterprises. Many older females travel more than their predecessors did and this has implications for tourism products and services. Owing to differences in life expectancy, older women will continue to outnumber older men in the future. This is an issue of which future tourism marketers should be aware. Gender also has an influence on the perceptions of tourism services. Certain products and services, such as safety, cleanliness and good housekeeping, are factors likely to be more important to women than to men.

A gender and family issue is the 'left alone single' older traveller, the great majority of whom are women. They tend to look for travel opportunities appropriate to single persons and to travel either alone or as part of an organised tour. Traditionally, the tourism industry has not been sensitive to the needs of the single traveller. Room rates and the price for a cabin on a cruise ship, for example, are commonly based on double occupancy. While the policy of charging supplementary fees for singles can be understood from the hotel's viewpoint, it may also be regarded as discriminatory and unfair. Restaurants often have the tables for single persons in less attractive locations, for instance near the kitchen. As for special needs, safety and security issues are more important for the single traveller. The issue of how gender influences the expectations of older tourists is generally not well understood. Women travelling on their own report that they are often treated as second-class citizens on planes, in restaurants and in hotels (McCleary et al. 1994).

■ 17.4.3 Travel motivations *of the older consumer*

There is a misconception in the travel industry that all people holiday with the intention of escaping from their daily routines. This may be the case with younger people and stressed workers, but older people are looking more for experience and personal growth. Stuart (1992) notes that the older people become, the less interested they are in acquiring possessions and the more interested they become in simply 'experiencing'. He suggests that while the younger traveller seeks 'to escape', the older traveller wishes to become 'involved' in the travel experience.

For many modern people, the reasons for travel are often influenced by a 'work to live' instead of a 'live to work' attitude. Motives based on this attitude include to experience something different; to explore; to have a change; to have fun; to increase enjoyment; to play and be active; to be with others; to relax without stress; to do as you please; and to be close to nature and the intact environment. Poon (1994) estimates that the above motives apply to 45 per cent to 60 per cent of the population in the developed world including a large proportion of the older traveller segment. Other elements important to the older traveller are interesting venues that provide learning and/or cultural experiences, good architecture, pleasant countryside, peace and quiet, participation, opportunities to develop and support friendship and good weather experienced in a comfortable but simple environment. Further wants may include indulgence and receiving respect (Badinelli et al. 1991; Calver et al. 1993).

■ 17.4.4 Travel patterns *of senior tourists*

Older travellers have the freedom to travel when they want. They do not have family commitments that reduce the choice of when to travel. Older people have acquired a greater propensity to travel and take longer holidays because they have more leisure time and are able to take holidays during off-peak seasons when travel and accommodation costs are considerably lower. This flexibility is of great importance to tourism industries. Owing to demand fluctuations, these industries often have unused capacity, the cost of which has to be recovered from sales at busier times. The older traveller market offers the potential to fill this capacity. It must be stressed that capitalising on the seniors market should not be seen as a stop-gap measure for breaking the deadlock of seasonality, since surveys show that many older travellers still prefer to travel in the peak season, particularly if they are travelling with younger members of the family (Hart 1994).

Older Australian travellers have no strong preference for a particular time to travel, although they prefer to avoid the 'clutter' of school holidays. But one thing is clear: they seek out the warmer regions of Australia. Having more leisure time allows older travellers to enjoy more and longer trips. Domestic trips of four to seven nights and eight to fourteen nights are increasing while one- and two-night trips are static or decreasing (Wei & Ruys 1998).

Where to travel?

Many older Australian travellers prefer one or two rather than multiple destinations in any one trip. They travel to their friends and relatives wherever they live. If they travel for a break or a holiday to relax, many seek the coastal regions. If they travel for a more active trip or a tour, many forgo the eastern seaboard in favour of geographically remote areas (Environmetrics 1991). The latter suggests that tourism service providers in rural destinations could benefit from increasing interest in their region among older travellers (Ruys 1997). While seniors express the desire to travel more within Australia, a lack of information on domestic transport and a lack of well-promoted, nationwide discounts is making overseas travel more attractive to older Australians.

SPECIAL INTEREST INVESTIGATION
Seniors and holiday transport

In a recent survey by Wei and Ruys (1998) to identify if there are gaps between what seniors and providers perceive to be of importance to seniors, one of many findings, based on responses from 1200 Australian seniors, rated the following means of transport as often or always used when travelling to their holiday destination: car (57.3 per cent), plane (37.4 per cent), public transport (16.4 per cent), tour coach (15.4 per cent) and long-distance train (13 per cent). In a parallel study of 499 providers, their perceptions of the same issue rated tour coach (76 per cent), car (57.1 per cent), long-distance train (54 per cent), public transport (40 per cent) and plane (34 per cent) as often or always used by seniors.

These findings indicate that service providers have not fully prioritised the transport preferences of seniors when travelling on holiday. With respect to the reasons why seniors travel, the opinions of the seniors matched well with those of service providers. The findings also suggested that tourism providers overestimated the frequency with which seniors travel, the duration of the trips they take and their purchasing ability.

Seniors can find travel information from many different sources, such as the *Australian Travel Guide for Seniors* published by Queensland Seniors Card, *The Australian Senior* newspaper, National Seniors Tours, automobile clubs, travel agents and coach tour operators that specialise in senior travel.

When author and media personality Tim Bowden joined the so-called grey nomads camping and driving their way around Australia, he had no intention of roughing it.

Most people have a dream of just taking off and living the gypsy life. But when can you do it? There are two main windows in life. First, when you are very young but generally broke — the backpacking era with fruit-picking and odd jobs along the way and grotty sleeping bags in budget hostels. Second, in retirement, when you are hopefully fit enough to enjoy it and almost certainly more able to afford it.

There is an enormous sense of freedom in not knowing exactly where you are going to stop and where you might go — changing plans on a whim is half the fun. Which is why, when we reach the Eyre Peninsula in South Australia, we turn back on our tracks at Streaky Bay and run down the coast to Venus Bay, stopping in a delightful little waterfront camping and caravan park. The caravans around us are sheltering cheerful couples of mature years, most of whom have been slowly circulating around Australia for 12 months or more.

The TV documentary *Grey Nomads*, screened on ABC TV just before we left, is constantly in our thoughts. After all, we have joined them. Hordes of age-challenged Australians circling the continent in a variety of caravans, mobile homes, cars and camping trailers, Kombis, vans and even one venerable psychiatrist on a motorcycle without sidecar. He was the ultimate minimalist camper, rejoicing whenever he found something in his lightly packed saddle-bags that he could throw away and do without.

The camping rigs of other travellers are an endless source of interest to us nomads. Norm and Jean are camped nearby. They are in their mid-60s. They have a huge caravan towed by a four-wheel-drive with a 'tinny' (aluminium dinghy) strapped to the roof. Norm is a fanatical fisherman. He has circled Australia on the coastal route, Highway 1, in a ceaseless quest for the ultimate fishing opportunity. They are from Fremantle, Western Australia, have been headed around Australia clockwise for nearly a year, and are almost home . . .

Source: The Weekend Australian, *June 5–6, 1999, Review, p. 24.*

■ **Figure 17.4**
Queensland's coastal resorts are popular with 'Grey Nomads'.

Source:
Queensland Office of Ageing

■ *17.4.5* **Segmenting** *the Australian senior travellers market*

As with other market segmentation attempts, the seniors market can be segmented by demography, geography, psychography or behaviour. Because travel involves activities, interests and preferences, psychographic segmentation is often preferred over other criteria. By understanding what makes seniors travel, the tourism industry will be better positioned to meet the wants of the older traveller. For example, based on travel motivations, the seniors market could be segmented into groups like 'enjoying later life travellers', 'self-fulfilment travellers' and 'comfort and familiarity travellers'. Enjoying later life motives include 'to go now while my health is good', 'to visit places I have always wanted to visit' and 'to enjoy quality facilities and services'. Self-fulfilment motives include 'to be adventurous and try new things', 'to meet new people' and 'to have personal growth and enrichment'. Comfort and familiarity motives include 'to spend time with family and friends', 'to feel comfortable and secure in a comfortable location' and so on (Wei & Ruys 1998).

Because of the heterogeneity of the mature market, it might be easier and more practical to speak about this market in general terms, using its similarities as opposed to its differences. This is often the case when the physiological aspects of ageing are taken into account in designing tourism products. However, when making references to the motives or behaviour of the mature market, its heterogeneity has to be kept in mind to cater for the needs of different market segments (Moschis 1992).

17.5 SOME EUROPEAN GOVERNMENT POLICIES ON TRAVEL

Among the closing resolutions agreed upon during the European Tourism Commission (ETC) and International Hotel Association (IHA) seminar in November 1985 in Cannes on 'The Senior Tourist: Solution or Seasonality' was that the ETC and the IHA should develop closer links with seniors' welfare. By the mid-1980s it was becoming obvious to many that there was a large unsatisfied demand for more travel among the European elderly. This resulted in many welfare organisations becoming actively involved in travel arrangements, often in partnership with a professional travel agent or tour operator. The industry developed the Euro Senior Pass, which allowed rebated travel (including reduced entry to tourist attractions and museums) throughout Europe (Viant 1993). In several European Union countries governments have demonstrated political sensitivity to the social consequences of ageing by taking steps to support the older person. For example, government-owned and -subsidised public transport systems offer 'senior citizens' special fare reductions or periods of free travel.

A few countries subsidise the travel accommodation of seniors under the banner of 'social tourism'. While these programs are on the wane in most member countries, Spain continues to support such an approach. The main welfare thrust now is to stimulate the older segment of the population by improving income rather than by providing particular subsidised services, so that every individual can choose how to use the available resources (Wheatcroft & Seekings 1992).

17.5.1 Australian governments' initiatives in tourism for seniors

Federal and state governments have developed policies addressing travel and leisure for the older population. Travel activities by older people are presently supported by the government with four free annual rail journeys for Australians. Concessions for local and long-distance train travel for pensioners and Seniors Card holders are also available; however, these concessions are not always usable in different states and are not available to overseas senior travellers.

Seniors Card offices in different states work actively together and carry out and support research projects to better develop work plans and other strategies that would benefit seniors. Many have a strong tourism focus. Each state has a 'Framework for Ageing' document that highlights tourism as a beneficial strategy for healthy ageing. In 1997–98 the Australian state and territory governments responded to the United Nations International Year of Older Persons by initiating the National Healthy Ageing Strategy. One publication to come out of this is a travel guide, *Get up & go, Australian travel guide for seniors 2000*. This is a joint effort by the Commonwealth Government, Department of Families, Youth and Community Care Queensland and the Northern Territory Office of Senior Territorians (Wiseman 1999). It is the first travel guide written specifically for Australian seniors and includes travel tips, exciting destinations, money-saving ideas, transport suggestions and so on.

We will now examine selected issues that are relevant to the market of older Australian tourists. These issues are important not only to older Australian tourists but also to older travellers from other countries who visit Australia.

17.6 THE ACCOMMODATION INDUSTRY AND THE SENIOR TOURIST

Many older travellers visit friends and relatives (**VFR travellers**) during their holidays. They like spending time with their relatives and friends, but staying with them in their houses may not appeal (Environmetrics 1991). Many select conveniently located commercial accommodation so they can be independent and combine VFR with pleasure travel. Another segment of older tourists travel purely for pleasure purposes. These pleasure travellers usually belong to the younger seniors, those in the 60 to 69 age bracket who have retired and are married or in a de facto relationship (Golik 1999). Both groups, the VFR and the pleasure traveller, offer the accommodation industry in particular more opportunities than the industry currently perceives or exploits.

Mid-priced accommodation is preferred by older tourists over budget or luxury accommodation since it provides the comforts they find at home at a relatively consistent level of acceptable quality. They also see a senior discount as a welcoming gesture for a valued guest. Older people who use hotel accommodation when travelling with a group tour can often create special demands for hotel staff, such as the need for pre-registration with assigned rooms and keys and special luggage-handling arrangements to facilitate orderly rooming of the older guests. Catering for coach tours has considerable benefits for the hotel: one sale can mean the rental of a large number of rooms and the sale of many meals. But this advantage has to be balanced against the commission the tour operator expects and the possible low occupancy of the hotel during the days before and after the tour booking.

Accommodation attributes that older travellers consider important include ensuite bathrooms, ease of access (stairs often create difficulties), facilities for people with disabilities and a porter or similar luggage-handling service. Many seniors who drive their own car prefer a room near to where the car is parked. Those seniors who do not drive their own car appreciate courtesy pick-up services. Some who may be concerned about becoming ill when travelling, consider the availability and proximity of medical assistance an important factor. Also, since the older traveller is often health conscious, non-smoker rooms and dining areas are in high demand.

When Australian seniors were asked to select the five most important attributes that would affect their repeat choice for accommodation, the selected attributes were:

• cleanliness
• the friendliness of staff
• security
• comfort
• the condition and maintenance of the room.

Note that the cost of accommodation, which was also listed as a choice, does not feature in this list. Older guests are particular about the cleanliness and maintenance of the rooms. Therefore, rigorous cleaning and maintenance programs should be in place to ensure the standards the older guest wants. They also like rooms that are well lit and sound proofed. Other important attributes are physical design features including easy-to-handle door knobs, lever taps in the bathroom, a supportive mattress and non-slip mats in the bath area. Safety and security features should be explained in person where possible (Ruys & Wei 1998). Personal touches are appreciated. Guests are aware that friendliness doesn't cost money. Professionalism is valued too. This can be promoted through proactive service such as assisting with luggage, bookings and the supply of information such as attractions and historical events. Many older travellers prefer accommodation in rural or suburban environments to city accommodation. There is, however, little preference for accommodation near an airport (Golik 1999).

BREAKTHROUGH TOURISM
Hotels and the seniors market

Choice Hotels International was one of the first hotel operators to recognise the growing importance of the seniors market. Initiatives taken by Choice Hotels to build up its image in this market included giving its staff 'senior awareness' training, including pictures in promotional materials, of seniors enjoying themselves and building hotels with 'seniors friendly' features. Seniors responded positively and Choice Hotels published a free *Tips for travellers over 50* booklet to further nurture this market. The booklet contains tips for seniors travelling by air, train, cruise ship and rental car. It also gives a quick course on travel photography for better photos. Finally, it lists toll-free phone numbers for airlines, car rental businesses, state tourism offices and foreign government tourism offices in the United States. Choice Hotels understands that travel satisfaction is closely linked to senior tourists' every experience during a trip, starting from planning, booking and interacting with tourism service providers, through to taking photos home. In Australia and New Zealand Choice Hotels International is known as Flag Choice Hotels. The following illustrates the approach taken by them to senior customers.

Special rooms. If you don't want the hassle of using stairs and elevators, request a room on the first floor — they are much easier to get to. Better yet, when you stay at a Rodeway Inn, request a 'Choice' room. This room is specifically designed to meet the needs of the mature traveller. It includes 'convenience items' such as coffee makers [*authors' comment: this is not common in the US*], full-length mirrors, large button television control, and brighter lighting. Instead of door knobs, there are levers to make it easier to open doors.

Grandchildren stay free. Many hotels allow children to stay free if they share the same room as a parent. Choice Hotels Family Plan allows children and grandchildren who are under 18 to stay free when they share the same room as a parent or grandparent (Choice Hotels nd).

Most hotel chains and many independent hotels in Australia and New Zealand now have senior-specific strategies. As with Choice Hotels, many operators now have distinctive brochures that feature seniors. Promoting special discounts for accommodation and meals is also a strategy for targeting seniors. The Accor group of hotels and the South Pacific Hotels Corporation group promote this strategy through targeted advertising. Best Western rewards seniors with discounted accommodation and Fly Buys points. The Youth Hostel Association attracts Seniors Card holders from some states with a two years' membership for the price of one. Members receive reduced rates in the YHA accommodation network. While competitive pricing is the most commonly used marketing tool to attract seniors, equally important are services and design features that recognise the special needs and expectations of seniors.

17.7 RESTAURANTS PATRONISED BY SENIOR TOURISTS

Restaurants patronised by seniors during travel may not be actively selected by seniors themselves. Often a package deal includes a restaurant selected by the tour company, or the restaurant may be part of the facilities supplied by the accommodation provider. On the other hand, the older persons market has been recognised by many restaurants as a vital part of their business and programs have been developed to capture and retain the older customer (Harris & West 1995). Older people may require special needs to be met before they give a restaurant their approval. Many older people experience physical changes that include loss of smell and taste. Digestive functions may also affect appetites and eating habits. An important expectation, for example, is that food should be well cooked, meaning that it should be soft and tender. Restaurant meals should be supplied at the lowest possible price and many seniors would expect a restaurant to serve smaller meal portions. Those meals should be served early — for example, at 6 p.m. Other restaurant attributes of importance to seniors include cleanliness of the facilities, waiting time for the meal, the atmosphere of the restaurant and staff friendliness (Wei & Ruys 1998).

17.8 TRANSPORT AND THE SENIOR TOURIST

Most older Australian travellers prefer to use a private car or van rather than a plane or coach as a means of transport during their vacation. The older the traveller, the more likely a coach is selected as a means of transportation. Seniors actively seek more information on transport than on any other travel-related service. In a survey that asked what types of travel information older persons found most useful, transport-related topics were prominent. They included discounted fares for long-distance travel, discounted fares for public transport in other cities, tips for stretching your travel dollar further, how to get to and from airports, railway and bus stations and availability of courtesy pick-ups (Golik 1999).

■ 17.8.1 Private car *travel and the senior tourist*

Older persons who drive themselves are among the most frequent senior travellers. As 60 per cent of seniors own at least one motor vehicle, the main contributing factor to regular travel is the ability to go on a trip when it suits them, without having to make transport bookings well in advance. These self-drive holidays provide the older person with independence and flexibility. They can escape from the crowd if they wish to and plan their trip at a pace that suits them. Some are more adventurous and keen to get off the beaten track; trips to the Outback and through the bush are popular. In this type of trip some self-drive travellers prefer to travel in convoy to benefit from the safety of numbers.

Government bodies and Automobile Associations can better serve this market segment by designing road and touring maps with the needs of the older traveller in mind. These could include locations that have medical facilities and accommodation that has the attributes that older people value. Furthermore, self-drive holidays could be facilitated by initiatives such as Australian Self Drive Tours, which supplies a driver to take people on holiday in their own car. There is also a perceived need to organise and promote coordinated convoys of private cars to remote destinations to help senior drivers feel safe and supported. However, insurance restrictions placed on persons over a certain age mean that car hire is not a popular alternative for some older travellers.

■ 17.8.2 **Rail transport** *and the senior tourist*

Older Australians see rail transport as a pleasant, affordable means of travel. It has a number of other attractive qualities that they appreciate. In comparison with coach travel, travel by train is considered more comfortable; people can move around to stretch their legs, visit the dining car and are able to socialise in the lounge. Train travel gives the passenger a good view of the scenery and the rhythm of driving over the tracks creates a sense of nostalgia.

Several aspects of train travel services could be improved for older travellers as well as the general public. Many platforms are poorly lit and not well signposted. Many seniors find the meals and the sleepers too expensive and are disappointed with the restricted availability of discounted seats and the lack of porters to help with luggage at the beginning and end of their trip. Because sleepers are too expensive, many sleep in their seats and later discover them to be extremely uncomfortable.

Many older people would travel when there is a low demand for train services by other travellers. Again, a more proactive approach by service providers could be applied, such as the development of a comprehensive travel package that included pointing out places of interest on the journey, a review of the food service and its costs and the availability of other rail products such as discounts.

■ 17.8.3 **Coach travel** *and the senior tourist*

The stereotypical view holds that the majority of older travellers take guided tours — especially guided bus tours — when they venture away from home. This is not necessarily the case and depends on the age of the traveller: older travellers are more likely to take a guided tour than the younger end of the senior sector (Loverseed 1993). Because of the relatively low costs, coach transport is a very popular means of travel for many single seniors and full pensioners. Coach travel does not require booking long in advance, which makes it suitable for impulsive travel decisions. Also, on-board entertainment such as video and driver commentary helps to pass the time.

What older people do not like about coach travel is that the steps are too high, making access to the coach difficult. The restricted room on board and, in particular, limited leg room can make travel uncomfortable. Many older travellers do not like to use the on-board restroom; neither do they like the price and quality of food at rest stops and roadhouses. They also feel that the rest stops are too infrequent.

Using these opinions, tourism marketers could not only stress the cost competitiveness of coach travel, but also make the coach travel part of the entire travel/holiday experience. For example, the technical skills of the driver should be supplemented by hospitality skills, with travellers treated as guests rather than passengers. The physical attributes of coaches such as the steps, seats and on-board restrooms should be better designed to satisfy the needs and wants of the older person.

■ 17.8.4 Air transport *and the senior tourist*

It is understandable that air transport is the most popular means of covering long distances, but it is not always used because of the costs involved. Older travellers are not always aware of the special deals available to them. However, many of these special deals are on inconvenient flights. Because airfares to some overseas destinations are cheaper than domestic airfares, many older travellers travel overseas, even though many would like to travel more within Australia. They also feel insecure when travel involves transfers and when information is supplied through the paging system. Cabin and ground staff should be aware of these insecurities and act to overcome them. Lack of leg room is also a negative experience of the older air traveller, although in this case seniors are not alone.

■ 17.8.5 Public transport *at destination*

Many older Australian travellers indicate that they want to use public transport when they visit other cities during their holidays. However, the lack of information about transport availability and special deals deters them from doing so. In particular, reciprocity of discounts when travelling outside of their home state is generally not available for them. Some of them have found it easier to obtain seniors discounts overseas than in Australia. Currently only 15 per cent of travelling seniors use local public transport at their holiday destination. There is potential to expand this market by developing low-cost public transport that suits older travellers as well as others. This potential is demonstrated by the popularity among older tourists of the public transport harbour ferries in Sydney and the Citycat and other ferries in Brisbane. Other initiatives may include special seniors tourist tickets that allow them to travel all day (including seniors from interstate), promoting public transport as part of their trip and training staff in information centres and on public transport to be sensitive to the needs of seniors.

17.9 GUIDED TOURS AND THE SENIOR TOURIST

Guided tours are the natural alternative for seniors beginning to experience difficulty with self-drive holidays. Seniors who enjoy guided touring like handing over the responsibility for transport, accommodation and leisure activities to the tour operator. They select a tour company on the range of attractions, learning opportunities and staff expertise. In particular, they value the sharing of knowledge by tour staff of places and sites visited. They feel safe in a large group of people and know that if help is needed it is readily available. Seniors prefer touring with people who have the same interests over travelling with people of the same age. They also prefer to stop at fewer places that can be more fully experienced than to have many brief stops where information cannot be absorbed (Wei & Ruys 1998).

17.10 TRAVEL AGENTS AND THE SENIOR TOURIST

Older persons find assistance by travel agencies valuable when planning breaks and holidays to unfamiliar destinations or when planning a major trip. They find some information from government travel bureaus but generally use travel agents to make bookings. A reputable travel agency with knowledgeable, courteous and friendly staff who have expertise in senior travel activities would attract senior travellers. Very reasonable prices would also help! Satisfied seniors will be loyal customers who will spread the word. Older persons are critical of travel insurance they perceive as discriminating against them. Travel agents should be able to recommend a senior-friendly travel insurer.

17.11 THE SENIOR TOURIST AND INFORMATION SOURCES

Many seniors plan their longer trips (three weeks or more) about three months before departure, much earlier than younger age groups. Most seniors do not seek information on where to travel as they already have a wish list of desired destinations. But they seek information on when to go, how to get there and what other experiences may add value to their trip. They draw on a wide range of information resources including guides, pamphlets, word of mouth, directories, travel brochures, newspapers, television, travel agents, visitor information centres, government information centres and the Seniors Card business discount directory. Other sources of lesser importance include radio, the Internet, commercials, non-travel magazines, travel shows and expos and frequent flyer/rewards programs (Golik 1999). Word of mouth is a highly valued source of travel information that may add or delete entries from the seniors' wish list of destinations.

17.12 SUMMARY

Given the recognised beneficial effects associated with travel by older people, both the Australian governments and the international community have endorsed and promoted travel activities for older people. Clearly, seniors have the propensity and desire to travel. Many of them also have the time and means to do so. However, economic, health and social issues all influence their travel motivation, patterns and activity. The older traveller has the freedom to travel longer at off-peak periods, providing an excellent opportunity for tourism service providers.

Since older people of this generation differ from the previous generation in their travel motivations and activities, tourism service providers should identify the needs and wants of the older traveller by market segments. Lifestyle changes have an impact on the ageing process, so the next cohort of older tourists will also differ from the present one, offering a continuing challenge for the tourism industry.

Issues that should be addressed by tourism service providers include accommodation, restaurants, transport, guided tours and travel agents. While older people are generally healthier than ever, many of those who still travel are less agile. There are many areas in which tourism service providers can improve their performance. Although some improvements are costly, such as more leg room in coaches and planes, many others, such as better lighting on train platforms, more thoughtful facilities in hotels and the serving of smaller portions of food in restaurants, would cost relatively little. These improvements would benefit not only the older travellers but also the public in general.

Questions

17.1 Even though the population of Australia is ageing, many older people perceive themselves as younger than their chronological age. Offer at least two explanations.

17.2 What do you see as the benefits of travel for older people? Do they differ from those for younger people? Do the benefits of travel for older people outweigh the costs of such travel? Justify either answer.

17.3 Summarise the incentives and disincentives for older people to travel. Brainstorm in a group how the disincentives to travel might be overcome by the appropriate tourism service providers.

17.4 Do you think the government should provide more assistance for older people to travel, such as discounts or free travel for train transport? Why?

17.5 The **single surcharge** for accommodation has been an issue for younger and older single travellers alike. In many tour brochures accommodation prices are quoted for double occupancy. Single travellers must share a room with a stranger or pay a surcharge for having a private room. Older single travellers often perceive this as unfair. Can the single traveller reach a compromise with the accommodation service providers? How?

17.6 Talk to one or more older persons who have travelled recently and ask:

- their travel motives
- where and how they obtained travel information
- what they consider important when travelling, in the areas of accommodation, transport and packaged tours.

Use the issues discussed in this chapter as a guideline for your questions.

REFERENCES

Australian Bureau of Statistics. 1995. *Household Expenditure Survey 1993–4*. Canberra: Commonwealth of Australia.

Australian Bureau of Statistics. 1996. *Australian Social Trends*. Canberra: Commonwealth of Australia.

Australian Bureau of Statistics. 1997. *Population Projections: 1997–2051*. Canberra: Commonwealth of Australia.

Australian Bureau of Statistics. 1998. *Time Use Survey*. Canberra: Commonwealth of Australia.

Australian Tourist Commission. 1999. *Brand Australia. A New Image for the New Millennium*. Sydney: Australian Tourist Commission.

Badinelli, K., Bavis, N. & Gustin, L. 1991. 'Senior Traveler study: America's Mature Market Not Content to While Away Their Days'. *Hotel and Motel Management* 206 (15): 31–34.

Barwick, N. J. 1984. 'Leisure Services for an Ageing Population'. *Australian Journal of Aging* 3 (3).

Berndt, R. M. & Berndt, C. H. 1984. *The World of the First Australians*. Sydney: Ure Smith.

Blazey, M. A. 1987. 'The Differences between Participants and Non-participants in a Senior Travel Program'. *Journal of Travel Research* 26 (1): 7–12.

BTR. 1999. *Domestic Tourism Monitor*. Canberra: Bureau of Tourism Research.

Calver, S., Vierich, W. & Phillips, J. 1993. 'Leisure in Later Life'. *International Journal of Contemporary Hospitality Management* 5 (1): 4–9.

Choice Hotels. nd. *Tips for Travellers over 50*. Silver Springs, New York: Choice Hotels International.

Dychtwald, K. & Flower, J. 1989. *Age Wave: The Challenges and Opportunities of an Aging America*. New York: St. Martin's Press.

Environmetrics. 1991. *Needs and Expectations of Tourists Aged over 55 Years*. Sydney: NSW Tourism Commission.

Golik, B. 1999. *Not Over the Hill. Just Enjoying the View*. Brisbane: Office of the Ageing, Department for Families, Youth and Community Care of the Queensland Government.

Hall, E. 1980. 'Interview with Bernice Neugarten: Acting on One's Age: New Rules for Old'. *Psychology Today*, April, pp. 66–80.

Harris, K. & West J. 1995. 'Senior Savvy: Mature Diners' Restaurant Service Expectations'. *Florida International University Hospitality Review* 13 (2): 35–44.

Hart, M. 1994. 'How to Use a Mature Tourism Mix Towards the Healthy Redevelopment of the Traditional Sun and Sand Resorts'. In Seaton, A. V. (Ed.). *Tourism: The State of the Art*. Chichester, UK: John Wiley & Sons.

Leinberger, P. 1992. 'Highlights from the ARM: Quantum Mature Market Study'. Paper presented at the symposium 'Targeting the Mature Market', Gazebo Hotel, Sydney, December.

Loverseed, H. 1993. 'Market Segments; US Mature Travellers Market'. *Economic Intelligence Unit Travel and Tourism Analyst* 1: 51–64.

McCleary, K., Weaver, P. & Lan, L. 1994. 'Gender-based Differences'. *The Cornell Hotel and Restaurant Administration Quarterly* 35 (2): 51–8.

McInerney, J. A. 1992. 'Getting More for Less?'. *Lodging*, March, pp. 39–40.

McIntosh, R. & Goeldner, C. 1986. *Tourism, Principles, Practices, and Philosophies*. Fifth Edition. New York: John Wiley & Sons.

Moschis, G. P. 1992. Marketing to the Older Consumer: A Handbook of Information for Strategy Development. Westport, USA: Quorum Books.

Muller, T. & O'Cass, A. 1998. *Using Travel Motives to Segment the Australian Seniors Market: Working Paper*. Griffith University: School of Marketing and Management.

Pederson, B. 1994. 'Future Seniors and the Travel Industry'. *Florida International University Hospitality Review* 12 (2): 59–70.

Poon, A. 1994. 'The "New Tourism" Revolution'. *Tourism Management* 15 (2): 91–92.

Queensland Department of Family Services. 1989. *Action for the Ageing: The Report of the Task Force on the Ageing*. Brisbane: Queensland Department of Family Services.

Rowland, D. T. 1991. *Aging in Australia*. Melbourne: Longman Cheshire.

Ruys, H. 1997. Survey of Mature Domestic Travellers. Master's thesis. Victoria University of Technology.

Ruys, H. & Wei, S. 1998. 'Accommodation Needs of Mature Australian Travellers'. *Australian Journal of Hospitality Management* 5 (1): 51–60.

Small, Frank & Associates. 1986. 'Aged Travellers Research'. A marketing research presentation prepared for Qantas Airways Ltd.

Stuart, J. E. 1992. Lessons from the US. Paper presented at the Second European Conference on the Senior Travel Market, 'Europe's Senior Travel Market'. Paris: European Travel Commission, pp. M25–M27.

Viant, A. 1993. 'Enticing the Elderly to Travel'. *Tourism Management* 14 (1): 52–60.

Wei, S. & Ruys, H. 1998. *Seniors and Industry Perception Survey.* Report prepared for the Seniors Card Office. Brisbane: University of Queensland.

Wheatcroft, S. & Seekings, J. 1992. The ATI Report: The Action Plan Reviewed. Paper presented at the Second European Conference on the Senior Travel Market, 'Europe's Senior Travel Market'. Paris: European Travel Commission.

Wiseman, H. (Ed.). 1999. *Get Up & Go, Australian Travel Guide for Seniors 2000.* Sydney: Mahlab Cramb Media.

Zimmer, Z., Brayley, R. & Searle, M. 1995. 'Whether to Go and Where to Go: Identification of Important Influences on Seniors' Decisions to Travel'. *Journal of Travel Research* 33 (3): 3–10.

Mr and Mrs Cassidy's story

In 1998 the Bureau of Tourism Research reported that 3.18 million persons aged 55 years and over participated in overnight domestic travel (BTR 1999). Ageing brings with it a reduction in motor functions of the individual. It becomes more difficult to turn on a tap or there is a feeling of insecurity when getting in or out of a bathtub. The ability of hotels to cater for these additional demands, which may be as simple as installing lever handle taps or handrails, will be an increasingly significant factor in capturing the seniors market. Although many accommodation providers have not yet recognised the special needs of older persons, a growing number have. The Grand Mercure Hotel on the Gold Coast is one example. The story of Mr and Mrs Cassidy's experiences at the Grand Mercure illustrates the impact that such recognition can have on the individual.

Mr and Mrs Cassidy were regular guests of the Pan Pacific Hotel in Broadbeach, Queensland. They had used the hotel for a weekend escape for several years and were satisfied with the hotel products and services. They continued to be patrons when the hotel was taken over by the Accor group and the hotel was re-branded the Grand Mercure. Over the years they had seen staff come and go but the atmosphere stayed the same; they really felt at home. As they aged their mobility and agility began to decline. Their beach walks took longer and using the hotel's swimming pool became more difficult. They did not stop using it, but simply getting in and out of the pool became more demanding.

When they checked out after a recent stay, the front office staff member asked the usual question, 'Was everything to your satisfaction?' expecting a positive answer. Mrs Cassidy said she did not have any complaints but did have a suggestion. She mentioned that getting in and out of the pool had become more difficult for them and perhaps the hotel could make it a little easier. She also said that they were not the only guests who had difficulties; she had seen several others having the same problems and felt her remark was worth taking into consideration.

The staff member must have done her job well. Some days later the General Manager of the Grand Mercure telephoned the Cassidys and asked them for suggestions for improving the pool. The Cassidys suggested, among other things, that they place handrails near the steps. On their next visit to the Grand Mercure they were delighted to see that handrails had been installed. Not only was it now easier for them to use the pool, but the fact that their opinion was valued made them feel recognised and appreciated. They discovered that they were not the only ones to benefit, as they saw guests of all ages using the handrails.

A relatively inexpensive modification greatly enhanced the Cassidys' (and other guests') enjoyment of the hotel.

Questions

1 What mechanisms does the Grand Mercure have for recognising the needs of its customers?

2 Do you think that the outlay of installing the handrails, mentioned in the text, was worthwhile for the hotel?

3 What can those employed in the tourism industry learn from this case study? What can senior tourists learn from it?

4 'Customers have endless needs and wants. We cannot satisfy everybody.' Comment on this statement. Develop a set of criteria as part of the hotel policy to guide whether customer complaints/suggestions ought to be acted upon when there are costs (tangible or intangible) involved. Justify your criteria. For example, should wheelchair access be available throughout the hotel? Should a non-slippery mat be provided for all bathroom tubs? Should seats be provided in lifts?

Peter Schofield

CHAPTER 18

Urban tourism
and small business

LEARNING OBJECTIVES

After reading this chapter, you will have an appreciation of:

- the post-industrial transformation of cities and the role of tourism in the restructuring of urban areas

- the comparative neglect of research on small tourism businesses operating in urban areas

- the difficulties of establishing the exact contribution of small tourism businesses to the economy of cities

- the role of small businesses in the urban tourism 'product'

- the multi-functional and multi-experiential nature of post-industrial cities

- the complexity of both the tourism industry and the tourist experience of cities

- the importance, from the small business perspective, of tourists' secondary motivations and their needs regarding secondary facilities

- the strategic and operational importance of information and communications technology for small businesses operating in an urban context

- the need for inter-organisational partnerships to encourage cooperation between sectors and to avoid both inefficient use of resources and ineffective promotions.

𝓘NTRODUCTION

Tourism is a major social and economic activity in a variety of destinations throughout the world. One of its distinguishing characteristics as a commercial activity, along with its intangible products, the inseparability of their production and consumption and the role of coordinating intermediaries, is the important contribution made by large numbers of small businesses at each tourist destination. If a destination's infrastructure represents the foundations of its tourism industry and its primary attractions are its building blocks, then it is the small businesses that cement the structure together and provide an augmented destination product by adding breadth, interest, originality and even authenticity to the visitor experience.

The aim of this chapter is to outline the nature, role and significance of *small tourism enterprises* (STEs) in the contemporary tourist experience of urban areas. Within this context, we will consider the complexity of the urban tourism product and the extent to which small businesses can be described as tourist resources with respect to providing urban attractions, amenities and facilities. We will also address the role of government policy in the development and management of STEs. To this end, the chapter draws heavily on both the urban tourism literature and the general small business literature because of the limited availability of sources pertaining to small tourism businesses in urban areas.

A variety of urban tourism destinations have been recognised, ranging from capital cities and large historic cities through cultural or art cities and industrial cities to revitalised waterfront areas, seaside resorts and tourist-entertainment complexes like EuroDisney (Page 1995). While recognising the importance of all of these types of destination, we will focus on cities as tourist attractions and examine the role of STEs in the city 'product' and in the tourist experience of these places.

𝓣HE TRANSFORMATION OF CITIES: FROM PRODUCTION TO CONSUMPTION

Ever since people first lived in cities, they have attracted visitors for a wide variety of purposes and have had a fundamental influence on, and been influenced by, a range of social and economic activities. In the last 40 years, the post-industrialisation of the western world has brought about the most significant changes both in the structure and character of cities and in the way in which they are used. Traditional industries have declined to the point where economic regeneration, particularly in the central areas, is high on the political agenda and many governments have used tourism as a primary force in inner-city rejuvenation because it is a desirable and feasible means of employment and income generation with positive social, cultural and environmental effects.

Urban societies have now become more diversified, individualistic, globally aware and oriented to lifestyles based upon fashion-conscious and rapidly shifting consumerism (Ashworth & Voogd 1994). The result is that cities, formerly centres of production, have been reconstructed into centres of consumption. In this context, cities are now evaluated according to a set of attributes formerly considered to be of marginal consequence. They are judged by post-industrial society on the basis of their 'amenity value' in terms of their physical environmental quality and the human experience of place.

Cities are usually characterised by high concentrations of visitor attractions and amenities that serve both the tourist and local resident markets. They may therefore have a comparative advantage with respect to this central resource base, because smaller centres cannot attain either the requisite critical mass of attractions and facilities or the desired 'product' that results from their synergy. This multifunctional nature is reflected by the volume and value of the tourist trade, which, notwithstanding the difficulties of calculating its positive spin-off, are considered to be of significant benefit to the wider economy. Whether visitors desire spectacle, excitement, authenticity, fun or entertainment — both legal and illegal — the contemporary city can accommodate their needs, but cities now compete against each other in an increasingly competitive marketplace and must therefore promote themselves effectively, because the public's image of the city 'product' is a critical factor in the destination choice process and in the subsequent evaluation of their experience.

18.3 THE SMALL BUSINESS ENIGMA: A CITY'S HIDDEN ASSETS

The economic and social significance of urban tourism are undeniable, yet much of the general tourism literature neglects the urban context in which a great deal of this activity is set, while the urban studies literature tends either to omit discussion about tourism or to underestimate its impact. A similar argument can be made for the subject of small businesses in tourism, because although their importance is widely recognised, there has also been a comparative neglect of research in this area. A number of authors, notably Ashworth (1989), Ashworth and de Haan (1986), Ashworth and Tunbridge (1990), Ashworth and Voogd (1990), Law (1993) and Page (1995), have begun to redress this imbalance with respect to the urban tourism literature, while important contributions to the STE literature have been made by Williams et al. (1989), Shaw and Williams (1987; 1990; 1994), Morrison et al. (1998), Ng (1997), Thomas (1998), Wanhill (1999) and Page et al. (1999). There is, however, a gap in the literature concerning small tourism businesses in *urban* tourism.

Figure 18.1
Urban tourism has revived older areas, such as the Rocks in Sydney, but brought an increase in traffic.

Source: *Norman Douglas*

■ *18.3.1* **A neglected** *area of study*

The neglect of STEs in urban tourism is not surprising given that it is only relatively recently that both urban tourism and small tourism businesses have become of interest to academics and that very few cities have access to comprehensive information about either the nature of their tourism industry or small tourism businesses. As a result, the specific nature and scope of their activities are neither explicitly recognised nor fully understood by key decision makers; their essential qualities remain an enigma and perhaps they can best be described as a tourist destination's hidden assets. They remain hidden because of the following reasons.

1. The complexity of both the tourism industry in urban areas and the tourist experience (and consequently, the role of small businesses) means that data collection and impact measurement are problematic, making it difficult for planners and other decision makers to understand the nature of urban tourism. In turn, this may explain why they often consider tourism as subordinate and incidental to other commercial and industrial activities and why relevant data are not collected and/or research is not commissioned, so that a vicious circle is created.

2. Because of this complexity and, in particular, the multiple motivations of visitors, it is difficult to establish definitions of urban tourism. They are often restrictive and exclude *visiting friends and relatives* (VFR) and certain business categories. Many studies have tended to focus on particular aspects of urban tourism (for example, the primary attractions) while ignoring other details of visitors' experience of place that bring them into direct contact with small businesses. Research is needed to determine the

tourist needs that are satisfied through their interaction with small businesses and whether the interaction is an essential, incidental or even accidental element of the experience.

3. Even assuming agreement about definitions, it is difficult to measure the number and flow of tourists and the breakdown of their expenditure because the requisite statistical basis for the analysis is not available. Secondary data sources do not distinguish between tourism businesses on the basis of their size, survey evidence is fragmented, time-budget research is practically nonexistent and other short-cut methods provide unreliable data (Law 1993). As a result, only an elementary examination can be made. Additionally, because of these problems, it is difficult to estimate the number of jobs being created in small businesses.

4. Because urban areas are multifunctional and small 'tourism' businesses are also used by a wide range of other consumers such as residents, people who work in the area and students, it is difficult to disaggregate the touristic and non-touristic aspects of small business operations.

5. The absence of an accepted classification of STEs to a large extent precludes a structured analysis of these businesses in an urban context. Much of our existing knowledge of small tourism firms has been gleaned from generic studies of small enterprises. This general small business literature is strewn with a wide range of definitions of 'small firms' that relate to market share, influence on either market prices or the level of supply, organisations independent of central control, owner-managers, turnover or number of employees (Stanworth & Gray 1991; Storey 1994; Burns 1996; Thomas 1996). The tourism and hospitality literature is also characterised by its variable use of small business definitions using similar criteria (see Morrison 1996; Thomas et al. 1997) and as yet there is no published material relating to small businesses in an urban environment.

6. There have been varying estimates of the number of small businesses in Britain (Wedgwood & Markham 1994), which further complicates the issue. Many small tourism businesses, particularly in the accommodation sector in the UK, may not be registered for value added tax (VAT) because they operate in the informal economy; because they operate below the threshold at which they are required to register; or because they do not have the required number of rooms (Thomas 1998).

7. The use of British census and employment data in an analysis of small firms is also problematic because the census covers pay as you earn (PAYE) schemes and therefore excludes the self-employed who do not employ others and organisations that do not use these schemes (Bannock & Daly 1994). Moreover, data based on PAYE schemes may include employees from a number of locations or companies with more than one scheme in operation. As a result, there may be considerable inaccuracies in the data.

Therefore, although it is widely acknowledged that the tourism industry is 'largely made up of small firms' (DNH 1996:16), the lack of reliable statistics makes the task of analysing the precise contribution of STEs, not to mention their role in an urban context, a particularly difficult one.

■ 18.3.2 The small business *contribution to the urban tourism product*

Jansen-Verbeke's (1986) notion of the **leisure product** provides a useful conceptual framework within which to examine the contribution of small businesses to tourism in urban areas, because it facilitates a discussion of both their leading and their supporting roles while recognising the contribution of the state and, in particular, public–private sector partnerships in the establishment and maintenance of an appropriate operating environment. Small businesses form an integral part of the urban 'leisure product'. They may contribute to the *primary elements* comprising the main attractions while also enhancing the *leisure setting*, consisting of the architectural and topographical features and the sociocultural characteristics of place. They are, however, more likely to be part of the *secondary elements* of the product. These have been traditionally referred to as the 'supporting' facilities and services, such as tourist accommodation, transportation, food and beverage outlets and retail establishments.

The primary attractions, symbols and icons of cities are usually their most memorable traits and few people would be prepared to travel a great distance to visit the secondary elements of city tourism products. Nevertheless, the secondary elements can be critical to whether a city is successful or not as a tourist destination, not least because for many visitors they constitute the main form of expenditure — primarily on accommodation, food and beverage, which normally account for more than 50 per cent of the spend. This injection of cash into the local economy can stimulate a significant multiplier effect. Accommodation is particularly important in this respect because, in a European context, small, independent hotels dominate the market (Sheldon 1993). Moreover, accommodation is considered by many visitors who stay overnight in a city to be one of the most important components of their visit; it may in fact be the key element in the decision to visit one destination over another and the most important element of the 'product' from the consumer's point of view. However, it has traditionally been classified as a 'secondary' element from the perspective of the tourism industry. Given its importance, the general maxim that the demand for accommodation is a derived demand is untenable.

This is not to say that other 'secondary' elements are insignificant. The availability of a wide variety of good quality food in a range of international restaurants is essential for a successful urban tourism product. This is particularly effective where they are clustered in or near the central area or in cultural districts. Law (1993) argues that the right mix of retail facilities can also increase the attractiveness of a city to tourists; they are particularly attracted to 'speciality' retailing — for example, art and craft goods and luxuries such as unusual household items and designer clothes. Indeed, for some tourists like 'leisure shoppers' these so-called secondary facilities may be the primary motivation for the visit (Page 1995). In some cases, a combination of secondary elements can form an interchangeable symbiotic relationship, For example, the Trafford Centre in Greater Manchester and the Darling Harbour complex in Sydney are spectacular retail attractions with supporting food and beverage outlets, but for some visitors the restaurants are the main attraction and shopping is the secondary element of the product. In both cases and whether shopping is planned or spontaneous, the small business contribution to the visitor experience is significant.

Numerically, STEs dominate the tourism sector of a city and provide visitors with a point of direct contact with the destination and its residents. An enjoyable evening in a restaurant, a friendly and helpful shop assistant, a well-structured and -delivered guided tour or live music in an atmospheric pub may all contribute significantly, along with a wide range of other factors, to a positive experience of place. Many of the small businesses that provide these services may offer an additional reason for a visit to one city rather than another. Alternatively, their absence could deter a prospective visitor. Poor quality service in any of these elements of the 'product' may result in a 'halo' effect that could spoil a visitor's overall experience of the city, deter that person from revisiting the destination and result in negative word-of-mouth publicity. Additionally, small businesses may also play an important indirect role in visitor motivation and experience because of their contribution to the overall character and image of a place. This may be the case even where the visitor does not use a particular business during his or her stay.

18.4 THE MULTI-EXPERIENTIAL NATURE OF CITIES: OPPORTUNITIES FOR STEs

Cities like Sydney, New York, London and Paris are among the world's most popular tourist attractions. Clearly, they have unique characteristics that differentiate them from other city 'products', but all cities share a number of common characteristics that explain the large numbers of visitors they receive each year. Some of these are outlined below.

- Cities are concentrations of commerce, industry and services; they are major transportation hubs; and they have high population densities.
- As a result, they are centres of intensive human interaction and it is not surprising that so much of contemporary tourist activity has contact, in one form or another, with urban areas.
- Cities serve as gateways for tourists entering a country.
- Cities are 'centres of accommodation' and may be a base for excursions to rural areas as well as being destinations in their own right (Law 1993).
- Recent trends in tourist activity, such as the growth in the short break and day trip sectors, have also increased the number of visits to large cities, so that they are undoubtedly one of the most important types of tourist destination.

A wide variety of motivations for visiting cities have been cited in the urban tourism literature. These motivations range from VFR, business, conference and exhibition, education and culture to heritage, religion, hallmark events and leisure shopping. This standard classification is useful as a basis for a priori segmentation of the market and clearly demonstrates the diversity of use and the simultaneous functions within the urban tourism sector. A survey of urban tourism in 34 European cities carried out in 1993 by KPMG consultants (cited in Wober 1997) showed that the purpose of visit for 46 per cent of visitors was 'business and professional' compared with leisure (27 per cent), VFR (8 per cent), health treatment (2 per cent) and other (18 per cent). The mix of business and leisure visitors did, however, vary markedly from one destination to another. The mix is an important consideration because business trips are less prone to seasonal fluctuation and business visitors tend to spend more, on average, than leisure visitors. Moreover, factors such as accessibility and business facilities may be higher priorities than the city's visitor attractions, which are likely to be the important pull factors from the perspective of the leisure traveller. Because the character of the city may be either secondary or irrelevant to its use by business and conference tourists, Ashworth and Tunbridge (1990) have described them as 'incidental users' compared with the 'institutional users' — leisure tourists who are motivated by the character of the city.

Clearly, the purpose of the visit and the mix of market segments have important implications for small tourism businesses, particularly with respect to developing effective targeting and product development strategies in order to reduce the potential threat of fluctuations in demand over the year resulting in cash flow problems. On the one hand, an urban location may be a key factor in reducing small business vulnerability to hostile environmental factors when, for example, business visitors, day excursionists and local markets represent important segments that provide stability in off-peak periods. On the other hand, competition is fierce in relation to the commercially attractive segments and effective product differentiation is a crucial factor in the survival of small firms. This issue is explored in more detail in the case study at the end of the chapter.

■ 18.4.1 'Urban tourism' — *a restrictive definition?*

The standard classification of urban tourists is based on the primary motivation for a visit. On this basis, it is perhaps more relevant to primary attractions and organisations that relate directly to this motivation than to small businesses that are more likely to provide either secondary facilities for a wide range of user types (for example, the accommodation sector) or attractions that satisfy the secondary needs of visitors, such as specialist guided tours. Indeed, many visits to the city are multipurpose or have a secondary motivation (Law 1993) and even when the tourists' needs are few, the expressions of these needs, in terms of the paths individual tourists tread across a city during their visit, are many and varied. Consequently, the pattern of interactions with a range of primary and secondary elements at various times is extremely complex and without detailed accounts of tourist time-budgets, it is difficult to determine the role small businesses play in visitor activities.

The term *urban tourism* has a tendency to bring to mind its more mainstream and conventional activities, including visits to art galleries, theatres, museums, heritage attractions and shopping. This begs the question, has the use of this umbrella term conjured up a stereotypical image of the urban tourist while neglecting the variety of activities and experiences they seek and enjoy? This question is particularly relevant in this context because these other aspects of the visit — typically, low-key leisure activities — are likely to be provided by small businesses.

The temporal dimension of the visit experience is an important consideration in this respect. Clearly, over long periods of time the nature of cities can change dramatically, but even in the short term the character of a city, district or street can alter significantly through the seasons or between night and day. During the day, a street or area can be attractive because of its buildings, specialist shops, markets, cafes, trees, street furniture and overall colour and vitality. By night, the atmosphere may be very different because of the way it is lit, its bars, its restaurants and mix of diners and its street entertainers and their music. Examples can be found in most cities, from the Ramblas in Barcelona to the Rocks in Sydney.

Even from the perspective of the individual visitor on one day or night of their visit, the city provides new experiences in rapid succession, so that initial needs relating to primary motivations may be satisfied quickly and as a result, other facets of the city experience are then engaged. A conference delegate, business person or cultural tourist may enjoy a football match, an evening at the theatre, stand-up comedy in a local pub or specialist leisure shopping in addition to their main activity. The multi-experiential nature of the tourist experience can therefore create a number of opportunities for small businesses in both the secondary attractions and facilities components of the city's tourism 'product'.

SPECIAL INTEREST INVESTIGATION
Tourism and dance club culture

San Antonio on the island of Ibiza is probably one of the best known examples of a tourist destination in which the primary attraction is the dance club scene — the more contemporary mainstream incarnation of **'acid house'** — and its associated activities. However, many cities throughout the world also have an established dance club culture with its attendant demand for supporting facilities such as accommodation and food and beverage. Clubbers fit into the short break market, often travelling considerable distances to experience the alternative face of the contemporary Jekyll and Hyde city.

Despite its association with drugs, club culture is moving away from its 'folk devil' status not least because of its financial respectability; the youth market is characterised by high levels of discretionary income and early adoption of new concepts and products (Nowicka 1995). Many clubs and cafe bars have emerged as important business enterprises. Cafe bars fill the gap between pubs and clubs because they are often designed by contemporary architects and provide the sought benefits of style, comfort and high quality service reminiscent of upmarket clubs. In Britain the relaxation in licensing laws has allowed cafe bars to serve alcohol until the early hours of the morning and permit dancing so that young people are spared the high entrance fees that clubs charge. Many cafe bars and clubs also employ door staff who exclude groups of drunken males; as a result, young women are not subjected to the harassment they may encounter in a less regulated pub setting (Stewart-Smith 1997).

The imagery borrowed from club culture is now being used to market a range of goods and services to the youth market, including tourism products. For example, in 1996 the British Tourist Authority, having recognised the touristic potential of club culture, launched a campaign to target international visitors in the 18 to 30 age group by highlighting dance clubs in their *UK Guide*. The promotional literature even featured a guide to drug-inspired slang like 'sorted', 'bangin' and 'mad for it' (Collin 1997). This is tantamount to official endorsement of club culture on an international scale, and yet recreational drug consumption, which is inextricably bound up in it, is part of a broader problem that costs the British government £1.4 billion a year, with the additional social and economic costs of drug-related crime, sickness and absenteeism estimated to be between £3 and £4 billion a year more (Travis 1998). On the other hand, drug-related deaths and problems are relatively few when compared with those connected with alcohol consumption (*ABC of Drugs* 1998), and yet the latter is considered to be an established part of the tourist experience at a destination.

In Australia the 'rave' or dance parties are still on the fringe of society despite their rapidly spreading popularity. Highly publicised police raids and the occasional death either from poor quality drugs or from overdose reinforce the negative aspect of these events in the public mind. But organised entertainments of this nature, which consistently attract well over 5000 people to a single event, cannot be ignored for too long when the business flow-on implications are considered.

Clearly, dance club or party culture means big business for many small businesses that service the needs of this market. However, the link between club culture and recreational drug consumption also means that the trade in illegal drugs, increasingly class 'A' drugs, is developing in parallel. The ethics of endorsing tourism based on club culture and recreational drug consumption clearly requires further consideration.

Having considered some of the temporal dimensions of the tourist experience, it is also important to address the spatial aspects. The multifaceted tourist experience of the city has complicated the analysis of tourist functional areas such as the **tourist-historic city** (Ashworth & de Haan 1986). This complexity not only results from the fact that the tourist shares the use of these areas with residents, workers and students, but because what little we know about urban tourist behaviour suggests that it would be inaccurate to classify a visitor simply as a culture or history tourist. Myriad combinations are possible and likely, depending on a range of variables including the inclination of the individual, the available attractions, the nature and duration of the visit, the season and the time of day. Clearly, the multi-motivational and multi-experiential nature of urban tourist behaviour has muddied the waters for those who have attempted to classify visitors in terms of their primary or specific use of the city.

Perhaps a special case can be made for urban tourism within the context of special interest tourism (SIT) because of the sheer breadth of a city's attractions and facilities, which cater for a range of interests and sought experiences, from the reality of Sydney's Kings Cross district to the hyperreality of Edinburgh's ghost tours. Every visitor to the city is, arguably, involved in their own SIT because they uniquely interpret the city's stimulating environment and its features and mould them into their personalised 'soft city' — that is, their own desired tourism experience of place. In this respect, the term *tourism in urban areas* would seem more appropriate than urban tourism.

18.5 THE ROLE OF THE STATE

Urban tourism can be an important generator of income, employment and taxes and many states receive a greater return from urban tourism than from other types of tourist destinations. One of the most commonly cited economic benefits of tourism development in urban areas is the creation of entrepreneurial opportunities. This is not surprising, given that innovation and entrepreneurship lie at the heart of the wealth-creating process. Traditionally, the study of small firms has focused on the entrepreneur from three disciplinary perspectives: economics, sociology and psychology; but within this research framework, small tourism businesses have received very little attention in terms of either the behavioural characteristics of tourism entrepreneurs or their economic impact. The available evidence suggests that many tourism owner-managers may lack either relevant tourism industry experience or general management experience, which may explain their inability to both innovate and react to uncertainty (Shaw & Williams 1990).

In recent years, British urban policies have been characterised by support for increasing private sector led initiatives, a reduction in government control and financial support and a growing interest in various forms of cooperation between public and private sectors, including a small business policy. State support for small businesses is not a new phenomenon (see Stanworth & Gray 1991) but it is now an established feature of the political landscape in the UK and yet there has been very little research into the impact of the policy on the behaviour of tourism organisations (Thomas 1998).

The issue of small business failure is central to the identification of relevant needs. It is a complex area and a large number of endogenous and exogenous factors have been found to be relevant. The high business failure rate among small tourism organisations is primarily due to undercapitalisation, high gearing, a weak local economy and poor management at strategic and operational levels. Much of the research has focused on the accommodation and food and beverage sectors of the industry. In this context, the comparatively high investment in fixed assets and the high break-even point in hotels and restaurants means that only a small amount of funding is available for working capital, resulting in operations with a tendency to be highly geared and, at times, undercapitalised (Boer 1998). By comparison, success results from the synergistic effect of four factors:
1. suitable financial resources
2. a specific set of ownership characteristics
3. appropriate features of an organisation
4. an organisation's strategy (Webster 1998).

■ 18.5.1 **Small business** *policy: its relevance for tourism firms*

The four key objectives of Britain's small business policy address the main concerns facing small businesses in most international urban areas. They seek to:
1. implement policy that will create an economic environment appropriate for the development of small businesses. Key policy goals are reduced taxation, control of inflation and the elimination of unnecessary rules and regulations that represent a considerable burden on small businesses and may discourage enterprise.
2. develop initiatives such as the Loan Guarantee scheme to encourage financial investment
3. provide appropriate business information and support for both start-up and subsequent operations
4. sponsor programs to encourage training and development for small business managers.

From the perspective of STEs, however, there are a number of key issues. First, despite the availability of business loans, many small tourism businesses rely solely on personal sources of capital to fund business initiatives (Shaw & Williams 1990; Thomas et al. 1997). Second, only a small proportion of small businesses make use of the Business Link Services (or the equivalent Business Enterprise Centres in Australia) even though firms are disadvantaged without it, in terms of their access to relevant data and their subsequent development of business strategies (Costa & Teare 1996). Moreover, there is a high level of satisfaction and some evidence for enhanced business performance among organisations that use the services on offer (Storey 1994; Molian & Birley 1995). Third, there is a relatively low level of participation by many managers of small tourism organisations in management development programs despite the benefits. This may result from a failure to recognise sector-specific issues. In the case of tourism, there are a number of relevant factors (Wynarczyk et al. 1993; Storey & Westhead 1995; Thomas et al. 1997).

- Managers of small tourism organisations are motivated by a wide range of factors, many of which are prioritised over profit and growth.
- The absence of internal labour markets in STEs means that there is a risk of trained employees leaving to join other organisations.
- Small tourism firms have short-term horizons, whereas training offers longer-term benefits.
- STEs may have reduced awareness about training opportunities or may experience difficulties in finding training opportunities tailored to their specific needs.
- There is an additional opportunity cost in employees being absent from work while being trained.

The British Government's **training and enterprise councils (TECs)** have been praised for their role in filling important niches and addressing local market failure while being criticised for failing to attract the attention of the majority of their target organisations. Authorities in the field argue that TECs and Business Links have penetrated only between 3 and 10 per cent of the sector. Consequently, there is some agreement that support agencies can improve the services they offer through more effective targeting strategies and through initiatives that have a more sector-specific focus (DNH 1995; DTI 1996). In Australia, the equivalent organisations are the business enterprise centres and although no formal study exists to date, it is quite reasonable to suggest that the above comments could be directed to these as well.

BREAKTHROUGH TOURISM
Small business networking

City tourism is to a large extent an 'information business' (Schertler 1994) and although technology can't replace human engagement in the provision of tourism services, it is clearly an important element in the success of tourism organisations operating in an urban environment. This is one area in which an initiative by the British Government's Department of Trade and Industry (DTI) has proved to be successful, after their international benchmarking study identified that although the UK compared favourably with the majority of European countries in using information and communication technologies, small businesses lagged far behind larger companies and needed more expert advice. The DTI's Information Society Initiative (ISI) Programme for Business has raised awareness about, and encouraged the use of, relevant technology by small businesses through the national network of local business partnerships in England — the Business Link. There are 85 Business Links with 240 outlets, which provide an integrated Innovation and Technology Service tailored to the needs of small businesses. Innovation and Technology Counsellors (ITCs) help small businesses to recognise the benefits of information and communications technologies and innovative practice and to develop and apply relevant skills (DTI 1998).

The technology is being used extensively in certain sectors such as tourism agencies and accommodation organisations. Most information technology applications are predominantly database applications that support a particular organisation and enable its management to focus more on people-oriented activities and strategic issues. An increasing number of small businesses are finding significant benefits from their use of the Internet. For example, the Enterprise Zone, launched by the DTI in 1997, is the definitive Internet site for small business information. It provides rapid, easy and cost-effective access to high quality information on relevant topics such as regulation, sources of finance, innovation and technology and managing new businesses. Internet services can also facilitate the market environmental scanning and analysis functions of organisations and increase the efficiency and effectiveness of communication with suppliers and consumers.

This technology offers significant potential for promotion — an area that often causes difficulties for small tourism businesses. Ad-hoc, sector and integrative World Wide Web–based city information systems offer opportunities for small businesses to promote their individual or specialist product or service. If we take the accommodation sector as an example, most sites currently display only top class hotels or budget accommodation in line with the requests of two major groups of Internet users — high-income business persons and low-income students (Maier, 1997). There is, however, significant potential for small tourism businesses as Internet use increases across a wider range of city visitor market segments and because of meta information systems such as 'City.Net', which combine links to all relevant Web pages and can therefore potentially increase consumer exposure. It is important to note in this respect that those countries that spend most on tourism — the United States, Germany, Japan and the UK — account for 79 per cent of the world's present Internet population, and that more and more consumers are adopting online distribution channels as their preferred way of buying tourism products. Use of this new infrastructure by small businesses may therefore be an effective way of reaching potential visitors in both existing and new market segments.

■ 18.5.2 Inter-organisational *cooperation*

Visitors' consumption of the city involves a series of experiences involving interactions with people and 'product' elements that occur to a large extent in public places and facilities. As a result, most of the visitors' overall experience of the city lies outside the immediate control of individual small businesses. In these circumstances, and given the intense competition between cities and the need for effective promotion, inter-organisational relationships with other tourism organisations and external relations with the host community increase in importance.

The development of a coordinated approach to the management of the tourism product is necessary in order to encourage cooperation between sectors and avoid the risk of both inefficient use of scarce resources and ineffective promotions, which can confuse the potential visitor. Partnerships between the public and private sectors have therefore been forged in the form of destination associations, marketing oganisations and visitor and convention bureaus that often perform functions such as the acquisition and dissemination of relevant information, cooperative marketing, business planning, setting service standards and training. They may also produce tourism statistics at an appropriate scale of aggregation. The Greater Glasgow Tourist Board is a good example of this type of cooperative structure. There is no general, universally applicable model, however, because the situation in each destination is sufficiently different to warrant the development of a tailored plan.

An important task for destination marketing organisations or supporting agencies is to develop the STEs' understanding of the multilevel competitive environment within which they operate. Most STEs tend to concentrate on the competition among local providers and ignore the direct and indirect competitive forces in the global marketplace and the threat of online distribution channels. Buhalis and Cooper (1998) have identified five levels of competition for small and medium-sized tourism enterprises: from similar products at a destination, from similar or undifferentiated destinations, from differentiated destinations, from the distribution channel and from alternative leisure activities. The role of information technology is vital in this respect and supporting agencies have a key role to play in both demonstrating its potential benefits and providing consultation and support.

Competition between small tourism businesses is often fierce, although their interests converge on the subject of promotion, which is widely regarded as one of the most important tasks of tourism organisations. Small tourism businesses are particularly vulnerable to changes in visitor or potential visitor perceptions of the overall tourism product or of its component parts. Changes in consumers' images of a destination can result in economic success or failure. This is a particular area of concern for small businesses, because although they make a significant contribution to an urban tourism product, they may not be in a position to influence the creation and projection of an appropriate image and may instead be reliant on the effectiveness of a destination's 'official' image, which is primarily based on the key benefits or primary attractions.

Given the large number of small tourism businesses that contribute to the tourist experience of place, it is not practicable to promote their distinctive individual characteristics and effectively retain the image of a cohesive tourism product without overcomplicating matters from a consumer perspective in terms of destination attribute overload. Nevertheless, the promotional literature should provide a flavour of the characteristics that small businesses lend to a city. This is often absent because the agencies responsible for creating the 'official' image of the product lack the necessary information about the diversity of products and services on offer. As a result, a 'composite view' is often adopted (Page 1995).

SUMMARY

This chapter has sought to outline the main characteristics of, and the key issues relating to, STEs in urban destinations. In doing so, it has discussed the problems of defining and categorising small urban tourism businesses and the difficulties of measurement with respect to their number, contribution and role in urban tourism.

The urban tourism literature and the general small business literature have provided useful indications that certain factors may be relevant to small tourism organisations currently operating in urban areas. The fact remains, however, that there is still a sizeable gap in our knowledge and understanding about these businesses. The overriding problem is the complexity of both the tourist experience of these places and the urban tourism industry that services the requirements of visitors. Consequently, the contribution to, and impact of, small tourism businesses in this environment are difficult to examine.

In drawing on a body of research that is limited compared with other areas of tourism, any conclusions are inevitably tentative. However, small businesses appear to make an important contribution, in a number of different roles, to both the tourism industry in cities and urban regeneration because visitors undertake activities in addition to those associated with the primary motivation for their visit and the expenditure on these secondary elements is significant. Moreover, although visitors are unlikely to be attracted to a city because of the attractions or amenities provided by small businesses, the absence of these organisations can make a significant difference to their overall experience of the destination and could influence their decision about whether to visit one destination over another.

Clearly, there is a need both for further study of tourism firms within the small business research and for a greater emphasis on small businesses within tourism research. Given the reasons for the neglect of this subject hitherto, however, it is likely that small businesses in tourism will continue to be a difficult topic to research and, on that basis, they are likely to remain the hidden assets of urban tourist destinations.

Questions

18.1 How do small tourism businesses contribute to the tourists' overall experience of a city?

18.2 What are the practical problems associated with examining the role and importance of small tourism businesses in urban areas?

18.3 Under what circumstances could a component of the urban 'leisure product' such as accommodation, which has traditionally been classified as a 'secondary' element, be considered to be a 'primary' element of that product, from the consumer perspective? How does this distort the concept of 'derived demand' for tourism products?

(*continued*)

18.4 To what extent can the state influence the performance of small tourism businesses in urban areas?

18.5 Evaluate the proposition that the impacts from small tourism businesses cannot be comprehensively assessed because of the complexity of the urban tourism product and the absence of an appropriate methodology.

18.6 Discuss the proposition that because small tourism businesses have a crucial role to play in the creation of a country's wealth and prosperity, governments have a responsibility to develop and maintain a supportive economic environment that fosters a culture of enterprise and encourages entrepreneurs and investors.

18.7 Evaluate the ethics of promoting dance club culture as part of a city's tourism product.

18.8 Outline a proposal for a research project to examine the contribution of small tourism businesses to the tourist experience of a city with which you are familiar.

REFERENCES

ABC of Drugs. 1998. London: Channel 4 Television.

Ashworth, G. J. 1989. 'Urban Tourism: An Imbalance in Attention'. In Cooper, C. P. (Ed.). *Progress in Tourism, Recreation and Hospitality Management.* London: Belhaven Press.

Ashworth, G. J. & de Haan, T. Z. 1986. 'Uses and Users of the Tourist–Historic City'. *Field Studies* 10. Groningen: Faculty of Spatial Sciences.

Ashworth, G. J. & Tunbridge, J. 1990. *The Tourist–Historic City.* London: Belhaven Press.

Ashworth, G. J. & Voogd, H. 1990. *Selling the City: Marketing Approaches in Public Sector Planning.* London: Belhaven Press.

Ashworth, G. J. & Voogd, H. 1994. 'Marketing of Tourism Places: What Are We Doing?'. In Uysal, M. (Ed.). *Global Tourist Behaviour.* New York: International Press, pp. 5–20.

Ayto, J. 1991. *The Longman Register of New Words.* Volume 2. London: Longman.

Bannock, G. & Daly, M. 1994. *Small Business Statistics.* London: Paul Chapman Publishing/Small Business Research Trust.

Boer, A. 1998. An Assessment of Small Business Failure'. in Thomas, R. (Ed.). *The Management of Small Tourism and Hospitality Firms.* London: Cassell, pp. 39–57.

Buhalis, D. & Cooper, C. 1998. 'Competition or Co-operation? Small and Medium Sized Tourism Enterprises at the Destination'. In Laws, E., Faulkner, B. & Moscardo, G. (Eds.). *Embracing and Managing Change in Tourism.* London: Routledge.

Burns, P. 1996. 'Introduction: The Significance of Small Firms'. In Burns, P. & Dewhurst, J. (Eds.). *Small Business and Entrepreneurship.* Second Edition. Basingstoke, UK: Macmillan.

Collin, M. 1997. 'Mad for It'. *The Guardian*, 28 March, p. 14.

Costa, J. & Teare, R. 1996. 'Environmental Scanning: A Tool for Competitive Advantage'. In Kotas, R., Teare, R., Logie, J., Jayawardena, C. & Bowen, J. (Eds.). *The International Hospitality Business.* London: Cassell, pp. 12–20.

DNH. 1995. *Tourism: Competing with the Best.* London: Department of National Heritage.

DNH. 1996. *Tourism: Competing with the Best. People Working in Tourism and Hospitality.* London: Department of National Heritage.

DTI. 1996. *Small Firms in Britain Report 1996.* London: Department of Trade and Industry.

DTI. 1998. *Small Business Action Update 1998.* London: Department of Trade and Industry.

Featherstone, M. 1988. 'In Pursuit of the Postmodern'. *Theory, Culture and Society* 5: 211.

Jansen-Verbeke, M. 1986. 'Inner City Tourism, Resources, Tourists and Promoters'. *Annals of Tourism Research* 13: 79–100.

Law, C. M. 1993. *Urban Tourism: Attracting Visitors to Large Cities.* London: Mansell.

Maier, G. 1997. 'Exploiting New Media: City Tourism and the Data Highway'. In Grabler, K., Maier, G., Mazanec, J. A. & Wober K. (Eds.). *International City Tourism.* London: Pinter, pp. 213–35.

Molian, D. & Birley, S. 1995. 'Decoding a Black Box? Evaluating Marketing Consultancy Schemes for SMEs'. In Birley, S. & Mason, C. (Eds.). *International Entrepeneurship.* London: Routledge, pp. 273–302.

Morrison, A, Rimmington, M. & Williamson, C. 1998. *Entrepreneurship in the Hospitality, Tourism and Leisure Industries.* Oxford, UK: Butterworth-Heinemann.

Morrison, A. 1996. 'Marketing the Small Tourism Business'. In Seaton, A. V. & Bennet, M. (Eds.). *Marketing Tourism Products: Concepts, Issues, Cases.* London: International Thomson Publishing.

Ng, S. 1997. Tourism business use of the Internet: survey results, http:// www.vuw.ac.nz-samuel/thesis/survey/results/int.html, 1 October. Cited in Page, S. J., Forer, P. & Lawton, G. R. 1999. 'Small Business Development and Tourism: Terra Incognita?'. *Tourism Management* 20: 435–59.

Nowicka, H. 1995. 'The Market: He Who Pays the Piper'. *The Independent*, 29 October, p. 20.

Page, S. 1995. *Urban Tourism.* London: Routledge.

Page, S. J., Forer, P. & Lawton, G. R. 1999. 'Small Business Development and Tourism: Terra Incognita?'. *Tourism Management* 20: 435–59.

Schertler, W. 1994. 'Tourism 2000 — An Information Business'. In Schertler, W., Schmid, B., Tjoa, A. M. & Werthner, H.(Eds.). *Information and Communication Technologies in Tourism.* Proceedings of the International Conference in Innsbruck, Austria, 1994. Vienna: Springer.

Shaw, G. & Williams, A. M. 1987. 'Firm Formation and Operating Characteristics in the Cornish Tourism Industry — The Case of Looe'. *Tourism Management*, December, pp. 344–8.

Shaw, G. & Williams, A. M. 1990. 'Tourism Economic Development and the Role of Entrepreneurial Activity. In Cooper, C. P. (Ed.). *Progress in Tourism, Recreation and Hospitality Management.* Volume 2. London: Belhaven Press, pp. 67–81.

Shaw, G. & Williams, A. M. 1994. 'Tourism and Entrepreneurship'. In Shaw, G. & Williams, A. M. (Eds.). *Critical Issues in Tourism: A Geographical Perspective.* Oxford: Blackwell, pp. 120–37.

Sheldon, P. 1993. 'Destination Information Systems'. *Annals of Tourism Research* 20 (4): 633–49.

Stanworth, J. & Gray, C. (Eds.). 1991. *Bolton 20 Years on: The Small Firm in the 1990s.* London: Paul Chapman Publishing.

Stewart-Smith, S. 1997. 'Called to the Bar'. *The Telegraph*, 29 March, p. 16.

Storey, D. J. 1994. *Understanding the Small Business Sector.* London: Routledge.

Storey, D. & Westhead, P. 1995. 'Management Training in Small Firms: A Case Study of Market Failure?' *SME Centre Working Paper No. 29.* Warwick, UK: University of Warwick.

Thomas, R. 1996. (Ed.). *The Hospitality Industry, Tourism and Europe: Perspectives on Policies.* London: Cassell.

Thomas, R. 1998. 'An Introduction to the Study of Small Tourism and Hospitality Firms'. In Thomas, R. (Ed.). *The Management of Small Tourism and Hospitality Firms.* London: Cassell, pp. 1–16.

Thomas, R., Friel, M., Jameson, S. & Parsons, D. 1997. *The National Survey of Small Tourism and Hospitality Firms: Annual Report 1996–1997.* Leeds, UK: Leeds Metropolitan University.

Travis, A. 1998. '$5m Extra for War on Drugs'. *The Guardian*, 28 April, p. 2.

Wanhill, S. 1999. 'Small and Medium Tourism Enterprises'. *Annals of Tourism Research* 27 (1): 132–47.

Webster, M. 1998. 'Strategies for Growth'. In Thomas, R. (Ed.). *The Management of Small Tourism and Hospitality Firms.* London: Cassell, pp. 207–18.

Wedgewood Markham. 1994. *Hotels and Guesthouses.* London: Wedgewood Marham Associates Ltd. Cited in Thomas, R. 1998. 'An Introduction to the Study of Small Tourism and Hospitality Firms'. In Thomas, R. (Ed.). *The Management of Small Tourism and Hospitality Firms.* London: Cassell, pp. 1–16.

Williams, A. M., Shaw, G. & Greenwood, J. 1989. 'From Tourist to Tourism Entrepreneur, from Consumption to Production: Evidence from Cornwall, England'. *Environment and Planning A* (21): 1639–53.

Wober, K. 1997. 'Local Tourism Organisations in European Cities'. In Grabler, K., Maier, G., Mazanec, J. A. & Wober, K. (Eds.). *International City Tourism.* London: Pinter, pp. 3–12.

Wynarczyk, P., Watson, R., Storey, D., Short, H. & Keasey, K. 1993. *Managerial Labour Markets in Small and Medium-sized Enterprises.* London: Routledge.

Reconstructing the City of Manchester
in the image of popular culture

Tourism is becoming an increasingly important element in the economy of most cities and a great deal of emphasis is being placed on the development of traditional urban tourist attractions and high-profile projects at the more prestigious end of the spectrum. Manchester, Britain's third most popular city for staying visitors, with more than 7 million each year, is no exception to this general rule. Recent developments have included the Bridgewater Hall — home of the Hallé Orchestra, the Lowry Centre and Imperial War Museum on Salford Quays together with the preparations for the 2002 Commonwealth Games, which are expected to attract a visitor spend of £7 million.

Urban tourists are no longer interested in seeing only great works of art, relics from distant historical periods or sport, however. The market has become highly segmented and developments such as those listed above tend to overshadow other aspects of a city's tourism product that have a considerable and increasing significance because of the value being placed on a range of other activities and experiences. Contemporary urban tourist activities are being sought in a wider variety of places than ever before, as less traditional subjects have become of interest and are being packaged and presented for tourist consumption through a process of **postmodern** anti-elitism.

This essentially *postmodern tourism* is characterised by *post tourists* who 'move through liminal urban spaces in search of spectacles in a simulational world' (Featherstone 1988:211), often in the form of guided tours. They are receptive to an eclectic mix of high culture, low culture and historic references of all sorts and are not so much concerned with accurate details as with the creation of visually interesting and entertaining 'products'. In short, they require popular images of preferred histories the value of which is symbolic, associated with a nostalgic or representational quality and related to the satisfaction of an emotional need. The new products that have been developed to satisfy the demands of this market include specialist city tours that reconstruct the urban landscapes through a process of imaginative interpretation of selected aspects of a destination's heritage or culture.

This type of alternative new product development epitomises the entrepreneurial skill of successful small tourism businesses operating in an urban environment. Moreover, by presenting a new perspective on the urban environment, it can contribute to a more balanced representation of a district's or city's heritage or culture so that local and/or regional relevance need not be sacrificed on the altar of more traditional or elitist histories. Nostalgia has lengthened and deepened to the extent that a more existential history — a heritage of popular culture, of everyday work and childhood, of age and other aspects of life that people can more readily identify with — is beginning to reshape our images of urban landscapes. Residents and workers, who represent important secondary markets for urban tourism products, may also be more interested in these alternative, often media-themed, reconstructions of their city.

An example of one of these alternative tourism products is provided by Jonathan Schofield, a self-employed official tourist guide for England and Wales, or 'Blue Badge Guide', who offers both traditional and unconventional tours of Manchester and the north-west of England. After gaining a degree in Law and pursuing an early career in various retail jobs together with some tour guiding, Jonathan turned his 'background knowledge and feel for the region' and a particular interest in the cotton industry, local architecture and popular music into a full-time tour guiding occupation. He is now one of Manchester's best-known tour guides, because of his innovative and hugely entertaining style, which could best be described as a nostalgic pastiche of factual and anecdotal material using a wide range of historical and contemporary references. He has been described by Jim Gilchrist of *The Scotsman* as 'a walking repository of local history who should be declared a Mancunian national treasure'.

Jonathan's other income streams include lecturing and public speaking, writing articles for the press and providing training courses to increase the local knowledge of receptionists in a range of tourist outlets in addition to the guided tours. He comments that 'you simply can't do enough jobs in Manchester if you want to live off it full time; the city is not a mass tourism destination. ... It's different in London, you can do Jack the Ripper tours 'til you're blue in the face'.

Jonathan's portfolio of tour products includes general tours of Manchester, educational tours, ghost tours, a full range of historical tours including Chinatown, 'cottonopolis', 'underworld Manchester' and 'Romans in the north', together with pub walks, coffee crawls, 'sporting city' tours, a 'bizarre tour', which involves a 'madcap excursion around the city looking at the crazy stories it has generated', and the ever popular and unique 'pop capital tour' featuring sites associated with the city's music scene. The latter includes such Manchester bands as the Hollies, the BeeGees, 10CC, the Buzzcocks, Joy Division, New Order, the Smiths, Simply Red, the Stone Roses, Happy Mondays, Take That and Oasis. Along with Manchester United, the Smiths are one of the most popular aspects of the city for tours.

Tours can also be tailormade to suit the needs of individual clients or groups. For example, every two years a large group of Canadian women travels to Manchester for a tour featuring Simply Red that simply must include the Barca bar in the Castlefield district, which is owned by Mick Hucknell, the lead singer!

The key markets for the tour guiding aspect of the business, which represents 70 per cent of his income, are established tour operators, local government, corporate clients and direct bookings mainly from regulars and popular music fans representing a wide variety of customers from 42 different countries. There is no marked seasonality in demand for the tours, compared with more traditional tourist centres such as York or Chester. A combination of Manchester's size and character together with Jonathan's broad customer base, varied portfolio and flexible approach keeps business on an even keel with an average of three to five tours a week, although August and December are difficult months. In August, local authority, corporate and regular group business is minimal although tour operator patronage and direct bookings from music fans remain. In December, daytime business is limited apart from the 'Manchester United' tours; most of the work is done in the evenings on the 'ale trails', which provide an amusing narrative, an insight into aspects of local history and the 'basic facts about boozing in Manchester'. The size and character of each group also varies according to the particular tour and the source of the booking. Tour party sizes range from one to 55 for coach tours of the city, from 15 to 25 for the popular culture tours and from three (in winter) to 30 (in summer) for the ale trails.

The pricing strategy is simple but effective. There are standard rates for all the tours based on the duration of the tour rather than the number of participants. A two-hour tour costs £55, a four-hour tour costs £75 and a full-day (8 hours) tour costs £100. A £10 discount is available for educational groups. The prices are agreed by the Manchester Guild of Blue Badge Guides, which regulates the rates charged by the city's official guides.

The promotional mix includes both above- and below-the-line elements. Fifteen thousand leaflets per year are distributed in the city's libraries and tourist information centres and occasionally desktop published posters are used to advertise a particular tour. The business has been able to generate a considerable amount of free publicity through its media exposure; Jonathan's other income streams such as public speaking and writing also help in this respect. In addition, a website is currently being developed. By far the most important aspect of the business's promotion is, however, the positive word-of-mouth publicity generated by the tours. Each time Jonathan regales his audience with amusing anecdotes and interesting tales of Manchester's unsung heroes, he is promoting his business; he is inseparable from the product. His successful formula is a function of his customer service background, the application of the 'same service standards as any good business', a flexible, anecdotal approach and a clear understanding that the product is '20 per cent knowledge and 80 per cent presentation'. In many tours, he claims, there is 'too much emphasis on days, dates and bricks and mortar'; it is important to 'make history immediate'.

This type of new product development, through its process of selection, interpretation and emphasis on certain aspects of the city's heritage in its commercial presentation, can create a more romantic image of the city. Most of us can conjure immediate cognitive responses to names such as Paris, Sydney, Venice, London or Rome, but what of Manchester? One is tempted to merely add '. . . United' or '. . . Ship Canal'! It would appear that, despite a considerable amount of redevelopment in the city in recent years and an aggressive promotional effort, the public's perception of Manchester continues to reflect its stereotypical 'cloth cap and clogs' image — negative aspects of its industrial past. Jonathan is always surprised by the number of visitors who expect the city centre to be 'full of chimneys' and are pleasantly surprised to find that it is not. This type of product can therefore make a positive contribution to the development of a more favourable image for the city. This is important in a competitive marketplace where a prospective visitor's city image is a significant factor in the destination choice process.

Questions

1 Evaluate the strengths of, and opportunities for, Jonathan's business.

2 How does this business differentiate itself from competitor products?

3 Evaluate the way in which the business is marketed and suggest alternative pricing and promotional strategies.

4 Why are the inherent characteristics of tourism 'products' such as perishability and inseparability such critical issues for small tourism businesses?

5 What is meant by the expression a 'mixed blessing of heritage' in the context of developing an appropriate image for a city?

GLOSSARY

Aboriginal tourism Tourism product that is Aboriginal owned or operated, employs Aboriginal people and/or provides consenting contact with Aboriginal people, culture or land.

acid house At The Warehouse music venue in Chicago, Frankie Knuckles began using electronics to create a new sound by re-editing records on reel-to-reel tape and adding pre-programmed rhythms from drum machines. His style of mixing was referred to as 'house music'. 'Acid house' probably derives from the Chicago slang 'acid', meaning 'steal', referring to the way in which 'house music' appropriates snatches of other recordings (Ayto 1991). According to another school of thought, 'acid' here refers to the recreational drug LSD.

amenity spa A resort in which the spa experience is only one of a range of recreational activities and facilities offered.

appellation A designation awarded to a wine or food product guaranteeing that it was produced in the specified region using specified and regulated methods.

Australian Heritage Commission The Commonwealth statutory authority charged with responsibility for the National Estate – that is, Australia's natural and cultural heritage.

authenticity Relates to the accurate and genuine manifestation of traditions, cultures and items.

Burra Charter A document setting out principles, processes and standards for the conservation of the cultural environment. Also known as the Australian ICOMOS Charter for the Conservation of Places of Cultural Significance. Based on the 1966 Venice Charter and named after the 1979 meeting in Burra, South Australia, at which it was adopted.

carrying capacity A tool for tourism planning in the consideration of both ecological and social impacts. Ecological carrying capacity in relation to tourism is the level of visitation beyond which unacceptable ecological impacts will occur. For the visitor, the social carrying capacity is the level of visitation beyond which satisfaction is no longer experienced because of excessive crowding or noise or limited access to services. For the host community, the social carrying capacity is the level of visitation beyond which unacceptable change occurs – this can be physical, cultural, economic, ecological or psychological.

commoditisation (Also called commodification.) Changing traditions, cultures or artefacts from their original forms into saleable products in response to (tourist) market demand.

community-based festival or event A themed public occasion designed to occur for a limited duration and to celebrate valued aspects of a community's way of life.

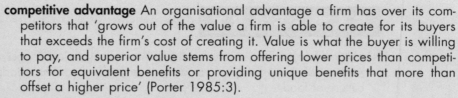

competitive advantage An organisational advantage a firm has over its competitors that 'grows out of the value a firm is able to create for its buyers that exceeds the firm's cost of creating it. Value is what the buyer is willing to pay, and superior value stems from offering lower prices than competitors for equivalent benefits or providing unique benefits that more than offset a higher price' (Porter 1985:3).

conservation All the processes of caring for a place so as to retain its fundamental values and significance.

cruise A ship voyage taken wholly for reasons of leisure and recreation.

cruise director Individual responsible for the organisation and presentation of public activities and entertainment on board a cruise ship.

cultural authenticity The perceived legitimacy of a site or experience that reflects its traditional form as closely as possible. The transparency or genuineness of simulacra or encounters and the honesty with which a site, event or experience is constructed or portrayed.

cultural exchange Interaction between tourists and host communities that ideally leads to enhanced understanding and respect for different value systems and traditions.

cultural heritage significance Aesthetic, historic, scientific or social value for past, present or future generations.

cultural sustainability The maintenance of cultural practices and values that also recognises the dynamic nature of culture and the aspirations of communities to ensure their cultures remain creative and vigorous.

demonstration effect The effect of the host community's exposure to the different lifestyles of visitors and its tendency to imitate them.

destination mix The combination of attractions, facilities, accommodation, forms of transport and accessibility, together with hospitality services, offered by a destination.

destination spa A facility with a single purpose, which is the spa experience itself.

discounted services Opportunities offered by tourism service providers that are a particularly important stimulus to the seniors market segment.

diversified indigenous tourism Tourism ventures controlled by indigenous people that do not have indigenous culture as their main theme.

drawing power The capacity of an attraction or destination to attract tourists from their point of origin and away from alternative attractions and destinations. Because of travel distances and times involved, rural attractions and destinations must have considerable drawing power to compete successfully for tourists.

entrepreneurship 'The process of creating or seizing an opportunity and pursuing it regardless of the resources currently controlled. Entrepreneurship involves the definition, creation and distribution of value and benefits to individuals, groups, organizations and society' (Timmons 1990:5).

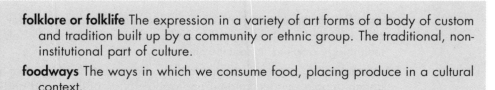

folklore or folklife The expression in a variety of art forms of a body of custom and tradition built up by a community or ethnic group. The traditional, non-institutional part of culture.

foodways The ways in which we consume food, placing produce in a cultural context.

gross registered tonnes (GRT) A measurement of a ship's capacity, not of its weight.

hallmark event A major festival or event designed to promote awareness and appeal of particular aspects of a destination.

host community The people who live and work in the places tourists visit.

hot interpretations Engaged forms of interpretation in which tourists are invited or obliged to 'read', or make their own sense of, a tourist site or experience, often relating it to their personal experiences or memories.

ICOM International Council of Museums, a non-government organisation that acts as the governing body of member museums around the world.

ICOMOS International Council on Monuments and Sites, a professional non-government conservation organisation concerned with the care and protection of places of cultural significance. Advises UNESCO on World Heritage matters.

indigenous cultural tourism Cultural tourism centred on an indigenous or First Peoples culture, site or experience. Typically involves indigenous ownership or joint-venture enterprise emphasising authenticity, cultural maintenance and self-determination.

indigenous peoples Those peoples who belong to the land – its aboriginal inhabitants, as opposed to later settlers.

indigenous tourism See *Aboriginal tourism*.

in-kind support Contributions, other than financial, towards an event. May take the form of goods or services.

infrastructure All forms of construction and services relating to transportation (road, rail and air), utilities (electricity, gas, water, communications), health care and security services needed by tourist destinations and other inhabited areas.

inseparability Tourists come into contact with a tourism organisation in order to experience a 'performance' by the organisation's personnel. The organisation cannot produce this performance in advance and store it in preparation for the next service encounter. As a result, tourism personnel are inseparable from production, which, in turn, is inseparable from consumption by tourists.

intangible Unlike manufactured products, tourism's 'service products', such as package holidays, are essentially non-material things; they are an experience of place at a particular time. As such, they cannot be tasted, touched or sampled prior to purchase and are difficult to evaluate objectively.

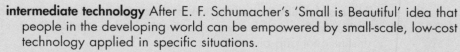

intermediate technology After E. F. Schumacher's 'Small is Beautiful' idea that people in the developing world can be empowered by small-scale, low-cost technology applied in specific situations.

interpretation A way of communicating ideas and feelings that can help enrich people's understanding and appreciation of the world and their role in it. Also 'adds value' to a heritage site.

leakage The loss of potential profits derived from tourism as these flow out of the destination to other areas – for example, as payments for goods and services that must be imported to meet the needs and demands of tourists, and as government taxes. The extent of leakage greatly influences the true value of tourism development for any destination.

leisure product That which attracts visitors to a place – its cultural, sports and amusement facilities, its physical and socio-cultural features (primary elements), its accommodation, food and beverage, and shopping facilities (secondary elements), and its accessibility, parking and information facilities (additional elements).

liminal person Someone who occupies a marginal social position. People in the mainstream may feel challenged by the existence of marginal people, who represent alternative modes of life.

limits of acceptable change (LAC) Related to *carrying capacity*. From the perspective of the resource, the point beyond which change brought about by encroaching tourism enterprises or infrastructure has unacceptable negative impacts.

line voyage A way of getting from port A to port B by ship.

living history Applied to heritage sites or interpretive centres where static displays are embellished by interactive exhibits and activities – for example, costumed actors playing roles, re-creations of past activities and customs, or participatory activities and learning experiences for visitors.

management plan A plan for the management, care and maintenance of the natural and cultural heritage and non-heritage features of a site. May contain a conservation plan and/or its components.

market segment A homogeneous sector of the community that shares particular characteristics.

McDonaldisation of culture Alludes to the homogenisation of global tourist culture and commodities, and the reduction of diversity that accompanies it.

multiplier effect A measure of the economic activity generated by tourism expenditure. The more money is retained and circulated within an economy, the larger the multiplier effect.

National Estate Defined in the *Australian Heritage Commission Act 1975* as 'those places, being components of the natural environment of Australia or the cultural environment of Australia, that have aesthetic, historic, scientific or social significance or other special value for future generations as well as for the present community'.

opportunity cost The opportunity that is lost by choosing a particular course of action.

positioning voyage A practice by which a company temporarily locates a ship in another part of the world in order to take advantage of the season there.

postmodern Postmodern society is generally described as being relatively unstructured and characterised by highly processed communication, simulated pleasure and spectacle and by the consumption of products, the image and exhibition value of which, is more important than their utility value.

product development Transforming natural and cultural phenomena into activities and experiences that can be sold to tourists.

propensity to travel Higher among seniors than other age groups in developed countries such as Australia and New Zealand because of fewer time constraints and greater discretionary income among older people.

quality of life Relates to the physical and social attractiveness of a place. A range of factors contribute to making us feel good about being – and staying – in a place.

REAL travel Derived from Read (1980), REAL travel relates to the demand-side definitions of tourism and refers to various experiences that tourists find **R**ewarding, **E**nriching, **A**dventuresome and an opportunity for **L**earning.

regional economic development Creation of new wealth by strengthening existing economic activity or creating new economic activity in regional areas. May be achieved through economic diversification, new enterprise development, income and employment creation, infrastructure development and investment.

regional tourism Tourism activity centred outside capital cities. Defined by the place tourism occurs rather than the featured activities or experiences.

senior One of many descriptors for an older person. As the general population ages, seniors become an increasingly important market segment.

senior tourism Distinctive aspects of tourism in which older tourists have specific needs and wants – e.g., travel motivations, means of transport, food requirements, accommodation, access.

sense of place A perception that includes factors that together contribute to a place's identity. It has tangible elements like buildings, streetscape and landscape, and intangible elements such as history, sentiment, memory, familiarity, civic pride, and emotions that come from knowledge and caring for the place.

single surcharge Charge applied to a single traveller that is usually much more than half that of a couple of travellers.

small business A business in which 'one or two persons are required to make all the critical management decisions – finance, accounting, personnel, purchasing, processing or servicing, marketing, selling – without the aid of internal specialists and with specific knowledge in only one or two functional areas' (Wiltshire Committee Report, cited in Johns, Dunlop & Sheehan 1989).

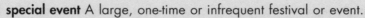

special event A large, one-time or infrequent festival or event.

special interest tourism Customised leisure and recreational experiences driven by the specific expressed interests if individuals and groups.

sponsor Individual or organisation contributing in-kind or financial support to promotion and/or running of an event.

staged sets Term used by MacCannell to refer to contrived spaces established for tourists. *Fronts* refer to areas deliberately set up for tourists to experience the legitimated tourist experience. *Backs* refer to private, off-limits areas 'off-stage', which are often of greater interest to more curious, adventurous tourists. *Backs* may include the less salubrious, seedier aspects of a destination.

stakeholders Individuals or organisations with an interest or investment in tourism products or the outcome of a festival or event.

strategic fit 'An effective combination of the firm's objectives; internal resources; resource application; management capabilities; external threats and changing market opportunities; strategic analysis, decision making and implementation' (Morrison, Rimmington & Williams 1999:193).

strategy 'The pattern or plan that integrates an organisation's major goals, policies, and action sequences into a cohesive whole. A well-formulated strategy helps to marshal and allocate an organisation's resources into a unique and viable posture based on its relative internal competencies and shortcomings, anticipated changes in the environment, and contingent moves by intelligent opponents' (Quinn 1980, in Mintzberg, Quinn & Voyer 1995:5).

sustainability Applied to tourism, it may relate to environmental, ecological or socio-cultural values of destinations. Sustainability is maintained so long as the impacts of tourism do not compromise these values.

sustainable tourism development Generates positive social and economic outcomes while protecting important features of the natural and cultural environment.

tourism service provider Any individual or organisation that supplies services to tourists, such as food, accommodation, transport, travel and leisure facilities.

tourist-historic city Refers to those parts of a city where the tourist areas, characterised by the provision of visitor facilities, overlap with the historic areas of the city.

training and enterprise councils (TECs) Not-for-profit organisations, operating under performance-related government contracts, who work in partnership with local authorities, chambers of commerce, visitor and conventions bureaux, local universities, colleges and schools, voluntary organisations and training providers to enhance workforce competence and business competitiveness.

UNESCO United Nations Education and Scientific Organisation.

VFR travellers Those who travel mainly in order to visit friends and relatives.

viticulture The science of wine-grape production.

volunteer A person who contributes time and energy to the promotion, organisation or running of an event for no financial reward.

winescape A human landscape marked by the impacts of wine-grape production.

wine tourism Tourism activity centred on the physical, social and cultural dimensions of the winescape and its components.

FURTHER READING

Bacon, W. 1998. 'Economic Systems and Their Impact on Tourist Resort Development: The Case of the Spa in Europe'. *Tourism Economics* 4 (1): 21–32. The author identifies factors facilitating the success of spa resorts and those associated with their business failure. He argues convincingly that the British spa declined primarily because it relied on private sector entrepreneurship while the European spa flourished because it was regarded as an important component of the public sector.

Bishop, R. & Robinson, L. S. 1998. *Night Market: Sexual Cultures and the Thai Economic Miracle.* London: Routledge. An analysis of the socioeconomic constructs of sex tourism in Thailand.

Bureau of Tourism Research. 1999. *Tourism Expenditure by International Visitors in Regional Australia.* Occasional Paper No. 29, Canberra. A useful source of data on international tourism activity in regional Australia.

Butler, R. W. 1990. 'Alternative Tourism: Pious Hope or Trojan Horse?'. *Journal of Travel Research*, Winter, p. 40. Brings together the early discussion of the role of alternative tourism and gives a framework for evaluating the distinctions between old/new and mass/special interest tourism.

Butler, R. C., Hall, C. M. & Jenkins, J. M. (Eds.). 1998. *Tourism and Recreation in Rural Areas.* Chichester: John Wiley & Sons. A useful reference work on rural tourism, with an international perspective.

Chai, P. P. & Skene, J. 1996. 'Attracting the Older Visitor: A Market Segmentation Study'. Canberra: Bureau of Tourism Research, Commonwealth of Australia. The authors discuss the importance of the senior tourist and the use of the CD-MOTA (Compact Disk-Monitor of Tourism Data).

Dodd, T. H. 1995. 'Opportunities and Pitfalls of Tourism in a Developing Wine Industry'. *International Journal of Wine Marketing* 7 (1): 5–16. A useful article highlighting some of the advantages and disadvantages of wine tourism in the American context.

Douglas, N. & Douglas, N. 1999b. 'Cruise Consumer Behaviour: A Comparative Study'. In Pizam, A. & Mansfeld, Y. (Eds.). *Consumer Behaviour in Travel and Tourism.* New York: Haworth Hospitality Press, pp. 369–92. A comprehensive description and assessment of what cruise passengers do and why, from research on three different vessels.

Dwyer, L. & Forsyth, P. 1998. 'Economic Significance of Cruise Tourism'. *Annals of Tourism Research* 25 (2): 393–415. A useful analysis of the economic benefits and otherwise to be derived from the port visits of cruise ships.

European Travel Commission. 1992. *Europe's Senior Travel Market.* Proceedings of the Second European Conference on the Senior Travel Market. Paris: ETC. Features a large collection of case studies on senior tourism.

Federation of Nature and National Parks of Europe. 1993. *Loving Them to Death?: Sustainable Tourism in Europe's Nature and National Parks. Grefenau: FNNPE.* Offers recommendations on how natural resources can be managed in a sustainable way. Highlights 16 projects from protected landscapes in Europe; case studies include initiatives on cycle tourism.

France, L. (Ed.). 1997. *The Earthscan Reader in Sustainable Tourism.* London: Earthscan Publications. Offers theory and case study papers on special interest tourism, sustainability and tourism development issues. Includes seminal observations from Valene Smith, Jost Krippendorf, Brian Wheeler, Aurelia Poon and Colin Michael Hall.

Frechtling, D. 1993. *Annotated Bibliography on Health and Tourism Issues.* USA: Pan American Health Organisation. A useful resource from which to begin a literature search.

Goodrich, J. N. & Uysal, M. 1994. 'Health Tourism: A New Positioning Strategy for Tourist Destinations'. In Uysal, M. (Ed.). *Global Tourist Behaviour.* Birmingham: International Business Press, pp. 227–38. Focuses on the Caribbean in particular but is a very good general discussion of this sector.

Haigh, R. 1993. 'Keeping Australians at Home'. Occasional Paper No. 17. Canberra: Bureau of Tourism Research, Commonwealth of Australia. Presents an overview of the factors that encourage people to travel overseas and gives suggestions on nurturing domestic tourism.

Hall, C. M. & Weiler, B. 1992. 'What's Special About Special Interest Tourism?'. In *Special Interest Tourism.* London: Belhaven Press. An attempt to draw together early writing on the segments of the special interest tourism market. Includes material on adventure, heritage and events tourism.

Hall, C. M. & Mitchell, R. 2000. 'Wine Tourism in the Mediterranean: A Tool for Restructuring and Development'. *Thunderbird International Business Review* 42 (4): 445–65. Provides a useful basis of comparison between the European and Australasian experience of wine tourism.

Hall, C. M., Sharples, L., Cambourne, B., Macionis, N., with Johnson, G. & Mitchell, R. (Eds.). 2000. *Wine Tourism around the World: Development, Management and Markets.* Oxford: Butterworth-Heinemann. The first book written on wine tourism from a research and business perspective. Uses both a regional approach (e.g., wine tourism in Australia, Canada, France, New Zealand and the United States) and a thematic approach (e.g., chapters on consumer behaviour, marketing and regional development).

Hembry, P., Cowie, L. W. & Cowie, E. E. 1997. *British Spas from 1815 to the Present: A Social History.* London: Athlone Press. A detailed social history of the rise and fall in popularity of the British spa and the British devotion to the seaside.

Hunt, S., Prosser, G., Braithwaite, R. & Bonnet, G. 2000. *The Significance of Regional Tourism.* Occasional Paper No. 2. Lismore: Centre for Regional Tourism Research. Draws together recent research on the benefits of tourism for regional communities, and presents recent data on domestic and international tourism activity in regional Australia.

Law, C. M. 1993. *Urban Tourism: Attracting Visitors to Large Cities.* London: Mansell. A useful examination of the role and significance of tourism in urban areas, with a focus on key components of supply, organisation, funding, strategy and impact.

Legge, J. & Hindle, K. 1997. *Entrepreneurship: How Innovators Create the Future.* Melbourne: Macmillan Education Australia. A perspective that can be usefully applied to the Australian context; documents each step in the journey from idea to enterprise.

MacCannell, D. 1976. 'Staged Authenticity'. In *The Tourist: A New Theory of the Leisure Class.* New York: Schocken, pp. 91–107. Tourism encourages historical or cultural representation through 'staged' events, which often tend to commodify and trivialise past events and our (and others') cultural heritage.

McAuley, R. 1997. *The Liners: A Voyage of Discovery.* London: Boxtree. As up-to-date as a history of this fast-developing subject can be.

O'Connell Davidson, J. 1998. *Prostitution, Power and Freedom.* London: Routledge. Although not specifically about sex tourism, the author draws on research from sex tourism locations to examine gender issues of power.

Page, S. 1995. *Urban Tourism.* London: Routledge. A well-written introductory text on urban tourism that provides comprehensive coverage of relevant concepts, issues and problems, with a wide range of international case studies.

Page, S. J., Forer, P. & Lawton, G. R. 1999. 'Small Business Development and Tourism: Terra Incognita?'. *Tourism Management* 20: 435–59. A useful review of the small business literature as it relates to tourism. Highlights the need for both a greater tourism focus and a more explicit contribution to methodological development than currently exists. Also reports the results of a project assessing the role of STEs in Northland, New Zealand.

Peisley, T. 1999. 'The Cruise Business in Asia Pacific'. *Travel and Tourism Analyst* 2: 1–20. A quite thorough examination of a fairly recent phenomenon.

Ringer, G. (Ed.). 1998. *Destinations: Cultural Landscapes of Tourism.* London: Routledge. These essays examine the utility of cultural landscape as a framework for understanding, planning and formulating tourism policy.

Rojek, C. & Urry, J. (Eds.). 1997. *Touring Cultures: Transformations of Travel and Theory.* Routledge: London. The contributors bring together observations on the significance of tourism in contemporary society.

Rowland, D. T. 1991. *Aging in Australia.* Melbourne: Longman Cheshire. Outlines issues associated with the ageing of the population.

Russell, R. & Faulkner, B. 1999. 'Movers and Shakers: Chaos Makers in Tourism Development'. *Tourism Management* 20: 411–23. Proposes a new framework for the study of entrepreneurship and applies this to tourism development on Australia's Gold Coast.

Ryan, C. & Hall, C. M. 2001. Sex Tourism: Liminalities and Marginal People. London: Routledge. A review of heterosexual and gay sex tourism written from the perspective of socio-psychological theory and addressing gender issues.

Shaw, G. & Williams, A. M. 1994. 'Tourism and Entrepreneurship'. In Shaw, G. & Williams, A. M. (Eds.). *Critical Issues in Tourism: A Geographical Perspective.* Oxford: Blackwell, pp. 120–37. A good discussion of the importance of entrepreneurship in tourism and its impact on economic development. Focuses on both the role of entrepreneurship in tourism development and the nature and characteristics of tourism entrepreneurs.

Thomas, R. 1998. 'An Introduction to the Study of Small Tourism and Hospitality Firms'. In Thomas, R. (Ed.). *The Management of Small Tourism and Hospitality Firms.* London: Cassell, pp. 1–16. By far the best first point of reference for students, researchers and practitioners interested in the development and management of small tourism organisations. It consolidates the existing knowledge and provides a comprehensive analysis of the key issues.

Urry, J. 1990. *The Tourist Gaze: Leisure and Travel in Contemporary Societies.* London: Sage. The first book to tackle the important issues of vision/observing/looking within the touristic experience. It asks the reader to consider how the notion of viewing is socially constructed and affected by economic, gender, ethnicity and other social factors.

Wanhill, S. 1999. 'Small and Medium Tourism Enterprises'. *Annals of Tourism Research* 27 (1): 132–47. A thorough examination of the growing interest in community tourism development in Europe and the role of SMEs in underpinning entrepreneurship and job creation in outlying regions, with particular reference to Wales.

Weaver, D. & Oppermann, M. 1999. *Tourism Management.* Brisbane: John Wiley & Sons. Broadly and clearly explores the environments in which tourism operates and explains how it is managed. Chapter 11 deals with sustainable tourism development and practice.

Wiseman, H. (Ed.). 1999. *Get Up & Go: Australian Travel Guide for Seniors 2000.* Sydney: Mahlab Cramb Media. A special travel guide containing a wealth of case studies to help the reader gain an insight into the needs and wants of senior travellers.

World Travel & Tourism Council. 1998. *Rural Tourism — Real or Imagined Economic Potential.* World Travel & Tourism Council — Econett, http://www.wttc.org/ecodiscuss.nsf. An international tourism industry perspective on rural and regional tourism.

Websites

http://www.adventuresports.com/mtnbike A comprehensive source of adventure sports opportunities and resources around the world.

http://www.ageofreason.com The Age of Reason website offers various resources and links for seniors.

http://www.budgettravel.com The Budget Travel website presents comprehensive domestic and international information on travel destinations and travel information.

http://www.butterfield.com Butterfield & Robinson describe cycle tours in Europe, the Americas and Asia.

http://www.cota.org.au The website of the Council of the Ageing, an independent consumer organisation run by and for older Australians.

http://www.manchester.com A Web guide to the city of Manchester, including community information, business news, sports and travel tips.

http://www.marketing-guild.com Offers training programs to improve advertising, direct mail, exhibition, telemarketing, sales and marketing strategies.

http://www.nzway.co.nz/contents.html The website of the New Zealand Way provides a good illustration of the interrelationships between wine, food and tourism in place promotion and marketing.

http://www.seniornet.com The website of a nonprofit organisation providing education about computer technology and the Internet for seniors.

http://www.seniorresource.com An informative website presenting material on housing options, retirement planning, finance, insurance and care for seniors.

http://www.seniortraveltips.com Provides information on destinations, travel packages and itinerary ideas for the mature travel market.

http://www.thirdage.com Features a variety of information relevant to seniors. Includes information on computers, health, money, news and travel.

http://www.worldexpeditions.com.au Provides information on cycle tours worldwide.

INDEX